Conscious Mind, Sleeping Brain

Perspectives on Lucid Dreaming

Conscious Mind, Sleeping Brain

Perspectives on Lucid Dreaming

Edited by

Jayne Gackenbach

University of Northern Iowa
Cedar Falls, Iowa

and

Stephen LaBerge

Stanford University
Stanford, California

Plenum Press • New York and London

Library of Congress Cataloging in Publication Data

Conscious mind, sleeping brain.

Includes bibliographies and index.
1. Lucid dreams. I. Gackenbach, Jayne, 1946-   . II. LaBerge, Stephen. [DNLM:
1. Consciousness. 2. Dreams. 3. Sleep. WL 108 C755]
BF1099.L82C66   1988   154.6'32   88-6034
ISBN 0-306-42849-0

To the pioneers who brought the
light of consciousness into the dream

Contributors

Sue Blackmore, Brain and Perception Laboratory, University of Bristol, Bristol, England

David B. Cohen, Department of Psychology, University of Texas at Austin, Austin, Texas

Robert Dentan, Departments of American Studies and Anthropology, State University of New York, Amherst, New York

Peter Fellows, Centre for Inner Learning, Toronto, Ontario, Canada

Peter Fenwick, London, England

Jayne Gackenbach, Department of Psychology, University of Northern Iowa, Cedar Falls, Iowa

Patricia Garfield, San Francisco, California

George Gillespie, Department of Oriental Studies, University of Pennsylvania, Philadelphia, Pennsylvania

Mary Godwyn, Boston, Massachusetts

Gordon Halliday, The Center for Individual and Family Services, Mansfield, Ohio

Robert Hoffmann, Department of Psychology, Carleton University, Ottawa, Ontario, Canada

Harry T. Hunt, Department of Psychology, Brock University, St. Catharines, Ontario, Canada

Harvey J. Irwin, Department of Psychology, University of New England, Armidale, New South Wales, Australia

Stephen LaBerge, Departments of Psychology, Stanford University, Stanford, California

Judith R. Malamud, Bronx, New York

Alan Moffitt, Department of Psychology, Carleton University, Ottawa, Ontario, Canada

Janet Mullington, Department of Psychology, City College of New York, New York, New York

Robert D. Ogilvie, Department of Psychology, Brock University, St. Catharines, Ontario, Canada

Ross Pigeau, Human Factors, Defense and Civil Institute of Environmental Medicine, Toronto, Ontario, Canada

Robert F. Price, Department of Psychology, University of Texas at Austin, Austin, Texas

Sheila Purcell, Department of Psychology, Carleton University, Ottawa, Ontario, Canada

Morton Schatzman, London, England

Wynn Schwartz, Department of Psychiatry, Harvard Medical School at the Cambridge Hospital, Cambridge, Massachusetts

Thomas J. Snyder, Developmental Disabilities Center, University of Alberta, Edmonton, Alberta, Canada

Charles T. Tart, Department of Psychology, University of California at Davis, Davis, California

Paul Tholey, Psychological Institute, Johann Wolfgang Goethe University, Frankfurt, West Germany

Roger Wells, Department of Psychology, Carleton University, Ottawa, Ontario, Canada

Alan Worsley, London, England

Preface

A conscious mind in a sleeping brain: the title of this book provides a vivid image of the phenomenon of lucid dreaming, in which dreamers are consciously aware that they are dreaming while they seem to be soundly asleep. Lucid dreamers could be said to be awake to their inner worlds while they are asleep to the external world.

Of the many questions that this singular phenomenon may raise, two are foremost: What is consciousness? And what is sleep? Although we cannot provide complete answers to either question here, we can at least explain the sense in which we are using the two terms. We say lucid dreamers are *conscious* because their subjective reports and behavior indicate that they are explicitly aware of the fact that they are asleep and dreaming; in other words, they are reflectively conscious of themselves. We say lucid dreamers are *asleep* primarily because they are not in sensory contact with the external world, and also because research shows physiological signs of what is conventionally considered REM sleep. The evidence presented in this book—preliminary as it is—still ought to make it clear that lucid dreaming is an experiential and physiological reality. Whether we should consider it a paradoxical form of sleep or a paradoxical form of waking or something else entirely, it seems too early to tell. Terms like *sleep, waking,* and *dreaming* may be too crude to capture usefully the fine structure of consciousness. Our vocabulary for describing states of consciousness is still too undeveloped. But for now (*pace* William James), lucid dreaming should remind us not to close our accounts on the possibilities of human consciousnesss and the sleeping brain prematurely.

This book addresses the subject of lucid dreaming in an interdisciplinary manner. It contains chapters providing historical and cultural perspectives on lucid dreaming in Western literature, Tibetan Buddhism, and Senoi culture; reviews of empirical investigations on dream control, individual differences, induction, psychophysiology, and content of lucid dreams; discussions of clinical applications and accounts of personal experiences with lucid dreaming; and theoretical chapters relating lucid dreaming to the out-of-body experience, meditation, descriptive psychology, and cognitive psychology. The level at which the material is presented varies from general to technical, although it should all be readable by nonspecialists. Prospective readers should include scholars in fields as diverse as clinical and experimental psychology, neuroscience, religion, anthropology, and philosophy. The book should also appeal to the educated public, especially those with an interest in dreaming and the nature of human consciousness.

We gratefully acknowledge the assistance of Lori Cook, Albert Gilgen, Mushkil Gusha, Lynne Levitan, K. Romana Machado, Mark Rosekind, Vera Sullivan, Mary Tuttle, and Eliot Werner. Thanks also to our families and friends, who endured the usual hardships associated with the writing of a book.

Finally, there are people who played a part (known to us or not) in making this book possible who must remain unnamed. Obviously, without the material contributed by the chapter authors, we would have had no book. But without the contributions of many previous workers, we would have had no field of lucid dreaming research. We thank them all.

Jayne Gackenbach
Stephen LaBerge

Cedar Falls and Stanford

Contents

Chapter 10

Individual Differences Associated with Lucid Dreaming 221
Thomas Snyder and Jayne Gackenbach

Introduction

STEPHEN LaBERGE and JAYNE GACKENBACH

After many years of neglect during the behaviorist period of modern psychology, the past decade has seen the reemergence of interest in consciousness as a topic of legitimate scientific inquiry (Natsoulas, 1978). Researchers interested in consciousness as well as sleep and dreaming have naturally turned increasing attention to a new field of study: consciousness during sleep and the phenomenon of lucid dreaming (van Eeden, 1913), in which people are consciously aware that they are dreaming while they are dreaming. Lucid dreamers can apparently be in full possession of their waking faculties (this is the meaning of the adjective *lucid*) while continuing to dream vividly. Both subjective reports and physiological evidence indicate that these experiences take place during sound sleep.

While being fully asleep to the external world, lucid dreamers are conscious of and, in a certain sense, are fully awake to their inner worlds. This paradoxical fact challenges traditional beliefs about "sleep" and the presumed limitations of sleep mentation. The discovery of REM sleep (also originally called "paradoxical sleep") required the expansion of our concept of sleep. The evidence associating lucid dreaming with REM sleep seems to require a similar expansion of our concept of dreaming and a clarification of our concepts of sleep and consciousness.

This introduction will provide an outline and orientation to the book and the field of lucid dreaming. The field is very young, and much of what is presented here should be regarded as speculative. Consequently, much of this book is closer to a record of works in progress than a collection of final and definitive statements. The book is divided into four sections that describe a variety of approaches to lucid dreaming, which are not necessarily mutually exclusive.

STEPHEN LaBERGE • Department of Psychology, Stanford, CA 94305.   JAYNE GACKEN-BACH • Department of Psychology, University of Northern Iowa, Cedar Falls, IA 50614–0505.

The first section deals with the historical, anthropological, philosophical, and religious perspectives on lucid dreaming in several different cultural contexts. The significance attributed to dreams and lucid dreams varies tremendously with the assumptions of the culture in question. Stephen LaBerge surveys lucid dreaming in Western literature, tracing the changing view of lucid dreams during the development of Western culture, from the fourth century B.C. to the mid-1960s. His review reveals that lucid dreaming has been known in the West at least since the time of Aristotle but remained an academic curiosity until very recently.

We often find well-developed systems of applied psychology in the East in areas we in the West are just beginning to explore. Lucid dreaming is no exception. In "Lucid Dreams in Tibetan Buddhism," George Gillespie discusses lucid dreaming in the literature of Tibetan Buddhist meditation. Remarkably, for a thousand years, Tibetan Buddhists have been practicing a form of yoga aimed at the maintenance of full waking consciousness during sleep and the control of the dream state.

Sometimes, however, it seems we find it all too easy to believe in the marvelous ways of the East. The writings of Kilton Stewart led many Westerners to believe the Malaysian Senoi tribe had a widely cultivated proficiency in dream control and that the emphasis on dreams in their culture was responsible for their peaceful way of life. Robert K. Dentan's chapter, "Lucidity, Sex, and Horror in Senoi Dreamwork," suggests that this is a misconception. Dentan notes that "recent publications have made it plain that much of the 'Senoi' ethnography with which Western dreamworkers are familiar is of dubious reliability." He points out that, although the Senoi do place a high value on dreams, dream control expertise in the culture is the province of the few rather than the many.

The second section of the book presents empirical approaches to the study of lucid dreaming. In 1969, Charles T. Tart reprinted Frederik van Eeden's (1913) classic essay on lucid dreaming in *Altered States of Consciousness*, giving many their first exposure to the concept of lucid dreaming. Part II begins with an updated version of Tart's "From Spontaneous Event to Lucidity: A Review of Attempts to Consciously Control Nocturnal Dreaming" (1979). Tart discusses dreaming and lucid dreaming from a systems perspective and reviews studies using, among other techniques, various forms of suggestions to affect the content of dreams, including overt presleep and posthypnotic suggestions. He concludes that lucidity may present the greatest potential for the control of dreams.

Lucid dreaming has been shown to be a learnable skill (LaBerge, 1980; Tholey, 1983). However, as with all skills, the ease with which it is learned varies with the individual. For the purpose of laboratory investigation of the lucid dream state and to make any potential applications of lucid dreaming practical, it would be desirable for subjects to be able to have lucid dreams on demand. Consequently, there has been great interest in developing methods of inducing the lucid dream state reliably. In the chapter, "Lucid Dream Induction: An

Empirical Evaluation,'' Robert F. Price and David B. Cohen present a theoretical framework based on the concept of duality of thought, which they apply to lucid dreaming. After reviewing presleep, physiological, and dream-content conditions associated with lucid dream initiation, Price and Cohen divide induction techniques into categories and examine them in detail. They conclude that "lucid dreaming appears to be an experience widely available to the highly motivated."

Additional research on lucid dream induction has been conducted since the Price and Cohen chapter was written. Sheila Purcell has found that in a comparison of the effectiveness of a hypnotic induction to a waking cue (i.e., a wristband worn by the subjects during the day to remind them of the intention to recognize when they are dreaming) that the latter was more successful in inducing dream lucidity (A. Moffitt, personal communication to J. G., June 1987). Jayne Gackenbach and her colleagues in Iowa, building on Henry Reed's (1977) finding of a positive relationship between the practice of meditation and subsequent dream lucidity, have found a significantly higher incidence of lucid dreams among the practitioners of transcendental meditation relative to nonmeditating controls (Gackenbach, Cranson, & Alexander, 1986). And, recent findings suggest that a device developed by LaBerge, using light as a lucidity cue given to subjects during REM sleep, may be effective for inducing lucid dreams; in one study more than half of 28 subjects had lucid dreams on their first night in the laboratory (LaBerge, 1987). The work on the problem of reliably inducing lucid dreams continues.

Ten years ago the orthodox view in sleep and dream research was that anecdotal accounts of "lucid" dreams must be somehow spurious. The situation is different today because of laboratory proof of the occurence of lucid dreams during unequivocal REM sleep described in "The Psychophysiology of Lucid Dreaming,'' by Stephen LaBerge. He characterizes the lucid dream state as being associated with periods of highly activated physiology within the REM state and reviews studies of psychophysiological relationships found during REM lucid dreaming, concluding that lucid dreaming offers great potential as a tool in the study of mind–body relationships.

The next chapter, "Correspondence during Lucid Dreams between Dreamed and Actual Events,'' by Morton Schatzman, Alan Worsley, and Peter Fenwick, directly addresses the question of the relationship between deliberate actions performed in lucid dreams and their physiological manifestations. Their subject (Worsley) was able to execute a variety of complex dream acts planned before sleep, and observable physiological effects of his dream actions were as predicted. Additionally, he was able in certain circumstances to accurately perceive and respond to external stimuli, a fact that demonstrates the difficulty in unambiguously classifying all mental states as either "waking" or "sleep."

Lucid dreams differ in content from nonlucid dreams in one obvious way— as a matter of definition. But the question remains of whether and how dream lucidity affects other aspects of dream content. Is the only difference between lucid and nonlucid dreams that in the former dreamers know they are dreaming? Jayne Gackenbach explores this question in ''Psychological Content of Lucid versus Nonlucid Dreams.'' She begins by reviewing past research with dreamer evaluations of the content of lucid and nonlucid dreams and then presents new results, using the Hall and Van de Castle (1966) system of analyzing manifest content. Gackenbach concludes that lucid dreams are more similar to than different from nonlucid dreams but that there are some significant differences. Lucid dreams are statistically likely to contain more auditory perception and cognitive activities and have fewer characters than nonlucid dreams.

A major procedural consideration not addressed in Gackenbach's work has been brought up by recent findings presented by Price (1987) of a content analysis of a single subject's lucid dreams, pointing out the importance of separating lucid from nonlucid scenes in a dream sequence. Making this distinction is likely to result in a decrease in similarity between lucid and nonlucid dreams.

Although most people report having had at least one dream in which they knew they were dreaming, few people have lucid dreams with any regularity. Discovering ways in which those who frequently have lucid dreams differ from those who do not could reveal something of the nature of the mental processes involved in lucidity as well as the potential benefits of lucid dreaming to the individual. In the last chapter of Part II, ''Individual Differences Associated with Lucid Dreaming,'' Thomas Snyder and Jayne Gackenbach approach the question of individual differences and lucid dream frequency by examining four sets of variables from different functional domains of psychology. Correlations were found between the incidence of dream lucidity and classical personality measures, but this line of inquiry proved less productive than the consideration of the spatial skills of the dreamers. Snyder and Gackenbach review Witkin's model of psychological differentiation, from which the construct of field independence is derived, and find numerous parallels between it and the individual differences found to be associated with lucid dreaming ability. They interpret their widely ranging findings as generally supporting the model of the gifted lucid dreamer as field independent, relying on internal rather than external cues in perceptual and spatial judgments.

The third part discusses applications of lucid dreaming to self-growth and therapy and includes two personal accounts of lucid dreaming.

In ''A Model for Lucidity Training as a Means of Self-Healing and Psychological Growth,'' Paul Tholey argues that the usual nonlucid dream state should be regarded as ''a form of consciousness disorder'' and that the mere induction of lucid dreaming is ''a step towards healing.'' Tholey considers lucid dreaming an important tool in therapy because it allows the dreamer to ''find his own way to the unconscious and its integration into the personality'' without the need for interpretation by the therapist. He notes that in lucid dreams, unconscious conflicts can be resolved through conscious behavior without the dreamer needing to understand the root of the conflict or the logic behind the dream. The basis of Tholey's technique is nonaggressive, courageous interaction with hostile dream figures. He advises that, for the purposes of self-growth, we should seek out threatening situations in our lucid dreams and reports that the majority of clients treated with his lucid dreaming therapy experienced "positive effects on their subsequent dreaming and waking lives."

In the next chapter, Patricia Garfield, Peter Fellows, Gordon Halliday, and Judith R. Malamud individually present their ideas on clinical applications of lucid dreaming. In her introductory comments, Garfield lists 10 different potential benefits of lucid dreams and proposes that lucidity can enable one to deliberately draw on the creative power of dreams. Fellows outlines a therapeutic approach and introduces his concept of the "dream speaker"; Halliday describes his use of lucidity as a treatment for nightmares; and finally, Judith R. Malamud offers a model for therapy using lucidity training in waking and dreams.

An important source of information about the phenomenology of lucid dreaming is individuals who have kept careful records of their experiences over an extended period of time. In "Without a Guru: An Account of My Lucid Dreaming," George Gillespie describes some of his personal experimentation within lucid dreams and their philosophical and religious significance to him. Gillespie's material derives from 435 lucid dreams he recorded over a 9-year period. He provides a unique account of his experiences with conscious "dreamless sleep" that followed his study of the Upanishads while teaching in India.

In the final chapter of Part III, "Personal Experiences in Lucid Dreaming," Alan Roy Worsley, the first person to signal from a lucid dream, describes his laboratory and home experiments and relates his childhood and adolescent experiences with lucid dreaming. He has had thousands of lucid dreams in his 35 years of personal experimentation; here he focuses on the results of a fascinating variety of experiments testing his capacities for voluntary control of dream content.

The fourth section of this book presents theoretical implications of lucid dreaming in several related areas. First are two chapters treating the controversial relationship of lucid dreams and out-of-body (OBE) experiences. LaBerge (1985) proposed that OBEs were hallucinated dream experiences misinterpreted as reality and warned that a strong feeling that "this is real!" is in no way proof of the objective reality of an experience, especially in the face of clear evidence to the contrary. In "Out-of-the-Body Experiences and Dream Lucidity: Empirical Perspectives," Harvey J. Irwin searches for an explanation for the statistical dependence between the occurrence of OBEs and lucid dreams and for the fact that, though this relationship is highly stable, the overlap in occurrence of the two phenomena is small, accounting for only 12% of the variance in the strongest case. He argues that the nature of the association cannot adequately be explained by hypothesizing a "functional connection" (that many OBEs are initiated from lucid dreams), or by proposing that the two experiences are phenomenologically equivalent and are simply interpreted differently at different times, or by the idea of a neurophysiological equivalence between the two subjective experiences. He suggests that OBEs and dream lucidity are sometimes reactions to high levels of cortical arousal that can be evoked by stress and that this accounts for the small but stable correlation between the incidence of these phenomena.

The one common factor between OBEs of all kinds, and lucid dreams, which seems to be most often overlooked in comparisons of the states, is the relative lack of sensory input to an awake and activated mind. Thus the cortical arousal theory proposed by Irwin is incomplete without noting that, at the same time as the arousal, the subject experiences loss of contact with his or her normal experience of reality. Sue Blackmore's "A Theory of Lucid Dreams and OBEs" describes how our way of developing cognitive maps and models of reality based on sensory input and our dependence on these models can account for OBEs, dreams, dream lucidity, and other altered states of consciousness. She answers Irwin's question of why the relationship between OBEs and lucid dreams is as small as it is, considering their similarity, by explaining that, though the two states "are both ways of entering a world of thought and memory unconstrained by sensory input and the restrictions of the body," they are constrained in different ways by the availability or lack of input from the senses and memory.

In "Lucid Dreams in Their Natural Series: Phenomenological and Psychophysiological Findings in Relation to Meditative States," Harry T. Hunt and Robert D. Ogilvie, rather than treating lucid dreaming as an isolated phenomenon of human experience, attempt to place it into a "natural series" composed of related phenomena, including out-of-body experiences, near-death experiences, autoscopic hallucinations, hypnagogic autosymbolism, and particularly "mindfulness" meditation. Hunt and Ogilvie also describe their conception of the role of lucid dreams in experience and review their psychophysiological and phenomenological program of research relating lucid dreaming to meditation. Hunt argues here and elsewhere that dream lucidity may represent the sleep equivalent of waking meditation.

A current topic of interest is the relationship of lucid dreaming to other forms of consciousness in the dream state. For example, Gackenbach and colleagues have recently begun investigations of the relationship of lucid dreaming to "witnessing the dream state," a phenomenon reported as a by-product of meditation in which the meditator is encouraged to "witness" the true nature of the waking, sleeping, and dreaming states. They argue that consciousness is present during sleep in both dream lucidity and dream witnessing but that there are qualitative differences in the role of consciousness in the two phenomena. Preliminary data (Gackenbach, Moorecroft, Alexander, & LaBerge, 1987) suggest that dream witnessing may be, psychologically and physiologically, a less active state than lucid dreaming.

In "Action and Representation in Ordinary and Lucid Dreams," Wynn Schwartz and Mary Godwyn probe the fundamental question of the difference between waking and dreaming reality from the perspective of descriptive psychology. They assert that the central difference between dreaming and waking activity is that, while awake, our action is constrained by the demands of external reality; while we dream, we are limited only by semantic or pictorial constraints of what we can coherently imagine. Others (e.g., LaBerge, 1985) have emphasized that lucid dreams are less constrained than waking reality but constrained nevertheless by psychophysiological limitations on what the dreamer's brain can do as well as the dreamer's expectations about what is possible. On the other hand, the Tibetan yogis of the dream state assert that complete control of dreaming is possible, suggesting that the observed limitations of dream control are ultimately mental, not physiological. Which of these points of view is closer to the truth is one of the many questions remaining for future research.

In the final chapter of the volume, "Dream Psychology: Operating in the Dark," Alan Moffitt, Robert Hoffmann, Janet Mullington, Sheila Purcell, Ross Pigeau, and Roger Wells discuss the scientific significance of lucid dreaming for cognitive psychology, suggesting that the self-reflectiveness of lucidity is especially important to understanding the function of dreaming. They point out two important consequences of lucid dreaming: first, the phenomenon of lucid dreaming renders our understanding of what it is to be awake relative rather than absolute, and second, it enables the development of unique forms of perception and intentional action in the dream state, facilitating "the creation of knowledge based on experience and of experience based on knowledge." Moffitt *et al.* make a strong case for the idea that dream self-reflectiveness and lucid dreaming comprise an essential part of any complete picture of human consciousness.

As we noted at the beginning of this chapter, the field of lucid dream research is still very young; the scientific study of lucid dreaming has been in progress for only a decade. But in that short time, lucid dreaming has shown potential for application in a variety of fields: research on the nature and function of sleep and dreaming, investigation into the relationship of mind and body, studies of the nature of consciousness and cognition, self-improvement, and psychotherapy. With development of more reliable methods of inducing lucid dreams, the accessibility of the lucid dream state will increase, and even more applications will likely be developed. Hopefully, this book will inspire a new generation of researchers to investigate this unique and fascinating state of consciousness and help to fulfill Tart's (1979) prediction that "given a few years of development and refinement of techniques for control of the content of dreams, especially the development of lucidity, we may enter an era of deliberate and controlled phenomenological and scientific exploration of dreaming . . . which promises great excitement as well as great significance" (p. 264).

REFERENCES

Gackenbach, J., Cranson, R., & Alexander, C. (1986). Lucid dreaming, witnessing dreaming, and the transcendental meditation technique: A developmental relationship. *Lucidity Letter, 5,* 34–40.

Gackenbach, J. I., Moorecroft, W., Alexander, C., & LaBerge, S. (1987). Physiological correlates of "consciousness" during sleep in a single TM practitioner. *Sleep Research, 16,* 230.

Hall, C., & Van de Castle, R. (1966). *The content analysis of dreams.* New York: Appleton-Century.

LaBerge, S. (1980). Lucid dreaming as a learnable skill: A case study. *Perceptual and Motor Skills, 51,* 1039–1042.

LaBerge, S. (1985). *Lucid dreaming.* Los Angeles: J. P. Tarcher.

LaBerge, S. (1987, June). *Seeing the light in dreams.* Paper presented at the annual meeting of the Association for the Study of Dreams, Arlington, VA.

Natsoulas, T. (1978). Consciousness. *American Psychologist, 33,* 906–914.

Price, R. (1987, June). Dream content within the partially lucid REM period: A single subject content analysis. In H. Hunt, J. Gackenbach, & S. LaBerge (Co-chairs), *Lucid Dreaming Satellite Symposium* held in conjunction with the annual meeting of the Association for the Study of Dreams, Arlington, VA.

Reed, H. (1977). Meditation and lucid dreaming: A statistical relationship. *Sundance Community Dream Journal, 2,* 237–238.

Tart, C. T. (1979). From spontaneous event to lucidity: A review of attempts to consciously control nocturnal dreaming. In B. Wolman, M. Ullman, & W. Webb (Eds.), *Handbook of dreams: Research, theories, and applications* (pp. 226–268). New York: Van Nostrand Reinhold.

Tholey, P. (1983). Techniques for inducing and manipulating lucid dreams. *Perceptual and Motor Skills, 57,* 70–90.

van Eeden, F. (1913). A study of dreams. *Proceedings of the Society for Psychical Research, 26,* 431–461.

Historical and Cultural Perspectives on Lucid Dreaming

Lucid Dreaming in Western Literature

STEPHEN LaBERGE

Although Plato wrote that the faculty of reason is suspended during sleep, his pupil, Aristotle, was the first to state clearly, in his treatise *On Dreams,* that often, when we are asleep, there is something in our consciousness that tells us that what we are experiencing is only a dream. Beyond merely describing lucid dreaming, the "first scientist" also sought to explain how such a thing could happen. He argued that if someone were to place his finger directly in front of your eyes without your observing his doing it, the resulting double image would cause you to believe that you were seeing two fingers. If on the other hand, you were to observe his finger as it nears your eye, you would not be misled by your double vision into believing that there actually were two fingers. "Exactly so it is in the states of sleep," Aristotle continued, "if the sleeper perceives that he is asleep, and is conscious of the sleeping state during which the perception comes before his mind, it presents itself still, but something within him speaks to this effect: 'The image of Koriskos presents itself, but the real Koriskos is not present'" (Aristotle, 1952, pp. 702–706).

In other words, if we know we are asleep, it should be but a small step to the conclusion that we are dreaming. Although this is true enough, unfortunately for the philosopher's argument, the order of events is usually the other way around: We first recognize we are dreaming, and then, consequently, that we must therefore be asleep.

Aristotle's testimony tells us that lucid dreaming was not unknown to the Athenian philosophers of the fourth century B.C. However, because the ancient Greeks left no actual reports of lucid dreams, we can only surmise what the

---

STEPHEN LaBERGE • Department of Psychology, Stanford University, Stanford, CA 94305.

experience may have meant to them. The ancient Greeks believed that dreams were messages of divine will. So lucid dreams might have had not only the supernatural significance often attributed to them by archaic humanity but a religious aspect as well.

The first actual lucid dream report in Western history is preserved in a letter written in A.D. 415 by St. Augustine. While arguing for the possibility of having experiences after death when the (physical) senses no longer function, he quoted the dream of Gennadius, a physician of Carthage. Augustine explained that Gennadius was suffering from doubts as to whether there was an afterlife. Consequently, he dreamed that a youth "of remarkable appearance and commanding presence" accosted him with the order: "Follow me!" Obediently following the angelic youth, Gennadius came to a city where he heard singing "so exquisitely sweet as to surpass anything he had ever heard." Inquiring what the music was, he was informed that "it is the hymn of the blessed and the holy." Thereupon he awoke and thought of it as "only a dream." Yet the next night, Gennadius dreamed of the same youth, who asked him whether he recognized him. When Gennadius replied, "Certainly!", the young man questioned where he had made his acquaintance. Again, Gennadius's memory "failed him not as to the proper reply," and he recounted the events of the previous dream. The youth then inquired whether these events had taken place in sleep or wakefulness. To Gennadius's reply, "in sleep," the youth declared, "You remember it well; it is true that you saw these things in sleep, but I would have you know that even now you are seeing in sleep."

Gennadius was persuaded of the truth of his dream companion's assertion and thus became conscious of the fact that he was dreaming. The lucid dream continued with the youth proceeding with the next of his leading questions: "Where is your body now?" To Gennadius's proper response, "in my bed," his inquisitor pursued his argument with a rhetorical question: "Do you know that the eyes in this body of yours are now bound and closed, and that with these eyes you are seeing nothing?" Gennadius replied, "I know it." At this the youth set up the conclusion of his argument, demanding, "What then are the eyes with which you see me?" Gennadius, unable to solve this puzzle, remained silent, and his dream tutor "unfolded to him what he was endeavoring to teach him by these questions, triumphantly exclaiming, "As while you are asleep and lying on your bed these eyes of your body are now unemployed and doing nothing, and yet you have eyes with which you behold me, and enjoy this vision, so, after your death, while your bodily eyes shall be wholly inactive, there shall be in you a life by which you shall still live, and a faculty of perception by which you shall still perceive. Beware, therefore, after this of harboring doubts as to whether the life of man shall continue after death" (Kelsey, 1974, pp. 264–265). Augustine tells us that thereby the dreamer's doubts were removed completely.

The force of the argument within Gennadius's lucid dream is diminished by the fact that the reassuring youth was no more able than Gennadius himself to explain the nature of the eyes with which we see in dreams. Seeing was still believing in Augustine's time. Dreaming of seeing something implied that the dream object seen actually existed somewhere outside of the dreamer. Equally, seeing something in a dream implied the existence of dream eyes and a dream body analogous to the physical organs and body but somehow independent of them. Thus, in the fifth century, lucid dreaming must have been considered a kind of conscious "out-of-body" experience (OBE), with the lucid dreamer experiencing what seemed like a foretaste of the afterlife condition of the soul.

There are indications that as early as the eighth century, the Tibetan Buddhists were practicing a form of yoga designed to maintain full waking consciousness during the dream state (Evans-Wentz, 1935). The Tibetans were the first to reach the understanding that dreams were solely the mental creation of the dreamer—a sophisticated concept consistent with current scientific thought. To the Tibetan yogis, the lucid dream presented an opportunity to experiment with and realize the subjective nature of the dream state and by extension, all experience.

In the flowering of Islamic civilization several centuries later, we again find reference to lucid dreaming. In the twelfth century, Ibn El-Arabi, the famous Spanish Sufi known in the Arab world as "the Greatest Master," is reported to have asserted that "a person must control his thoughts in a dream. The training of this alertness will produce great benefits for the individual. Everyone should apply himself to the attainment of this ability of such great value" (Shah, 1964, p. 141).

A century later, in Christendom, St. Thomas Aquinas mentioned lucid dreaming in passing, citing Aristotle's supposition that the senses may occasionally show relatively little attenuation during sleep. Aquinas wrote that this happens especially "towards the end of sleep, in sober man and in those who are gifted with a strong imagination." He went on to explain that in this event "not only does the imagination retain its freedom, but also the common sense is partly freed; so that sometimes while asleep a man may judge that what he sees is a dream, discerning as it were, between things and their images" (Aquinas, 1947, p. 430). Medieval Europe evidently knew of lucid dreaming. But dreams were generally held in some disrepute during the Middle Ages and were more frequently considered the inventions of demons than of God. Perhaps lucid dreaming was the sort of risky talent that might have resulted in the dreamer's being burned at the stake.

Although all but unknown today, Pierre Gassendi was considered by his seventeenth-century contemporaries as "one of the three greatest living philosophers, Descartes and Hobbes being the other two" (Brush, 1972, p. vii). Though Descartes had apparently heard of lucid dreaming, his entire skeptical philosophy was founded on his own inability to distinguish wakefulness from sleep; Hobbes likewise was unable to tell the difference between the two states. Gassendi, however, not only recognized the fact that these two states are fundamentally different but also knew from personal experience that it is possible at times to realize one is dreaming. Having his own lucid dreams to reflect upon no doubt aided Gassendi's understanding of the phenomenon. In fact, his insightful explanation of lucid dreaming represented a very significant advance over Aristotle's. Aristotle believed that the sleeper perceives by means of an external sense that he or she is asleep and thereby infers that he or she must be dreaming. Gassendi contradicted this idea, explaining that the fact that the understanding "can realize that it is dreaming, or understand that it is imagining, is nothing more than the fact that it can think that it is thinking, which is the privilege of the internal faculty and is not granted to the external senses." Gassendi also argued against the sort of reasoning that convinced Gennadius he could have experiences after death without his corporeal senses, because, he believed, he did not need them while dreaming. Gassendi considered the understanding to be a function of the brain rather than being independent of it. Because the brain possesses within itself the power of reflection or consciousness

> when it is dreaming it can recognize and scrutinize to a certain extent the things it is imagining with the same facility that it can recognize and scrutinize them when it is awake. And since we are often amazed when we are awake at the absurd things we think in dreams, it is not surprising that sometimes when these incongruities occur in a dream, the same sort of amazement is stimulated and consequently these things appear absurd although we are dreaming. [Gassendi knew this from his personal experience with lucid dreaming; he testified,] This is precisely what happens to me when I seem to see men at the same time I remember they are dead. Immediately the thought occurs to me that I am dreaming since dead men do not come back. (Brush, 1972, p. 195)

Here, at the threshold of the Age of Reason, lucid dreaming was viewed as a product of the sleeper's brain rather than as journeys of the soul or messages from God. Around the same time, the English author Robert Burton expressed this sentiment wit the phrase, "The Gods send not our dreams, we make our own" (MacKenzie, 1965, p. 81), thereby essentially stating the modern conception of dreams. Nevertheless, a few centuries would pass before the idea of dreams as a creation of the sleeper's brain would gain universal acceptance in the scientific world.

In a letter written in 1779, Thomas Reid, the philosopher, recounted how, as a youth, he was plagued by nightmares that not only disturbed his sleep but left a "disagreeable impression" on him during the followng day. Finally it occured to him that

> it was worth trying whether it was possible to recollect that it was all a dream, and that I was in no real danger. I often went to sleep with my mind as strongly impressed as I could with this thought, that I never in my lifetime was in any real danger, and that every fright I had was a dream. After many fruitless endeavors to recollect this when the danger appeared, I effected it at last, and have often, when I was sliding over a precipice into the abyss, recollected that it was all a dream, and boldly jumped down. The effect of this commonly was that I immediately awoke. But I awoke calm and intrepid, which I thought a greater acquisition. (Seafield, 1865, p. 194)

Reid added that "after this my dreams were never uneasy, and in a short time I dreamed not at all." Given the findings of modern sleep research, we have to assume that, actually, Reid merely ceased to remember his dreams, presumably because they no longer frightened him awake.

The Marquis d'Hervey de Saint-Denys was the nineteenth-century's great innovator in the field of lucid dream research. He was a professor of Chinese literature and language at the College de France, and an industrious and ingenious experimenter who recorded his dreams from the time he was 13 years old. Sigmund Freud described him as "the most energetic opponent of those who seek to depreciate psychical functioning in dreams" (Freud, 1900/1965, p. 93).

The Marquis documented more than 20 years of dream research in his remarkable book, *Dreams and the Means to Direct Them*, published anonymously in 1867. Unfortunately, the book never seems to have been widely available (until recently; see Saint-Denys, 1982). Freud was unable to obtain a copy "in spite of all efforts" (Freud, 1900/1965, p. 93), with the regrettable consequence that the founder of psychoanalysis never gained more than the most superficial acquaintance with the possibilities of dream control.

In the first part of his book, Saint-Denys describes the development of his ability to control his dreams: first, increasing his dream recall; next, becoming aware that he was dreaming; then, learning to awaken at will; and finally, being able, to a certain extent, to direct his dream dramas. The second part of *Dreams and the Means to Direct Them* reviews prior dream theories and presents his own ideas based on extensive self-experimentation. A notion of the Marquis's experimental approach to dreaming can be gained from the following extract:

> I fell asleep. I could see clearly all the little objects which decorate my study. My attention alighted on a porcelain tray, in which I keep my pencils and pens, and which has some very unusual decoration on it. . . . I suddenly thought: whenever I have seen this tray in waking life, it has always been in one piece. What if I were to break it in my dream? How would my imagination represent the broken tray? I immediately broke it in pieces. I picked up the pieces and examined them closely. I observed the sharp edges of the lines of breakage, and the jagged cracks which split the decorative figures in several places. I had seldom had such a vivid dream. (McCreery, 1973, p. 88)

Many of Saint-Denys' experiments can be criticized for failing to control for expectation, an important factor in lucid dreams. However, the Marquis is to be commended without qualification for demonstrating that it is possible to learn to dream consciously.

Not everyone who has made the effort to learn this skill has had such success. Frederic W. H. Myers, a classical scholar at Cambridge and one of the founders of the Society for Psychical Research, complained that, by "mere painstaking effort," he succeeded on only 3 nights out of 3,000 in realizing that he was dreaming. Although Myers himself attributed his small gains to his "poor endowments" as a dreamer, he may serve as a reminder of the fact that what is needed is not "painstaking," but effective effort. In an article on automatic writing and other psychic phenomena, Myers briefly digressed to explain that

> I have long thought that we are too indolent in regard to our dreams; that we neglect precious occasions of experiment for want of a little resolute direction of the will. . . . We should constantly represent to ourselves what points we should like to notice and test in dream; and then when going to sleep we should impress upon our minds that we are going to try an experiment;—that we are going to carry into our dreams enough of our waking self to tell us that they *are* dreams, and to prompt us to psychological inquiry. (Myers, 1887, pp. 241)

Myers then quoted a "curious dream" of his own, hoping that "its paltry commonplaceness may perhaps avert the suspicion that it has been touched up for recital":

> I was, I thought, standing in my study; but I observed that the furniture had not its usual distinctness—that everything was blurred and somehow evaded a direct gaze. It struck me that this must be because I was *dreaming*. This was a great delight to me, as giving the opportunity of experimentation. I made a strong effort to keep calm, knowing the risk of waking. I wanted most of all to see and speak to somebody, to see whether they were like the real persons, and how they behaved. I remembered that my wife and children were away at the time [which was true], and I did not reason to the effect that they might be present in a dream, though absent from home in reality. I therefore wished to see one of the servants; but I was afraid to ring the bell, lest the shock would wake me. I very cautiously walked downstairs—after calculating that I should be more sure to find someone in the pantry or kitchen than in a workroom, where I first thought of going. As I walked downstairs I looked carefully at the stair-carpet, to see whether I could visualise better in dream than in waking life. I found that this was *not* so; the dream-carpet was not like what I knew it in truth to be; rather, it was a thin, ragged carpet, apparently vaguely generalised from memories of seaside lodgings. I reached the pantry door, and here again had to stop and calm myself. The door opened and a servant appeared,—quite unlike any of my own. This is all I can say, for the excitement of perceiving that I had created a new personage woke me with a shock. The dream was very clear in my mind; I was thoroughly awake; I perceived its great interest to me and I stamped it on my mind—I venture to say—almost exactly as I tell it here. (Myers, 1887, pp. 241–242)

A few more brief references complete our understanding of the nineteenth-century view of lucid dreaming. These are primarily little more than testimonials for or against the existence of lucid dreams. Among the doubters, two were of sufficient renown to require mention here. The first was the French psychologist Alfred Maury. Although a pioneer in the scientific investigation of dreams, he was evidently personally unacquainted with the phenomenon of lucid dreaming. He was quoted as claiming in regard to lucid dreams that "these dreams could not be dreams" (van Eeden, 1913, p. 433). The other skeptic was an English psychologist of even greater eminence—Havelock Ellis. Ellis declared his disbelief in lucid dreams by stating that "I do not believe that such a thing is really possible, though it has been borne witness to by many philosophers and others from Aristotle . . . onwards" (Ellis, 1911, p. 64).

Among the believers, we find Ernst Mach of the University of Vienna, who footnoted his discussion of what he considered the characteristic inertness of attention in dreams with the following qualification: "The intellect often sleeps only in part . . . we reflect, in the dream-state, concerning dreams, recognize them as such by their eccentricities, but are immediately pacified again." The eminent psychologist showed his personal acquaintance with the exceptional case presented by lucid dreams, recounting in the same note that "at a time when much engrossed with the subject of space-sensation, I dreamed of a walk in the woods. Suddenly I noticed the defective perspective displacement of the trees, and by this recognized I was dreaming. The missing displacements, however, were immediately supplied" (Mach, 1900, pp. 114–115).

Charles Dickens, in a letter written in 1851, demonstrated his insight into the intricacies of dream thought that can lead to the onset of lucidity. He wrote,

> We all fall off the Tower, we all skim above the ground at a great pace and can't keep on it, we all say "this must be a dream, because I was in this strange, low-roofed, beam constructed place once before, and it turned out to be a dream" . . . we all confound the living with the dead, and all frequently have a knowledge or suspicion that we are doing it. (Edel, 1982, p. 178)

Friedrich Nietzsche, one of the most famous philosophers of the nineteenth century, while arguing that we use dreams to train ourselves to live, explained that "the whole 'Divine Comedy' of life, and the Inferno" pass before the dreamer "not merely . . . like pictures on the wall—for he lives and suffers in these scenes—and yet not without," the philosopher added in apparent reference to lucid dreaming, "that fleeting sensation of appearance. And perhaps many a one will, like myself, recollect having sometimes called out cheeringly and not without success amid the dangers and terrors of dream life: 'it is a dream! I will dream on!'" (deBecker, 1965, p. 139). Thus we see that Nietzsche, "the prophet of the modern age," had lucid dreams. He was also considered the prophet of psychoanalysis by the founder of the movement, Sigmund Freud.

The first edition of Freud's *The Interpretation of Dreams* made no overt reference to lucid dreaming at all. However, in the second edition, Freud noted,

> there are some people who are quite clearly aware during the night that they are asleep and dreaming and who thus seem to possess the faculty of consciously directing their dreams. If, for instance, a dreamer of this kind is dissatisfied with the turn taken by a dream, he can break it off without waking up and start it again in another direction— just as a popular dramatist may under pressure give his play a happier ending. (Freud, 1909/1965, p. 611)

Freud continued with what he considered an example of the usefulness of consciousness in dreams: "Or another time, if his dream had led him into a sexually exciting situation, he can think to himself, 'I won't go on with this dream any further and exhaust myself with an emission; I'll hold back for a real situation instead'" (Freud, 1909/1965, p. 611). It is likely that the subject of

Freud's remarks—the unnamed dreamer of the 1909 edition—was Freud himself. This interpretation leads to the conclusion that Freud apparently had erotic dreams upon occasion and "under pressure" from his moralistic superego was compelled to give his dream plays more "acceptably upright" endings. Victorian prudishness, or guilt about enjoying sexual fantasies, seems a much more plausible explanation for his holding back from wish fulfillment in his dreams than does the fear of exhausting himself.

In all his voluminous writings, Freud added but a single paragraph to what he had already said about lucid dreaming. In the fourth edition of *The Interpretation of Dreams*, he wrote:

> The Marquis d'Hervey de Saint-Denys claimed to have acquired the power of accelerating the course of his dreams just as he pleased, and of giving them any direction he chose. It seems as though in his case the wish to sleep had given place to another preconscious wish, namely to observe his dreams and enjoy them. Sleep is just as compatible with a wish of this sort as it is with a mental reservation to wake up if some particular condition is fulfilled (e.g. in the case of a nursing mother or wet-nurse). (Freud, 1900/1965, p. 611)

Thus Freud admitted that consciousness in dreams can not only provide the dreamer with a means of escape from negative, embarrassing, or "immoral" dreams but also can promote a positive attitude toward dreams—allowing one to enjoy them with full awareness.

To Frederik Willems van Eeden, a Dutch psychiatrist and well-known author, we owe the term *lucid dream*. Van Eeden kept a diary of his own dreams for many years, noting with particular care those cases in which he had "full recollection of [his] day-life, and could act voluntarily," yet was fast asleep; it was these lucid dreams that aroused his "keenest interest" (1913, p. 437). Van Eeden at first veiled his observations in a novel called *The Bride of Dreams*, because, as he later admitted, the fictional guise allowed him "to freely deal with delicate matters." In 1913, he presented a paper to the Society for Psychical Research, reporting on 352 of his lucid dreams, collected between 1898 and 1912. "In these lucid dreams," van Eeden declared, "the re-integration of the psychic functions is so complete that the sleeper reaches a state of perfect awareness and is able to direct his attention, and to attempt different acts of free volition. Yet the sleep, as I am able confidently to state, is undisturbed, deep and refreshing" (van Eeden, 1913, p. 437).

By a curious coincidence, van Eeden's first lucid dream was quite similar to the experience of Mach's quoted previously. "I obtained my first glimpse of this lucidity," wrote van Eeden, "in the following way. I dreamt that I was floating through a landscape with bare trees, knowing that it was April, and I remarked that the perspective of the branches and twigs changed quite naturally. Then I made the reflection, during sleep, that my fancy would never be able to invent or to make an image as intricate as the perspective movement of little twigs seen in floating by" (van Eeden, 1913, p. 438).

Van Eeden, like Saint-Denys, whom he quotes, took an experimental approach to his dreams, as is illustrated by the following report:

> On Sept. 9, 1904, I dreamt that I stood at a table before a window. On the table were different objects. I was perfectly well aware that I was dreaming and I considered what sorts of experiments I could make. I began by trying to break glass, by beating it with a stone. I put a small goblet of glass on two stones and struck it with another stone. Yet it would not break. Then I took a fine claret-glass from the table and struck it with my fist, with all my might, at the same time reflecting how dangerous it would be to do this in waking life; yet the glass remained whole. But lo! when I looked at it again after some time, it was broken. (van Eeden, 1913, p. 439)

"It broke all right," van Eeden continued, "but a little too late, like an actor who misses his cue." He explained that "this gave me a very curious impression of being in a fake-world, cleverly imitated, but with small failures. I took the broken glass and threw it out of the window, in order to observe whether I could hear the tinkling. I heard the noise all right and I even saw two dogs run away from it quite naturally. I thought what a good imitation this comedy-world was" (van Eeden, 1913, p. 439). At about the same time that van Eeden was carrying out his investigations in The Netherlands, the biologist Yves Delage was engaged in a similar study of his own lucid dreams in France. Delage characterized his lucid dreams in the following terms:

> I say to myself: here I am in a situation which may be troublesome or pleasant, but I know very well that it is completely unreal. From this point of my dream, knowing that I cannot run any risk, I allow scenes to unfold themselves before me. I adopt the attitude of an interested spectator, watching an accident or catastrophe which cannot affect him. I think: over there are waiting for me people who want to kill me; I then try to run away; but suddenly, I realize that I am dreaming and I say to myself: since I have nothing to fear I am going to meet my enemies, I will defy them, I will even strike them in order to see what will happen. However although I am sure enough of the illusory character of the situation to adopt a course of action which would be unwise in real life, I have to overcome an instinctive feeling of fear. Several times, I have in this way thrown myself on purpose into some danger in order to see what would come of it. (Green, 1968, pp. 142–143)

On the other side of the English Channel, Mary Arnold-Forster was also exploring the world of dreams. Drawing from her own experience she wrote: "There are dreams and dreams, and we must get rid of the assumption that they all resemble each other" (Arnold-Forster, 1921, p. x), a fact well worth remembering. Some of the dreams described in her book were lucid, though most were not. Of relevance here is that she, too, describes how she learned to deal with her frightening dreams by recognizing that they were "only dreams." She also seems to have had success with teaching this method to children, a practice surely deserving wider application. It does not appear, however, that Arnold-Forster developed her dream consciousness very extensively, perhaps due to the fact that her only source of information on lucid dreams seems to have been the very few experiences of Myers quoted before.

At about the same time, Hugh Calloway, a countryman of Mary Arnold-Forster, undertook much more extensive experimentation with lucid dreams and closely related states. Publishing his occultist writings under the pen name of Oliver Fox, he apparently discovered lucid dreaming completely on his own, developing nonetheless a high degree of proficiency in the area. In the summer of 1902, when Calloway was a 16-year-old college student of science and electrical engineering in London, he dreamt a lucid dream that he said marked "the real beginning" of his research. "I dreamed" he wrote,

> that I was standing on the pavement outside my home. The sun was rising behind the Roman wall, and the waters of Bletchingden Bay were sparkling in the morning light. I could see the tall trees at the corner of the road and the top of the old grey tower beyond the Forty Steps. In the magic of the early sunshine the scene was beautiful enough even then. Now the pavement was not of the ordinary type, but consisted of small, bluish-grey rectangular stones, with their long sides at right-angles to the white curb. I was about to enter the house when, on glancing casually at these stones, my attention became riveted by a passing strange phenomenon, so extraordinary that I could not believe my eyes—they had seemingly all changed their position in the night, and the long sides were now parallel to the curb! Then the solution flashed upon me: though this glorious summer morning seemed as real as real could be, I was dreaming! With the realization of this fact, the quality of the dream changed in a manner very difficult to convey to one who has not had this experience. Instantly, the vividness of life increased a hundred-fold. Never had sea and sky and trees shone with such glamourous beauty; even the commonplace houses seemed alive and mystically beautiful. Never had I felt so absolutely well, so clear-brained, so inexpressibly *free!* The sensation was exquisite beyond words; but it lasted only a few minutes and I awoke. (Fox, 1962, pp. 32–33)

Calloway called his lucid dreams, dreams of knowledge, "for one had in [them] the *knowledge* that one was really dreaming." With a certain ostentation, he pictured himself in his dreams of knowledge "free as air, secure in the consciousness of my true condition and the knowledge that I could always wake if danger threatened, moving like a little god through the glorious scenery of the Dream World" (Fox, 1962, p. 34).

As we have seen, the experience of lucid dreaming can pose some formidable paradoxes for the philosophically minded. In the 1920s, Ram Narayana, an Indian physician and editor, widely circulated a 14-item questionnaire on dreaming "to a broad spectrum of representative men, Eastern and Western, from classes of religion, philosophy and science, including the so-called materialists, realists, idealists, and dogmatic theologians" (Narayana, 1922, Vol. 2, p. xii). The question relevant to the present context was number 8: "Is it possible for a dreamer to remain cognizant during his dream state of the fact that he is dreaming? If so, what are the means to acquire this power?" (Narayana, 1922, Vol. 2, p. 530).

Given the extreme range of world views represented by the respondents to Narayana's questionnaire, a similar extremity of answers was only to be expected. The following is a sample of some of the opinions expressed by Westerners on point 8: "No, it is not possible," some flatly stated. Or, on the contrary, "It is quite possible for the dreamer to be cognizant during his dream state that he is actually dreaming" asserted another. "But such power can come only through intense and prolonged concentration on things spiritual." A psychiatrist contended that "it often happens, especially in relatively shallow sleep." But, he added, "It is undesirable to spoil good sleeping habits for this purpose." Another conceded that in "rare cases," lucid dreaming occurs "where one has diligently cultivated real spirituality." A professor held the view that while there is no "peculiar means of acquiring this power," it is in any case "common and worthless." Another declares, on the contrary, that gaining this power is "a task of utmost difficulty, and involves the development of every other faculty to its full expression." One respondent asserts, rather cryptically, that "one who could attain this power has far more important matters to occupy him" (Narayana, 1922, Vol. 2, p. 190ff.).

The previously enumerated fragments convey a clear enough picture of the confused state of educated opinion concerning lucid dreaming in the West during the first part of the twentieth century. In general, the Eastern responses showed a far greater degree of direct and indirect acquaintance with the phenomenon, as is well illustrated by the answer of Babu Bhagavan Das to point 8:

> For a dreamer to remain cognizant of the fact that he is dreaming is to begin to "wake up" on that plane, i.e., to begin to exercise his will deliberately, and to pass, on that plane and in that world, from the condition of the helpless infant to that of the adult, and to convert that state and plane from "dreaming" into an extension of the waking plane and state, by a corresponding extension of faculty. (Narayana, 1922, Vol. 2, p. 248)

The Babu continued with a survey of the techniques for developing lucid dreaming, explaining that

> The idea running through most of such methods seems to be to put the body to sleep, but keep the mind awake. The continuous mental repetition of a mantra, particularly the Om (a-u-m) sound, whatever the work one may be engaged in, is said to be one of the most frequent of such devices; thereby, gradually, the mind comes to remain awake, repeating that sound, even when the body has fallen asleep. (Narayana, 1922, Vol. 2, p. 238).

An awareness of the further potential of lucid dreaming can be found in Thomas Mann's great novel, *The Magic Mountain* (1927/1969). Here we have the protagonist, Hans Castorp, whose initiation into life's mysteries takes the form of a lucid dream that resolves all his questions about the seeming contradictions of life and death. Mann's hero is described as "searching for the Grail— that is to say, the Highest: knowledge, wisdom, consecration, the philosopher's stone . . . the elixir of life" (p. 726). Lost in the perilous mountains in a deadly blizzard, Hans loses consciousness of his surroundings and collapses in the snow. He now dreams himself a world—a delightful vision of sunshine, comfort, and harmony—in direct contrast to his true surroundings of harshness, elemental chaos, and violence. Hans joyously walks through this idyllic scene, enjoying the friendliness and courtesy of the happy, yet serious and noble people of his dream. But soon, he discovers a horrible temple of human sacrifice in which he witnesses two hideous old hags tearing apart a child over a cauldron. The shock of this vision awakens him.

Upon awakening, Hans says to himself, "I felt it was a dream, all along . . . lovely and horrible dream. I knew all the time I was making it up myself." (p. 495). He reflects on his "dream poem of humanity" that brings him to the knowledge that "It is love, not reason, that is stronger than death." He declares, "My dream has given [this insight] to me, in utter clearness, that I may know it forever" (p. 497). Mann says of Castorp: "If he does not find the Grail, yet he divines it, in his deathly dream" (p. 727). In this fictional work we see the possibility that conscious dreams can be revelations by which to guide our lives.

The Russian philosopher, Piotr D. Ouspensky, wishing "to verify a rather fantastic idea" that he said occurred to him as an adolescent, asked himself the question, "*Was it not possible to preserve consciousness in dreams,* that is, to know while dreaming that one is asleep and *to think consciously* as we think when awake?" (Ouspensky, 1931/1971, p. 243). Ouspensky found, as others had, that the answer was yes. Ouspensky's main interest in lucid dreaming, or "half-dream states," as he called them, was simply to observe the formation and transformation of ordinary dreams. He claimed that

> the fact is that in "half-dream states" I was having all the dreams I usually had. But I was fully conscious, I could see and understand how these dreams were created, what they were built from, what was their cause, and in general what was cause and what was effect. Further, I saw that in "half-dream states" I had a certain control over dreams. I could create them and could see what I wanted to see, although this was not always successful and must not be understood too literally. Usually I only gave the first impetus, and after that the dreams developed as it were of their own accord, sometimes greatly astonishing me by the unexpected and strange turns they took. (Ouspensky, 1931/1971, p. 245)

Here is Ouspensky's description of one of his "half-dream states":

> I remember once seeing myself in a large empty room without windows. Besides myself there was in the room only a small black kitten. "I am dreaming," I say to myself. "How can I know whether I am really asleep or not? Suppose I try this way. Let this black kitten be transformed into a large white dog. In a waking state it is impossible and if it comes off it will mean that I am asleep." I say this to myself and immediately the black kitten becomes transformed into a large white dog. At the same time the opposite wall disappears, disclosing a mountain landscape with a river like a ribbon receding into the distance.
>
> "This is curious," I say to myself; "I did not order this landscape. Where did it come from?" Some faint recollection begins to stir in me, a recollection of having seen this landscape somewhere and of its being somehow connected with the white dog. But I feel that if I let myself go into it I shall forget the most important thing that I have to remember, namely, *that I am asleep and am conscious of myself.* (Ouspensky, 1931/1971, p. 249)

A. E. Brown, in an article reporting his having nearly 100 experiences of lucid dreams also showed himself familiar with most of the earlier writings with the significant exception of Saint-Denys. Apart from testifying to the existence of the phenomenon, Brown was chiefly concerned with countering the notion that lucid dreaming is a variety of daydreaming. He introduced a valuable and subsequently widely used method for deciding whether or not one is dreaming: jumping into the air and testing the sensation of gravity (Brown, 1936). The main interest of the article is that it is one of the only two papers devoted to the topic of lucid dreaming to be found in the mainstream of scientific psychology until the last several years.

The second paper appeared in a German psychological journal 2 years later. The author, Harold von Moers-Messmer, reported and commented on 22 of the lucid dreams he had between 1934 and 1938. That Moers-Messmer possessed an unusually logical mind can be seen from the following report:

> From the top of a rather low and unfamiliar hill, I look out across a wide plain towards the horizon. It crosses my mind that I have no idea what time of year it is. I check the sun's position. It appears almost straight above me with its usual brightness. This is surprising, as it occurs to me that it is now autumn, and the sun was much lower only a short time ago. I think it over: the sun is now perpendicular to the equator, so here it has to appear at an angle of approximately 45 degrees. So if my shadow does not correspond to my own height, I must be dreaming. I examine it: it is about 30 centimeters long. It takes considerable effort for me to believe this almost blindingly bright landscape and all of its features to be only an illusion. (Moers-Messmer, 1938, pp. 299–300)

When Moers-Messmer became conscious within his dreams, he made use of the opportunity to satisfy his scientific curiosity, carrying out a variety of experiments. After his "indestructible intellectualism" had emerged in one lucid dream, he continued:

> Reflecting upon what I should do now, it suddenly gets dark. After a little while, it grows light again. After some consideration, the word that I have long borne in mind occurs to me: "Magic!" I find myself in a city, on a large, relatively uncrowded street. Next to one of the houses I see nearby an entrance gate; the doors are closed, and flanked to right and left by two wide, jutting pillars. These are composed of five squared-stone blocks piled on top of each other, upon which there is projecting relief work in the shape of garlands. I cry out, "This will all grow much larger!" At first nothing happens, even while I fixedly imagine that the gateway is larger than the way I see it. All at once, a great number of little pieces of stone come crumbling out of the second highest block on the left, which is set in slightly towards the inside. More and more keep coming, mixed with sand and larger stones, until there is nothing left of the block, while on the ground there now lies a whole pile of rubble. Through the open space that has thus resulted, I can see a gray wall towards the back. (Moers-Messmer, 1938, pp. 304–305)

The preceding illustrates Moers-Messmer's use of key words (i.e., "magic") in the extract to remind him of what he wanted to do in the dream. In another lucid dream, he sought to test whether people really speak in dreams:

> I am in a large street, with people passing by. I repeatedly feel that I want to address myself to someone, but I always hesitate at the last moment. Finally I gather up all my courage, and say to a male personage who is just passing by, "You're a monkey." I chose this particular phrase in order to provoke him into a harsh reply. He remains standing there and looks at me. It is so uncomfortable for me that I would have most liked to have apologized. Then I hear his voice saying, "I've been waiting for that; you've been weighing it over in your mind for a long time." Whether I even saw him speaking, I do not recall. He continues speaking with the intonations of a preacher; however, I realize that I will soon have forgotten everything. I therefore grab for my notebook and pull it out of my pocket. Then I realize the absurdity of my intentions, and I throw it aside. (Moers-Messmer, 1938, p. 296)

Ten years after Moers-Messmer's all but unknown article, Nathan Rapport, an American psychiatrist, extolled the delights of lucid dreaming in an article entitled "Pleasant Dreams!" According to Rapport, "the nature of dreams may be studied best on those rare occasions when one is aware that he is dreaming." His method for lucid dream induction appears to be similar to that used by Ouspensky: "While in bed awaiting sleep, the experimenter interrupts his thoughts every few minutes with an effort to recall the mental item vanishing before each intrusion by that inquisitive attention." This habit of introspection is cultivated until it continues into sleep itself. The degree of enthusiasm Rapport had for lucid dreaming is clearly conveyed by the terms in which he concluded his article:

> As to the mysterious glories all too seldom remembered from dreams—why atı mpt to describe them? Those magical fantasies, the weird but lovely gardens, these luı,inous grandeurs; they are enjoyed only by the dreamer who observes them with active interest, peeping with appreciative wakeful mind, grateful for glories surpassing those the most accomplished talents can devise in reality. The fascinating beauty found in dreams amply rewards their study. But there is a higher call. The study and cure of the mind out of touch with reality can be aided by attention to dreams. And when secrets are wrested from the mystery of life, many of them will have been discovered in pleasant dreams. (Rapport, 1948, p. 317)

Lucid dreams can convey a sense of such phenomenal significance to the dreamer that they seem "more real than real." An experience of this order led J. H. M. Whiteman, a lecturer in mathematics at the University of Capetown, to exclaim, "I have never been awake before!" (Whiteman, 1961, p. 186). Whiteman's extraordinary world is revealed by his book, *The Mystical Life,* which drew on the almost 3,000 personal experiences that he had recorded over a 40-year period. With a mathematician's zeal, he classified his miscellany of lucid and nonlucid dreams, hypnagogic imagery, daydreams, "out-of-body experiences," and so on, according to a complicated set of criteria compounded from a mixture of experiential characteristics and metaphysical assumptions.

In 1966, a Czechoslovakian psychiatric journal published an article by Z. Havlczek entitled "A Contribution to the Dynamics of 'Lucid' Dreams" (Havlczek, 1966). It made reference to a 1951 work by S. Nevole, whose Czech title translates as "On So-Called Lucid Dreams." These few references suggest the possible existence behind the Iron Curtain of a body of knowledge on lucid dreaming unknown to the West.

We have seen in this chapter that lucid dreaming has been known since antiquity. But like electricity—a phenomenon also known to the Greeks—it was not until recently that lucid dreams have received serious scientific attention. The last 20 years have witnessed a great expansion of both scientific and popular interest in lucid dreaming. One important instigator of this was Celia Green's *Lucid Dreams,* published in 1968. Her book was based upon the published accounts we have reviewed here, as well as case material.

For accounts of the extensive literature that has amassed since Green's seminal work, see LaBerge (1985) and LaBerge and Gackenbach (1986).

REFERENCES

Aquinas, St. Thomas. (1947). *Summa theologica* (Vol. 1). New York: Benziger.

Aristotle. (1952). *On dreams.* In R. M. Hutchinson (Ed.), *Great books of the Western world: Vol. 8* (pp. 702–706). Chicago: Encyclopedia Briticannica.

Arnold-Forster, M. (1921). *Studies in dreams.* London: Allen & Unwin.

Brown, A. E. (1936). Dreams in which the dreamer knows he is asleep. *Journal of Abnormal Psychology, 31,* 59–66.

Brush, C. B. (1972). *The selected works of Pierre Gassendi.* New York: Johnson Reprint Corp.

deBecker, R. (1965). *The understanding of dreams.* London: Allen & Unwin.

Edel, L. (1982). *Stuff of sleep and dreams.* New York: Avon.

Ellis, H. (1911). *The world of dreams.* London: Oxford University Press.

Evans-Wentz, W. Y. (1935). *Tibetan yoga and secret doctrines.* London: Oxford University Press.

Fox, O. (1962). *Astral projection.* New York: University Books.

Freud, S. (1965). *The interpretation of dreams.* New York: Avon Books. (Original work published 1900)

Green, C. (1968). *Lucid dreams.* Oxford: Institute for Psychophysical Research.

Havliczek, Z. (1966). Contribution to the dynamics of "lucid" dreams. *Cekoslovenska Psychiatrie, 62,* 309–318.

Kelsey, M. T. (1974). *God, dreams and revelation.* New York: Augsburg.

LaBerge, S. (1985). *Lucid dreaming.* Los Angeles: Tarcher.

LaBerge, S., & Gackenbach, J. I. (1986). Lucid dreaming. In B. B. Wolman & M. Ullman (Eds.), *Handbook of states of consciousness* (pp. 159–198). New York: Van Nostrand Reinhold.

Mach, E. (1900). *The analysis of the sensations* (2nd ed.). Jena: Fisher.

MacKenzie, N. (1965). *Dreams and dreaming.* New York: Vanguard.

McCreery, C. (1973). *Psychical phenomena and the physical world.* Oxford: Institute of Psychophysical Research.

Mann, T. (1969). *The magic mountain.* New York: Vintage. (Original work published 1927)

Moers-Messmer, H. von (1938). Traume mit der gleichzeitigen Erkenntnis des Traumzustandes [Dreams with concurrent knowledge of the dream state]. *Archives fur Psychologie, 102,* 291–318. (Translated by Beth Mugge).

Myers, F. W. H. (1887). Automatic writing—3. *Proceedings of the Society for Psychical Research 4(Part II).*

Narayana, R. (Ed.). (1922). *The dream problem and its many solutions in search after ultimate truth* (Vols. 1 & 2). Delhi, India: Practical Medicine.

Ouspensky, P. (1971). *A new model of the universe*. New York: Random House. (Original work published 1931)

Rapport, N. (1948). Pleasant dreams. *Psychiatric Quarterly, 22*, 309–317.

Saint-Denys, H. (1982). *Dreams and how to guide them*. London: Duckworth.

Seafield, F. (1865). *The literature and curiosity of dreams*. London: Chapman & Hall.

Shah, I. (1964). *The Sufis*. London: Octagon Press.

van Eeden, F. (1913). A study of dreams. *Proceedings for the Society for Psychical Research, 26*, 431–61.

Whiteman, J. H. M. (1961). *The mystical life*. London: Faber & Faber.

3

Lucid Dreams in Tibetan Buddhism

GEORGE GILLESPIE

Lucid dreaming is discussed in centuries-old Tibetan Buddhist texts. A simple definition that comes out of our present scientific studies is that lucid dreaming is "awareness of dreaming while in the dream state" (Gackenbach, 1980, p. 253). Traditional Tibetan religion and modern psychology are very diverse contexts for discussions of lucid dreaming. To show that the Tibetans are discussing the same subject that our contemporary dream researchers describe, I quote (in translation) a sample statement from a Tibetan text.

> If . . . the dream be about fire, think, "What fear can there be of fire which occurreth in a dream!" Holding to this thought, trample upon the fire. In like manner, tread under foot whatever be dreamt. (Evans-Wentz, 1958, p. 220)

It is clear that the text is talking about lucid dreaming as we understand it.

Nevertheless, in the texts, the teaching about lucid dreams is thoroughly mixed with traditional Buddhist metaphysics and religion and is based largely upon an esoteric understanding of the body and the universe. Through applying the teaching, the Buddhist sees the truth of the doctrine of illusion, uses dreams as a means of worship, and progresses toward liberation by using dream meditation.

THE SIX TOPICS OF NĀROPĀ

The teaching on lucid dreaming is one of the six topics (or laws or yogas) attributed to the Indian teacher Nāropā. Nāropā was a Tantric Buddhist of the tenth (Tucci, 1980) or eleventh (Guenther, 1963) century A.D. in India, where he

GEORGE GILLESPIE • Department of Oriental Studies, University of Pennsylvania, Philadelphia, PA 19104.

27

was known as Nāḍapāda. Nāropā was the pupil of Tīlopā. The late twelfth-century biography of Nāropā (Guenther, 1963) describes how Tīlopā taught the six topics to Nāropā. There is the tradition mentioned in two sixteenth-century biographies of Tīlopā and in Tīlopā's own *Ṣaḍdharmopadeśa* (see Heruka, 1982) that Tīlopā learned the substance of the six topics from four different individuals. He received the teachings on heat yoga and dreaming from Kṛṣṇācārya, the academic "gatekeeper" at the southern gate of Nalanda University.

Marpa, the first Tibetan to receive the six topics, studied under Nāropā in the lamasery of Phullahari, not far from Nalanda. Because Nāropā, the Indian, transmitted the six topics, including the teaching on dreams, to Marpa, the Tibetan, the knowledge about lucid dreams must have entered Tibet with the third return of Marpa to Tibet in the eleventh century. According to Nāropā's biography and also Marpa's (Heruka, 1982), Nāropā passed the six topics to Marpa orally, because these teachings were of the most secret nature.

The six topics of Nāropā, which form the context for the teaching on lucid dreams, are (1) *Heat yoga,* the creation of bodily heat through yogic practices. There are instructions for yogic postures, breathing practices, and visualizations. The practice actually makes the yogin hot and may lead to the experience of great light. This "clear light" is the sign of the universal void and is said to lead to *nirvāṇa,* release from repeated births in this world of suffering. (2) *The illusory body.* Here are yogic postures and visualizations designed to show that all phenomena are like dreams and are void. Through this practice, it is said, one experiences voidness or even the light. (3) *Lucid dreaming.* (4) *The clear light.* There are practices used in yoga initiated while awake or while dreaming to achieve the experience of clear light. The manifestations of light that precede the clear light are also described. (5) *The death state.* This teaching describes how to proceed when dying, how to recognize that one has died, how to choose a womb for one's next birth, and how to progress toward liberation upon dying. (6) *Consciousness transference.* Instructions are given on how to transfer one's consciousness to divine realms or into a living or even a dead body.

THE TEACHING ON LUCID DREAMS

Because of new interest in Tibetan studies in the West, we have available a number of English translations of old Tibetan texts on lucid dreams. We have the biography of Nāropā, previously mentioned. Longchenpa (1308–1363), a writer and translator of the Nyingmapa school, has discussed lucid dreams in a text called in translation *Wonderment* (Guenther, 1976). Tsongkhapa (1357–1410), the founder of the Gelukpa school, wrote a commentary on the six topics of Nāropā (in Musès, 1961). Tucci (1935) says that Tsongkhapa is one of the best commentators on the six topics. Padma Karpo (1526–1569), of the Kagyü-pa school, compiled a text on the six topics. This is available to us as "Herein Lieth

the Epitome of the Abridged Six Doctrines'' (in Evans-Wentz, 1958). A composition by Drashi Namjhal on the six topics has been translated from Chinese
versions (Chang, 1963). My description of lucid dream practice will come
largely from these sources.

The original writers did not intend to expose these teachings to the general
public. They did not write even for Buddhist monks and nuns as a whole but for a
restricted number of qualified yogins within certain traditions. Undoubtedly in a
country where relgous life centered around extensive monastic communities and
secluded hermitages, these yogins were for the most part male, and the texts are
male-oriented. However, we know that there were occasional women disciples
of gurus, and there is no reason to believe that the practices were restricted to
males.

The texts are largely guides for teaching yogins already familiar with extensive Buddhist teaching. The teachings are to be practiced only with the help of an
instructor, not only because the learner needs personal help step by step but
because the writings themselves are intentionally incomplete and must be supplemented by the knowledge of the instructor. Garma C. C. Chang, who has
translated for English readers more than one text on the six topics of Nāropā,
warns us that

> the translator declines all responsibility for readers who may rashly experiment with
> these Six Yogas. A mere reading of these texts can never replace a living Guru from
> whom a serious Bodhi-seeker should first receive initiation and guidance before he can
> start the actual practice. (Chang, 1963, p. 15)

The texts describe certain types of yogins who will have difficulty having
lucid dreams or will find it impossible to induce them. These are yogins who
violate Tantric precepts, have little faith in their guru, are greedy for material
gains, lose certain bodily secretions or become ritually unclean, are full of
distracting thoughts, or yearn very little to have lucid dreams. Above all, the
texts stress, the yogin cannot achieve lucid dreams without adequate preparation
in heat yoga, the first of the six topics.

The texts offer procedures for bringing about lucid dreams. During the day,
the yogin should maintain the realization that all things are of the substance of
dreams. He should think, ''This is a dream.'' Tsongkhapa explains that desires
during the day tend to appear in dreams; therefore, one should also desire during
the day to recognize the dream.

It is recommended that when the yogin lies down to sleep, he rest on his
right side on a comfortable bed and use a thin quilt and a high pillow. He should
press his throat arteries with the thumb and ring finger of the right hand, stop his
nostrils with the left hand, and let saliva collect in his throat. This can be done
upon falling asleep either at night or in daytime. A prayer to one's guru upon
going to sleep should also help to bring about lucidity. Visualization practices are
also helpful when going to sleep. To specifically bring about lucid dreaming, the
yogin is to first think of himself as the goddess Vajra-Yoginī, then visualize the

syllable *āḥ,* bright red, as being in his throat. He should think of the syllable as the embodiment of "Divine Speech" and concentrate upon it. As it is difficult to recognize a dream after midnight and before dawn, so the texts say, visualizations for achieving lucid dreaming are most effective after daybreak.

At dawn, the texts recommend, the yogin should practice 7 times certain breathing exercises called "pot-shaped" breathing. He should resolve 11 times to realize he is dreaming. Then he should concentrate upon a dot as being between the eyes. The dot is to be seen as white, red, or green, according to the yogin's temperament. If that does not work, he is to meditate upon the dot at night. In the morning, he does 21 "pot-shaped" breathing exercises and makes 21 resolutions to recognize the dream. He then concentrates on a small black dot as being at the base of the sex organ. There are a variety of methods for achieving lucid dreaming, but the practice of heat yoga is considered to be the best help.

If, when the yogin is just about to realize he is dreaming, he wakes up because he is too intent upon recognizing the dream, the texts recommend that he eat good food and work hard during the day so that he will sleep more soundly. If he has a recurring dream, he should meditate on it often with resolve to recognize it the next time it occurs. Here, "pot-shaped" breathing and visualization of the dot also help. If he remembers nothing when he awakes, he is to avoid places, people, and food that are unclean (in a religious sense). He should take religious initiation and visualize the dot as being at the sex organ. If dreams do not come, he should meditate upon "pot-shaped" breathing, visualize the dot at the sex organ, and worship certain heroes and female deities. If lucid dreams are short, concentration on the throat helps. Lucid dreaming is easier to accomplish in clear dreams. Tsongkhapa recommends certain visualizations and concentration practices along with resolve during the day and dwelling in a solitary place to make dreams clearer. If sleep is too heavy for lucid dreaming, then only heat yoga will help.

Once the yogin has learned to bring about lucid dreams, he can set about to change the dream, the texts say. For instance, if there is a fire in the dream, he need have no fear for he may tread it out. If a beast threatens him, he may change himself into a fireball and fly into it and burn it up. He can change ominous dreams to auspicious ones. He may even transform himself into a Buddha or Boddhisattva and again into a person. Or he may create realms where the Buddhas live, visit the Buddhas, and listen to the Buddhas' messages, all the time knowing, of course, that the Buddhas and their messages are creations of his own mind. Visiting the Buddhas is difficult to achieve. So, when he is about to sleep, the yogin should visualize a red dot as being in his throat and resolve to see whichever Buddha realm he has in mind. Tsongkhapa suggests that it is only through power produced by mastering certain yogic practices that one may transform or create a dream at will.

The dreamer can use the lucid dream experience to demonstrate the doctrine of illusion. He can change fire into water, small objects into large objects, and large objects into small objects. He can change single objects into many and many into a single. Through changing the dream, the texts indicate, he will clearly see the dream to be an illusion. He will see that he has created the images that appear, including the image of his own body. This observation is supposed to carry over to waking life and help the yogin to see that all physical experience is as unreal as dreams and is one's own creation and thus an illusion.

DREAM MEDITATION

Tsongkhapa recognizes that lucid dreaming is not in itself a form of meditation. The lucid dreamer may not even use the lucid dream for religious purposes. He or she may use it simply to fly or to go to the sun or the moon. Yet the lucid dreamer may not only use the dream to learn the doctrine of illusion or to create Buddhas to listen to but may set about to practice meditation in the dream. The use of meditation in a dream is considered to be a combination of the teaching on dreams and the teaching on light. The ultimate aim of meditation is to experience the light and achieve *nirvāṇa*. Nirvāṇa is the transcendence of one's illusory awareness of individuality and liberation from repeated rebirths. Yogic meditation plays a large role in efforts to achieve this goal.

Most descriptions of yogic procedure deal with yoga initiated while the yogin is awake. But in the teachings of Nāropā, the possibility of dream meditation is disclosed. Dream meditation parallels waking meditation. It is only in the first steps that the procedures differ.

When awake, the yogin sits in a posture that is conducive to meditation. He then regulates his breathing by specific procedures taught by the guru. Then, by force of will, he creates an image that he sees. This visualization is to be accurate and detailed and substantial enough to touch. The yogin then concentrates on the created image. By controlling his body and his breathing and by concentrating on the image, he loses contact with outer objects. Through concentration, he experiences what is taken to be union with the visualized image. His mind stops functioning. The object then vanishes and is forgotten. He has reached what is called "dreamless sleep,"[1] sometimes called deep sleep or simply sleep (as opposed to dream). If successful, he will then see a series of visions said to be experiences of the void that underlies the physical world. These visions lead to the experience of the clear light, which is the experience of the universal void. If he holds onto the light, he achieves nirvāṇa. This is only a simplified description

[1]The state beyond both waking and dream experience is considered to be dreamless sleep, regardless of whether it is reached through waking-initiated or dream-initiated meditation. *Dreamless sleep* is a term with a long history in Hindu and Buddhist thought. No present-day psychological understanding of such a term should be inferred.

of the process. The texts go into great detail, and the reader can find numerous variations in the accounts.

In a lucid dream, the dreamer has already lost awareness of outer objects. So, in order to meditate, he or she need not proceed with the bodily postures and breathing exercises of waking yoga. The dreamer proceeds to create a dream image to concentrate on. The image is seen as part of the dream. It is in the form of a deity, a syllable, or symbolic physiology of the dreamer's body. The dreamer–yogin concentrates on the image, trying to remain free of all mental content other than the image. When all other sense and mental activities are inhibited, new dream images stop arising.

Just as the yogin who began awake reaches a union with the visualization, the dream yogin reaches a union with the dream image. The experiences are the same. This is the beginning of quiescence. The image then vanishes, and the dreamer enters what is considered to be the state of dreamless sleep, in which a series of phenomena begin to appear. These visions are not considered to be dreams. They are signs that one's meditation, whether begun awake or while dreaming, is leading toward the goal of the clear light.

The first four of these visions are minor signs. The last four are considered to be experiences of voidness. All are visions of some form of light or darkness. The first four are thought of as successively brighter. The texts are not uniform when they describe the first four signs, but there tends to be a majority opinion. The first vision is called a mirage, for it resembles the haziness of an apparent lake in a desert. The second resembles the billowing of smoke. The third looks like fireflies or sparks within smoke. The fourth vision resembles the sputtering light of a butter lamp, or, according to others, a steady lamplight. One source speaks of light rays appearing in the first and fourth visions.

The four experiences of voidness that follow are visions of solid light or darkness. The first is a vision as if of a clear and cloudless moonlit night sky. The second is a vision as of a glaring, sunny sky. The sky is clear; the sun itself is not present. The third is complete darkness. There is no conscious activity whatever in this darkness. There is no memory or mental content. This third experience is qualitatively different from the first two visions of voidness, for, during the first two, awareness is maintained. From this complete darkness, there can survive no remembered awareness of the darkness. This is the deepest of dreamless sleep.

It is believed that the visual manifestations of the minor signs and of voidness are due to the gradual dissolution of the contents of consciousness. The components of materiality dissolve one into the other step by step, until all forms dissolve into the pure light from which they have originated. Thus the last experience is of the clear light, a very bright, lasting light, compared to the light of dawn. The light is clear of all content. It is the light of the universal void. If the dreamer–yogin holds onto this light, he or she experiences nirvāṇa—liberation. All the experiences of voidness are associated with feelings of bliss, but the greatest bliss is found in the final experience of light.

The yogic steps to eliminate dreaming and reach dreamless sleep are not easy, and nirvāṇa may very well not be achieved in one's present lifetime. However, the practice of dream yoga and the experience of the signs have great value, it is believed, because they prepare one for death. For the eight visions are also experienced upon dying and are the signs of death. Upon death, the yogin can again try to hold onto the clear light and thus not take birth again. However, it is said that achieving the clear light upon dying is more difficult than during meditation.

Although the teachings on lucid dreams are not a noticeable part of the Tantric literature before the time of Tīlopā and Nāropā, discussions of the minor signs, the voids of cloudless sky, and the clear light reach back centuries before Tīlopā. They form an essential part of the earliest Tantric literature. There is very esoteric discussion of the experiences as early as the composition of the *Guhyasamāja Tantra* in the third or fourth century A.D. (Shastri, 1984; Wayman, 1977). This tantra has been of primary importance to the Buddhism of Tibet. Its discussion of the minor signs, the voids, and the clear light supplements for us the discussion of the same in the later texts on the six topics of Nāropā.

DISTINGUISHING METAPHYSICS FROM PHENOMENA

We might question whether in these discussions of dream meditation, the void, and the clear light we are still talking about reportable lucid dream experience or whether we have flown off into the realm of esoteric Tibetan speculation and mysticism. It is useful, therefore, for us to try to separate the metaphysical interpretations from the phenomena of the experiences described. We can consider as metaphysical interpretation the views that the visual signs occur in (a) a state of dreamless sleep (b) the visual signs indicate the progressive dissolution of forms into their original light (c) experiences of voidness are evidence of a void underlying all worldly manifestation and (d) liberation from rebirth occurs through the experience of clear light.

In the Tibetan accounts, we find descriptions of experience and phenomena, such as (a) the creation of dream images by the dreamer, (b) the cessation of ordinary dream images due to the dreamer's concentration, (c) visions of what look like a mirage, smoke rising, fireflies (or sparks), a lamp burning, and rays of light, (d) visions of darkness and of light as in a clear sky, (e) the loss of awareness in darkness, (f) the experience of brilliant clear light, and (g) the feeling of bliss.

When reading religious texts, we should be prepared to find that descriptions of psychological experience may be molded to conform to doctrine. Yet experiences as described by the Tibetans have been reported by contemporary lucid dreamers. Just as a Tibetan yogin may create a Buddhist image in a dream for meditation, there are reports by lucid dreamers of creating dream images by will (Gillespie, 1983; Green, 1968). In lucid dream reports, we find examples of minor effects of light comparable to sparks, lamps, rays, and such, and visions of formless light and darkness, as of the sky (Gillespie, 1983; Green, 1968; Sparrow, 1976). These visual effects often follow the dreamer's deliberate elimination of the visual environment by closing dreamed eyes or follow the incidental elimination of a scene, as happens when the dreamer flies, falls, or simply looks off into the sky, or when the dreamer concentrates on something. There are reports also of loss of awareness in darkness, a brilliant overwhelming light that at times follows darkness, and feelings of bliss (Gillespie, 1986).

The visual experiences have not all been reported to have happened on the same occasion. Nor have they occurred necessarily in the same sequence as described in the Tibetan accounts. Judging from the variety in the Tibetan texts, particularly concerning the minor signs, differences can be expected. Namjhal says that because there are individual differences in capacities and karma, "it is . . . difficult to predict the definite sequence of the various experiences that a yogi must go through" (Chang, 1963, pp. 77–78). It is quite possible, besides, that a yogin trying to proceed step by step according to the guidelines of a text will come closer to achieving all the steps in the order specified in the text than would someone who occasions upon the phenomena without trying for them.

We still do not have a great quantity of contemporary lucid dream accounts, and among what we have, we do not have many dreamers reporting the kinds of phenomena described in the Tibetan texts. Nor do we yet have in English translation much of the vast and complex literature belonging to Tibetan Buddhism. But in what we have, we can see that Tibetan accounts of lucid dreaming are relevant to our understanding of this new area of study, particularly if we are able to distinguish between the phenomena of lucid dreams and their metaphysical and religious interpretation.

REFERENCES

Chang, G. C. C. (Ed.). (1963). *Teachings of Tibetan yoga.* Secaucus, NJ: Citadel Press.
Evans-Wentz, W. Y. (Ed.). (1958). *Tibetan yoga and secret doctrines.* London: Oxford University Press.
Gackenbach, J. (1980). Lucid dreaming project. *The A. R. E. Journal, 15*(6), 253–265.
Gillespie, G. (1983). *Dreamer's progress: A record of experiments made while dreaming.* Unpublished manuscript.
Gillespie, G. (1986). Ordinary dreams, lucid dreams and mystical experience. *Lucidity Letter, 5*(1), 27–31.
Green, C. (1968). *Lucid dreams.* Oxford: Institute of Psychophysical Research.
Guenther, H. V. (1963). *The life and teaching of Nāropa.* Oxford: Oxford University Press.
Guenther, H. V. (Ed. & trans.). (1976). *Kindly bent to ease us: Part 3. Wonderment.* Emeryville, CA: Dharma.
Heruka, T. N. (1982). *The life of Marpa the Translator* (Translated by Nālandā Translation Committee). Boulder: Prajñā Press.
Musès, C. A. (Ed.). (1961). *Esoteric teachings of the Tibetan tantra.* York Beach, MA: Samuel Weiser.

Shastri, D. (Ed.). (1984). *Guhyasamāja Tantra or Tathāgataguhyaka*. Varanasi: Bauddha Bharati.

Sparrow, G. S. (1976). *Lucid dreaming: Dawning of the clear light*. Virginia Beach, VA: A. R. E. Press.

Tucci, G. (1935). A propos the legend of Nāropā. *Journal of the Royal Asiatic Society*, pp. 677–688.

Tucci, G. (1980). *The religions of Tibet* (G. Samuel, Trans.). Bombay: Allied.

Wayman, A. (1977). *Yoga of the Guhyasamājatantra: The arcane lore of forty verses*. Delhi: Motilal Banarsidass.

4

Lucidity, Sex, and Horror in Senoi Dreamwork

ROBERT K. DENTAN

INTRODUCTION

Aims of This Chapter

This chapter is a description and analysis of aspects of the dream praxis of the Senoi, a Malaysian people whose way of interpreting and responding to dreams has had much influence on Europeans and Americans interested in the psychotherapeutic use of dreams. Recent publications have made it plain that much of the "Senoi" ethnography with which Western dreamworkers are familiar is of dubious reliability. This chapter indicates, by example, that the differences between the familiar version of Senoi life (by Stewart) and the accounts given by anthropologists are not merely matters of interpretation.

Why are Senoi Important to Students of Dreams?

Probably more American students of dreams have heard of Senoi dream praxis than have heard of any other "primitive" oneirology. Accounts of the way in which Senoi teach children to have lucid dreams and thus to attain mental and physical health are widely disseminated. This chapter is an interpretive account of the way in which actual Senoi dream praxis manifests Senoi social reality.

The Senoi owe their American notoriety to the work of Kilton Riggs Stewart, a colorful Rankian psychologist who spent 8 to 10 months traveling through

ROBERT K. DENTAN • Departments of American Studies and Anthropology, State University of New York, Amherst, NY 14260.

Senoi Temiar territory in the mid-1930s (Dentan, 1983c, pp. 6–8; Domhoff, 1985; Stewart, 1953/1954, 1954b, 1962, 1972a, 1972b). Like his brother, the distinguished anthropologist Omer C. Stewart (e.g. 1944, 1964), Kilton was interested in dreams/visions and in popularizing anthropology. These interests stemmed from a remembered Mormon childhood in which visionary faith and radically democratic praxis was salient. He was consciously looking for a community that matched this idealized reconstruction of a communitarian, dream-based childhood (1954a, pp. 17, 20–21). His failure to reside with the Senoi in any one place long enough to learn the language, establish rapport, or get a sense of quotidian life left him free to project these fancies onto what he observed (Dentan, 1978, 1983a,b,c, 1984; Faraday & Wren-Lewis, 1983, 1984; Howell, 1983; Rainwater, 1979, p. 127; Robarchek, 1983). His account is substantially wrong. Therefore, this chapter is in part a corrective measure.

There are four sets of reasons that people interested in dreams, particularly in lucid dreams, can learn from studying the Senoi case. First, the documentation is voluminous. (1) Although Stewart's popularized work misrepresents Senoi reality, his thesis (1948), read carefully, contains valuable material. (2) The belated attempt to correct his misconceptions seems to be producing a multi-faceted analysis of actual Senoi dream praxis, so that the corpus now emerging promises to be one of the most comprehensive anywhere. (3) Moreover, the various analytical perspectives of such different people as Benjamin, Dentan, Faraday, Gomes, Roseman, Wren-Lewis, and, perhaps in years to come, Anthony Williams-Hunt, who is a Senoi, should enrich each other and compensate for each other's stress on particular issues.

The second set of reasons for becoming familiar with Senoi dream praxis is so that one can evaluate ethnographic accounts of dreams by becoming familiar with how ethnographers work (Dentan, 1984; Faraday & Wren-Lewis, 1984). *Thick description,* in ethnographers' jargon, refers to piling up contextual details in order to make sense of local categories of reality. This piling up is not to see how many pages you can make people read but rests on the premise that ''meaning is context,'' so that ''glosses'' (rough translations) without context can be misleading, as I have argued happens in Stewart's case (Dentan, 1983c). To get these details, one needs to reside with the people one is observing for a year or more.

The third set of reasons involves professional responsibility. (1) A barely recognizable version of Senoi reality has affected the lives of thousands of Americans, who should know that what they are asked to do is *not* validated by a cure-all praxis among Malaysian hill peoples (cf. Johnson, 1978; McGlashan, 1987; Rovics, 1983; Williams, 1980). (2) As Rovics acknowledges (1984), calling the ''Senoi'' of American theory a ''mythic'' people is no loophole (cf. Faraday & Wren-Lewis, 1984; Stimson, 1983; Williams, 1980, pp. 281–284). The Senoi deserve to be known as who they are, not as whom we may wish them to be. If we have distorted their lives, we need to set the record straight. (3) Professional students of dreams need to show that we can keep our own house in order (Dentan, 1987, 1988; Domhoff, 1985; Faraday, 1986). Some ethnographic accounts of dreams have been marred by charlatanry and fraud. That makes our colleagues wary. Preferring facile myth to laborious fact is a sign of immaturity.

The final, and perhaps for me most important, set of reasons has to do with proper professional humility. As Western scientists, we sometimes in our arrogance think our own theories are immune from the cosmological preconceptions and the economic and social constraints that restrict our "primitive contemporaries." The rapid dissemination of Stewart's account in the 1970s, when "the time was ripe," seems to me precisely due to such nonscientific factors. Thus, examination of how Senoi oneirology fits the Senoi conditions may shed light on the tacit limitations of our own praxis and suggest the origin of the modifications Americans made to Senoi theory.

Fieldwork

Ethnographers have to describe their fieldwork briefly to allow readers to evaluate their reports (Dentan, 1986, pp. 318–321). I lived in West Malaysia among the Senoi Semai for 14 months in 1961–1963 and another couple of months in 1975. In 1976, I lived 7 months with the Btsisi', a related people. I speak 4 of the 40 Semai dialects well enough to eavesdrop and find the jokes and wordplay funny as well as a couple of rural Malay dialects rather fluently and Btsisi' well enough to carry on ordinary conversations or interviews.

The Peoples

A comparison of Senoi data with data from cognate or historically connected peoples may shed light on both. The dominant people of West Malaysia are Malays, lowlanders speaking Austronesian languages related to Hawaiian. The dream praxis of the Malays in the state of Kelantan seems cognate with that of the Senoi Temiar, the aboriginal inhabitants (Benjamin, 1966, p. 5; Cuisinier, 1936, p. 38; K. M. Endicott, 1970, pp. 21–22, 81). The indigenous hill peoples speak Austroasiatic (Aslian) languages related to Cambodian.

Aslian Languages

Aslian includes north, central, and southern families (see maps in Benjamin, 1976a; Jimin, 1968). Of the peoples this chapter mentions, the Batek and Che Wong speak North Aslian, which is associated with the term *Semang;* the Semnam, Sabum, Temiar, Semai, and Jah Hut speak central Aslian, which is

Table 1. Aslian Peoples

Languages	Traditional economies	
	Foraging	Horticulture
	(*Semang*)	
North Aslian	Batek[a]	Che Wong
Central Aslian	Semnam	Temiar (Senoi)
	(Lanoh)[b]	
	Sabum	Semai (Senoi)
	(Lanoh)[b]	
		Jah Hut
South Aslian		Btsisi'
		Semelai

[a]There are several dialects of Batek.
[b]Lanoh comprises at least four languages.

associated with *Senoi;* and the Btsisi' and Semelai speak South Aslian. Benjamin's (1976a) linguistic overview is standard (see Table 1).

Aslian Economies

Traditionally, ethnographers called West Malaysian hunter-gatherers and foragers *Semang* or *Negritos.* Aslian genetic and phenotypic variability render the latter term stultifying (Dentan, 1979, pp. 8–11, 1981; Fix, 1982; Fix & Lie-Injo, 1975; Noone 1936, p. 1; Stewart, 1948, p. 48). The word *Senoi,* which can cover all Aslian horticulturalists (Dentan, 1964) in this chapter refers only to Stewart's "Senoi," that is, Temiar and "East Semai" (Dentan, 1979, 1983c; Stewart, 1948). Dentan (1964), Jimin (1968), and Lebar (1964) have surveyed Aslian ethnology in a few pages. Carey (1976), Skeat and Blagden (1906), and Williams-Hunt (1952) give more detail. Benjamin's Temiar studies (e.g., 1966, 1967, 1968a,b, 1976b) are exemplary, and Roseman (e.g., 1984) is beginning to write up her work on music and trance. A special issue of the *Federation Museums Journal* summarizes recent Aslian studies (e.g., Azizah, 1979, Baharon, 1979, Dahlan, 1976; "Librarian," 1979, Walker, 1979), and the *Orang Asli Newsletter,* edited by Kirk Endicott at Dartmouth, gives current bibliographies.

Aims of This Section

Interpreting Ambiguities

Recapitulating this wealth of material or my own 1983 writings on Senoi dream praxis seems unnecessary. Because it seems important to show that ethnographers' unanimous rejection of Stewart's popularized work is *not* merely a matter of interpretation (cf. Stimson, 1983), this section presents an account of Senoi dreamwork that is an alternative to Roseman's (1984) study of Temiar ethnomusicology. The difference between Roseman's work and Stewart's is that Roseman's falsifiable assertions hold. The question is how to interpret them. Because the phenomena in question—gender relations, mystic powers, and the semblances that appear in altered states of consciousness (ASCs)—are inherently complex, ambivalent, and ambiguous, I would argue that my interpretation here complements hers; that both are equally correct and incomplete; and that no final or definitive interpretation is possible.

GENDER AND DREAMS

Are Senoi Women Oppressed?

The Problem

Roseman raises the question why Temiar women report dreams that legitimize "adept" (*halaa'*) status more rarely than men do. She proceeds to analyze Temiar trance rituals as a way of restoring gender equality. To deal with her sophisticated and careful account requires some notion of how the Senoi define "gender," the cultural edifice people everywhere construct to define the social implications of biological "sex."

Studying Gender

As Americans, anthropologists have trouble studying gender relations, particularly distinguishing equal from unequal gender roles. Traditional American notions of gender involve not symmetry or complementation (Leacock 1978) but systematically different access to "rewards, prestige or power" (Schlegel, 1977, p. 3), so that, to equalize gender statuses, Americans adopt "unisex" garb, try to switch roles, and classify pregnancy as just another "disease"; for any distinction is invidious (e.g., Dyer, 1980; Kennedy, 1979; Tocqueville, 1835/1951, pp. 254–270). No *vive la différence* for Uncle Sam! Specifying structural or behavioral criteria that constitute a "women's position" combats such biases (e.g., Friedl, 1975; Kennedy, 1979; Nowak, 1979; Sacks, 1975; Sanday, 1981; Schlegel, 1977). The problem with such positivist stipulation is that its radical simplification of the issue sloughs off the ambiguous context that makes gender meaningful to those who live it. Roseman properly resists this temptation to premature closure. In fact, Senoi gender relations resist simplistic analysis.

Senoi Notions of Sex and Gender

Sexual Activity

Everyday Senoi sexual relations seem free and casual (Dentan, 1979, pp. 61–63), shading gradually into marriage, but the Senoi are aware that desire can easily get out of hand (Robarchek & Dentan, 1987). They can get upset enough about sex to contemplate doing violence to themselves or others. The pervasive Senoi concern that loss of self-control dissolves the limits that define the mundane universe, releasing supernatural horrors, makes sex ambivalent. Initial sexual intercourse can be terrifying, and dream sex is a perilous form of -*yayah* "nightmare" (Dentan, 1968b).

The same mingling of fear and desire permeates the songs Jelai River Semai sing to lure familiar spirits, for example: Dugout is ferrying; grasp strongly; cutting [circumcized] Malay penis; hill box; spurts come from Malay penis. The words *tangkol* ("carry on the shoulder"?) and *cntig* in another Jelai River song refer, people said, to "vagina" (Semai *leed,* Temiar *kyed*). The song, each line of which is repeated by the chorus, runs as follows:

> *Tangkol*
>   Choking-up ("with effort"; -*wɔɔg*)
> *Cngtig*
>   Blockage, grunt
>   Penetrate, grunt
>   Penetrate, groan
>   Portal Manglaw

Manglaw is the second of the seven dimensions, tiers, layers, or "portals" of the universe, to which the singer "penetrates," a gloss for the Semai word for planting seeds with a long pointed dibble stick. Since melodies rather than texts lure gunig, interpreting seance songs is harder than understanding other Semai or Temiar songs. Nevertheless, sexuality among Senoi is a focus of both pleasure and fear, at least initially. The texts seem to make intromission of the penis a metaphor for entering other dimensions of reality (for Senoi music, see Baskaran, 1963; Blacking 1954/1955; Singam 1961, p. 88; Wilkinson, 1926, p. 22).

Gender Rules

Few rules constrain gender behavior. Unlike English, Senoi gender words involve no marking, so that no value judgments are implicit in the language (Brown, 1982; Brown & Witkowski, 1980; Dentan, 1983a). Rules governing gender relations tend to be reciprocal or to have "mirror images," that is, to apply to otherwise similar situations in which the genders are reversed. For instance, sons-in-law should avoid mothers-in-law, who should reciprocally avoid them; and daughters-in-law should avoid fathers-in-law (Benjamin, 1967, p. 10; Carey, 1961, pp. 159–160; Dentan, 1979, pp. 73–75). Similarly, the most formal Senoi marriages may involve a brief bride service, in which the man lives with the woman's family, contributing to their household. But such services are reciprocated; they are "not payments but proofs of equality in status" (Collier & Rosaldo, 1981, p. 279); and, unlike the peoples Collier and Rosaldo discuss, Senoi newlyweds shuttle between their parents' households, so that a mirror-image groom service alternates with bride service (Benjamin, 1967, p. 4; Dentan, 1964, 1979, p. 73). The Senoi have expectations about how women or men will act but lack the means and will to impose conformity. In short, jurally and structurally, men and women are equal.

Gender Behavior

> Behaviorally, roles are flexible, with no really clear cut distinction between male and female activities other than obvious ones such as nursing babies but even then I have seen father with a feeding bottle. Once I lived in a *Semai* ladang for a month and tried to note down every day what tasks were done by men and by women but I found that so many tasks were shared or that there were so many exceptions to the general rule that my observations were relatively valueless. (Williams-Hunt, 1952, p. 51).

Nevertheless, women statistically tend to predominate in some activities, men in others. I know of only one Senoi woman who hunts with a blowpipe, the salient Senoi virility symbol (Dentan, 1979, p. 31), although in principle Senoi women are as free as Batek ones to do so (Endicott, 1979). Unlike the Batek, this West Semai woman also reputedly wore a man's loincloth and had a female wife. Senoi marriages are much more often polygynous than polyandrous. Indeed, the Semai say that only Temiar women take more than one husband. Women rarely become headmen (Benjamin, 1968a, p. 42), but Senoi headmanship evolved quite recently, to accommodate the interests of non-Aslian peoples for whom political power entailed male gender (Benjamin, 1968a; Carey, 1961; Dentan, 1979, pp. 67–68; Noone, 1936, pp. 61–73). Aslian women in principle can become leaders by speaking out forcefully and wittily at the public meetings that set group policy by consensus (e.g., Evans, 1937, pp. 30–31; Nowak, 1983, 1984a,b). Although there was a Semai woman headman in the 1980s, Senoi women usually speak up but shun public leadership roles (Robarchek, 1977; cf. Sacks, 1975, pp. 568; Sanday, 1981, pp. 113–114; Stacey, 1953, p. 110; Stewart, 1948). The congruence of this statistical underrepresentation of women with the infrequency of "adept" women underlies Roseman's interpretation of the prevalence of "female" familiars among the Temiar as a symbolic restoration of gender equality.

Learning to Trance

Senoi go through recognized states in growing up (Manssor, Rashid, Jaafar, Tan & Nagata, 1973; Dentan, 1978, pp. 116–120; 1979, pp. 65–67). Young women (*mnaleh*) and men (*litaw*), from 10 or 11 years old to their mid-20s, start off fearful of sex and wind up fairly promiscuous until finally they grow out of that stage and settle into adulthood in a fairly stable relationship with a person by whom they have had a couple of children. They have erotic nightmares (-*yayah*) but no familiars. Before or after the serious parts of sing seances (see Dentan, 1978), which are held in the dark, they dance in fancy dress, urged on by the audience, often ribaldly, and are paced by adepts.

East Semai litaw dance more often than mnaleh. They fool around a lot at first, but after half an hour to an hour, they start stumbling and reeling in step, a sign that they are "dizzy" (-*lwig*), showing that their "beautiful bodies" have attracted spirits. Older men and women or the singing adept himself keeps the dancers on their feet, perhaps singing into their ears until half a dozen litaw fall prostrate, usually within a few minutes of each other, 10- or 12-year-olds falling first. As they lie twitching rhythmically, onlookers stretch their arms at their sides so that other dancers will not trip. The doors are barred so that when their possessing spirit makes them dash for the dark rainforest outdoors, the onlookers have a chance to subdue the struggling bodies until the spirit departs and the bodies collapse. After 5 or 10 minutes, the adept sprinkles them with a special water, from his whisk, crying "*L'ap!*" (supernatural cool). They rise and dance for a few minutes, then quit.

One adult man, not an adept, said that, as a litaw, he always faked his trances and noted accurately that a "trancer" with lice will scratch his head (i.e., is not oblivious to his surroundings). Some litaw camp up trancing outrageously, clowning for mnaleh. In an East Semai example, the serious part of the song seance had begun around 8 P.M., the fires were out, and three adepts were taking turns leading the singing. My edited notes read:

> 10:20. Fires relit. Adept continues singing.
> 10:25. Cong, a dancing 15-year-old *litaw*, gets the adepts' bowl of neutralizing water and hams up sprinkling and crying "*L'ap!*" His *mnay* (an in-law with whom joking and flirting is proper), a *mnaleh*, whacks him playfully with one of the bamboo stampers with which women set the rhythm. Cong grabs his right buttock and raises his right leg at her, continues dancing. She tries to trip him. Onlooker: "He's having erotic fantasies" (-*yayah*), jokingly.
> 10:30. Another adept takes over singing. Cong staggers around dizzily, faking -*lwig*. Adult man yells, laughing, "Dance it right, Cong, don't goof around!" Cong falls, "unconscious," twitching exaggeratedly. His *mnay*, laughing, taps him again with the bamboo stamper.
> 10:40. Ceremony over.

Mnaleh sometimes join in litaw dances, but I never saw a woman in trance, even in the women's circle dance described by Roseman (1984) and Stewart (1948, 1972a) which is supposed to make women as adept as men. The question is important enough that another edited fragment of field notes seems appropriate. The ceremony started around 8 P.M.

9:10 Rhythm picks up.
9:20 Men stop dancing.
9:22 Three *mnaleh* pluck at Cong's wornout shirt, giggling.
9:26 A *mnaleh* starts the circle dance, bowing and swinging her arms in rhythm. Other women and a girl toddler join in.
9:30 Adept, who whirled himself dizzy an hour earlier, joins in dancing. Toddler makes the steps of the dance, at least the leaps, but keeps tripping on her overlong sarong. Dancers get "dizzy" (*-lwig*) and break.
9:35 Adept *-lwig* again, lurching into onlookers.
9:40 Another adept takes over singing, with choral reprise.
9:45 One woman dancing by herself.
9:46 Another woman joins in, following her in a circle.
9:50 Four women dancing.
10:00 Stampers increase tempo until dance becomes an oval run, with much laughter.
10:03 Everyone *-lwig* and collapses.
10:04 Resume at much slower tempo.
10:06 Quit.

As trance faking, this performance was not very convincing, nor was it supposed to be.

Even the faking and parodizing are a sort of rehearsal. Eventually, some litaw go into deep possession trance. It took a couple of much larger adults to restrain little Cong from tearing up the floor or walls to get "back" to the rainforest when he was possessed. These dances, not "dream clinics" (Stewart, 1972a), seem to be where men learn how to trance. From a Senoi viewpoint, such rehearsal trancing is part of being litaw, not learning or being taught (Dentan, 1978). Litaw trances are not lucid. Only "great adepts" have lucid trances, and the lucidity may be a mythical attribute, like the ability to turn into a tiger.

SENOI CATEGORIES OF ALTERED STATES OF CONSCIOUSNESS

Dreams

Mpo'

Senoi dream typology is too complex to discuss in detail here (see Dentan, 1983a,c). *Mpo'* refers both to dreams in general and in particular to culture pattern dreams in which a familiar gives a dreamer a tune that thereafter he can sing to summon its aid, making him "adept" (*-halaa'*). In linguists' useful jargon, *mpo'* denotes an "unmarked" category, both generic and specific, like English *man* or *he*, which likewise refers both to humans in general and adult male humans in particular. Culturally less significant categories must be marked off from the "unmarked" ones by adding modifiers or other constructions, so that marked words tend to be longer, like English "wo-man," than unmarked ones.

Possible Etymologies

Mpo' seems to be an ancient Austroasiatic word, perhaps cognate with Malay *mimpi* or (rarely) *impi,* "dream" (Benedict, 1975, p. 274; Iskandar, 1970, p. 388; Means & Means, 1986; Skeat & Blagden, 1906, II, p. 584). Unmarked words normally resist change this way (Brown, 1982). By contrast, other words for dream seem cognate with words for deception. East Semai - *bibooy* (West Semai *-pipuuy*), "dream meaninglessly," seems to be a redupli- cated form of central Aslian *-booy,* glossed "be false" (Means and Means, 1986; Skeat & Blagden, 1906, II, 597). The West Semai noun form *pnipuuy* may owe something to Malay *tipu,* "cheat," *penipu(i),* "cheater," which is found as a loan word in Central Aslian (Skeat & Blagden, 1906, p. 577). East Semai words for "nightmare" (Dentan, 1968b, pp. 141, 145, 150; 1983c, 29, 32–33) are puzzling. The etymology of *-rayeh* is unknown (but cf. Skeat & Blagden 1906, II, p. 596). *-Yayah,* "erotic nightmare," seems to be a reduplication of a North Aslian word for "be false" (Carey, 1961, 91; Skeat & Blagden, 1906, II, 597). These distinctions imply that significant dreams are true but that many dreams are deceptive. Senoi are as skeptical about dreams as about other received wisdom (Dentan, 1979, pp. 93–94).

Other ASCs

Malays and some North Aslians refer to all ASCs as "dreams" (Endicott, 1979, pp. 94–95; Wilkinson, 1956), but the Senoi lexicon for ASCs seems more extensive than English. It treats ASCs as whole-body states that involve forces only metaphor can describe—supernatural entities for the Senoi or "unconscious forces" for Americans. *-Wɔɔl,* for example, glossed as "choking up" or "the 'forgetting' of trance" (Roseman, 1984) involves (1) a physical state akin to nausea but not producing vomiting and (2) obliviousness of one's surroundings.

Unconsciousness

Several Semai words refer to clonic spasms and/or losing consciousness. Semai gloss Malay *pingsan,* "to faint," as *-pucug* (Temiar *-hilud,* Carey, 1961, p. 91), a sort of *dnnan,* "dying". *-Nylap* involves losing consciousness, falling, and clonus, as in the "dying" of epilepsy (Dentan, 1968b; Means & Means, 1986). North and Central Aslian *saban* (Malay *sawan*) refres to infants' convul- sions, attributed to the parent's eating *pila'* food. *Pila'* (Malay *pilak, pelak*) animals fall into two groups, those associated with tree spirits and those associ- ated with bird spirits. Tree spirits appear in the daytime as gibbons and siamangs or, rarely, macaques; in dreams, as ruminants, which are associated with incest (Dentan, 1983a). Barking deer, sambar, mousedeer, and pygmy deer may cause *saban;* the larger gaur and serow may cause epilepsy as well. Bird spirits may appear as pheasants (argus, redeye, and *huhaw;* Dentan, 1978, 101–102, 136; Dentan, in press; cf. Schebesta, 1926, pp. 231–232).

Lngwig

"Intoxicated" (Semai *-buul*) people often suffer *lngwig mad* (Malay *mata pusing,* "eye spin"), that is, visual dizziness (Means & Means, 1986; Robarchek & Dentan, 1987). Choking-up nausea (*-wɔɔl*) and vomiting may follow. The same sequence affects people who break off trance dancing before going into trance, say the East Semai. Otherwise, the trancing sequence runs as follows: *lngwig mad,* "choking-up," *lngwig,* trance. Roseman glosses *-lwig* as "transform," which is correct as far as it goes, but it is too aseptic, I think, to give an idea of the lurking horror to which *lngwig,* in the Senoi metaphor, opens the "door."

Tree spirits (*nyani' jhuu'*), euphemistically the "long-handed ones," cause *lngwig,* East Semai say. They look a lot like gibbons (*Hylobates* spp.), especially the huge siamangs (*H. syndactylus*), which are found eating *wɔɔl* fruit (*Ochanostachys amentacea, Homalium* spp.) and the fruits of strangler figs (Semai *jri'* and *wig*). A large male siamang stands 3 ft tall and has a pouch that booms when the male barks. Thus one form of Thunder, one of the powerful entities that bring cataclysm, is a siamang "the size of King Kong" (Baharon, 1966; Dentan, 1979, pp. 22–23; Schebesta, 1927, pp. 22, 25–27).

Tree spirits have long black fur, very long arms, white chests, and 5-in. claws. They travel in couples, one male and one female, like people, and dwell in *bdɔ'* trees (*Dyera* spp.), which have blood-red sap. They string invisible wires between trees, which cause headaches and dizziness of the sort Semai treated for TB suffer. They will tear a house apart to devour its inhabitants, then each make sexual partners of the ghosts that form from the shadows of their prey. Early symptoms of an attack are drowsiness, headache, pains in the nape of the neck, and talking in one's sleep or incoherence. A lethal strike makes the victim insanely violent and causes dizziness (*lngwig mat*), choking-up nausea, epileptiform seizure, and death within 15 minutes (Dentan, in press).

Lngwig thus involves not only blurred perceptions, "transformation," and trance but also, potentially or implicitly, supernatural viciousness, obscene eroticism, insanity, and violent death. My guess is that lngwig transformation may be a blurring and deliquescence of the boundaries of the categories into which Senoi divide the cosmos. Maintenance of those boundaries is all that prevents the irruption of chaos and cataclysm into the tidy Senoi world, people seem to feel. Disorder always threatens, in the form of volcanic eruptions, thundersqualls, floods, earthquakes, or vaguer cosmic upheavals, often as a result of human failure to observe limits (e.g., Dentan, 1978, pp. 132–133; 1979, pp. 21–24, 61–62; 1983c, p. 33; Schebesta, 1926, pp. 215, 221–223; 1927, 22–27; cf. Guenther, 1979, 1986). Everyday rituals maintain cosmic order by keeping disparate things separate and shielding people from anomaly (e.g., Dentan, 1970). Yet there are always entities that do not quite fit. Most animals of a particular species, for example, are just animals; but "one in a hundred" is something entirely different, through which shapeless extradimensional horror can irrupt into the orderly Senoi world. Semai and Btsisi' stories repeatedly adjure things to keep a single form: "If you are a so-and-so, *stay* a so-and-so; if something else, *stay* something else."

The immanence of supernatural chaos, violence, and obscenity does not preoccupy the Senoi. The rituals that keep metaphysical order are as automatic as keeping kosher and as likely to change. Reasonably secure within the intellectual limits, they impose on cosmic disorder; Senoi in the clean, well-lighted world of everyday life worry no more about the polymorphous horror at the heart of darkness than Americans worry in their daily lives about looming nuclear holocaust or *Fimbulwinter*. But the terror is there.

Form (Malay *Peruman*) created the world, say the Jah Hut (Werner, 1975, pp. 31–32, 34–36, 622, 625). The dissolution of form in lngwig opens the door, in the Senoi metaphor, to chaos, *peruman cukup lngri'*, or "forms from all dimensions" as one Ulu Telom Semai song begins. I know no English term for the state of consciousness in which all the limits human intellect and language impose upon the world blur and dissolve, unleashing nameless obscenity, shapeless horror and unspeakable truth. "Transformation" or "lucid dreaming" seems overintellectual.

Familiars

Br-gunig and Bergending

A Senoi *gunig* is a familiar whose spirit gives a person, usually a man, a tune with which he can thereafter summon the gunig's spirit to help him in the diagnosis and treatment of problems that involve entities from outside the orderly human world. A Kelantanese Malay *bergending*, a cognate word, is a "principal assistant" of a medium who is in touch with tiger spirits. This assistant "during the seance questions the medium while he is possessed and in trance" (Shaw, 1973, pp. 75, Pl. XIb; cf. Couillard, 1980, p. 44; Hood, 1979, pp. 110, 116). He guides, interprets, and invokes for the medium but remains an assistant whose job is to make sense of visions that only the medium can have. In this sense, bergending–medium relations are as ambiguous with respect to power as the mutually contradictory teacher–student and child–parent relations Roseman (1984) finds in the ties between Temiar gunig and "adept" (*halaa'*).

I have some reservations about Roseman's interpretation because teacher–student relations are alien to the Senoi and Senoi parents deny they have power over their children (Dentan, 1978), but concur that the adept–gunig partnership is uneasy and ambivalent. Stewart (1948) suggests that Temiar "adepts" develop from having no gunig, through an adolescent period of having -*yayah* erotic nightmares, into a stage of depending on gunig to do their spiritual traveling and seeing, followed by traveling themselves with gunig as "friend, protector, guide, and representative in the world of spirits". "Great" adepts can travel spiritually without gunig help and may finally become gunig themselves. The contradictions Roseman finds might result from her synchronic treatment of a mutually complementary dyad that develops over time, the power relations shifting as the adept's skill increases.

Adepts

Kelantanese Malay praxis may again shed light on the related Temiar one, from which it derives and which it influences (Roseman, 1984). Most Kelantanese familiars are tigers (Cuisinier, 1936, pp. 38–73; Endicott, 1970, pp. 21–23, 81, 106n, 154–155; Skeat, 1900, pp. 436–444). Tiger familiars are common among all West Malaysian hill peoples (Dentan, 1979, p. 91, 99n; Embun, 1959, I, pp. 24–27; Endicott, 1970, pp. 81–82; 1979, pp. 44–47, 112–115, 124–126, 130–141, 150, 154; Evans, 1923, pp. 210–211; Karim, 1981, pp. 87–88, 175; Schebesta, 1926, pp. 215, 222; 1927, p. 15; 1928/1973, pp. 163, 189, 223–229; Skeat, 1900, pp. 70–71, 104, 157–163; Skeat & Blagden, 1906, II, pp. 227–229). Still, say the Semai, they are so common among the Temiar that you have to be careful about waking a Temiar up, lest they transmute into tigers, and some Temiar are furry, with claws between their fingers (Semai xenophobia aside, see Carey, 1961, pp. 101–113, 200–203; Faraday & Wren-Lewis, 1984; Noone, 1936, p. 28; Stewart, 1948, pp. 23, 143–149, 186–187, 203–207). Tigers, the most terrible animals Aslian peoples know, are an appropriate symbol for the terror of ASC experiences. Kelantanese Malays call tiger familiar spirits *halak* or *hala* (Cuisinier, 1936, p. 63; Endicott, 1970, p. 21; Shaw, 1973, pp. 77, 84), which is cognate with Senoi *halaa'*, "adept," and perhaps with Malay *hala*, "course" or "direction." On the evening the halak is to appear, the medium's assistant describes the journey of the first halak, a magician, through the world after Creation. For the Senoi, dream melodies are "paths" (Roseman, 1984), so that a *br-halaa'* person, "one with adept powers," would be a guide who knows the way to go, a pilot who sets a course, a melodic direction finder.

Mpo' and Gunig

Roseman (1984) suggests that the prevalence of women *gunig* counterbalances the relative rarity of women adepts. I cannot document or deny that prevalence for the Semai, for reasons discussed later, and Stewart's massive corpus of dream narratives (1948) is useless because he uses unmarked "he" and does not specify dreamers' sex. If Temiar men dream about women oftener than they dream about men, then, cross-cultural studies suggest, Temiar women may be of greater ideological or political significance than women elsewhere (Dentan, 1986, p. 325).

Stewart avers that the Temiar, like the Semai, interpret attractive young women in adolescents' -*yayah* dreams as semblances of sexual frustration (1948, pp. 151–153) but as semblances of gunig in the dreams of older men (cf. Dentan, 1979, p. 85; 1983a; 1983c, pp. 31–33, 39; cf. Herdt, 1981, 142–144, 165n; Krohn & Gutmann, 1971; Marshall, 1971). Stewart thought this change had to do with lucid dreaming, whose occurence the Temiar and Semai deny (Dentan, 1983c; Faraday & Wren-Lewis, 1984). My collection of Semai dreams, not much smaller than my collection of Chinese college student dreams, shows none of the spontaneous lucid dreams the students reported (Walters & Dentan, 1985a,b). I think, but am not sure, that the maturational change in Senoi dream interpretation results from the different sorts of trances each go through during seance dances. The -*yayah* eroticism persists, but Roseman's interpretation of adept–familiar relations as an inverse form of man–woman power relationships downplays the persistence of erotic ambivalence.

Now, gunig dream semblances seem timid and harmless. They take adepts as their "parents." Any attempt to constrain their behavior, like an attempt to discipline a child (Dentan, 1978), would scare them off. Lights, loud noises, or the presence of strangers frighten them away from song seances to which adepts try to entice them. Lucid dreaming, in the sense of establishing control over dream semblances, would be fruitless. This seeming timidity, however, stems from the fact that gunig attend dreams and seances as apparitional souls (*ruwaay* or *kloog;* Dentan, 1979, pp. 82–86; 1983a,c; Roseman, 1984). Semai say that "one in a hundred" natural phenomena in a particular category has an apparitional soul; Temiar say all do (Roseman, 1984). Such souls are always shy and timid.

The gunig itself, however, is not the same thing as its dream semblance. The latter is *mpo'*, "dream." Gunig exist independently of dreams, sometimes in the mundane world and sometimes elsewhere. They are erotically attracted to their "parent" adepts, a sort of incestuous lust. Hence they appear to adept men as seductive women, much as in -*yayah* mightmares. But these semblances are not "real" women. Here, for instance, from my edited field notes, are the female mpo' and corresponding gunig of an East Semai adept man (cf. Dentan, 1978).

1. A thumbsized black woman rustling through the leaves is in the real world a hideous spiny grub. Such grubs belong to the anomalous natural/supernatural class *smēd*, of which an evil gryllid cricket is the unmarked synecdoche (Dentan 1970). A similar stridulating insect (Temiar '*enraal*, Semai '*engreel*) became the familiar of a

Temiar woman; a Temiar adept drew me a picture of one that seemed to be all eyes, fangs, and sharp-angled legs; its call makes people fidget and fall quiet.

Smēd are associated with women, in that they originate from the blood of the dead, particularly from the blood of women dead during their first childbirth. The grubs follow the milk smell of pregnant women because they thirst for breast milk "like leeches for blood." Moreover, stridulating insects and sex go together in Senoi metaphor, as in the Ulu Telom seance song line *-Llweel, -llweel tniweel rayɔd, hari' bi-duui,* glossed as "Linger, linger, lingering the cicada, as day becomes dusk." The lingering, people said, is that of lovers who cannot bear to part, and the cicada is a teenage girl. Mantises, called "flirting grasshoppers," embrace other grasshoppers before eating them, so that eroticism and death remain allied (see Dentan, in press).

Among Malays and Semelai, women have evil cricket familiars (*polong*) oftener than men do; these familiars often take on the semblance of beautiful long-haired vampire women like Senoi bird spirits. Childbirth also arouses bird spirits' bloodlust. 2. A red highland Semai woman *mpo'* is in reality a fish-poison vine (*Strychnos ovalifolia,* Senoi *lguub*), whose "spirit" also manifests itself in other ways. Menstruating women should not go fish poisoning lest they turn into tigers; the sap is thus an objective correlative of menstrual fluids.

3. An old woman from the "mountains above the sky" is cloud, Senoi *rahuu'.* Semelai shamans and Semai midwives are in frequent contact with powerful female entities above the sky.

4. A Malay girl is in reality a black-shelled river turtle, an ambiguous semblance, because Semai, Btsisi', Chinese, and Malays associate turtle heads with shrinking penises, although the Semai interpret turtles in dreams as standing for women. Again, sex is present, but in a threatening form.

In a pragmatic sense, these female dream semblances stand for disturbing real-world entities for which gender is irrelevant (cf. Herdt, 1977, pp. 157–158; 1981, pp. 139–144, 153, 207). Familiars may assume human form but remain part of the supernatural as in many other societies (e.g., Herdt, 1981, p. 229n; Schieffelin, 1977). If Stewart's account of their ontogeny is correct, they may symbolize the perilous seductiveness of the shape-changing cosmos outside human definitions. Relationships with them involve sex, all right, but of the most dangerous kind. Their relationship to blood, moreover, merits further examination, for it inverts the relationship of human women to blood.

GENDER AND SACRED FLUIDS

Introduction

Magical Fluids

Roseman (1984) describes Temiar *kahyek* as a "cool" spiritual liquid, resembling branch water, rain, or dew. During song seances, it flows from the rain forest into the hanging leaf ornaments and spirit lures (for which, see Dentan, 1978), cooling them for the spirits. Thence, it flows into all the participants. Because most adepts are men, kahyek seems a male resource for the Senoi.

The corresponding female fluid, I think, is blood (cf. Karim, 1981, pp. 35–38), a cross-culturally common emblem of women's spiritual power (e.g., Herdt, 1981, p. 170; Hogbin, 1970; Lowie, 1948, pp. 205–217; Read, 1965, p. 166; Underhill, 1939; Whitehead, 1981, pp. 82, 91–92). Blood has cropped up as a concern throughout the foregoing discussion of dreams and trance. Tree spirits haunt bloody trees. The smell of blood attracts the physical avatars of bird spirits, as kahyek attracts the spiritual ones. The same entities that as gunig confer the ability to attract kehyek seek to devour mother's milk, blood, menstrual fluid, and puerperal discharge. In this sense, they are reverse women-images that destroy what women's bodies create. The erotic ties these vampire mirror-women establish with adepts threaten incestuous madness, violence, and death. They are simultaneously erotically desirable women, as Roseman's analysis stresses, and the obscene reverse, unimaginable in human terms. The balance of kahyek and blood, coupled with the antagonism towards blood that kahyek creatures show, suggests an initial tentative answer to Roseman's question: Why, in egalitarian Senoi society, do women become adepts less often than men do? Perhaps, in blood, women have naturally a power that offsets the power men attain only at their peril.

Creative Blood

Childbirth

Childbirth (Dentan, 1978, pp. 110–116) exemplifies the power of blood. Puerperal blood requires particular care. A midwife wraps the placenta (*nsoob*, "nesting," from *soob*, "nest") in a banana leaf and stores it with the navel cord for the husband to take into the "cool" rain forest and store in the fork of a tree, so that the smell will not trickle into the groundwater and attract bird/water spirits. For the same reason, people suspend a platform of earth beneath the slatted floor where the birth takes place, so that the discharge (East Semai *trɔg; cpah,* Wilkinson. 1915, p. 55) does not drip on the ground (Cerruti, 1906/1908, pp. 116–117). Men may attend childbirth, but few do, fearing "all that blood" (Williams-Hunt, 1952, p. 64). Because "they have looked at the blood," attendent midwives and adepts require ritual bathing along with the mother and newborn baby.

Menstruation

Semai euphemisms protect people from invoking feared entities (Dentan, 1967). The proliferation of euphemisms for menstruation suggests that menstrua-

Table 2. East Semai Euphemisms for Menstruation

Euphemism	Root	Gloss
Gnoy	-goy	Sitting
La'na'	-la'	Restriction (on food)
Lngnong	-log	Tying up
Prmbu'	-prbu'	Avoid? (cf. bu, "female" [Means and Means, 1986, p. 23])
Crntoh	-ctoh	Making to perform blood sacrifice

tion is a dangerous condition. The first four euphemisms in Table 2 refer to the restrictions on menstruents' activities (cf. Skeat & Blagden, 1906, II, p. 54). Girls menstruating for the first few times should sit quietly in their sleeping compartments, leaving only to urinate or defecate. Individuals test the limits of these tabus, as the Senoi check all tabus, to see whether minor infractions have ill effects. If not, they relax their observance. Still, menstruating women should not take long walks or overexert themselves. If they sleep next to their husbands, they move away a little (Williams-Hunt, 1952, p. 71). If they bathe with other women, they undress separately, to conceal the leaf or pad of cloth with which they staunch the flow. As already noted, they run the risk of turning into tigers, from eating large animals or striped-bee honey, or, because menstrual fluids are like the fish poison whose apparitional soul can become a gunig, from poisoning fish. The only men who ever change into tigers are "great adepts." Tigers are the ultimate symbol of spiritual power. Menstruating women thus seem to be on the verge of attaining the highest spirit power, without benefit of gunig intermediaries.

Blood Sacrifice

Aslian "blood sacrifice" to placate/drive away thundersqualls has attracted a lot of ethnographic attention (e.g., Dentan, 1979, pp. 21–24, 36–37, 61–62; Endicott, 1979; Evans, 1923, pp. 81–82, 87–88, 199–206, 271–272; Karim, 1981, pp. 61–63; Needham, 1965; Schebesta, 1926, 1927; Singam, 1939/1961, p. 150; Skeat & Blagden, 1906, II, pp. 204–206; Williams-Hunt, 1952, pp. 72–75). Thundersqualls are the objective correlative of the dissolution into chaos which always threatens Senoi order and into which adepts tap. People, mostly women, respond to thundersqualls by slashing their shins, mixing the blood with rainwater and throwing the mixture into the shrieking winds, crying "Alas!" (to show that they are in pain) or "Go away!" Giving the storm riding agents of chaos the blood they seek, the sacrifices preserve the tidy Senoi world. The blood has creative and protective power to control the uncontrolled.

In short, the power of women's blood, although it may stem from the same source as the power of men's kahyek, can counteract the amorphous horrors that men's relations with gunig always threaten to unleash. Women make the ordinary world run properly, whereas men risk messing it up.

Spiritual Powers

Midwives

Midwifery (details in Dentan, 1978) is in some ways a mirror image of adepthood. People address their midwives (Senoi *bidat,* Malay *bidan*) by the same polite term, *tuhat,* they use for adepts (Dentan, 1983b). Men can become midwives but rarely do. Like adept skill, midwife ability varies from person to person and requires ritual bathing to keep it from going *jah,* "insipid, flat." Adepts attend some births, but people give midwives better presents for helping. Adepts and midwives should be buried with their heads to the sunrise, not to the sunset like ordinary people. Midwives may have significant dreams and are in touch across the dimensions with the Seven Original Midwives (Dentan, 1978; cf. Hood, 1976, pp. 109–111; Couillard, 1980, pp. 29–31). Fittingly, adepts and midwives often marry each other.

The main difference is that midwives "just grow." They need not study nor acquire familiars. They should be sturdy, so that "their" babies will be strong. Detractors sometimes allege that their adept husbands rely on their wives' supernatural sensitivity. The forceful behavior of Temiar adepts' wives in local affairs (Roseman, 1984) may be connected with midwifery.

Most recognized midwives are postmenopausal or sterile (cf. Harner, 1982, p. 55; Whitehead, 1981, p. 93). Perhaps their long experience with "creative blood" is the equivalent of adepts' long practice with calling gunig, so that Senoi recognize midwife ability as in a sense to be the equivalent of adepthood.

Sorcerers (Pracōo')

As midwives, mostly women, bring life, so sorcerers, usually men, may destroy it. Sorcery (*pnacōo'*) is not nearly as salient in Senoi life as midwifery or adepthood, and all my information comes from a few Semai men, none of whom were, or knew any, sorcerers. People from distant settlements, especially Temiar, practice sorcery. (Temiar can also turn into pigs or tigers). Sorcerers are "like adepts but different," relying heavily on spells, typically of Malay origin, rather than on dream familiars. A sorcerer puts a bit of a victim's food or lime (for chewing betelnut) in a bamboo internode or tin can. East Semai add stones, mud, sand, and a pair of crossed sticks (*hnunjam*). The sorcerer buries the container kneedeep, "like manioc to be leached," and curses the victims. They

suffer horrible pain from their shoulders to buttocks (-cpʉg crʉʉs) and succumb
to raging fever. If the sorcerer digs a channel from a stream to the buried
container, the victim swells up with water. Such sorcery can wipe out a settle-
ment "like an A-bomb." A west Semai "expert" (malib) in Malay spells may
avenge himself on a woman who has rejected his erotic advances by going to her
bathing spot and reciting a spell over some benzoin, bitter lemon (Citrus hystrix),
and some of the victim's possessions—a scrap of cloth, a hank of hair. Bird
spirit(s) will fly downstream to drive her mad (sasaw).

Thus, normally, sorcery involves no dreams at all, let alone lucid ones.
Rarely, however, a gunig will attack an enemy for an adept. Such gunig are
usually bird spirits or smēd insects of the sort already described (see also, for bird
spirits, Dentan, 1968a, pp. 23, 26–27; 1978, in press; Embun, 1959, II, pp. 1–
8; K. M. Endicott, 1970, pp. 57–59; Gimlette, 1971, pp. 47–51, 103–104;
Hood, 1976, pp. 112–116; McHugh, 1959, p. 64, 68–73; Schebesta, 1927, pp.
5–6, 26; Skeat, 1900, pp. 320–321, 329–331; Swettenham, 1895, pp. 197–198;
Werner, 1975, pp. 191–196, 514; Zainal, 1976, p. 80). Lowland West Semai
had heard of an adept in the Cameron Highlands who could breathe on a strip of
matting and turn it into a large poisonous centipede (ke'eb, Scolopendra sp.) that
attacked his enemies; and of another who could make his knife invisible and send
it out to kill. Temiar gunig may steal things for their adepts, Semai say. Nevertheless, although adepthood is an amoral condition, adepts use gunig to heal
the sick and help those otherwise in trouble far oftener than to do harm.

Great Adepts: Lucidity and Transformation

Introduction

For Senoi, the culmination of all these ASCs and spiritual experiences is
"great adeptness," which only "one in a hundred" adepts attain. Information is
so scarce that definitive statements are impossible, but my impression is that,
although women become ordinary adepts less often than men, there are almost as
many greatly adept women as men. Ordinary adepts depend on gunig to travel
and diagnose for them. "He doesn't see what's the matter with a person. It's as if
he's drunk (-buul), and gunig do the seeing." Great adepts travel themselves, see
for themselves, turn themselves into tigers, and, after death, become kraad (a
West Semai version of Malay keramat), local supernaturals that themselves can
become gunig.

Generalized accounts of "great adeptness" suggest phenomena like lucid
trancing. Untangling fact from myth is so difficult, however, that I will reproduce from my field notes the short accounts of adepts he has known that I got
from Ngah Hari bin Kulop, in whom a generation of American anthropologists
found their intellectual father. Readers can then judge for themselves.

Case Histories of West Semai "great adepts".

1. *To' Sang* (fl 1920s) had 7 hairs on his tongue and could scare away Malay slavers by yelling at them. He became a *kraad* elephant which haunts *Rngway,* a large limestone outcrop in Sahum parish.

2. *Kulop Lalu'*, Ngah Hari's grandfather, told kinsmen before he died around 1954 on Gn. Batu ("Stone Mt."): "If the day I die it doesn't rain, I'll become *kraad*. Bury me on a lofty peak. If you do, you can rely on my help. I won't live here but on Cnan Lumut (Malay Gn. Bubu). Don't forget me." His descendents gather to feast him every February, not naming him except euphemistically as the *kraad* of Stone Mountain. Attendance is optional.

3. *Johor* (d. ca. 1955) of Teiw Galah (Malay Sg. Galah) near Teluk Anson requested no special burial but in life would literally disappear for four or five days at a time, spending them with his supernatural wife, one of Those Beneath the Earth (for which, see Dentan 1970). People would think he had walked back from the market with them, only to find that he had stayed behind.

4. *Jaju' Glag* ("Granny Bracelet") of Teiw Grig (Malay Sg. Geriang), still alive in 1963, also vanished often, without explanation, especially while bathing. "We'd go calling for her, and then she'd pop out of the water. Of course, we might have been looking in the wrong direction."

5. *Bah Uca' bin Bah Lupeh,* also still alive in 1963, had several miraculous escapes, once when a Land Rover in which he was riding overturned and once when a raft capsized. His immunity may be due to his visiting the powerful *kraad* of Cba' Sungkay (Malay K. Sungkai).

These cases, of whom Ngah Hari knew the last four personally, do not match the generalized description of great adepts Senoi give. It is easy to see, however, how lives like the last four could give rise to such descriptions. Lucid trances seem to play no role in these cases.

Becoming *Kraad*

It seems fitting to conclude this fruitless search for lucidity in Senoi ASCs with a summary account from my field notes of events following the death of Din, a man who wanted to be remembered as a great adept. It shows how the notion of great adept arises in a particular case.

> Din (not his real name), chief adept in the West Semai settlement of Mncaak, died on April 7, 1963. He had asked for *pnasar*. Until the 1950s or 1960s, Senoi *pnasar* involved tree burial, as described by Kirk Endicott (1979), in cool primary rain forest with no undergrowth, often in a cotton tree (*Caryota mitis*). West Semai men build a little shed with a two-pitch attap roof and a bamboo or attap-palm floor 1½' to 4' off the ground, which they deck with the usual accoutrements of an adept's seance: spirit lure, asperger, whisk, brazier, etc. The dead man's helper (*assisten*) or heir apparent to his *gunig* "prays" briefly (*-cagɔh*). The burial party returns home dry-eyed, prays again and feasts. Seven days later, when they seal the grave, they imagine that the corpse will have vanished, leaving behind its shrouds. Pug marks around the shed show that the adept has become a *kraid* tiger. The men deposit food at the spot, *cagɔh,* and return home, hoping to dream that the adept has returned, telling the survivors to call on him in case of trouble and promising to help them.
>
> Mncaak elders, worried about offending the Malays who lived nearby, professed

themselves unsure about how to *-pasar* and buried Din in the usual way. On April 13, the day of the grave-sealing feast, Alang, Din's daughter's best girlfriend, was staying with the daughter in the house of Din's son, Blor. Alang dreamed that Din wanted a farewell feast of the sort given people about to depart on a long journey. She told Blor about the dream on April 14. Blor was upset (*-sngɔh*, "was afraid") because there was no way to tell whether the dream semblance was his father's spirit (*kloog*) or a deadly supernatural (*nyani'*).

Blor found Ngah Hari in a coffee shop and asked him to summon (*-panggil*) Din's *kloog*. Blor did not know how to summon spirits, but he knew better than to invoke (*-trlɔh*) any extradimensional being which was not already a familiar. (*Trnglɔh,* "calling into being," also means innovation or novelty, something never done before; the root *Hɔh* means alien, foreign, unknown, strange.) Ngah Hari agreed to help by praying (*-cagɔh*) but, not being himself adept, thought Blor should conduct a song seance, since Blor had heard Din's *gunig* songs often enough to know them by heart.

That evening the two men went to Blor's house on the hill, away from their Malay neighbors. Beside myself, only Blor's wife and children were there. Hearing Din's songs, Blor said, would just make people "miss" him (*-riaak*). Ngah Hari prayed but, atypically, became possessed (*-mʉit ya maay,* "was entered by others") and went on for an hour. Blor went into adept's shaking (*-krɔg*). Later he said that Bah Kuali', one of Din's male familiars, told him that Kuali' and the other *gunig* were at Blor's disposal. That night, however, the others remained outside, because Blor would have been unable to bear the memories of his father the familiars would recall. The next night's seance, Kuali' told Blor that *kraad* were purifying (*-'asoh*) Din to make him *kraad*.

Blor went to Din's grave to look for "signs," e.g., a piece of quartz or *srpeeg* rattan, but found only a tin can, left over from the grave offering. "He [Din] threw it away from the grave; probably didn't like it." He did find "footprints like those of cats and dogs," probably *gunig*. Blor hoped, if he had appropriate dreams, to hold another song seance in a month or so, when he was more resigned to his father's death. He badly wanted familiars and even tried to get some from a Geruntom River adept. The Geruntom familiars, however, had not "liked his body," and the dreams did not occur before I left Mncaak.

In short, although becoming kraad and a familiar oneself is in a sense the culmination of the spiritual odyssey of men or women, it seems no more particularly associated with lucid trance (or any sort of trance) than it is with creative blood or midwifery.

SUMMARY AND CONCLUSIONS

Who Needs Trance?

Traveling In and Out of Dreams

Semai say travel can substitute for dreams: One West Semai man explained that he was too footloose to dream much. Nowak found no Btsisi' who would want to be reborn a woman. Their reason was one familiar to Senoi: Women cannot move about as freely as men (Nowak, 1984a). The resulting inexperience makes them diffident: "Men's loincloths are long, women's loincloths are short" (Dentan, 1979, p. 68). Because Senoi weaning takes years, women young enough to travel or hunt often have infants, toddlers, or young children to impede them. To scare off dangerous animals, they go into the forest or town in groups large and noisy enough to scare off dangerous animals or "Malay" rapists (e.g., Dentan, 1979, pp. 62–63; K. L. Endicott, 1979, pp. 22, 35–36, 41, 88–90; Nowak, 1984a).

How much of Senoi women's immobility is due to fear of rape is imponderable. As a folk explanation, applicable when there are no Malays for miles around, it expresses traditional Senoi fear of (formless) violence in a concrete way. Since homosexuality is an alien notion to Senoi, let alone homosexual rape, this expression necessarily applies only to women victims but to both male and supernatural assailants.

This is where the sexual component of mpo' and trance becomes important. The violent eroticism of supernaturals may arouse the same anxieties that express themselves as fear of rape by "Malays." In other words, women may find men's powers not only undesirable but frightening and obscene. Aslian women do occasionally reject importunant supernaturals (Couillard, 1980, p. 47). Trance may not be worth its nastiness for people with access to a complementary source of power like blood. Indeed, perhaps, as in nearby Melanesia and New Guinea, male salience in adepthood simply reflects men's uneasy sense that women have the really significant powers and men's symmetry, however fearful, will never burn as bright.

Conclusion

Interpretion

Roseman's meticulous and insightful study of Temiar magical-musical praxis is a major contribution to Senoi ethnography. My quibbles have only been about emphasis. I think the genders are somewhat more equal than she does. My impression is that, like many secularized Americans, she does not fully recognize that, for most of the world's peoples, including the Senoi, the sacred is not merely pure and "nice" but also in many ways repellent and terrifying. Positivist criteria do not apply, so that no final interpretation is possible. The two versions of Senoi life can coexist comfortably.

Lucidity

Neither can coexist with Stewart's "Senoi dream theory," however. The foregoing lengthy examination of all Senoi ASCs known to me or recorded in the literature uncovers no phenomenon unequivocally like the lucidity postulated in Stewart's account. Faraday and Wren-Lewis (1984), explicitly looking for such lucidity, elicited only denials from their Temiar informants.

Yet a similarly close examination of shamanic activity elsewhere may turn up some clear cases of lucid dreaming/trancing. Michael Harner is already conducting shamanic sessions based on Jivaro praxis (e.g., 1973, 1982; Cowan, 1984), much like American versions of Senoi dream therapy. More research, as always, is needed.

REFERENCES

Azizah, K. (1979). Research of the Orang Asli in the University of Malaya. *Federation Museums Journal, 24,* 219–232.

Baharon A. bin Raffiei. (1966). Engku—spirit of thunders. *Federated Malay Museums Journal, 11,* 34–37.

Baharon A. bin Raffiei. (1979). Research on the Orang Asli and its relevance to the Department of Orang Asli Affairs Malaysia. *Federation Museums Journal, 24,* 219–232.

Baskaran, K. (1963, August 8). The cool, cool cats deep in the jungle. *Straits Times,* p. 7.

Benedict, P. K. (1975). *Austro-Thai language and culture with a glossary of roots.* New Haven: Human Relations Area Files.

Benjamin, G. (1966). Temiar social groupings. *Federation Museums Journal, 11,* 1–25.

Benjamin, G. (1967). Temiar kinship. *Federation Museums Journal, 12,* 1–25.

Benjamin, G. (1968a). Headmanship and leadership in Temiar society. *Federation Museums Journal, 13,* 1–43.

Benjamin, G. (1968b). Temiar personal names. *Bijdragen tot de Taal-, Land- en Volkenkunde, 124,* 99–134.

Benjamin, G. (1976a). Austroasiastic subgroupings and pre-history in the Malay Peninsula. In Philip N. Jenner, Laurence C. Thompson, & Stanley Starosta (Eds.), *Austroasiastic Studies, Part I* (pp. 37–129). Honolulu: University Press of Hawaii.

Benjamin, G. (1976b). An outline of Temiar grammar. In Philip N. Jenner, Laurence C. Thompson, & Stanley Starosta (Eds.), *Austrosiastic Studies, Part I* (pp. 129–188). Honolulu: University Press of Hawaii.

Blacking, J. A. R. (1954/1955). Musical instruments of the Malayan aborigines. *Federation Museums Journal, 1/2,* 35–52.

Brown, C. H. (1982). Folk zoological life-forms and linguistic marking. *Journal of Ethnobiology, 2(1),* 95–112.

Brown, C. H., & Witkowski, S. R. (1980). Appendix B. Language universals. In D. Levinson & M. J. Malone (Eds.), *Toward explaining human culture* (pp. 359–384). New Haven, CT: Human Relations Area Files.

Carey, I. Y. (1961). *Tengleg kui serok.* Kuala Lumpur: Dewan Bahasa dan Pustaka.

Carey, I. Y. (1976). *Orang asli. The aboriginal tribes of peninsular Malaysia.* Kuala Lumpur: Oxford University Press.

Cerruti, G. B. (1908). *My friends the savages* (I. Stone Sapietro Trans., Como) (original work published in 1906).

Collier, J., & Rosaldo, M. Z. (1981). Politics and gender in simple societies. In S. B. Ortner & H. Whitehead (Eds.), *Sexual meanings: The cultural construction of gender and sexuality* (pp. 275–329). Cambridge: Cambridge University Press.

Couillard, M.-A. (1980). *Tradition in tension: Carving in a Jah Hut community.* Penang: Penerbit Universiti Sains Malaysia.

Cowan, T. D. (1984). Dreamwatch. *Dream Network Bulletin, 3*(3), 19–20.

Cuisinier, J. (1936). *Danses magiques de Kelantan.* Paris: Institut d'Ethnologie.

Dahlan, H. M. (1976). Penyelidikan terhadap masyarakat Orang Asli masakini. *Federation Museums Journal, 24,* 211–216.

Dentan, R. K. (1964). Senoi. In Frank M. Lebar, Gerald D. Hickey, & John K. Musgreave (Eds.), *Ethnic groups of mainland Southeast Asia* (pp. 176–181). New Haven: Human Relations Area Files.

Dentan, R. K. (1967). The mammalian taxonomy of the Sen'oi Semai. *Malayan Nature Journal 20,* 100–106.

Dentan, R. K. (1968a). Notes on Semai ethnoentomology. *Malayan Nature Journal, 21,* 17–28.

Dentan, R. K. (1968b). The Semai response to mental aberration. *Bijdragen tot de Taal-, Land- en Volkenkunde, 124,* 135–158.

Dentan, R. K. (1970). Labels and rituals in Semai classification. *Ethnology, 9,* 16–25.

Dentan, R. K. (1978). Notes on childhood in a nonviolent context. In A. Montagu (Ed.), *Learning non-aggression.* London: Oxford University Press.

Dentan, R. K. (1979). *The Semai* (Rev. ed.). New York: Holt, Rinehart & Winston.

Dentan, R. K. (1981). Review of Kirk M. Endicott, Batek Negrito religion. *Journal of Asian Studies, 40,* 421–423.

Dentan, R. K. (1983a). Senoi dream praxis. *Dream Network Bulletin, 2*(5), 1–3, 12.

Dentan, R. K. (1983b). Hit and run ethnograph [*sic*]: Reply to Alexander Randall. *Dream Network Bulletin, 2*(8), 11–12.

Dentan, R. K. (1983c). *A dream of Senoi.* Council on International Studies, State University of New York at Buffalo, (Special Study 150).

Dentan, R. K. (1984). Techniques and antecedents: A response to Gieseler. *Lucidity Letter, 4*(2–3), 5–7.

Dentan, R. K. (1986). Ethnographic considerations in the cross-cultural study of dreaming. In J. Gackenbach (Ed.), *Sleep and dreams: A sourcebook* (pp. 317–358). New York: Garland.

Dentan, R. K. (1987). You can never find a cop when you need one: A response to Faraday. *Association for the Study of Dreams Newsletter, 4*(2), 14–16.

Dentan, R. K. (1988). Rejoinder to McGlashan. *Parabola 13*(1).

Dentan, R. K. (in press). Ambiguity, polymorphism and transmutation in Semai medical praxis. *Social Science and Medicine.*

Domhoff, G. W. (1985). *The mystique of dreams. A search for utopia through Senoi dream theory.* Berkeley: University of California Press.

Dyer, T. G. (1980). *Theodore Roosevelt and the idea of race.* Baton Rouge: Louisiana State University Press.

Embun, Ahmad bin. (1959). *Hantu dengan kerja-nya. 2 vv.* Penang: Sinaran Bros.

Endicott, K. L. (1979). *Batek Negrito sex roles.* Unpublished master's thesis, Australian National University, Australia.

Endicott, K. M. (1970). *An analysis of Malay magic.* Oxford: Clarendon Press.

Endicott, K. M. (1979). *Batek Negrito religion. The world-view and rituals of a hunting and gathering people of peninsular Malaysia.* Oxford: Clarendon Press.

Evans, I. H. N. (1923). *Studies in religion, folk-lore* [sic] *custom in British North Borneo and the Malay peninsula.* Cambridge: Cambridge University Press.

Evans, I. H. N. (1937). *The Negritos of Malaya.* Cambridge: Cambridge University Press.

Faraday, A. (1986). Review of G. W. Domhoff, *The mystique of dreams. Association for the Study of Dreams Newsletter, 3*(4), 12–13.

Faraday, A., & Wren-Lewis, J. (1983). Reply to Randall. *Dream Network Bulletin, 2*(8), 10–11.

Faraday, A., & Wren-Lewis, J. (1984). The selling of the Senoi. *Lucidity Letter, 3*(1), 1–3.

Fix, A. G. (1982). Genetic structure of the Semai. In M. H. Crawford & J. H. Mielke (Eds.),

Current developments in anthropological genetics. Ecology and population structure. New York: Plenum Press.

Fix, A. G., & Lie-Injo, L. E. (1975). Genetic microdifferentiation in the Semai Senoi of Malaysia. *American Journal of Physical Anthropology, 43,* 7–55.

Friedl, E. (1975). *Women and men: An anthropological view.* New York: Holt, Rinehart & Winston.

Gimlette, J. D. (1971). *Malay poisons and charm cures.* Kuala Lumpur: Oxford University Press. (Original work published 1915)

Guenther, M. G. (1975/1976). The San trance dance: Ritual and revitalization among the farm Bushmen of the Ghanzi District, Republic of Botswana. *Journal of the South West African Scientific Society, 30,* 45–53.

Guenther, M. G. (1979). Bushman religion and the (non) sense of anthropological theory of religion. *Sociologus, 29,* 102–132.

Guenther, M. G. (1986). From foragers to miners and bands to bandits: On the flexibility and adaptability of Bushman band societies. *Sprache und Geschichte in Afrika, 7,* 133–159.

Harner, M. J. (1973). *The Jivaro. People of the sacred waterfalls.* New York: Anchor.

Harner, M. J. (1982). *The way of the shaman: A guide to power and healing.* New York: Bantam.

Herdt, G. H. (1977). The shaman's "calling" among the Sambia of New Guinea. In B. Juillerat (Ed.), *Madness, possession and shamanism in New Guinea, Journal de la Societe des Oceanistes* (Special ed.), *33,* 153–167.

Herdt, G. H. (1981). *Guardians of the flutes. Idioms of masculinity. A study of ritualized homosexual behavior.* New York: McGraw-Hill.

Hogbin, I. (1970). *The island of menstruating women.* Scranton, PA: Chandler Publishing Co.

Hood, H. M. S. (1976). Morality and restraint among the Semelai of Malaysia. In H. M. Dahlan (Ed.), *The nascent Malaysian society: Developments, trends and problems* (pp. 53–69). Siri Monograf Jabatan Antropologi dan Sosiologi Universiti Kebangsaan Malaysia.

Hood, H. M. S. (1979). The cultural context of Semelai trance. *Federation Museums Journal, 24,* 107–124.

Howell, S. (1983). Kilton Stewart failed to understand what he saw. *Dream Network Bulletin, 2*(11), 8.

Iskandar, T. (1970). *Kamus Dewan.* Kuala Lumpur: Dewan Bahasa dan Pustaka.

Jimin I. B. (1968). Distribution of Orang Asli in West Malaysia. *Federation Museums Journal, 13,* 44–48.

Johnson, J. (1978). Elements of Senoi dreaming applied to a Western culture. *Sundance Community Dream Journal, 2*(1), 50–61.

Karim, W. J. begum. (1981). Ma' Betisek concepts of living things. *London School of Economics Monograph on Social Anthropology 54.*

Kennedy, E. L. (1979). Discussant's comments for the second half of this volume: A perspective of feminist studies. In Ann McElroy & Carolyn Matthiasson (Eds.), *Sex-roles in changing cultures. SUNY/Buffalo Occasional Papers in Anthropology, 1,* 189–193.

Krohn, A., & Gutmann, D. (1971). Changes in mastery style with age. *Psychiatry, 34,* 289–300.

Leacock, E. (1978). Society and gender. In Ethel Tobach & B. Rosoff (Eds.), *Genes and gender* (pp. 75–85). New York: Gordian Press.

Lebar, F. M. (1964). Semang. In *Ethnic groups of mainland Southeast Asia* (pp. 181–186). New Haven: Human Relations Area Files.

"Librarian." (1979). Checklist on materials on the Orang Asli available in the University of Malaya library. *Federation Museums Journal, 24,* 245–265.

Lowie, R. H. (1948). *Primitive religion.* New York: Liverwright.

Manssor, Ahmad Ezanee, Modh. Razha Razha, Syed Jamal Jaafar, Tan Chi Beng, & Shuichi Nagata. (1973). Peringkat-peringkat umur di kalangan Orang-orang Kensiu di Kedah dan Orang-orang Kintak dan Temiar di Ulu Perak—satu lapuran pendahuluan. *Manusia dan Masyarakat, 2,* 117–125.

McGlashan, Alan (1987). The dream people. *Parabola 12*(3), 11–15.

McHugh, J. N. (1959). *Hantu hantu: An account of ghost belief in modern Malaya.* Singapore: Eastern Universities Press.

Means, N., & Means, P. B. (1986). *Sengoi-English and English-Sengoi dictionary.* Gordon Means, ed. Toronto: Joint Center on Modern East Asia, University of Toronto and York University.

Needham, R. (1965). Blood, thunder and mockery of animals. *Sociologus, 14,* 136–149.

Noone, H. D. (1936). Report on the settlements and welfare of the Ple-Temiar Senoi of the Perak-Kelantan watershed. *Journal of the Federated Malay States Museums, 19,* 1–85.

Nowak, B. S. (1979). Women's roles and status in a changing Iroquois society. In Ann McElroy & Carolyn Matthiasson (Eds.), *Sex-roles in changing cultures. SUNY/Buffalo Occasional Papers in Anthropology, 1,* 95–110.

Nowak, B. S. (1983). *Cooperation and partnership: A look at gender relations among Hma' Btsisi' of West Malaysia.* Paper presented at the 82nd annual meeting of the American Anthropological Association, Chicago, IL.

Nowak, B. S. (1984a). *Ideal versus real: Practicality in the sexual division of labor among Hma' Btsisi'.* Paper presented at 11th annual congress of the Canadian Ethnology Society, Montreal, Quebec.

Nowak, B. S. (1984b). Can the partnership last? Marital partners and development. *Cultural Survival Quarterly, 8*(2), 9–11.

Rainwater, J. (1979). *You're in charge! A guide to becoming your own therapist.* Culver City, CA: Peace Press.

Read, K. E. (1965). *The high valley.* New York: Charles Scribner's Sons.

Robarchek, C. (1977). *Semai nonviolence: A systems approach to understanding.* Unpublished doctoral dissertation, University of California at Riverside.

Robarchek, C. (1983). Senoi anthropologist speaks up. *Dream Network Bulletin, 2*(8), 8.

Robarchek, C., & Dentan, R. K. (1987). "Blood drunkenness" and the bloodthirsty Semai: Unmaking another anthropological myth. *American Anthropologist, 89,*356–365.

Roseman, M. (1984). The social structuring of sound: An example from Temiar of peninsular Malaysia. *Ethnomusicology, 28,* 411–445.

Rovics, H. (1983). American Senoi dreamwork. *Dream Network Bulletin, 2*(11), 1–2, 6–7, 13–14.

Sacks, K. (1975). Engels revisited: The organization of production and private property. In Rayna Reiter (Ed.), *Toward an anthropology of women.* New York: Monthly Review Press.

Sanday, P. R. (1981). *Female power and male dominance. On the origins of sexual inequality.* Cambridge: Cambridge University Press.

Schebesta, P. (1926). Religiose Anschauungen der Semang uber die Orang Hidop (die Unsterblichen). *Archiv fur Religionswissenschaft, 24,* 209–233.

Schebesta, P. (1927). Religiose Anschauungen der Semang uber die Orang Hidop (die Unsterblichen). *Archiv fur Religionswissenschaft, 25,* 5–35.

Schebesta, P. (1973). *Among the forest dwarfs of Malaya.* Kuala Lumpur: Oxford. (Original work published in 1928)

Schieffelin, E. L. (1977). The unseen influence: Tranced mediums as historical innovators. In B. Juillerat (Ed.), *Madness, possession and shamanism in New Guinea, Journal de la Societe des Oceanistes* (special ed.), *33,* 169–178.

Schlegel, A. (1977). Toward a theory of sexual stratification. In A. Schlegel (Ed.), *Sexual stratification: A cross-cultural view* (pp. 1–40). New York: Columbia University Press.

Shaw, W. (1973). Aspects of spirit-mediumship in peninsular Malaysia. *Federation Museums Journal, 18,* 71–176.

Singam, S. D. R. (1961). *Malayan tit bits* (4th ed.). Singapore: Liang Khoo Printing Company. (Original work published in 1939)

Skeat, W. W. (1900). *Malay magic: Being an introduction to the folklore and popular religion of the Malay peninsular.* London: Macmillan.

Skeat, W. W., & Blagden, C. O. (1906). *Pagan races of the Malay peninsula.* London: Macmillan.

Slot, J. A. (1935). Koro in Zuid-Celebes. *Geneeskundig Tijdschrift voor Nederlandsch-Indie, 75,* 811–820.

Stacey, T. (1953). *The hostile sun. A Malayan journey.* London: Gerald Duckworth.

Stewart, K. R. (1948). *Magico-religious beliefs and practices* [sic] *in primitive society–A sociological interpretation of their therapeutic aspects.* Unpublished doctoral dissertation, London School of Economics.

Stewart, K. (1953/1954). Culture and personality in two primitive groups. *Complex, 9,* 3–23.

Stewart, K. (1954a). *Pygmies and dream giants.* New York: W. W. Norton.

Stewart, K. (1954b). Mental hygiene and world peace. *Mental Hygiene, 38,* 387–403.

Stewart, K. (1962). The dream comes of age. *Mental Hygiene, 46,* 230–237.

Stewart, K. (1972a). Dream theory in Malaya. In C. T. Tart (Ed.), *Altered states of consciousness* (pp. 161–170.). Garden City, NY: Anchor.

Stewart, K. (1972b). Dream exploration among the Senoi. In Theodore Roszak (Ed.), *Sources* . New York: Harper & Row.

Stewart, O. C. (1944). Washo-Northern Paiute peyotism. *University of California Publications in American Archaeology and Ethnology, 40,* 63–142.

Stewart, O. C. (1964). The need to popularize basic concepts. *Current Anthropology, 5,* 431–442.

Stimson, W. R. (1983). Anthropology of the dream people. *Dream Network Bulletin, 2*(8), 1, 14–15.

Swettenham, F. H. (1895). *Malay sketches.* London: John Lane.

Tocqueville, A. de. (1951). *Democracy in America* (The Henry Reeve text as revised by Francis Bowen. Phillips Bradley, Ed., Vol. 1.). New York: Alfred A. Knopf. (Original work published in 1835)

Underhill, R. M. (1939). *The social organization of the Papago Indians.* New York: Columbia University Press.

Walker, A. R. (1979). Orang Asli studies at Universiti Sains Malaysia, 1971–1979. *Federation Museums Journal, 24,* 235–243.

Walters, M. & Dentan, R. K. (1985a). Are lucid dreams universal? Two unequivocal cases of lucid dreaming among Chinese university students in Beijing, 1985. *Lucidity Letter, 4*(1), 12–14.

Walters, M., & Dentan, R. K. (1985b). ''Dreams, illusions, bubbles, shadows'': Awareness of 'unreality' while dreaming among Chinese college students. *Association for the Study of Dreams Newsletter, 2*(3), 10–12, 16.

Werner, R. (1975). *Jah-het of Malaysia, art and culture.* Kuala Lumpur: Penerbit University Malaya.

Whitehead, H. (1981). The bow and the burden strap: A new look at institutionalized homosexuality in native North America. In Sherry B. Ortner & Harriet Whitehead, (Eds.), *Sexual meanings: The cultural construction of gender and sexuality* (pp. 80–115). Cambridge: Cambridge University Press.

Wilkinson, R. J. (1915). A vocabulary of central Sakai (dialect of the aboriginal communities in the Gopeng Valley). *Papers on Malay Subjects* (2nd series #3).

Wilkinson, R. J. (1926). Supplement: The aboriginal tribes. *Papers on Malay Subjects* (2nd series #5).

Williams, S. K. (1980) *Jungian-Senoi dreamwork manual* (Rev. ed.). Berkely, CA: Journey Press.

Williams-Hunt, P. D. R. (1952). *An introduction to the Malayan aborigines.* Kuala Lumpur: Government Press.

Zainal, K. (1976). Magical Practices in a rural Malay community in Sarawak. In H. M. Dahlan (Ed.), The nascent Malaysian society: Developments, trends and problems. *Siri Monograf Jabatan Antropologi dan Sosiologi.* Universiti Kebangsaam. Malaysia *3,* 71–97.

II

Empirical Approaches to the Study of Lucid Dreaming

5

From Spontaneous Event to Lucidity

A Review of Attempts to Consciously Control Nocturnal Dreaming

CHARLES T. TART

Within Western culture, dreams have been and are still generally regarded as events that just happen to people, bizarre nocturnal events that seldom bear any discernible relation to the waking life of the dreamer. If dreams are given any positive value, they are seen as unsolicited gifts. When not particularly valued, the more usual situation in our culture, they are seen as mostly meaningless, chance events. The occasional relationships between life events and dreams tend to be fitted into what Hadfield (1954) charmingly called the "pickled walnut theories" of dreaming: If you ate something that disagreed with you, it might result in the bizarre mental activity of dreaming.

A major shift in the attitude in our culture resulted from Freud's claim, in 1900, that dreams are valuable clues to our unconscious mental life (Freud, 1954). He argued that rather than being spontaneous happenings, dreams are reliably and lawfully related to recent events (day residue), as modified by our fundamental drives and personal developmental history. Life events influence dreams in a transformed, rather than a direct way. Freud argued that the technique of free association could be used to trace the subtle connections between daily life and dream experience, showing that life experience, interacting with unconscious dynamics, makes the dream a lawfully determined, rather than a spontaneous event. Although most of the evidence supporting Freud's claim is a

This is an updated version of a chapter of the same title that originally appeared in B. Wolman, M. Ullman, & W. Webb (Eds.), *Handbook of dreams: Research, theories and applications:* New York: Van Nostrand Reinhold, 1979. It is reprinted here by permission of the original publishers.

CHARLES T. TART • Department of Psychology, University of California at Davis, Davis, CA 95616.

*post*dictive fitting of life events and dream content together from association in analytic sessions, and so open to alternative explanations, some studies have claimed *pre*dictive validation of this theory.

With the birth of the modern era of sleep research, starting in 1953 with the publication of Eugene Aserinsky and Nathaniel Kleitman's "Regularly occurring Periods of Eye Motility and Concommitant Phenomena during Sleep," more direct tests of whether the content of nocturnal dreams could be directly influenced by presleep operations, such as specific suggestions as to what to dream about, began to be carried out. These studies showed that some direct, untransformed *presleep control of dream content* was possible. Further, publication of Kilton Stewart's paper, "Dream Theory in Malaya," and Frederick van Eeden's "A Study of Dreams" in my widely read *Altered States of Consciousness* (Tart, 1969a) dovetailed with extensive professional and public interest in altered states of consciousness and suggested to many individuals that they could learn to achieve an altered state of consciousness termed "lucid dreaming," a state in which they could exercise conscious control over the events of their dreams *while they were dreaming,* what I shall term *concurrent control of dream content.*

Rather than viewing dream content as either a spontaneous activity or one postdictable (but seldom predictable) only through complex and subtle Freudian dynamics, evidence now demands that we view it as an activity that can be clearly influenced to at least some extent by an individual's presleep desires. Indeed, the psychological quality of dreaming can sometimes be transformed into a discrete state of consciousness (d-SoC)[2] in which direct, volitional control of content is possible.

I shall review the literature on the control of the content of nocturnal dreaming, with special emphasis on methodological considerations relevant to creating a sound scientific knowledge of this area. This review will not deal with ways of affecting the more general process of dreaming, such as shifts in the timing of Stage 1-REM periods but will focus on content changes. Some of this material has been reviewed from other perspectives also in the last 14 years, and the interested reader should see review papers by Arkin (1966), Evans (1972), Garfield (1974b), Moss (1967), Tart (1965a,b; 1967; 1969b), and Walker and Johnson (1974).

Almost all of the laboratory studies reviewed in this chapter have accepted the widely held theory that the d-SoC we call dreaming (a *psychological* construct) is uniquely associated with Stage 1-REM periods, or at least that "dream-

---

[2]The term discrete state of consciousness (d-SoC) will be used throughout this chapter as a scientific term to cover the stabilized patterns of interacting psychological factors called by such common names as "waking state," "hypnosis," "dreaming" "hypnagogic state," and so on, in accordance with its definition and usage in my systems approach to consciousness (see primarily Tart, 1975). The more common term, "state of consciousness," has been used in too general a manner to be scientifically useful.

like'' reports of mental activity are far more frequently associated with awakenings from Stage 1-REM periods than with awakenings from NREM stages of sleep. The latter kinds of awakenings often yield either no recall or reports of more "thoughtlike" activity.

Although this assumption will not be explicitly questioned in this review, we should be aware that there are data contradicting this dichotomy (see Rechtschaffen, 1973, for a review). Some subjects report quite dreamlike activity from NREM awakenings. As an especially striking example, Brown and Cartwright (1978) instructed subjects to press a microswitch taped to one hand whenever they were aware, during sleep, of experiencing visual images. The experimenter than awakened the subject for a report. Eight subjects' reports were scored for their dreamlike quality on a reliable (judges correlated .90) 5-point scale. There were as many switch presses by the subjects in NREM sleep as in Stage 1-REM sleep, and the ratings of the reports on dreamlike quality showed that the subjects' own judgments as to when they were experiencing visual imagery in sleep were almost twice as dreamlike as control awakenings initiated on other nights by the experimenter, for both Stage 1-REM and NREM awakenings. A further case study of one high-responding NREM signaler again obtained very dreamlike reports from his NREM awakenings. I believe the next decade of research will have to focus much more closely on the question of just what are the physiological correlates of the psychological d-SoC of dreaming, as our current conceptions are probably too simplistic; but in this review I shall generally use the assumption that the psychological d-SoC we label *dreaming* is rather uniquely associated with the discrete physiological state we label *Stage 1-REM periods*.

METHODOLOGICAL CONSIDERATIONS

As we shall see in some detail later, there are a very large number of variables that can potentially affect how attempts to influence nocturnal dream content eventually succeed. The vast majority of these variables have only been studied infrequently and unsystematically. Affecting dream content is a complex, multistep process, but most of the steps are very poorly specified and understood.

Partially, this is due to the nature of laboratory sleep research: It is an expensive undertaking, and not many variables can be manipulated at one time. Owing to the ambiguous specifications of most of these many variables, I can do little more in the present review than indicate what sorts of things are important to look out for, rather than reach any kind of firm conclusions about the effects of various variables on affecting dream content. Thus the empirical studies later reviewed can, at this date, do little more than roughly outline *possibilities* about dream content control.

To begin our discussion of the many variables affecting the way attempts to

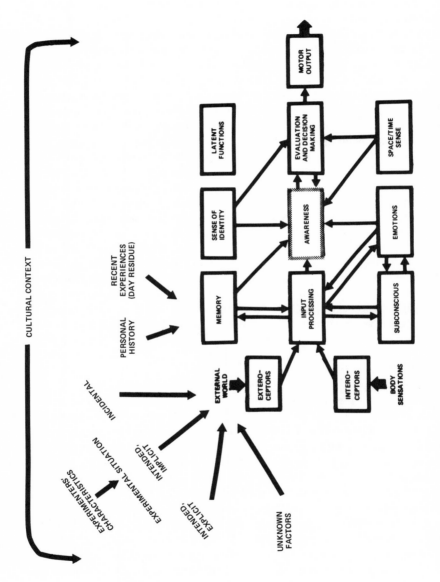

Figure 1. External psychological factors affecting later dream content, as modified by constituents of waking consciousness.

influence dream content exert their effect, consider Figure 1. This diagram is deliberately complex in order to illustrate the many variables involved only at the start of the process we consider, namely the giving of some kind of specific presleep suggestions as to what a subject should dream about, either in the context of the sleep laboratory or at home. We shall consider other variables that occur if an altered d-SoC such as hypnosis is added to the process and the physiological/psychological state transitions inherent in the process of sleeping later.

Figure 1 has two major sections. The lower-right-hand series of labeled psychological process blocks and interconnecting arrows represents a systems approach to understanding the major functioning of ordinary, waking consciousness, as described elsewhere (Lee, Ornstein, Galin, Deikman & Tart, 1975; Tart, 1974a, 1975, 1976, 1987). The variables at the upper left, shown as impinging on the subject through his or her exteroceptors (eyes, ears, and, to some extent, touch, in the laboratory situation), represent the external experimental variables.

To begin with, any experiment is never carried out in isolation, but within a cultural context. Both the experimenters and the subjects have been enculturated within a specific culture to share a relatively common set of views, including attitudes about the importance of dreams, their nature, and the degree to which they can be deliberately manipulated. Although we have some historical and anthropological data on different cultural attitudes toward dreams and volitional control of them, I know of no direct experimental data on possible differences; so the most we can do with those cultural variables at the present time is be sensitive to the fact that in many important ways any results we have may be culture-bound. This is a particularly hard point to keep in mind: We tend to think we are investigating basic biological culture-free aspects of man because we are taking physiological measures.

Within the overall cultural context of the experiment, we have a quite complex specific situation that we have long been fooling ourselves into believing is quite simple. We have liked to believe that (a) the laboratory is a rather neutral setting; (b) a clearly defined experimental manipulation, the independent variable, is applied to a subject; and (c) the behaviors observed, the dependent variables, are either exclusively functions of the independent variable or of the independent variable and random variation. In the latter case, we believe that by running a number of subjects this random variation cancels out, so that we can ascertain the true relationship between the independent and dependent variables. This oversimplified view has now been amply demonstrated to be incorrect for most experimental studies; I recommend Silverman's review book (1977) for an excellent overview of the complexities inherent in running a subject in a psychological or physiological) laboratory. A more realistic view is to assume that any subject is an active problem solver, forming his or her own conclusions about what is expected in an experiment. Thus many unknown, covert, or even incidental variables can be potentially more important than formal independent variables.

Demand Characteristics

Among the main variables influencing the subject, we must consider the experimenter (or experimenters) and the experimental situation they create. The experimenter's personal characteristics and manner can generally affect the way he treats subjects and probably thus affect their dreams. Experimenter characteristics are almost never described in the reports. What is likely to be described in an experimental report is the formal experimental variable, labeled the "intended, explicit" stimulation that the subject receives in Figure 1. Perhaps even more important, experimenters usually have an intellectual and oftan an emotional investment in verifying a particular hypothesis, and so implicitly and covertly *deliberately* (rather than randomly) affect subjects in ways likely to make this hypothesis come true. This influence is what Orne (1962) has called so nicely the "demand characteristics" of the experimental situation, a covert demand on the subject to please the experimenter by verifying the experimenter's hypothesis. Let us consider a specific example.

Stern, Saayman, and Tougy (1978) carried out a sophisticated study of the effects of implicit demand characteristics of the type likely to be commonplace in sleep research. Both laboratory (2 nights) and home dream reports (12 nights) were collected from 12 subjects. All subjects filled out a form asking specific questions about the *settings* of their dreams in addition to asking for a general account of the dream. Half the subjects had forms asking about outdoor/nature settings, half about urban settings: This was the only experimental treatment. The experimenter who interacted with the subjects in the laboratory was blind as to which report-form treatment group the subjects were in. Postexperimental inquiry revealed that none of the subjects consciously guessed that the report form was designed to affect the content of their dreams. A statistically significant effect was found, however, equally spread over the home and laboratory dreams.

The effects of the report forms were assessed both in a global rating of outdoor/nature versus urban environment, on which two independent judges correlated .80, and with two setting-relevant word-count indexes, on which the independent judges correlated .91 and .70. Both types of measures showed a significant increase in suggested settings in the groups receiving each of the two reporting forms, compared to their own baseline dreams. The absolute sizes of the changes were small by the overall rating, about a 1-point change on a 7-point scale. The word index measure change was stronger, indicating a three- to fourfold increase in appropriate setting-relevant words.

Although the absolute magnitude of the significant changes in the Stern, Saayman, and Tougy study does not seem large, the potential importance of demand characteristics in affecting other studies about the effects of various presleep suggestions on dream content may become clearer when we realize the magnitudes of Stern, Saayman, and Touyz's changes were larger than what is reported in many of these other studies.

General Situational Effects

There are many incidental aspects of the experimental situation not directly related to the formal independent variable or the experimenters' covert demands, which have been labeled "incidental" in Figure 1. As some examples, the so-called first night effect was recognized early in the era of modern sleep research (Agnew, Webb, & Williams, 1966; Domhof & Kamiya, 1964; Kales, Jacobson, Kales, Kun, & Weissbuch, 1967; Mendels & Hawkins, 1967; Rechtschaffen & Verdone, 1964), and sleep researchers have routinely treated the first laboratory night as an adaptation one without analyzing its data as a consequence. The particulars of a laboratory situation may affect dream content for more than a single night, however (see, e.g., Dement, Kahn, & Roffwarg, 1965; Hall, 1967; Whitman, Pierce, Maas, & Baldridge, 1962). The general characteristics of the experimenter who works with a subject may directly or indirectly affect dream content (Fox, Kramer, Baldridge, Whitman, & Ornstein, 1968; Keith, 1962; Tart, 1964a; Whitman, Kramer, & Baldridge, 1963). Further, it is not clear how much the content of dreams reported in the laboratory is representative of home dream content, and there have been some demonstrations that content characteristics of laboratory and home dreams differ (see, e.g., Domhof & Kamiya, 1964; Hall & Van de Castle, 1966).

Day Residue

Subjects do not enter the sleep laboratory from a vacuum: They have had a whole developmental history of their own that is likely to influence the kind of dreams they have, and, even more specifically, they have had a variety of experiences over the past few days that may influence their dreams. We may lump these influences together as "day residue," understanding that it is not necessarily limited to only the previous 24 hours. There is typically no specification or attempts to even assess what kinds of day residues subjects may bring to the laboratory with them; so this is a very uncontrolled variable. As with the other variables discussed, it is a poor (albeit common) assumption to believe that the particulars of subjects' day residues cancel out in a random fashion, given the small number of subjects in most dream studies.

The Subject's Internal Processes

Considering now the subject himself, the lower-right-hand portion of Figure 1 is a diagram of my systems approach to understanding ordinary consciousness.

No attempt will be made to explain it in full here, but it will simply be used to illustrate several important points. First, consciousness is not simply "there"; it is an active, ongoing, constructive process. Second, although we can identify components of it for convenience of analysis (for instance the various labeled processes in Figure 1), we must also recognize that, as in any system, consciousness as a whole has emergent system properties that are not straightforward predictions from a knowledge of component psychological processes. Thus the subject is in the laboratory situation, and a variety of stimuli are impinging on his exteroceptors, but this in no way results in a "simple perception" of what we naively assume is there. Our sensory input goes through complex, nonconscious, automated construction processes, processes resulting from our personal socialization. The complex constructions we naively take as simple perceptions thus reflect our personal history and are influenced by the total system properties, including our needs, at the moment. Thus Figure 1 shows all stimuli passing through the input processing subsystem before they result in any kind of awareness. Input processing itself is influenced by our permanent characteristics as embodied in memory, by various kinds of processes we call subconscious or unconscious, by our emotions, by our sense of identity, and so forth. This highly processed construction of what is going on may sometimes bear little resemblance to what an outside observer or the experimenter would say is going on in the laboratory.

In terms of experimental design, what we as experimenters think is the essential nature of the stimuli applied to the subject may not be the way the subject perceives these things at all; so our interpretation of results may be very misleading. Further, it must be emphasized how *active* this process is: Although much of the construction/perception of the experimental situation and experimental demands is automated, the subject also actively attempts to understand it, evaluates the situation, and makes some decisions about how he should behave. Usually there is no motor output, as the subject does not actively behave at the time he is getting sleep suggestions, but only later in reporting dream content.

By and large, most experiments have been done with an implicit assumption that the "ordinary consciousness" of each subject, the results of this complex systems interaction, is pretty much the same and/or is lawfully related to a few specifiable personality variables. Considering the number of emergent system properties that can occur, given just what we know currently about psychology, this is a grossly oversimplified assumption.

At the start of the process of attempting to influence nocturnal dreaming then, what we have, as sketched in Figure 1, is a quite complex situation, full of implicit demands and many important unknowns as well as an overtly described experimental procedure, to which quite unique individual subjects actively react in ways for which there are usually not even attempts at assessment, much less assessment in any adequate detail. The simple question, "What did you believe we really expected from the laboratory procedure?", for example, is distinguished in sleep research by its rarity. Familiarity with the research on experimenter bias and demand characteristics, excellently reviewed in Silverman's (1977) book, will reveal that this kind of question is a necessary even if a minimal start; and we must move toward sophisticated postexperimental inquiry in this area, toward specifying what the laboratory situation is and what the subjects have made of it.

The Addition of an Altered State Procedure

We shall now consider the additional complexities introduced into affecting dream content when an altered state of consciousness, such as hypnosis, is used to influence the subject. We shall simplify the systems diagram of consciousness used in Figure 1 into four more global processes, namely input processing, cognitive processes, memory processes (the effects of the various experimental variables and particularly the presleep suggestions must be carried in memory for some time before they become effective), and motor output to represent some sort of final behavior, typically the reporting of mental activity during sleep. In the simplest situation, the conscious, overt presleep suggestion/stimulation is given; the subject is, in his own constructed way, aware of what it is that is expected of him, such as "Dream about X tonight in all your dreams"; and he stores this suggestion/expectation in memory. A varying period of time then passes in which no other major events (as far as the *experimenter* is concerned) happen, and the subject is told to go to sleep. Subjects, however, are probably trying various types and intensities of procedures to influence their later dreams. Typically, there is no experimental assessment at all of what subjects do during this time!

A large class of experiments, which will be discussed briefly later, is what we might call nonconscious or implicit presleep suggestion/stimulation, in that a subject is not overtly told that he or she is expected to dream about certain kinds of stimuli which have been presented to him or her before he or she goes to sleep. Here the stored content is represented as dissociated from what a subject *presumably* could consciously verbalize about the purpose of the experiment: Dissociation is represented as a partial wall in the memory subsystem. Note that I emphasize the "presumably" here: Given what we have looked at about demand characteristics and the active, problem-solving approach of many subjects, subjects might quite often be able consciously to verbalize what the experiment was about if they thought it was all right to do so; but here we consider the special case where a subject is not consciously aware of the presleep stimulation pattern that is intended to affect him, but, nevertheless, it has some kind of effect. I shall give a few examples later on. As with overt presleep suggestion, there are no other experimental manipulations carried out before the subject is told to go to sleep.

Now let us consider the case where hypnotic suggestion is used to give a suggestion about dream content that is intended to be acted upon posthypnotically during sleep. The subject starts the experiment in his ordinary state of consciousness. A hypnotic induction procedure is carried out. In terms of my systems approach, this consists of applying various psychological stimuli, which disrupt the stability of the subject's ordinary d-SoC. Patterning stimuli are also applied, which, following successful disruption of the ordinary d-SoC, restructure the subject's conscious functioning into the d-SoC we call *hypnosis*. There is a brief transitional period between this disruption and the formation of the hypnotic d-SoC, whose nature is largely unknown. If the hypnotic induction is successful, the altered d-SoC of hypnosis results, with its stabilized but altered psychological functioning.

Presleep suggestions as to what to dream about are then given to the subject in the hypnotic d-SoC. If, as is often the case, amnesia for these presleep suggestions is also suggested, the presleep content suggestion is stored in memory in a dissociated fashion. A procedure is then gone through to dehypnotize the subject, the deinduction procedure. This is similar to the induction procedure in that disrupting stimuli to destabilize the hypnotic state are given, and patterning stimuli to reinduce the ordinary state of consciousness are applied. A poorly understand transitional period results, and the subject's ordinary state of consciousness is reinduced. If amnesia has been suggested, the presleep suggestions exist in memory, but in a dissociated form. The nature of the process of inducing any altered state of consciousness, especially hynposis, is discussed at greater length elsewhere (Lee *et al.*, 1975; Tart, 1974a, 1975, 1976, 1987). The subject is now ready to go to sleep.

State Changes Resulting from Sleep

We will now consider the various states and transitions in sleep that may affect the action of the presleep content suggestion. Once a subject is told to go to sleep, after a varying period of time he or she will enter a hypnagogic period, which, in the systems approach, is usually viewed as a transition into sleep rather than as a stabilized d-SoC itself. The quality we call "sleepiness" as well as other factors such as lying down in a quiet place and deciding to go to sleep, constitute disrupting and patterning forces that destabilize the waking state and produce the hypnagogic state. Motor output is blocked, as a subject lies still in order to go to sleep. The EEG shows a pattern of mixed alpha and theta, and eventually a clear Stage 1 pattern.

A "successful induction," successfully going to sleep, leads to the d-SoC of "dreamless" sleep, usually associated with Stages 2, 3, and 4 of the EEG with no rapid eye movements (NREM). The EEG is characterized by theta, spindles, and delta, depending on the stage. Note that in both the hypnagogic transition into sleep and the NREM sleep that results, the presleep content suggestion is still being carried along in memory, in a dissociated form if amnesia has been suggested.

Although possible physiological correlates of this have not been established yet, the systems approach predicts a brief transition period in going from NREM sleep into Stage 1-REM sleep where the psychological activity of dreaming usually occurs. Then a physiological and psychological state change occurs, and the Stage 1-REM state associated with nocturnal dreaming occurs (is induced), stabilizes, and persists for some period of time. Rapid eye movements, usually correlated with dream imagery, characterize this state, although other motor output is actively inhibited by a paralysis of neuromuscular junctions. Sensory input is rather strongly blocked from the d-SoC of dreaming. If it is effective, the presleep content suggestion is now not only active in the memory subsystem but active in various cognitive and emotional subsystems where the experienced dream content is created and reacted to.

In order to find out to what extent the presleep suggestion has been effective, we usually deliberately awaken the subject or allow the subject to awaken himself. We apply some stimulus to awaken a subject, or it happens naturally; there is again some kind of brief transitional period where the system properties of the dreaming d-SoC become unstable and break down; and the system goes through a reorganization to produce the waking d-SoC where we request a dream report. The presleep suggestion and/or its effects are now active in memory and cognitive processing and are being expressed via the motor output subsystem to produce the dream report that we observe.

A large number of changes have taken place prior to our getting our *first* dream report. Memory, which we tend implicitly to assume holds the presleep suggestion rather steadily, has had to carry the presleep suggestion through a variety of transitions, a variety of physiological state and psychological d-SoC changes, any one of which might presumably have some effects on it. Each of the various state changes may also have effects on how the experimental task is perceived, the subject's desires as to how to react to it, how to understand it, and so on. We do not have sufficient knowledge even to begin to speculate on the various effects of this wide variety and number of state changes, but clearly we shall have to be sensitive to them in future experimental research. Later awakenings involve even more of these changes. The major point here is that it is relatively easy at the current state of our knowledge to conceptualize a very large number of variables that may affect our results, and we cannot even begin to specify or speculate on the effects of many of them at this stage of our knowledge.

Inquiry Variables

The action of asking the subject for a report of mental activity preceding an awakening is not the simple one it seems to be. Early in the era of modern sleep research, for example, it was discovered that "simply" asking "Were you dreaming?" was a complex question, involving *simultaneously* asking (1) whether any mental activity could be remembered, and (2) whether the subject would then classify that mental activity as "dreaming," according to his own, idiosyncratic norms. Asking the more neutral question "Was anything going through your mind just before I awakened you?" produced different sorts of answers, such as a much higher percentage of recall from NREM awakenings. Similarly, the questioning process designed to elicit whether there was compliance with the presleep content suggestion can introduce many variables. Practically all experiments now start with a relatively neutral question on the order of "What was going through your mind just before I awakened you?", as it would be obviously biased to ask "Were you dreaming about X?" Almost all of the experiments, however, ask for "clarification" and "further details" on dream reports, and there is considerable possibility of subtly and implicitly exerting psychological pressure on subjects to distort their report to comply here. This was an obvious problem with the early psychoanalytically oriented studies in this area (Fisher, 1953, 1954, 1960; Malamud & Linder, 1931; Nachmansohn, 1951; Poetzl, cited by Ramsey, 1953; Schrötter, 1951). Full reporting of experimental inquiry procedure here is a must, and further specification of possible implicit demands in this procedure is in order. Outside observers' evaluation of demands would be a methodological advance. By and large, there is no standardization of the way requests for greater detail and clarification are carried out from experiment to experiment.

Analysis Variables

Experiments never stop with reports of mental activity, the raw data. They are *analyzed* as to what they "mean," especially in terms of the presleep content suggestions. Except for all-too-occasional repetitions of an experiment in the same laboratory (see, e.g., Tart, 1964b, 1966; Tart & Dick, 1970), there are no standardized analysis procedures for judging how well the subject has complied with the presleep content suggestions. Two general types of analysis procedures have been used, one a general measure of overall thematic compliance, the other an attempt to count the number of times specific elements of the suggestion appear in the reports. Sometimes the degree of reliability of the analysis/judging procedures is not specified. Questions of the validity of the analysis procedures, reliable or not, have seldom even been raised. In reviewing specific studies later, I shall try to make some comparisons of the strength of the content suggestion effect, but these must be very rough because of this lack of standardization or comparability of analysis procedures.

To reiterate the main point of this section on methodological considerations, the number of actual studies of control of the content of dreams is far too small to assess adequately the effects of even a small number of the many variables that are probably important in affecting the content control process. The empirical studies that we now turn our attention to, then, must be seen as illustrating possibilities rather than drawing conclusions.

CONTROLLING DREAM CONTENT BY IMPLICIT SUGGESTION

Many studies have been carried out in which the experimental treatment consisted of exposing subjects to some stimulus condition before they went to sleep, with later awakenings for reports, in order to see if the stimulus condition affected their reported dream content. Subjects were not overtly instructed to have dreams about the experimental treatment, nor were they overtly told that the purpose of the experiment was to see if the experimental treatment would affect their dreams; so the investigators have usually conceptualized these studies as being about relatively direct and nonconscious effects on dreams content. Many of them seem to be based on implicit stimulus-response or physiological models, where a treatment, like giving a drug, is conceptualized as having a direct effect on the biological organism, which is then reflected in dream content reports or physiological variables. From our modern understanding of the active, problem-solving orientation of many experimental subjects, however, it is clear that it may be more profitable to view these kinds of studies as ones involving *implicit presleep suggestion* to dream about a particular topic, the experimental treatment. The effects of such implicit suggestion, mixed with varying (and almost always unassessed) degrees of conscious understanding of and reaction to the suggestion by the subjects, are thus confounded with any more direct effects the experimental treatments may have had. In terms of the methodological points, we have unknown degrees of reactive responses to the treatment: How much, for example, might a subject have self-instructed himself to dream about the specified topic while falling asleep?

I shall make no attempt to review this quite large literature here but merely give two examples to illustrate the procedures.

In a study by De Koninck and Koulack (1975), 16 subjects slept 3 nonconsecutive nights in the laboratory. They viewed a stressful film of industrial accidents before sleep. The film showed two workers losing fingers in machine accidents and another killed by a flying board shot from a circular saw because of another worker's carelessness. Half the subjects saw only the film before sleep; the other half had the sound track from the film played softly to them during Stage 1-REM periods as well as a presleep viewing of the film. Mood assessment showed the film was an effective stressor. No overt suggestions to dream about the film were made.

Only subjects in the film-plus-sound group showed statistically significant incorporation of the film in their reported dreams (baseline mean of .27 identifiable film elements vs. a mean of .89 elements on the experimental night). The magnitude of the effect is quite small, even if statistically significant. This very small magnitude of effect is typical of the implicit suggestion studies.

Although most of the implicit suggestion studies seem blithefully unaware of experimenter effects, a series of studies by Roffwarg and his colleagues (Roffwarg, Herman, Bowe-Anders, & Tauber, 1978) shows a fine sensitivity to the implicit demands of the laboratory situation. Subjects wore red goggles for prolonged periods before sleep in order to test the hypothesis that this prolonged change in the quality of visual input would affect the visual qualities of reported State 1-REMP dreams. The goggle effects were quite strong, producing many visual dream worlds that were tinted the way the ordinary world was experienced while wearing the goggles. Roffwarg and his colleagues realized that the subjects would undoubtedly make some kind of connection between wearing the goggles and being asked about color in their dreams, and so the subjects were asked to keep track of their expectations about the experiment as it progressed. The goggle effect was shown as strongly by subjects who formed incorrect hypotheses as to what the purpose of the studies really was as by those who correctly stated its purpose. As a further control, one or more subjects (the rough version of the chapter available to me at this time is ambiguous as to how many subjects were actually used) were deliberately biased to expect the greenish *afterimage* experienced after removing the goggles while awake to dominate the colors of their dreams, but the usual, reddish goggle effect was seen in the dream reports. This study is reassuring in showing that effects on dream content do not necessarily have to be mediated through suggestion!

OVERT PRESLEEP SUGGESTION STUDIES

We shall now review a number of studies in which subjects were overtly told to try to dream about a specific, suggested topic just before they went to sleep.

Cartwright (1974) had 17 college student subjects rate various self versus ideal self characteristic traits with a *Q* sort. A discrepant trait was individually selected for each subject, and, after being wired for physiological recordings, the subject was instructed to try to dream about having a valued (or in other conditions *not* having a *non*valued) trait by repeating over and over to himself as he fell asleep a suggestion to that effect. After each Stage 1-REM period awakening for dream recall, the subjects were reminded to repeat the suggestion again as they went back to sleep.

Judges averaged 87% agreement on rating the presence or absence of the experimental traits in the dream reports. Two control traits were also scored for, one of about equal discrepancy between self and ideal self, the other of zero discrepancy: Neither had any suggestions given to dream about it.

Fifteen of the 17 subjects showed at least one instance of the appearance of the experimental trait in their four Stage 1-REM period dream recalls. Control traits also appeared rather frequently, however, and Cartwright comments that the incorporations of the suggested traits were typically weak and indirect.

In the same year, Garfield (1974a) reported a case study of self-conditioning of home-recalled dream content in a practiced dream recaller who could regularly awaken several times per night and recall dreams. The subject tried to increase the frequency of images of his hands appearing in dreams (I presume this was inspired by the technique for *dreaming* described by Castaneda, 1971, 1973, 1974, 1977) for 5 months, and the frequency of flying dreams for 12 months. Compared to a baseline month, the frequency of hand images stayed about the same (14%), but a subset of them took on a quality of extraordinary vividness. The frequency of flying dreams went from 2% in a 1-month baseline period to 4% in the experimental period, again with a marked qualitative change involving intense kinesthetic sensations as part of the dreams of flying.

In a brief clinical note, Garfield (1975a) reports teaching students in "creative dreaming" (Garfield, 1974b) classes to "confront or conquer danger in your dreams." If threatened or attacked by a dream character, students were to move toward it and/or counterattack. The presleep suggestion is here a general admonition, carried out by the subjects at home over many nights. Although no quantitative data are presented, Garfield reports that a large majority of her students found themselves occasionally able to recall these instructions while dreaming and were thus able to confront and master fearful dream images. She recommends this as a tool for assertion training, as there was some carryover of a more positive attitude into threatening waking life situations. Other clinicians (Greenleaf, 1973; Latner & Sabini, 1972) have reported similar observations from this kind of active, group-dream discussion work.

Foulkes and Griffin (1976), stimulated by Garfield's (1974a,b) work, attempted to see how much subjects could deliberately influence their dream content working under their usual sleep-at-home conditions. Twenty-three college students who professed an interest in dream control along the lines outlined in Garfield's (1974b) popular book each submitted a list of six dream topic suggestions of a simple subject–verb–object type. The experimenters randomly selected one of the six as a constant dream goal for a given subject for all his or her 10 consecutive nights of attempting to influence dreams. For a subgroup of 10, the randomly selected suggestion came from the submitted list of a like-sexed peer. These measures controlled for dreaming about a selected topic resulting primarily from personal preoccupations.

Each subject's collection of home dream reports, ranging from 1 to 10 dreams each, was carefully edited for contaminating information (such as reference to the presleep topic suggestion) and given, along with the list of six possible suggestions, to each of two psychologist judges with long experience in dream research. The judges' task was to identify which suggestion was intended to influence a particular subject's dream reports.

For 23 subjects and a sixfold matching task like this, we would expect about four correct matches by chance alone. One judge got six correct, and the other got three, with only one common correct match between them; so there was no evidence for deliberate control of reported dream content among this group of subjects.

Griffin and Foulkes (1977) repeated the Foulkes and Griffin (1976) study with several improvements that they believed would make successful dream control more likely. With 29 new subjects and 4 judges, we would expect about 7.25 correct matches per judge by chance alone. The 4 judges got nine, six, five, and five correct matches, with only two joint hits among the 4 judges; so the replication again gave no evidence for conscious dream control.

These two studies, questioning the reality of deliberate presleep control, bear an interesting parallel to two studies by Foulkes and his colleagues (Belvedere & Foulkes, 1971; Foulkes, Belvedere, Masters, Houston, Krippner, Honorton & Ullman, 1972) in which they failed to replicate the rather successful ostensibly telepathic content control effects reported from the Maimonides Medical Center laboratory and elsewhere (see Van de Castle, 1977, and Child, 1986, for a recent review of that literature). Foulkes (as reported in Van de Castle, 1977, p. 491) reports that he and his staff had an air of aggressive skepticism that might have inhibited possible telepathic effects in those studies: Could a similar bias have existed in the studies of deliberate presleep content control? Although space considerations preclude further consideration of ostensible telepathic effects on dreams here, it should be noted that the magnitude of that effect often seems to exceed the magnitude of the effects of presleep suggestion through ordinary sensory channels; so it deserves a careful examination.

A number of other studies have given postive evidence for deliberate presleep content control. Hiew (1976a) had 16 college student subjects try to influence the content of their dreams at home. Student experimenters who were acquaintances of the subjects gave one of four possible topic suggestions (riding a bicycle; going on a fishing trip; involvement in a car accident; hearing about a world war breaking out) on 3 consecutive nights, following an adaptation night. The subjects recorded their own dreams in the morning. Control subjects recorded their dreams but received no suggestion of a topic. Four judges worked independently to score the presence or absence of each suggested topic in the dream reports. They collaborated on final scoring, but no data are presented on their initial degree of agreement.

Ten of the 19 dreams reported by the experimental subjects contained the suggested topics, whereas only one of the 15 dreams reported by the control group did. Seven of the compliant experimental dreams were about the pleasant suggested topics, and only 3 about the unpleasant ones. Subjects who reported themselves as likely to linger in bed after awakening in the morning, to waken by themselves, and to be introspective tended to show more compliance with the experimental suggestions. No data are given that would allow the magnitude of the experimental effect to be assessed.

In another study, Hiew (1976b) requested 70 subjects to suggest to themselves as they fell asleep at home that they would dream about eating a pleasant meal. Each subject recorded his own dreams on alarm-clock-initiated arousal in the morning. Hiew presents no data on the degree of content control *per se* but rather on the relation of degree of control to other variables, studied through correlational and factor analytic techniques. Because significant relationships are reported, there must have been some content control. He found that those better at dream control generally recalled dreams more frequently and with higher vividness and considered dreaming to be a meaningful activity. They tended to introspect about their own life and to daydream more frequently. Immediate presleep factors like mood or degree of activation were not related to success in dream control.

Hiew's study is important in highlighting the importance of subjects' attitudes toward the task of controlling dreaming: we probably should not expect very good results from subjects who do not consider the task very important. Hiew's finding here may be stronger than was empirically found, as the correlations obtained would probably underestimate the true population correlations, owing to a fair number of dreams about such a common topic as eating a pleasant meal probably occurring by chance.

Hiew and Short (1977) investigated the effects of suggested dream topics on dreams reported from laboratory awakenings. Although they woke subjects from NREM as well as Stage 1-REM periods, for a total of four awakenings per subject, their initial analyses do not segregate reports from these different kinds of awakenings; so we will simply call them sleep awakenings here. Twenty-four subjects were used with 4 subjects each in a 3×2 factorial design. The three main conditions were a positive affective tone to the suggested topic (dream about eating a pleasant meal) versus an unpleasantly toned suggestion (eating an unpleasant meal and getting sick from it) versus no specific topic suggestion. All of the subjects heard a repeated tone every 30 seconds as they were falling asleep: Half of them were instructed that it was a reminder for them to think about the suggested topic; the other half were told it was merely a timing signal they could ignore.

Although details on the scoring of content compliance are sparse, each dream could apparently receive 0 to 4 points, depending on the number of elements of the suggested topic incorporated. No data on judging reliability are presented. The suggestion of eating was apparently something likely to be dreamed about anyway, and so a poor choice as a stimulus, as half of the subjects who had no topic suggested to them dreamed about it at least once, as I suggested earlier. The count of the number of suggested elements in the sleep awakening reports clearly discriminated the positive affect suggestion group from both the negative affect and no suggestion groups (total elements of 30, 7, and 9, respectively, over all subjects). The highest number of elements scored for a single subject was 7: over a total of four awakenings, this is not quite 2 elements of the suggested topic per report. The tone cue did not seem to have any clear effect on compliance with the suggested topic, but the affective dimension did, with positive affect eliciting much more compliance. Because Hiew and Short report that all the suggestions were given in a permissive, nonauthoritarian manner, the subjects might have not tried very hard to dream about the unpleasant topic.

Brunette and De Koninck (1977) had 24 female subjects who strongly disliked snakes sleep for 4 nonconsecutive nights in the laboratory. After an adaptation and baseline night, presleep content suggestions were administered on the last 2 nights, and dream reports were obtained from Stage 1-REM awakenings. Six subjects received suggestions to have pleasant dreams involving a snake, 6 to have pleasant dreams involving a neutral object, 6 to have unpleasant dreams involving a snake, and 6 to have unpleasant dreams involving a neutral object. Dream reports were analyzed with the Hall and Van de Castle (1966) scales. The two pleasant dream suggestion groups reported dreams that had significantly higher levels of tranquility, happiness, friendliness, surgency, and social affection, and significantly lower levels of anxiety, sadness, and aggression. While the authors report statistically significant ($p < .05$) incorporation of the elements of the suggestion. no quantitative data on its magnitude are given, but we can guess that it was probably small and in line with other studies averaging one element or less per dream. No data are reported on differences between the neutral and snake condition.

Reed (1976) reports what is probably the most active attempt to influence dream content, a modern form of ancient *dream incubation* rituals. Many ancient and traditional cultures had special ceremonies, usually in conjunction with healing needs, where, after ritual preparation, a person (the incubant) would have a specially meaningful dream that would give indications for working through his physical or psychological health problems. Reed carefully selected potential incubants, largely on the basis of their current recalled dreams suggesting they could profit from this kind of treatment. After several days of preparation, involving growth- and therapeutic-oriented discussions of current problems, as well as symbolic preparations reinforcing the expectation that the incubant would receive dream help from his own inner resources, the incubant spent the night alone in a special setting, a tent set aside for these incubation procedures. Reed's report of results is preliminary, but he reports important growth benefits obtained by almost all incubants, especially as the dreams recalled on the special night were worked through and integrated into daily living.

Many incubants also reported what seemed like altered d-SoC experiences which they labeled "visions," rather than dreams. One of these was so profound that Reed temporarily discontinued using the dream incubation technique until better understanding of the basic processes was available. It is instructive to quote Reed's description of this "vision," which occurred in addition to a number of meaningful dreams:

She awoke, startled to find that a strong wind was blowing, and that the tent had blown away. A small, old woman appeared, calling out the incubant's name, and commanded her to awaken and pay attention to what was about to happen. The woman said that she was preparing the incubant's body for death, and that the winds were spirits which would pass through her body to check the seven glands. The incubant was at first afraid, then took comfort in the old woman's aura of confidence and authority, and finally yielded her body to the experience, almost pleased with the prospect of death. During this time the incubant saw before her a large luminous tablet, containing many columns of fine print, detailing her experiences in her past and future lives. The vision ended abruptly, and the incubant found herself lying within the tent as if she had awakened from a dream. She reported that this experience was qualitatively different, however, from any of her other dreams or psychedelic experiences. (Reed, 1976, pp. 22–23)

I am impressed with the remarkable similarity of this experience to anthropological accounts of the initiatory and training visions of shamans in traditional cultures (see, e.g., Eliade, 1964). There may have been idiosyncratic factors in this particular case, but Reed's general experiences suggest that quite powerful and personally meaningful control can be exercised over dreams.

One additional study of overt presleep content suggestion, a group in the Barber, Walker, and Hahn (1973) study, will be discussed in the next section.

POSTHYPNOTIC CONTROL OF DREAM CONTENT

A number of older studies carried out within a psychoanalytic framework (Fisher, 1953, 1954, 1960; Malamud & Linder, 1931; Nachmansohn, 1951; Poetzl, cited by Ramsey, 1953; Schrötter, 1951) took it for granted that hypnotic suggestion was a highly effective method for implanting a posthypnotic dream suggestion in the unconscious, and thus used hypnosis primarily as a tool for studying the specifics of dream formation along psychoanalytically predicted lines. A modern example of this approach is that of Whitman, Ornstein, and Baldridge (1964). Their procedure used trained hypnotic subjects, capable of posthypnotic amnesia. On an experimental day, a subject was hypnotized in the morning, and 1 of 25 structural conflicts was randomly selected from a prepared list and suggested as a dream stimulus. A hypnotic dream was sometimes immediately elicited, but it was expected that the suggested structural conflict would influence later sleep dreams. Amnesia was suggested and tested for effectiveness. Following an immediate psychiatric interview, the subject went about his daily routine until reporting to the sleep laboratory that evening. Stage 1-REM dream reports and associations to them were collected during the night. The dream reports and associations were later examined blind by the research team to see if the focal conflict suggestion could be identified and the mechanisms of dream formation discovered. The technique is in principle quite interesting, but only an initial case report has been published. Other results obtained with it were complex and contradictory, although clinically useful; so the study was discontinued (Whitman, personal communication, 1978).

As I suggested in my earlier review of attempts deliberately to control dream content (Tart, 1965a), the appearance of classic psychoanalytic transformations in the posthypnotically suggested dreams of the older studies could very likely have been due to the implicit demand characteristics of the experiments. The older studies thus present evidence that presleep content suggestions *can* be transformed along classic psychoanalytic dream work lines, affecting the latent rather than the manifest content, but they do not prove that this is a "normal" mechanism. In the more modern studies to be reviewed later, experimenters who were not analysts seem to have expected to affect dream content *directly* with posthypnotic suggestions, and they got direct effects.

Stoyva (1965), in a 1961 dissertation, was the first to investigate the effects of posthypnotic suggestion of content on dreaming with modern sleep laboratory procedures. Using 16 college student subjects who showed at least a moderate degree of hypnotic responsiveness, Stoyva would hypnotically suggest that they would posthypnotically dream about some simple topic, such as climbing a tree, or beating a drum, on a specified laboratory night. The subjects were generally awakened for dream reports near the estimated end of early Stage 1-REM periods. Seven of his 16 subjects reported dreams that were clearly influenced by the posthypnotic suggestions between 71% and 100% of the time, with some subjects dreaming about the suggested topic in every one of their Stage 1-REM periods. All but 2 of the 16 subjects had at least an occasional dream about the suggested topics. Stoyva also found some influence of the suggested topics on the "thinking" reports obtained from NREM periods. Because Stoyva usually used single-element suggestions, we may estimate a peak effect of about one element per dream.

Tart (1964b) trained 10 selected college student subjects to reach a deep hypnotic state, defined by successful posthypnotic amnesia and high reports on a self-report scale of hypnotic depth (see Tart, 1970, 1972a, for a review of such scales). Each subject's response to hypnotic suggestions to dream in the hypnotic state as well as posthypnotic suggestions to dream during sleep for a single night was studied. We shall focus on the responses from Stage 1-REM awakenings here, as the study conclusively showed that dreams in the hypnotic state were not the same physiologically as Stage 1-REM nocturnal dreams (see Tart, 1965b, for a review of the literature on hypnotic dreams).

Subjects received either of two complex dream narratives as a posthypnotic suggestion. Each narrative was exciting, had a fearful affective tone, and contained 23 scorable elements. Two blind judges correlated .99 on element scoring. Five of the 10 subjects showed at least one Stage 1-REM dream report with at least one suggested element appearing in it, with one individual having all five of his Stage 1-REM reports contain at least seven suggested elements in each. The highest number of suggested elements in a single dream report was 13.

This study was also concerned with whether Freudian-type transformations of the suggested content occurred, as had been reported in the older studies: This was the reason for the strong, negative affective tone of the suggestions. No indication of any such transformations occurred in the obvious ways it had been reported in the older studies. Stoyva (1965) made the same observation.

Data on content effects in an additional, selected subject are presented by Tart as part of a study primarily designed to study the effects of posthypnotic suggestion on the process, rather than the content, of Stage 1-REM dreaming (Tart, 1966). On 3 laboratory nights, this subject averaged 45% of the suggested elements from the complex (23-element) dream suggestions in his reported dreams. He tended to dream quite literally along the lines of the suggestions. The affective tone of the suggestions (strong negative affect as in the earlier study vs. two netural topics added for this study) had no obvious effect.

The most extensive exploration of the posthypnotic content effect and its relation to hypnotizability was carried out by Tart and Dick (1970). Thirteen highly hypnotizable subjects, initially selected to be in the upper 16% of the population by the norms for Form C of the Stanford Hypnotic Susceptibility Scale (Weitzenhoffer & Hilgard, 1962), received several hypnotic training and assessment sessions prior to spending 2 nights each (after an adaptation night) in the sleep laboratory. A different stimulus narrative was used each night. Both were very positive in tone and contained 40 and 43 scorable elements, respectively. Judges counted the number of these elements in dreams reported from Stage 1-REM awakenings: They correlated .98 with each other.

To illustrate more concretely the way posthypnotic suggestion can influence dream content, what follows is the text of one of the stimulus narratives, and two dreams in response to it:

> It had been raining continuously for a week: The earth is soggy, and there are large puddles all along the path you are walking along. The water level has risen in the wells, and the frogs had been having a splendid time, croaking tirelessly all night long. Now, however, it is slowly clearing up. There are patches of blue sky just overhead, and the morning sun is scattering the clouds. It will be months before the leaves of the newly washed trees will again be covered with fine, red dust. The blue of the sky is so intense that it makes you stop and wonder. The air has been purified, and in one short week the earth has suddenly become green. In this morning light, peace lies upon the land, as you walk along the forest path.
>
> A single parrot is perched on a dead branch of a nearby tree and you stop to look at it. It isn't preening itself, and it sits very still, although its eyes are moving and alert. Its color is a delicate green with a brilliant red beak and a long tail of paler green. You want to touch it, to *feel* the color of it, but if you move it will fly away, so you, too, stand perfectly still, eyes fixed upon the parrot. Though it is completely still, a frozen green light, you can feel that it is *intensely* alive, and it seems to give life to the dead branch on which it sits. It is so astonishingly beautiful that it takes your breath

away, and you dare not take your eyes off it, lest in a flash it be gone. You have seen parrots before, but this single bird seems to be the focus of all life, of all beauty, of all perfection. There is nothing but this vivid spot of green on a dark branch against the blue sky. There are no words, no thoughts in your mind; you aren't even conscious that you aren't thinking. You hardly even blink, although the intensity of it almost brings tears to your eyes. Even blinking might frighten the bird away!

But it remains there, unmoving, so sleek, so slender, with every feather in its place.

Five minutes pass as you stand completely still yourself, never taking your eyes from this still vision, but these minutes cover the day, the year, all time: In these few minutes all life is, was, will be, without an end, without a beginning. It is not an experience to be stored up in memory, a dead thing to be kept alive by thought, which is also dying: It is totally alive and so cannot be found among the dead.

And after this 5 minutes of eternity someone calls from a house near the path, and the dead branch is suddenly bare.

Then you awaken.

The following dream report was rated as containing 3.25 elements in the averaged rating of the two judges:

TECHNICIAN: Martha, can you recall any dreams?

S: Yes. We went to—my grandfather and I went to a field—to pick up wood to bring for the fire, and as we were going away we got chased by some cattle that lived on the farm, and it was kind of fun because they were just calves, and they were fooling around with us, but they were sort of frisky and everything. And as we were carrying the firewood away, there was a bird in the trees. A green bird—I didn't look at it—but it just kept saying, "Oh, you're taking it away," and it just kept announcing the fact that we were taking the firewood and we wanted it to be quiet because we weren't really sure it was all right for us to be taking this firewood off this land, but this bird just kept saying, "Oh, they're taking it away," and my grandfather was unconcerned, but it bothered me in a way because I was afraid of being caught by a farmer or something like that. There was—the fields were in this—the land was relatively barren. It was kind of dry and the trees had no foliage on them and the fields were dry and there was a lot of dead wood about and everything was rather still—there was no life really around except there was this cattle— there were two calves who were kind of fooling around and running about, but they were kind of far away and we left them. As we were walking away from them to take the firewood to the truck we encountered the bird as we were almost to the truck. And the farmhouse was nearby— that's why I was worried about being caught. But it wasn't really an unpleasant feeling—it was just sort of let's hurry because here's the bird announcing that we were taking firewood. I think that's about it.

TECHNICIAN: Okay, fine. Did you have any feelings or anything like that? You mentioned fright— anything else about the day or anything?

S: Oh, I really felt free. It was such a nice feeling because it was such a nice day, even though there was no foliage in the trees and it was kind of a barren atmosphere. It was just so pleasant. I don't know how to explain it. Everything was so clear and really crisp—not crisp, like crisp and cold, but like sharp outlines and everything like that. It was really beautiful to be there. That's why it was so pleasant, I think. I just had this feeling of real happiness there. I think that's all.

This report also illustrates a shortcoming of the element-counting type of measure of compliance, for thematically this report is clearly centered around the posthypnotic suggestion.

The second example illustrates just how detailed and pervasive an effect the posthypnotic suggestion can have: The averaged rating of the judges was 14 elements.

TECHNICIAN: Peggy, can you remember any dream?

S: It's really broken. There I was talking to my roommate and then I was looking at bugs, and then there were things about legs and sticks, then I was walking along the path and there were puddles on each side—it had been raining for a long time, and the frogs were croaking, and it was getting sunny and the sky was all blue and I walked along and there was a parrot, and I just watched the parrot and he was so green, I just got lost, and I started thinking—oh, then I thought of something else and I never went back to the parrot. I wasn't finished dreaming when you called me, was I?

TECHNICIAN: I think so, Peggy. Maybe not, but I think so. Can you think of anything else?

S: Because I can't remember if there was anything, maybe it just stopped. Oh, I guess it was just green. I was watching the parrot and it was just the greenness and either I went on from there or I just stopped there at green. That's about the last thing I can remember.

TECHNICIAN: Okay, and how did you feel?

S: Really disoriented. I felt—it was really kind of strange—skipping around from talking to my roommate in one scene and then seeing bugs and legs and sticks—I don't even know how I got on the path and it was [long pause].

TECHNICIAN: Are there any other details you want to mention before you go back to sleep?

S: No.

Overall for the 13 subjects, there was a range of 0 to 25 of the suggested stimulus elements appearing in reported individual Stage 1-REM dream reports. There was considerable variation across subjects, with the mean effect per subject running between 2½ and 4½ elements, depending on the narrative. The effects were quite comparable to the earlier Tart (1964b) study, in spite of some differences in experimental procedure. The peak effect of 25 elements in a single dream suggests great potential for posthypnotic content control. Tart and Dick also note that after other laboratory work on the effects of posthypnotic suggestion on dream process, some of the subjects reported that they had learned to control the content of their home dreams on their own.

Because quite extensive measures of hypnotic susceptibility had been given to all the subjects, useful correlations with the extent of content effect in the reported dreams could be carried out. They suggested that the more deeply hypnotizable the subject in general (hypnotic *susceptibility*) and/or the more deeply hypnotized a subject felt at about the time the posthypnotic suggestions were given (hypnotic *depth*, a momentary state measure), the greater the degree of content control seen. The "ability" aspects of hypnotizability seemed more related to the content effect than the "compulsion" qualities of hypnosis.

One of the most extensive studies of the effects of posthypnotic suggestion on dream content was by Barber, Walker, and Hahn (1973), using 77 student-nurse subjects who slept 2 nights each in the laboratory. For each subject there were a sleep onset awakening, two Stage 1-REM awakenings, and two NREM awakenings. After each report the subject herself classified it as a "thought" or a "dream." We shall deal only with the reports classified as "dreams" here. In a 2 × 3 factorial design, the effects of (1) administering versus not administering a standardized hypnotic induction *procedure* and (2) permissive topic suggestions versus authoritarian topic suggestions versus no specific topic suggestions were studied on the second night. The suggested topic was dreaming about the death of President Kennedy.

Neither of the no-suggestion topic groups dreamed about this topic. One quarter of the subjects in the other four groups had at least one report they called a dream from their several Stage 1-REM and NREM awakenings that was reliably (99% agreement between two judges) judged as about Kennedy's death. For three of the four treatment groups, this broke down to 2 or 3 of the 13 subjects in each group giving at least one (but not more than two) report about this; so the suggestions were effective for about a quarter of the subjects. They suggested topic affected 6 of the 13 subjects in the permissive suggestion-no hypnotic induction procedure group.

The magnitude of the effect was assessed by counting the number of elements in the dream reports clearly related to Kennedy's death. In the groups administered the hypnotic induction procedure, authoritative suggestions seemed more effective (a total of 16 elements over three subjects) than permissive suggestions (3 elements over two subjects), whereas in the groups not administered the hypnotic induction procedure, the permissive suggestion procedure seemed superior (a total of 21 suggested elements over six subjects) to the authoritarian suggestions (3 elements over two subjects). This gives a maximum average effect (in the hypnotic induction group) of about 5 elements per subject from five awakenings, about 1 element per report on the average. Because no subject gave more than two dream reports containing suggested elements, the magnitude may have averaged more like 2 or 3 elements in a particular dream: These are my rough estimates.

Barber *et al.*'s data analysis does not discriminate Stage 1-REM awakenings from NREM awakenings, although it does discriminate between reports labeled as "thoughts" or "dreams" by the subjects themselves.

It should be noted that this study's procedure was quite different from most other studies of the effects of posthypnotic suggestions on dreaming in several major ways. First, the "hypnosis" variable is the experimenter's administration of a standardized induction *procedure,* rather than the presence or absence of a diagnosed hypnotic *state* resulting from that procedure. Barber has frequently argued that there is no hypnotic d-SoC, but other hypnosis researchers note that carrying out an induction procedure does not necessarily do anything to a subject; so some of Barber *et al.*'s subjects in the hypnotic induction procedure group *might* have been hypnotized, whereas some might not (see, e.g., Tart, 1977). Second, subjects in the hypnotic induction procedure group apparently did not know they were going to be hypnotized until after they were in the sleep laboratory, and this might have been an upsetting procedure for subjects who did not know they were volunteering for more than sleep research. Third, although the experimenters administered five suggestibility test items following the hypnotic induction procedure and reported that this measure did not correlate with sleep performance, this is a rather small number of items to measure hypnotizability with and so may be unreliable. Fourth, any comparison of the effectiveness of presleep dream content suggestion in subjects' waking d-SoC versus the administration of a hypnotic induction procedure might be biased to an unknown degree by Barber's well-known conviction that "hypnosis" does not increase suggestiility. Thus it is difficult to compare the Barber *et al.* findings with other studies of the effects of posthypnotic suggestion on dreaming.

Some researchers (Barber, 1962; Moss, 1967) have expressed doubt as to whether Stage 1-REM dreams apparently affected by posthypnotic suggestion are what they seem to be: Perhaps the subjects (with or without momentarily entering a hypnotic state) fabricate the dreams they report just after they are awakened from a Stage 1-REM period and before reporting. Stoyva and Budzynski (1968) tried to investigate this by correlating the length of the Stage 1-REM period before awakening and the length of the reported dream: A high correlation would argue for the geniuneness of the report. They worked with eight subjects who were preselected to report dreams in compliance with simple posthypnotic content suggestions in at least 50% of their Stage 1-REM awakening reports. They found no correlation between Stage 1-REM time and the length of the reported dreams. However, they did note that short reporting latencies yielded long dream narratives, exactly the opposite of what would be expected if the subjects needed time to confabulate or hypnotically dream the suggested narrative. This finding was completely consistent across all eight subjects and supports the hypothesis that posthypnotic content suggestions affect Stage 1-REM mental activity.

In two yet unpublished studies, I investigated concurrent content alteration of Stage 1-REM dream content by giving tape-recorded suggestions as to what to dream about while the subjects were in Stage 1-REM sleep, after posthypnotic priming. The subjects were preselected for high responsiveness to posthypnotic dream content control, being the more successful ones from the Tart and Dick (1970) study reviewed before. The content suggestions in each study consisted of three element suggestions (such as "Being with a famous person as you smell perfume in an arena," or "Being with some aunts who are carrying beams around on an airfield," or "Being with a group of men who are digging up mounds in a railroad yard") with each element having been picked from the Hall and Van de Castle (1966) norms on home dreaming to have a frequency of occurrence in ordinary dreaming of less than 1%. Thus the priori probability of dreaming about all three elements of the suggestion by chance alone was about one in a million.

In the first study, the subjects were given posthypnotic suggestions just before going to sleep that they would hear the content suggestion that would be played to them during their dreams that night without waking up and would dream about the suggested topics. Although some clear compliance with the suggestions resulted, there were frequent awakenings when the suggestions were presented, thus invalidating some of the trials. In the second study, basically the same procedure was used except that the tape-recorded suggestions were introduced at an almost inaudible volume and then slowly raised to a soft, but clearly audible level. The awakening problem disappeared, and a very high level of compliance appeared. The dream reports obtained from awakenings a few minutes after the suggestions indicated that spontaneous (unrelated to the experiment) dreaming would be going on and then the dream action would rather suddenly change to be about the suggested topic. The following dream report, in response to the suggestion to dream about "Being with a group of lady welders who are applying ointment to the hull of a submarine," is illustrative of typical responses:

> . . . had to do with Dolores, who is my friend from home, I think. She and I were planning to go to some little dinky town to see her grandmother (she really doesn't have a grandmother in a dinky town). Anyway, like it was some place that was real far away. We decided that we were going to do it, but we didn't have a chance to tell her. So we decided to call, and for some reason we called the operator and decided just to talk to her. Because we thought her grandmother wouldn't be there or something. We called the operator and we talked to her for a while. But the funny thing is we talked to her about submarines, not about Dolores' grandmother. I don't know why, but we just did. It cost $5.40. Then we figured out that her grandmother still wouldn't know we were coming. We were going on Mother's Day, so we decided that she wouldn't be doing anything anyway. That is all I can remember about the second part, and I still can't remember the first part.
> (Q: What about submarines? What did you say about them?)
> Something about how if they were welded properly they were safe, but otherwise they just fell apart like the *Thresher* and the other one that was lost.
> (Q: Was this a long conversation?)
> No. It was just very short and really out of context with the rest of the dream.

Classic psychoanalytic theory predicts that the more threatening a suggested presleep dream topic is, the more need for dream work to make the manifest dream content innocuous and so preserve sleep, even though the latent dream content must deal with the threatening material. As discussed in a previous section, the early studies purporting to demonstrate this experimentally seemed to have strong implicit demand characteristics forcing this sort of result. In recent years, Witkin and his colleagues (Witkin, 1969; Witkin, & Lewis, 1965, 1967) have carried out a number of experiments in which subjects are shown one of several highly threatening films before sleep in what I have earlier described as an implicit presleep suggestion procedure: There are no formal instructions to dream about the films, but it must be obvious to the subjects that this is expected. A stimulus film of particular interest is an anthropological documentary film showing subincision rites of Australian aborigines, with close-ups of quite bloody operations performed with sharp stones on the penises of adolescent boys being initiated into manhood. Witkin and his colleagues have reported many transformed elements of the film appearing in dream reports but, as expected from psychoanalytic theory, no direct incorporations of the film.

In a still unpublished study, designed to test the potential power of posthypnotic suggestion to control dream content, I asked my selected hypnotic subjects described before if they would volunteer for an unpleasant but scientifically meaningful experiment in dreaming about unpleasant material. Several volunteered, received a posthypnotic suggestion to dream explicitly about the film they were to see, and were then shown the subincision film. Most of the subjects dreamed directly about the film, despite its threatening nature.

LUCID DREAMING

Lucid dreaming is an altered d-SoC characterized by the lucid dreamer experiencing himself as located in a world or environment that he intellectually knows is "unreal" (or certainly not ordinary physical reality) while *simultaneously* experiencing the overall quality of his consciousness as having the clarity, the lucidity of his ordinary waking d-SoC. As discussed at length in my systems approach to understanding altered states of consciousness (Lee *et al.*, 1975; Tart, 1972b, 1974a, 1975, 1976, 1987), this characterization of the overall configuration of his consciousness as practically identical to his waking state by the lucid dreamer is the crucial defining element of lucid dreaming.

If you were to answer seriously the question, "Are you dreaming right now?" (to which I assume most, if not all readers' answers will be no), and examine the process(es) by which you arrive at your answer, two basic types of experiential examination processes can be discerned. You might look at some particular quality of consciousness/experience, such as continuity of memory, for example, and say that because you can continuously remember all of your day up to the present moment, but one of your criteria of dreaming is a lack of such continuity, then you must be awake. Or you might simply scan the gestalt, holistic, pattern qualities of your ongoing experience and well nigh instantly classify that pattern as characteristic of your waking state. Either or both of these basic experiential examination operations can occur when a dreamer questions whether he or she is dreaming.

A dreamer decides he or she is experiencing a lucid dream by the results of either or both of these two basic classifications operations: The overall, gestalt quality of his or her conscious functioning is that of ordinary waking, even though he or she is located in a dream world, and/or he or she notices specific aspects of his or her mental functioning that are characteristic of his or her waking state and not of his or her dream state. It is important to note in the latter case that, whereas a particular aspect of mental functioning may trigger the *recognition* that he or she is having a lucid dream, the lucid dreamer then usually goes on to notice that the overall pattern or his or her mental functioning, many aspects of it, are more like waking. The appearance of an isolated characteristic of waking thought is *not* the criterion of lucid dreaming, even though it may serve as a convenient indication of the presence of the lucid dream d-SoC to the dreamer. Lucid dreaming is a d-SoC involving a complex pattern change where many of the components of mental functioning we feel characterize waking consciousness come into play together. These methodological aspects of defining a d-SoC are discussed further in Tart (1975).

The feeling of a lucid dream, judging from my own few experiences of them as well as the descriptions of others, is that it feels just like your mental functioning feels right now, except that you know the world you perceive around you is some sort of clever imitation, no matter how real it seems, because you know you are asleep and dreaming.

Lucid dreaming often (but not always) starts from an ordinary dream when the dreamer (in ordinary dream consciousness) notices that some dream event does not "make sense" by ordinary consciousness standards, leading to the realization that he is dreaming. Following this realization, a major change in his or her pattern of mental functioning, usually quite rapid, is felt, and the dreamer "wakes up" in terms of his or her general pattern of consciousness; but he or she still experiences himself as located in the dream world.

I find that a frequent confusion about the concept of lucid dreaming centers around the realization that the dreamer has that he or she is dreaming. Simply experiencing the dream thought, "This is a dream," or some variant of it, is a necessary but not a sufficient condition for a lucid dream to occur. This thought can be a part of the ordinary dreaming d-SoC. A reorganization of the state of consciousness into a d-SoC pattern that feels like or is experienced as "waking" consciousness is the crucial defining pattern of a lucid dream.

In terms of the systems approach to altered states, a lucid dream is of special theoretical interest. The "higher" mental processes that we think of as characterizing waking consciousness, such as memorial continuity, reasoning ability, volitional control of cognitive processes, and volitional control of body actions (at least for the dream body), all seem to be functioning at a lucid, waking level. Yet the physiological/psychological mechanisms that serve to construct the ordinary dream world are also still functioning; so the lucid dreamer experiences himself or herself in an "external world," one that usually is as vidid and real-seeming as the world of ordinary consciousness, in spite of his or her intellectual knowledge that it is unreal. Lucid dreamers often make minute examinations of the texture of the dream world to see how closely it resembles (their apparently clear memory of) the ordinary physical world.

The following description of one of his lucid dreams by the Dutch physician, Frederick van Eeden, gives the flavor of a typical lucid dream:

> On Sept. 9, 1904, I dreamt that I stood at a table before a window. On the table were different objects. I was perfectly well aware that I was dreaming and I considered what sorts of experiments I could make. I began by trying to break glass, by beating it with a stone. I put a small tablet of glass on two stones and struck it with another stone. Yet it would not break. Then I took a fine claret-glass from the table and struck it with my fist, with all my might, at the same time reflecting how dangerous it would be to do this in waking life; yet the glass remained whole. But lo! when I looked at it again after some time, it was broken.
>
> It broke all right, but a little too late, like an actor who misses his cue. This gave me a very curious impression of being in a *fake-world*, cleverly imitated, but with small failures. I took the broken glass and threw it out of the window, in order to observe whether I could hear the *tinkling*. I heard the noise all right and I even saw two dogs run away from it quite naturally. I thought what a good imitation this comedy-world was. Then I saw a decanter with claret and tasted it, and noted with perfect clearness of mind: "Well, we can also have voluntary impressions of taste in this dream-world; this has quite the taste of wine." (Tart, 1969a, p. 154).

Lucid dreams are generally considered pleasant and important by those who have them, although they are sometimes initiated as a response to unpleasant or threatening situations in ordinary dreaming. The lucid dreamer frequently has volitional control over this lucid dream world to some extent, frequently performing actions that are "magical" by waking-life standards, such as willing changes in the "physical" qualities of the dream world, a kind of "experiential psychokinesis." Unpleasant dream situations, for example, can be conquered or turned into friendly ones along the lines of Senoi dreamwork discussed later (Stewart, 1953–1954, 1954, 1962, 1969). Note that whereas control over dream situations and characteristics is a frequent aspect of lucid dreaming, control of a dream situation is not *per se* a sufficient indicator of lucidity. Dreamers can sometimes learn partially volitional control in dreams without experiencing the overall shift in state of consciousness that constitutes the d-SoC of lucid dreaming. The high degree of apparent volitional control of content often manifested in lucid dreaming suggests it is the ultimate form of concurrent content control.

Experience in lucid dreams can seem as real or even more vivid and real than ordinary experience. Unlike ordinary dream experience, which may seem real at the time but is rapidly discounted on waking, lucid dream experience usually retains its feeling of reality. This can lead lucid dreamers to entertain serious philosophical questions about the nature of reality. One of the best illustrations of this was the lucid dreams of Ram Narayana, a British-educated editor of Indian medical periodicals. In numerous lucid dreams, for example, he engaged other dream characters in debates about the nature of reality, even though he knew at the time that they were only dream characters! An interesting and amusing example is the following:

> One night when he [Narayana] went to sleep, the dreamer found that during the dream he was walking in a street which appeared quite new to him, and while enjoying this beautiful scene and knowing full well that it was his dream experience he thought of finding out the name of the place he was walking in. He stopped a passerby and

enquired of him the name of the street. The man simply laughed and went away, saying that he was in a hurry to go to his office and had no time to waste in idle gossiping. The dreamer then stopped another person and put the same question. This man replied by addressing the dreamer by name: "Don't you recognise this street, it is the same in which you have your own house? Are you mad, what is the matter with you?" Thus speaking, he laughed and went away. The dreamer on hearing the name of the street at once recognised it, but he could not trace his own house. He then approached another person who appeared to be a well-known friend and thus addressed him: "Friend, I feel giddy at this time, would you oblige by taking me to my house?" The man took the dreamer by the arm, left him outside his house and went away. On entering the house, the dreamer did not recognise it as his own and began to talk aloud: "What a fine building I am looking at in my own dream." He then saw the inmates of the house in a group, weeping with downcast faces. The dreamer wondered why were they all weeping and when he enquired the cause of it none of them spoke. He then forcibly raised up the face of one of them, when to his great surprise, he recognised in him the face of his own son, and being very angry the dreamer said, "Why are you so silent my son, and why do you not tell me the cause of all this weeping?" The boy said, "We are weeping, father because you have become mad, and not only do you not recognise us—your own family members—but say that it is a dream." The dreamer then understood why they were weeping and thought it foolish of him to talk of its being a dream scene in their presence. He pacified them by telling that he was all right and that it was his mistake to call it a dream. However, he felt grieved over his people's condition and tried to put an end to that unpleasant dream, but could not succeed in wakening himself. He now fully recognised his home and went to his own room, where he found all the articles exactly in the same condition in which they were in his waking state. He touched and held them up in his hand to see if they were real and found nothing unusual in them. (Narayana, 1922, pp. 10–11)

An important comment about lucid dreams, which this example illustrates, is in order. Note that the dreamer did not recognize some familiar aspects of the dream, such as the street his own house was on at first, a fact that seems to contradict the notion of (complete) lucidity. For clarity of presentation, I have oversimplified the concept of the d-SoC of lucid dreaming so far, as if were a quite stable, all-or-none phenomenon. It is not. There are variations in the degree of lucidity and the components of lucidity from time to time within a lucid dream, often but not always recognized by the lucid dreamer. Reports are typical, for example, in which a dreamer reports a minute or so of lucid dreaming and then reports he slipped back into ordinary dreaming, without recognizing this while it happened, but recognizing it a minute later when lucid dreaming resumed. Thus although we can postulate a "pure case" of lucid dreaming at an extreme, one in which *all* cognitive functions work at waking levels while the dream world still seems real in spite of the dreamer's intellectual knowledge that it is not real, future research will have to deal with some variation within this category and the fact of rapid transitions between ordinary dreaming and lucid dreaming. I have dealt elsewhere with the methodological problems of researching the "depth" or "intensity" dimension of a d-SoC (Tart, 1972a, 1975).

I shall not review the literature on lucid dreaming in this chapter but refer the reader to the rest of this book.

WHY IS DREAM CONTROL IMPORTANT?

Developing presleep control over the content of nocturnal dreams and/or developing the concurrent control that occurs with lucidity is scientifically interesting; but would such development be of any practical importance?

In considering this question, we must remind ourselves that we typically do not ask from a neutral position: Our general cultural bias is that dreams are trivial mental aberrations, of no practical importance, and probably tainted with the pathological. Even within our psychotherapeutic and psychoanalytic subcultures, dreams are seen primarily as a *reflection* or indicator of important unconscious processes, rather than as important processes themselves.[3] We are aware that other cultures have often regarded dreams as important, but we usually consider them "primitive" cultures; indeed, the importance they give to dreams is usually considered one of the marks of "primitivity"! Most of this cultural bias we have against considering dreams important is not a scholarly or scientific attitude based on study or data but simply a result of irrational and arational historical processes that affected our socialization; so we must be especially aware of the possible distorting effects of our biases here.

I shall not attempt to survey the many cultures that have assigned a positive function to nocturnal dreaming but shall focus on one culture that seems to have had the most positive attitude toward and most developed "technology" for dream control, the Senoi of Malaysia. I regretfully use the past tense in describing this culture. The Senoi were a peaceful and isolated series of small, related groups, protected by their isolation in the jungles of Malaysia; but their culture was largely destroyed by successive waves of modern, mechanized warfare, with both Japanese and Allied invasions of their territory in World War II, as well as consequent continuous guerrilla warfare and accompanying forced conscription of the Senoi. Our knowledge of Senoi dream control techniques is thus historical knowledge, taken from a few articles written by Kilton Stewart (now deceased) a number of years after he actually visited them before world War II (Stewart, 1943–1954, 1954, 1962, 1969), and some tangentially relevant writings by some travelers (Holman, 1958; Noone & Holman, 1972).

Since Stewart's writings have become popular, there has been considerable fieldwork intended to find out more about the Senoi (see Dentan's chapter in this book). It now seems clear, as Domhoff (1985), among others, has pointed out, that the "Senoi" Stewart wrote about had little resemblance to real Senoi who can be found today. Much of what Stewart attributed to the Senoi may have been his own (quite ingenious) ideas, projected on to the Senoi.

I was concerned about this when I popularized Stewart's ideas in 1969 in

---

[3]A partial exception is the psychoanalytic theory that dreams serve a "safety valve" function by allowing discharge of unconscious tension, but this is seen as an automatic function, beyond conscious control.

my *Altered States of Consciousness* book (Tart, 1969a). No one else had de-scribed the Senoi as Stewart had: Was it basically accurate reporting? As de-scribed next, I had independently found the basic principles to work in my own dream life, and others have also found them to work, so I decided to publish. It is very worthwhile to review Stewart's writings, although the reader should bear in mind that we may be talking about "Stewart dreamwork" rather than "Senoi dreamwork."

Briefly, Stewart reports that the Senoi believed all normal persons could attain lucidity in many of their dreams and thus exercise volitional control over dream events. Because dreams were viewed as representing real events in some nonphysical continuum and/or as representing deep psychological events (Stew-art interprets their beliefs as the latter), dreams were seen as both reflecting ongoing life events and as presaging developing life events. Dreaming of a quarrel with a known friend in an ordinary dream, for example, would be seen as reflecting unconscious psychological tensions between the dreamer and his friend, even if those tensions were not yet manifested overtly in ordinary life. The proper response to such a dream would include discussing the dream with the dreamer's family group and with the friend, giving a gift to the friend to make up for any slights that might have occurred but not been recognized in ordinary life and attempting to have a lucid dream in which friendship would be man-ifested to the dream image of the friend. Stewart believed the Senoi had a basic understanding of the dynamics of the unconscious but had gone beyond Western understanding by developing dream control and lucid dreaming so that they dealt *directly* with potential conflicts on the unconscious level as they arose, thus efficiently dealing with them *before* they reached the stage of overt problems in everyday life.

I can attest to the validity of one aspect of Senoi dream technique through personal experience. The Senoi teach their children that any unpleasant, frighten-ing, or threatening image in a dream represents a part of themselves that they have not come to grips with, and rather than run from it or wake up, they should confront it. The child should try to dream about the frightening image again in his or her next dream, and either fight and conquer it, make friends with it, or allow himself or herself to be conquered by and absorbed by it, as a third way of healing the split. I discovered this technique myself as a young child of about 8, when I was troubled by nightmares. Feeling that the nightmares were *my* dreams and so should be responsive to me instead of frightening, I taught myself to go back to sleep and into the dream as quickly as possible, and either conquer the frightening image or make friends with it. After fewer than a dozen dreams where I did this, nightmares became a very rare occurrence with me, and my dreams took on a very positive, happy tone. I taught the technique to my son when he was having frightening dreams around age 4, and it quickly worked for him. Students in my classes who have heard of the technique from me have also reported that they taught it to their children with successful results.

Many other sophisticated techniques of dream control, as well as uses for dreams (e.g., creative inspiration), were employed by the Senoi but cannot be reviewed here. The reader is referred to Stewart's writings.

Stewart describes the Senoi as an incredibly civilized people, with practically no obvious cases of mental illness, and with warfare unheard of. His description is idyllic enough to make some people wonder if the Senoi were really like that or whether Stewart exaggerated his material. The destruction of Senoi culture makes any definitive answer impossible, but regardless of the literal truth of Stewart's reports, the central ideas of dream control and lucidity in dreams have taken hold in our culture. Several therapists (Corriere & Hart, 1977; Garfield, 1975; Green-leaf, 1973; Johnston, 1978; Latner & Sabini, 1972; Reed, 1976; Sabini, 1972; Wallin, 1977) have applied these ideas in their therapeutic practice and report quite positive results, not only in patients occasionally showing control over difficult or unpleasant situations in their dreams (with or without accompanying lucidity), but in terms of positive carryovers to their life situations.

It is difficult to draw any precise conclusions from a few anthropologi-cal/psychological reports and clinical reports; but even if the claims made are scaled down considerably, deliberate control of dream content, with or without lucidity, will have considerable therapeutic use.

CONCLUSIONS

In reviewing the literature on various techniques for affecting the content (and the process) of nocturnal dreaming almost 14 years ago (Tart, 1965a), I concluded that sleeping and dreaming were not passive states where things "just happened" to people but rather that sleepers could respond selectively to external stimuli, both in terms of incorporation into dreams and in making overt motor responses, with some control over dream content being possible as well. The studies reviewed in this chapter, almost all published subsequent to that earlier review, further confirm that some control over the content of Stage 1-REM dreaming (and, in some cases, NREM activity) is quite possible.

I further concluded in the earlier review that posthypnotic suggestion seemed to be the most powerful technique for content control via presleep sug-gestion, and that conclusion is now stronger than ever. Studies using implicit or overt presleep suggestion with subjects in their ordinary waking state seem to have a peak effect of about one or two suggested content elements per dream, whereas the studies utilizing posthypnotic suggestion have reported peak effects of up to 25 elements in a single dream, and average effects in the 5–15 element range. A very high degree of control is possible with posthypnotic suggestion.

Lucid dreaming is a form of concurrent content control, rather than presleep control. It may be the most powerful form of content control, although the sparse data we have on lucid dreaming at present are too qualitative to allow any precise comparison with presleep suggestions in the waking or hypnotic d-SoCs.

As I emphasized in the methodological section, our present data allow only a pointing out of possibilities rather than any firm drawing of conclusions about effects of specific parameters. Yet these possibilities are very intriguing: Posthypnotic suggestion and lucid dreaming, for example, are clearly large effects of great potential psychological significance, not just statistically significant trivia that are only of arcane scholarly interest. Given a few years of development and refinement of techniques for control of the content of dreams, especially the development of lucidity, we may enter an era of deliberate and controlled phenomenological and scientific exploration of dreaming (including the development of state-specific sciences of dreaming (Tart, 1972b, 1975)) that promises great excitement as well as great significance.

REFERENCES

Agnew, H., Webb, W., & Williams, R. (1966). The first night effect: An EEG study of sleep. *Psychophysiology, 3,* 263–266.

Arkin, A. (1966). Sleep-taking: A review. *Journal of Nervous and Mental Disease, 143,* 101–122.

Aserinsky, E., & Kleitman, N. (1953). Regularly occurring periods of eye motility and concomitant phenomena during sleep. *Science, 118,* 273–274.

Barber, T. (1962). Toward a theory of "hypnotic" behavior: The "hypnotically induced dream." *Journal of Nervous and Mental Disease, 135,* 206–221.

Barber, T., Walker, P., & Hahn, K. (1973). Effect of hypnotic induction and suggestions on nocturnal dreaming and thinking. *Journal of Abnormal Psychology, 82,* 414–427.

Belvedere, E., & Foulkes, D. (1971). Telepathy and dreams: A failure to replicate. *Perceptual and Motor Skills, 33,* 783–789.

Brown, J., & Cartwright, R. (1978). Locating NREM dreaming through instrumental responses. *Psychophysiology, 15,* 35–39.

Brunette, R., & De Koninck, J. (1977). *The effect of presleep suggestions related to phobic object on dream affect.* Paper presented at the annual meeting of the Association for the Psychophysiological Study of Sleep, Palo Alto, California.

Cartwright, R. (1974). The influence of a conscious wish on dreams: A methodological study of dream meaning and function. *Journal of Abnormal Psychology, 83,* 387–393.

Castaneda, C. (1971). *A separate reality: Further conversations with Don Juan.* New York: Simon & Schuster.

Castaneda, C. (1973). *Journey to Ixtlan: The lessons of Don Juan.* New York: Simon & Schuster.

Castaneda, C. (1974). *Tales of power.* New York: Simon & Schuster.

Castaneda, C. (1977). *The second ring of power.* New York: Simon & Schuster.

Child, I. L. (1986). Psychology and anomalous observations: The question of ESP in dreams. *American Psychologist, 40*(11), 1219–1230.

Corriere, R., & Hart, J. (1977). *The dream makers: Discovering your breakthrough dreams.* New York: Funk & Wagnalls.

De Koninck, J., & Koulack, D. (1975). Dream content and adaptation to a stressful situation. *Journal of Abnormal Psychology, 84,* 250–260.

Dement, W., Kahn, E., & Roffwarg, H. (1965). The influence of the laboratory situation on the dreams of the experimental subject. *Journal of Nervous and Mental Disease, 140,* 119–131.

Domhof, G. W. (1985). *The Mystique of Dreams.* Berkeley: University of California Press.

Domhof, B., & Kamiya, J. (1964). Problems in dream content study with objective indicators. *Archives of General Psychiatry, 11,* 519–524.

Eliade, M. (1964). *Shamanism: Archaic techniques of ecstasy.* New York: Pantheon.

Evans, F. (1972). Hypnosis and sleep: Techniques for exploring cognitive activity during sleep. In E. Fromm & R. Shor (Eds.), *Hypnosis: Research developments and perspectives*. Chicago: Aldine-Atherton.

Fischer, C. (1953). Studies on the nature of suggestion: Part 1. Experimental induction of dreams by direct suggestion. *Journal of the American Psychoanalytic Association, 1*, 222–255.

Fischer, C. (1954). Dreams and perception: The role of preconscious and primary modes of perception in dream formation. *Journal of the American Psychoanalytic Association, 2*, 389–445.

Fischer, C. (1960). Subliminal and supraliminal influences on dreams. *American Journal of Psychiatry, 116*, 1009–1017.

Foulkes, D., & Griffin, M. (1976). An experimental study of "creative dreaming." *Sleep Research, 5*, 129.

Foulkes, D., Belvedere, E., Masters, R., Houston, J., Krippner, S., Honorton, C., & Ullman, M. (1972). Long distance "sensory bombardment" ESP in dreams: A failure to replicate. *Perceptual Motor Skills, 35*, 731–734.

Fox, P., Kramer, M., Baldridge, B., Whitman, R., & Ornstein, P. (1968). The experimenter variable in dream research. *Diseases of the Nervous System, 29*, 298–301.

Freud, S. (1954). *The interpretation of dreams*. London: Allen & Unwin.

Garfield, P. (1974a). *Self-conditioning of dream content*. Paper presented at the annual meeting of the Association for the Psychophysiological Study of Sleep, Jackson Hole, Wyoming.

Garfield, P. (1974b). *Creative dreaming*. New York: Ballantine.

Garfield, P. (1975). *Using the dream state as a clinical tool for assertion training*. Paper presented at the annual meeting of the Association for the Psychophysiological Study of Sleep, Edinburgh.

Greenleaf, E. (1973). Senoi dream groups. *Psychotherapy: Theory, Research, and Practice, 10*(3), 218–222.

Griffin, M., & Foulkes, D. (1977). Deliberate presleep control of dream content: An experimental study. *Perceptual Motor Skills, 45*, 660–662.

Hadfield, J. (1954). *Dreams and nightmares*. Baltimore: Penguin.

Hall, C. (1967). Representation of laboratory setting in dreams. *Journal of Nervous and Mental Disease, 144*, 199–208.

Hall, C., & Van de Castle, R. (1966). *The content analysis of dreams*. New York: Appleton-Century-Crofts.

Hiew, C. (1976a). *The influence of pre-sleep suggestions on dream content*. Paper presented at the annual meeting of the Brunswick Psychological Association, Bathurst, NB, Canada.

Hiew, C. (1976b). *Individual differences in the control of dreaming*. Paper presented at the annual meeting of the Association for the Psychophysiological Study of Sleep, Cincinnati, Ohio.

Hiew, C., & Short, P. (1977). *Emotional involvement and auditory retrieval cues in presleep dream suggestion*. Paper presented at the annual meeting of the Association for the Psychophysiological Study of Sleep, Houston, TX.

Holman, D. (1958). *Noone of the Ulu*. London: Heinemann.

Johnston, J. (1978). Elements of Senoi dreaming applied in a Western culture. *Sundance Community Dream Journal, 2*(1), 50–61.

Kales, A., Jacobson, A., Kales, J., Kun, T., & Weissbuch, R. (1967). All-night EEG sleep measurements in young adults. *Psychonomic Science, 7*, 67–68.

Keith, C. (1962). Some aspects of transference in dream research. *Bulletin of the Menninger Clinic, 26*, 248–257.

Latner, J., & Sabini, M. (1972). Working in the dream factory: Social dreamwork. *Voices: The Art & Science of Psychotherapy, 8*(3), 38–43.

Lee, P., Ornstein, R., Galin, D., Deikman, D., & Tart, C. (1975). *Symposium on consciousness*. New York: Viking.

Malamud, W., & Linder, F. (1931). Dreams and their relationship to recent impression. *Archives of Neurological Psychiatry, 25*, 1081–1099.

Mendels, J., & Hawkins, D. (1967). Sleep laboratory adaptation on normal subjects and depressed patients (first night effect). *EEG Clinical Neurophysiology, 22,* 556–558.

Moss, C. (1967). *The hypnotic investigation of dreams.* New York: Wiley.

Moss, C. (1969). Innovations in the experimental manipulations of dreams. *Progress in clinical psychology.* New York: Grune & Stratton.

Nachmansohn, M. (1951). Ueber experimentell erzeugte Traeume nebst kritischen Bemerkungen ueber die psychoanalytische Methodik. (Reprinted from *Zeitschrift fur die gesamte Neurologie und Psychiatrie,* 1925, *98,* 556–586.) In D. Rapaport (Ed.), *Organization and pathology of thought.* New York: Columbia University Press.

Narayana, R. (1922). *The dream problem and its many solutions in search after ultimate truth* (Vol. 2, 1). Delhi, India: Practical Medicine.

Noone, R., & Holman, D. (1972). *In search of the dream people.* New York: William Morrow & Sons.

Orne, M. (1962). On the social psychology of the psychological experiment: With particular reference to demand characteristics and their implications. *American Psychologist, 17,* 776–783.

Ramsey, G. (1953). Studies of dreaming. *Psychological Bulletin, 50,* 432–455.

Rechtschaffen, A. (1973). The psychophysiology of mental activity during sleep. In F. McGuigan, & R. Schoonover (Eds.), *The psychophysiology of thinking.* New York: Academic Press.

Rechtschaffen, A., & Verdone, P. (1964). Amount of dreaming: Effective incentive, adaptation to the laboratory, and individual differences. *Perceptual and Motor Skills, 19,* 947–958.

Reed, H. (1976). Dream incubation: A reconstruction of a ritual in contemporary form. *Journal of Humanistic Psychology, 16*(4), 53–70.

Roffwarg, H., Herman, J., Bowe-Anders, C., & Tauber, E. (1978). The effects of sustained alterations of waking visual input on dream content. In A. Arking, J. Antrobus, & S. Ellman (Eds.), *The mind in sleep* (pp. 295–350). New York: Lawrence Erlbaum Associates.

Sabini, M. (1972). *The dream group: A community mental health proposal.* Unpublished doctoral dissertation, California School for Professional Psychology.

Schrötter, K. (1951). Experimentelle Traume. (Reprinted from *Zentralblatt fur Psychoanalyse, 2,* 638–648). In D. Rapaport (Ed.), *Organization and pathology of thought.* New York: Columbia University Press.

Silverman, I. (1977). *The human subject in the psychological laboratory.* New York: Pergammon Press.

Stern, D., Saayman, G., & Tougy, S. W. (1978). A methodological study of the effect of experimentally induced demand characteristics in research on nocturnal dreams. *Journal of Abnormal Psychology, 87*(4), 459–462.

Stewart, K. (1953–1954). Dream theory in Malaysia. *Complex, 9,* 3–30.

Stewart, K. (1954). Culture and personality in two primitive groups. *Mental Hygiene, 38,* 387–403.

Stewart, K. (1962). The dream comes of age. *Mental Hygiene, 46,* 230–237.

Stewart, K. (1969). Dream theory in Malaya. In C. Tart (Ed.), *Altered states of consciousness: A book of readings* (pp. 161–170.). New York: Wiley.

Stoyva, J. (1965). Posthypnotically suggested dreams and the sleep cycle. *Archives of General Psychiatry, 12,* 287–294.

Stoyva, J., & Budzynski, T. (1968). *The nocturnal hypnotic dream: Fact or fabrication?* Paper presented at the annual meeting of the Association for the Psychophysiological Study of Sleep, Denver, CO.

Tart, C. (1964a). The influence of the experimental situation in hypnosis and dream research: A case report. *American Journal of Clinical Hypnosis, 7,* 163–170.

Tart, C. (1964b). A comparison of suggested dreams occurring in hypnosis and sleep. *International Journal of Clinical and Experimental Hypnosis, 12,* 263–28.

Tart, C. (1965a). Toward the experimental control of dreaming: A review of the literature. *Psychological Bulletin, 64,* 81–91.

Tart, C. (1965b). The hypnotic dream: Methodological problems and a review of the literature. *Psychological Bulletin, 63,* 87–99.

Tart, C. (1966). Some effects of posthypnotic suggestion on the process of dreaming. *International Journal of Clinical and Experimental Hypnosis, 14,* 30–46.

Tart, C. (1967). The control of nocturnal dreaming by means of posthypnotic suggestion. *International Journal of Parapsychology, 9,* 184–189.

Tart, C. (Ed.). (1969a). *Altered states of consciousness: A book of readings.* New York: Wiley.

Tart, C. (1969b). Influencing dream content: Discussion of Witkin's paper. In M. Kramer (Ed.), *Dream psychology and the new biology of sleep* (pp. 344–360.). Springfield, IL: Charles C Thomas.

Tart, C. (1970). Self-report scales of hypnotic depth. *International Journal of Clinical and Experimental Hypnosis, 18,* 105–125.

Tart, C. (1972a). Measuring the depth of an altered state of consciousness, with particular reference to self-report scales of hypnotic depth. In E. Fromm & R. Shor (Eds.), *Hypnosis: Research developments and perspectives.* Chicago: Aldine/Atherton.

Tart, C. (1972b). States of consciousness and state-specific sciences. *Science, 176,* 1203–1210.

Tart, C. (1974a). On the nature of altered states of consciousness, with special reference to parapsychological phenomena. In W. Roll, R. Morris, & J. Morris (Eds.), *Research in parapsychology*. Metuchen, NJ: Scarecrow Press.

Tart, C. (1975). *States of consciousness.* New York: Dutton. Reprinted by Psychological Processes: El Cerrito, California, 1983.

Tart, C. (1976). The basic nature of altered states of consciousness: A systems approach. *Journal of Transpersonal Psychology, 8*(1), 45–64.

Tart, C. (1977). *Psi: Scientific studies of the psychic realm.* New York: Dutton.

Tart, C. (1980). A systems approach to altered states of consciousness. In J. Davidson, R. Davidson, & G. Schwartz (Eds.), *Human consciousness and its transformation: A psychobiological perspective* (pp. 243–269). New York: Plenum Press.

Tart, C., & Dick, L. (1970). Conscious control of dreaming: I. The posthypnotic dream. *Journal of Abnormal Psychology, 76,* 304–315.

Van de Castle, R. (1977). Sleep and dreams. In B. Wolman, L. Dale, G. Schmeidler, & M. Ullman (Eds.), *Handbook of parapsychology* (pp. 473–499.). New York: Van Nostrand Rheinhold.

van Eeden, F. (1913). A study of dreams. *Proceedings of the Society for Psychical Research, 26,* 431–461.

Walker, P., & Johnson, R. (1974). The influence of presleep suggestions on dream content. *Psychological Bulletin, 81,* 362–370.

Wallin, D. (1977). *Intentional dreaming: An active approach to the imagery of sleep.* Unpublished doctoral dissertation, Wright Institute.

Weitzenhoffer, A., & Hilgard, E. (1962). *Stanford Hypnotic Susceptibility Scale, Form C.* Palo Alto, CA: Consulting Psychologists Press.

Whitman, R., Pierce, C., Mass, J., & Baldridge, B. (1962). The dreams of the experimental subject. *Journal of Nervous and Mental Disease, 134,* 431–439.

Whitman, R., Kramer, M., & Baldridge, F. (1963). What dream does the patient tell? *Archives of General Psychiatry, 8,* 277–282.

Whitman, R., Ornstein, P., & Baldridge, B. (1964). An experimental approach to the psychoanalytic theory of dreams and conflicts. *Comprehensive Psychiatry, 5,* 349–363.

Witkin, H. (1969). Influencing dream content. In M. Kramer (Ed.), *Dream psychology and the new biology of dreaming.* Springfield, IL: Charles C Thomas.

Witkin, H., & Lewis, H. (1965). The relation of experimentally induced presleep experiences to dreams: A report on method and preliminary findings. *Journal of the American Psychoanalytic Association, 13,* 819–849.

Witkin, H., & Lewis, H. (1967). *Experimental studies of dreaming.* New York: Random House.

6

Lucid Dream Induction
An Empirical Evaluation

ROBERT F. PRICE and DAVID B. COHEN

INTRODUCTION

> Don Juan's praxis of *dreaming* was an exercise that consisted of finding one's hands in
> a dream . . . by simply dreaming that one lifted one's hands to the level of the eyes.
> (Castaneda, 1974, p. 18)

With these words, anthropologist Castaneda describes a technique for developing the art of *dreaming*. By focusing attention on the objects of one's dreams, according to the Yaqui shaman Don Juan, one can learn to "awaken" within the dream, thereby transcending the limited world of the senses. Similar accounts of attaining "waking" consciousness within the dream state and exerting willful control over dream events are sprinkled throughout ancient philosophical and religious treatises (Chang, 1977; de Becker, 1968; Evans-Wentz, 1967). These writings describe a state of expanded dream awareness remarkably similar to what we now call "lucid dreaming."

Numerous people experience such a state on rare occasions, and a few claim to achieve it almost at will; for most, however, the lucid dream remains elusive (Blackmore, 1982). The recent emergence of lucid dreaming as an object of scientific investigation has been heralded by significant advances in validating and communicating from the state (Hearne, 1978; LaBerge, 1980a). However, these advances have not been paralleled by the development of proven strategies for eliciting the experience. In order to utilize the lucid dream in psychotherapy, personal development, or research, we must first learn how to induce the state consistently; this is the major task currently facing lucid dream research.

ROBERT F. PRICE and DAVID B. COHEN • Department of Psychology, University of Texas at Austin, Austin, TX 78712–7789.

The main question addressed throughout this chapter will be, "Which particular techniques, if any, promise to induce lucid dreaming reliably?" Growing out of this question are several others concerning the limits of the skill: How often can a proficient lucid dreamer attain lucidity? Once achieved, how much control can the dreamer exert over the events of the dream, and how long can the state be maintained? Although the ability to lucid dream with consistency has been reported by a handful of individuals (Garfield, 1976; LaBerge, 1980a,b), is the potential to develop this ability universal or exceptional? Beyond identifying useful induction techniques, lucidity induction studies must eventually address these questions.

THEORETICAL FRAMEWORK

Answers to such questions should have major implications for any attempt to assimilate the lucidity concept into theories of dreaming and consciousness. A good theory of lucid dreaming should in turn guide our efforts to induce the state. In an effort to place the lucid dream in a context of dreaming and consciousness we will examine (1) duality of thought; (2) relationship between the dual thought processes; and (3) duality of lucid dreaming.

Duality of Thought

Most dreams are characterized by pervasive nonreflectiveness, what Rechtschaffen (1978) calls "single-mindedness." The single-mindedness of dreams becomes particularly salient "when their contents are such that would ordinarily inspire very active, conscious, critical reflection during wakefulness" (1978, p. 100). When confronted with bizarre content, why do we not question the reality of the dream? For Rechtschaffen (1978), the question is not why we occasionally have lucid dreams, but rather, "Why are not all dreams lucid as is most of conscious experience?" (p. 100).

The answer to this question may well be found in the long-standing tradition of conceiving the human brain as capable of two qualitatively different modes of thought. Ideas about duality of thought have echoed throughout history in philosophy, literature, and psychology. In 1763, Jerome Gaub wrote:

> If you yourselves have never been taught by a certain interior sense nor agree with my
> previous assertion that the mind contains two very different principles of action I
> hope that you will believe Pythagoras and Plato, the wisest of ancient philosophers,
> who, according to Cicero, divided the mind into two parts, one partaking of reason
> and the other devoid of it. (Rather, 1965, p. 123)

The best-known modern version of the dualistic notion is Freud's distinction between "primary" and "secondary" processes. Freud's dichotomy of thought has often reappeared in the concepts of others: Varendonck's (1921) "fore-conscious" versus "conscious" thought; McKellar's (1957) "A-thinking" versus "R-thinking;" Hilgard's (1962) "impulsive" versus "realistic" thought; and Berlyne's (1965) "autistic" versus "directed" thought. Klinger (1978) uses Skinnerian terms to distinguish between "operant" and "respondent" thought:

> In very general terms, operant thinking appears to differ from respondent thinking in that it is accompanied by a sense of volition, is checked against feedback concerning its effects, is evaluated according to its effectiveness in advancing particular goals, and is protected from drift and distraction by the thinker's deliberately controlling his or her attention. (p. 235)

Operant thought (OT) involves deliberate focused attention governed by rules of reality and logic. In contrast to OT, respondent thought (RT) is experienced as a continuous stream of hallucinatory perceptions, usually of a visual or auditory nature. They flow spontaneously and effortlessly as in daydreams or nocturnal dreams. While free of normal conscious constraints, RT is steered by various unconscious motivations and "current concerns" (Klinger, 1971).

The terms *operant* and *respondent* capture major distinctions between the two modes of thought: deliberate goal-directed mentation utilizing feedback versus involuntary ideation independent of goals. Rather than introduce yet another set of terms to describe this duality, we will adopt Klinger's (1978) as a convenient starting point in our attempt to develop a model of lucid dreaming.

Relationship between the Dual Thought Processes

Even while engaged in an operant task such as reading, it is not uncommon to experience frequent brief lapses into RT. If attempting to read while feeling drowsy, one might often "catch" oneself daydreaming rather than continuing to process the text for meaning. One's associations seem to have been proceeding automatically, freed from the constraints of the written material. As alertness and motivation decline, these RT detours become more frequent.

Two alternative hypotheses may be posited to explain this "interruption" process (Klinger, 1971). A *switching* hypothesis proposes that OT and RT alternate; only one mode would thus be active at any one time. On the other hand, a *suppression* or *masking* hypothesis assumes that, whereas RT is continuous, OT periodically becomes activated, masking RT with focal attention.

The masking hypothesis best explains the relationship between OT and RT (Klinger, 1971; Singer, 1975; West, 1975). RT can be viewed as a baseline process, the ongoing "stream" of consciousness that continues during both sleep and wakefulness. Sensory input and/or ascending arousal of the reticular activating system stimulates awakening and OT. Because OT sustains focal awareness, it is dominant in highly aroused waking states. However, linked closely to OT but unencumbered by its rules of logic, RT continues its parallel processing outside of awareness. This RT flow activates associated memories and affective responses, adding collateral enrichment and meaning to OT. With simultaneous reduction of both exogenous stimulus input and endogenous arousal, as during periods of drowsiness or sleep onset, OT relinquishes its hold on consciousness with the consequent emergence of RT.

During the periodic high cortical activation of REM sleep, ongoing RT becomes apparent in the form of vivid dreams:

> Our dreams, like the stars, are there all the time. We do not often see the stars because by day the sun shines brightly, and by night we sleep. Suppose, however . . . that we awaken from time to time on a clear night to look at the sky; then the stars, like our dreams . . . may always be seen. . . . The dream is an experience during which, for a few minutes, the individual has some awareness of the stream of data being processed. (West, 1975, p. 302)

Duality of Lucid Dreaming

Although dreams are primarily RT creations, some include the partial emergence of OT, for example, when the dreamer questions the reality of a bizarre event. Rossi (1972) postulated that the dreamer's level of awareness and self-reflection fluctuates on a continuum. The expansion of self-awareness may lead the dreamer to question the reality of the experience. Dreams involving a critical subjective attitude even to the point of the dreamer asking, "Am I dreaming?" are called "prelucid" (Green, 1968; Tholey, 1983).

Nowhere does the dual nature of human thought become more apparent than during the lucid dream state. Occasionally the dreamer goes beyond mere suspicions to a compelling realization that "this is a dream!" The onset of lucidity appears to be marked by a discrete phenomenological breakthrough into a qualitatively different state of consciousness. With the sudden activation of OT akin to that of waking consciousness, the dreamer is free to observe and marvel at the unfolding RT production. However, the degree of OT seems to fluctuate even in the lucid dream, occasionally resulting in "quasi-logic," as when the lucid dreamer saves a dream sandwich to eat after awakening.

The lucid dreamer may attempt to modify the dream's course or content, but the results of such efforts appear somewhat limited and unpredictable. For example, the dreamer may succeed in a wish to become airborne only to be startled by an onlooker's angry reaction. Although practice may increase one's level of success, the RT dream "generator" always maintains ultimate control over dream production (Dane, 1984). The focused nature of OT apparently makes it incapable of the spontaneous imagery creation required to produce a dream in all its hallucinatory complexity; it may be limited to observing and modifying the RT flow.

Here we may have a clue into the single-mindedness of dreams with which we began our discussion. The lucid dreamer appears to walk a tightrope between nonlucidity and awakening. Too little OT induces the dreamer to slip into non-lucidity. Too much OT disrupts the dream, prompting it to fade and awakening to ensue, much as sudden awareness of a daydream causes it to dissipate. OT overactivation could account for the high frequency of spontaneous awakenings following lucidity initiation. Lucid dreaming may be the exception rather than the rule because of the difficulty involved in activating and then regulating OT during sleep.

CONDITIONS ASSOCIATED WITH LUCID DREAM ONSET

Examining the circumstances accompanying the emergence of lucidity may provide clues concerning the conditions most likely to facilitate the state. The conditions examined here will include (1) presleep and pre-REM conditions; (2) electrophysiological variables; and (3) dream content.

Presleep and Pre-REM Conditions

High levels of physical activity during the day appear to precede lucidity at night (Gackenbach, Curren, & Cutler, 1983; Garfield, 1976). In addition, heightened daily affective arousal seems associated with the emergence of lucidity, but the evidence regarding the type of emotion is inconsistent (Gackenbach *et al.*, 1983; Sparrow, 1976).

Several authors reported that after awakening from sleep during the night and carrying out various activities, lucid dreams would ensue during their subsequent REM period (Garfield, 1976; LaBerge, 1980a,b; Sparrow, 1976). The suggested activities include meditation (Sparrow, 1976), sexual intercourse (Garfield, 1976), and reading (LaBerge, 1980b). The diversity of these activities led LaBerge (1980b) to suggest that the important aspect is not the particular behavior but the period of intervening wakefulness. He found early-morning wakefulness to be especially effective in promoting lucidity. Because REM sleep becomes more frequent as sleep progresses, the short REM latency following wakefulness in the latter half of the night may lower the threshold necessary to stimulate OT in the form of dream lucidity.

Electrophysiological Variables

Electrophysiological correlates of lucidity initiation support a three-way classification (LaBerge, Nagel, Taylor, Dement, & Zarcone, 1981). Polysom-

nogram analysis of seven subjects' ocular signal-verified lucid dreams suggested
that they occurred either (1) within 2 minutes of REM period onset (21%); (2)
following momentary wakefulness within a REM period (30%); or (3) in association with elevated phasic REM activity (49%).

All three of these conditions are assumed by LaBerge *et al.* (1981) to share a
unifying feature—elevated cortical activation—resulting in a transient arousal
overshoot necessary to initiate lucidity. The finding is consistent with the OT/RT
view. Cortical arousal manifested in phasic activity may set the stage for the
emergence of OT during REM sleep, culminating in the lucid dream. Lucid
dreams following momentary arousal from REM sleep, like lucidity subsequent
to early-morning activity, may be primed by coming on the heels of waking OT.

The initiation of lucidity is often marked by indications of orienting responses including respiratory pauses, biphasic heart rate responses, and skin
potential responses (SPR) (LaBerge, Levitan, Gordon, & Dement, 1983). The
current authors found lucid dream onset to be strongly associated with a slow
high-voltage (.25–.35 Hz; 100–150 μV) biphasic SPR wave in the EEG channels (see Figure 1). This finding was based on examination of the REM period
polysomnograms from a single subject's 13 consecutive laboratory nights. The
SPR occurred during each of the subject's 16 lucid REM periods but less than
half of the nonlucid REM periods. Within the former, the wave generally occurred at the time of lucidity onset and was frequently (16 times) followed within
1 minute by the ocular signal. A range of vivid bodily sensations often accompanied the SPR. These were described by the subject as numbness, paralysis,
bodily vibration, nonpainful electric shock, or floating.

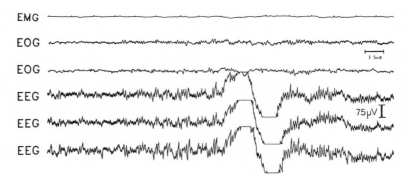

Figure 1. REM sleep polysomnogram record of the initial skin potential response (SPR) "lucid
wave" (clearly seen in EEG channels). The wave frequently coincides with both lucidity onset
and the dreamer's experience of vivid physical sensations.

The dramatic first appearance of this ''lucid wave'' during the subject's first laboratory REM period was accompanied by the following false awakening report:

> I dreamt that I woke up and I'm in the sleep lab. . . . I'm starting to write and . . . I just got this big electrical shock all through my body. ZZZZZZZZZZ . . . . I'm getting zapped, paralyzed, shocked all through my body as I'm trying to write. And so I'm starting to fall out of bed and trying to wake up, trying to go, ''Bob, get in here!'' And then you come running in, shaking me, trying to wake me up. And I finally sit up and ask you if you got that, and you say you've never seen brain waves like that.

Along with other elevated phasic REM sleep activity, SPR waves and related sensations may together be correlates of the arousal overshoot associated with lucidity onset. A striking similarity exists between sensations accompanying the SPR wave and those often reported in out-of-body experience. This resemblance suggests that both experiences may spring from common underlying neurophysiological processes. Because of the wave's potential for serving as a marker and illuminating the mechanisms of lucidity onset, further investigation into its specificity, generality, and origin appears warranted.

Dream Phenomenology

What is occurring in the dream immediately preceding lucidity onset that might serve to trigger lucidity? At least three dream conditions have been found to precede the majority of lucid dreams: (1) heightened anxiety or stress; (2) detection of incongruities; and (3) recognition of a ''dreamlike'' quality (Gackenbach, 1982; Green, 1968; Hearne, 1982a).

In the first condition, after being filled with anxiety or fear, the dreamer typically realizes that such a frightening scenario could only be a dream. In the second, the dreamer detects some element within the dream to be incongruent with the laws of waking reality, such as flying without mechanical aids. In the third category, lucidity onset occurs following the dreamer's recognition of a subtle dreamlike quality, following examination of a detail of dream experience.

The dream conditions described here are often assigned causative status in the initiation of lucidity (Garfield, 1976; Hearne, 1982a). However, the tendency to search for causation within the dream may be misguided. Green (1968) cautions us that

> although the subject may appear to examine the texture of the dream just before deciding that it is a dream, we should be cautious in saying that the realization arises from this examination of texture . . . . There is obviously a temptation for subjects to say: ''I examined the texture of my experience and concluded from it that I was dreaming,'' rather than ''I examined the texture of my experience, and realized that I was dreaming.'' (p. 36)

Discussion: Lucid Dream Onset

The three lucidity initiation categories—presleep, electrophysiological, and dream content—appear to converge on one quality: activation. Days preceding lucidity have been tentatively characterized as physically active and emotionally aroused (Gackenbach *et al.*, 1983; Garfield, 1976; Sparrow, 1976). In addition, the onset of lucidity tends to occur during dreams of high cognitive and/or affective intensity (Gackenbach, 1982; Green, 1968; Hearne, 1982a) that are accompanied by elevated neurophysiological activation (LaBerge, Nagel, Taylor, Dement, & Zarcone, 1981). The emotional intensity and critical thought often present during the dream at lucidity onset may be the phenomenological correlate of brain arousal, as observed via increased phasic activity.

Despite the correlational nature of the relevant data, we may speculate about the mechanisms of lucidity initiation. Individual trait and state factors set the presleep stage for neurophysiologically active REM sleep and perceptually, cognitively, and emotionally intense dream experiences. This cortical activation and corresponding dream intensification work together to facilitate initiation of lucidity. Heightened critical faculties of an aroused brain confronted with incongruous, bizarre, or frightening imagery can sometimes overcome dream single-mindedness. Subsiding neurophysiological activation during tonic REM sleep then necessitates intense concentration to maintain the lucid state. This speculative model is of course overly simplistic; it fails to explain those prelucid dreams that appear to lack both critical thought and intensified content.

How might these various conditions be enhanced to maximize the chance of triggering lucidity? Techniques designed to initiate lucidity during ongoing dreams may be grouped into three broad classes: (1) lucid-awareness training; (2) intention and suggestion techniques; and (3) cue "REM-minding" techniques.

LUCID-AWARENESS TRAINING

Can the development of a particular attitude in waking life facilitate the emergence of dream lucidity? Tholey (1983) claims that it can:

> If a subject develops while awake a critical-reflective attitude toward his momentary state of consciousness by asking himself if he is dreaming or not, this attitude can be transferred to the dream state. The unusual nature of dream experiences as a rule makes it possible for the subject to recognize that he is dreaming. (p. 80)

Cultivating the proper waking attitude to promote lucidity involves frequently posing the *critical question:* "Am I dreaming or not?" (Tholey, 1983, p. 80). When this self-questioning becomes habitual in the waking state, it might carry over into dreams and be answered affirmatively, initiating lucidity.

Tholey (1983) emphasized three factors affecting the success of this technique: frequency, similarity, and temporal proximity. First, the critical question should be posited as frequently as possible, initially from 5 to 10 times daily. Furthermore, it should be asked in waking situations or conditions that resemble dream experiences. Lastly, the question should be asked as close to sleep onset as possible, particularly for experienced lucid dreamers wishing to induce lucidity on a particular night. This *reflection technique* was found by Tholey to be especially useful with subjects lacking prior lucidity experience.

Personal Accounts

Personal accounts of similar techniques may help distill critical elements of the proper waking attitude to facilitate lucid dreaming. Self-reports have emphasized the development of two types of OT: (1) an active critical attitude; or (2) a passive receptive focus on current experience.

Among the proponents of an active OT attitude, Dane (1982) combined Tholey's emphasis on repetition of the critical question with Castaneda's (1974) description of focusing on one's hands during the dream. By setting a wristwatch alarm every 90 minutes during the day, Dane reminded himself to hand-focus while asking, ''Do I have a lucid dream in hand now?'' Although Dane's success was minimal—one brief lucid dream following 20 days of hand focusing—the technique is notable as an example of the active approach. Garfield (1974) also stressed developing a critical waking attitude to trigger lucidity.

In contrast, proponents of a passive or receptive OT attitude emphasize development of a waking state of heightened *perceptual awareness* rather than *critical reflection*. For example, Peth (1983) practiced quieting his mind and increasing his level of waking perceptual awareness by ''balance walking'' along a rail. He reasoned that the task was sufficiently demanding physically to require perceptual/kinesthetic concentration and yet intellectually simple enough to encourage mental quieting. Peth found his balance practice in perceptual awareness to be useful in maintaining dream lucidity.

To become ''conscious during the day,'' Clerc (1983) advocated a type of receptive ''awareness training,'' during which one constantly reminds oneself to focus on ongoing sensorimotor, cognitive, and emotional experiences *as one's own creation*. Utilizing a simple cue technique similar to Dane's (1982), Clerc initially wrote a large C (for conscious) on his hand that frequently reminded him to focus on his current experience. Clerc reported experiencing his first lucid dream after following this procedure for 1 week.

Although these self-reports promote apparently dichotomous waking states, the development of lucidity may require their synthesis—a simultaneously active yet receptive OT attitude. Waking practice in developing both an active critical attitude toward reality and concurrent passive observation of ongoing experience may carry over into REM sleep and make recognition of the dream state more likely.

Each stage of the unfolding lucid dream may require both active and passive aspects of OT. Lucidity initiation appears to call for a receptive perceptual focusing as well as a critical evaluation of unusual dreamlike percepts culminating in the critical question. Once lucidity is achieved, receptive OT allows the detached observation of RT dream production needed to prevent overarousal and awakening. However, to avoid submergence in nonlucidity, periodic critical evaluation may become necessary. Clearly, active OT is primarily involved in attempts to manipulate dream content, but the receptive mode may be operative in this endeavor as well, allowing the dreamer to accept calmly whatever surprises those attempts might evoke. In general then, both active and receptive OT elements act together in a balanced fashion to stimulate, preserve, and expand lucidity. What evidence supports the development of an active yet receptive waking attitude as a tool in inducing lucidity?

Alpha Feedback Training

Noting the cognitive and phenomenological similarities linking lucid dreams, out-of-body experiences, and the insight meditation traditions, Ogilvie, Hunt, Tyson, Lucescu, and Jeakins (1982) reasoned that

> all involve a tenuous balance between an active participating effort and a detached, observational, "receptive" attitude that is hard to achieve under any circumstances and maintain, and in all three, one is preoccupied by feelings of special mental clarity, freedom, and release. Various of the meditative traditions . . . have cultivated lucid dreaming as the form of meditation naturally available in dreaming. (p. 806)

Phenomenological and electrophysiological similarities between lucidity and meditative states have been noted, but it is not clear whether practice in meditation facilitates lucid dreaming. Some lucid dreamers have reported increases in dream lucidity following meditation (Sparrow, 1976). Based on a sample of 300 meditators and 9,810 dreams, Reed (1977) found that lucid dreams were more likely to occur following a day that included meditation; however, the statistical effect accounted for only a small portion of the variance between groups. McLeod and Hunt (1983) reported that among meditators, years of meditative practice correlated with lucid dream frequency. However, the number of lucid dreams in the meditators was not significantly higher than in a group of good dream recallers. Gackenbach (1978) reported that lucid dreamers are in fact less likely to be involved in meditative practices than nonlucid dreamers.

Early reports (Ogilvie, Hunt, Sawicki, & McGowan, 1978; Ogilvie et al., 1982) suggested that lucid REM dreams are accompanied by increased alpha activity characteristic of certain meditative states. Although since challenged by LaBerge (1980a), this observed link led Ogilvie et al. (1982) to attempt lucidity induction by experimental enhancement of REM alpha via presleep biofeedback training. They selected 10 good dream recallers with high waking alpha, each of whom spent 2 nights in the sleep laboratory. For 45 minutes immediately preceding sleep, 5 of the 10 were given alpha feedback. All subjects were subsequently awakened from REM sleep under conditions of both high and low alpha production. Although arousals from high alpha REM yielded significantly higher lucidity ratings, alpha feedback training had no effect on either REM alpha levels or lucid dream frequency. Although this study provides no support for the use of alpha feedback training as a potential induction technique, the similarity between lucid dreaming and meditation in the maintenance of an active/receptive OT balance is intriguing and deserves further investigation.

Waking Fantasy Training

By focusing on the interplay between OT and RT during wakefulness, Malamud (1979) extended the concept of lucidity to encompass expanded awareness in waking life as well as in sleep. Out of an ongoing dialogue between researcher and subjects, a lucidity training procedure gradually evolved. Malamud's six participants corresponded with her for 12 to 17 weeks regarding their progress in lucidity training. In her principal procedure, subjects "redreamed" their ordinary dreams during waking fantasy. While thus engaged, participants attempted to transform the problems and opportunities of their previously nonlucid dreams into "lucid waking dreams" with more satisfactory outcomes.

Malamud (1982) hypothesized that practicing the "lucid" attitude—the "awareness of the subjective aspects of a seemingly objective reality" (p. 8)— would expand the subjects' capacity for satisfaction in both dreams and waking life. The most frequent result was greater "lucidity" in *waking fantasies*. Subjects "became more aware of their imaginative power and creativity, they behaved more freely, fearlessly, and uninhibitedly during their fantasies, and they gained insight into themselves by recognizing the self-reflecting nature of their own imagery" (Malamud, 1982, p. 9). Although Malamud did not assess change in the frequency of lucid dreams during sleep, two subjects incidentally reported increases in this activity. Perhaps in the confines of an experimental induction study, her technique would prove useful in lucid dream induction.

Sparrow (1983) conducted such a study. His main induction strategy, *dream reliving*, is strikingly similar to Malamud's (1979, 1982) principal training procedure. By reexperiencing during waking fantasy their previously unpleasant dreams *as if* they were now lucid, Sparrow's subjects were in essence rehearsing new roles and attitudes for the ensuing dream production. In addition, by reliving the dream immediately prior to sleep the subjects were providing a waking model of the state they were attempting to achieve in sleep. In a 1978 study (cited in Sparrow, 1983), involving 91 subjects, Sparrow compared the effectiveness of dream reliving with that of merely trying to have a lucid dream. Both groups experienced an increase in lucid dreaming over their baseline levels.

In a better controlled study, Sparrow (1983) compared his original induction strategy with a motivational control. Several methodological features of this study are noteworthy as a model for future induction research. First, to determine whether achievement of lucidity is a realistic goal for a wide range of persons, Sparrow studied 161 volunteers who varied greatly in lucid dream experience. Second, he used a "placebo" control for both motivation and cognitive task; subjects in this group wrote a *motivational essay* describing their motivation for dreaming lucidly. Third, an uninformed delayed treatment group controlled for spontaneous lucidity in the absence of motivation. Finally, besides allowing for between-group comparisons, Sparrow utilized a pretreatment dream reporting period, thus permitting within-group analyses.

Considering within-group changes over baseline measures, the dream-reliving subjects achieved significant increases in their lucidity scores, whereas the motivational essay subjects experienced only nonsignificant increases. Collapsed across induction strategies, 25% of the participants reported experiencing a fully lucid dream during the week-long induction phase; 42% reported achieving either lucidity or prelucidity. Subjects with little if any previous lucidity experience also demonstrated an ability to induce lucid dreams. Ten of these inexperienced subjects achieved full lucidity, and 13 more experienced some degree of prelucidity.

Sparrow (1983) concluded that the study tentatively demonstrated the superiority of the dream-reliving exercise over the motivational essay technique as a tool for inducing greater lucidity. Noting the poor performance of the motivational essay subjects, he suggested that desire alone may not be sufficient; lucid dream induction is much more effective when motivation is coupled with an appropriate cognitive strategy. Sparrow's study lends tentative support for the use of waking fantasy training as a lucid dream induction strategy, particularly when practiced just prior to sleep.

Discussion: Lucid Awareness

When we "catch" ourselves daydreaming, we are generally unaware of the preceding course of our thoughts. This is because when RT takes hold of our mentation, we totally relinquish our grasp on OT, thus allowing RT to operate unmonitored. The fact that we maintain OT awareness to observe RT flow during the lucid dream suggests that the same feat may be possible during wakefulness. Capturing this parallel awareness while awake is admittedly not an easy undertaking, particularly for the inexperienced:

> Trying to watch our psycho-mental flux without interfering in it or becoming attached
> to its contents (and thereby losing awareness) and yet to still be receptive to it, is one

> of the hardest possible things—perhaps because of the paradox of activity embodied in the principle of action through non-action. We must sacrifice what seems to us to be a sense of control on our part, but . . . in a sense we gain actual control through the crystallization of our awareness. (Watkins, 1976, p. 21)

If this process of "aware participation in the imaginal" (Watkins, 1976, p. 18) can be developed during wakefulness, it may facilitate emergence of the analogous lucid state during sleep. Waking fantasy techniques (Malamud, 1979; Sparrow, 1983) are intended to familiarize the dreamer's conscious mind with the potential range and power of RT as an active creator of perceptual experience. Through this process of discovery, the dreamer learns to maintain receptive OT during the fantasy/dream process and trustingly observe emerging RT creations previously perceived as alien and threatening. By becoming familiar with this dual state during wakefulness, one can then foster and experience it during REM sleep with relish rather than fear.

Developing a critical-reflective attitude during wakefulness may also help the individual muster a similar state in the dream. Merely positing the critical question throughout the day may not be enough, however, because this may be done without involving the receptive aspect of OT or the emergence of RT. The key to the effectiveness of the critical question may lie in *how* it is asked. This is why Tholey (1983) stresses that the awake subject try "to imagine intensely that he is in a dream state . . . that everything he perceives, including his own body, is merely a dream" (p. 81). This point may help illustrate the similarity and the distinction between Tholey's reflection technique and waking fantasy procedures (Malamud, 1979; Sparrow, 1983). The subject maintains an active yet receptive OT state in both. In the former, however, OT is used to observe the world *as though* it were an RT creation, whereas in the latter RT is actually allowed to emerge under the aegis of OT.

INTENTION AND SUGGESTION TECHNIQUES

Can one trigger a lucid dream through an act of will or suggestion? Tholey (1983) has distinguished between "intention" techniques, in which one resolves to achieve lucid awareness during the dream, and "auto-suggestion" techniques, wherein one initiates the lucid state with nonwillful suggestion. The difference between these techniques lies in their varying emphasis on *will*. In practice, a fine line separates willful intention and nonwillful suggestion.

Waking intention has been proposed as an effective lucidity induction strategy (Saint-Denys, 1982; Garfield, 1974; LaBerge, 1980a,b). In her popular account of techniques for creatively influencing dreams, Garfield (1974) describes lucidity as the type of dream control most difficult to achieve and maintain, yet as a skill realizable with intention and practice. In a deliberate attempt to self-induce lucid dreams at home, Garfield (1976) reported obtaining a classical

learning curve, increasing the frequency of prolonged lucid dreams from a baseline of zero to a high of three per week.

Action-Specific Intention

Because the intention to become lucid is a rather vague goal, the would-be
lucid dreamer may be more successful intending instead to carry out specific
actions while dreaming (Garfield, 1974; Tholey, 1983). An association between
the action and the recognition of dreaming is forged prior to sleep so that if the
behavior occurs in the dream, lucid awareness will accompany it. *Action-specific*
intention techniques thus rest on two assumptions: first, through intention, the
dreamer must remember to perform the action; and second, the action must then
trigger the emergence of lucidity. Don Juan's advice to focus on one's hands
during the dream is an example of such a technique (Castaneda, 1974).

Because certain dream events, especially flying and false awakenings, appear universally associated with lucid dreaming, they may be especially well-
suited to serve as target actions in these intention procedures. Flying appears to
be a learnable dream skill, each dream flight making the next attempt easier
(Garfield, 1974; Green, 1968). Lucid dreams often appear to be initiated by or
involve the dream act of flying. Not surprisingly then, habitual lucid dreamers
frequently experience flying dreams. Because flying flagrantly violates laws of
waking reality, conscious intention to fly in dreams may be a useful induction
technique.

Why would the act of flying be more prevalent during lucid dreams? Several
lines of speculation may be advanced. On a psychological level, the act of flying
elegantly captures the essence and spirit of the lucid experience. The lucid
dreamer makes a leap of faith and rises above ordinary dream consciousness with
feelings of freedom, adventurousness, and an openness to whatever novel experience the dream may bring. On a physiological level, the sensations of floating,
rolling, or flying rapidly through space may be linked with phasic activation of
the vestibular nuclei during REM sleep (Pompeiano, 1974). This connection
would be in keeping with the generally high phasic activation associated with
lucidity onset (LaBerge, Nagel, Taylor, Dement, & Zarcone, 1981) and with the
positive association between lucidity experience and vestibular sensitivity
(Gackenbach, Snyder, Rokes, & Sachau, 1986).

A second dream event that may be particularly well-suited for action-specific intention is the "false awakening" (Garfield, 1974; Green, 1968; Hearne,
1982b). Rather than actually waking during a false awakening, the dreamer
dreams of waking up, often then recalling preceding lucid or nonlucid dream
experiences. Several times within a REM period, the dreamer may mistakenly
feel that awakening has taken place, recognize the preceding segment as a
dream, but fail to perceive the nonreality of the ongoing experience.

Why does the false awakening appear to be associated with dream lucidity? Both the false awakening and the lucid dream may be looked upon as means to maintain sleep. The lucid dreamer achieves a state similar to waking consciousness and with it insight into the illusory nature of the ongoing dream experience; yet the dreamer remains in REM sleep. During a false awakening, on the other hand, one correctly recognizes the preceding as a dream but is deceived about the nature of current experience. Falsely believing oneself to be awake, there is no longer any reason to question the perceived reality. The false awakening can be understood as a self-deceptive alternative to the perceptually accurate state of lucidity. Because the false awakening often results in loss of lucid awareness, it provides the dreamer with a convenient unconscious device to terminate the difficult balancing act of lucidity without actually awakening. But if the dreamer becomes skilled in recognizing the false awakening for what it really is, its occurrence could serve to initiate or maintain lucidity.

Hearne (1982b) proposed an experimental method to induce lucidity by producing false awakenings in the sleep laboratory. After having been repeatedly awakened momentarily by the experimenter, the sleeper develops a psychological set for anticipated sleep disturbance that theoretically triggers false awakenings. This technique, which Hearne has dubbed "false awakening with state testing" (FAST), also includes a set of procedures with which the dreamer may test reality immediately upon apparent awakening at any point during the day or night:

1. Do not speak or make any gross body movements but simply try to move a hand or a foot.
2. Keep generally still but attempt to push your hand through the bed.
3. Listen for inappropriate, incongruous, or distorted sounds.
4. Assess the realism of the quality of light and details of the scene.
5. Attempt to float up slowly from the bed or even sink through the bed.
6. "Will" yourself to be in another room in the house. (Adapted from Hearne, 1982b)

Any unusual results from these tests should in principle initiate lucidity. Because no data are yet available concerning efficacy, the technique remains suggestive only. Although this procedure involves testing reality during the dream state, it requires the dreamer's firm waking intention to perform these tests after any apparent awakening.

Mnemonic Induction of Lucid Dreams (MILD)

Throughout the foregoing discussion of intention techniques, a general problem with these methods becomes apparent: If one practices the waking intention to perform an action or achieve lucidity in the dream state, how does one later "remember" these intentions during the dream? LaBerge (1980a,b) has applied the following mnemonic device to the problem of transferring waking intention to the dream: "When X, do Y." This method is based on the ability to remember to perform future actions by establishing a mental association between the desired behavior (Y) and the future circumstances in which one intends to act (X). In this case the desired behavior is to become lucid while dreaming, and the situational cues are the psychophysiological concomitants of the dream (e.g., REMs or vivid imagery). This association is fixed in long-term memory by both visualizing oneself carrying out the intention and verbally rehearsing the pre-scribed formula. LaBerge reported having found the mnemonic to be most effec-tive when practiced during a period of wakefulness following early morning awakening from a dream.

LaBerge (1980b) outlined his "mnemonic induction of lucid dreams" (MILD) procedure as follows:

1. During the early morning, the subject awakens spontaneously from a dream.
2. After rehearsing the dream, the subject engages in 10 to 15 min of reading or other activity demanding full wakefulness.
3. Then, while lying in bed and returning to sleep, the subject says to himself, "Next time I'm dreaming I want to remember I'm dreaming."
4. The subject visualizes his body lying asleep in bed, with rapid eye movements indicating that he is dreaming. At the same time, he sees himself being in the dream just rehearsed and realizing that he is dreaming.
5. The subject repeats Steps 3 and 4 until he feels his intention is clearly fixed. (p. 1041)

LaBerge (1980a,b) developed the MILD technique over a period of 2 years using himself as subject. During the first 16 months (Figure 2, Phase I) he used auto-suggestion alone (i.e., "Tonight I *will* have a lucid dream"), reporting an average of 5.4 lucid dreams per month during this period, results comparable to Garfield's (1976). With increasing experience, LaBerge realized the importance of the presleep intention to *remember* to dream lucidly. Following this realization and clarification of intention (Figure 2, Phase II), he experienced an immediate increase in his monthly frequency of lucid dreaming. Further refinement led to the development of the more specific MILD technique. With MILD, LaBerge achieved an average of 21.5 lucid dreams per month, with as many as 4 in 1 night (Figure 2, Phase IV and last 4 months of Phase II). A 4-month withdrawal period during which MILD was discontinued (Figure 2, Phase III) was accompanied by a decrease in lucid dream frequency.

LaBerge (1980a) succeeded in developing a promising induction technique and in substantiating his main premise: that volitional access to lucid dreaming— in one subject at least—is a learnable skill. However, because fluctuations in motivation may well have been partly responsible for LaBerge's results, the efficacy of MILD cannot be established from this case study. No controlled study has yet demonstrated the effectiveness of MILD beyond motivation. In two unpublished studies with college students, Gackenbach and LaBerge (cited in

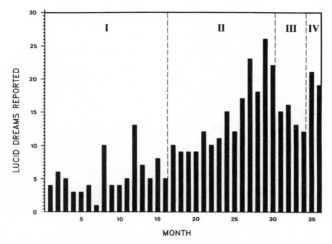

Figure 2. Monthly rate of lucid dreaming reported by the subject during the 3-year experimental period (LaBerge, 1980a,b). During the first 16 months (I), lucid dreams were induced by auto-suggestion. During the next period (II), the subject developed the mnemonic method for induction of lucid dreams (MILD) as described in the text. For the next 4 months (III), he discontinued regular practice of MILD; the resulting extinction is clearly evident. During the last 2 months (IV), the subject used MILD to produce lucid dreams for polysomnographic recordings.

Gackenbach, 1985–1986) found no differences between MILD and either simple presleep visualization (Study 1) or the combination of presleep visualization, high motivation, and presleep mental arithmetic (Study 2). S. Blackmore (personal communication, February 24, 1984) attempted a comparison of LaBerge's MILD and Hearne's FAST techniques, both of which were substantially modified to allow presleep induction rather than early-morning awakening. After a month of practice, six highly motivated subjects experienced no increase in lucidity with either technique. In this case, the modifications may have been at least partly responsible for the lack of positive results.

In summary, although intention procedures have been among the most widely promoted induction methods, data supporting their effectiveness come from uncontrolled case studies of highly selected and motivated subjects.

Posthypnotic Suggestion (PHS)

In contrast to intention procedures, suggestion procedures avoid conscious effort (Tholey, 1983). The suggestion to become lucid may be made by the experimenter or by the subject (i.e., "auto-suggestion"). The efficacy of suggestive formulas may be improved by employing special relaxation techniques such as autogenic training (Tholey, 1983). But how does the presleep suggestion become activated during subsequent REM sleep?

Posthypnotic suggestion (PHS) offers one possible solution. A PHS implanted during hypnosis does not become effective until a predetermined time after the subject has been dehypnotized. A specific cue originally introduced in conjunction with the PHS may later be employed to trigger the desired behavior. Subjects under hypnosis may therefore be given either a direct suggestion to become lucid or to dream about specific content, the appearance of which would be intended to trigger lucidity.

Speaking of dream control, Tart (1979) stated that PHS may offer "the most powerful technique for content control of dreams via presleep suggestion" (p. 263). Early pilot data from his laboratory indicated that PHS may have some potential for inducing lucid dreams. After receiving a PHS to have a lucid dream on three occasions, LaBerge (1980a, 1981) was twice successful.

Encouraged by these results, Dane (1984) formulated a two-part strategy for using PHS. His action-specific PHS technique proceeds thusly: (1) give subjects under hypnosis the direct command to become lucid in their dreams; and (2) supplement this command with suggestions to dream about specific topics or events. Subjects' recognition of these dream events in subsequent sleep is designed to cue lucidity.

In a pilot study (cited in Dane, 1984) comparing PHS versus MILD in 20 frequent lucid dreamers, baseline frequency of lucid dreaming predicted the number of lucid dreams better than either experimental condition. Dane (1984) subsequently conducted a better controlled study comparing the effectiveness of waking instruction plus PHS versus waking instruction alone during a single night in the sleep laboratory. Because subjects' prior experience with lucid dreaming is difficult to control, Dane chose as subjects 30 females who reported no prior experience with lucidity.

Two groups of 15 females each were matched for level of hypnotic susceptibility and dream recall. As part of susceptibility assessment, all subjects were instructed to have a dream about the personal meaning of hypnosis when hypnotized. On the laboratory night, subjects in the PHS group developed a personal dream symbol from their hypnotic dream imagery. After being rehypnotized, these subjects visualized their symbol while requesting assistance in eliciting a lucid dream during subsequent sleep. Strong verbal encouragement to achieve lucidity was provided to all subjects. The only treatment difference between groups was the presence or absence of PHS induction utilizing the subjects' personal symbolism.

All subjects were given waking instructions specifying the sleep conditions under which to attempt ocular signaling. Originally, these instructions were simply to attempt ocular signaling whenever dreaming and to signal every minute or so thereafter while lucid. During the study, these instructions were broken down into three stages to increase the subjects' sensitivity to sleep and dream onset. Subjects progressed through these stages by signaling initially when suspecting they might be asleep, later when experiencing visual imagery, and finally only when truly dreaming. Modification of the waking instructions necessitated subdivision of the two original groups into four comparable conditions, two of which included PHS.

The original waking instructions alone produced significantly fewer lucid dreamers. Although the revised waking instructions alone were as effective as PHS, lucid dreams associated with PHS were longer and personally more relevant and involving. Moreover, follow-up indicated that the PHS groups maintained greater lucidity both in the proportion of subjects continuing to dream lucidly and in the number of lucid dreams per subject.

Dane's (1984) results suggest that both PHS and his revised waking instructions are effective tools for inducing the lucid state in otherwise nonlucid dreamers. However, qualitative differences would favor the use of PHS when dreams of high personal relevance and involvement are desired. The superiority of PHS in terms of lucidity duration suggests that it may lend a certain stability to an experience that is typically unstable and fleeting, especially in inexperienced lucid dreamers. The higher lucidity frequency during follow-up in the PHS subjects also indicates that hypnosis may have a more lasting and durable influence on dream activity than waking suggestion. Further work would be required to identify which particular aspect of Dane's PHS procedure was most responsible for his results: hypnotic induction, suggestion, personal symbolism, or the entire procedure.

Discussion: Intention and Suggestion

Despite some preliminary support for both intention and suggestion techniques, the evidence remains quite limited. Intention procedures have been described in several case studies (Garfield, 1974; LaBerge, 1980a,b), but have not been the focus of controlled research. Suggestion procedures have been supported in one controlled study utilizing PHS (Dane, 1984). It is not yet clear that one class is truly superior or that there is really any substantive difference between them.

Within our theoretical framework, intention techniques may be understood as the reiteration of a waking self-command—"I *will* lucid-dream"—in order to empower OT to emerge during the dream. Suggestion techniques, on the other hand, can be conceptualized as an attempt to prompt the emergence of OT by promoting the appearance of specific cues in the RT flow. The problem common to both classes involves the transfer of intention or suggestion into the subsequent REM period. The utilization of mnemonic cues, such as the MILD visualization process, lends a respondent component to the intention procedures, but the efficacy of intentional memory associations in dream formation remains unclear (Tholey, 1983).

Dane's (1984) use of personal dream images initially generated in the respondent hypnotic dream to trigger the emergence of the operant mode has intuitive appeal. Hypnosis seems to share some kinship with the lucid state in that both appear dominated by RT. During both hypnosis and the lucid dream, operant awareness observes and mediates, yet is somehow held in abeyance. By evoking a state sharing some of the quality of the lucid dream and utilizing PHS, hypnosis may provide a practical solution to the transfer problem with hypnotizable subjects.

CUE "REM-MINDING" TECHNIQUES

Both lucid-awareness training and intention/suggestion suffer from the lack of a reliable "trigger" during REM sleep. One may continually question reality during wakefulness or fix the intention to become lucid firmly in mind but then fail to remember these intentions during the single-mindedness of the dream state. However, could an external stimulus presented at low intensity during REM sleep "*REM-mind*" the dreamer to become lucid? This is the main question addressed by external cue studies. Although olfactory cuing was anecdotally reported by Moers-Messmer (cited in Gackenbach, 1985–1986), these studies have focused primarily on the use of tactile and auditory cues.

Tactile Cues

In an attempt to induce lucidity with tactile stimulation, Hearne (1978) directed a fine spray of water at the face or hands of 10 subjects during REM sleep. Prior to sleep, the subjects had been informed that they would receive this cue during the night. They were told to be particularly aware of any water-related imagery in their dreams that should remind them that they were dreaming. Although 60% of the reported dreams displayed incorporation of the water stimulus into the dream content, there were no reports of lucidity. Apparently the cue was often perceived, but the association between the liquid stimulus and the realization of dreaming was not firm enough to stimulate lucidity.

Hearne (1978, 1983) reported that the most reliable cue method he tried involved the application of mild electrical shocks given through the skin to the median nerve at the wrist. Subjects were given presleep instructions to recognize the impulses and at that point to consider whether they were dreaming. Two initial applications with one experienced lucid dreamer were unsuccessful in producing fully lucid dreams but did result in two false awakenings (Hearne, 1978). In a follow-up sleep laboratory study, Hearne (1983) found the technique to be effective for inducing sustained ocular signal-verified lucidity in 6 of 12 subjects.

Based on the success of this study, Hearne (1983) devised a portable "dream machine" for home use. The mechanism detects REM sleep by means of changes in breathing rate and automatically emits electrical stimulation. Hearne stated that in some cases there was an intrusion of alpha activity after stimulation, but that REM reentry occurred without waking. No data were provided, however, on the number of nonlucid awakenings resulting from the stimulation or the number of electrical impulse sets followed by bursts of alpha activity. Data concerning alpha production would be valuable to ascertain whether lucidity was caused by the electrical impulses *per se* or by partial arousals evoked by the impulses. Venus (1982) reported that after attempting to induce lucid dreams with Hearne's dream machine for approximately 3 weeks, only two shock incorporations and no instances of lucidity were obtained by three subjects.

Auditory Cues

The most common method utilized to induce lucidity with external stimuli has involved auditory cues (Kueny, 1985; LaBerge, 1980a; LaBerge, Owens, Nagel, & Dement, 1981; Ogilvie, Hunt, Kushniruk, & Newman, 1983; Price & Cohen, 1983; Tholey, 1983). Encouraged by successful auditory cuing pilot work (cited in LaBerge, 1980a, 1981), LaBerge, Owens *et al.* (1981) monitored four subjects for 1 or 2 nights each. A tape recording repeating the phrase "this is a dream" in the subject's own voice was played at gradually increasing volume 5 to 10 minutes after the beginning of each REM period. The subjects were instructed to signal with a distinct pattern of eye movements whenever they heard the tape or recognized that they were dreaming. The tape stimulus was introduced a total of 15 times, producing lucidity in one-third of those cases.

Four distinct audio cues were tested by Kueny (1985) for their ability to induce lucidity. Forty subjects completed a 3-week home training period during which they practiced specific induction techniques on at least 14 nights. The home training involved a wide variety of procedures, including aspects of MILD (LaBerge, 1980a,b), as well as Tholey's (1983) reflection and hypnagogic image techniques. Sixteen subjects each reporting at least 2 lucid dreams during this training period were selected for the sleep laboratory phase of the study.

Each subject spent 4 nights in the laboratory. During the first two, spontaneous lucid dreaming was assessed under conditions of nonintervention. During the third and fourth, a taped audio stimulus was delivered via headphones every REM period. Each subject received two of four possible cues: (1) a male voice repeating the sentence, "Remember, this is a lucid dream," (cf. LaBerge, Owens *et al.,* 1981); (2) a 3-second musical phrase delivered every 20 seconds; and (3) and (4) cues corresponding to the first two respectively but increasing 5 db at each interval. Prior to sleep, the subjects had 15 minutes to associate the cue with becoming lucid and were instructed to make a specific ocular signal upon achieving lucidity.

Two-fifths of the original subjects reported success during the home training period, although the validity of these lucid reports cannot be substantiated. Because a variety of induction techniques were practiced at home, it is impossible to tell which were most effective. Out of 41 lucid dreams reported during the laboratory phase, 11 were sleep- and signal-verified. These lucid dreams were evenly divided between nonintervention and intervention nights; apparently, the various audio cues produced no more lucid dreaming than would have occurred spontaneously. In addition, there was no significant efficacy difference among the various cues. Could the audio cues have been more effective had the exposures continued for additional nights? Price and Cohen (1983) addressed this question in the following study.

Inspired by the demonstrated ability of subjects to make instrumental responses during REM sleep (Oswald, Taylor, & Treisman, 1960; Salamy, 1971), Cohen and Webberman (Price, 1982; Webberman, 1981) reasoned that sleeping subjects could unconsciously attend to and, by varying their eye movement frequency, control the intensity of tones presented during REM sleep. In a pilot study, subjects were trained prior to sleep in an auditory biofeedback procedure. This same procedure was later initiated during the subject's REM sleep; a low decibel 1,000-Hz tone was introduced that gradually increased in volume until the subject produced a rapid eye movement that automatically terminated the tone. In an opposite contingency used on alternate nights, the subject's eye movements resulted in an increase in the tone, whereas cessation of eye movements terminated it. Results suggested that a subject could successfully avoid the tone by either increasing or decreasing rapid eye movements without arousal from REM sleep.

Price and Cohen (1983) used this biofeedback technique to examine the effect on dream content of variations in eye movement frequency prompted by the tone. The study focused on a single subject over a period of 28 nights to maximize within-subject reliability of measurement. The subject reported experiencing REM period lucidity on the fifth and thirteenth nights. During the sixteenth night, the subject produced several uncharacteristic rapid and large saccades (see Figure 3). Upon awakening from this REM period, he described both the experience of lucidity and the conscious attempt to communicate with the experimenter using rapid eye movements as signals:

> I became conscious of the tone as I was floating around in the room. . . I moved my eyes around to try to signal you, so you would come in, and I could tell you how I did it. I gave this big eye burst consciously. But I was asleep. Is that contradictory?

This spontaneous use of eye movements to communicate with an experimenter was startling because, up to that point, neither lucidity nor its communication via eye movements had been a research goal.

Scoring for the presence of lucidity in each REM report was based on individual "scenes" defined by location of the dreamed events; each change in

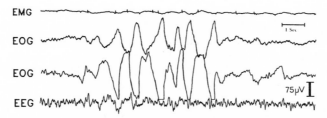

Figure 3. Polysomnogram record of the subject's initial use of eye movements to communicate with the experimenter (EOG channels). The recording was accompanied by the dreamer's report of intentional signaling (see text).

dream location constituted a change in scene. This method of defining the scene as the basic unit of analysis is in keeping with the authors' view that REM mentation is often composed of several dream scenes whose relatedness is an empirical question (Cohen, 1981; Price, 1982). Because lucidity is often not maintained throughout a REM period, scoring by scene yields a relatively conservative estimate of lucidity as a percentage of total dreams. The accompanying figure (Figure 4) illustrates the dramatic increase in lucidity over the course of the study. From the sixteenth through the twenty-eighth nights, the subject reported lucidity at least once a night. In all but two of those REM periods, his report of lucidity was accompanied by distinct ocular signals. After the twenty-second night, the subject had become so proficient at lucid dreaming that the tone

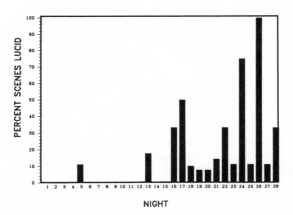

Figure 4. Percentage of dream "scenes" in which subject reported lucidity over course of 28 weekly sleep-monitored nights. All but two of the lucidity reports were verified with ocular signals.

had become an unnecessary annoyance and was therefore eliminated from the remainder of the study. Although based on different units of measurement, the similarity between this lucidity learning curve and the one obtained by LaBerge (1980a) and LaBerge, Owens et al. (1981) (Figure 2) is noteworthy.

Several different hypotheses may be advanced to account for the dramatic rise in this subject's lucid dream frequency. First, the tone itself may have served as an external cue for the subject, "REM-minding" him that he was sleeping (much like Hearne's dream machine). In addition, the tone may have stimulated lucid awareness by partially arousing the subject, as evidenced by occasional increases in alpha activity associated with the tone. Alternatively, the biofeedback-induced involvement of the subject with his environment may have been primarily responsible for his rapid gains in lucid ability.

The results of this study can be seen as providing only tentative support for the use of the auditory biofeedback procedure as a lucidity induction tool. The subject of this pilot study, although not accustomed to experiencing frequent lucidity, had prior exposure to both lucid dreaming and out-of-body experience. Also, once this subject had achieved lucidity, he was thereafter very motivated to recapture the state. Prior experience and motivation play an important if not vital role in the development of lucidity (Garfield, 1974; LaBerge, 1980a,b); clearly, they need to be controlled in any study examining the efficacy of a specific technique. One further factor requiring control in cue induction studies is the repeated awakenings either for dream reports or inadvertently caused by stimuli that may facilitate the appearance of false awakenings and lucid dreams (Hearne, 1982b).

Discussion: Cue "REM-Minding"

Several studies suggest that external cues may be effective in "REM-minding" the subject to become lucid (Hearne, 1983; LaBerge, Owens, Nagel, & Dement, 1981; Price & Cohen, 1983). Cue induction methods offer one possible solution to the major problem inherent in the lucid awareness and intention/suggestion techniques—transfer into the dream state. Potentially meaningful stimuli perceived during REM sleep elicit the emergence of OT processing, directly triggering the lucid dream.

A difficulty frequently encountered in cue studies is modulating the amplitude of the stimuli so they are high enough to elicit operant consciousness without producing awakening (Hearne, 1983; LaBerge, 1980a). The delicate balance of lucidity is reflected in the narrow band of stimulus intensities that promote the state. This difficulty is further complicated by evidence of varying threshold levels to external stimuli within REM sleep (i.e., differences between tonic and phasic REM sleep intervals), between REM periods across the night, and among individuals (Cohen, 1979). Finally, there is the problem of optimal stimulus presentation timing; because REM bursts typically precede lucidity onset, the preferable time to introduce the stimulus appears to be during high phasic REM (Gackenbach, 1985–1986; LaBerge, 1980a). If external stimulation is to become a reliable induction tool, the most effective intensity levels and presentation times must be carefully specified.

Special considerations are uniquely applicable to the use of external stimuli as an induction method. Besides introducing a "foreign" element into the individual's dreams (Tholey, 1983), most of the external cue techniques require laboratory monitoring and special equipment, limiting their general applicability. These two factors suggest that external cue techniques may be best suited to acquaint inexperienced subjects with their initial lucid dreams, after which they may no longer be necessary (Tholey, 1983).

ADDITIONAL TECHNIQUES

Two additional procedures for lucidity induction that do not fit into the three major classes are (1) combined techniques and (2) hypnagogic lucidity techniques.

Combined Techniques

Combinations of induction techniques may prove to be more effective than individual methods in isolation; each may prime lucidity in a unique way and reinforce the effects of complementary procedures. Tholey (1983) has proposed a "combined technique" that stresses the development of a critical-reflective frame of mind, but also includes elements of intention and suggestion. It is presented here as an example of a combined technique:

1. Ask the critical question, "Am I dreaming or not?", at least 5 to 10 times per day, especially
   (a) while imagining intensely everything perceived as a dream creation.
   (b) while concentrating on recent unusual happenings or lapses of memory.
   (c) whenever something surprising or improbable occurs.
   (d) when experiencing recurrent or very rare events.
2. Employ methods of improving dream recall.
3. Go to sleep thinking you will attain awareness of dreaming but avoid a conscious effort of will.
4. Resolve to carry out a particular action while dreaming; simple motions are sufficient. (adapted from Tholey, 1983, pp. 81–82)

Tholey (1983) believes that anyone consistently following this advice can learn to dream lucidly. He suggests that individuals who practice this combined technique will experience their first lucid dream after an average of 4 to 5 weeks and that most will eventually experience one every night.

Hypnagogic Lucidity Techniques

Following the literature, our review has focused primarily on attempts to induce lucidity during an ongoing dream. However, it appears that some lucid dreams may be entered directly from the waking state at sleep onset (Evans-Wentz, 1967; Green, 1968; LaBerge, 1980a; Ouspensky, 1960; Tholey, 1983). This brings us to a second major type of induction technique: retaining continuous reflective consciousness while falling asleep, thus inducing hypnagogic lucid dreams.

LaBerge (1980a) reported that 8% of his own lucid dreams were of the sleep-onset variety, typically following a period of early morning wakefulness. A subject reporting vivid hypnagogic imagery was studied by LaBerge for three sessions in the sleep laboratory. After attempting to retain OT while entering hypnagogic states, the subject would spontaneously awaken and record a mentation report. Out of 42 such dream reports, the subject claimed to have been lucid in 25. All of these brief hypnagogic lucid dreams occurred during Stage 1 sleep. LaBerge (1980a, p. 101) described the specific procedure: "the subject repeatedly rested quietly, but vigilantly, and counted (1, 2, 3, . . .) while drifting off to sleep until she began to dream."

Tholey (1983) has described various methods for maintaining conscious awareness into sleep onset, reporting only those techniques successfully utilized by at least five subjects. In keeping with previous findings (Garfield, 1976; LaBerge, 1980a,b; Sparrow, 1976), Tholey found these techniques to be most successful when employed following awakening from a dream in the early morning hours.

Tholey (1983) distinguished the techniques on the basis of whether one concentrates while falling asleep on hypnagogic images, one's body, or one's "thinking ego." He utilizes evocative metaphorical language in an attempt to capture these phenomenological experiences. In the "image" technique, the subject concentrates while falling asleep only on visual images that gradually transform from indistinct blurs into stabilized dream scenes. The subject then attempts to be carried passively into the scene. In the "body" technique, the subject concentrates on the immobile physical body and then either psychologically separates from the body or imagines being in a different location than the physical body. In the "image–body" technique, the subject concentrates not only on the visual images but also on the physical and phenomenal body. After initially perceiving a moving visual pattern that solidifies into dream scenery, the subject then experiences the sensation of gliding into the scene. A final lucidity retention technique is the "ego-point" technique, wherein the subject has the self-perception of being an ego-point in space that floats freely into a dream.

Retaining OT during sleep onset has several practical advantages over evoking that state in the dream. First, retaining consciousness into sleep removes the main difficulty inherent in the awareness and intention methods: the need to trigger lucidity, whether through mnemonic device, PHS, or external cue. By not fully relinquishing OT while falling asleep, the dreamer has no need to trigger its reemergence. Second, the practice of maintaining consciousness has the advantage—like MILD—of producing lucid dreams during a specific sleep period, obviously a benefit in terms of both individual lucidity development and laboratory investigation.

Hypnagogic lucid dreams initiated by these techniques may be compared with their REM-sleep counterparts. By comparing these lucid states in terms of both phenomenology and electrophysiology, we may gain insight into the conditions necessary to initiate and sustain lucidity. Their similarities and differences may add to our knowledge about the full spectrum of mentation across the range of sleep stages (LaBerge, 1980a). Eventually, this work could investigate the extent to which qualities of dream phenomenology are dependent upon underlying neurophysiological factors.

CONCLUSION

Each major class of technique may play a unique role in the development of the lucid-dreaming skill. Lucid-awareness training prepares the individual for dream lucidity through practice in attaining a similar state during wakefulness. By questioning the reality of waking experience, as though it were a dream, with the reflection technique, one may begin to do the same during actual dreams. Likewise, as one learns to maintain receptive OT while allowing RT to emerge in waking fantasy, one's chances of capturing the analogous state during REM sleep may greatly increase.

Intention procedures, on the other hand, strengthen OT, empowering it to breakthrough during the dream as lucidity. In contrast, suggestion techniques promote the appearance of specific dream content in the RT channel that elicits the emergence of OT. Finally, external cues trigger OT directly in response to a potentially meaningful stimulus, ''REM-minding'' the individual that the perceived world is the dream world.

Lucid dreaming appears to be an experience widely available to the highly motivated. The induction research performed to date has established a broad range of techniques and laid the groundwork for controlled comparison studies. Our review of the three major classes of induction indicates that at this point, none of these promising techniques stands out as superior to the others. We await future research to determine whether the long-ignored and elusive lucid dream can be evoked consistently enough to shed new light on dreaming and consciousness.

REFERENCES

Becker, R. de (1968). *The understanding of dreams*. New York: Allen & Unwin.

Berlyne, D. E. (1965). Structure and direction in thinking. New York: Wiley.

Blackmore, S. J. (1982). Have you ever had an OBE?: The wording of the question. *Journal of the Society for Psychical Research, 51*, 292–301.

Castaneda, C. (1974). *Tales of power*. New York: Simon & Schuster.

Chang, G. C. C. (Ed.). (1977). *Teachings of Tibetan yoga*. Secaucus, NJ: Citadell Press.

Clerc, O. (1983). Natural induction of lucid dreams. *Lucidity Letter, 2*(1), 4–5 (available from Lucidity Assoc., Department of Psychology, University of Northern Iowa, Cedar Falls, IA 50614-0505).

Cohen, D. B. (1979). *Sleep and dreaming: Origins, nature and functions*. New York: Pergamon Press.

Cohen, D. B. (1981, June). *Functional significance and heterogeneity of REM dreaming*. Paper presented at the annual meeting of the Association for the Psychophysiological Study of Sleep, Hyannis, MA.

Dane, J. (1982). A possible "new" technique for lucid dream induction. *Dream Network Bulletin, 1*(5), 7. (Available from Sally A. Shute, editor of 'Lucidity & Beyond,' P. O. Box 746, Maywood, NJ 07607)

Dane, J. (1984). *An empirical evaluation of two techniques for lucid dream induction*. Unpublished doctoral dissertation, Georgia State University, Atlanta.

Evans-Wentz, W. Y. (Ed.). (1967). *Tibetan yoga and its secret doctrines*. New York: Oxford University Press. (Original work published 1935)

Gackenbach, J. I. (1978). A personality and cognitive style analysis of lucid dreaming (Doctoral dissertation, Virginia Commonwealth University, 1978). *Dissertation Abstracts International, 39*, 3487B. (University Microfilms No. 79-01560)

Gackenbach, J. I. (1982). Differences between types of lucid dreams. *Lucidity Letter, 1*(4), 11–12.

Gackenbach, J. I. (1985–1986). A survey of considerations for inducing conscious awareness of dreaming while dreaming. *Imagination, Cognition, and Personality, 5*(1), 41–55.

Gackenbach, J., Curren, R., & Cutler, G. (1983). Presleep determinants and postsleep results of lucid versus vivid dreams. *Lucidity Letter, 2*(2), 4–5.

Gackenbach, J. I., Snyder, T. J., Rokes, L. M., & Sachau, D. (1986). Relationship of lucid dreaming ability to vestibular sensitivity as measured by caloric nystagmus. *Cognition and Dream Research: Special Issue of Journal of Mind and Behavior, 7*(2,3), 277–298.

Garfield, P. (1974). *Creative dreaming*. New York: Ballantine.

Garfield, P. (1976). Psychological concomitants of the lucid dream state. *Sleep Research, 4*, 183.

Green, C. E. (1968). *Lucid Dreams*. London: Hamish Hamilton.

Hearne, K. M. (1978). *Lucid dreams: An exploratory study of consciousness during sleep*. Unpublished doctoral dissertation, University of Liverpool.

Hearne, K. M. (1982a). Settings and causes of lucidity. *Lucidity Letter, 1*(3), 2–3.

Hearne, K. M. (1982b). A suggested experimental method of producing false-awakenings with possible resulting lucidity or O.B.E.—The 'FAST' (false-awakening with state testing) technique. *Lucidity Letter, 1*(4), 12–13.

Hearne, K. M. (1983). Lucid dream induction. *Journal of Mental Imagery, 7*(1), 19–24.

Hilgard, E. R. (1962). Impulsive versus realistic thinking: An examination of the distinction between primary and secondary processes in thought. *Psychological Bulletin, 59*, 477–489.

Klinger, E. (1971). *Structure and functions of fantasy*. New York: Wiley.

Klinger, E. (1978). Modes of normal conscious flow. In K. S. Pope & J. L. Singer (Eds.), *The stream of consciousness: Scientific investigations into the flow of human experience* (pp. 225–258). New York: Plenum Press.

Kueny, S. (1985). *Auditory cueing in REM sleep for the induction of lucid dreaming.* Unpublished doctoral dissertation, Pacific Graduate School of Psychology, Menlo Park, CA.

LaBerge, S. P. (1980a). Lucid dreaming: An exploratory study of consciousness during sleep (Doctoral dissertation, Stanford University, 1980). *Dissertation Abstracts International, 41,* 1966B. (University Microfilms No. 80-24691)

LaBerge, S. P. (1980b). Lucid dreaming as a learnable skill: A case study. *Perceptual and Motor Skills, 51,* 1039–1042.

LaBerge, S. P. (1981). Lucid dreaming: Directing the action as it happens. *Psychology Today, 15,* 48–57.

LaBerge, S. P., Nagel, L. E., Taylor, W. B., Dement, W. C., & Zarcone, V. P. (1981). Psychophysiological correlates of the initiation of lucid dreaming. *Sleep Research, 10,* 149.

LaBerge, S. P., Owens, J., Nagel, L. E., & Dement, W. C. (1981). ''This is a dream'': Induction of lucid dreams by verbal suggestion during REM sleep. *Sleep Research, 10,* 150.

LaBerge, S. P., Levitan, L., Gordon, M., & Dement, W. C. (1983). The psychophysiology of lucid dream initiation. *Psychophysiology, 20,* 455.

Malamud, J. R. (1979). The development of a training method for the cultivation of ''lucid'' awareness in fantasy, dreams, and waking life (Doctoral dissertation, New York University, 1979). *Dissertation Abstracts International, 40,* 5412B. (University Microfilms No. 80-10380)

Malamud, J. R. (1982). Training for lucid awareness in dreams, fantasy, and waking life. *Lucidity Letter, 1*(4), 7–12.

McKellar, P. (1957). *Imagination and thinking.* New York: Basic Books.

McLeod, B., & Hunt, H. (1983). Meditation and lucid dreams. *Lucidity Letter, 2*(4), 6–7.

Ogilvie, R. D., Hunt, H. T., Sawicki, C., & McGowan, K. (1978). Searching for lucid dreams. *Sleep Research, 7,* 165.

Ogilvie, R. D., Hunt, H. T., Tyson, P. D., Lucescu, M. L., & Jeakins, D. B. (1982). Lucid dreaming and alpha activity: A preliminary report. *Perceptual and Motor Skills, 55,* 795–808.

Ogilvie, R., Hunt, H., Kushniruk, A., & Newman, J. (1983). Lucid dreams and the arousal continuum. *Lucidity Letter, 2*(2), 1–2.

Oswald, I., Taylor, A., & Treisman, M. (1960). Discriminative responses to stimulation during human sleep. *Brain, 83,* 440–453.

Ouspensky, P. (1960). *A new model of the universe.* London: Routledge & Kegan Paul. (Original work published 1931)

Peth, W. M. (1983). Response to Gackenbach. *Lucidity Letter, 2*(1), 5–6.

Pompeiano, O. (1974). Vestibular influences during sleep. In H. H. Kornhuber (Ed.), *Handbook of sensory physiology: Vol. 6. Vestibular system: Part 1. Basic mechanisms* (pp. 583–622). New York: Springer-Verlag.

Price, R. F. (1982). *The narrative organization of REM dreams: Effect of eye movement biofeedback.* Unpublished manuscript, Psychology Department, University of Texas at Austin.

Price, R. F., & Cohen, D. B. (1983). Auditory biofeedback as a lucidity induction technique. *Lucidity Letter, 2*(4), 1–3.

Rather, L. J. (1965). *Mind and body in eighteenth-century medicine: A study based on Jerome Gaub's De regimine mentis.* Berkeley: University of California Press.

Rechtschaffen, A. (1978). The single-mindedness and isolation of dreams. *Sleep, 1,* 97–109.

Reed, H. (1977). Meditation and lucid dreaming: A statistical relationship. *Sundance Community Dream Journal, 2,* 237–238.

Rossi, E. L. (1972). *Dreams and the growth of personality: Expanding awareness in psychotherapy.* Elmsford, NY: Pergamon Press.

Saint-Denys, H. de (1982). *Dreams and the means of directing them.* (N. Fry, Trans.; M. Schatzman, Ed.). London: Duckworth. (Original work published 1867)

Salamy, J. (1971). Effects of REM deprivation and awakening on instrumental performance during Stage 2 and REM sleep. *Biological Psychiatry, 3,* 321–330.

Singer, J. L. (1975). Navigating the stream of consciousness: Research in daydreaming and related inner experience. *American Psychologist, 30*(7), 727–738.

Sparrow, G. S. (1976). A personal testimony: Developing lucidity in my dreams. *Sundance Community Dream Journal, 1,* 4–17.

Sparrow, G. S. (1983). *An exploration into the inducibility of increased reflectiveness and "lucidity" in nocturnal dream reports.* Unpublished doctoral dissertation, College of William and Mary, Williamsburg, VA.

Tart, C. T. (1979). From spontaneous event to lucidity: A review of attempts to consciously control nocturnal dreaming. In B. B. Wolman (Ed.), *Handbook of dreams: Research, theories and applications* (pp. 226–268). New York: Van Nostrand Reinhold.

Tholey, P. (1983). Techniques for inducing and manipulating lucid dreams. *Perceptual and Motor Skills, 57,* 79–90.

Varendonck, J. (1921). *The psychology of daydreams.* New York: Macmillan.

Venus, S. (1982). Early results with Hearne's dream machine. *Lucidity Letter, 1*(2), 3.

Watkins, M. M. (1976). *Waking dreams.* New York: Harper & Row.

Webberman, J. (1981). *Instrumental responsivity to auditory stimuli during REM sleep.* Unpublished manuscript, Psychology Department, University of Texas at Austin.

West, L. J. (1975). A clinical and theoretical overview of hallucinatory phenomena. In R. K. Siegel & L. J. West (Eds.), *Hallucinations: Behavior, experience, and theory* (pp. 287–311). New York: Wiley.

7

The Psychophysiology of Lucid Dreaming

STEPHEN LaBERGE

LUCID DREAMING PHYSIOLOGICALLY VERIFIED

Although we are usually unaware of the fact that we are dreaming while we are dreaming, at times a remarkable exception occurs, and our consciousness becomes lucid enough for us to realize that we *are* dreaming. Lucid dreamers report being able to freely remember the circumstances of waking life, to think clearly, and to act deliberately upon reflection, all the while experiencing a dream world that seems vividly real (Green, 1968; LaBerge, 1985a). This is all in contrast to the usual characterization of dreams as typically lacking any reflective awareness or true volition (Rechtschaffen, 1978).

Indeed, the concept of *conscious sleep* can seem so self-contradictory and paradoxical to certain ways of thinking that some theoreticians have considered lucid dreams impossible and even absurd. Probably the most extreme example of this point of view is provided by Malcolm (1959), who argued that if being asleep means experiencing nothing whatsoever, "dreams" are not experiences during sleep at all but only the reports we tell after awakening. This concept of sleep led Malcolm to conclude that the idea that someone might reason while asleep is "meaningless." From here, the philosopher reasoned that

> If "I am dreaming" could express a judgment it would imply the judgment 'I am asleep,' and therefore the absurdity of the latter proves the absurdity of the former." Thus "the supposed judgement that one is dreaming" is "unintelligible" and "an inherently absurd form of words (Malcolm, 1959, pp. 48–50)

The point of this example is to show the skeptical light in which accounts of lucid dreaming were viewed before physiological proof of the reality of the

---

STEPHEN LaBERGE • Department of Psychology, Stanford University, Stanford, CA 94305.

phenomenon made philosophical arguments moot. As for the occasional reports in which dreamers claimed to have been fully conscious that they were dreaming *while* they were dreaming, the orthodox view in sleep and dream research assumed (until very recently) that anecdotal accounts of lucid dreams must be somehow spurious.

Nevertheless, people still reported dreaming the impossible dream, so the question was raised: "Under what presumably abnormal physiological conditions do reports of 'lucid' dreams occur?" In the absence of empirical ence bearing on the question, speculation largely favored two answers: either wakefulness or NREM sleep. Most sleep researchers were apparently inclined to accept Hartmann's "impression" that lucid dreams were "not typical parts of dreaming thought, but rather brief arousals" (Hartmann, 1975, p. 74; cf. Berger, 1977). Schwartz and Lefebvre (1973) noted that frequent transitory arousals were common during REM sleep and proposed these "microawakenings" as the physiological basis for lucid dream reports. Although no one had put forward any evidence for this mechanism, it seems to have been the received opinion (cf. Foulkes, 1974) up until the last few years. A similar view was put forward by Antrobus, Antrobus, and Fisher (1965) who predicted that recognition by the dreamer of the fact that he or she is dreaming would either immediately terminate the dream or continue in NREM sleep. Likewise, Hall (1977) speculated that lucid dreams may represent "a transition from Stage-1 REM to Stage-4 mentation" (p. 312). Green (1968) seems to have been alone in reasoning that, because lucid dreams usually arise from nonlucid dreams, "we may tentatively expect to find lucid dreams occurring, as do other dreams, during the 'paradoxical' phase of sleep" (p. 128).

Empirical evidence began to appear in the late 1970s supporting Green's speculation that lucid dreams occur during REM sleep. Based on standard sleep recordings of two subjects who reported a total of three lucid dreams upon awakening from REM periods, Ogilvie, Hunt, Sawicki, and McGowan (1978) cautiously concluded that "it *may* be that lucid dreams begin in REM" (p. 165). However, no proof was given that the reported lucid dreams themselves had in fact occurred during the REM sleep immediately preceding the awakenings and reports. Indeed, the subjects themselves were uncertain about when their lucid dreams had taken place. What was needed to unambiguously establish the physiological status of lucid dreams was some sort of on-the-scene report from the dream, an idea first suggested by Tart (1965).

LaBerge and his colleagues at Stanford University provided this verification by arranging for subjects to signal the onset of a lucid dream immediately upon realizing that they were dreaming by performing specific patterns of dream actions that would be observable on a polygraph (i.e., eye movements and fist clenches). Using this approach, LaBerge, Nagel, Dement, and Zarcone (1981) reported that the occurrence of lucid dreaming during unequivocal REM sleep had been demonstrated for five subjects. After being instructed in the method of lucid dream induction (MILD) described by LaBerge (1980b), the subjects were recorded from 2 to 20 nights each. In the course of the 34 nights of the study, 35 lucid dreams were reported subsequent to spontaneous awaking from various stages of sleep as follows: REM sleep 32 times, NREM Stage-1, twice, and during the transition from NREM Stage-2 to REM, once. The subjects reported signaling during 30 of these lucid dreams. After each recording, the reports mentioning signals were submitted along with the respective polysomnograms to a judge uninformed of the times of the reports. In 24 cases (90%), the judge was able to select the appropriate 30-second epoch on the basis of correspondence between reported and observed signals. All signals associated with lucid dream reports occurred during epochs of unambiguous REM sleep scored according to the conventional criteria (Rechtschaffen & Kales, 1968).

A replication of this study with two additional subjects and 20 more lucid dreams produced identical results (LaBerge, Nagel, Taylor, Dement, & Zarcone, 1981). LaBerge et al. argued that their investigations demonstrated that lucid dreaming usually (though perhaps not exclusively) occurs during REM sleep. This conclusion is supported by research carried out in several other laboratories (Dane, 1984; Fenwick et al., 1984; Hearne, 1978; Ogilvie, Hunt, Kushniruk, & Newman, 1983).

Ogilvie et al. (1983) reported the physiological state preceding 14 spontaneous lucidity signals as unqualified REM in 12 (86%) of the cases; of the remaining 2 cases, 1 was "ambiguous" REM and the other appeared to be wakefulness. Keith Hearne and Alan Worsley collaborated on a pioneering study of lucid dreaming in which the latter spent 50 nonconsecutive nights in the sleep lab while the former monitored the polygraph. Worsley reported signaling in eight lucid dreams, all of which were described by Hearne (1978) as having occurred during unambiguous REM sleep.

Brylowski, LaBerge, Levitan, Booth, and Nelson (1986) monitored a single skilled lucid dreamer for four nights while measuring the subject's H-reflex. The reflex was evoked every 5 seconds and later measured and analyzed for differences in suppression between lucid and nonlucid REM. They found that the H-reflex was significantly suppressed during lucid REM as compared to nonlucid REM ($p < .001$). Because H-reflex suppression is often considered a unique hallmark of REM sleep, this finding should finally lay to rest the notion that lucid dreams do not occur during REM.

However, demonstrations that signaling of lucid dreams occurs during REM sleep may raise another kind of question for some readers: What exactly do we mean by the assertion that lucid dreamers are "asleep?" Perhaps these "dreamers" are not really dreamers, as some argued in the last century; or perhaps this "sleep" is not really sleep, as some have argued in this century. How do we know that lucid dreamers are "really asleep" when they signal? If we consider perception of the external world as a criterion of being awake (to the external world), we can conclude that they are actually asleep (to the external world) because, although they know they are in the laboratory, this knowledge is a matter of memory, not perception. Upon awakening, they report having been totally in the dream world and not in sensory contact with the external world. It might be objected that lucid dreamers might simply not be attending to the environment; rather than being asleep, perhaps they are merely absorbed in their private fantasy worlds as, for example, when deeply immersed in a novel or daydream. However, according to the reports of lucid dreamers (LaBerge, 1980a, 1985a), if they deliberately attempt to feel their bedcovers they know they are sleeping in or try to hear the ticking of the clock they know is beside their bed, they fail to feel or hear anything except what they find in their dream worlds. Lucid dreamers are conscious of the *absence* of sensory input from the external world; therefore, on empirical grounds, they conclude that they are asleep. If, in a contrary case, subjects were to claim to have been awake while showing physiological signs of sleep, or vice versa, we might have cause to doubt their subjective reports. However, when—as in the present case—the subjective accounts and objective physiological measures are in clear agreement, it is embarrassingly awkward to assert (as some critics have done) that subjects who reported being certain that they were asleep while showing physiological indications of unequivocal sleep were actually awake (cf. LaBerge, Nagel, Dement & Zarcone, 1981). The evidence is clear: Lucid dreaming is an experiential and physiological reality; though perhaps paradoxical, it is clearly a phenomenon of sleep.

PHYSIOLOGICAL CORRELATES OF THE INITIATION OF LUCID DREAMS

The preceding studies have shown that lucid dreams typically occur in REM sleep. However, this is not as precise a characterization as we would like. REM sleep is a heterogeneous state exhibiting considerable variations in physiological activity, of which two distinct phases are ordinarily distinguished. In its most active form, REM is dominated by a striking variety of irregular and short-lived events such as muscular twitching, including the rapid eye movements that give the state one of its most common names. This variety of REM is referred to as "phasic," whereas the relatively quiescent state remaining when rapid eye movements and other phasic events temporarily subside is referred to as "tonic." Thus, to more precisely characterize the lucid dream state, we need to ask whether lucid dreams take place in tonic or in phasic REM. Pivik (1986) predicted that lucid dreams should be associated with decreased phasic activity. However, research by the Stanford group, detailed later, has shown lucid dreaming to be associated with, on the contrary, *increased* phasic activity.

LaBerge, Levitan, and Dement (1986) physiologically analyzed 76 signal-verified lucid dreams (SVLDs) derived from 13 subjects. The polysomnograms corresponding to each of the SVLDs were scored for sleep stages, and every SVLD REM period was divided into 30 sec epochs aligned with the lucidity onset signal. Up to 60 consecutive epochs of data from the nonlucid portion preceding the SVLD and 15 epochs from the lucid dream were collected. For each epoch, sleep stage was scored and rapid eye movements (EM) were counted; if scalp skin-potential responses were observable as artifacts in the EEG, these were also counted (SP). Heart rate (HR) and respiration rate (RR) were determined for SVLDs recorded with these measures.

For the first lucid epoch, beginning with the initiation of the signal, the sleep stage was unequivocal REM in 70 cases (92%). The remaining 6 SVLDs were less than 30 sec long and hence technically unscorable by the orthodox criteria (Rechtschaffen & Kales, 1968). For these cases, the entire SVLD was scored as a single epoch; with this modification, all SVLDs qualified as REM. The lucid dream signals were followed by an average of 115 seconds (range: 5 to 490 s) of uninterrupted REM sleep.

Physiological comparison of EM, HR, RR, and SP for lucid versus nonlucid epochs revealed that the lucid epochs of the SVLD REM periods had significantly higher levels of physiological activation than the preceding epochs of nonlucid REM from the same REM period.

In order to study the temporal variations of physiology as they correlated with the development and initiation of lucidity, for each SVLD REM period the physiological variables were converted to standard scores and averaged across dreams and subjects. Figure 1 is a histogram of the resultant mean standard scores for the 5 minutes before and the 5 minutes after the initiation of lucidity. Note the highly significant increases in physiological activation during the 30 seconds before and after lucidity onset.

Physiological data (EM, RR, HR, and SP) were also collected for 61 control nonlucid REM periods, derived from the same 13 subjects, in order to allow comparison with SVLDs. Mean values for EM and SP were significantly higher for REM periods with lucid dreams than nonlucid control REM periods (RR and HR did not differ).

LaBerge reasoned that if lucid dream probability were constant across time during REM periods, lucid dreams should be observed most frequently in the first few minutes of REM. This is because, out of 10 REM periods, there will be nearly 10 minutes of total REM time for the first minute of REM, but less for the second minute, and much less for the twentieth minute (because some REM periods are only a few minutes in length). On this hypothesis, lucid dream probability should be a monotonically decreasing function of time into REM, following the survivor function of mean REM period lengths. Although this survivor function proved to be an excellent predictor of lucid dream probability ($r = .97$, $p < .005$), the data show that lucid dream probability does not reach its maximum before about 5 to 7 minutes into REM.

Given the finding that lucid dreams reliably occur during activated (phasic)

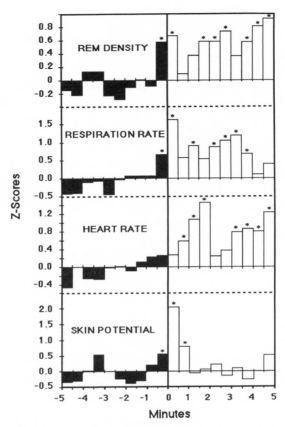

Figure 1. Histograms of mean Z-scores for EM, RR, HR, and SP. Bins are 30 sec in length with t = 0 representing the signaled onset of lucidity. Ns vary with variable and bin, but all values are averaged across lucid dreams and subjects. Note that REM density values do not include voluntary eye movement signals that, if counted, would further increase observed values (*$p < .05$).

REM, measures of central nervous system activation, such as eye movement density, should partially determine the distribution of lucid dreams. Because it has been reported that eye movement density starts at a low level at the beginning of REM periods and increases until it reaches a peak after approximately 5 to 7 minutes (Aserinsky, 1971), LaBerge hypothesized that lucid dream probability should follow a parallel development and accordingly found that mean eye movement density correlated positively and significantly with lucid dream probability ($r = .66$, $p < .01$). In a regression of lucid dream probability on eye movement density and the survivor function of mean REM period lengths, both variables entered significantly, giving an adjusted multiple $R = .98$ ($p < .005$), and demonstrating that CNS activation is an important factor in determining when in REM periods lucid dreams are initiated.

As was mentioned earlier, momentary intrusions of wakefulness occur very commonly during the normal course of REM sleep, and it had been proposed by Schwartz and Lefebvre (1973) that lucid dreaming takes place during these microawakenings. However, LaBerge *et al.*'s data indicated that while lucid dreams do *not* occur during interludes of wakefulness within REM periods, lucidity is sometimes *initiated* from these moments of transitory arousal, with the lucid dreams themselves continuing in subsequent undisturbed REM sleep. The subjects were normally conscious of having been awake before entering this class of lucid dream. More commonly, lucid dreams are initiated from the dream state without an awakening (Green, 1968; LaBerge 1985a).

Because lucid dreams initiated in these two ways would be expected to differ physiologically, the SVLDs were dichotomously classified as either "wake-initiated" (WILD) or "dream-initiated" (DILD), depending on whether or not the reports mentioned a transient awakening in which the subject consciously perceived the external environment before (consciously) reentering the dream state. Fifty-five (72%) of the SVLDs were classified as DILDs, and the

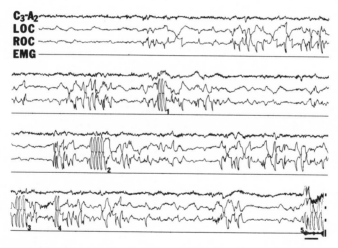

Figure 2. A typical dream-initiated lucid dream (DILD). Four channels of physiological data (central EEG [C_3-A_2], left and right eye movements [LOC and ROC], and chin muscle tone [EMG]) from the last 8 min of a 30-min REM period are shown. Upon awakening, the subject reported having made five eye movement signals (labeled 1-5 in figure). The first signal (1,LRLR) marked the onset of lucidity. Skin potential artifacts can be observed in the EEG at this point. During the following 90 seconds, the subject "flew about" exploring his dream world until he believed he had awakened, at which point he made the signal for awakening (2,LRLRLRLR). After another 90 seconds, the subject realized he was still dreaming and signaled (3) with three pairs of eye movements. Realizing that this was too many, he correctly signaled with two pairs (4). Finally, upon awakening 100 seconds later, he signaled appropriately (5,LRLRLRLR). Calibrations are 50 μV and 5 seconds.

remaining 21 (28%) as WILDs. For all 13 subjects, DILDs were more common than WILDs (binomial test, $p < .0001$). Compared to DILDs, WILDs were more frequently immediately preceded by physiological indications of awakening (Chi-squared $= 38.3$, 1 df, $p < .0001$), establishing the validity of classifying lucid dreams in this manner. See Figures 2 and 3 for illustrations of these two types of lucid dreams.

The distributions of DILD and WILD latencies from the onset of REM are significantly different (LaBerge, Levitan, & Dement, 1986). A Wald-Wolfowitz test demonstrated that WILDs do not occur as early or late in REM periods as DILDs do ($p < .0015$). This difference may be simply explained: As a matter of definition, a necessary condition for a WILD to occur is a transitory awakening followed by a return to REM sleep. If the awakening were to happen too near to the beginning of REM, the REM period might simply be aborted. Similarly, if the awakening were to occur too near to the "natural" end of the REM period, it would be more likely that REM would not resume but that wakefulness would persist or a NREM sleep stage would ensue.

To summarize, an elevated level of CNS activation seems to be a necessary condition for the occurrence of lucid dreams. Were this condition unnecessary,

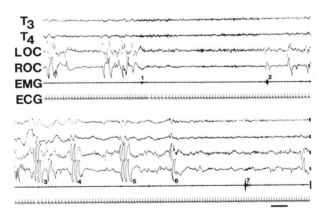

Figure 3. A typical lucid dream initiated from a transient awakening during REM (WILD). Six channels of physiological data (left and right temporal EEG [T_3 and T_4], left and right eye movements [LOC and ROC], chin muscle tone [EMG], and electrocardiogram [ECG]) from the last 3 min of a 14-min REM period are shown. The subject awoke at 1 and after 40 seconds returned to REM sleep at 2, and realized he was dreaming 15 s later and signaled at 3. Next he carried out the agreed-upon experimental task in his lucid dream, singing between signals 3 and 4, and counting between signals 4 and 5. This allowed comparison of left and right hemisphere activation during the two tasks (LaBerge & Dement, 1982b). Note the heart-rate acceleration-deceleration pattern at awakening (1) and at lucidity onset (3) and the skin potential potential artifacts in the EEG (particularly T_4) at lucidity onset (3). Calibrations are 50 μV and 5 seconds.

lucid dreams would be found randomly distributed within REM periods and perhaps every stage of sleep. Why then is CNS activation necessary for lucid dreaming? Evidently the high level of cognitive function involved in lucid dreaming requires a correspondingly high level of neuronal activation. In terms of Antrobus's (1986) adaptation of Anderson's (1983) ACT* model of cognition to dreaming, working memory capacity is proportional to cognitive activation, which in turn is proportional to cortical activation. Becoming lucid requires an adequate level of working memory to activate the presleep intention to recognize that one is dreaming. This level of activation is apparently not always available during sleep but normally only during phasic REM.

THE TEMPORAL DISTRIBUTION OF LUCID DREAMS

St. Thomas Aquinas mentioned "that sometimes while asleep a man may judge that what he sees is a dream, discerning as it were, between things and their images" and that this happens especially "towards the end of sleep, in sober men and those who are gifted with a strong imagination." (Aquinas, 1947, p. 430). Van Eeden (1913) stated that his lucid dreams invariably occurred between 5 and 8 o'clock in the morning. By way of explanation, he quoted Dante's characterization of these hours as the time "when swallows begin to warble and our mind is least clogged by the material body." Garfield (1975) exactly agreed with van Eeden's observation, though perhaps not with his poetic explanation. LaBerge (1979) plotted the times of 212 of his lucid dreams and found their pattern of occurrence closely fit the usual cyclic distribution of REM periods. He suggested that the fact that most REM sleep occurs toward the end of the night provided a plausible explanation for Van Eeden's and Garfield's observations. Later, LaBerge (1980a) tested this hypothesis by comparing the temporal distribution of his lucid dreams with that expected on the basis of normative data from Williams, Karacan, and Jursch (1974). A chi-square test indicated that the observed distribution of lucid dreams in the first three REM periods was not significantly different from what would be expected on the basis of mean REM period lengths at different times of the night.

Cohen (1979) argued that the left hemisphere shows a gradual increase in dominance across the night (but see Armitage, Hoffmann, Moffitt, & Shearer, 1985). Since left-hemisphere abstract symbolic functions are undoubtedly crucial for lucid dreaming, Cohen's GILD hypothesis led LaBerge (1985b) to predict that the probability of dream lucidity should increase with time of night.

This hypothesis was tested by LaBerge et al. (1986). For each of their 12 subjects, a median split for total REM time was determined; 11 of their subjects had more lucid dreams in the later half of their REM than in the earlier (binomial test; $p < .01$). For the combined sample, relative lucidity probability was calculated for REM periods 1 through 6 of the night by dividing the total number of lucid dreams observed in a given REM period by the corresponding total time in stage REM for the same REM period. A regression analysis clearly demonstrated that relative lucidity probability was a linear function of ordinal REM period number ($r = .98, p < .0001$). No measure of activation (EM, RR, HR, SP) even approached significance when entered into the regression equation, indicating that the increase in lucid dream probability is not explained by a general increase in CNS activation across the night. These results strongly support the conclusion that lucid dreams are more likely to occur in later REM periods than in earlier ones—provided, of course, that sleep is continued long enough.

Another factor influencing the temporal distribution of lucid dreams is initiation type. LaBerge's (1987) personal record of lucid dreams indicates that, for him, W-type lucid dreams are over 10 times more frequent during afternoon naps than they are during the first REM period of the night ($p < .0002$).

EEG ALPHA ACTIVITY DURING REM LUCID DREAMS

The fact that lucid dreaming occurs during REM sleep partially defines the sort of EEG activity characteristic of lucid dreams. However, the standard criteria for determining REM sleep (Rechtschaffen & Kales, 1968) are quite general when referring to the EEG, being simply "relatively low voltage, mixed frequency," without specifying how much of which frequencies might be mixed. As noted previously, REM sleep is a labile and heterogeneous state. For example, during REM, the EEG sometimes shows predominant 2 to 3 Hz "sawtooth" waves, whereas at other times it may exhibit prominent 8 to 10 Hz alpha waves. Consequently, the question arises: Does the range of EEG activity characteristic of lucid dreams reliably differ in any way from that of nonlucid dreams?

In a series of studies, Ogilvie and colleagues have pursued the hypothesis that lucid dreams are associated with high levels of alpha activity. In the first of these investigations, they came to the initial "impression that alpha is the dominant EEG frequency during lucid dreams" on the rather shaky grounds of a comparison of "percent alpha in the EEG" of just two lucid dream REM periods with percentage alpha for six nonlucid dream REM periods for a *single* subject (Ogilvie, Hunt, Sawicki, & McGowan, 1978, p. 165).

Ogilvie, Hunt, Tyson, Lucescu, and Jeakins (1982) followed up their preliminary work with a larger study in which 10 subjects (all good dream recallers, with a wide range of lucid dreaming ability) were recorded 2 nights each in the sleep laboratory, during which they were awakened four times per night from REM sleep: half of the time during periods of relatively high alpha and half of the time during relatively low alpha. Dream reports were collected and rated on a lucidity scale by a judge blind to the awakening condition. Significantly higher lucidity ratings were obtained for high-alpha compared to low-alpha awakenings.

Several methodological problems of this study cast doubt on Ogilvie *et al.*'s

(1982) conclusion that lucid dreams are associated with high alpha activity. One is that the differences found between low and high alpha reports were based primarily on the degrees of *pre*lucidity in the reports. Even more important, we have no assurance of whether, in either condition, the episode of prelucidity or lucidity occurred in association with the final 20 to 30 second period of either high or low alpha activity that determined the awakening condition. Moreover, because none of the dreams classified as lucid were marked by any signals, we have no proof that they were in fact lucid dreams, nor in any case do we have any way of determining what the degree of alpha activity was *during* the frequently brief episodes of lucidity.

Because of Ogilvie *et al.*'s (1982) design, we cannot exclude the possibility that what their study may actually have demonstrated is that the tendencies of subjects to retrospectively judge themselves to have been briefly or partially lucid vary with the amount of alpha activity either just before or during the process of awakening. Support for this interpretation comes from an earlier study, which concluded that mentation reports collected from REM periods showing EEGs with a high proportion of alpha waves were associated with "some feeling of control over the content" and were frequently labeled by subjects as "thoughts" rather than "dreams" (Goodenough, Shapiro, Holden, & Steinschriber, 1959).

There is another possible design problem with the Ogilvie *et al.* (1982) study that seems serious enough to merit mention: The judges' lucidity ratings were based not upon the spontaneous dream reports but on the subjects' answers to rather leading questions subsequently posed by the interviewer, such as "Was there any point when you wondered whether or not you might be dreaming?" and "Was there any point at which you knew you were dreaming while the dream was going on?" The demand characteristics should be obvious. Additionally, there is a problem that retrospective judgments about earlier states of mind are likely to be confounded by our current mental state. Cognitive capacities we currently possess are likely to be mistakenly remembered as having been present in an earlier state. A conservative approach should perhaps put more weight on the original dream reports; in the present context, one would like to know how many subjects spontaneously mentioned in their reports that they had been prelucid or lucid.

In a more recent study, Ogilvie *et al.* (1983) remedied several of these methodological problems and arrived at a conclusion regarding alpha activity and lucidity unsupportive of their earlier work. They studied eight lucid dreamers for 1 to 4 nights in a sleep lab. The subjects were awakened from REM following spontaneous or cued eye movement signals. The cue buzzer sounded after 15 minutes of REM during periods of either high or low alpha activity. The subjects were to signal at the cue and again 30 seconds later if in a lucid dream. Reports were elicited 30 to 60 seconds after cued or spontaneous signals and rated for lucidity. Contrary to their earlier findings, the low-alpha condition yielded slightly more lucid dreams than the high-alpha condition; however, this difference was not statistically significant. Addressing this same issue, LaBerge (1980b) performed a Fourier analysis on EEG activity (C3/A1) for a single lucid dream REM period. Comparison of the spectral profiles for the lucid and nonlucid portions of the REM period revealed alpha activity for the nonlucid portion to more closely resemble the waking EEG spectrum than did that in the lucid portion; however, the two REM samples did not significantly differ.

In summary, it would seem that at this point no reliable association of lucid dreaming with alpha activity (whether high or low) has been established. A more productive approach to the question of EEG in lucid versus nonlucid REM would probably involve quantifying whole-band EEG frequency spectra from several electrode placements and comparing signal-verified lucid dreams with nonlucid controls.

NREM LUCID DREAMS

The findings summarized here indicating that lucid dreams typically occur in REM sleep should not be misconstrued to suggest that lucid dreams never occur in NREM sleep. In fact, in LaBerge, Nagel, Dement and Zarcone's initial study (1981), lucid dreams were reported by two subjects after spontaneous awakening from NREM sleep (Stage-2 once; Stage-1, twice). The Stage-2 report indicated only a brief moment of lucidity before awakening; because the subject was unable to signal while lucid we cannot be certain that her experience took place during Stage-2 sleep and not while awakening. As for the NREM Stage-1 reports, although the subject reported signaling before awakening on these occasions, no signals could be verified on her polysomnogram.

LaBerge (1980a) polysomnographically recorded a single trained subject during sleep onset on 3 consecutive nights. The subject reported a rich history of hypnagogic imagery. On the experimental nights, she made an effort to retain consciousness while entering sleep-onset dream states. "Dreaming" was distinguished from other sleep-onset mentation by the two requirements that (1) the subject was subjectively asleep (i.e., unaware of the actual position of her body in bed) and (2) that she hallucinated her body within the dream scene.

On each of the experimental sessions (lasting about 2 hours), the subject repeatedly rested quietly, but vigilantly, and while drifting off to sleep counted to herself ("One, two, three, . . .") until she began to dream, at which point she awakened and tape-recorded a mentation report. In 25 of the 42 resultant dream reports (all of which were very short), the subject claimed to have been lucid. The following is a typical report: "I am in the grocery store, going down an aisle; only I am standing on a cart. It is whizzing real fast. As I go by the Coke and Pepsi bottles, I realize that I am dreaming. I think to look at my hands, but they won't move up to eye level" (p. 101). Note the absence of voluntary control over the body image, a very unusual condition for REM lucid dreams. Visual inspection of the polygraph record showed all of these "dreamlets" to have occurred during Stage-1 sleep, with slow eye movements.

This pilot study makes it clear that the observed frequency of NREM lucid dreaming will depend on experimental demand characteristics. The same point is made by Dane (1983), who found a high proportion of lucid dream reports deriving from NREM under conditions of heightened attention during sleep onset and explicit instructions that "dreams occur during NREM as well as during REM sleep" (p. 249). A comparative study of REM versus NREM (and "waking") lucid dreaming clearly needs to be done.

PSYCHOPHYSIOLOGICAL RELATIONSHIPS DURING REM SLEEP

One of the major obstacles impeding the development of human consciousness as a topic of rigorous scientific study has been that the only direct account available of the private events occurring in a person's mind is his or her own subjective report. Subjective reports, unfortunately, are not subject to objective verification—at least not directly. To make matters worse, of all the "bad witnesses"—as Heraclitus called the senses—"introspection" appears to be the least reliable. Introspection is not really even a sense: We do not simply "look and see" the contents of our minds; what we "see" there is largely dependent on what we *expect* to see based on our theories of ourselves. These theories tend to portray ourselves as more consistent and rational than we really are (Nisbett & Wilson, 1977). Given that the only witness is of uncertain reliability, what we need in order to study consciousness more objectively is a means of corroborating the testimony of the "I-witness," and this is precisely the role of the psychophysiological approach. A key element in this new strategy is the idea of making full use of the subject's cooperativeness and intelligence. A frequent practice in experimental psychology requires the deception of subjects about the true nature of the experiment. This has the advantage of minimizing the effect the subject's knowledge might have on the experiment. But this particular methodology is inappropriate when the object of the investigation is the subject's own consciousness. In this case, a more suitable approach is one in which the dichotomous subject/experimenter relationship is modified: Perhaps subjects should be regarded as—to borrow an anthropological term—participant–observers.

What about the problem of the uncertain reliability of introspective accounts of consciousness? There are two strategies likely to increase our confidence in the reliability of subjective reports: In the first place, it helps to study highly trained (and lucid) subjects who are skillful reporters. Second, we can make use of the fact that the convergent agreement of physiological measures and subjective reports provides a degree of validation to the latter (Stoyva and Kamiya, 1968).

The fact that lucid dreamers can remember to perform predetermined actions and signal to the laboratory suggested to LaBerge (1980a) a new approach to dream research: Lucid dreamers, he proposed,

> could carry out diverse dream experiments marking the exact time of particular dream events, allowing the derivation of precise psychophysiological correlations and the methodical testing of hypotheses. (LaBerge, Nagel, Dement, & Zarcone, 1981, p. 727)

This strategy has been put into practice by the Stanford group in a number of studies summarized by LaBerge (1985a).

LaBerge first of all pointed out that the data reported in LaBerge, Nagel, Dement, and Zarcone (1981) and LaBerge, Nagel, Taylor, Dement, and Zarcone (1981) indicate that there is a very direct and reliable relationship between gaze shifts reported in lucid dreams and the direction of polygraphically recorded eye movements. It should be noted that the results obtained for lucid dreams (see also Dane, 1984; Fenwick *et al.*, 1984; Hearne, 1978; Ogilvie, *et al.*, 1982) are much stronger than the generally weak correlations demonstrated by earlier investigations testing the notion that the dreamer's eyes move with his or her hallucinated dream gaze, which had to rely on the chance occurrence of a highly recognizable eye movement pattern that was readily matchable to the subject's reported dream activity (e.g., Roffwarg, Dement, Muzio, & Fisher, 1962). This would seem to illustrate the methodological advantage of using lucid dreamers.

LaBerge (1980a, 1985a) reports having straightforwardly approached the problem of dream time by asking subjects to estimate various intervals of time during their lucid dreams. Signals marking the beginning and end of the subjective intervals allowed comparison with objective time. In all cases, LaBerge reported, time estimates during the lucid dreams were very close to the actual time between signals.

In another study, LaBerge and Dement (1982a) demonstrated the possibility of voluntary control of respiration during lucid dreaming. They recorded three lucid dreamers who were asked to either breathe rapidly or to hold their breaths (in their lucid dreams), marking the invertal of altered respiration with eye movement signals. The subjects reported successfully carrying out the agreed-upon tasks a total of nine times, and in every case, a judge was able to correctly predict on the basis of the polygraph recordings which of the two patterns had been executed ($p < .002$).

Evidence of voluntary control of other muscle groups during REM was found by LaBerge, Nagel, Dement, and Zarcone (1981) while testing a variety of lucidity signals. They observed that a sequence of left and right dream-fist clenches resulted in a corresponding sequence of left and right forearm twitches as measured by EMG. However, the amplitude of the twitches bore an unreliable relationship to the subjective intensity of the dreamed action. Because all skeletal muscle groups except those that govern eye movements and breathing suffer a profound loss of tone during REM sleep, it is to be expected that most muscular responses to dreamed movements will be feeble. Nonetheless, these responses faithfully reflect the motor patterns of the original dream. One might say that the dreamer's body responds to dreamed actions with movements that are but shadows of the originals.

Further support of this notion comes from a study (Fenwick *et al.*, 1984) of a single highly proficient lucid dreamer (Alan Worsley, who had also been Hearne's [1978] subject) who carried out a variety of dreamed muscular movements while being polygraphically recorded. In one experiment, Worsley executed movements during lucid dreams involving finger, forearm, and shoulder muscle groups (flexors) while EMG was recorded from each area. The results were consistent: The axial muscles showed no measurable EMG activity, whereas the forearm EMG "consistently showed lower amplitude and shorter bursts" compared to the finger EMG. A similar experiment with the lower limbs yielded similar results. In addition to the finding that REM atonia shows a central-peripheral gradient with motor inhibition least for the most distal muscles, Fenwick *et al.* reported that similar experiments comparing EMG response to dreamed arm and leg flexions and extensions suggested that flexors were less inhibited than extensors. In addition to EMG, an accelerometer was utilized in several experiments demonstrating that Worsley was able to produce minor movements of his fingers, toes, and feet during REM, though not of his legs. Fenwick *et al.* also presented the results of a single experiment suggesting that dream speech may be initiated in the expiratory phase of respiration just as it usually does during waking. In still another experiment they demonstrated the voluntary production of smooth pursuit eye movements during a lucid dream. LaBerge (1986) has carried out related experiments in which two subjects tracked the tip of their fingers moving slowly left to right during four conditions: (1) awake, eyes open; (2) awake, eyes closed mental imagery; (3) lucid dreaming; and (4) imagination ("dream eyes closed") during lucid dreaming. The subjects showed saccadic eye movements in the two imagination conditions (2 and 4), and smooth-tracking eye movements during dreamed or actual tracking (conditions 1 and 3).

Fenwick *et al.* also showed that Worsley was able to perceive and respond to environmental stimuli (electrical shocks) without awakening from his lucid dream. This result raises a theoretical issue: If we take perception of the external world to be the essential criterion for wakefulness (LaBerge, Nagel, Dement, & Zarcone, 1981), then it would seem that Worsley must have been at least partially awake. On the other hand, when environmental stimuli are incorporated into dreams without producing any subjective or physiological indications of arousal, it appears reasonable to speak of the perception as having occurred during sleep. Furthermore, it may be possible, as LaBerge (1980c) has suggested, for one sense to remain functional and "awake" while others fall "asleep." As long as we continue to consider wakefulness and sleep as a simple dichotomy, we will lie in a Procrustian bed that is bound at times to be most uncomfortable. There must be degrees of being awake just as there are degrees of being asleep (i.e., the conventional sleep stages). Before finding our way out of this muddle, we will probably need to characterize a wider variety of states of consciousness than those few currently distinguished (e.g., dreaming, sleeping, waking, and so on).

Because many researchers have reported cognitive task dependency of lateralization of EEG alpha activity in the waking state, LaBerge undertook a pilot study to determine whether similar relationships would hold in the lucid dream state. The two tasks selected for comparison were dreamed singing and dreamed counting, activities expected to result in relatively greater engagement of the subjects' left and right cerebral hemispheres, respectively.

Integrated alpha band EEG activity was derived from electrodes placed over right and left temporal lobes while four subjects sang and counted in their lucid dreams (marking the beginning and end of each task by eye movement signals). The results supported the hypothesized lateralization of alpha activity: The right hemisphere was more active than the left during singing; during counting the reverse was true. These shifts were similar to those observed during actual singing and counting (LaBerge & Dement, 1982b).

Sexual activity is a rather commonly reported theme of lucid dreams (Garfield, 1979; LaBerge, 1985a). However, at this point, only a single physiological investigation of lucid dream sex has been published. LaBerge, Greenleaf, and Kedzierski (1983) undertook a pilot study to determine the extent to which subjectively experienced sexual activity during REM lucid dreaming would be reflected in physiological responses. Their subject was a highly proficient lucid dreamer who spent the night sleeping in the laboratory. Sixteen channels of physiological data, including EEG, EOG, EMG, respiration, skin conductance level (SCL), heart rate, vaginal EMG (VEMG), and vaginal pulse amplitude (VPA), were recorded. The experimental protocol called for the subject to make specific eye movement signals at the following points: when she realized she was dreaming (i.e., the onset of the lucid dream); when she began sexual activity (in the dream); and when she experienced orgasm. The subject reported a lucid dream in which she carried out the experimental task exactly as agreed upon. Data analysis revealed a significant correspondence between her subjective report and all but one of the autonomic measures; during the 15-second orgasm epoch, mean levels for VEMG activity, VPA, SCL, and respiration rate reached their highest values and were significantly elevated compared to means for other REM epochs. Contrary to expectation, heart rate increased only slightly and nonsignificantly.

LaBerge (1985a) reports replicating this experiment using two male subjects. In both cases, respiration showed striking increases in rate. Again, there were no significant elevations of heart rate. Interestingly, although both subjects reported vividly realistic orgasms in their lucid dreams, neither actually ejaculated, in contrast to the "wet dreams" commonly experienced by adolescent males. The mechanism of nocturnal emissions is probably local reflex irritability because wet dreams do not necessarily involve dream content of a sexual nature, again in contrast to lucid dream orgasms, which are obviously sexual; it appears we have two extreme cases: "bottom-up" versus "top-down" orgasms.

All of these results support the conclusion that the events we experience while asleep and dreaming produce effects on our brains (and to a lesser extent, bodies) remarkably similar to those that would be produced if we were actually to experience the corresponding events while awake. The reason for this is probably that the multimodal imagery of the dream is produced by the same brain systems that produce the equivalent perceptions (cf. Finke, 1980). Perhaps this is why dreams seem so real: To our brains, dreaming of doing something is equivalent to actually doing it.

REFERENCES

Anderson, J. R. (1983). *The architecture of cognition.* Cambridge: Harvard University Press.

Antrobus, J. S. (1986). Dreaming: Cortical activation and perceptual thresholds. *Journal of Mind and Behavior, 7,* 193–212.

Antrobus, J. S., Antrobus, J. S., & Fisher, C. (1965). Discrimination of dreaming and nondreaming sleep. *Archives of General Psychiatry, 12,* 395–401.

Aquinas, St. Thomas. (1947) *Summa theologica* (Vol. 1). New York: Benziger Brothers.

Armitage, R., Hoffmann, R., Moffitt, A., & Shearer, J. (1985). Ultradian rhythms in interhemispheric EEG during sleep: A disconfirmation of the GILD hypothesis. *Sleep Research, 14,* 286.

Aserinsky, E. (1971). Rapid eye movement density and pattern in the sleep of young adults. *Psychophysiology, 8,* 361–375.

Berger, R. (1977). *Psyclosis: The circularity of experience.* San Francisco: W. H. Freeman.

Brylowski, A., LaBerge, S., Levitan, L., Booth, F., & Nelson, W. (1986). *H-reflex suppression in lucid vs. non-lucid REM sleep.* Manuscript submitted for publication.

Cohen, D. B. (1979). *Sleep and dreaming: Origins, nature and functions.* Oxford: Pergamon.

Dane, J. (1984). *An empirical evaluation of two techniques for lucid dream induction.* Unpublished doctoral dissertation, Georgia State University.

Fenwick, P., Schatzmann, M., Worsley, A., Adams, J., Stone, S., & Backer, A. (1984). Lucid dreaming: Correspondence between dreamed and actual events in one subject during REM sleep. *Biological Psychology, 18,* 243–252.

Finke, R. A. (1980). Levels of equivalence in imagery and perception. *Psychological Review, 87,* 113–132.

Foulkes, D. (1974). Review of Schwartz and Lefebvre (1973). *Sleep Research, 3,* 113.

Garfield, P. (1975). Psychological concomitants of the lucid dream state. *Sleep Reserach, 4,* 183.

Garfield, P. (1979). *Pathway to ecstasy.* New York: Holt, Rhinehart, & Winston.

Goodenough, D. R., Shapiro, A., Holden, M., & Steinschriber, L. (1959) A comparison of "dreamers" and "nondreamers": Eye movements, electroencephalograms and the recall of dreams. *Journal of Abnormal Psychology, 59,* 295–302.

Green, C. (1968). *Lucid dreams.* London: Hamish Hamilton.

Hall, J. A. (1977). *Clinical uses of dreams.* New York: Grune & Stratten.

Hartmann, E. (1975). Dreams and other hallucinations: An approach to the underlying mechanism. In R. K. Siegal & L. J. West (Eds.), *Hallucinations* (pp. 71–79). New York: Wiley.

Hearne, K. M. T. (1978). *Lucid dreams: An electrophysiological and psychological study.* Unpublished doctoral dissertation, University of Liverpool.

LaBerge, S. (1979). Lucid dreaming: Some personal observations. *Sleep Research, 8,* 158.

LaBerge, S. (1980a). *Lucid dreaming: An exploratory study of consciousness during sleep.* (Doctoral dissertation, Stanford University, 1980). (University Microfilms International No. 80-24,691).

LaBerge, S. (1980b). Lucid dreaming as a learnable skill: A case study. *Perceptual and Motor Skills, 51,* 1039–1042.

LaBerge, S. (1980c). Induction of lucid dreams. *Sleep Research, 9,* 138.

LaBerge, S. (1985a). *Lucid dreaming.* Los Angeles: J. P. Tarcher.

LaBerge, S. (1985b). The temporal distribution of lucid dreams. *Sleep Research, 14,* 113.

LaBerge, S. (1986). Unpublished data.

LaBerge, S. (1987). Unpublished data.

LaBerge, S. & Dement, W. C. (1982a). Voluntary control of respiration during REM sleep. *Sleep Research, 11,* 107.

LaBerge, S., & Dement, W. C. (1982b). Lateralization of alpha activity for dreamed singing and counting during REM sleep. *Psychophysiology, 19,* 331–332.

LaBerge, S., Greenleaf, W., & Kedzierski, B. (1983). Physiological responses to dreamed sexual activity during lucid REM sleep. *Psychophysiology, 20,* 454–455.

LaBerge, S., Nagel, L., Dement, W. C., & Zarcone, V., Jr. (1981). Lucid dreaming verified by volitional communication during REM sleep. *Perceptual and Motor Skills, 52,* 727–732.

LaBerge, S., Nagel, L., Taylor, W., Dement, W. C., & Zarcone, V., Jr. (1981). Psychophysiological correlates of the initiation of lucid dreaming. *Sleep Research, 10,* 149.

LaBerge, S., Levitan, L. X., & Dement, W. C. (1986). Psychophysiology of lucid dreams. Unpublished data.

LaBerge, S., Levitan, L., & Dement, W. C. (1986). Lucid dreaming: Physiological correlates of consciousness during REM sleep. *Journal of Mind and Behavior, 7,* 251–258.

Malcolm, N. (1959). *Dreaming.* London: Routledge.

Nisbett, R. E., & Wilson, T. D. (1977). Telling more than we can know: Verbal reports on mental processes. *Psychological Review, 84,* 231–259.

Ogilvie, R., Hunt, H., Sawicki, C., & McGowan, K. (1978). Searching for lucid dreams. *Sleep Research, 7,* 165.

Ogilvie, R., Hunt, H., Tyson, P. D., Lucescu, M. L., & Jeakins, D. B. (1982). Lucid dreaming and alpha activity: A preliminary report. *Perceptual and Motor Skills, 55,* 795–808.

Ogilvie, R., Hunt, H., Kushniruk, A., & Newman, J. (1983). Lucid dreams and the arousal continuum. *Sleep Research, 12,* 182.

Pivik, R. T. (1986). Sleep: Physiology and psychophysiology. In M. G. H. Coles, E. Donchin, & S. Porges (Eds.), *Psychophysiology: Systems, processes, and applications* (pp. 378–406). Guilford Press: New York.

Rechtschaffen, A. (1978). The single-mindedness and isolation of dreams. *Sleep, 1,* 97–109.

Rechtschaffen, A., & Kales, A. (Ed.). (1968). *A manual of standardized terminology, techniques and scoring system for sleep stages of human subjects.* Bethesda: HEW Neurological Information Network.

Roffwarg, E., Dement, W. C., Muzio, J., & Fisher, C. (1962). Dream imagery: Relationship to rapid eye movements of sleep. *Archives of General Psychiatry, 7,* 235–238.

Schwartz, B. A., & Lefebvre, A. (1973). Contacts veille/P.M.O. II. Les P.M.O. morcelees [Conjunction of waking and REM sleep. II. Fragmented REM periods.]. *Revue d'Electroencephalographie et de Neurophysiologie Clinique, 3,* 165–176.

Stoyva, J. & Kamiya, J. (1968). Electrophysiological studies of dreaming as the prototype of a new strategy in the study of consciousness. *Psychological Review, 75,* 192–205.

Tart, C. (1965). Toward the experimental control of dreaming: A review of the literature. *Psychological Bulletin, 64,* 81–91.

Van Eeden, F. (1913). A study of dreams. *Proceedings of the Society for Psychical Research, 26,* 431–461.

Williams, R., Karacan, I., & Jursch, C. (1974). *Electroencephalography (EEG) of Human Sleep: Clinical Applications.* New York: Wiley.

8

Correspondence during Lucid Dreams between Dreamed and Actual Events

MORTON SCHATZMAN, ALAN WORSLEY, and
PETER FENWICK

INTRODUCTION

Previous research (Fenwick *et al.*, 1984; Hearne, 1978; LaBerge, Nagel, De-ment, & Zarcone, 1981; LaBerge, 1985) has shown that, during REM sleep, certain subjects can signal that they are dreaming lucidly by means of volitional eye movements (recorded by the electro-oculogram) and forearm muscle con-tractions (recorded by the electromyogram). If confirmed, these results suggest the possibility of a new method for examining experimentally the long-standing assumption that a dream report of a subject awakened from REM sleep corre-sponds to what the subject really dreamed. These results suggest, too, that if, while dreaming lucidly, a subject can perceive external sensory stimuli and, in response to them, can signal volitionally—thereby in effect engaging in two-way communication—then the ability in dreams to perceive incoming stimuli and respond to them (for example, by counting them) could be experimentally exam-ined. Our experiments were designed to provide data relevant to these issues and, further, to explore the relationship in lucid dreams between the dream body and the physical body.

This report presents our previous findings (Fenwick *et al.*, 1984), together with our subject's hitherto unpublished dream accounts from our experiments and an expanded discussion of our conclusions.

MORTON SCHATZMAN, ALAN WORSLEY, and PETER FENWICK • 35 Croftdown Road, London NW5 1EL, England.

METHODS

The experiments reported here took place between December 1980 and January 1982 in the EEG laboratory at St. Thomas's Hospital. The subject was Alan Worsley, a university psychology graduate in his early 40s, who for years had been cultivating an ability to dream lucidly. Throughout this chapter, except in the dream accounts, we refer to our subject as "Worsley" or "he", rather than as "I"; the dream accounts, which are direct quotations, are told in the first person. Besides being our subject, Worsley is an author of this chapter.

By history and polysomnogram, Worsley's sleep was normal, and he had no psychiatric or neurologic disorder. During periods when the experiments took place, instead of pursuing his usual sleep pattern, he slept from about 3 A.M. until about 7A.M., then came to the laboratory where EEG electrodes were applied. In the laboratory, before going to sleep, Worsley wrote out what he planned to do while asleep. He slept from about 10 A.M. until about 12 noon, and frequently dreamed lucidly. This unusual sleep pattern suited the laboratory technicians, who preferred daytime to nighttime experimentation, and it was also intended to increase the yield of lucid dreams: having experimented, on his own, informally with various sleep patterns, Worsley had observed that, if he interrupted his nighttime sleep after a few hours, stayed awake and returned to sleep, the incidence of lucid dreams in the last sleep period would be particularly high. This observation requires objective confirmation.

The electrodes were placed according to the 10-20 system, together with two channels for horizontal and vertical eye movements, which were recorded with AC-coupled electrodes, a submental EMG, and additional channels for each particular experiment. Sleep stages were scored according to the criteria of Rechtschaffen and Kales (1968).

RESULTS

Except where indicated otherwise, all experiments reported here occurred during stage REM, as shown by the absence of submental EMG, by spontaneously occurring rapid eye movements preceding and following the volitional eye movements that signaled lucidity onset, by a theta-dominant EEG, and by power spectral analysis, which for epochs immediately following lucidity onset showed the usual REM spectral profile.

Eye-Movement Signals and Hand Movements

In one experiment, Worsley planned to signal lucidity onset with eye movements and to dream of drawing large triangles on a wall or on another suitable surface, while watching his hand move.

After waking, he related that in a dream he had become lucid and performed the tasks successfully. This is the account of his dream, which, upon waking, he narrated into a tape recorder:

> I seemed to be in a room in the EEG Department at St. Thomas's. [In fact, I was sleeping in a room of the EEG Department, so in this regard the dream resembled a false awakening.] After a few moments, perhaps half a minute, I signaled lucidity onset with 5 eye movements.
>
> I searched for something to draw triangles on. There were several pieces of paper but most of them looked too small and had things written on them. I shouldn't use them, I thought, in case they were somebody's valuable notes. [Insofar as I was supposing that the notes were real and valuable to someone, I was not completely lucid.] I walked through two [I think] rooms and found a blackboard with writing on it and some red chalk. I hesitated to use the blackboard, again in case somebody had left the writing there for further use.
>
> Nevertheless, I started to draw the triangles on the blackboard. The chalk seemed greasy and didn't write very well, which momentarily concerned me. [Had I been more lucid, I might have realized sooner that it wasn't necessary for the chalk to write well.]
>
> I tried to mark each attempt to draw a triangle with eye flicks: one flick for the first attempt, two flicks for the second, and so on. [I'm confident that I had considereable success with this routine.] I drew five triangles altogether. Between the second and third triangles, I had to pause briefly—a man was in the way, and I took a few seconds to move round him. Each triangle was about a foot high or a bit more, so I needed plenty of room. Between the third and fourth triangles—or maybe the fourth and fifth—I ran out of space on the blackboard and moved across the corner of the room to another blackboard.
>
> After finishing drawing these five triangles, I wondered what else to do. I wandered round the EEG Department, looking at things. I noticed a fair amount of detail, pieces of equipment and so on, but somehow nothing struck me enough for me to remember anything significant about it. People were around too.
>
> I'd say the whole dream took about 5 minutes.

The dream account corresponded well with the polygraph record. On that record, the vertical and horizontal eye-movement channels showed the lucidity-onset signals (five eye movements) occurring after a half minute of REM. From REM onset until waking took 5 minutes and 15 seconds, which approximates closely Worsley's subjective estimate, upon waking, that "the whole dream took about 5 minutes." The electro-oculogram record showed the planned pattern of eye-movement markers: one eye flick, followed by two eye flicks, followed by three and so on, up to five eye flicks. The three intervals between the beginnings of the first four sets of eye-flick markers were 9, 9, and 8 seconds respectively, and the interval between the beginnings of the fourth and fifth sets was 20 seconds, which apparently corresponded to Worsley's memory of having run out of blackboard space and having looked for another blackboard. The right forearm EMG showed groups of spikes, which began 2, 1½, 2½, 2½, and 6 seconds respectively after the ends of the eye-flick markers, so that these spikes apparently corresponded to the drawing of the triangles. Thus actions in a dream produced corresponding eye movements and electromyogram responses.

We planned another experiment to show that writing in a lucid dream would produce corresponding eye movements and forearm EMG potentials. Before going to sleep, Worsley outlined his intentions: to signal the onset of dream lucidity with five horizontal eye movements in quick succession (this, he estimated, would take about 3 seconds); to write large numbers—about 1 foot high—each number written with the same number of strokes as the number itself ($1, 2, 3, 4, 5$); before writing each number, to make horizontal eye movements equal in number to the number to be written; and to produce as large a forearm EMG as possible, by grasping the writing instrument tightly on each stroke. He thought of using an umbrella and writing with it on the ground, while he stood up and watched the tip of the ferrule as he wrote; and, if he made a mistake or wished to write a particular number again, to signal "error" by "scribbling" with his eyes—that is, by making a few rapid horizontal eye movements.

Upon waking up, he reported that he had managed to signal the numbers twice. This was his dream:

> I was at the university in Hull, walking round the campus. I'd been round the back of the administration building, which looked not quite as it does now, but more as it used to in 1956, when I'd first been there.
>
> I stood on a steeply sloping bumpy roadway that was paved with small square blocks of granite. I deliberately slipped down it—rather like the way that sometimes, when dreaming, I slip down steps, as if skiing down their edges. The slope was steep and led to a car park. "There's no need for me to go this way round," I thought, but I wasn't sure which way to go.
>
> I walked back from the campus towards the main exit. There was another bit of interesting road surface—very bumpy and composed of big stones stuck together with concrete that had shiny pebbles embedded in it for decoration. I noticed nearby a tree that resembled a rosebush—except that it was rather big, and the leaves didn't look like rose leaves. I couldn't work it out. I couldn't see if the base was that of a rosebush. No roses were at the top, but it looked as if at another time there might be some.
>
> I walked round to the front entrance of the administration buidling and, when I got near it, I became lucid. The scene didn't conform very well to reality—for instance, there were no steps leading up to the entrance. The double doors to the main entrance resembled the doors, which I normally use, at the entrance to the St. Thomas's Casualty Department.
>
> I saw hanging on one of the door handles an umbrella. [My umbrella is black, but this was a woman's umbrella and was brown]. It was very useful—just what I needed to write with. I took hold of it, and signaled lucidity onset with five eye movements.
>
> I looked for somewhere to write. I was standing on a paved area, which wouldn't have shown marks made by the umbrella, so I moved over to a grassy area. The ground was slightly muddy, and I thought the umbrella tip would leave marks that I'd be able to see. Quite a few people were walking around—it seemed to be about the middle of the day, but I ignored them and hoped they'd ignore me doing my strange routine.
>
> I started to draw numbers. I didn't do the series perfectly. I wasn't thinking properly. Number "2" I did as a plus sign. I wondered whether to use the "scribble" error signal, but decided not to. I thought, if possible, I'd do another series to produce

at least one perfect series. Between each number I took longer breaks than I'd expected. I'd intended to go straight through the series, but there were one or two hitches—such as walking around to find a new place to write. I don't know whether I remembered to track the tip of the umbrella as conscientiously as I'd planned to, but at least once I reminded myself to do it.

I doubt whether the eye movements can be easily resolved to show what I'd been tracking, but the number of strokes and their pattern should appear.

While doing the second series of five, I awoke—because, I think, I'd been paying too much attention to writing and not enough to the wider scene.

Perhaps the reason I dreamed about being at the university was that usually I go there on a Thursday—and this experiment was on a Thursday.

The polygraph record agreed very well with this account. According to that record, the dream clearly occurred during sleep, though whether it was in Stage 1 or REM sleep is not clear.

The first part of the record showed no EMG blips. Four seconds before the five eye movements that clearly signaled lucidity onset were the first EMG blips, which could correspond to the dreamer's taking hold of the umbrella. The lucidity-onset signal was present about 2¼ minutes before waking. About 3 seconds after the end of that signal, a single eye movement followed. Most of the subsequent eye-movement markers were clearly present and, in most cases, were followed by EMG blips. However, the number of blips did not correspond well with the dreamed strokes of the hand.

Scanning Movements

In another experiment, Worsley planned to dream of moving his finger smoothly from side to side and following it with his eyes to determine if he could produce slow scanning movements of his physical eyes. These eye movements are controlled by the frontal-lobe eye-movement center and are very difficult to produce in the absence of a "real" stimulus.

This is Worsley's report of his dream:

> I was with many rowdy people in a hall that seemed medieval. It resembled a demon's palace. I was struggling with a woman, who was skinny, dark, and a bit slippery, and who was clinging to me. I wanted to go, but she didn't want me to.
>
> I was concerned about whether or not the magnetic tape—which was supposed to record my eye movements—was running, in case I produced some good signals. I dreamed that I woke up to see if it was running, and that I went into the next room, which I found dark and full of cigarette smoke, and containing a piece of equipment that looked like a cinema projector. Three technicians—Ann, Sylvia and a young lad whose name I hadn't heard—were sitting around.
>
> "Is the tape running?" I asked.
>
> I saw they were winding the tape back. "How long is it since it was running?" I asked.
>
> I didn't get a straight answer.
>
> This went on for about 2 minutes.

Eventually, I thought, "This isn't right, I'm dreaming." I checked whether I was dreaming by trying to levitate—if I could levitate, I must be dreaming—and I did levitate. Having done so, immediately I started signaling with my eyes.

"What's he doing?" someone said.

Several times I went through the routine of following my finger with my eyes.

I was going to walk off or fly away, in order to leave the situation. I seemed to move through the air, mainly downwards, and felt on my lips a draft of air, which was strong enough to open my upper lip slightly. At the same time, I felt I was waking up.

I tried to get back into the room I'd come out of, which seemed to be the room I was actually sleeping in. I wanted to lie down there, so that I'd wake up in my physical body.

I actually woke up.

Immediately after waking, I went to see if the magnetic tape was running. I was anxious about this, as I'd been in my sleep, because the lab had been short of tapes, and I wanted to be sure that, while I'd been asleep, the tape hadn't run out before I'd signaled or, if it had, that the technicians had noticed in time and replaced it with an unused tape or an unused patch on a used tape.

I think that I dreamed of their sitting around and smoking, because, when awake, I'd worried that their attitude toward my experiment was too casual and that their lack of concern could result in my signals from my dream going unrecorded.

In fact, during the signaling, the magnetic tape had been running. The record showed that Worsley did tracking movements with his eyes (Figure 1). This indicates that volitional high-precision eye movements are possible during REM sleep, and that, when dream eyes follow the movements of a dream hand, the physical eyes move in the same way they would if the dreamer were awake and following slow to-and-fro movements of his hand.

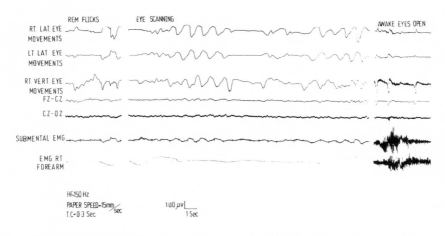

Figure 1. Eye-scanning movements that apparently corresponded to dreamer's report: "I went through the routine of following my finger with my eyes."

In this experiment, we lost no useful information by recording with AC--coupled electrodes because, in studying slow scanning movements, we found the frequency of the movements to be within the band pass of the EEG recording system.

Body Movements

We then studied body movements. It had been suggested (Guilleminault, 1976) that cataplexy is due to the same type of mechanism that produces loss of muscle tone in REM sleep, and there is evidence that, in cataplectic attacks. different muscle groups may be paralyzed unequally; the jaw muscles and knee extensors are paralyzed first. It has been reported (Jacobson, Kales, Lehmann, & Hoedemacher, 1964) that, in REM sleep, tonic activity is decreased markedly in some muscle groups but not in others. As well as recording tonic activity, the EMG records phasic spikes and bursts that may be below the threshold for visible displacement of a body part. We wished to see whether in lucid REM sleep the duration and amplitude of phasic spikes and bursts varied among different muscle groups.

To test this, in the first of a series of experiments, EMG electrodes were placed on the right upper and lower arm and on the right anterior and posterior calf and thigh (the anterior calf and posterior thigh muscles are flexor muscles, and the posterior calf and anterior thigh muscles are extensor muscles). Worsley, who is right-handed and right-footed, had the task of making six eye movements (in two groups of three each) to signal lucidity onset, and to produce simultaneous upper and lower extremity EMG blips in the pattern of 1, 2, 3 . . . up to six blips, by dreaming of alternately pushing and pulling something with his right arm and leg.

Here is his dream account:

> I'd been drifting in and out of sleep every minute or so for what seemed like 20 minutes [the record confirms this, except not for so long]. I didn't manage to do the structured series—one blip, two blips, three blips, and so on—in any of the minor dreams which occurred during this period.
>
> In the most interesting dream, the only one that I remember marking with the three-plus-three eye-movement lucidity signal, I was worried about the time.
>
> In the dream, Ann, the technician, came in. She said something about lunch.
>
> "Are you wondering," I asked, "if you can leave me unattended while you go for lunch?"
>
> In the dream I was lying on my back, and she was bending over me. [Before I'd gone to sleep, we'd been in this position during her taping on the submental chin electrodes.]
>
> Suddenly, she deliberately, a bit passionately, fell forward onto me. I reciprocated—though not quite so passionately—being covered with wires [as, in the dream, I imagined I was].

"When you said that," she said [referring to my expression of concern about interrupting her lunch break], "I knew you cared." She was now responding to my remark, I thought, by doing something she'd been wanting to do before but, not knowing how I felt about her, hadn't done. [I have no evidence that this is in fact what Ann would like to do, and in waking life I'd never considered how she might feel about me.]

She seemed to have brought some food in.

"How . . . what are you doing?", I said. "Are you? . . . you've brought me some food."

"Oh, wait a minute," I suddenly thought. "This is a dream."

At about this point, I gave the three-plus-three eye-movement lucidity signal.

I got up with all my wires attached. Being careful not to dislodge the electrodes, I placed the toes of my right foot against the base of a bench and my right heel on the floor. Standing with most of my weight on my left leg and holding the top edge of the bench with my hands, several times I pushed my right foot down against the base of the bench and against the floor. Each time I pushed down with my foot, I pulled upwards on the top of the bench with my hands. [Actually, in the lab next to the bed is a bench about 3 feet high, and in the dream the bench was there.] Instead of doing the arithmetic series—1,2,3,4,5—which I'd planned when awake, I did a plain series of about seven quick downward thrusts with my foot at a rate of nearly two a second.

I think I did the simple rather than the arithmetic series because I was in a hurry, the realization that it was a dream having taken me by surprise. A further consequence of my haste was, I think, that I didn't pay enough attention to the dream situation—which is probably why the imagery then changed.

At first, I thought I was waking. Then, I dreamed I was looking at the polygraph results of the previous dream. In this false awakening, I thought I saw on the chart paper a signal trace of three eye movements, and I checked off the channels. The paper was rather old, washed-out looking, and inky, about half the size it should be. Yet I didn't realise I was still dreaming—the lucidity was gone—nor did I manage to work out what was going on about the chart paper and what it meant.

After that, I think I had two or three more false awakenings—dreams about being in the department and talking to technicians.

The polygraph record agreed well with this dream account. Unfortunately, the upper-extremity electrodes had come off. However, clearly on the record were the lucidity-onset signals and, beginning 10½ seconds later, EMG from leg channels. On the posterior-calf channel, which produced the most distinct results, there were nine clear spikes (the dream report mentions "about seven" thrusts with his foot), over 5½ seconds (the dream report says they were done "at a rate of nearly two a second"). On the anterior-calf channel, there was simultaneous EMG activity with an amplitude roughly equivalent to that on the posterior-calf channel. During the same period of time, there was some low-amplitude activity on the anterior thigh channel and one high-amplitude spike on the posterior thigh channel. About 4 seconds after the last EMG activity was a 10-second increase in EEG alpha, which often seems to accompany the fading of imagery, a change of scene, and false awakenings.

In the dream, the main thrust of the dreamer's right leg was downwards, an action that, in waking life, would involve the lower-leg extensors more than the lower-leg flexors. However, our records showed approximately equal activity in flexors and extensors, suggesting that EMG activity from the flexors was less inhibited than from the extensors.

In another experiment, we wanted to find out whether dreaming of volitional whole-arm movements would produce EMG responses from all, or only some, arm muscles. Before Worsley went to sleep, electrodes were placed on his right forearm (to record finger flexors), right upper arm (to record forearm flexors), and right back shoulder (to record upper-arm flexors). The movements, which Worsley planned to make several times in his dream, were to pick up and put down his shoulder bag without letting go of the strap. Each time, he was to lift his shoulder bag from the ground, holding the strap by his right middle finger, put the strap over his head onto his left shoulder (leaving the bag on his right hip), and then reverse this procedure. His plan was to signal lucidity onset with five eye movements just before beginning the series of shoulder-bag lifts and, just before each lift, to signal its position in the sequence with a corresponding number of eye movements—one eye movement for the first lift, two for the second, and so on. Worsley expected that each lifting of the shoulder bag and putting the strap onto his left shoulder would take about 3 seconds, followed by about a 1-second pause, and then each lowering of the bag to the ground would take about another 3 seconds. Then there was to be a pause of about 2 seconds, followed by the next eye movement marker, and so on.

Here is the dream account:

> I was in a room with the laboratory technicians, I think. I don't remember what led up to this situation or what caused the lucidity.
>
> As planned, I picked up and put down my shoulder bag several times without letting go of the strap. Several times—I think about six altogether—I carried out movements that closely approximated the planned ones, each time labeling the lifting movement with the appropriate number of eye movements. I estimate that each lifting and putting down of the shoulder bag took about 10 seconds.
>
> Towards the end—I was up to about the seventh lift of the shoulder bag—I was losing the imagery and thought I was waking up, which I tried to prevent. "Come on, come on—where are you?", I imagined calling to the imagery, trying to recover it. Mentally, I searched around for it, and it came back.
>
> By this time I must have decided I'd carried out the prearranged task, and I tried, since I was still dreaming, to think of some other relevant task to do. I did a sort of dance, involving snapping my fingers.
>
> I went out of the room, and seemed to adopt a cavalier attitude to my situation. I found myself at No. 18 Carlton Road, Northwich [where I lived until I was 18 and where my father still lives; I visit him occasionally]. I was in the front bedroom [which used to be mine]. I wanted to get out of this room and decided [still lucid but apparently less involved than before with the experiment] to crash backwards through the window.
>
> I was in the road. I went past No. 16 [where my mother's parents used to live]. Many flowers were in the garden, and I thought how pleasant it was. From the angle of the sun, I judged that it was late morning (which corresponded to the actual time—

about 11 A.M., though the same flowers would not be out now—March—certainly
not in such profusion.

The EEG/EOG/EMG record showed a close correspondence to the dream
account. Clearly shown was the initial five eye-movements signal, just before he
first began to lift the shoulder bag, as well as the eye-movement markers for each
of seven lifts of the shoulder bag (the dream report mentions lifting the bag six
times and marking a seventh lift).

Of the EMG channels, only the finger-flexor one showed any activity. On
that channel, activity corresponding in time to lifting and lowering the bag
occurred after the first and second eye-movement markers—the amplitude corresponding to lifting being greater, as might be expected, than that corresponding
to lowering. After the third to the seventh eye-movement markers, activity on the
EMG channel corresponding in time to lifting, but not to lowering, occurred.

In two instances, it was possible to measure on the record the time between
the EMG corresponding to lifting the shoulder bag and the EMG corresponding
to putting it down, and in the first instance the time was about 8 seconds and in
the second instance about 9 seconds. These times approximated the estimate
made before going to sleep of 7 seconds to do these movements and the estimate
made after waking up of 10 seconds to have done them.

Later in the dream account is a report of finger snapping while dancing, and
EMG forearm flexor activity lasting about 15 seconds appeared in an appropriate
place on the polygraph—about 43 seconds after the last eye-movement marker of
a shoulder-bag lifting.

The record showed that altogether, REM sleep continued for about 2 minutes and 10 seconds after the last eye-movement marker.

For some minutes before the lucidity-onset signal of five eye-movements, no
REM flicks characteristic of phasic REM occurred (2½ minutes before the lucidity-onset signal, a microawakening occurred), though the EEG and submental
EMG were consistent with REM. Indeed, no rapid eye movements characteristic
of phasic REM occurred until after the last eye-movement markers, which accords
with the lack of rich imagery and the paucity of description in the account of the
early dream situation ''I was in a room with the technicians . . . ''

Worsley later speculated that perhaps, upon lucidity onset. his attention had
been taken up with the obligations of the experiment, and only after having
discharged these obligations could he relax and allow, so to speak, the dream
imagery to take its course.

What had brought about the lucidity? Was it Worsley's recognition that the
situation was suitable for carrying out the experiment? Or, on the contrary, did
his awareness, when awake, of a need for such a situation somehow bring about
the situation? Worsley recalled other occasions when, in the absence of lucidity,
a situation particularly suitable for the current experiment had appeared, without
his consciously, while asleep, having anticipated its appearance. Is there some
process that is independent of awareness that controls the contents of dreams so

that, at least sometimes, they relate to the dreamer's intended activity. If so, in these cases the lucidity could be brought about by the perception in the dream situation not of an incongruity (which, according to lucid-dream literature, is a frequent precipitant of lucidity) but of favorable circumstances for carrying out an intended activity.

In this particular case, the dream situation resembled one that had occurred more than once in the dreamer's waking life, which may have contributed to its occurrence in his dream. "Usually," Worsley said, "when I'm about to leave the EEG laboratory, I go to the technicians' room to tell them I'm going, and sometimes I spend a few moments talking to them. My bag is with me and, while I talk, I put it on the floor. Shortly afterwards, just before leaving, I pick it up again." He had had other dreams of being in the EEG Department and of contact with the technicians but did not recall handling his bag in any of them.

The results of several experiments to test muscle activity were consistent with each other and always manifested a clear hierarchy; no EMG activity was ever recorded from the axial muscles, and the EMG from the forearm flexors consistently showed lower amplitude and shorter bursts than the EMG from the finger flexors. The experiment was repeated for the lower limbs with similar results.

Thus, in the upper and lower extremities, the motor inhibition characteristic of REM sleep was strongest in the axial muscles and progressively weaker towards the peripheral muscles. It is interesting that the inhibition is not uniform and varies along a central-peripheral axis, rather than segmentally. It is also clear that there is a precise connection between the dream body and the physical body because a movement of a dream limb produces EMG potential in that limb.

Additional experiments comparing EMG responses in the flexors and extensors of the right arm and right leg suggested that flexor activity was higher than extensor activity. For instance, in experiments in which Worsley dreamed of moving his right leg, we recorded four times from the right lower leg and found a total of 27 flexor and 5 extensor bursts and once from the right hip and found 6 flexor and 3 extensor bursts. Nearly always the flexor burst exceeded in amplitude the extensor ones.

Digit Movements

It has been reported (Dement & Kleitman, 1957) that during REM sleep numerous very small distal limb and digital movements occur. It has been suggested (Dement & Wolpert, 1958) that, whereas eye movements sometimes seem to be specifically related to dream imagery, body movements are not. However, a subsequent report (Grossman et al., 1972) indicated that the account of a subject awakened from REM sleep after exhibiting fine distal limb movements generally indicated a dream in which the same limbs moved. In our experiments, an accelerometer to measure movement was placed on Worsley's right long finger. Before going to sleep, Worsley planned to dream in a lucid dream of wiggling that finger to and fro anterodorsally five times, then four times, then three times, then twice, then once, and to remain asleep afterwards.

Here is a report of Worsley's dream experience:

> I was dreaming that I was in the room where I really was, though the resemblance was imperfect. In the dream I was attached to a lot of wires—as I actually was. I considered I'd be able to get up, and I did. Funnily, I thought I could feel the real wires, as I sometimes do when I actually get up; they pull because their weight isn't taken by the floor. I wanted to disencumber myself from them before signaling, thinking that their pulling on me was distracting me from being able to concentrate on signaling. I unplugged the wires that were easy to unplug, but some I had to cut, and I used a pair of scissors I found. It took me a minute or two to get rid of the wires.
>
> I was going to carry some boxes with me, such as the head box, and perhaps the small sine-wave generator box [which is in the other room] and perhaps my tape recorder, and I think I may have picked up one or two of these boxes.
>
> I opened a door and went outside. I found myself in a large yard similar to one that is actually immediately outside, on the floor below the lab. At this point, I signaled by finger wiggling, doing the reverse series 5-4-3-2-1.
>
> A few seconds after doing 5-4-3-2-1, I tried to do it again. This time I think I was less accurate, in that I did the *3* signal twice. On both occasions I wiggled my finger instead of, as originally intended, snapping it. This might've been because, before going to sleep, when I'd tested the accelerometer, Sylvia had told me to wiggle my finger, which I'd done. Thus perhaps I'd substituted the idea of wiggling for that of snapping.
>
> After these two lots of signaling, I decided to get onto an enormous foam-rubber mattress that was in this yard. I thought I'd bounce up and down on it, and then take off. I was doing that, but it didn't work—and I woke up.
>
> [This sort of playful activity often seems to occur after I've carried out my experimental task; it's as if after submitting to the discipline of carrying out the task, I'm glad to be finished with it and to feel free to amuse myself.
>
> My imagining that I was on a foam-rubber mattress could have caused my waking. It could've reminded me that I actually was on a foam-rubber mattress, and that the simplest way to "bounce" off it—that is to get up from it—was to wake up and sit or stand up.]

The polygraph record showed the 5-4-3-2-1 pattern on both the forearm EMG and accelerometer channels (Figure 2), meaning that the finger had moved as planned. Starting about 1¼ minutes before the 5-4-3-2-1 pattern and lasting about half a minute, there were EMG blips that could correspond to the dream action of unplugging the wires and cutting them with scissors. About 1¼ minutes before the 5-4-3-2-1 pattern, there were EMG and accelerometer blips that could correspond to Worsley opening the door to go outside.

The record was also consistent with the report that a few seconds after doing the 5-4-3-2-1 series, Worsley tried to do it again, and this time did the "3" signal twice.

A similar experiment involving the right lower extremity demonstrated that

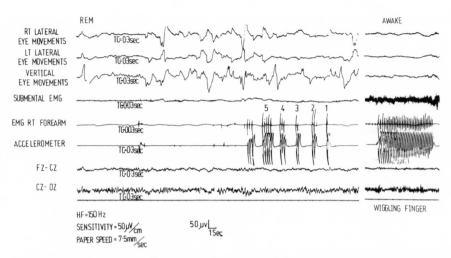

Figure 2. Finger movements that apparently corresponded to dreamer's wiggling his finger according to 5-4-3-2-1 pattern.

the dreamer could produce minor willed movements of the physical toes and feet, but not—at least not without waking up—of the legs.

Memory and Mentation

Next, we studied memory and mentation during REM. The dreamer was connected to a device that measures lateral eye movements recorded from an electro-oculogram and delivers an electrical stimulus if the amplitude of the eye movement exceeds a preset level. Stimulating electrodes were placed on the forearm, and 1 hour after Worsley went to sleep the machine was switched on. The task was to signal lucidity onset with forearm EMG bursts, to indicate with forearm EMG bursts how many stimuli he intended to administer to himself, to administer them by means of eye movements, counting the stimuli while he did so, and, after administering the intended number, to indicate that number with forearm EMG bursts.

In the event, the induction of stimuli by eye movements proved to be complicated. First, a stimulus was administered only if either the amplitude of one eye movement or the cumulative amplitude of several eye movements was high enough. Secondly, the gain and trigger-level controls of the machine happened to have been set so that the latent or refractory period during which the machine would not trigger again was a few seconds. As a result, the relationship between the number of eye movements and the number of stimuli was far from one to one. The long and unpredictably irregular intervals between the stimuli made it hard not only to induce them but to keep count of them, thus providing an unexpectedly severe test of the dreamer's ability to carry out the task. It meant that if he administered and counted the correct number of stimuli, it would be virtually certain that he had perceived the actual stimuli rather than merely dreamed stimuli.

Here is the report of the dream, which, just after waking up, Worsley narrated into a tape recorder:

> I seemed to be lying on the ground by a fence outside a building with my sleeping bag over me. [In fact, I did have a sleeping bag over me.] It was raining and a bit dark. Puddles of water were about. One or two people came through a gate just next to me and walked through puddles splashing water about, as if I wasn't there. I expected them to ask me what I was doing there, and I anticipated telling them—but they didn't ask.
>
> I thought I could see the light from my alarm clock next to me, which made me wonder whether I was awake; I'd be cheating, I thought, to do the experiment when awake. "However," I thought, "from past experience I know that whenever I've wondered whether I've been awake, it's turned out that I've been asleep. Probably I'm dreaming of seeing the light from the alarm clock."
>
> I was aware of the machine that was supposed to deliver the stimuli.

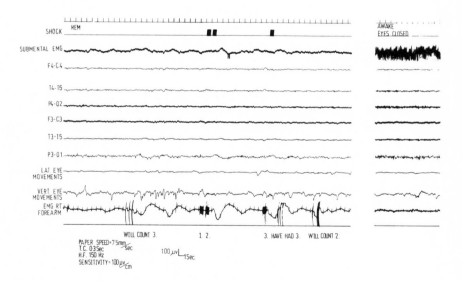

Figure 3. Dreamer signals that he will administer three electrical stimuli, he administers them, and he indicates that he has done so.

> I did the planned sequence of tasks. While I did, I worried about the machine getting wet in the rain.
>
> I think that the dream continued about a minute or two after the signaling.

His worry about the machine getting wet suggests that, while carrying out the planned experiment, he experienced the machine as part of the dream and, despite being aware that he was dreaming, he supposed the rain was real enough to wet the machine.

He performed the task successfully (Figure 3) and correctly indicated that he had received three stimuli. In the event, the interval between the first and second stimuli was 1 second and between the second and third stimuli was 10 seconds. That he did not signal receiving three stimuli until after the delivery of the third one—and that he signaled only 2 seconds afterward—is further evidence that he perceived the actual stimuli.

This result shows that, while dreaming, he remembered an experiment planned when he was awake, understood that the eye movements would produce stimuli, counted the stimuli as he made them, counted the number of stimuli he received (whether he actually perceived them or only dreamed he did), and remembered the number long enough to signal that number. The conclusion is that complex cerebral activity that relates to the concurrent waking-life situation is possible during REM sleep.

Speech

In another experiment, we investigated speech during lucid dreaming. Waking speech usually occurs at or near the start of expiration, and we wondered if dream speech also does. Before Worsley went to sleep, EMG electrodes were attached to the skin over his larynx, over his right-forearm flexors, over the flexors and extensors of his right upper arm, and over his right chest. He planned to count out loud in his dream and on each count to dream of moving his right hand—thereby synchronizing his speech with activity of his right-forearm muscles. The EMG electrode over his larynx was to record laryngeal muscle activity, so that we could determine whether the expiratory phase of actual respiration would be linked in time with the EMG indications from his right forearm of dream speech.

This was Worsley's report of his dream experience:

> I forgot how the dream started, but by lucid-dream standards it went on for a long time—maybe as long as 5 minutes.
>
> In the dream, Morty Schatzman and I were in a quiet street, a cul-de-sac. For perhaps 2 minutes after becoming lucid, I didn't start to draw the numbers. That was because we were interrupted by an old woman telling us a tale about something, and for a while I listened to her.

"Well," I thought eventually, "we've really got to get on with this experiment."

I looked around for something to use as a writing instrument and found a washing-up brush. I knew it wouldn't make marks very well on the hard road, but it would serve the purpose. I didn't want to use my hand directly, in case the thought that I might injure it would distract me.

While I was getting organized, Morty wandered off. He went to look at a poster on which someone had made little drawings of a rather relaxed uninhibited woman. It seemed as if he was looking for something to occupy his mind while waiting.

"Come on, Morty," I said, "you've got to watch me to see that I do these numbers right."

I thought that request was a good thing to do to fill in the situation, that is, to build up the richness of the dream, as well as to make sure, under the eyes of the "master", of doing it right.

"Come on," I said. "Pay attention. You're not the real Morty, so don't think there's any point in doing otherwise."

He grinned.

I drew the first series, I think, on top of a pile of new paving stones at the end of this cul-de-sac we were in.

I began to write the numbers about 15 to 18 in. high and about 15 in. across. Number 1 consisted of one stroke, number 2 two strokes and so on up to number 5, which consisted of five strokes (I, $\mathbf{2}$, $\mathbf{3}$, $\mathsf{'4}$, $\mathsf{5}$), and then, without regard to the number of strokes, I just continued up to 10. I did the numbers one on top of the other, which I knew was all right, since the point of the activity wasn't to leave visible traces, but to generate EMGs; anyway, there was no confusion, as the brush handle left no traces. On the first stroke of each number, in a loud voice, I said what number it was. Each number took on average about 3 seconds to draw, the numbers with more strokes taking more time, and I paused about 1 or 2 seconds between numbers.

After doing one series I decided to find another place to do the next series. [The reason was that I'd previously found that if I ignore the wider dream scene for too long, the imagery tends to fade away. In this particular case, it's likely, judging from previous experience, that I'd have been left in the dark, without visual imagery, with only tactile and kinesthetic imagery, which might have been insufficient to sustain the dream state.]

I walked along the street looking for a suitable surface, and saw a Rolls Royce. I considered writing on it but thought that perhaps I'd better not—not out of respect for Rolls Royces but in case somebody saw me and came out to complain, thereby interrupting things. [That sort of thing might happen just because I half-expected it to. While attending to the main task, I don't have enough spare attention to control these distracting expectations, and so it's better to prevent them.]

Later on, I didn't write on the side of a van, even though I thought it would bother no one.

I decided to write on the road surface itself. I knelt and began to write the numbers as before.

[I don't think that in either series I followed the numbers very closely with my eyes, although I'd planned to. I had a number of things to attend to, such as remembering to count loudly and distinctly and to draw the numbers the right size and at the right pace. While awake, I'd rehearsed the procedure but not enough to have made it automatic.]

The road surface was rather rough, and I found it difficult while writing on it to maintain a firm enough grip on the washing-up brush. My right arm seemed to get tired and to feel a bit weak. "Maybe I should use the other arm for a bit," I thought, but I remembered there were no electrodes on my left arm, so I perservered. At one point, near the end of the series, I lost my grip on the brush, and it fell from my hand. I carried on writing that number with my hand so as not to break the rhythm, though, unless absolutely necessary, I wouldn't have done that with my real hand, for fear of damaging it. This seems an indication that lucidity was continuing.

After waking up, Worsley found it interesting that he had experienced tiredness in an imaginary arm. "In reality," he observed, "my right arm had been lying alongside me, and my left arm, which had become numb before I fell asleep properly, was folded up alongside my chest. I was lying face down, and my head was slightly turned to the left. I might have expected that the tired arm would have been the left one, which was numb, but in the dream I got no real feeling of this. The tiredness in my right arm may have been just imaginary, that is, an unexpected authentic detail forming part of the rich sensory imagery that is typical of a proper dream."

Based upon his dream experience and before looking at the polygraph record, Worsley believed that he had been "completely successful" in carrying

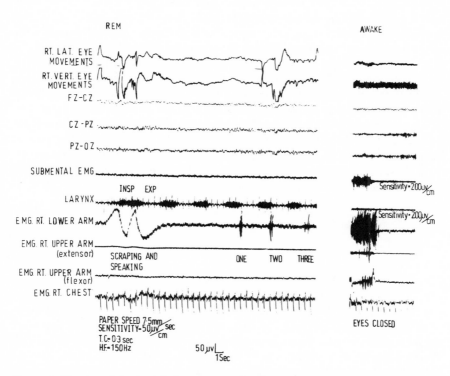

Figure 4. Muscle activity in right lower arm and in larynx that apparently corresponded to dreamer's report of drawing numbers on the ground and saying the numbers.

out the experimental task. "Two or possibly three times," he said, "I went through the agreed sequence, which was to count from 1 to 10 while writing the numbers with my right hand on a suitable surface."

The record showed about 10 minutes of REM until the first EMG activity. That activity was considerable from the forearm flexors and consisted of a few blips from the upper-arm flexors, while no activity was recorded from the upper-arm extensors or chest. The forearm EMG showed a clear pattern of activity, with one spike followed about 4 seconds later by two spikes, which were followed about 5 seconds later by three spikes. About 1⅓ seconds after the group of three spikes was the next group, consisting of four or five spikes. After that were several groups of spikes separated by varying intervals in which the individual spikes were difficult to count. The entire EMG sequence lasted about 33 seconds. That total time may correspond roughly to the dreamer's subjective estimate, after waking, that each number had taken on average about 3 seconds to write and was separated from others by about 1 or 2 seconds.

About 5 minutes after the end of this EMG activity and again about 6 minutes after it were two more periods of high EMG activity, each lasting about half a minute, and in both cases a clear pattern was difficult to discern. Again, activity in the forearm was much greater than in the upper arm, and activity in the upper-arm flexors was greater than in the extensors. Waking occurred about half a minute after the end of the last period of EMG activity.

In his dream he had counted 1, 2, and so on, while dreaming of scraping the numbers with the handle of a brush on a road surface. He had tried to make the EMG potentials from his forearm coincide with his dream speech: in the first series of EMG potentials, which were the only ones that clearly followed the planned pattern, the potentials did occur at or near the beginning of expiration, as they would have if he had carried out the same actions when awake (Figure 4).

No surface EMG activity suggestive of movement in the laryngeal muscles was recorded.

CONCLUSIONS

"Volitional" Actions in Lucid Dreams

It is apparent that Worsley, like other expert lucid dreamers is capable, while dreaming, of carrying out complex tasks (van Eeden, 1913) that were planned while he was awake (Fenwick *et al.,* 1984; LaBerge 1985; LaBerge, Nagel, Dement, & Zarcone, 1981; Saint-Denys 1982). It is apparent, too, that satisfactory evidence of his carrying out the tasks is produced only if the tasks are of a sort that can leave objective traces on recording equipment, such as an EMG or EOG. To produce that evidence, he did things in his dreams of such a sort that corresponding—and, presumably, simultaneous—events occurred in his physical body.

What relation do dreamed events have to physical—or "real" ones? Consider, for instance, the relation between dreamed and physical eye movements: As reported here, Worsley often signaled lucidity onset with eye movements. The eye movements left visible traces on the electro-oculogram, so that certainly his physical, or real, eyes moved. Did his dream eyes move too?

What, exactly, are "dream eyes"? And what is the "dream body"? Unlike the physical body, the "dream body" does not exist as an object in the world. It is experienced only by the dreamer and only insofar as it, or some part of it, plays a role in the dream. "My impression is," says Worsley, "that in ordinary dreams at least, I assume my body is there and that if any particular part of it becomes relevant to the dream, I become specifically aware of that part. In a lucid dream, if I ever check whether a part of my body is there, I find that it is. But it's there only insofar as it's required, so to speak, to be there."

While asleep and dreaming, he recalled the intention to signal with eye movements and, then, he willed his eyes to move. "I moved my eyes rapidly to signal," he says, "and had much the same visual experience, or lack of it, as if I'd carried out the same movements when awake." He was aware, too, of the sensations in his eye muscles that would, if he were awake, be associated with making extreme eye movements.

If the "dream eyes" are defined as his experience, while dreaming, of his eyes, then it is the case that he moved his dream eyes. However, as his physical eyes also moved, to what extent is it valid to distinguish in this case between two kinds of eyes? Are there two kinds of eyes between which there is a correspondence or only one kind? Why not simply say that he moved his eyes?

In this case, if there are two kinds of eyes, they seem inextricably combined. Perhaps the eyes that he was aware of moving included a component, as it were, of "dream eyes."

On several occasions, Worsley dreamed of slowly moving his finger across his visual field while tracking it with his eyes. The electro-oculogram showed eye movements similar to those that would have occurred had he been awake and tracking a real object. His experience in the dream of tracking his finger was similar to what it would have been had he been awake: He saw and felt his finger move and, at the same time, felt his arm move. Yet, as far as we know, his physical finger and arm did not move. In this case, we can speak of a "dream finger" as distinct from a physical finger.

In our experiments with arm movements, Worsley intended to dream, and did dream, of lifting and putting down his shoulder bag. In waking life, this set of movements would involve the flexor muscles of his fingers, forearm, and shoulder. In the dream, he felt his whole arm move; yet the EMG record coinciding with his doing so showed EMG responses from only the finger flexors. Assuming that, in the forearm and shoulder flexors, no significant EMG activity took place below the threshold of our recording instrument, we reckon that his experienced feeling of arm movement conformed to his intended movement, not to the presence of EMG activity in the corresponding muscles. If so, then movement of a "dream limb" can coincide with EMG activity in only part of the corresponding physical limb.

From the instances we have examined, we infer that, in lucid dreams, events in the "dream body" often coincide with corresponding events in the physical body. We also infer that parts of the "dream body" can move without there being movements or even recordable EMG activity in corresponding parts of the physical body. It may be that, so far as the dream experience is concerned, events in the voluntary muscles of the physical body that correspond to "dream-body" events are only incidental. It seems that the dream goes ahead, and so do the dreamer's dream activities, with or without detectable accompaniment by the physical body.

In another experiment, Worsley carried out his plan to stare at a fixed point in the dream imagery, such as a doorknob, and to keep his gaze fixed on that point, while dreaming of slowly turning his head from side to side. The resulting electro-oculogram resembled one that would have been produced if he had carried out the same movement when awake. Because of the well-known inhibition during REM sleep of the head and neck muscles, we believe that his physical head and neck did not move—although during the experiment we did not observe his head. To produce that electro-oculogram, Worsley's physical eyes must have moved relative to his physical head in much the same way that they would if they tracked a real object moving across his visual field while his physical head remained still. In fact this electro-oculogram was very similar to the one in the experiment in which he tracked his "dream finger."

In dreaming of staring at a fixed point and turning his head from side to side, he experienced simultaneous movements in his head and neck and, relative to them, in his eyes. Yet, presumably, his physical head and neck did not move, whereas his physical eyes did.

How can this result be explained? Some part of his brain, probably some part of his cerebral cortex, must have "assumed" that his head was going to move and then was moving and, accordingly, that his physical eyes would have to move relative to it, in order to maintain the fixation. This "assumption" was based not on proprioceptive information from head and neck movements, or from the vestibular apparatus, because, in fact, the head and neck were not moving. Upon what was the "assumption" based? Perhaps upon his intention to move his head and neck. Perhaps upon his experience in the dream of focusing on a visual image while turning his dream head and neck; in waking life, turning his physical head and neck would require movements of his eyes relative to them. Perhaps these psychological events, an intention and an experience, activated the mechanisms for smooth eye movements that are ordinarily activated when real head and neck movements occur. Normally, the mechanisms monitor and control the angular velocity of eye movements in such a way as to stabilize retinal images. Presumably, these mechanisms made possible, too, the smooth tracking movements of Worsley's physical eyes when he followed the movement of his "dream finger."

An alternative explanation for the movements of his physical eyes while he dreamed is that his dreaming of moving his head and neck and of fixing his gaze on a stationary object activated the vestibulo-ocular reflex. In waking life, that reflex is ordinarily activated by actual head and neck movements if they occur while the eyes are fixated upon an object; the reflex stabilizes the visual field in compensation for those movements.

We can conclude that, in a lucid dream, volitional movements of the "dream body" are possible because our results demonstrate coincident movements or EMG activity in at least some of the corresponding parts of the physical body. We can conclude, too, that in a lucid dream volitional movements or EMG activity in parts of the physical body are also possible.

It seems that during a lucid dream, true volitional activity in the physical body is possible because the dreamer is aware—or at least has available the awareness—of the correspondence between the "dream body" and the physical body. This awareness enables the lucid dreamer to know while dreaming that the part of the body that he or she is moving is, in at least some cases, actually moving.

Sensations in Lucid Dreams

In the experiment in which Worsley administered electrical stimuli to himself, he was aware of the machine that delivered the stimuli. Yet the delivered stimuli did not become part of his dream. By that we mean that they did not form part of the drama or scenario that comprised his dream situation.

"I didn't really think about where the stimuli were coming from," said Worsley. "I was too busy concentrating on inducing and counting them. But if I'd considered where they were coming from, I think I might have concluded they were coming from the actual machine outside the dream, not from the machine in the dream. That's because I was lucid and aware of what was happening."

In discussing that experiment, we explained why we think it preferable to suppose that he perceived actual stimuli rather than merely dreamed them. By "perceived" we mean that, while dreaming, he felt the actual stimuli. It is conceivable that at the same, or at virtually the same, time as the actual stimuli were being delivered, he dreamed, in response to their being delivered, that he was receiving them. However, this possibility is difficult to distinguish experimentally from his having felt the actual stimuli.

He not only felt the stimuli (or in response to their delivery dreamed of receiving them) but correctly identified their source. It is possible to experience stimuli in a dream in response to their actually being delivered and to misconstrue their source. For instance, before the present series of experiments, Worsley once was the subject in an experiment that involved his receiving electrical stimuli to his wrist during REM sleep. (In that experiment, there was no means of his controlling, while asleep, the delivery of the stimuli.) While awake, he knew the experiment involved stimuli to his wrist. "I went to sleep and had a nonlucid dream," he recalls, "during which I felt sensations on my wrist. I thought, 'These feel like electrical stimuli, but they can't be. I'm walking down the street unattached to the machine that delivers them. They must be muscle twitches.'" In his dream, he was aware of the stimulus-delivering machine and thereby, in a sense, of the experimental situation. Yet information in his memory about the true source of the stimuli and the consequent inference that he was dreaming did not reach his consciousness.

In the case in which a dreamer experiences sensations caused by stimuli without realizing their true source, is it correct to say that the actual stimuli are perceived? That depends on how the word *perceived* is defined. In the case in which, alternatively, the dreamer correctly interprets sensations caused by stimuli as originating in the real world, we can say with some assurance that the stimuli were perceived.

Perhaps it is possible to dream lucidly and still misconstrue the source of actual stimuli delivered during the dream, but we have no experimental evidence on this.

We conclude that, in a lucid dream, it is sometimes possible to infer correctly the source in the real world of a dreamed sensation. That inference is possible, it seems, because the dreamer is aware—or at least has available the awareness—of the correspondence between dreamed sensations and their true origin.

Consciousness in Lucid Dreams

When a person is asleep and dreaming, he or she is participating in or observing the dream events from a vantage point within the dream world. Among the images of that world are images of the "dream body." At the same time, the physical body is lying, or sitting, asleep somewhere in the real world. In a lucid dream, with which body does the dreamer identify? Who does the lucid dreamer think that he or she is? Someone who is a character in a dream? Someone asleep on, say, a bed? Being aware, while dreaming, of one's true situation could entail identifying either with the "dream body" or with the sleeping physical body.

By definition, in a lucid dream the dreamer is aware of dreaming. That implies an awareness that the experienced events are being dreamed. In a lucid dream where the dreamer understands well what is happening, the dreamer recognizes that the body and sense organs whereby he or she apparently experiences dream events are themselves being dreamed.

By definition, too, a dream, lucid or nonlucid, occurs during sleep. It is possible to be aware during a dream of dreaming, without being explicitly aware of being asleep. Is the lucid dreamer explicitly aware of his or her sleeping body? "Aware of" can mean either knowing about the existence of or having the immediate experience of. According to Worsley, in some of his lucid dreams, he is not—in either sense of the term—aware of his sleeping body. He does not experience his sleeping body directly, and it does not occur to him to consider whether the dream is taking place during sleep and whether, consequently, his body is lying in bed. In those dreams he is aware of dreaming but not of being asleep in bed. However, in other dreams he is aware, to some extent, of both his "dream body" and his sleeping body. In some of those dreams, he knows about his sleeping body, and in others he directly experiences it.

Consider, for instance, Worsley's lucid dream in which he experienced himself attached to electrode wires. In fact, his sleeping body was attached to electrode wires. In his dream, he said, he "got up" with all the wires attached and, "being careful not to dislodge the electrodes," performed the experimental task, which involved pushing a bench with his foot and pulling it with his hand. The body that "got up" was his "dream body", not his physical body—which remained horizontal—but the body that he initially experienced as attached to the wires could have been either body.

In another dream, he was dreaming that he was in the room where he really was, "though the resemblance was imperfect." In the dream he was "attached to a lot of wires"—as he actually was. He dreamed that he got up. "Funnily," he said, he thought he "could feel the real wires," as he sometimes did when he "actually got up." "They pull, because their weight isn't taken by the floor." He "wanted to disencumber" himself from them before signaling lucidity because he thought that their "pulling" on him was "distracting" him "from concentrating on signaling." In the dream, in order to "get rid" of the wires, he unplugged some of them and cut the others with scissors.

In this case, to which body were the wires attached, the "dream body" or the sleeping physical body? There seems here to be a tangle of levels. In a room in a laboratory in the real world, wires are attached to electrodes in order to record signals from a sleeping subject. The subject is dreaming of being in a room in a laboratory, which closely resembles the room in which he is actually sleeping. In his dream he is about to produce signals to be recorded. Apparently, in his dream, is a model that closely resembles the world that he is "really" in at that moment.

Are the wires only being dreamed or are the real wires actually being felt? The wires that he sees can only be dreamed wires. But the wires he experiences, at least initially, as pulling on and "distracting" him could be the real wires. (We say "initially" because the intensification of the pulling that he felt when dreaming of getting up could not have come from the real wires because he did not actually get up.) Similarly, the body upon which he initially experiences them pulling could be his physical body.

To what extent can it be said that Worsley was aware of his true situation? After waking up, he commented that, in getting ready to signal, he had been taking account of the aims of the experiment and in that regard was lucid. What about his unplugging and cutting the wires? In that regard, too, he was taking account of the aims of the experiment: He was trying to relieve himself of the "distraction" the wires were causing in order to get on with the experiment. Disconnecting the wires in the dream, he explained, was doing something concrete and practical as a means of persuading himself that he had got rid of the distraction.

However, if he was lucid, why did he go to the trouble of unplugging and cutting the wires? Why not just make them disappear—magically, so to speak—say, by spitting on them or staring them into nonexistence? "In a lucid dream I sometimes simply conform without much reflection to waking conventions," Worsley explains, "rather than involve myself in exploiting the freedoms of the lucid state, especially in regard to activities that are only incidental to my main task."

If the wires were the real wires, then disconnecting them would have aborted the experiment, whereas because they were only dreamed wires, his act did not prevent the signals being recorded.

Worsley's act of disconnecting the wires has different meanings, depending upon whether it is considered from the point of view of the dream world or of the real world. The one act encompasses requirements derived from both worlds. From the point of view of the dream world, he disconnects the wires with the conscious, dreamed, purpose of getting rid of a distraction. He can thereupon attend to carrying out a task that was planned in, and involves transmitting signals to, the real world. From the point of view of the real world, disconnecting the wires does not abort the experiment only because *those* wires are not the real wires. It is as if he has, at least implicitly, both points of view.

At the moment of cutting the wires, Worsley evidences an awareness that the model of the real world in his dream is only a copy of that world, that it is a fake and that it "nests" in that world.

In an ordinary dream, by contrast, the point of view of the dream world ordinarily predominates. Often, an external stimulus is represented in the dream in distorted form or is not represented at all.

It seems that the informed lucid dreamer is aware—or at least has available the awareness—of details of the correspondences between the dream situation and the real situation. That is useful in helping the lucid dreamer to carry out experiments that produce objectively recordable results.

REFERENCES

Dement, W., & Kleitman, N. (1957). Cyclic variations in EEG during sleep and their relation to eye movements, body motility, and dreaming. *EEG and Clinical Neurophysiology, 9,* 673–690.

Dement, W., & Wolpert, E. A. (1958). The relation of eye movements, body motility, and external stimuli to dream content. *Journal of Experimental Psychology, 55*(6), 543–553.

Fenwick, P., Schatzman, M., Worsley, A., Adams, J., Stone, S., & Baker, A. (1984). Lucid dreaming: Correspondence between dreamed and actual events in one subject during REM sleep. *Biological Psychology, 18,* 243–252.

Grossman, W. I., Gardner, R., Roffwarg, H. P., Fekete, A. F., Beers, L. & Weiner, H. (1972). Relation of dreamed to actual movement. *Psychophysiology, 9*(1), 118–119.

Guilleminault, C. (1976). Cataplexy. In Guilleminault, C., Dement, W. C., & Passonant, P. (Eds.), *Narcolepsy* (p. 125). Holliswood, NY: Spectrum Publications.

Hearne, K. M. T. (1978). *Lucid dreams: An electro-physiological and psychological study.* Unpublished doctoral dissertation, Liverpool University.

Jacobson, A., Kales, A., Lehmann, D., & Hoedemaker, F. S. (1964). Muscle tonus in human subjects during sleep and dreaming. *Experimental Neurology 10,* 418–424.

LaBerge, S. P. (1985). *Lucid dreaming.* Los Angeles: Jeremy P. Tarcher.

LaBerge, S. P., Nagel, L. E., Dement, W. C., & Zarcone, V. P., Jr. (1981). Lucid dreaming verified by volitional communication during REM sleep. *Perceptual and Motor Skills, 52,* 727–732.

Rechtschaffen, A., & Kales A. (Ed.) (1968). *A manual of standardized terminology, techniques and scoring system for sleep stages of human subjects.* Los Angeles: Brain Information Service/Brain Research Institute, U.C.L.A.

Saint-Denys, H. de. (1982). *Dreams and the means of directing them.* London: Duckworth. Edited by Schatzman, M., & translated by Fry, N., from the French *Les Rêves et Les Moyens de Les Diriger* (1867). Paris: Amyat.

van Eeden, F. W. (1913). A study of dreams. *Proceedings of the Society for Psychical Research, 26,* 431–461.

9

The Psychological Content of Lucid versus Nonlucid Dreams

JAYNE GACKENBACH

In a review of Stephen LaBerge's (1985) *Lucid Dreaming,* David Foulkes (1985) asked a key question: How are lucid and nonlucid dreams different? He pointed out that such a consideration may be the most interesting implication for ordinary dreaming. The issue is, Foulkes notes, what *else* changes when you change ordinary dreaming by adding a self that intends and reflects. The focus of this chapter is to review research relevant to these concerns. That is, beyond the obvious difference of awareness of dreaming while dreaming, do the psychological contents of lucid and nonlucid dreams differ in other respects?

The data presented in this chapter are, in the main, from the manifest or surface level of the dream. The bulk of the work to date comparing dream types is from dreams collected from home diaries, classroom exercises, and survey responses. In all cases, the dreamer made evaluations about aspects of the dream. Because these are self-evaluations of dreams, one can argue that, to some extent, latent content is obtained. That is, to the extent that dreamers rate the content of dreams with such considerations in mind.

Lucid and nonlucid dreamers self-evaluations of their lucid and nonlucid dreams will be offered first. These are available from reports of their long-term memory of these dream experiences by survey (Gackenbach & Shilling, 1983) as well as their short-term memory vis-à-vis self-evaluations taken from daily dream logs (Gackenbach, 1978; Gackenbach & Schillig, 1983; Gackenbach,

Thanks to Stephen LaBerge and Alan Worsley for providing the sleep laboratory dreams. Part of the funds for the collection of the adult dreams were supplied by a research grant to the author from the Graduate College of the University of Northern Iowa.

JAYNE GACKENBACH • Department of Psychology, University of Northern Iowa, Cedar Falls, IA 50614-0505.

Curren, LaBerge, Davidson, & Maxwell, 1983; Gackenbach, Curren, & Cutler, 1983).

After this review, the remainder of the chapter will be devoted to the reporting of a recently completed 4-year project aimed at the content analyses by independent judges of the manifest content of lucid and nonlucid dream experiences. Hall and Van de Castle's (1966) system of content analyses, with some modification, was utilized. Dreams gathered from college students and adults from their dream examples, their dream diaries, and from the sleep laboratory are included in this data base.

Although, case reports or the analyses of hundreds of lucid dreams from a single individual abound in the literature (LaBerge, 1980b; Moers-Messmer, 1938), they are subject to the biases of the single individual and consequently will not be considered herein. It is suggested that the reader consult the chapters by Gillespie, and Worsley for such a perspective. Finally, caution in interpretation is advised in the analysis of the psychological content of these dream experiences because, as Worlsey (1982) points out, surveys may include information from lucid dreamers who do not appreciate the subtleties involved. Furthermore, descriptive content analyses of these dreams are constrained by the limits of systems developed prior to the current research surge on lucidity. Finally, such an approach ignores the actual flow of the dream narrative, that is, the storylike quality.

SELF-EVALUATIONS OF CONTENT

The work of Gackenbach and Schillig (1983) on lucid versus nonlucid dreams demonstrates the conceptual difference between these dream experiences. They separately factor-analyzed self-evaluations of the content of lucid and nonlucid dreams recalled by adults for both morning-after dream logs and lucid dreaming questionnaires. Gackenbach and Shillig found that the structure of nonlucid dreams was primarily characterized by their perceptual qualities, whereas lucid dreams were characterized by a sense of being able to control the dream and a sense of intellectual, emotional, and physical balance. Differences between lucid and nonlucid dream experiences have been typically conceptualized in terms of three general types of contents: sensations and perceptions, cognitions, and emotions.

Sensations and Perceptions

A wide range of approaches to the question of whether sensations and perceptions differentially characterize the lucid from the nonlucid dream have been investigated. The primary waking sensory modality is vision, and its relative representativeness in lucid and nonlucid dreams has been examined from four perspectives: general vision, color, brightness, and clarity of imagery. In morning-after dream reports, subjects evaluated their lucid dreams as more visual than their nonlucid dreams (Gackenbach & Schillig, 1983). However, in two later studies using the same instrument but where the dream recall of each dream was controlled, no dream-type difference in vision emerged (Gackenbach, La-Bergen, Davidson, & Maxwell, 1983; Gackenbach, Curren, & Cutler, 1983). Long-term recall (i.e., information on dreams gathered by questionnaire) of this dream event evidenced the opposite, that is, nonlucid dreams were reported as more visual than lucid (Gackenbach & Schillig, 1983). The authors explain these discrepant findings by saying that, due to the infrequency of experiencing dream lucidity, it lacks the salience of nonlucid dreams for effective long-term recall.

Lucid dreams were determined to be more colorful than nonlucid dreams by Gackenbach and Schillig (1983) and Gackenbach, Curren, LaBerge, Davidson, and Maxwell (1983) in morning-after reports but less colorful as ascertained by long-term recall (Gackenbach & Schillig, 1983). No differences were noted by Gackenbach, Curren, and Cutler (1983). The latter is probably the most accurate estimate, as this study involved randomly selected student samples rather than the high dream interest adult samples used by Gackenbach and Schillig (1983) and Gackenbach, Curren, LaBerge, Davidson, and Maxwell (1983). Additionally, this study controlled for dream recall whereas Gackenbach and Schillig did not.

Relatedly, Hearne (1983) notes that an average of 73.4% of two samples of lucid dreamers report that colors in lucid dreams are the same or brighter than colors seen while awake, whereas only 54.75% said the same of nonlucid dreams. As regards brightness, Hearne (1978) reports no difference from prior to the dawning of dream lucidity to after its onset in one adept subject and later argued that there is a brightness ceiling in lucid dreams (Hearne, 1981). Worsley (1982) points out that such a ceiling may be a problem with functioning in different modalities and not with brightness *per se*.

Finally, as to the differential vividness or clarity of lucid versus nonlucid dreaming images, Hearne (1978) found no difference in students' self-reports of vividness of the dream taken from prior to lucidity onset and from during lucidity but notes elsewhere (Hearne, 1983) that 65.5% of his adult lucid dreaming sample report their lucid images as more vivid than their nonlucid images. In none of Hearne's (1978, 1983) work has dream recall as a covariate of the lucidity abilities been accounted for. Consequently, as regards vision, the better controlled studies clearly indicate no difference between lucid and nonlucid dreams.

The second major sensory modality is audition. With the exception of Gackenbach and Schillig's questionnaire data, lucid dreams have collectively been found to be perceived as more auditory than nonlucid dreams (Gackenbach, Curren, LaBerge, Davidson, & Maxwell, 1983; Gackenbach, Curren, and Cutler, 1983; Gackenbach & Schillig, 1983; Hearne, 1983).

Dream content differences in the minor sensations of taste, smell, kinesthesia, touch, pain, and temperature have also been investigated. Taste and
smell have generally evidenced no dream-type differences in morning-after reports (see the two Gackenbach *et al.* 1983 studies; Gackenbach & Schillig,
1983). However, in two survey studies with no dream recall control, nonlucid
dreams were reported as evidencing more of these senses (Gackenbach &
Schillig, 1983; Hearne, 1983). Likewise, these two surveys noted pain as being
reported more in nonlucid dreams. No dream-type differences have been noted as
regards temperature (Gackenbach & Schillig, 1983). The most often noted minor
sensations occurring more often in lucid than in nonlucid dreams are those of the
body sensations of touch and kinesthesia (Gackenbach & Schillig, 1983; Hearne,
1983; Moers-Messmer, 1938; and see the two Gackenbach *et al.*, 1983 studies),
although a lack of difference (Gackenbach & Schillig, 1983) has also been
reported.

In sum, of the two major waking sensory modalities—vision and audition—the latter shows a strong dream-type difference. When this is considered
with the findings of dream-type differences in touch/kinesthesia, the pivotal role
of "balance" in the lucid dreaming experience becomes evident. As noted, this
emerged in Gackenbach and Schillig's factor analysis and has since been supported by the work of Gackenbach, Snyder, Rokes, and Sachau (1986) and
Gackenbach, Snyder, Sachau, and Rokes (1986).

Cognitions

As with the sensory and perceptual components of lucid dreams, the cognitive components have been investigated from multiple perspectives using various techniques. Waking expectations, clarity of thought, memory of waking life,
dream control, and the ability to do experiments in the lucid dream are highly
interrelated. In order to do the dream experiments, which have been clearly
demonstrated in the sleep laboratory (Fenwick *et al.*, 1984; LaBerge, Nagel,
Dement, & Zarcone; 1981), and by individual adepts in their homes (LaBerge,
1980a; Moers-Messmer, 1938; see Gillespie, Chapter 13, in this volume) and
which have been reported in a general lucid dreaming population (Hearne,
1983), the dreamer needs the proper waking expectations and a clear dream mind
in order to be able to remember a waking suggestion to do the experiment. Upon
remembering, dream control is required to carry it out.

Gackenbach and LaBerge (1986) have pointed out that

> The waking assumptions that dreamers hold about what lucid dreams are like or could
> be like determine to an extent the precise form taken by their lucid dreams. For
> instance, the philosopher Ouspensky assumed on theoretical grounds that "man can-
> not in sleep think about himself *unless the thought is itself a dream*" (1931). From this
> premise, he reasoned that "a man can never pronounce his own name in sleep." It

should therefore come as no surprise that Ouspensky reported "as expected" that "if I pronounced my name in sleep, I immediately woke up." A generation later, a lucid dreamer referred to by Green (1968) had a similar experience as did Garfield (1974). However, LaBerge (1980a) wrote that when he read Ouspensky's account, he neither followed the philosopher's reasoning nor accepted his original premise about thinking in dreams. Consequently, he could see no reason why saying his name while dreaming should present any difficulty at all and was able to do so. This illustrates that the assumptions which the dreamer makes about what can happen during a lucid dream, may wholly or in part determine what *does* happen. (pp. 61–62).

Despite the pivotal role of waking expectations, there may be limitations to this dream experience for some. Although lucid dreams have been found to possess more voices or speech (see the two Gackenbach *et al.* 1983 studies; Gackenbach & Schillig, 1983) than nonlucid dreams, the understanding of such material received through either audition or vision (i.e., reading) has been reported as difficult (Moers-Messmer, 1938; Wilmes, 1983; Worsley, 1983). In these instances, there was no supposition of an inability to understand language; if anything, the waking expectation was the opposite. Yet in all three accounts, these lucid dreamers report difficulty in doing so. The light-level limitation notion of Hearne's (1981) is another illustration of this point.

As for thought clarity while lucid, Hearne (1978) found a significant increase in self-reported thought clarity by one proficient lucid dreamer in the sleep laboratory, from prior to lucidity onset to just after lucidity emerged. Similarly, in a survey study Hearne (1983) reported that over 80% of two adult lucid dream samples said that their lucid dreaming thoughts were the same or clearer than their waking thoughts. Gackenbach (1978) determined that lucid dreamers felt that their memory of waking life was clearer during lucid dreams than during other dreams. However, the aforementioned studies were done without dream recall control.

Dream control—that is, the ability of the dreamer while dreaming to consciously manipulate the dream experience—has consistently and repeatedly been shown to be higher in lucid dreams than in nonlucid dreams. This has been found by questionnaire (Gackenbach & Schillig, 1983; Hearne, 1983), by self-evaluation of an individual's dreams while keeping a dream journal (Hearne, 1978; see the two Gackenbach *et al.* 1983 studies;), and in the sleep laboratory by the successful completion of prearranged experiments (Fenwick *et al.*, 1984; LaBerge *et al.*, 1981).

The relative bizarreness of lucid versus nonlucid dreams is another cognitive aspect that has been the focus of considerable inquiry. Historically, lucid dreams have been perceived as more realistic and less bizarre than nonlucid dreams (Green, 1968), and some of the new wave of lucidity research has supported this perspective (Gackenbach, 1978; Hearne, 1983). However, other recent research has reported more bizarreness in lucid dreams (Hearne, 1978; Hoffman & McCarley, 1980; and see the two Gackenbach *et al.* 1983 studies;) or no difference (Gackenbach & Schillig, 1983).

These mixed findings may be due in part to the association of lucid dream initiation with bizarreness (Green, 1968) or with dream incongruities (Gackenbach, 1978, 1981). This has recently received experimental attention. For instance, Hoffman and McCarley (1980) tested the hypothesis that the degree of dream lucidity will be correlated with the amount of accompanying bizarreness by scoring 104 sleep laboratory dream reports for bizarreness and lucidity and found they were related. However, "lucidity" as operationally defined by their scale was essentially equivalent to "perception of anomaly." Furthermore, it may be that the Gackenbach, Curren, LaBerge, Davidson, and Maxwell finding of higher bizarreness evaluations for lucid dreams than for nonlucid dreams was due in part to the presence of an inconsistency or an oddity as the key device in the realization that one is asleep and dreaming. It would seem, as observed by Ogilvie, Hunt, Tyson, Lucescu, and Jeakins (1982), that bizarreness is needed for the dawning of dreaming awareness, but once achieved, the lucid dream scene is relatively realistic.

To summarize the cognitive components of dream lucidity mentioned herein, dream control is possible, given the appropriate waking expectations, yet inherent limitations beyond personal expectation may exist. Second, bizarreness seems to function as a key lucidity induction ingredient, but its role in the ongoing content of these dreams is unclear.

Emotions

Lucid dreams have historically been characterized as eliciting strong emotions (Green, 1968), and more recent survey data continue to support this contention (Hearne, 1983). However, they have been found to be emotionally both negative (Gackenbach & Schillig, 1983) and positive (Gackenbach, 1978; Gackenbach & Schillig, 1983; Gackenbach, Curren, LaBerge, Davidson, & Maxwell, 1983). A lack of dream-type differences for either emotion have also been reported (Gackenbach, Curren, & Cutler, 1983).

Summary of Self-Evaluations of Content

Several weaknesses are evident with these data. All the self-evaluations of dreams were done on dreams gathered in a home setting. Although, in some cases, verification of understanding of the concept of lucidity was determined without sleep laboratory signal verification (i.e., predetermined eye movements that serve as a signal from the dreamer to the experimenter that the former knows he or she is dreaming), one can never be certain if the subject is in fact talking about a REM-sleep phenomenon, a borderline state, or another experience. Second, all biases inherent in any self-report measure, such as underreporting, overreporting, halo effect, hostile reports (Feldman, 1985), or, as noted earlier (Worsley, 1983), the probable failure of inexperienced lucid dreamers to fully appreciate the subtleties of mentation in this state, are present in these reports.

With these cautions in mind, a general statement about the psychological content of these unique dream experiences can be made. Lucid dreams beyond the awareness of dreaming while dreaming seem to also be singularly characterized by a sense of bodily balance, as evidenced by their superiority in auditory and kinesthetic sensations, and control of the dream events.

JUDGES' EVALUATIONS OF CONTENT

Although in recent years there has been a shift from descriptive-oriented systems of dream content analysis to process-oriented systems (Foulkes, 1985), the bulk of the dream content analyses work to date is descriptive (Winget & Kramer, 1979). Certainly a process analysis of lucid versus nonlucid dreams is called for, but the first priority is for a descriptive analysis so comparisons can be made to previously collected normative data. Of the 150-plus content scales devised to date, Hall and Van de Castle's (1966) is one of the most widely used (Webb, 1979). Consequently, it is the scale of choice in the present investigation.

All but the Objects subscale were used in this inquiry. Additionally, four bizarreness scales and three of particular interest to dream lucidity (i.e., palpable sensations, balance, and control) were added. Hypotheses regarding the characters subscale are not possible as no previous content work has been done with dream characters and the lucid experience.

To the extent that dream lucidity emerges from nightmares (Green, 1968), one might expect a higher incidence of negative emotions, aggressive social interactions, failures in achievement, bad fortune from the environment, and negative descriptive elements as well as a lower incidence of positive emotions, friendly interactions, achievement success, good fortune from the environment, and positive descriptive elements in lucid than in nonlucid dreams. However, Gackenbach (1982) reported that only 15% of 313 lucid dreams reported over a 16-week period by college students were nightmare-initiated. If this is more accurate than Green's prediction of the majority coming from nightmares than the aforementioned data, differences would not emerge. Also, to the extent that these dream experiences are positive, one would predict the opposite of the previously mentioned.

With regards to the activities scoring category, based on the conclusion that lucid dreams are clearly characterized by auditory and kinesthetic sensations and a perception of dream control, it is predicted that there will be a higher incidence of verbal, physical, movement, auditory, and cognitive activities in lucid than in nonlucid dreams.

With regards to the Bizarreness subscales, lucid dreams should be less bizarre than nonlucid dreams. They should also evidence more palpable sensations, control, and balance than the nonlucid dream experience.

METHODOLOGICAL CONSIDERATIONS

Samples

Dream transcripts ($n = 421$) were obtained from 10 samples of either students or adults. They were collected in classroom exercises, from home dream diaries, or from the sleep laboratory. Table 1 shows the distribution of these dreams as a function of sample and dream type. The actual numbers included in subsequent statistical analyses were somewhat smaller for several reasons. Prelucid dreams were deleted. When samples were compared, dreams from samples with unclear or clearly inconsistent sample characteristics were deleted (i.e., elderly dreams deleted from the adult sample, as they were not highly interested in dreams, whereas the rest of the adult group was interested). Dreams used to calculate reliability information were not used, and dreams with duplicate dream numbers were omitted. The preferred statistical analyses would consider these variables: type of dream (lucid, nonlucid), type of sample (adult, student), method of dream collection (classroom, diary, laboratory), and sex of subject (male, female). The last variable in order to compare to the Hall and Van de Castle normative data. However, there were not enough dreams scored to fill all possible cells so two separate sets of analyses were calculated. In the first set of analyses, only the dream transcripts of college students were utilized. Because the dreams came from college students and could be classified as lucid or nonlucid and according to the sex of dreamer, they most closely paralleled the normative data of Hall and Van de Castle. It should be noted that, in a recent use of this sytem Hall, Domhoff, Blick, and Weesner (1982) report few if any differences as a function of sex of subject from the original 1947–1952 group of

Table 1. Number of Dreams Content-Analyzed as a Function of Sample Type and Dream Type

Dream type	Sample		
	Students	Adults	Sleep laboratory[a]
Lucid	144	117	36
Nonlucid	104	7	5

[a]The sleep laboratory dreams were collected from 13 subjects in two sleep laboratories (Stanford University and St. Thomas' Hospital, London).

college students. In this inquiry, four of the five student samples were from a midwestern univeristy, whereas one was from an eastern college. There were 236 dreams (male lucids = 44; female lucids = 88; male nonlucids = 42; female nonlucids = 62) included in this first set of analyses. The major reason for the second set of analyses was the inclusion of 41 dreams collected in the sleep laboratory, 36 REM-episode signal-verified lucid dreams, and 5 REM-episode nonlucid dreams. These were compared to students' nonlaboratory dreams collected by class exercise and home dream diary. However, because the laboratory dreams were from self-selected adults who were highly involved in their dreams, it was thought advantageous to also compare these to the dreams collected by home dream diaries or questionnaire of a parallel group of adults. Sample characteristics other than dream content were only available on the midwestern univeristy students. Consequently, in order to compare samples on variables other than dream content, the eastern college student dreams were dropped (lucid = 15; nonlucid = 9). Therefore, of the three samples compared, two are from high dream-interested adults and one is from students. The dreams of two of the samples were collected from dream diary or questionnaire (one adult and one student), and one sample was collected in the sleep laboratory (adults). Due to the small number of nonlucid dreams collected from the sleep laboratory sample ($n = 5$) and from the adult samples ($n = 7$), sex of dreamer was dropped from the second set of analyses. Consequently, the content of 117 student lucid, 104 adult lucid, 36 adult laboratory lucid, 95 student nonlucid, 7 adult nonlucid, and 5 adult laboratory nonlucid dreams were statistically analyzed.

Instrument

As noted, many of the scoring categories from the Hall and Van de Castle system of dream content analyses were used but were adapted for easier computer data entry. Specifically, dreams were scored for characters, social interactions, activities, achievement outcomes, environmental press, emotions, and descriptive elements. In all cases, dreams were scored in terms of the frequency of each element in the category. The character who was involved was not considered except in the case of the character's scoring category. Additionally, consequences of achievement outcome and environmental press were not considered. This resulted in a simplified scoring procedure. Specific variables scored can be found in Tables 3 to 9.

Additional scales were added. Four scales measuring bizarreness include Domhoff's (1962) metamorphoses as well as one measuring animate characters, inanimate environment, and dream transformations (see Table 10 for details of these scales). Finally, three scales of particular interest to dream lucidity and not covered directly in the aforementioned were also included. Previous research indicated the presence of palpable sensations (i.e., touch or body sensations) with dream lucidity as well as balance. Items assessing both were added to the judges' scoring sheets as was an item concerning dream control.

Procedure

Lucid and nonlucid dreams analyzed in this study were gathered over a 4-year period from participants in various lucid-dreaming research projects. The majority of the nonlaboratory lucid dreams were gathered when subjects thought

Table 2. Total Incidences of Dream Content Subscales for 10 Dreams Evaluated by Each Judge and Average Percentage Agreements

	Judges				Average percent agreement
Scales	1	2	3	4	
Characters					
Number	33	36	30	30	90%
Sex	33	34	30	27	88%
Identity	33	34	30	30	91%
Age	15	16	14	16	93%
Social interactions					
Aggresive	7	9	14	12	69%
Friendly	8	7	6	13	69%
Sexual	0	0	0	0	100%
Activities	38	36	34	58	78%
Achievement					
Success	2	4	4	4	75%
Failure	3	4	6	6	68%
Environmental press					
Misfortune	4	3	2	6	57%
Good Fortune	0	0	0	0	100%
Emotions	14	14	12	12	91%
Bizarreness					
Animate	2	2	2	4	75%
Inanimate	1	1	1	1	100%
Transformation	1	0	0	2	53%
Metamorphoses	1	0	0	0	75%
Descriptive elements					
Modifiers	18	71	23	41	49%
Temporal	2	12	4	3	45%
Negative	4	16	7	1	29%
Miscellaneous scales					
Palpaple	9	3	11	3	50%
Control	53	48	41	33	77%
Balance	8	33	52	42	47%

they were giving an example of a lucid dream (e.g., Gackenbach, Curren, LaBerge, Davidson, & Maxwell, 1983, report losing half of their sample when collecting illustrative lucid dreams due, typically, to confusion with morning-after dream recall). About half of the nonlucid dreams came from a 3-month dream diary project. The laboratory lucid dreams were from a sample of 114 dreams of 12 subjects provided by LaBerge (personal communication, 1985) and from a sample of seven lucid dreams of 1 subject sent by Worsley (personal communication, 1985). Lucid dreams selected for inclusion in subsequent data analyzes were only those obtained from unambiquous REM sleep where both the judge and the dreamer agreed that there had been lucidity accompanied by a clear eye-movement signal. The few nonlucid dreams were clearly identified as such by both the subject and the judge and also came from unambiguous REM episodes.

Four female judges were trained on a simplified version of the Hall and Van de Castle system of content analyses. In order to calculate scorer reliability, they all scored the same 10 randomly chosen dreams from the college students. Scorer reliabilities were expressed in percentage agreement. Specifically, as detailed in Table 2, total subscale incidences were calculated for each judge. For instance, for age of character, the total number of adult, teen, child, and infant characters for each judge was computed. Percentage agreement scores were then computed for every possible two-judge set, and the average of the six possible judge sets was then computed to obtain average percentage agreement scores for each scale listed in Table 2. These ranged from a low of 29% for the negative subscale of Descriptive Elements to 100% for several scales. The mean of these average percentage agreements was 73%. Considering the sample size (10 dreams) and the number of judges (4), this is an acceptable figure.

RESULTS

As pointed out by Winget and Kramer (1979), several solutions to the problem of differences in word length of dream transcripts have been offered. Hall and Van de Castle selected dreams of between 50 and 300 words in an attempt to address this problem. The method selected in this study was to determine if there were differences in word length as a function of the independent variables and, if so, to treat word length as a covariate. Results of the student analyses will be presented first, followed by those comparing samples, including the sleep laboratory dreams.

Students

In a Sex × Dream analysis of variance on number of words per dream, both a main effect for dreams ($F(1,232) = 7.36$, $p < .007$) and the Sex × Dream interaction ($F(1,232) = 5.57$, $p < .019$) reached significance. Nonlucid dream transcripts had more words in them ($\bar{x} = 82.16$) than lucid dream transcripts ($\bar{x} = 63.89$). This was entirely accounted for by the females (female lucids, $\bar{x} = 66.60$; female nonlucids, $\bar{x} = 100.00$; male lucids $\bar{x} = 58.48$; male nonlucids, $\bar{x} = 55.83$). Consequently, in all subsequent student sample analyses, word count was a covariate.

Results of most of the 102 2(type of dream: lucid and nonlucid) × 2 (sex of dreamer; male and female) analyses of covariance with number of words per dream as the covariate on Hall and Van de Castle's subscale scores are presented in Tables 4 to 10.[2] Tables 11 and 12 are results from the 24 types of Dream × Sex of dreamer analyses of covariance for the additional scales—bizzareness, palpable sensations, dream control, and dream balance. Finally, Table 3 gives the percentage of significant effects for both the proportional comparisons and the analyses of covariance from Tables 4 to 17.

Three types of information are presented in Tables 4 to 10—relative proportions from Hall and Van de Castle's sample and this sample and adjusted means and F-ratios for effects involving type of dream. In each case, proportions for this sample were calculated in the same manner as the Hall and Van de Castle normative sample. For instance, the total male characters for females proportion was calculated by dividing the total males ($n = 507$) by the total number of human characters for females ($n = 1,363$) to reach a proportion of .372. It should be noted that the proportions on the student sample are uncontrolled for word length. However, only about 10% of the 236 student dreams in the first set of analyses exceeded the Hall and Van de Castle limits. Finally, Tables 11 and 12 list adjusted means and F-ratios for the Bizzarreness subscales and the three additional subscales (Palpable Sensations, Control, and Balance).

Sample Comparisons

As with the student analyses, a Sample × Dream-type analysis of variance was computed on number of words in the dream transcripts. There was a sample main effect ($F(2,358) = 43.35$, $p < .0001$) as well as a Sample × Dream-type interaction ($F(2,358) = 11.50$, $p < .0001$). The dreams collected in the sleep laboratory were longer ($\bar{x} = 199.85$) than those from the highly interested in dreams adults ($\bar{x} = 108.95$) and both were longer than the student dreams ($\bar{x} = 75.18$). A posteriori tests on the means from the interaction showed that there was no difference as a function of sample for the length of nonlucid dreams.

---

[2]Ten analyses, six number-of-character units, two temporal reference scales, and two negative scale subscales are not included in these tables as there are not comparable normative proportions in Hall and Van de Castle and because they were all nonsignificant.

Consequently, the sample main effect was due, in the main, to sample differences in reporting lucid dreams.

Only significant dreamer effect findings and adjusted means of the 102 2(dream type; lucid or nonlucid) × 3(sample; student, adult, or sleep laboratory) analyses of covariance with number of words as the covariate on the Hall and Van de Castle scoring categories are offered in Tables 14 to 18. Table 18 lists the same type of information as with the student analyses for the 24 analyses involving Bizarreness scales and the additional scales. Finally, Table 13 gives information on the population from which the majority of each sample was drawn so that assessments of potential sample similarities and differences can be made.

DISCUSSION

The overwhelming finding of these numerous analyses assessing manifest content differences between lucid and nonlucid dreams is that *they are more alike than they are different*. Specifically (see Table 3), for the proportion tests as well as for the two sets of analyses of covariance, 70% to 80% of the tests resulted in *no dream type differences*. Although they are more alike than they are different, the differences occurred at greater than chance levels. That is, by chance alone, one would expect 5% of the total 612 proportional paired comparisons or 31 tests to be significant. In fact, 169 were significant. Likewise, with the 252 analyses of covariance, one would expect 13 to be significant by chance. Fifty-seven analyses had either a main effect and/or an interaction involving dream type. Consequently, although the similarities outnumber the differences, the differences are significant and not due to chance fluxuations. That is, there is a substantive difference between lucid and nonlucid dreams. The nature of these differences will be taken up next, first for student analyses and then for the sample analyses.

Students

Because many of the hypotheses are tied to whether or not lucid dreams are more (Green, 1968) or less (Gackenbach, 1982) likely to be initiated by nightmares, the incidence of various triggers of dream lucidity was examined for the student sample. Consistent with Gackenbach's finding, only 18% of the 136 lucid dreams analyzed were judged to have arisen out of a nightmare. This was slightly more likely to occur with women than with men. Also relatively consistent with Gackenbach was the finding that 11% (vs. her 19.2%) of these dreams arose out of the recognition of an incongruent element and 67% (vs. her 48%) as a function of the "dreamlike sense" of the dream.

Table 3. Percentages of Significant Differences for Both Proportional Paired Comparisons and Analyses of Covariance for Hall and Van de Castle Subscales

				Subscales			
Tests	Overall	Characters	Social interaction	Activities	Achievement and environmental press	Emotions	Descriptive elements
Student proportions[a]							
Numbers of tests	102	37	22	8	8	5	22
Males							
Norms–lucid	27%	30%	5%	37%	37%	20%	41%
Norms–nonlucid	27%	24%	23%	25%	37%	0%	36%
Lucid–nonlucid	17%	8%	23%	37%	0%	0%	27%
Females							
Norms–lucid	45%	41%	27%	63%	50%	20%	68%
Norms–nonlucid	28%	24%	18%	37%	25%	60%	36%
Lucid–nonlucid	25%	8%	0%	50%	50%	60%	55%
All lucid–nonlucid[b]	29%	22%	14%	47%	22%	25%	48%
Analyses of covariance[c]							
Student sample only	20%	24%	5%	50%	25%	20%	14%
Student, adult, and sleep lab samples	26%	27%	9%	50%	25%	20%	36%

[a]With the exception of the number of tests, this section lists the percentage of significant differences obtained on the paired comparison tests between proportions. Three sets of proportions were compared within sex of subject. They were the Hall and Van de Castle norms (Norms) and lucid and nonlucid proportions from the current study.

[b]Percentage of significant defferences between all lucid-nonlucid paired comparisons for the student sample with nonlucids including those from this study and the Hall and Van de Castle norms.

[c]Percentage of analyses of covariance with either a significant dream-type main effect or a significant sex × dream interaction for the students only and the students, adults, and sleep lab analyses.

Table 4. Proportions, Adjusted Means, and F-Ratios for Sex, Number, and Age of Characters Subscales on the Student Sample

Subscale	Males Hall	Males Nonlucid	Males Lucid	Females Hall	Females Nonlucid	Females Lucid	Lucids (top)	Lucids M	Lucids F	Nonlucids (top)	Nonlucids M	Nonlucids F	F-ratios[a]
Number													
Single	$.687_a^b$	$.755_{ab}$	$.835_b$	$.719_{ab}$	$.681_a$	$.757_b$	1.24	0.66	1.78	2.06	1.83	2.21	$F_{(1,231)} = 3.70,\ p<.056$ / $F_{(1,231)} = 0.18$, n.s
Group	$.313_a$	$.225_b$	$.165_b$	$.281_b$	$.269_b$	$.180_a$	0.39	0.34	0.41	0.74	0.55	0.87	$F_{(1,231)} = 10.62,\ p<.001$ / $F_{(1,231)} = 0.54$, n.s
Sex													
Male	$.530_a$	$.566_b$	$.681_b$	$.372_a$	$.255_b$	$.221_b$	0.80	1.34	0.53	1.02	1.33	0.81	$F_{(1,231)} = 1.26$, n.s. / $F_{(1,231)} = 0.77$, n.s.
Female	$.258_a$	$.162_b$	$.132_b$	$.401_a$	$.464_b$	$.482_b$	0.84	0.27	1.13	1.03	0.38	1.47	$F_{(1,231)} = 6.65,\ p<.011$ / $F_{(1,231)} = 1.09$, n.s.
Joint	$.131_a$	$.071_b$	$.055_b$	$.133_a$	$.189_b$	$.059_c$	0.13	0.11	0.14	0.42	0.17	0.60	$F_{(1,231)} = 18.57,\ p<.0001$ / $F_{(1,231)} = 7.33,\ p<.007$
Indefinite	$.081_a$	$.202_b$	$.132_b$	$.093_b$	$.092_b$	$.239_{ab}$	0.45	0.27	0.55	0.37	0.48	0.29	$F_{(1,231)} = 1.24$, n.s. / $F_{(1,231)} = 7.97,\ p<.005$
Age													
Adult	$.973_a$	$.963_a$	$.987_a$	$.933_a$	$.955_a$	$.930_a$	1.66	1.61	1.68	2.19	1.88	2.40	$F_{(1,231)} = 9.40,\ p<.002$ / $F_{(1,231)} = 0.91$, n.s.
Teenager	$.006_a$	$.000_a$	$.000_a$	$.014_a$	$.019_a$	$.006_a$	0.01	0.00	0.01	0.03	0.00	0.05	$F_{(1,231)} = 1.35$, n.s. / $F_{(1,231)} = 0.81$, n.s.
Child	$.018_a$	$.024_a$	$.000_a$	$.042_a$	$.019_a$	$.041_a$	0.05	0.00	0.08	0.05	0.05	0.05	$F_{(1,231)} = 0.02$, n.s. / $F_{(1,231)} = 1.72$, n.s.
Baby	$.003_a$	$.012_a$	$.013_a$	$.011_a$	$.006_a$	$.023_a$	0.04	0.02	0.05	0.02	0.02	0.02	$F_{(1,231)} = 0.51$, n.s. / $F_{(1,231)} = 0.35$, n.s.

Columns: *Proportions* (Males: Hall, Nonlucid, Lucid; Females: Hall, Nonlucid, Lucid); *Adjusted means* (Lucids: M, F; Nonlucids: M, F); *F-ratios*.

[a]Top = dream main effect. Bottom = dream × sex interaction.

[b]Paired comparisons were computed within each sex between proportions. Significant ($p<.05$) differences are indicated by differing subscripts. Proportions that do not differ have the same subscript.

Table 5. Proportions, Adjusted Means, and F-Ratios for Character Identities Subscales on the Student Samples

Subscale	Proportions — Males Hall	Males Nonlucid	Males Lucid	Females Hall	Females Nonlucid	Females Lucid	Adjusted means — Lucids M	Lucids F	Nonlucids M	Nonlucids F	F-ratios[a]
Father	$.025_a$[b]	$.020_a$	$.011_a$	$.032_a$	$.020_{ab}$	$.005_b$		0.02		0.06	$F(1,230) = 2.68$, n.s. / $F(1,230) = 0.22$, n.s.
Mother	$.024_a$	$.010_a$	$.000_a$	$.046_a$	$.010_a$	$.009_b$	0.02	0.02	0.05	0.03	$F(1,230) = 1.01$, n.s. / $F(1,230) = 0.02$, n.s.
Parents	$.011_a$	$.000_a$	$.000_a$	$.013_a$	$.000_a$	$.005_a$	0.00	0.01	0.02	0.00	$F(1,230) = 0.80$, n.s. / $F(1,230) = 0.51$, n.s.
Brother	$.013_a$	$.011_a$	$.011_a$	$.015_a$	$.010_a$	$.009_a$	0.00	0.02	0.02	0.03	$F(1,230) = 0.23$, n.s. / $F(1,230) = 0.13$, n.s.
Sister	$.009_a$	$.000_a$	$.011_a$	$.025_a$	$.036_a$	$.027_a$	0.02	0.05	0.00	0.07	$F(1,230) = 0.11$, n.s. / $F(1,230) = 0.66$, n.s.
Husband	—	—	$.000_a$	$.009_a$	$.005_a$	$.014_a$	0.00	0.02	0.00	0.01	$F(1,230) = 0.49$, n.s. / $F(1,230) = 0.31$, n.s.
Wife	$.008_a$	$.000_a$	$.000_a$	—	—	—					—
Son	$.001_a$	$.000_a$	$.000_a$	—	$.000_a$	$.000_a$	0.00	0.02	0.00	0.00	$F(1,230) = 0.69$, n.s. / $F(1,230) = 0.43$, n.s.
Daughter	—	$.000_a$	$.000_a$	—	$.005_a$	$.004_a$	0.00	0.01	0.00	0.01	$F(1,230) = 0.00$, n.s. / $F(1,230) = 0.00$, n.s.
Child	$.018_a$	$.010_a$	$.000_a$	$.042_a$	$.020_{ab}$	$.018_b$	0.03	0.05	0.02	0.06	$F(1,230) = 0.00$, n.s. / $F(1,230) = 0.69$, n.s.

Infant							0.03		0.01		F(1,230) = 0.89, n.s.
	$.003_a$	$.000_a$	$.000_a$	$.011_a$	$.005_a$	$.018_a$	0.00	0.05	0.00	0.02	F(1,230) = 0.55, n.s.
Family							0.04		0.10		F(1,230) = 4.25, $p<.04$
	$.095_a$	$.020_b$	$.000_b$	$.147_a$	$.041_b$	$.023_b$	0.00	0.06	0.05	0.13	F(1,230) = 0.23, n.s.
Relative							0.03		0.04		F(1,230) = 0.13, n.s.
	$.023_a$	$.010_a$	$.011_a$	$.045_a$	$.015_b$	$.018_b$	0.02	0.03	0.02	0.05	F(1,230) = 0.07, n.s.
Known							0.41		0.67		F(1,230) = 4.37, $p<.038$
	$.313_a$	$.232_b$	$.220_b$	$.368_a$	$.240_b$	$.181_b$	0.41	0.41	0.55	0.76	F(1,230) = 0.30, n.s.
Prominent							0.00		0.03		F(1,230) = 2.63, n.s.
	$.016_a$	$.010_a$	$.000_a$	$.010_a$	$.010_a$	$.000_a$	0.00	0.00	0.02	0.03	F(1,230) = 0.00, n.s.
Occupation							0.08		0.19		F(1,230) = 2.99, n.s.
	$.171_a$	$.091_b$	$.044_b$	$.085_a$	$.056_a$	$.027_b$	0.00	0.07	0.21	0.18	F(1,230) = 0.20, n.s.
Ethnic							0.01		0.05		F(1,230) = 2.92, n.s.
	$.020_{ab}$	$.030_a$	$.000_b$	$.021_a$	$.010_a$	$.005_a$	0.00	0.01	0.07	0.03	F(1,230) = 0.90, n.s.
Stranger							0.21		0.21		F(1,230) = 0.00, n.s.
	$.232_b$	$.000_b$	$.121_c$	$.171_a$	$.112_b$	$.077_b$	0.25	0.20	0.00	0.35	F(1,230) = 8.85, $p<.003$
Uncertain							0.19		0.18		F(1,230) = 0.12, n.s.
	$.119_a$	$.091_a$	$.066_a$	$.133_a$	$.051_b$	$.086_b$	0.14	0.22	0.21	0.16	F(1,230) = 1.79, n.s.
Creature							0.03		0.04		F(1,230) = 0.04, n.s.
	$.001_a$	$.010_b$	$.011_b$	—	$.015_a$	$.018_a$	0.02	0.03	0.02	0.05	F(1,230) = 0.02, n.s.
Animal							0.08		0.11		F(1,230) = 0.42, n.s.
	$.060_a$	$.061_a$	$.022_a$	$.042_a$	$.026_a$	$.045_a$	0.05	0.09	0.14	0.08	F(1,230) = 1.74, n.s.

[a]Top = dream main effect. Bottom = dream × sex interaction.
[b]See footnote [b] on Table 4.

Table 6. Proportions, Adjusted Means, and F-Ratios for Social Interactions Subscales on the Student Sample

Subscale	Proportions						Adjusted means				F-ratios[a]
	Males			Females			Lucids		Nonlucids		
	Hall	Nonlucid	Lucid	Hall	Nonlucid	Lucid	M	F	M	F	
Aggression											
Murder (8)	$.06_a$[b]	$.13_a$	$.12_a$	$.02_a$	$.00_{ab}$	$.06_b$	0.05		0.03		$F(1,231) = 0.48$, n.s.
							0.07	0.03	0.07	0.00	$F(1,231) = 0.40$, n.s.
Attack (7)	$.22_b$	$.43_a$	$.15_b$	$.15_a$	$.13_a$	$.11_a$	0.07		0.13		$F(1,231) = 2.27$, n.s.
							0.07	0.07	0.24	0.06	$F(1,231) = 2.87$, n.s.
Chasing-confining (6)	$.15_a$	$.26_a$	$.27_a$	$.13_a$	$.33_b$	$.40_b$	0.21		0.15		$F(1,231) = 0.58$, n.s.
							0.16	0.24	0.14	0.16	$F(1,231) = 0.15$, n.s.
Destruction (5)	$.06_a$	$.00_a$	$.04_a$	$.04_a$	$.00_a$	$.06_a$	0.02		0.00		$F(1,231) = 2.05$, n.s.
							0.02	0.00	0.00	0.00	$F(1,231) = 0.01$, n.s.
Serious threat (4)	$.05_a$	$.00_a$	$.08_a$	$.04_a$	$.00_a$	$.06_a$	0.02		0.00		$F(1,231) = 2.89$, n.s.
							0.05	0.01	0.00	0.00	$F(1,231) = 1.10$, n.s.
Rejection (3)	$.18_a$	$.13_a$	$.12_a$	$.36_a$	$.27_{ab}$	$.15_a$	0.08		0.11		$F(1,231) = 0.00$, n.s.
							0.07	0.09	0.07	0.13	$F(1,231) = 0.01$, n.s.
Verbal (2)	$.18_b$	$.00_a$	$.15_b$	$.15_a$	$.17_a$	$.13_a$	0.08		0.05		$F(1,231) = 1.04$, n.s.
							0.09	0.08	0.00	0.08	$F(1,231) = 0.80$, n.s.
Covert (1)	$.10_a$	$.04_a$	$.08_a$	$.11_a$	$.10_a$	$.04_a$	0.03		0.04		$F(1,231) = 0.01$, n.s.
							0.05	0.02	0.02	0.05	$F(1,231) = 0.14$, n.s.
Total 5–8	$.50_b$	$.83_a$	$.58_b$	$.34_a$	$.47_{ab}$	$.62_b$	0.35		0.32		$F(1,231) = 0.04$, n.s.
							0.32	0.36	0.45	0.23	$F(1,231) = 1.89$, n.s.
Total 1–4	$.50_b$	$.17_a$	$.42_b$	$.66_a$	$.53_{ab}$	$.38_b$	0.22		0.19		$F(1,231) = 0.82$, n.s.
							0.25	0.20	0.10	0.26	$F(1,231) = 0.63$, n.s.

Friendly											
Marriage							0.01		0.01		$F(1,231) = 0.04$, n.s.
	$.04_a$	$.00_a$	$.00_a$	$.08_a$	$.02_a$	$.04_a$	0.00	0.01	0.00	0.02	$F(1,231) = 0.02$, n.s.
Physical inviting							0.02		0.04		$F(1,231) = 0.13$, n.s.
	$.09_a$	$.10_a$	$.14_a$	$.08_a$	$.07_a$	$.04_a$	0.02	0.01	0.02	0.05	$F(1,231) = 0.02$, n.s.
Dating							0.02		0.07		$F(1,231) = 1.64$, n.s.
	$.08_a$	$.30_b$	$.00_{ab}$	$.15_a$	$.10_a$	$.12_a$	0.00	0.03	0.07	0.06	$F(1,231) = 0.58$, n.s.
Helping, protecting							0.12		0.16		$F(1,231) = 0.30$, n.s.
	$.42_b$	$.30_b$	$.86_a$	$.32_a$	$.34_a$	$.40_a$	0.14	0.11	0.07	0.23	$F(1,231) = 1.72$, n.s.
Gift, loan							0.00		0.02		$F(1,231) = 1.57$, n.s.
	$.11_a$	$.10_a$	$.00_a$	$.10_a$	$.02_b$	$.00_b$	0.00	0.00	0.02	0.02	$F(1,231) = 0.34$, n.s.
Verbal							0.05		0.16		$F(1,231) = 5.02$, $p<.026$
	$.20_a$	$.10_a$	$.00_a$	$.19_a$	$.39_b$	$.24_{ab}$	0.00	0.07	0.02	0.26	$F(1,231) = 1.61$, n.s.
Covert							0.03		0.03		$F(1,231) = 0.00$, n.s.
	$.06_a$	$.10_a$	$.00_a$	$.08_a$	$.05_a$	$.16_a$	0.00	0.05	0.02	0.03	$F(1,231) = 0.75$, n.s.
Sexual											
Intercourse							0.02		0.02		$F(1,231) = 0.05$, n.s.
	$.27_a$	$.50_a$	$.99_a$	$.26_a$	$.00_a$	$.33_a$	0.02	0.01	0.05	0.00	$F(1,231) = 0.89$, n.s.
Petting							0.01		0.01		$F(1,231) = 0.05$, n.s.
	$.18_a$	$.25_a$	$.00_a$	$.26_a$	$.00_a$	$.33_a$	0.00	0.01	0.02	0.00	$F(1,231) = 1.79$, n.s.
Kissing							0.01		0.02		$F(1,231) = 0.70$, n.s.
	$.11_a$	$.00_a$	$.00_a$	$.21_a$	$.67_b$	$.33_{ab}$	0.00	0.01	0.00	0.03	$F(1,231) = 0.43$, n.s.
Sexual overtures							0.00		0.02		$F(1,231) = 2.67$, n.s.
	$.30_a$	$.25_a$	$.00_a$	$.16_a$	$.33_a$	$.00_a$	0.00	0.00	0.02	0.02	$F(1,231) = 0.05$, n.s.
Sexual fantasies							—		—		—
	$.14_a$	$.00_a$	$.00_a$	$.11_a$	$.00_a$	$.00_a$	—		—		—

[a]Top = dream main effect. Bottom = dream × sex interaction.
[b]See footnote [b] on Table 4.

Two types of descriptive information are presented for the various scoring categories in Tables 4 to 10: relative proportions of a variable in a content category (i.e., number of males relative to all human characters identified by sex) and the average number of each variable per dream adjusted for differences in dream word count (i.e., the adjusted for word count average number of dream males). The former is derived as per Hall and Van de Castle and presented in order to afford comparisons to their normative data. As per Hall, Domhoff, Blick, and Weesner (1982), paired comparisons between proportions within each sex were also computed. Because the proportions are not controlled for word count, there are more differences (also see Table 3) between lucid and nonlucid dreams for that type of measurement than there are for the analyses-of-covariance-generated means. Additionally, there is a conceptual difference between these measures. The proportions are based on all dreams (denominator) and the number *for which the category was present* (numerator). The adjusted means are the average incidence counted of a category *per dream*. This conceptual distinction resulted in a difference in the direction of the finding for only one variable (number of characters). In all other cases where there was a dreamer effect (main or interactive) for the analyses of covariance, the proportional tests reflected the difference in the same direction. However, there were many incidences where the paired comparisons on the proportions were significantly different, but no difference was found in the covariance analyses.

It can be seen in Tables 4 and 5 that, for the dream-type main effects for the analyses of covariance, there were fewer characters in the lucid dreams than in the nonlucid dreams. With some minor variations, the proportions parallel this finding. That is, there were proportionately fewer characters in lucid than in nonlucid dreams.

Contrary to expectation (see Table 6) for both types of analyses (proportion paired comparisons and analyses of covariance), there were generally no dream-type differences in the frequency of aggressive, friendly, or sexual social interactions. The one dream main effect for verbal friendly interactions could be attributed to chance variation. It favored nonlucid dreams.

In terms of the frequency of types of activities (see Table 7) as expected, for proportions and covariance, the lucid dreams of these students contained significantly more auditory and cognitive components than their nonlucid dreams or than the nonlucid dreams of the normative sample of students. In the previous literature, no dream-type differences have reliably been found for visual elements. However, in these analyses, an interaction from the analysis of covariance was significant such that for males only lucid dreams were significantly *less* visual than nonlucid dreams. The same was true with the proportions data.

Also, as expected but for the female proportion data only, lucid dreams were more physical than either type of nonlucid dream. Contrary to expectation, but for the female proportional data only, verbal and movement activities were less frequently judged to exist in lucid than in the normative nonlucid dreams

Table 7. Proportions, Adjusted Means, and F-Ratios for the Activities on the Student Sample

Subscale	Males			Females			Lucids		Nonlucids		F-ratios[a]
	Hall	Nonlucid	Lucid	Hall	Nonlucid	Lucid	M	F	M	F	
Verbal	$.216_a$[b]	$.133_b$	$.127_b$	$.262_a$	$.217_{ab}$	$.188_b$	0.57		0.72		$F(1,231) = 0.34$, n.s.
							0.39	0.66	0.43	0.92	$F(1,231) = 0.01$, n.s.
Physical	$.265_a$	$.252_a$	$.246_a$	$.195_b$	$.175_b$	$.239_a$	0.80		0.77		$F(1,231) = 1.79$, n.s.
							0.73	0.84	0.81	0.74	$F(1,231) = 2.91$, n.s.
Movement	$.248_a$	$.296_a$	$.209_a$	$.251_a$	$.243_{ab}$	$.196_b$	0.69		1.00		$F(1,231) = 2.43$, n.s.
							0.64	0.72	0.95	1.03	$F(1,231) = 0.38$, n.s.
Location change	$.082_a$	$.096_a$	$.045_a$	$.074_b$	$.175_a$	$.069_b$	0.19		0.57		$F(1,231) = 16.09$, $p<.0001$
							0.14	0.22	0.31	0.74	$F(1,231) = 2.67$, n.s.
Visual	$.118_{ab}$	$.141_a$	$.075_b$	$.124_a$	$.061_b$	$.094_{ab}$	0.34		0.35		$F(1,231) = 0.07$, n.s.
							0.20	0.33	0.45	0.26	$F(1,231) = 5.33$, $p<.022$
Auditory	$.016_b$	$.007_b$	0.37_a	$.014_a$	$.008_a$	$.024_a$	0.10				$F(1,231) = 4.62$, $p<.033$
							0.11	0.09	0.02	0.03	$F(1,231) = 0.17$, n.s.
Expressive	$.022_a$	$.015_a$	$.037_a$	$.034_a$	$.057_b$	$.015_b$	0.08		0.16		$F(1,231) = 1.15$, n.s.
							0.11	0.06	0.05	0.24	$F(1,231) = 3.54$, n.s.
Cognitive	$.032_a$	$.059_b$	$.224_c$	$.046_a$	$.065_b$	$.175_c$	0.64		0.24		$F(1,231) = 24.20$, $p<.0001$
							0.66	0.64	0.19	0.27	$F(1,231) = 0.05$, n.s.

[a]Top = dream main effect. Bottom = dream × sex interaction.
[b]See footnote b, Table 4.

Table 8. Proportions, Adjusted Means, and F-Ratios for Achievement and Environmental Press Subscales on the Student Sample

| | Proportions | | | | | | Adjusted means | | | | |
| | Males | | | Females | | | Lucids | | Nonlucids | | |
Subscale	Hall	Nonlucid	Lucid	Hall	Nonlucid	Lucid	M	F	M	F	F-ratios[a]
Achievement											
Success	$.15_a$[b]	$.69_b$	$.50_b$	$.08_b$	$.60_b$	$.30_a$	0.08	0.07	0.23	0.24	$F(1,231) = 5.84$, $p<0.16$
							0.11		0.21		$F(1,231) = 0.01$, n.s.
Failure	$.15_a$	$.31_{ab}$	$.50_b$	$.10_a$	$.40_b$	$.70_c$	0.14	0.16	0.13	0.16	$F(1,231) = 0.08$, n.s.
							0.11		0.10		$F(1,231) = 0.00$, n.s.
Environmental press											
Death	$.08_a$	$.13_a$	$.18_a$	$.10_a$	$.25_a$	$.13_a$	0.03	0.02	0.04	0.05	$F(1,231) = 0.07$, n.s.
							0.05		0.02		$F(1,231) = 0.83$, n.s.
Injured or ill	$.21_a$	$.00_a$	$.09_a$	$.25_a$	$.17_a$	$.13_a$	0.02	0.02	0.02	0.03	$F(1,231) = 0.00$, n.s.
							0.02		0.00		$F(1,231) = 0.56$, n.s.
Accident, distrust, loss of possession	$.25_a$	$.13_a$	$.09_a$	$.19_b$	$.25_b$	$.00_a$	0.01	0.00	0.04	0.05	$F(1,231) = 2.60$, n.s.
							0.02		0.02		$F(1,231) = 1.51$, n.s.
Threat from environment	$.13_a$	$.38_b$	$.18_{ab}$	$.13_a$	$.00_a$	$.13_a$	0.03	0.02	0.03	0.00	$F(1,231) = 0.01$, n.s.
							0.05		0.07		$F(1,231) = 0.91$, n.s.
Falling	$.05_a$	$.38_b$	$.27_b$	$.03_a$	$.25_b$	$.19_b$	0.05	0.03	0.06	0.05	$F(1,231) = 0.13$, n.s.
							0.07		0.07		$F(1,231) = 0.04$, n.s.
Obstacle	$.28_a$	$.00_b$	$.18_{ab}$	$.30_{ab}$	$.08_a$	$.44_b$	0.06	0.03	0.01	0.05	$F(1,231) = 3.90$, $p<.049$
							0.07		0.07		$F(1,231) = 0.03$, n.s.
Good fortune	$.06_b$	$.00_{ab}$	$.00_a$	$.06_a$	$.00_b$	$.00_b$	—	—	—	—	—
							—		—		—

[a]Top = dream main effect. Bottom = dream × sex interaction.
[b]See footnote b Table 4.

Table 9. Proportions, Adjusted Means, and F-Ratios for Emotions Subscale on the Student Sample

| Subscale | Proportions | | | | | | Adjusted means | | | | F-ratios[a] |
| | Males | | | Females | | | Lucids | | Nonlucids | | |
	Hall	Nonlucid	Lucid	Hall	Nonlucid	Lucid	M	F	M	F	
Happy (main effect)	.195$_a$[b]	.261$_a$	.176$_a$	.195$_a$	.341$_a$	.115$_b$	0.06		0.20		$F(2,231) = 5.99$, $p<.015$
Happy (dream × sex)							0.07	0.06	0.14	0.24	$F(1,231) = 0.53$, n.s.
Sad (main effect)	.094$_a$	.087$_a$	.000$_a$	.129$_a$	.045$_a$	.058$_a$	0.02		0.04		$F(1,231) = 0.36$, n.s.
Sad (dream × sex)							0.00	0.03	0.05	0.03	$F(1,231) = 1.42$, n.s.
Anger (main effect)	.156$_a$	.261$_{ab}$	.470$_b$	.126$_a$	.136$_{ab}$	.250$_b$	0.15		0.12		$F(2,231) = 1.00$, n.s.
Anger (dream × sex)							0.18	0.14	0.14	0.10	$F(1,231) = 0.08$, n.s.
Confusion (main effect)	.215$_a$	.130$_a$	.118$_a$	.178$_b$	.318$_a$	.173$_b$	0.08		0.16		$F(1,231) = 1.61$, n.s.
Confusion (dream × sex)							0.05	0.10	0.07	0.23	$F(1,231) = 0.36$, n.s.
Apprehension (main effect)	.340$_a$	.261$_a$	.235$_a$	.372$_b$	.159$_a$	.404$_b$	0.17		0.12		$F(1,231) = 0.63$, n.s.
Apprehension (dream × sex)							0.09	0.22	0.14	0.11	$F(1,231) = 2.02$, n.s.

[a]Top = dream main effect. Bottom = dream × sex interaction.
[b]See footnote b Table 4.

Table 10. Proportions, Adjusted Means, and F-Ratios of Descriptive Elements Subscale on the Student Sample

Modifies	Proportions — Males			Proportions — Females			Adjusted means — Lucids			Adjusted means — Nonlucids			F-ratios[a]
	Hall	Nonlucid	Lucid	Hall	Nonlucid	Lucid		M	F		M	F	
Chromatic	$.07_a^b$	$.21_b$	$.21_b$	$.11_a$	$.07_b$	$.04_b$	0.22	0.48	0.09	0.38	0.52	0.27	$F(1,230) = 0.26$, n.s. $F(1,230) = 0.05$, n.s.
Achromatic	$.04_b$	$.04_b$	$.00_a$	$.05_b$	$.06_b$	$.01_a$	0.01	0.00	0.01	0.19	0.10	0.26	$F(1,230) = 3.21$, n.s. $F(1,230) = 0.33$, n.s.
Large	$.18_a$	$.12_a$	$.13_a$	$.13_a$	$.05_b$	$.00_c$	0.18	0.30	0.11	0.25	0.31	0.21	$F(1,230) = 0.15$, n.s. $F(1,230) = 0.05$, n.s.
Small	$.09_a$	$.07_a$	$.11_a$	$.08_a$	$.06_{ab}$	$.04_b$	0.15	0.25	0.10	0.22	0.17	0.26	$F(1,230) = 0.13$, n.s. $F(1,230) = 0.74$, n.s.
Intense	$.29_a$	$.02_b$	$.00_b$	$.30_a$	$.11_b$	$.02_c$	0.02	0.00	0.03	0.28	0.05	0.44	$F(1,230) = 3.60$, $p<.05$ $F(1,230) = 1.37$, n.s.
Weak	$.05_a$	$.03_b$	$.01_b$	$.04_a$	$.02_a$	$.03_a$	0.05	0.02	0.07	0.09	0.07	0.10	$F(1,231) = 0.31$, n.s. $F(1,231) = 0.39$, n.s.
Filled	$.02_a$	$.01_a$	$.02_a$	$.01_a$	$.04_b$	$.17_c$	0.17	0.05	0.23	0.11	0.02	0.16	$F(1,231) = 0.35$, n.s. $F(1,231) = 0.13$, n.s.
Empty	$.01_a$	$.02_a$	$.01_a$	$.00_b$	$.00_b$	$.02_a$	0.04	0.02	0.05	0.02	0.05	0.00	$F(1,231) = 1.00$, n.s. $F(1,231) = 2.80$, n.s.

(Top row for each trait = dream main effect; bottom row = dream × sex interaction.)

Trait	Effect	1	2	3	4	5	6	A	B	F
Straight	main	$.00_a$	$.00_a$	$.00_a$	$.00_b$	$.00_b$	$.09_a$	0.17	0.01	$F_{(1,231)} = 2.45$, n.s.
	int.							0.00 0.25	0.00 0.02	$F_{(1,231)} = 1.72$, n.s.
Crooked	main	$.01_b$	$.04_a$	$.00_b$	$.01_a$	$.00_b$	$.09_c$	0.17	0.04	$F_{(1,231)} = 2.08$, n.s.
	int.							0.00 0.25	0.10 0.00	$F_{(1,231)} = 2.76$, n.s.
Hot	main	$.01_a$	$.03_b$	$.18_c$	$.01_b$	$.00_b$	$.07_a$	0.18	0.04	$F_{(1,230)} = 2.76$, n.s.
	int.							0.40 0.07	0.07 0.02	$F_{(1,230)} = 5.42$, $p<.02$
Cold	main	$.01_a$	$.00_a$	$.02_a$	$.01_b$	$.00_b$	$.06_a$	0.05	0.00	$F_{(1,230)} = 0.05$, n.s.
	int.							0.05 0.06	0.00 0.10	$F_{(1,230)} = 2.41$, n.s.
Fast	main	$.04_a$	$.00_b$	$.01_{ab}$	$.02_a$	$.02_a$	$.01_a$	0.02	0.06	$F_{(1,230)} = 3.37$, n.s.
	int.							0.02 0.01	0.00 0.05	$F_{(1,230)} = 0.00$, n.s.
Slow	main	$.01_a$	$.03_b$	$.04_b$	$.01_a$	$.01_a$	$.00_a$	0.04	0.05	$F_{(1,230)} = 0.26$, n.s.
	int.							0.09 0.01	0.07 0.03	$F_{(1,230)} = 3.60$, $p<.05$
Old	main	$.04_a$	$.23_b$	$.08_c$	$.04_a$	$.26_b$	$.11_c$	0.25	0.85	$F_{(1,230)} = 0.17$, n.s.
	int.							0.19 0.28	0.57 1.03	$F_{(1,230)} = 0.07$, n.s.
Young	main	$.05_a$	$.10_b$	$.01_c$	$.04_b$	$.03_b$	$.08_a$	0.13	0.18	$F_{(1,230)} = 1.54$, n.s.
	int.							0.02 0.18	0.26 0.13	$F_{(1,230)} = 0.42$, n.s.
Pretty, good	main	$.05_a$	$.03_a$	$.02_a$	$.07_a$	$.12_b$	$.37_c$	0.69	0.32	$F_{(1,230)} = 0.31$, n.s.
	int.							0.05 1.01	0.07 0.48	$F_{(1,230)} = 0.46$, n.s.
Ugly, bad	main	$.03_b$	$.04_b$	$.16_a$	$.06_a$	$.13_b$	$.16_b$	0.41	0.34	$F_{(1,230)} = 0.25$, n.s.
	int.							0.36 0.44	0.10 0.50	

[a] Top = dream main effect. Bottom = dream × sex interaction. [b] See footnote [b] Table 4.

Table 11. Adjusted Means and F-Ratios for Bizarreness Subscales on the Student Sample

Subscale	Lucids M	Lucids F	Nonlucids M	Nonlucids F	F-ratios[a]
A. Animate characters sum	0.16	0.23	0.43	0.34	$F(1,231) = 1.60$, n.s.
1. Appearance in a dream of monsters and alien beings	0.05	0.27	0.00	0.01	$F(1,231) = 3.85$, $p<.051$
2. Appearance of fictional, dead, or prominent characters unknown personally to dreamer	0.00	0.07	0.05	0.05	$F(1,231) = 1.99$, n.s.
3. Absence for inappropriate clothing, tools, or implements	0.02	0.02	0.05	0.04	$F(1,231) = 1.24$, n.s.
4. Distorted or disfigured body parts not present in reality	0.00	0.00	0.02	0.02	$F(1,231) = 0.43$, n.s.
5. Impossible acts or magic by animate characters	0.00	0.02	0.02	0.03	$F(1,231) = 0.12$, n.s.
6. Wrong or inappropriate role of dreamers or other characters	0.11	0.12	0.29	0.19	$F(1,231) = 5.81$, $p<.017$
B. Inanimate environment sum	0.05	0.06	0.10	0.08	$F(1,231) = 0.07$, n.s.
1. Violation of physical laws by inanimate objects	0.02	0.02	0.05	0.03	$F(1,231) = 0.08$, n.s.

Measure	Data values	F (dream main effect)	F (dream × sex interaction)
2. Realistic objects but in the wrong place	0.00, 0.01, 0.02, 0.03	$F(1,231) = 1.41$, n.s.	$F(1,231) = 0.02$, n.s.
3. Inappropriate or fantastic combination of environmental features	0.00, 0.02, 0.02, 0.02	$F(1,231) = 0.00$, n.s.	$F(1,231) = 1.26$, n.s.
C. Dream transformation sum	0.02, 0.02, 0.07, 0.11, 0.13	$F(1,231) = 2.11$, $p < .02$	$F(1,231) = 0.00$, n.s.
1. An object suddenly appears or disappears	0.00, 0.00, 0.02, 0.02	$F(1,231) = 1.99$, n.s.	$F(1,231) = 0.18$, n.s.
2. A sudden shift backward or forward in time	—	—	—
3. A person suddenly appears or vanishes, but the entire dream scene is unaltered	0.00, 0.01, 0.00, 0.01, 0.02	$F(1,231) = 0.11$, n.s.	$F(1,231) = 0.07$, n.s.
4. Scene shift where the entire environment is altered without the character having moved	0.02, 0.01, 0.05, 0.08, 0.10	$F(1,231) = 0.92$, n.s.	$F(1,231) = 0.00$, n.s.
D. Metamorphoses sum	0.00, 0.02, 0.00, 0.02, 0.03	$F(1,231) = 0.20$, n.s.	$F(1,231) = 0.15$, n.s.
1. From one person to another	0.00, 0.00, 0.00, 0.01, 0.03	$F(1,231) = 1.09$, n.s.	$F(1,231) = 0.66$, n.s.
2. Animal to person or vice versa	—	—	—
3. Inanimate to animate and vice versa	—	—	—
4. From one object to another	0.00, 0.02, 0.00, 0.01, 0.02	$F(1,231) = 0.83$, n.s.	$F(1,231) = 0.57$, n.s.

[a] Top = dream main effect. Bottom = dream × sex interaction.

with no difference with the student nonlucid dreams. A similar situation occurred for males with the verbal proportion data.

There was no hypothesis regarding the location change activity. Lucid dreams were found to have fewer location changes than nonlucid dreams in the covariance analysis.

Table 8 lists findings from both the achievement and enviromental-press scoring categories. Regarding the former, nonlucid dreams were significantly higher in success achievement outcomes than lucid dreams for the covariance analysis and for the proportions within this sample. Regarding environmental press, more obstacles were found in lucid dreams for both types of analyses.

Regarding emotions, as can be seen in Table 9, only one dreamer effect emerged for the analyses of covariance, with the frequency of happy emotions favoring the nonlucid dream. For all other emotions, the findings were ambiguous and not as strong.

The final Hall and Van de Castle scoring category used in the present study was descriptive elements (see Table 10). There were no dream-type differences for the negative or temporal scales and only a few for the modifiers. Lucid dreams had fewer intense and old modifiers but more cold modifiers than nonlucid dreams in the covariance analyses. For the proportional comparisons, among males, lucid dreams had fewer achromatic and young modifiers and more hot and ugly modifiers than either type of nonlucid dream. For females, lucid dreams had fewer achromatic, large, and intense modifiers and more filled, empty, straight, crooked, hot, cold, young, and pretty modifiers than either type of nonlucid dream. This sex difference in the number of modifiers implicated in dream-type differences may be explained by females superiority in verbal skills (Maccoby & Jacklin, 1974). Otherwise, there does not seem to be a positive or negative valenced tendency to these dream type differences.

Only 3 of the 21 analyses of covariance on bizarreness scoring categories had a significant effect involving dream type. It can be seen in Table 11 that these effects were from the animate characters and inanimate environment scales. However, as this occurred at chance levels, one must conclude that there was no difference as a function of bizarreness.

Finally, in Table 12, the finding of *less* balance associated with lucid than with nonlucid dreams was contrary to expectation as was the lack of a dream-type difference for palpable sensations and control.

To summarize the student sample findings regarding dream type differences, *across types of analyses and sex of subject* lucid dreams have fewer characters and more obstacles and auditory and cognitive activities than nonlucid dreams. One sex difference across types of analyses also emerged. Specifically, males had less visual activities in their lucid than in their nonlucid dreams. All other findings were attenuated by conflicts between proportional differences and the analyses of covariance. Consequently, caution in interpretation is advised.

Table 12. Adjusted Means and F-Ratios for Miscellaneous Scales on the Student Sample[a]

| Scale | Adjusted means | | | | F- ratios [b] |
| | Lucids | | Nonlucids | | |
	M	F	M	F	
Palpable sensations (touch and body	1.25		1.32		$F(1,231) = 0.07$, n.s.
sensations)	1.14	1.31	1.24	1.37	$F(1,231) = 0.09$, n.s.
Control over dream	6.06		5.69		$F(1,231) = 0.42$, n.s.
	5.32	6.43	5.69	5.69	$F(1,231) = 0.92$, n.s.
Balance (physical, psychological,	5.20		6.95		$F(1,231) = 4.07$, $p<.045$
and intellectual)	5.27	5.17	5.90	7.66	$F(1,231) = 0.88$, n.s.

[a]Unlike all of the other scales, which are frequency counts, with palpable dream control and balance the judge was asked to make an evaluation along a 10-point scale (3-point for palpable) with a high score representing a lot of that quality in the dream.
[b]Top = dream main effect. Bottom = dream × sex interaction.

Sample Comparisons

It will be recalled that this second set of analyses of covariance was primarily undertaken in order to examine the content of sleep laboratory, signal verified REM-sleep lucid dreams to REM-sleep nonlucid dreams also collected in the laboratory. It is advantageous to compare this sample to the sample just analyzed (students). The laboratory and the student dreams just analyzed differ in two major ways—type of dreamer (adults vs. students) and method of dream collection (laboratory vs. diary/questionnaire). Consequently, a third sample of adults was added who are highly interested in their dreams. Furthermore, they are more similar in other sample characteristics to the sleep laboratory adults as can be seen in Table 13, than to the students. However, these adults dreams were collected with the same procedures as were the student sample (diary/ questionnaire).

Only significant interactions and main effects and the relevant adjusted means involving dream type are listed in Tables 14 to 18. As with the student analyses, across-sample, lucid dreams were scored as having fewer characters than nonlucid dreams. As can be seen in Table 14, there were two interactions that evidenced the same dream-type direction but that were attenuated by sample.

Table 15 lists the significant dream-type effects for activities. Consistent with the student analyses findings and with the hypotheses, lucid dreams were judged to have more auditory and cognitive activities than nonlucid dreams. Also as hypothesized but not evidenced in the prior analyses, lucid dreams had more physical activities than nonlucid ones. Unexpectedly, lucid dreams were judged to evidence significantly fewer location change activities than their counterparts.

Table 13. Percentage of Valid Cases for Descriptive Information on Samples[a]

Variable			Sample		
Type	Name	Categories	Students	Adults	Sleep lab
General demographics	Sex of subject	Males	40%	40%	50%
		Females	60%	60%	50%
		Cases[b]	413	125	10
	Race	White	98%	97%	100%
		Nonwhite	2%	3%	0%
		Cases	275	122	10
	Age	≤16–19	69%	6%	0%
		20–25	29%	25%	20%
		26–30	5%	22%	10%
		31–40	1%	32%	60%
		41–55	<1%	13%	10%
		56+	0%	2%	0%
		Cases	407	122	10
	Community size	Rural	50%	33%	0%
		Urban	50%	67%	100%
		Cases	409	122	9
Family	Marital status	Married	6%	32%	50%
		Single	92%	55%	50%
		Divorced/widowed	2%	12%	0%
		Cases	404	121	10
	Number of children	0	95%	66%	80%
		1	2%	9%	10%
		2	1%	15%	10%
		3+	1%	10%	0%
		Cases	432	121	10

Birth order	First	28%	44%	30%
	Later	72%	56%	70%
	Cases	409	122	10
Education	College major			
	Social science	17%	15%	10%
	Education	20%	6%	10%
	Humanities	1%	10%	10%
	Business	40%	10%	0%
	Physical science	7%	26%	50%
	Arts	4%	17%	20%
	Cases	332	98	10
	Highest degree			
	High school	0%	14%	0%
	Some college	100%	35%	10%
	Vocational certificate	0%	6%	0%
	Bachelors	0%	20%	20%
	Some graduate	0%	9%	0%
	Graduate degree	0%	16%	70%
	Cases	403	120	10
Political/religious orientation	Political beliefs			
	Liberal	28%	52%	89%
	Moderate	53%	38%	11%
	Conservative	18%	10%	0%
	Cases	399	120	9
	Self-religiosity			
	High	50%	23%	30%
	Moderate	37%	42%	40%
	Low	13%	35%	30%
	Cases	405	122	10

(continued)

Table 13. (Continued)

| Type | Variable | | | Sample | | |
	Name	Categories		Students	Adults	Sleep lab
	Religious affiliation	Protestant		56%	24%	10%
		Catholic		36%	13%	10%
		Jewish		1%	3%	0%
		Agnostic/atheist		3%	19%	10%
		Other		5%	40%	70%
		Cases		385	123	10
	Currently meditating	Yes		6%	39%	44%
		No		94%	61%	56%
		Cases		398	122	9
Health	Colds frequency	Frequently		26%	6%	0%
		Infrequently		74%	94%	100%
		Cases		415	122	10
	Smoking	Never		82%	74%	90%
		Sometimes		17%	21%	10%
		Often		1%	5%	0%
		Cases		413	123	10
	Alcohol	Never		9%	19%	30%
		Sometimes		90%	80%	70%
		Often		1%	1%	0%
		Cases		414	123	10

Exercise	Never	12%	29%	10%
	Sometimes	65%	51%	60%
	Often	23%	20%	30%
	Cases	412	122	10
General	Good	86%	85%	100%
	Fair	14%	14%	0%
	Poor	<1%	1%	0%
	Cases	397	121	9

[a]It should be noted that, for the student and adult samples, these figures are for the population from which the dreams were drawn.
[b]Total valid cases for each sample for each variable.

Table 14. Selected Adjusted Means and F-Ratios for Character Subscales on Student, Adult, and Sleep Lab Samples

	Adjusted means						
	Lucid			Nonlucid			
	Lab	Adult	Student	Lab	Adult	Student	F-ratios[a]
Sex							
Female		0.85			1.07		$F(1,357) = 4.72, p<.031$
	0.89	0.86	0.83	1.20	1.29	1.04	$F(2,357) = 0.81$, n.s.
Joint sex		0.14			0.42		$F(1,357) = 20.47, p<.0001$
	0.19	0.13	0.13	0.00	0.43	0.44	$F(2,357) = 1.14$, n.s.
Number							
Single		1.77			2.08		$F(1,357) = 6.52, p<.011$
	2.28	1.63	1.74	3.00	1.57	2.07	$F(2,357) = 1.51$, n.s.
Group		0.50			0.77		$F(1,357) = 7.86, p<.005$
	1.03	0.42	0.40	0.20	0.71	0.80	$F(2,357) = 1.74$, n.s.
Age							
Adult		1.65			2.15		$F(1,357) = 8.54, p<.007$
	1.89	1.53	1.68	2.40	1.14	2.21	$F(2,357) = 1.77$, n.s.
Identity							
Father		0.02			0.07		$F(1,359) = 7.37, p<.007$
	0.03	0.03	0.01	0.20	0.00	0.07	$F(2,359) = 1.69$, n.s.
Mother		0.02			0.05		$F(1,359) = 3.89, p<.049$
	0.03	0.02	0.01	0.00	0.14	0.04	$F(2,359) = 1.39$, n.s.
Parent		0.01			0.01		$F(1,359) = 0.36$, n.s.
	0.00	0.01	0.01	0.00	0.14	0.00	$F(2,359) = 7.45, p<.001$
Son		0.01			0.01		$F(1,359) = 0.00$, n.s.
	0.00	0.00	0.02	0.20	0.00	0.00	$F(2,359) = 6.89, p<.001$
Family		0.02			0.11		$F(1,359) = 9.62, p<.002$
	0.00	0.01	0.03	0.00	0.14	0.12	$F(2,359) = 0.53$, n.s.

[a]Top = dream main effect. Bottom = dream × sample.

Significant dream-type effects for the scoring categories of social interactions, achievements, and emotions are presented in Table 16. Consistent with the student analyses, lucid dreams in these analyses were judged to have fewer friendly verbal interactions and happy emotions than nonlucid dreams. The dream-type-by-sample interaction for friendly covert interactions is entirely accounted for by the nonlucid dreams collected in the sleep laboratory. They were judged to be higher in this type of social interaction than any of the other types of dreams. As regards the achievement success and failure interactions, they were also virtually entirely encounted for by the sleep-laboratory-collected lucid dreams.

The next set of analyses of covariance resulted in many more significant effects involving dreams than those computed for the students alone. Specifical-

Table 15. Selected Adjusted Means and F-Ratios for Character Subscales on Student, Adult, and Sleep Lab Samples

	Adjusted means						
	Lucid			Nonlucid			
	Lab	Adult	Student	Lab	Adult	Student	F-ratios[a]
Physical		1.52			0.78		$F(1,357) = 8.39, p<.004$
	5.42	0.93	0.84	0.40	0.71	0.80	$F(2,357) = 15.30, p<.0001$
Location change		0.45			0.51		$F(1,357) = 6.48, p<.011$
	1.14	0.58	0.13	0.20	0.43	0.54	$F(2,357) = 2.72$, n.s.
Auditory		0.14			0.02		$F(1,357) = 5.26, p<.022$
	0.28	0.13	0.10	0.00	0.00	0.02	$F(2,357) = 0.16$, n.s.
Cognitive		0.96			0.32		$F(1,357) = 15.66, p<.0001$
	3.17	0.52	0.68	2.00	0.00	0.25	$F(2,357) = 0.66$, n.s.

[a]Top = dream main effect. Bottom = dream × sample.

Table 16. Selected Adjusted Means and F-Ratios for Social Interactions, Achievements and Emotions Subscales on Student, Adult, and Sleep Lab Samples

	Adjusted means						
	Lucid			Nonlucid			
	Lab	Adult	Student	Lab	Adult	Student	F-ratios[a]
Social interactions							
Friendly verbal		0.07			0.17		$F(1,357) = 6.15, p<.014$
	0.17	0.08	0.04	0.04	0.00	0.17	$F(2,357) = 1.93$, n.s.
Friendly covert		0.03			0.04		$F(1,357) = 0.11$, n.s.
	0.03	0.02	0.03	0.20	0.00	0.03	$F(2,357) = 3.05, p<.049$
Achievements							
Success		0.49			0.25		$F(1,357) = 0.07$, n.s.
	2.11	0.39	0.08	0.20	0.00	0.27	$F(2,357) = 13.20, p<.0001$
Failure		0.24			0.13		$F(1,357) = 1.18$, n.s.
	1.03	0.09	0.13	0.00	0.14	0.14	$F(2,357) = 5.02, p<.007$
Emotions							
Happy		0.13			0.21		$F(1,357) = 4.69, p<.031$
	0.22	0.18	0.06	0.20	0.00	0.22	$F(2,357) = 1.46$, n.s.

[a]Top = dream main effect. Bottom = dream × sample.

ly, as can be seen in Table 17, consistent with the previous analyses, fewer intense modifiers were judged to be present in the lucid than in the nonlucid dreams across sample. Additionally, lucid dreams were judged to have fewer achromatic modifiers and negative prefixes than nonlucid dreamers. Again, there does not appear to be a positive or negative valenced trend in these analyses. As before, the three interactions are accounted for by the sleep laboratory dreams.

Finally, Table 18 lists the adjusted means and F-ratios for the covariance analyses on Bizarreness scales and the three miscellaneous scales. The bizarreness findings are primarily sample × dream-type interactions such that the lucid dreams collected in the sleep laboratory were judged to be the most bizarre. This is surprising when one considers that the literature clearly indicates that dreams collected in the sleep laboratory are generally less bizarre than those collected at home (Cartwright & Kaszniak, 1978).

Interactions also dominated the miscellaneous scale analyses. For dream control and palpable sensations, sleep laboratory dreams accounted for the interactions with lucid dreams, evidencing more of each quality. Such was also the case for the adult dreams for dream control; in fact, the highest levels of dream control were judged to be for the lucid dreams collected from the adults. The interaction for balance was in the same direction for the student sample as occurred in the student analyses but was opposite, and in the expected direction,

Table 17. Selected Adjusted Means and F-Ratios for Descriptive Elements Subscales of Student, Adult, and Sleep Lab Samples

	Adjusted means						
	Lucid			Nonlucid			
	Lab	Adult	Student	Lab	Adult	Student	F-ratios[a]
Modifiers							
Achromatic		0.07			0.21		$F(1,356) = 4.46, p<.035$
	0.17	0.11	0.01	0.00	0.14	0.22	$F(2,356) = 0.19$, n.s.
Intense		0.04			0.20		$F(1,356) = 4.73, p<.03$
	0.08	0.06	0.02	0.20	0.00	0.21	$F(2,356) = 0.44$, n.s.
Weak		0.07			0.10		$F(1,357) = 1.11$, n.s.
	0.17	0.05	0.06	0.40	0.00	0.09	$F(2,357) = 3.04, p<.049$
Empty		0.11			0.02		$F(1,357) = 2.22$, n.s.
	0.58	0.01	0.04	0.00	0.00	0.02	$F(2,357) = 3.73, p<.025$
Fast		0.10			0.07		$F(1,356) = 0.07$, n.s.
	0.47	0.06	0.02	0.00	0.14	0.06	$F(2,356) = 3.34, p<.037$
Negatives							
Prefixes		0.44			1.39		$F(1,357) = 4.03, p<.046$
	2.33	0.23	0.04	2.20	0.00	1.45	$F(2,357) = 0.17$, n.s.

[a]Top = dream main effect. Bottom = dream × sample.

Table 18. Selected Adjusted Means and F-Ratios for Bizarreness and Miscellaneous Subscales of Student, Adult, and Sleep Lab Samples

| | Adjusted means | | | | | | F-ratios[a] |
| | Lucid | | | Nonlucid | | | |
	Lab	Adult	Student	Lab	Adult	Student	
Bizarreness							
Animate characters sum score	1.53	0.47	0.24	0.40	0.33	0.35	$F_{(1,357)} = 0.14$, n.s. $F_{(2,357)} = 4.64$, $p<.01$
1. Appearance in a dream of monsters and alien beings	0.06	0.07	0.05	0.00	0.00	0.00	$F_{(1,357)} = 4.00$, $p<.046$ $F_{(2,357)} = 0.07$, n.s.
2. Impossible acts or magic by animate characters	0.53	0.17	0.03	0.00	0.03	0.03	$F_{(1,357)} = 0.96$, n.s. $F_{(2,357)} = 4.54$, $p<.011$
Dream transformation sum score	0.89	0.19	0.03	0.20	0.11	0.12	$F_{(1,357)} = 0.02$, n.s. $F_{(2,357)} = 2.89$, $p<.057$
1. A person suddenly appears or vanishes, but the entire dream scene is unaltered	0.22	0.13	0.01	0.00	0.01	0.01	$F_{(1,357)} = 0.47$, n.s. $F_{(2,357)} = 3.03$, $p<.05$
Miscellaneous scales[b]							
1. Palpable sensations	2.19	1.42	1.16	0.00	1.21	1.27	$F_{(1,357)} = 0.63$, n.s. $F_{(2,357)} = 5.06$, $p<.007$
2. Dream control	5.22	6.66	5.41	0.00	5.67	6.16	$F_{(1,357)} = 0.64$, n.s. $F_{(2,357)} = 14.15$, $p<.0001$
3. Physical, emotional, or intellectual balance	3.94	4.98	5.13	0.20	6.56	7.32	$F_{(1,357)} = 2.75$, n.s. $F_{(2,357)} = 5.13$, $p<.006$

[a] Top = dream main effect. Bottom = dream × sample.
[b] Unlike the other scales, which are frequency counts, with palpable control and balance the judge was asked to make an evaluation along a 10-point scale (3-point scale for palpable) with a high score representing a lot of that quality in the dream.

for the adults and for the sleep-laboratory lucid dreams. That is, for the two adult samples, balance was more prevelent in their lucid than in their nonlucid dreams.

To summarize the results with the sample analyses, consistent with the student analyses, lucid dreams were evaluated as having fewer characters, friendly verbal social interactions, happy emotions, and intense modifiers and more auditory and cognitive activities than nonlucid dreams.

CONCLUSIONS

The purpose of this chapter was to review the research examining differences in content between lucid and nonlucid dreams. This review covered two types of data—self-evaluations of the content by the dreamer as well as content evaluations by independent judges. The latter were new data not presented elsewhere. Both approaches were largely descriptive of the manifest level of content, although it could be argued that the self-evaluations involve some part of the latent content through the subjects' need to describe their own experience.

Before considering the differences between lucid and nonlucid dreams, it should be pointed out that lucid dreams are more *like* nonlucid dreams than different. Although the differences are few, they are not due to chance variations but are consistent across a variety of studies.

Consistent differences from the self-evaluations involve auditory and kinesthetic dream sensations and dream control as particularly characteristic of the lucid dream experience. Consistent with these self-observations are the findings from independent judges of dream lucidity as having more auditory and cognitive activities. Not evaluated in the self-observation studies was the role of characters. In the judges' evaluations across samples, sex, and dream collection method, lucid dreams had fewer characters. Although other dream-type differences emerged in the various studies, the most compelling differences are clearly in the auditory/cognitive domain.

REFERENCES

Cartwright, R., & Kaszniak, A. (1978). The social psychology of dream reporting. In A. Arkin, J. Antrobus, & S. Ellman (Eds.), *The mind in sleep*. Hillsdale, NJ; Erlbaum.

Domhoff, G. W. (1962). *A quantitative study of dream content using an objective indicator of dreaming*. Unpublished doctoral dissertation, University of Miami.

Feldman, R. (1985). *Social psychology: Theories, research and application*. New York: McGraw-Hill.

Fenwick, P. B. C., Schatzman, M., Worsley, A., Adams, J., Stone, S., & Baker, A. (1984). Lucid dreaming: Correspondence between dreamed and actual events in our subject during REM sleep. *Biological Psychology, 18*, 243–252.

Foulkes, D. (1985). Dreaming: Lucid and non. *Lucidity Letter, 4*(1), 2–4.

Gackenbach, J. I. (1978). *A personality and cognitive style analysis of lucid dreaming.* Unpublished doctoral dissertation, Virginia Commonwealth University.

Gackenbach, J. I. (1981). [Mass testing]. Unpublished raw data.

Gackenbach, J. I. (1982). Differences between types of lucid dreams. *Lucidity Letter, 1*(4), 11–12.

Gackenbach, J. I., & LaBerge, S. (1986). An overview of lucid dreaming. In A. A. Sheikh (Ed.), *International review of mental imagery: Vol. 2* (pp. 57–89). New York: Human Sciences Press.

Gackenbach, J. I., & Schillig, B. (1983). Lucid dreams: The content of conscious awareness of dreaming during the dream. *Journal of Mental Imagery, 7*(2), 1–14.

Gackenbach, J. I., Curren, R., LaBerge, S., Davidson, D., & Maxwell, P. (1983, June). *Intelligence, creativity, and personality differences between individuals who vary in self-reported lucid dreaming frequency.* Paper presented at the annual meeting of the American Association for the Study of Mental Imagery, Vancouver.

Gackenbach, J. I., Curren, R., & Cutler, G. (1983, June). *Presleep determinants and post-sleep results of lucid versus vivid dreams.* Paper presented at the annual meeting of the American Association for the Study of Mental Imagery, Vancounver.

Gackenbach, J. I., Snyder, T. J., Sachau, D., & Rokes, L. (1986). *Lucid dreaming frequency in relation to static and dynamic gross motor balance.* Manuscript submitted for publication.

Gackenbach, J. I., Snyder, T. J., Rokes, L., & Sachau, D. (1986a). Lucid dream frequency in relationship to vestibular sensitivity as measured by caloric stimulation. *Cognition and Dream Research: The Journal of Mind and Behavior, 7*(2,3), 277–298.

Garfield, P. (1975). Psychological concomitants of the lucid dream state. *Sleep Research, 4,* 183.

Green, Celia. (1968). *Lucid dreams.* London: Hamish Hamilton.

Hall, C. S., & Van de Castle, R. (1966). *The content analysis of dreams.* New York: Appleton-Century-Crofts.

Hall, C. S., Domhoff, G. W., Blick, K. A., & Weesner, K. E. (1982). The dreams of college men and women in 1950 and 1980: A comparison of dream contents and sex differences. *Sleep, 5*(2), 188–194.

Hearne, K. M. T. (1978). *Lucid dreams: An electrophysiological and psychological study.* Unpublished doctoral dissertation, University of Liverpool.

Hearne, K. M. T. (1981). A ''light-switch'' phenomenon in lucid dreams. *Journal of Mental Imagery, 5,* 97–100.

Hearne, K. M. T. (1983). Features of lucid dreams: Questionnaire data and content analyses (1). *Journal of Lucid Dream Research, 1*(1), 3–20.

Hoffman, E., & McCarley, R. W. (1980). Bizarreness and lucidity in REM sleep dreams. A quantitative analysis. *Sleep Research, 9,* 134.

LaBerge, S. P. (1980a). *Lucid dreaming: An exploratory study of consciousness during sleep.* Unpublished doctoral dissertation, Stanford University.

LaBerge, S. P. (1980b). Lucid dreaming as a learnable skill: A case study. *Perceptual and Motor Skills, 51,* 1039–1042.

LaBerge, S. P. (1985). *Lucid dreaming.* Los Angeles: Jeremy Tarcher.

LaBerge, S. P., Nagel, L. E., Dement, W. C., & Zarcone, V. P. (1981). Lucid dreaming verified by volitional communication during REM sleep. *Perceptual and Motor Skills, 52,* 727–732.

Maccoby, E. E., & Jacklin, C. N. (1974). *The psychology of sex differences.* Stanford, CA.: Stanford University Press.

Moers-Messmer, H. (1938). Dreaming while knowing about the dream state. *Archiv fur dio Gesamte Psychologie, 102,* 291–318.

Ogilvie, R., Hunt, H., Tyson, P. D., Lucescu, M. L., & Jeakins, D. B. (1982). Lucid dreaming and alpha activity: A preliminary report. *Perceptual and Motor Skills, 55,* 795–808.

Ouspensky, P. (1931). *A new model of the universe.* London: Routledge & Kegan Paul.

Webb, W. B. (1979). A historical perspective of dreams. In B. B. Wolman (Ed.), *Handbook of dreams: Research theories and applications.* New York: Van Nostrand Reinhold Co.

Wilmes, F. (1983). Editor's note. *Lucidity Letter, 2*(3), 5.

Winget, C., & Kramer, M. (1979). *Dimensions of dreams.* Gainesville: University of Florida Press.

Worsley, A. (1982). Alan Worsley's work on lucid dreaming. *Lucidity Letter, 1*(4), 1–3.

Worsley, A. (1983). Comments on an investigation of the relative degree of activation in lucid dreams. *Lucidity Letter, 2*(4),5.

Individual Differences Associated with Lucid Dreaming

THOMAS J. SNYDER and JAYNE GACKENBACH

Lucid dreaming has been said to be within the capability of all individuals (LaBerge, 1985). Based on analyses of the incidence of this dream experience among university students and among persons with an expressed interest in dreaming, a majority have reported experiencing at least one lucid dream during their lifetime, and about 20% have reported experiencing lucid dreams with relative frequency. Our goal in this chapter is to describe and to integrate what has been learned through research about individuals who experience lucid dreams. To this end we will present data derived from the study of four separable but not unrelated functional domains for which subject differences associated with lucid dreaming, or lucidity, have been found. These functional domains are (1) oculomotor/equilibratory; (2) visual/imaginal; (3) intellectual/creative, and (4) personal/interpersonal. The extent of individual differences in lucid dreaming and the methods by which these differences have been investigated will also be discussed. Because methodology is an integral part of research into individual differences, methodological considerations will first be presented.

METHODOLOGY

There are two general methodological considerations that pertain to individual differences associated with lucid dreaming. The first is conceptual and is related to the definition of lucid dreaming, the extent to which subjects understand that definition, and the measurement of lucidity. The second is procedural

THOMAS J. SNYDER • Developmental Disabilities Center, University of Alberta, Edmonton, Alberta, Canada 76G 2EI. JAYNE GACKENBACH • Department of Psychology, University of Northern Iowa, Cedar Falls, IA 50614–0505.

and has to do with the research designs by which individual differences in lucidity have been investigated as well as with subject factors that, if not taken into account, can obscure these differences. In Tables 1 and 2 can be found the methodological details of many of the studies referred to in this chapter.

In the study of individual differences in lucid dreaming, it has been useful to identify and rank persons according to the prevalence and frequency of their lucidity. Such classification has been accomplished through various self-report measures and is based on the belief that lucidity is best conceptualized as a function of act frequency, an approach that has been utilized by Buss and Craik (1983) to conceptualize individual differences in personality. Gackenbach (1978), for example, has classified subjects according to their frequency of lucidity as frequent lucid dreamers ($>$ one/month), infrequent lucid dreamers ($<$ one/month), or nonlucid dreamers and has then compared these groups for an assortment of behavioral characteristics. Because classification of subjects into dreamer groups has usually been based on subject self-report of lucidity frequency, there are two questions that must be addressed if such a classification scheme is to be used. First, how can researchers be confident that subjects who self-report lucidity have, in fact, experienced lucid dreaming? Second, how comparable are the different means that have been used to assess lucidity?

As our research into the differential psychology of lucid dreamers was pursued, it quickly became apparent that potential subjects often misunderstood the nature of lucid dreams (Gackenbach, 1986). Confusion with morning-after dream recall was frequently encountered, and we consequently formulated a process by which it could be verified that persons who reported lucidity had indeed experienced lucidity, that is, demonstrated "content" validity. Verification was accomplished by gathering from all potential subjects a very recent or especially salient dream transcript that ostensibly exemplified a lucid dream. Persons were instructed to be certain to include information about how they, in fact, knew they were dreaming lucidly. A recognition phrase, such as "then I realized it was only a dream," was judged as evidence of verification. Illustrative of the "hit rate" with this verification process is a mass testing of 707 university students of whom 344 were disqualified because their dream transcripts were judged to include dreams that were questionably lucid, partially lucid, or clearly not lucid (Gackenbach, Sachau, & Rokes, 1982; Gackenbach, 1980).

Although a verification process addresses the issue of the quality of self-reported lucid dreams, the classification of persons according to the frequency of lucid dreaming raises the issue of concurrent validity, that is, to what extent is the frequency of self-reported lucidity related to other indexes of lucid dreaming? Two indexes of lucidity other than self-report have been studied—signaled lucidity in the sleep laboratory and lucidity recorded in dream diaries. As in the general dream recall literature (Cartwright, 1978), correlations between the different indexes of dreaming, in this case lucid dreaming, have been found to be variable. Gackenbach (1978), for high dream recall adults, compared self-reported lucidity with dream diary lucidity and found that persons who reported that they frequently dreamed lucidly recorded more lucid dreams than did persons who reported infrequently or never experiencing lucidity. Though these three groups did not differ with regard to the total number of dreams reported, frequent lucid dreamers were found to record more information per dream, that is, to demonstrate greater dream recall than infrequents and nonlucids.

In a more recent study with self-selected adult subjects, Gackenbach, Curren, LaBerge, Davidson, and Maxwell (1983) have found significant positive correlations between self-reported estimates of lucidity and dream diary frequency of lucidity (males $r = .79$, females $r = .55$). Similarly, Kueny (1985), using self-selected adults for whom dream recall and verification of understanding were controlled, has reported a significant positive correlation between one self-report estimate of lucidity and frequency of lucidity in a dream diary ($r = .54$). The results from these studies enable us to conclude that, for self-selected adults, the relationship between self-report estimates of lucid frequency and dream diary lucid frequency is clearly positive, provided dream recall and verification are controlled for. In contrast, among randomly selected university students, Gackenbach, Curren, and Cutler (1983) obtained equivocal results when they compared lucid frequency as measured with three self-report scales to that reported in dream diaries. Using extent of dream recall as a covariate, significant positive correlations that ranged from .20 to .60 were found; however, reanalysis after subjects were screened for verification of understanding revealed that only one self-report scale correlated positively with dream frequency.

Kueny (1985) is the only investigator who has examined the relationship between self-report, dream diary, and laboratory-signaled estimates of lucidity frequency. For a small sample of adults ($N = 16$), she has reported that neither self-report nor dream diary frequencies were predictive of the frequency of signal-verified lucid dreams in the laboratory, though, as previously stated, self-report and dream diary estimates were found to be significantly correlated ($r = .54$). Despite the absence of a significant correlation between self-report indexes and sleep laboratory lucid dreaming in Kueny's data, it should be kept in mind that in most (LaBerge, 1985; Fenwick et al., 1984; Ogilvie, Hunt, Kushniruk, & Newman, 1983) but not all (Dane, 1984) sleep laboratory studies of lucidity, subjects who have been selected according to self-reported lucidity have successfully signaled the lucidity process.

In addition to these issues involving the validity of subject reports of lucidity, there are a number of procedural considerations that must be taken into account in order to study individual differences in lucid dreaming ability. Several subject characteristics (dream recall efficiency, sex) and sampling procedures (random, self-selected) have already been referred to. The confounding nature of general dream recall with self-reported lucidity frequency has been noted by many investigators (Belicki, Hunt, & Belicki, 1978; Gackenbach, 1978;

Table 1. Methodological Comparisons of Lucid Dreaming Frequency Estimates and Controls for Selected Individual Difference Studies

Reference	Lucid dreaming frequency estimate	Understanding verification	Controls[a]	
			Dream recall	Other
Belicki & Hunt, 1978	Self-report frequency	No[b]	No[c]	
Blackmore, 1984	Self-report frequency	No	No	
Gackenbach, 1978	(1) Dream diary. (2) Self-report frequency	No[b]	No	
Gackenbach, 1980	Self-report frequency	Yes	Self-report frequency	Social desirability
Gackenbach, 1983	Self-report frequency	Yes	Self-report frequency	Social desirability
Gackenbach, 1984a	Self-report frequency	Yes	Self-report frequency	Self-report religiosity, Self-report creativity
Gackenbach, 1984b	Self-report frequency	Yes	Self-report frequency	Social desirability
Gackenbach, 1985a	Self-report frequency	Yes	Self-report frequency	Handedness, Related physical
Gackenbach, 1986	Study 1: Self-report frequency, Study 2: Self-report frequency	No[b], Yes	No, No	
Gackenbach, Curren, LaBerge, Davidson, & Maxwell, 1983	(1) Dream diary. (2) Self-report frequency	Yes	(1) Dream diary; (2) Self-report frequency	Social desirability, educational attainment and sex-role identity (as appropriate)
Gackenbach & Hammons, 1983	Self-report frequency	No	No	
Gackenbach, Heilman, Boyt, & LaBerge, 1985	Study 1: Self-report frequency, Study 2: Self-report frequency, Study 3: Self-report frequency	No, Yes, Yes	No, No, Self-report frequency	Handedness
Gackenbach, Snyder, Rokes, & Sachau, 1986	Self-report frequency	Yes	Self-report frequency	Handedness, related physical problems, eye-movement direction

Study				
Gackenbach, Sachau, Rokes, & Snyder, 1986	Self-report frequency	Yes	Self-report frequency	Handedness; Related physical
Gackenbach, Snyder, & Esbeck, 1981	Self-report frequency	Yes	Self-report frequency	Handedness
Gackenbach, Snyder, McKelvey, McWilliams, George, & Rodenelli, 1981	Self-report frequency	Yes	No	
Gackenbach, Snyder, & Vognsen, 1981	(1) Dream diary. (2) Self-report frequency	Yes	Self-report frequency	Handedness
Hearne, 1978	Ch. 15: Self-report frequency Ch. 16: Self-report frequency	No No No	No No No	
Hearne, 1983	Self-report frequency			
Kueny, 1985	(1) Signal verified in sleep lab. (2) Dream diary. (3) Self-report frequency	Yes	(1) Dream diary; (2) Self-report frequency	Motivation to learn to dream lucidly
LaBerge & Gackenbach, 1982	(1) Dream diary. (2) Self-report frequency	Yes	Self-report frequency	
Reed, 1977	Dream diary	No[b]	No	
Snyder & Gackenbach, 1981	Self-report frequency	No	No	Consistency in right or left handedness

[a] Although information may have been obtained on these variables, it is only indicated as present if it was used as control in either experimental design or statistical evaluation.
[b] Due to the nature of the sample or procedures, it is unlikely that the degree of confusion over what is a lucid dream, often found, was present here.
[c] Although recall was not used as a control, lucid-nonlucid differences in dream diary dream recall were found.

Table 2. Methodological Comparisons of Type of Subject, Procedure, and Statistical Analyses for Selected Individual Difference Studies

Reference	Type of subject Sex/N	Type of subject Sample	Procedure	Major type of statistical analyses
Belicki & Hunt, 1978	$N=58$	Canadian college students	Personally administered questionnaire	t-test
Blackmore, 1984	$N=314$	English adults	Mail survey with untimed questionnaire	Chi-square
Gackenbach, 1978	$M=22$ $F=68$	Adults highly interested in dreams	Mail survey with both timed and untimed scales. Several years earlier other scales filled out and month-long dream diary kept.	Factor analysis followed by one-way analyses of variance on factor scores.
Gackenbach, 1980	$M=186^a$ $F=174$	Students at a midwestern university	Administration of a packet of questionnaires to groups.	Analysis of variance
Gackenbach, 1983	$M=47^a$ $F=117$	Students at a midwestern university	Administration of a packet of questionnaires to groups.	Partial correlation
Gackenbach, 1984a	$M=51^a$ $F=84$	Students at a midwestern university	Administration of timed and untimed questionnaires to groups	Partial correlation
Gackenbach, 1984b	$M=17$ $F=22$	Students at a midwestern university	Administration of a packet of questionnaires in one group	Partial correlation
Gackenbach, 1985a	$M=40$ $F=40$	Students at a midwestern university	10 trials of eye dominance; administration of eye-movement questions from behind subject and scored from videotape	Analysis of covariance
Gackenbach, 1986	$M=22$ $F=68$	Adults with high dream interest	Mail survey with timed scales	Factor analysis followed by one-way analysis of variance on factor scores
	$M=34$ $F=92$	Students at eastern college	Administered scales in groups	Analysis of variance

Study	Sample size	Population	Measure	Analysis
Gackenbach, Curren, LaBerge, Davidson, & Maxwell, 1983	M=81, F=102	Adults responding to magazine articles on lucid dreaming	Mail survey with both timed and untimed scales and 7- to 10-day dream diary	Partial correlation
Gackenbach & Hammons, 1983	M=59, F=93	Students at a midwestern university	Group administered timed and untimed tests	Analysis of variance
Gackenbach, Heilman, Boyt, & LaBerge, 1985	M=22, F=68	Adults with high dream interest	Mail survey on timed test	Analysis of variance
	M=40, F=41	Students at an eastern college	Experimenter-administered scale	Analysis of variance
	M=54, F=53	Students at a midwestern university	Experimenter-administered scale and task	Analysis of covariance
Gackenbach, Snyder, Rokes, & Sachau, 1986	M=24, F=24	Students at a midwestern university	Caloric irrigation to measure electronystagmography response	Analyses of covariance
Gackenbach, Sachau, Rokes, & Snyder, 1986	M=72, F=72	Students at a midwestern university	Balance beam and stabilometer performance under different visual conditions	Analyses of covariance
Gackenbach, Snyder, & Esbeck, 1981	M=57, F=58	Students at a midwestern university	Performance on a visual maze	Analysis of covariance
Gackenbach, Snyder, McKelvey, McWilliams, George, & Rodenelli, 1981	M=45[a], F=45	Students at an eastern college	Admin. of paper-and-pencil and performance-based perceptual tasks	Analysis of variance
Gackenbach, Snyder, & Vognsen, 1981	M=58, F=60	Students at a midwestern university	Performance on a tactile maze, trail-making task and form board	Analysis of covariance
Hearne, 1978	M=24[a], F=24	Students at an English university	Individually administered questionnaires	Correlation
	M=10, F=10	Students at an English university	Individually administered questionnaire and task	t-test

(continued)

Table 2. (Continued)

Reference	Type of subject		Procedure	Major type of statistical analyses
	Sex/N	Sample		
Hearne, 1983	$M=63$ $F=16$	English adults with high lucidity interest	Mail survey with untimed questionnaire	Descriptive
Kueny, 1985	$M=13^a$ $F=27$	West Coast adults with high lucidity interest	Group-administered hypnotic induction and other timed and untimed scales	Partial correlation
LaBerge & Gackenbach, 1982	$N=23$	Students at a West Coast university	Administration of untimed questionnaire to a group	Partial correlation
Reed, 1977	$N=300$	English adults with high dream interest	Mail survey of month-long dream diary	Chi-square
Snyder & Gackenbach, 1981	$F=48$	Students at an eastern college	Sequence manual tapping	Analysis of variance

^{a}Number of males and females varied with this figure as a maximum for each task/questionnaire.

Gackenbach, Heilman, Boyt, & LaBerge, 1985; Gackenbach, Sachau, & Rokes, 1982; Gackenbach & Schilling, 1983; Hearne, 1978; Palmer, 1974). Use of dream recall as a covariate with lucid frequency, preferably with parallel estimates of both, for example, self-reported or dream diary counts for both, is essential. Other covariates will be needed according to the types of evaluation techniques employed. Personality measures that can be biased in terms of social desirability may require measures of social desirability as controls (Crowne & Marlowe, 1961), whereas cognitive measures may need to be covaried with relevant variables like extent of education in order to assure accurate statements about individual and group differences. Because the studies reported in the remainder of this chapter differ in the extent to which these methodological controls have been incorporated, these studies should not be viewed comparably. Methodological incongruances will be pointed out as relevant.

LUCID DREAMING INCIDENCE

The incidence of lucid dreaming has been measured in terms of prevalence (how many people have ever had at least one lucid dream) and frequency (how often does an individual experience lucid dreams). The prevalence of lucid dreaming among students (Palmer, 1974; LaBerge, 1985; Gackenbach, Snyder, Rokes, & Sachau, 1986) and adults (Palmer, 1974; Kohr, 1980; Blackmore, 1983, 1984; Gackenbach, Curren, LaBerge, Davidson, and Maxwell, 1983) is reported in seven surveys. For adults, estimates have ranged from 100% (Gackenbach, Curren, LaBerge, Davidson, & Maxwell, 1983) to 47% (Blackmore, 1983, 1984). This variability can be attributed to differences in sampling procedures. Kohr (1980), Gackenbach (1978), and Gackenbach and associates (Curren, LaBerge, Davidson, & Maxwell, 1983), who reported percentages of 70, 76, and 100, respectively, surveyed highly motivated adults with an expressed interest in dreaming. Palmer (1974) and Blackmore (1983, 1984), who reported that 55% and 47%, respectively, of the persons they surveyed stated they have had at least one lucid dream during their lifetime, randomly selected subjects from an alphabetized public record. It may be notable that Palmer and Blackmore did not verify their subjects' understanding of lucidity.

The prevalence of lucid dreaming among university students is similarly variable according to the sampling and validation procedures utilized. LaBerge (1985) has reported a 77% prevalence for students enrolled in a sleep and dreams class (i.e., nonrandom) with verified understanding of lucidity. Palmer (1974), for a randomly selected but nonverified sample of students, found a prevalence of 71.5%. If random sampling and verification of understanding as judged by independent raters is used, then a more conservative estimate of prevalence, 57.5%, has been obtained (Gackenbach, Snyder et al., 1986).

The frequency of lucid dreaming as a measure of incidence has been evaluated either through self-reported ratings or through the percentage of lucid dreams in dream diaries compiled in the laboratory or at home. To date, too few dream laboratory subjects have been studied in order to derive meaningful estimates of frequency from this source. Only self-report and at-home dream diary estimates are therefore reported. As for estimates of the prevalence of lucid dreaming, estimates of frequency will vary according to sample characteristics and validation procedures.

Self-report estimates of the frequency with which individuals dream lucidly have been reported for groups of adults and students. Gackenbach (1978) and associates (1987) have estimated that about 15% of adults surveyed dream lucidly more than once per month (13.5% and 16%, respectively), whereas 20.75% of students have been found to report this frequency (Gackenbach et al., 1987). Palmer (1974), using a random but nonverified sample, estimated that 28.5% of adults experience lucidity more than once a month, whereas Kohr's (1980) nonverified and nonrandom sample showed 21% experienced dreams more than monthly. For persons who self-report dreaming lucidly less often, that is, once or more in their lifetimes but less than once a month, estimates have varied from 36.55% to 60%. Gackenbach, Snyder et al. (1986) found that 36.55% of a randomly selected and verified student sample were classifiable as infrequent lucid dreamers; Palmer (1974) has reported a similar value (41%) for his random sample. Gackenbach's (1978) high estimate of 60% was found for self-selected adults for whom verification of lucidity understanding was not procured.

When the frequency of lucid dreaming is estimated by counting the number of lucid dreams in a dream diary, values relatively comparable to those obtained through self-report ratings have been found. For adults with decided interests in dreaming and for whom it had been verified that they understood the concept of lucidity, 13% of dreams in a log maintained for 7 to 10 days were judged to be lucid (Gackenbach, Curren et al., 1983). This same frequency has been reported for randomly selected and concept-verified university students who recorded dreams on a weekly basis for a 16-week period (Gackenbach, Curren, & Cutler, 1983).

In conclusion, conservative estimates of the incidence of lucid dreaming indicate that about 58% of the population have experienced a lucid dream at least once in their lifetime and that some 21% report such dreams more often (one or more per month). Additionally, about 13% of dreams recorded in dream diaries are likely to be lucid. The remainder of this chapter will be a review of what has been learned about the behavioral and personal characteristics of persons who do or do not dream lucidly.

OCULOMOTOR/EQUILIBRATORY DIFFERENCES

Oculomotor activities are a complex set of diverse movements subserved by cortical and subcortical structures involved in cognitive, sensoriperceptual, visuopractic, equilibratory, and affective functions. They include reflexive and non-reflexive movements, are signals of neural processing during sleep and wakefulness, and *in toto* are a window through which the afferent and efferent worlds of a person can be viewed. LaBerge (1985) has described the importance of eye movements for studying subject awareness of the lucid process in the sleep laboratory. Our concern, and that of others, has been whether eye movements might be indirectly used to view individual differences associated with the dream process, especially with lucidity. This concern has been engendered by consideration of the content of lucid dreams, by how lucidity events are experienced, and by the fact that eye movements have been useful for studying the cognitive and personal characteristics of persons during wakefulness. Our concern has also derived from the hypothesis that lucid dreaming is an organismic response, a response that is typical of some persons but not others because of psychophysiological differences between these persons. To what extent lucidity is an emergent process, that is, one that can be developed in any individual, is a question open to empirical investigation. Claims have been made that lucid dreaming is a unique process, that it can be exhilarating and uplifting, that it is an experience that can be clinically useful, that it affords a path to spirituality, greater self-awareness, and higher consciousness, and that it is a step in a hierarchy of out-of-body experiences. We believe that these claims can also be investigated scientifically. Hendricks and Cartwright (1978) have asked: "Are there stable individual differences in the cognitive style of the night as there are in waking mental activity?" (p. 292). They have answered in the affirmative. Our subsequent question: Is lucid dreaming a particular cognitive style of the night that is associated with stable individual differences in waking mental activity? The study of eye movements and postural orientation have provided some data for answering this question—also in the affirmative.

Two variations of eye movements have been studied with reference to lucid dreaming. Gackenbach, Snyder, Rokes, & Sachau (1986) have investigated differences in nystagmoid movements during rest and following vestibular stimulation of lucid and nonlucid dreamers, whereas these same investigators (Gackenbach, 1985a) have studied differences between dreamer groups for conjugate lateral eye movements during reflective mentation. In response to directions to look leftward, rightward, or forward with eyes opened or closed, a procedure that is used to establish baselines for nystagmographic analyses, frequent lucid dreamers have been shown to demonstrate leftward eye movement preference as measured by the average amplitude per beat on electronystagmographic (ENG) records; nonlucid dreamers and infrequent lucid dreamers were found to exhibit no directional preference (Gackenbach, Snyder *et al.*, 1986). This result, which is based on recordings of 16 lucid, 16 infrequently lucid, and 16 nonlucid dreamers, half of each sex and all prescreened for handedness, balance-related disorders, oculomotor/noncorrectable visual disturbances, and an understanding of lucidity, is suggestive that lucid dreamers may have asymmetrical activation of the brain, whereas nonlucid dreamers and persons who seldom experience lucid dreams tend to demonstrate bilaterally symmetrical activation in this circumstance.

In recent years, differential activation of the right and left sides of the brain, sometimes referred to as brainedness, or hemisphericity, has received much attention (sometimes too much!) and has been related to a host of organismic variables. Bakan (1971) has proposed that consistently directed conjugate lateral eye movements are indicative of disproportionate activation of the hemisphere contralateral to the direction of eye movements. Persons with a tendency to move their eyes leftward, that is, left movers, would accordingly tend to be subject to greater activation of the right hemisphere. Because we have found that lucid dreamers during a baseline nystagmographic procedure are left movers whereas other dreamer types are not, we have begun to investigate how this difference varies according to subject characteristics and experimental conditions. There is already an extensive literature in which ocular movements have been related to individual differences in cognitive processing, affect, and personal attributes. Most of this literature, which has been reviewed by Ehrlichman and Weinberger (1978), Gur and Gur (1980), and Owens and Limber (1983), among others, deals with the conjugate lateral eye movements that occur as a person reflects on questions asked of him or her. Although there is controversy about the usefulness of conjugate lateral eye movements for studying individual differences, controversy in part engendered by methodological differences and by the probability that these eye movements derive from more than one level of brain activation, such movements have been directly related to dreamer characteristics, for example, dream recall (Van Nuys, 1984), and indirectly to a set of personal characteristics associated with lucid dreamers. Persons who shift their gaze leftward following questioning have been shown to be sensitive to hypnotic susceptibility (Bakan, 1969; Dewitt & Averill, 1976; Gur & Gur, 1974), to clear mental imagery (Bakan, 1969), to daydreaming (Meskin & Singer, 1974), to high verbal abilities (Bakan, 1971), and to interference on the Stroop Test (Kaban & Shotland, 1969). Persons who experience lucid dreaming have been found to have these same sensitivities (Dane, 1984; Hearne, 1978; Gackenbach, Snyder, McKelvey, McWilliams, George, & Rodenelli, 1981; Gackenbach, Curren, La-Berge, Davidson, & Maxwell, 1983).

Convergent associations between the characteristics of lucid dreamers and those found for left movers would predict that persons who frequently experience lucid dreams should tend to direct their eyes leftward in response to questioning. However, because the direction of conjugate lateral eye movements of a person involved in reflective mentation can differ according to whether questions are asked by an examiner facing a person or by an examiner behind a person, this predicted leftward movement of lucid dreamers could vary according to circumstances. Lateral eye movements in response to inquiries by a confronting examiner probably are an intrapersonal response pattern with an affective component. These lateral eye movements can be modulated by the types of questions asked, for example, those that necessitate visualization rather than linguistic processing, and can be superceded if a confronting examiner is not present and eye movements are recorded inobtrusively. Some of the confusion over the validity of eye movements for making inferences about brain activity is due to the fact that the moderating effects of question type and examiner location have not been controlled or accounted for. To do so may allow for a more precise understanding of the cognitive-style dimensions encompassed by lateral eye movements. When university students who report frequently lucid dreaming ($n = 40$) have been compared to those who are nonlucid dreamers ($n = 40$) for the direction of gaze in response to a set of prototypic questions, it has been found that the videotaped eye-movement pattern of the nonlucids was bidirectional, whereas that for the lucid group was biased to the right (Gackenbach, 1985a). We are now in the process of comparing this result with eye-movement patterns evoked by confrontive examination. Inasmuch as some eye movements are an endogenous response pattern characteristic of an individual, that is, have the properties of a trait, whereas others in part derive from exogeneous factors like the type of question a person is asked to process, we would expect, according to our hypothesis that a proclivity for lucid dreaming is an organismic response pattern, that frequently lucids display a leftward eye-movement bias to confrontive questioning but not to nonconfrontive questioning. To date, our results with regard to this variant of eye movements are promising but inconclusive. Less ambiguous and more revealing have been the findings of a study in which the eye movements of lucid and nonlucid dreamers in response to caloric stimulation have been compared.

Gackenbach *et al.* (1982) and Gackenbach, Snyder *et al.* (1986) using bithermal caloric irrigation of the tympanic membranes, a procedure that is used clinically to induce nystagmus via stimulation of the vestibular system (McCabe & Ryu, 1979), have found frequent lucid dreamers to be more responsive to caloric irrigation than persons who never dream lucidly. This greater responsivity was manifest for two graphic measures of nystagmus (amplitude per beat and speed in the slow phase) and for three measures that imply diminished vestibular integrity (dysrhymthmia, directional preponderance, and canal paresis). It was also found that the onset and duration of self-reported vertigo in response to caloric irrigation differed for these dreamer groups in the same direction. Calorically induced nystagmic eye movements have particular relevance to dreaming because they are believed to be generated by a neural system that also subserves REM. McCarly and Hobson (1979) have proposed that intense vestibular activation of this system can be reflected in dream experiences, especially with regard to sensations of spinning and floating. These types of movement sensations have been specifically related to lucidity (Green, 1968; LaBerge, 1985) and Gackenbach, Sachau *et al.* (1986) and Gackenbach, Snyder *et al.* (1986) have proposed that the vestibular system of lucid dreamers is uniquely subject to intense activation during sleep, an activation that in part explains the saliency that the self-observations of pleasurable motility have in lucidity. Divergent validation of this proposal is afforded by the negative correlation between lucid frequency and the prevalence of signs of vestibular dysfunction (Gackenbach, Snyder et al., 1986) and by the aversive motion experiences reported for persons with known vestibular dysfunctions (Doneshka & Kehaiyov, 1978; Eisinger & Schilder, 1929).

The vestibular system is a multimodal one in which receptors in the eyes, skin, and joints, in addition to those in the vestibular apparatus, play an essential role in orientation and balance. Evidence that lucidity might involve a balance or postual component first became apparent to us through the factor analysis of the content of collected lucid dreams (Gackenbach, 1978). We subsequently undertook studies in which three manifestations of equilibratory functioning were investigated: (1) static balance, (2) dynamic balance, and (3) vestibular responsiveness to caloric irrigation. Because the field dependence–field independence construct was an individual difference variable known to be related to spatial orientation, we reasoned that measures of this cognitive-style construct could also be helpful for understanding the lucid process. The static balance of persons grouped according to their frequency of lucid dreaming was assessed with a stabilometer, whereas dynamic balance was assessed with a balance beam. Both tasks were performed under conditions of light, darkness, and distorted visual fields. After controlling for dream recall, body weight, balance-related dysfunctions, and the validity of lucidity, Gackenbach et al. (1982, 1986) determined that lucid dreamers spent more time in balance on a stabilometer than did infrequently lucid or nonlucid dreamers but that dreamer types did not differ for the speed and accuracy with which they walked a balance beam. Static balance is distinguished from dynamic balance by the latter's requiring translocation. One interpretation of the finding that lucidity may be related to static balance but not dynamic balance is that static balance more closely simulates the physical conditions of the dream state, one in which no physical displacement in space is objectively determinable. An alternative interpretation is that use of a balance beam precluded detection of differences because walking a balance beam is an easier task than maintaining stabilometer balance. Theoretically, we prefer the former interpretation, but methodologically we are not justified in our preference.

In relation to studies in which balance, orientation, and lucid dreaming have been investigated electronystagmographically and with the use of stabilometer and balance beam, is a positive association that has been found between field independence and the frequency of dreaming lucidly, an association that we have found particularly semiotic for viewing the lucid process from an holistic, organismic perspective. Witkin and his many collaboraters over the past 30 years have sought to understand the basis for the perception of the upright. This perception has been attributed to apprehension through vision, coordinated with apprehension through the vestibular, tactile, and kinesthetic senses, that is, with reference to the visual field around us and with reference to the direction of gravity (Witkin & Goodenough, 1981). Initial research with the Body Adjustment Test (BAT), the Rod and Frame Test (RFT), and the Rotating Room Test (RRT) indicated that, across these three situations, subjects tended to be self-consistent with regard to degree of reliance on the external visual field or on their own body for perception of the upright. As Witkin has pointed out (Witkin & Goodenough, 1981), primary reliance on the external field (field dependence) or on the body (field independence) could be advantageous under some circumstances but not others. For example, in the RFT, reliance on cues from the body leads to relatively accurate adjustments of the rod to the gravitational vertical, whereas in the RRT, reliance on bodily cues leads to relatively inaccurate adjustments. As research into field dependence/independence progressed, this construct was extended beyond its initial confines, first to be conceived as a perceptual-analytical ability that pervades an individual's perceptual functioning, then to include elements of intellectual functioning, then to encompass personality characteristics like self-control and body concept, and finally to incorporate the social behavior of individuals. Integral to this elaboration into a psychological differentiation construct have been results from numerous studies with the Embedded Figures Test (EFT) in which subjects were asked to differentiate components in a complex visual field. In our own laboratory, we have used the EFT and the RFT as measures of spatial-visualization functions and with reference to the broader confines of psychological differentiation. This latter construct is presumed in a wealth of diverse studies that are potentially applicable to lucid dreaming, including those involving body image, psychopathology, visual imagery, hemispheric specialization, impulse control, sensory deprivation, social conformity, reactions to stress, and cross-cultural comparisons (Witkin, Goodenough, & Oltman, 1979).

With specific reference to dreaming, Witkin (Witkin, Dyk, Faterson, Goodenough, & Karp, 1962) has proposed that field-independent persons would demonstrate greater frequency of dream recall than persons who were more field-dependent. He has also noted that Linton (personal communication to Witkin) has found evidence that nightmares of falling are more common among field-dependent than among field-independent persons (Witkin *et al.*, 1962). Furthermore, more active participation in the dream experience has been attributed to field independents, whereas field-dependent subjects have been found to be more passive observers (Hendricks & Cartwright, 1978; Witkin *et al.*, 1962). Based on the results of our studies with caloric stimulation and the stabilometer, studies in which lucid dreamers have been found to be more reliant on cues from their own body than nonlucids for maintaining orientation, we would expect individuals who dream lucidly to be relatively field independent. Results with the Embedded Figures Test (EFT) have confirmed this expectation for males and females (Gackenbach *et al.*, 1985); results with the Rod and Frame Test (RFT) have clearly supported such a relationship for males and to a lesser degree for female lucid dreamers. As will be discussed later, sex differences among lucid dreamers are not uncommon. Whether these differences are attributable to variations in lucidity ability or to task-related sex differences is unclear. For example, it is well known that male adults tend to be more field-independent than females on the RFT (e.g., Witkin *et al.*, 1962). It is therefore not surprising that group differences for dreamer types would be more evident for males than females for the RFT.

Three additional studies of dreamer types have been done in our laboratory that are relevant to the issue of individual differences in bodily orientation. The first also demonstrates a sex difference. Kinesthetic feedback is an important component of the body's system for maintaining equilibrium and orientation. We have found that male lucid dreamers perform more accurately for the reproduction of arm placements without visual feedback than do nonlucid males; females manifested no differential performance on this measure of kinesthetic sensitivity when grouped according to dreamer type (Gackenbach, Snyder, McKelvey *et al.*, 1981). Another study in which kinesthetically related differences have been demonstrated for lucids and nonlucids implements a dual task paradigm (Snyder & Gackenbach, 1981). In this experiment, female subjects were asked to sequentially tap a set of four telegraph keys during silence and concurrent with recitation of a nursery rhyme. This type of task is especially interesting because it has been used as a measure of hemispheric specialization (Kinsbourne & Hicks, 1978), an area of research that has also been pursued with regard to field dependence–independence. In the study by Snyder and Gackenbach (1981), both right- and left-handed female lucid dreamers were found to evince greater hemispheric specialization than did nonlucid dreamers, that is, they gave evidence of more interference during concurrent tasks. Witkins *et al.* (1979) have proposed that greater specialization in the psychological domain, in other words, greater psychological differentiation as characterized by field independence, will be linked to greater specialization in the neurophysiological domain. According to the Snyder and Gackenbach (1981) results and those from studies in which lateralized eye movements have been investigated, lucid dreaming ability may be associated with a greater degree of disproportionate hemispheric activation. Because frequent lucid dreaming is also associated with field independence, indirect evidence for an interrelationship between lucid dreaming ability, degree of brain lateralization, and field independence is apparent. It should be noted that Witkin *et al.* (1979) emphasize degree of lateralization with regard to types of processing in the two hemispheres; they do not propose that field independence will be related to the preferred or prepotent use of one hemisphere versus the other across all tasks.

The final study that is relevant to our discussion of individual differences among lucid dreamers for functions that involve spatial orientation is one in which university students classified as frequent or infrequent lucid dreamers or nonlucids were compared on a set of tactual measures that included a pencil maze and a Sequin form board (Gackenbach, Snyder, & Vognsen, 1981). Analyses done with dream recall as the covariate for right-handers time to completion and errors made on the pencil maze over eight trials, four with each hand, revealed no differences among dreamer types for time and a marginal ($p < .06$) interaction for errors between dreamer type and the direction of errors made (right vs. left). These results do not clearly indicate differences in tactual maze performance for lucid and nonlucid dreamers. Comparable analyses of times to completion in placing geometric forms in a board without visual feedback also indicated no differences; however, analyses of the drawings by subjects done after these forms had been placed with the preferred, nonpreferred, and both hands, a procedure that is part of the Halstead-Reitan Tactual Performance Test, did reveal that lucid dreamers more accurately located shapes than did nonlucids ($p < .04$), though groups did not differ in terms of the number of shapes recalled. This measured difference is suggestive that lucid dreamers are able to better recall haptically learned spatial relationships than are persons who are not lucid dreamers. Because a comparable measure of recall was not obtained for the pencil maze, we cannot say whether this difference generalizes beyond form board performance.

Conclusions

Based on the results of the different studies reviewed in this section, studies in which various aspects of balance, bodily orientation, and personal style have been investigated, it can be concluded that lucid dreaming ability is related to the efficient use of one's own body as a referent during the experience of changes in orientation. On one level of interpretation, this can be said to demonstrate that lucidity is related to field independence, a statement that is substantiated by direct measures of the field dependence–independence construct. On a higher level of inference would be the statement that lucidity is also related to the broad construct of psychological differentiation. We could therefore expect to find evidence of this relationship on an organismic level as well as on a systemic level. There is also suggestive evidence that lucid dreaming ability and psychological differentiation involve a higher degree of intrahemispheric specialization, that is, neurophysiological differentation.

VISUAL/IMAGINAL DIFFERENCES

Evidence to date from studies of eye movements, kinesthesis, caloric stimulation of the vestibular apparatus, and field dependence/independence supports a functional role for the vestibular system during the experience of lucid dreaming. This role is not surprising, given the known relationships between sleeping, dreaming, eye movements, the vestibular apparatus, and the rotational movements reported for lucidity. Because dream mentation experientially involves visual imagery, as do other types of waking experiences that have been related to lucidity, for example, out-of-body experiences, it is of interest to determine if lucid dreamers differ from nonlucids for susceptibility to experiencing certain types of imagery. It is also of interest to determine if differences between lucids and nonlucids can be demonstrated for visual-perceptual tasks performed during the waken state. Because Shepard (1984) has established that imagery and perception appear to have similar mechanisms, information for both phenomena will be interrelated. The forms of imagery that will be considered include spontaneous waking images as experienced in hallucinations, daydreams, hypnogogery, and psychic experiences. Some qualitative aspects of waking imagery like vividness and control will also be reviewed relative to lucid dreaming. In addition to the information already presented for differences between lucid and nonlucid dreamers on the Rod-and-Frame and Embedded Figures tests, both of which entail visualization, results will be presented from a series of studies in which the performance of dreamer types on visual-perceptual tasks was compared. Measures of mental rotation, perceptual completion, visual maze learning, and susceptibility to visual illusion were included in these studies.

Spontaneous Waking Imagery

Lucid dreaming in relation to the imagery that is experienced in hallucinations, daydreams, hypnogogery, and psychic phenomena has not been thoroughly investigated. However, we would expect some interrelationship between lucidity and these waking imaginal experiences for several reasons. Because lucidity is by definition characterized by self-awareness during the dream process, an awareness that is typically attributed to a waken state, the imagery experienced in the lucid dream may have features in common with the imagery that can be induced by various means in persons who are not asleep. Siegel (1977) has described a number of conditions in which hallucinatory waking imagery occurs, including falling asleep, waking up, insulin hypoglycemia, the delirium of fever, epilepsy, psychotic episodes, advanced syphilis, sensory deprivation, photostimulation, crystal gazing, migrane headaches, dizziness, and various drug intoxications. To this list could be added meditation and hypnosis (Tart, 1972, 1975) as well as other altered states of consciousness. The descriptions of persons experiencing visual imagery during these different conditions appear to follow a common pattern with an initial stage in which four types of simple form constants, for example, spirals, are described. This is followed by a second stage in which the images become more complex and incorporate people, objects, and recognizable scenes, some of which represented improbable experientially derived images such as aerial perspectives (Siegel, 1977). Included in these subject descriptions of complex images were some that are congruent with the descriptions of lucid experiences, and one could consequently hypothesize that persons who do frequently experience lucid dreams more often experience other forms of spontaneous waking imagery than do nonlucid dreamers.

Hypnogogic imagery with reference to lucidity has been reported on by Hearne (1978, 1983) and Gackenbach (1978), though none of these studies may be generalizable because of inadequate controls. Hearne (1978) has found for women only that the frequency of experiencing dream lucidity is positively correlated with the frequency of experiencing hypnogogic images. In a more recent but selective study, he has reported that 82% of lucid dreamers experience images and 77% experience sounds while falling asleep (Hearne, 1983). The similarity between hypnogogic imagery and lucid dream imagery has been investigated by Gackenbach (1978). She found that adult high dream recallers perceived hypnogogic images as more similar to nonlucid than lucid imagery; however, for persons who did view lucid and hypnogogic imagery as similar, it was likely that their lucidity would be initiated by dreamlike or incongruent elements. As for hypnogogic imagery, the relationship between hallucinatory imagery and lucid imagery is equivocal. Hearne (1978) has found no relationship between the frequency of dreaming lucidly and the frequency of a body–schema hallucination, whereas Blackmore (1983) has reported a positive association between the quantity and quality of lucidity with waking hallucinations. In turn, the frequency of daydreams has been positively correlated with lucid frequency for males, but no relationship has been found for the vividness of daydreams and lucidity (Hearne, 1978) or for the emotionality and realism of daydreams and lucidity (Gackenbach, 1978).

In two investigations of self-reported experiences of PK and lucidity, no relationships have emerged (Gackenbach, 1978; Kohr, 1980), nor have there been consistent findings interrelating lucidity with seeing apparitions, with experiences and beliefs about survival of bodily death, or with having a near-death experience. Hearne (1978) and Gackenbach (1978) reported no relationship between lucidity and apparitional sightings, whereas Kohr (1980) has reported that lucid dreaming is positively correlated with such sightings. Among persons grouped according to whether or not they have had a near-death experience as a deep, moving personal episode, Kohr (1982) has described an experiencing group that reported a greater frequency of unusual dream states like lucidity, a higher incidence of dreaming in color, and greater multimodal dreaming than did a nonexperiencing group and a group for which death had come close but with ambiguous poignancy. Relatedly, Greyson (1982) notes that

> I have already asked about the occurrence of lucid dreams in one questionnaire (a shortened version of John Palmer's Survey of Psychic Experiences) administered to self-selected members of the International Association for Near-Death Studies (IANDS). Among the "controls" (i.e., IANDS members who have not had NDEs), 83 out of 155 respondents (54%) reported having had lucid dreams, which is roughly what Palmer found among his sample from the general population. Among near-death experiencers, 13 out of 62 respondents (21%) reported having had lucid dreams *prior* to their NDEs, and 33 (53%) reportedly had lucid dreams *since* their NDEs. Thus, a fairly low percentage of near-death experiencers had lucid dreams before their NDEs, while after the NDE, this percentage rises to the level among the IANDS controls and the population Palmer sampled. (p. 6)

Beliefs about survival have also been investigated as they relate to the lucid dreaming experience. Palmer (1974) found a positive relationship, whereas Blackmore (1983) found no relationship. Irwin, in Chapter 15 in this book, has summarized the empirical relationship between OBEs and lucidity as being consistent but weak.

> Where the relationship was at its strongest, less than 12% of the variance between the two variables is explained. The meta-analysis of the 10 results also puts the combined effect size at . . . .20 only. Thus, whereas the association between the occurrence of the two experiences is statistically significant and a fairly reliable finding, it is of meager predictive value.

Induced Waking Imagery

In addition to the data that have been collected about the shared frequencies of lucid dreaming and types of spontaneous waking imagery, there is a body of information in which the quality of images has been related to lucidity, especially with regard to the vividness and control of imagery. Hearne (1978) found no relationship between lucid dreaming and three vividness questionnaire items, whereas Blackmore (1982) has reported no differences between lucid and non-lucid dreamers for Bett's vividness of imagery scores (Richardson, 1969). In contrast, Gackenbach, Prill, and Westrom (1983) did find that when dream recall and social desirability were controlled and an understanding of lucidity was verified (cautions not taken by Hearne, 1978, or Blackmore, 1982), males who reported frequently dreaming lucidly also reported more vivid tactile images according to responses on the Bett's Inventory. In unpublished follow-up data from our laboratory, both male and female students showed a positive relationship between lucidity frequency and the Auditory and Tactile subscales of the Bett's, provided dream recall, social desirability, and lucidity verification were controlled. Suggestive evidence of a sex difference for vividness and lucidity was also found for the Kinesthetic (females) and smell (male) subscales (Gackenbach, 1984a).

Kueny (1985), taking into account dream recall, motivation for lucidity, and verification of lucid dreaming, has also found a positive association between lucidity and items designed to sample the vividness of imagery in the tactile, olfactory, kinesthetic, and gustatory modalities. Hearne (1983), too, has stated that the majority of his lucid dreamers report moderate-to-clear vividness for visual and auditory imagery tasks. Finally, Blackmore (1983) has obtained a significant positive correlation between lucidity and the vividness of visual imagery. In sum, when moderator variables are taken into account, there is consistent evidence that self-reported imagery vividness is positively correlated with an ability to dream lucidly—a correlation that is demonstrable for males and females.

Unlike the vividness of imagery, control of imagery has not been shown to relate to lucid dreaming. Blackmore (1982) and Gackenbach, Prill, and Westrom (1983), both using Gordon's Control of Imagery Questionnaire (Richardson, 1969), found no relationship, as did Hearne (1978, 1983) using several imagery questions invoking control. In unreported data (Gackenbach, 1984a), we have detected a marginally significant positive association between these two variables, but clearly the bulk of evidence argues against a very meaningful association. In summary, the frequency of experiencing dream lucidity can be said to be related to the frequency with which two forms of spontaneous waking imagery (sleep transition hallucinations and waking hallucinations) are experienced. Daydreaming and imagery vividness also appear to be associated with lucidity frequency.

The performance of persons classified according to lucid dreaming frequency has already been shown to differ for two perceptual measures of visualization, the Rod-and-Frame Test (RFT) and the Embedded Figures Test (EFT); according to Gackenbach et al., (1985), lucid dreamers rely less on the immediate visual field than do nonlucid dreamers. Because of suspected differences between dreamer types in their susceptibility to experiencing certain types of waking imagery (sleep transition hallucinations and waking hallucinations), a series of other studies of visualization comparisons between lucids and nonlucids have been undertaken. As Ley (1983) has pointed out, imagery is integral to the performance of many visuospatial tasks, including some for which sex differences have variably been reported (Harris, 1978). Before presenting our results, we would emphasize that visualization is a very general process that can undoubtedly be influenced by many experimental and personal variables. It is also but one part of an integrated organismic system.

Because personal accounts of lucid dreams have included imagery of rotational movements (Green, 1968; LaBerge, 1985), we have studied the abilities of lucid dreamers on mental rotation tasks. For a simple two-dimensional mental rotation task (Golden, Hemmeke, & Purisch, 1979), Gackenbach and associates, after controlling for dream recall, have found that lucidity frequency is unrelated to level of performance (Gackenbach, Curren, LaBerge, Davidson, & Maxwell, 1983; Gackenbach, Prill, & Westrom, 1983). However, for a more difficult two-dimensional rotation task (Hakstain & Cattell, 1975) as well as for a three-dimensional task (Vandenberg & Kuse, 1978), female lucid dreamers have been shown to perform better than nonlucid females. Interestingly, for a select sample of males performing these same tasks, a negative relationship between lucid dreaming frequency and level of performance was found.

The fact that lucid dreaming ability has been found to be related to higher level visuospatial performance is mirrored in a study in which the visualization of persons who have had out-of-body experiences (OBE) has been investigated (Cook & Irwin, 1983). Although OBEers and non-OBEers were not found to differ on a measure of visual imagery (Richardson's Necker Cube Fluctuations

Task), they were found to differ on a more complex, Piagetianlike visuospatial task that required the allocentric localization of three-dimensional block sketches within a simulated room. This task could also be interpreted as one that measures field independence. Because a relationship between lucid dreaming and OBEs has long been purported (Green, 1968; Irwin, 1985), it is particularly interesting with regard to this study that the occurrence of an OBE was not found to depend on an individual's skills in vividness and controllability of waking visual imagery. A comparable lack of dependence on visual vividness and controllability has been reported for lucid dreaming (Gackenbach, 1978; Gackenbach, Prill, & Westrom, 1983; Hearne, 1978).

If lucid dreaming ability is specifically related to higher level visualization skills that involve spatial orientation, evidence for which is discernable in the results obtained for dreamer types on figural rotational tasks and field-dependence/independence tasks, then we would expect no differences to be found between lucid and nonlucid dreamers on a visual perceptual task with minimal spatial demands. This hypothesis has not been tested extensively; however, no differences for dreamer types have been found for Mueller-Lyer illusion and Necker Cube tasks and for a perceptual completion task (Gackenbach et al., 1981). This last finding also serves to illustrate the need for controlling relevant variables when analyzing individual differences. In a study done by Gackenbach et al. (Gackenbach, Curren, LaBerge, Davidson, & Maxwell, 1983), in which the Perceptual Completion subscale of the Comprehensive Ability Battery (Hakstain & Cattell, 1975) was administered to adults highly interested in lucid dreaming, it was found that the performance of females was positively correlated with lucidity frequency $(r = .45)$. Dream recall and extent of education were controlled for in this study, as was lucidity verification. In a subsequent administration of this same measure (Gackenbach, 1984a) to college students, an opposite result was obtained after controlling for dream recall, college GPA, and lucidity verification. Lucidity ability was found to be negatively correlated with perceptual completion $(r = -.29)$ among university women. For both studies, there was no relationship between perceptual completion scores and lucidity for males. At this time, the inconsistency between these two studies for females is viewed as due to different sample characteristics. Cross-validation with this task and other visual perceptual tasks, however, is needed to confirm that visualization differences between lucids and nonlucids are not demonstrable for tasks with limited spatial demands.

Additional support for a visuospatial functional difference between lucid and nonlucid dreamers is afforded by the performance of dreamer types on a visual "stepping stone" maze used by Milner (1965) and Newcombe and Russell (1969) to study the effects of lateralized brain damage on visuospatial learning. In these studies, persons who had incurred right hemisphere lesions were found to perform poorer than persons with left hemisphere lesions or controls. Unlike Porteus Mazes, variants of which are included in the Wechsler Scales of

Children's Intelligence, the visual mazes used by Milner (1965) and by New-combe and Russell (1969) and us do not provide ongoing visual feedback as to the path already followed. Rather, self-generated auditory feedback occurs in the form of a click or buzzer whenever a deviation from the correct path takes place. Subjects are therefore required to initially discover the correct path by trial and error and subsequently to reproduce their correct movements over multiple trials. Visual imagery for movement through space is a part of this process:

> The subject's task is to discover this series of points [stepping stones] and to remember their order and direction so that he can select them correctly; in other words, he is asked to follow the imaginary path (Barker, 1931, p. 282).

When university students who were grouped according to lucid dreaming frequency were administered a version of a visual maze, persons who experience lucid dreams more than once per month were found to perform differently than those who reported never or infrequently experiencing lucid dreams (Gacken-bach, Snyder, & Esbeck, 1981). This difference was manifest in terms of speed of performance, with frequent lucid dreamers completing a predetermined number of trials (four per hand) more slowly than "infrequents" and "nevers" ($p < .04$). A marginal difference ($p < .06$) was also found for errors made, once more with frequents doing poorer than other dreamer types. Unlike for the tactual form board task (Gackenbach, Snyder, & Vognsen, 1981) in which lucid dream-ers were determined to more accurately recall the respective spatial location of different shapes, analyses of drawings of the maze path following eight trials did not indicate better recall for lucids versus nonlucids. These findings do not support the hypothesis that lucid dreamers can use imagery more effectively than others when performing a set number of trials on a visual maze of this type. They do, however, support the existence of differences between persons classified according to lucid dreaming ability, differences that parallel those already de-scribed for other visual tasks that rely to varying degress on external visual referrents, that is, field dependence or independence.

Conclusions

Several tentative conclusions can be reached based on the information pre-sented in this section. First, lucid dreaming frequency appears to be positively associated with the frequency with which sleep transition hallucinations, waking hallucinations, and daydreaming are experienced. An enhanced vividness of imagery across several sense modalities (auditory, tactile/kinesthetic, olfacto-ry/gustatory) also appears to be positively related to lucidity frequency. Perfor-mance on visualization tasks with limited spatial demands has not been useful for discriminating between lucid and nonlucid dreamers, nor has performance on a visual maze for which a visual field is delineated. However, as the visualization tasks increase in spatial complexity and/or there is less need to rely on visual field referents for successful performance, lucid dreamers become distinguishable from persons who do not dream lucidly. These findings are compatible with those reported in the section on oculomotor/equalibratory differences and fit into the stage pattern of imagery described by Siegel (1977). Visualization or imagery *per se* can therefore be said to not be essential for understanding the lucid process. Rather, selective nonvisual imagery in combination with internally oriented perspectives would appear to be keys for opening the portal to lucidity.

INTELLECTUAL/CREATIVE DIFFERENCES

Many of the differences between dreamer types that have been presented thus far can be said to primarily involve perceptual abilities rather than abilities that are largely intellectual. In this section the results from studies of individual differences of cognitive functioning, as apparent in measures of intelligence and creativity, will be reviewed. If lucid dreaming ability has manifestations on an organismic level, then we would expect to find evidence of lucidity differences in the cognitive as well as perceptual domains. Witkin and associates (Witkin *et al.*, 1962) have followed a similar rationale with regard to the field-dependence/independence construct. Because their construct was found to be useful for characterizing a person's problem-solving activities and perception, Witkin referred to self-consistent ways of experiencing as cognitive styles. Within this broader framework, field-dependence/independence was once said to represent the perceptual component of experience, with an analytical-global dichotomy being delineated in order to describe differences across intellectual and perceptual abilities. As already demonstrated, frequent lucid dreamers tend to be field independent rather than field dependent. Field independence as a cognitive style entails psychological differentiation in which a person tends to approach problems or situations by experiential restructuring rather than dealing with them as a given whole. If psychological differentiation is related to a tendency to dream lucidly, then we would expect to find differences between lucid and nonlucid dreamers consistent with those described by Witkin. We might also be in a position to better understand the experience of lucid dreaming as an active restructuring of the dream experience in which the ''unconsciousness'' of dreaming and the ''consciousness'' of waking is comingled.

Early investigations of intellecutal functioning of persons who were field-dependent and/or independent revealed that field independence might be associated with superior general intelligence (Witkin *et al.*, 1962). Subsequent research has shown that this superiority may be limited to performance on spatial-visualization types of intellectual tasks (Witkins *et al.*, 1979) and is unrelated to verbal ability (Witkin & Goodenough, 1981). If the relationship which we have postulated between lucid dreaming and the cognitive restructuring of field independence is a reliable one, we would expect differences between lucid and nonlucid dreamers to be apparent for some measures of intellectual functioning but not others. Specifically, lucid dreamers should do better than nonlucids for self-oriented nonverbal types of intellectual tasks. The data to date are inconclusive with regard to this hypothesis, in part because of poor experimental designs. Hearne (1978) and Gackenbach, Snyder, McKelvey *et al.* (1981), respectively, have found no difference between dreamer types for solving Raven's Advanced Progressive Matrices or the pyramid puzzle, both of which are measures of visually based problem-solving ability. However, neither study controlled for lucid vertification, and Hearne did not control for dream recall. In another study in which dream recall also was not taken into account (Gackenbach, 1986), lucid male adults and students were found to differ from nonlucids on a measure of verbal intelligence included in Cattell's Sixteen Personality Factor Questionnaire (16PF; 1969); lucid dreaming frequency, as would be expected, correlated negatively with Factor B scores. In a study in which dream recall, education, and sex role identification were accounted for, Gackenbach, Curren, LaBerge, Davidson, and Maxwell (1983) found that high lucid dreaming frequency among women was associated with high verbal and numerical abilities as measured with the Comprehensive Abilities Battery (CAB; Hakstain & Cattell, 1975); male frequent lucids scored comparably lower than male nonlucids for numerical abilities. This study, unfortunately, was exclusively a mail survey accomplished with self-selected adults with an expressed interest in lucid dreaming. More representative but unreported data (Gackenbach, 1984a) from our laboratory for the CAB administered to university students and analyzed with regard to dream recall and grade point average do indicate no differences for male or female dreamer types for the Verbal and Numerical CAB subscales. Although this last finding is as hypothesized, it is clear that more adequately controlled and more comprehensive studies of intellectual differences between dreamer types remain to be done before any conclusions can be reached.

Studies of lucid dreaming frequency in relation to the cognition of creative activities have been few in number but more substantive than those in which measures of intelligence have been employed. Relatedly, creativity with regard to field dependence/independence has been examined by a number of investigators (Bloomberg, 1971, 1976; Leftcourt & Telegdi, 1971; Noppe & Gallagher, 1977; Ohrmacht & McMorris, 1971; Spotts & Mackler, 1976). As for intelligence, different cognitive styles could be expected to involve their own forms of creative thought (Forisha, 1978). The same is to be expected for dreamer types, an expectation that has been met on the basis of three studies from our laboratory. Gackenbach and Hammons (1983), using the Remote Association Test (RAT), a measure of verbal reasoning, have found no differences in performance relative to lucid dreaming frequency. This finding was replicated by Gackenbach, Curren *et al.* (1983) for men, whereas frequent lucid dreaming women were found to show some evidence of higher verbal (RAT) and nonverbal (Torrance Non-verbal) creativity. In an unreported follow-up to these studies (Gackenbach, 1984a), male lucids were again determined to be no more creative than male nonlucids, but female dreamer types were determined to differ on two of four Torrance (Torrance, 1972) measures of nonverbal creativity. These findings are consistent in indicating that female lucid dreamers differ from their nonlucid counterparts in terms of their success at solving some types of nonverbal tasks. The results for males indicate no differential abilities. With reference to lucidity, much research is needed for both the intellectual and creative dimensions of cognition.

PERSONAL/INTERPERSONAL DIFFERENCES

In keeping with our contention that lucid dreaming ability involves multiple functional systems working in concert on an organismic level, we would expect to find that persons who frequently experience lucid dreams self-consistently differ from other persons on personal and interpersonal dimensions as well as on the equilibratory, perceptual, and cognitive dimensions already discussed. The personal and interpersonal characteristics of lucid dreamers studied to date include the demographic variables of gender, race, age, and family status, and the personality variables of risk taking, self-perception, anxiety, sex-role identity, and extroversion. Because individual differences for personal/interpersonal behaviors and attitudes have been demonstrated for the psychological differentiation construct of field dependence/independence, we will also review these demonstrated differences in order to relate them to hypothesized differences for dreamer types.

Demographic Differences

Demographic studies with regard to gender, age, birth order, and family status have been carried out by several researchers. Although not entirely consistent, these studies, if properly designed (Gackenbach, 1985b), have generally indicated no differences in lucid dreaming frequency according to gender (Blackmore, 1982; Gackenbach, 1978. 1980, 1983, 1984b, 1986, Gackenbach, Curren, LaBerge, Davidson, & Maxwell, 1983; Hearne, 1978; Palmer, 1974) but demonstrable differences according to age, birth order, and family variables. Overall, younger persons have been determined to dream lucidly more often than older persons (Blackmore, 1983; Gackenbach, 1980; Kueny, 1985; Palmer, 1974). Whether a cohort effect is operative for this age-related difference has not been studied, though Gackenbach (1978) has shown that among adult women with an expressed interest in dreaming, older women reported a higher frequency of lucidity than did younger women. Regarding birth order, Gackenbach *et al.*

have reported that firstborns report a higher incidence of lucid dreaming than later borns. In that same study, as well as in Palmer (1974), single adults have reported more frequently dreaming lucidly than married persons, though Gackenbach (1978) has also found no difference for another sample. Finally, with regard to deaths of family members, paternal and sibling deaths were statistically unrelated to the frequency of lucidity, but maternal deaths have been found to favor its frequency (Gackenbach, 1978).

Cultural differences in lucid dreaming frequency have not been systematically studied. Palmer (1974) has examined race differences in Virginia and found that 76% of blacks reported having had a lucid dream experience, whereas only 53% of whites reported such an experience. In the same study, Palmer reported that occupation and family income variables did not appear to affect lucid dreaming frequency. Educational levels have also not been found to influence the frequency of lucidity in quasi-normal (Palmer, 1974) or well-educated (Gackenbach, 1978; Gackenbach, Curren, LaBerge, Davidson, & Maxwell, 1983) samples. Regarding cultural factors, it may be notable that Gackenbach (1978) has reported, for an adult sample, differences between lucids and non-lucids for interests in Yoga:

> Frequent lucid dreamers . . . are much less likely to be involved in Yoga than members of the other two groups (infrequents and nevers).. . . In addition, nonlucid dreamers were slightly more likely to be involved with followers of Eastern gurus. Although frequent lucid dreamers may not be interested in Yoga, they are slightly more likely to be involved in Silva Mind Control than infrequent or non-lucid subjects. (pp. 176–177).

Administration of the Eastern and Western Scale (Gilgen & Cho, 1979) to university students has suggested an association between lucid frequency and east–west values for females only. Overall, these results provide suggestive evidence of racial differences in lucid dreaming frequency, no evidence that socioeconomic status influences lucidity frequency, and contradictory evidence of an association between an interest in non-Western ideologies and lucid dreaming. Although gender does not appear to influence the frequency with which a person dreams lucidly, being younger, firstborn, and unmarried may influence the likelihood of experiencing lucidity. Better controlled, longitudinal studies are needed, however, before we can be confident of these findings.

Personality Differences

In addition to the study of these demographic variables, there have been several studies of the personality characteristics of lucid and nonlucid dreamers. Because many of these same characteristics have been studied with reference to psychological differentiation, we will first review the personality differences between field-dependent and field-independent persons before discussing dif-

ferences between dreamer types. The cognitive styles of field depen-
dence/independence, which are now defined as "contrasting tendencies to rely
primarily on external referents or on the self in psychological functioning"
(Witkin *et al.*, 1979, p. 1131), have been studied with reference to three dimensions of personal attributes: (1) one's body concept, (2) one's sense of identity,
and (3) one's use of controls and defenses in dealing with impulses and potentially
disturbing experiences. The body concept of field-independent persons has been
said to be an impression of the body as having definite boundaries with the parts
within as discrete yet interrelated. In view of the self-reference of field independents to visuopatial, kinesthetic, cutaneous, and vestibular cues, it is not unexpected that they would develop a more articulated body concept than less ego-
centrically oriented persons. This is especially true when one considers the
measures that have been employed to study both body articulation (e.g., human
figure drawings and self-perceptual tests like Thurstone's Hands Test) and body
boundary (e.g., 2-point discrimination and tactile localization). Relatedly, but of
probably more meaning for understanding the personal attributes of lucid dreamers, is the imputed relationship between field independence and a sense of separate
identity. Whereas field-dependent persons tend to have an interpersonal orientation that enhances their social interactions with others, field independents are said
to function more autonomously and to have an impersonal orientation (Witkin *et
al.*, 1979). This dichotomy appears to be comparable to that described by Gardner
(1981) for persons who differ in terms of their interpersonal versus intrapersonal
abilities. We would expect that these differently oriented people would also vary
with regard to their ideation and their manner of dealing with impulses and
psychological conflict. Such differences have been established for field-depen-
dent/independent persons, for example, field independents have been shown to
rely on specialized defenses like isolation, intellectualization, and projection,
whereas field dependents have tended to use global defenses like denial and
repression (Witkin *et al.*, 1979).

Inasmuch as lucid dreaming ability is associated with field independence for
the personal/interpersonal domain, we could expect that persons who frequently
dream lucidly would evince differences from nonlucids along the three dimensions
of personal attributes studied with regard to cognitive styles. We have already
discussed lucid frequency in relation to self-image, or one's body concept, as
measured for tactile/kinesthetic localization. Frequent lucid dreamers have most
accurately drawn the relative location of form board figures previously placed
without visual feedback. They have also more accurately duplicated visually
unobserved angular displacements of their arms than have nonlucid dreamers. No
studies have been done in which human figure drawings of lucid and nonlucid
dreamers have been compared for differences in body articulation, but we are now
analyzing data derived from the administration of a variant of Thurstone's Hands
Test and a test of left–right orientation for upright and inverted figures to determine if differences will be demonstrable for these self-perceptual tasks that Witkin
and others have used as measures of body articulation. Although we are now

unable to state that lucid dreamers have a more articulated body concept than other persons, evidence does support a more distinct awareness of body boundary among lucid dreamers than among others.

With regard to an individual's sense of identity and personal and social manifestations of that sense of identity, there has been a set of studies carried out with dreamer types in which risk taking, self-perception, sex-role identity, extroversion, and anxiety have been assessed.

Risk Taking

Risk taking was originally conceived by Dane (personal communication, 1980) as related to lucidity. He developed eight items that described situations of either internal (e.g., develop your telephatic powers) or external (e.g., taking skydiving classes) risk and found that frequently lucid individuals expressed an interest in these potentially risky situations. Gackenbach (1980) administered Dane's scale to 707 students during a mass testing at a midwestern university and found that when dream recall and understanding were controlled, there was no dreamer difference for the external risk items. However, frequently lucid individuals reported themselves as significantly more interested in internally risky situations than their infrequently lucid or nonlucid counterparts.

In a follow-up with adults (Gackenbach, Curren, LaBerge, Davidson, & Maxwell, 1983) and with the additional control of social desirability, both internal and external risks were significantly correlated with lucidity frequency for females only. In a subsequent study (data unpublished; Gackenbach, 1984a), two traditional measures of risk proclivity were administered with Dane's scale—the Choice Dilemma Questionnaire (CDQ; Stoner, 1961) and the Sensation Seeking Scale (SSS; Zuckerman, 1979). High scores on the latter are defined by Zuckermann, Bone, Neary, Mengelsdorff, and Bustman (1972) as characterizing "a person who needs varied, novel, and complex sensations and experiences to maintain an optimal level of arousal" (p. 308). The CDQ was developed by Stoner (1961) to measure the "risky shift" phenomenon, or the finding that groups make riskier decisions than individuals. Among college students, the CDQ and the Dane scale were significantly positively correlated to the SSS, whereas the CDQ and Dane scale were unrelated. For the association between lucid dreaming frequency and these measures of risk taking, we found nothing for the Dane scale and a negative correlation for the SSS most evident for males but significant across sex. In contrast, the CDQ correlated positively across sex with lucid frequency. The SSS finding was replicated in males but not females in the final study in this sequence (data unpublished; Gackenbach, 1984b). Using the same design, scores on the external subscale of the Dane also showed a significant negative correlation for males with lucidity frequency. However, the SSS and Dane scale were not significantly correlated.

Although the three measures used in these studies all claim to measure risk, the interelationship between scales is moderate. Where significant correlations did occur, risk taking was positively associated with lucidity frequency for the Dane scale and for the CDQ, but for the SSS the inverse was found. This somewhat contradictory finding can be explained by making a distinction between internal and external risks. The Dane scale has both Internal and External Risk subscales and the CDQ clearly deals with external risk (i.e., all the items describe hypothetical situations involving other people and not the subject). As for the SSS, although there are a few items that deal with internal risk (i.e., "I have tried marijuana or would like to"), that is, experiencing or exploring inside the self as opposed to outside the self, the vast majority are external risk items. With this distinction in mind. except for the adult women in Gackenbach *et al.* (1983a) and the CDQ results, the rest of the significant findings (and the direction of the nonsignificant findings) are consistent in indicating that lucid dreaming is associated with a preference for internal risk and avoidance of external risk. Regarding the inconsistency of the CDQ research, Cartwright (1971) has noted that "the assumption that CDQ scores measure a unitary disposition to take risks is no longer tenable" (p. 375). The negative finding for adult women (Gackenbach, Curren, LaBerge, Davidson, & Maxwell, 1983) may, in turn, be accounted for by the fact that this sample reported themselves as being significantly more interested in externally risky situations than did the student samples used. As Goldenberg (1979) and Nussdorf (1975) point out, the traditional sex difference for risk taking favoring males is attenuated by sex-role identity. The adult women in the previously mentioned Gackenbach *et al.* study were found to be significantly less feminine than the women in the normative data provided by Spence and Helmreich (1978).

Sex-Role Identity

Integral to a person's self-concept is one's sex-role identity, or the extent to which one exhibits characteristics typically attributed to men or women. For example, men have typically been found to be less attentive to social cues, to favor solitude, to be less open about feelings, and to display greater internal locus of control in comparison to females. Sporros, Stam, Radtke, and Nightingale (1980) have reported that femininity, especially among men, is associated with enhanced dream recall. Gackenbach *et al.* (1985), on the other hand, have reported that field independence, a stereotypically masculine cognitive style (Witkin & Goodenough, 1981) is characteristic of frequent lucid dreamers. Although others have found a positive association between field independence and masculinity (Hulfish, 1978; Rosenberg, 1976), this support has diminished in recent years (Chatterjea & Bhaskar, 1980). Gackenbach (1978), however, has reported that a factor labeled *masculinity* was positively and moderately correlated with a factor defined by the frequency of lucid dreams experientially associated with the hypnogogic and hypnapompic states.

In order to directly compare lucidity frequency and sex-role identity, Gackenbach, Curren, LaBerge, Davidson, and Maxwell (1983) administered the Personal Attributes Questionnaire (PAQ) of Spence and Helmreich (1978) to adults with an expressed interest in dreaming. After controlling for dream recall, understanding of lucidity, and social desirability, it was determined that masculinity was positively related to lucid frequency for men and marginally for women. A positive relationship was also found between femininity and lucid frequency for men but none for women. Finally, Kueny (1985), using the Femininity subscale of the California Psychological Inventory (CPI), found a positive relationship for males and females between femininity and the number of lucid dreams signal-verified in the sleep laboratory but no relationship between femininity and several self-report and dream log indexes of lucid frequency.

In summary, there is evidence that both masculinity and femininity are related to lucidity. This evidence is consistent with the reconceptualizations of sex-role identity as a multidimensional trait rather than a monolithic one (Bem, 1974; Constantinople, 1973). We would therefore suggest that frequent lucid dreamers tend toward an androgenous sex-role identity. Some data in support of this suggestion are afforded by Gackenbach, Curren, LaBerge, Davidson, and Maxwell (1983), a study in which subjects were assigned to one of four sex-role identities: (1) androgynous (high masculine, high feminine); (2) masculine (high masculine, low feminine); (3) feminine (low masculine, high feminine); or (4) undifferentiated (low masculine, low feminine), according to Spence, Helmreich, and Stapp's (1975) median split method. Regardless of lucid dreaming frequency, women proved to be equally classified in the four identities; however, 49.1% of the frequently lucid males were androgynous—a difference that resulted in a significant chi-square value.

Self-Perception

Lucid dreaming history as it relates to self-perception, self-monitoring, and self-consciousness is relevant both to risk taking and sex-role identity and to studies of the personal and interpersonal characteristics of field-dependent and independent individuals. Our research has indicated that frequent lucid dreamers tend to be persons who are willing to take internal risks but who avoid external risks. In other words, their reference for risk is themselves. Sex-role characteristics that have been associated with high lucidity incidence, primarily for males but for some masculinely oriented females, also have favored intrapersonal rather than interpersonal abilities, including less self-disclosure, being less attentive to social cues, having an internal locus of control, favoring solitude, and being less socially conforming. Witkin has spoken of a field-independent person as being more differentiated than others, by which he meant that there is a greater self-nonself segregation than for field-dependent persons who display a greater connectedness between self and others. Because self-awareness of dreaming during the dream process is the defining characteristic of lucid dreaming, knowledge of the role that the self plays in this dream experience may be essential for an understanding of lucidity.

Belicki, Hunt, and Belicki (1978), taking into account neither dream recall nor lucidity verification, did not find that lucid dreaming history was related to typical, ideal, or private self-perception. In several, more recent studies, it has been found that lucidity is not positively related to an interpersonal orientation. Kueny (1985), taking into account dream recall, lucidity verification, and motivation to dream lucidly, reported that several indexes of lucidity were uncorrelated with a Self-Control (freedom from impulsivity and self-centeredness) measure derived from the California Psychological Inventory and marginally correlated with a Good Impression (concern for how others react to them) measure. Gackenbach (1978), using the Self-Sentiment Control (Q3) factor from the Sixteen Personality Factor Questionnaire (Cattell, 1969), also found no positive association between this measure and several indexes of lucidity. High scorers on Q3 are controlled and socially precise, whereas low scorers follow their own urges and are careless of social protocol. The Self-Consciousness Inventory (SCI), of Fenigstein, Scheier, and Buss (1975), has been used in three studies of lucid dreamer characteristics. The SCI is a measure of the extent to which persons habitually reflect upon themselves and includes two major components of self-consciousness—private self-consciousness and public self-consciousness. Private self-consciousness involves habitual attendance to one's thoughts, motives, and feelings, whereas public self-consciousness involves concern for social appearance and the impressions one makes on others. According to our hypothesis that persons who frequently dream lucidly tend toward an intrapersonal orientation whereas others tend toward a more interpersonal orientation, we could expect that lucid dreaming frequency would be positively associated with private self-consciousness but not public self-consciousness. In a pilot study, in which LaBerge and Gackenbach (1982) administered the SCI to students enrolled in a dreams class, both males and females who scored high for private self-consciousness self-reported frequently dreaming lucidly. In a follow-up study (Gackenbach, Curren, LaBerge, Davison, & Maxwell, 1983), the SCI was administered to adults, and multiple stepwise regression analyses done separately for males and females showed that private self-consciousness was the single best predictor of lucid frequency among males. Kueny (1985), also working with adults, some of whom attempted to signal lucidity in the sleep laboratory, found a significant negative relationship between private self-consciousness and the number of signal-verified lucid dreams. In one sense, Kueny's results with the SCI contradict the results of

Gackenbach and her associates. It is possible, however, that lucidity signaled in the sleep laboratory is an interpersonal act that is not comparable to self-reported or diary-recorded lucid frequency.

Extraversion and Anxiety

In the study by Kueny (1985) in which two CPI Class II scales (Self-Control and Good Impression) were found to have low correlations with lucid frequency, one of the Class I scales, Social Presence, was determined to be negatively correlated with the frequency of signal-verified lucid dreams in the sleep laboratory. According to Gough (1968), Class I scales pertain to "interpersonal effectiveness, style, and adequacy." These Class I scales, excluding Sense of Well-Being, have also loaded highly on a factor (Factor 2; Megargee, 1972) sometimes designated a measure of extraversion. We have proposed that frequent lucid dreamers tend toward an intrapersonal orientation. We would therefore expect them to tend toward introversion rather than extraversion, and we would emphasize that introversion, in turn, has been related to level of arousal (Corcoran, 1981). In addition to the finding by Kueny, which was obtained with few subjects and was accounted for principally by males, there are two studies in which lucidity frequency has been related to the dimension of introversion-extraversion. Hearne (1978), administering the Eysenck Personality Inventory (EPI), found no differences between lucid and nonlucid dreamers for the dimension of extraversion. Gackenbach (1978), using Form C of the 16 PF and scoring it for the second-order factor of Extraversion, did find that Extraversion loaded on two factor-analytic variables ("Masculinity" and "Joining") that were moderately and positively correlated with a lucid dream factor associated with hypnagogic and hypnapompic states. In a subsequent reanalysis of this adult data and other student data, Gackenbach (1986) reports a marginally significant correlation between extraversion and self-report lucid frequency for students but no relationship for adults. Finally, in an unpublished study (Gackenbach, 1984a), the Self-Monitoring Scale (Snyder, 1974), including a subscale purported to measure extraversion, was administered to students for whom dream recall, social desirability, and lucid verification were controlled. No relationship between lucid frequency and extraversion emerged. In general, these different studies do indicate that lucid frequency is not positively associated with various measures of extraversion.

Over the years, a body of literature has accumulated in support of arousal differences for persons who differ along the introversion–extraversion dimension. Introverts have been said to maintain a higher level of arousal than extraverts due to constitutionally determined properties of the central and autonomic nervous systems (Eysenck, 1982), though there is uncertainty about the locus of the arousal difference between introverts and extraverts and these differences

appear to vary with the time of day (Corcoran, 1981). It is interesting to speculate that lucid dreaming, which involves a high level of arousal during sleep,
occurs in individuals who tend toward introversion. We might also expect that
these individuals while awake might be more susceptible to stress than less
aroused individuals, that is, nonlucid dreamers. To date, six studies have been
carried out in order to assess the relationship between susceptibility to anxiety
and lucid dreaming frequency. The results from these studies are inconsistent,
though procedural and sampling differences may account for this inconsistency.
Gackenbach (1978) and Gackenbach (1986) used the 16 PF, Gackenbach, Curren, LaBerge, Davidson, and Maxwell (1983) and Kueny (1985) used the social
anxiety subscale of the Self-Consciousness Inventory (SCI), and two unpublished studies (Gackenbach, 1980; LaBerge & Gackenbach, 1982) used the
Zuckerman Affect-Adjective Checklist and the SCI, respectively, to derive measures of anxiety. Although high anxiety has been found to be associated with
high lucid frequency for males, the converse has been found for females if all the
data are combined and weighted according to methodological differences. We
are not sure why this gender difference has been found but do believe that this
issue merits further study. We also plan to investigate if persons who dream
lucidly differ from others with regard to how they deal with stress, for example,
with regard to the use of specialized versus global defense mechanisms when
faced with actual or potential conflict situations.

IN REVIEW

The studies that we have marched before you in this chapter have not always
been in step, and some are attired in rather shabby scientific uniforms. This state
of affairs can largely be attributed to the recency of scientific inquiry about lucid
dreaming. At times, we ourselves have groped in the dark trying to make this
dream process more understandable. Our investigations have consequently been
vitiated by imprecision and false steps. Nonetheless, we do believe that there is
an emerging conceptualization of the lucid dreamer within the ranks of the
studies in which individual differences have been investigated. In this emerging
conceptualization, lucid dreaming is viewed as typically experienced by some
individuals but not others. Evidence has been presented that supports that individuals who do frequently dream lucidly tend to rely primarily on the self in
psychological functioning rather than on external referents. Manifestations of
this intrapersonal orientation have been found for different domains of psychological functioning, including the reflexive, perceptual, cognitive, and personal.
As a group, persons with a propensity to dream lucidly can be described as
sensitive to tactile/kinesthetic and vestibular cues, as less reliant on an external
visual field, as relatively field-independent, as having a well-delineated body
boundary, as being androgenous in sex role and open to internal but not external

risks, as being more self- rather than socially oriented, and as tending toward introversion and a relatively high level of arousal. The data reviewed would also lead us to believe that the lucid experience is a cognitive style of the night in which nonvisual imagery plays an essential role. To what extent the characteristics described for lucid dreamers as a group are applicable to persons of different age, gender, race, and experiential background remains to be demonstrated. Only now is the quality and quantity of empirical evidence beginning to amass so that the individual characteristics associated with lucid dreaming can be seen in full review.

REFERENCES

Bakan, P. (1969). Hypnotizability, laterality of eye movements and functional brain asymmetry. *Perceptual and Motor Skills, 41,* 85–86.

Bakan, P. (1971). The eyes have it. *Psychology Today,* pp. 64–68.

Bakan, P., & Shotland, R. (1969). Lateral eye movement, reading speed, and visual attention. *Psychonomic Science, 15,* 93–94.

Barker, R. G. (1931). The stepping-stone maze: A directly visible space problem apparatus. *Journal of General Psychology, 5,* 280–285.

Belicki, D. A., Hunt, & Belicki, K. (1978). An exploratory study comparing self-reported lucid and non-lucid dreamers. *Sleep Research, 7,* 166.

Bem, S. (1974). The measurement of psychological androgyny. *Journal of Consulting and Clinical Psychology, 42,* 155–162.

Blackmore, S. J. (1982). More sex differences in lucid dreaming frequency. *Lucidity Letter, 1*(2), 5.

Blackmore, S. J. (1983). A survey of lucid dreams, OBE's, and related experiences. *Lucidity Letter, 2*(3), 1.

Blackmore, S. J. (1984). A postal survey of OBE's and other experiences. *Journal of the Society for Psychical Research, 52,* 225–244.

Bloomberg, M. (1971). Creativity as related to field independence and mobility. *The Journal of Genetic Psychology, 118,* 3–12.

Bloomberg, M. (1976). An inquiry into the relationship between field independence-dependence and creativity. *The Journal of Psychology, 67,* 127–140.

Buss, D. M., & Craik, K. H. (1983). The act frequency approach to personality. *Psychological Review, 90*(2), 105–126.

Cartwright, D. (1971). Risk taking by individuals and groups: An assessment of research employing choice dilemmas. *Journal of Personality and Social Psychology, 20*(3), 361–378.

Cartwright, R. D. (1978). *A primer on sleep and dreaming.* Reading, MA: Addison-Wesley Publishing Company.

Cattell, R. (1969). *16PF.* Champaign, IL: The Institute for Personality and Ability Testing.

Chatterjea, R. G., & Bhaskar, P. (1980). Field dependence, sex, introversion, extroversion, and social desirability. *Journal of Psychological Researches, 24,* 115–120.

Constantinople, A. (1973). Masculinity-femininity: An exception to a famous dictum? *Psychological Bulletin, 80,* 389–407.

Cook, A. M., & Irwin, H. J. (1983). Visuospatial skills and the out-of-body experience. *Journal of Parapsychology, 47,* 23–35.

Corcoran, D. W. J. (1981). Introversion-extroversion, stress, and arousal. In D. E. Broadbent & R. Lynn (Eds.), *Dimensions of personality: Papers in honour of H. J. Eysenck.* New York: Pergamon Press.

Crowne, D. P., & Marlowe, D. (1964). *The approval motive.* New York: Wiley.

Dane, Joe. (1984). *A comparison of waking instructions and post hypnotic suggestion for lucid dream induction.* Unpublished doctoral dissertation. Georgia State University, Atlanta.

DeWitt, G. W., & Averill, J. R. (1976). Lateral eye movements, hypnotic susceptibility and field independence-dependence. *Perceptual and Motor Skills, 43,* 1179–1184.

Doneshka, P., & Kehiyov, A. (1978). Some peculiarities of the dreams of patients with vestibular diseases. *Acta Medica (Irregular), 32*(1), 45–50.

Ehrlichman, H., & Weinberger, A. (1978). Lateral eye movements and hemispheric asymmetry: A critical view. *Psychological Bulletin, 85,* 1080–1101.

Eisinger, K., & Schilder, P. (1929). Dreams and labyrinth lesions. *Psychiatria et Neurologia, 73,* 314–329.

Eysenck, H. J. (1982). *Personality, genetics, and behavior: Selected papers.* New York: Praeger Publishers.

Fenigstein, A., Scheier, M. F., & Buss, A. H. (1975). Public and private self-consciousness: Assessment and theory. *Journal of Consulting and Clinical Psychology, 43*(4), 522–527.

Fenwick, P. B. C., Schatzman, M., Worsley, A., Adams, J., Stone S., & Baker, A. (1984). Lucid dreaming: Correspondence between dreamed and actual events in one subject during REM sleep. *Biological Psychology, 18,* 243–252.

Forisha, B. L. (1978). Mental imagery and creativity: Review and speculations. *Journal of Mental Imagery, 2,* 209–238.

Gackenbach, J. I. (1978). *A personality and cognitive style analysis of lucid dreaming.* Unpublished doctoral dissertation. Virginia Commonwealth University.

Gackenbach, J. I. (1980). [Fall mass testing]. Unpublished raw data.

Gackenbach, J. I. (1983). [Fall mass testing]. Unpublished raw data.

Gackenbach, J. I. (1984a). [Spring mass testing]. Unpublished raw data.

Gackenbach, J. I. (1984b). [Summer mass testing]. Unpublished raw data.

Gackenbach, J. I. (1985a, June). *Eye movement direction and the lucid dreaming ability.* Paper presented at the annual meeting of the Association for the Study of Dreams, University of Virginia, Charlottesville, VA.

Gackenbach, J. I. (1985b). Sex differences in lucid dreaming frequency: A second look. *Lucidity Letter, 4*(1), 11.

Gackenbach, J. I. (1986). *Personality differences between individuals varying in lucid dreaming frequency.* Manscript submitted for publication.

Gackenbach, J. I., & Hammons, S. (1983). Lucid dreaming ability and verbal creativity. *Dreamworks, 3*(3), 219–223.

Gackenbach, J. I., & Schillig, B. (1983). Lucid dreams: The content of conscious awareness of dreaming during the dream. *Journal of Mental Imagery, 7*(2), 1–14.

Gackenbach, J. I., Snyder, T. J., & Esbeck, S. (1981). [Visual maze task]. Unpublished raw data.

Gackenbach, J. I., Snyder, T. J., McKelvey, K., McWilliams, C., George, E., & Rodenelli, B. (1981). Lucid dreaming: Individual differences in perception. *Sleep Research, 10,* 146.

Gackenbach, J. I., Snyder, T. J., & Vognsen, E. (1981). [Tactile maze task]. Unpublished raw data.

Gackenbach, J. I., Sachau, D., & Rokes, L. (1982). Vestibular sensitivity and dynamic and static motor balance as a function of sex and lucid dreaming. *Sleep Research, 11,* 104.

Gackenbach, J. I., Curren, R., LaBerge, S., Davidson, D., & Maxwell, P. (1983, June). *Intelligence, creativity, and personality differences between individuals who vary in self-reported lucid dreaming frequency.* Paper presented at the annual meeting of the American Association for the Study of Mental Imagery, Vancouver.

Gackenbach, J. I., Curren, R., & Cutler, G. (1983, June). *Presleep determinants and post-sleep results of lucid versus vivid dreams.* Paper presented at the annual meeting of the American Association for the Study of Mental Imagery, Vancouver.

Gackenbach, J. I., Prill, S. & Westrom, P. (1983). The relationship of the lucid dreaming ability to mental imagery experiences and skills. *Lucidity Letter, 2*(4), 4–6.

Gackenbach, J. I., Heilman, N., Boyt, S., & LaBerge, S. (1985). The relationship between field independence and lucid dreaming ability. *Journal of Mental Imagery, 9*(1), 9–20.

Gackenbach, J. I., Sachau, D., Rokes, L., & Snyder, T. J. (1986). *Lucid dreaming ability as a function of gross motor balance.* Manuscript submitted for publication.

Gackenbach, J. I., Snyder, T. J., Rokes, L., & Sachau, D., (1986). Lucid dreaming frequency in relationship to vestibular sensitivity as measured by caloric stimulation. In R. Haskel (Ed.) *Cognition and Dream Research: The Journal of Mind and Behavior* (special issue), *7*(2/3), 277–298.

Gardner, H. (1983). *Frames of mind: The theory of multiple intelligence.* New York: Basic Books.

Gilgen, A. R., & Cho, J. H. (1979). Questionnaire to measure Eastern and Western thought. *Psychological Reports, 44,* 835–841.

Golden, C. J., Hemmeke, R. A., & Purisch, A. D. (1979). *The standardization Luria-Nebraska Neuropsychological Battery: A manual for clinical and experimental use.* Lincoln: University of Nebraska Press.

Goldenberg, Y. M. (1979). *The relationship of sex, sex-role orientation, and self-esteem to attitudes toward risk-taking.* Unpublished doctoral dissertation, Adelphi University.

Gough, H. G. (1968). An interpreter's syllabus for the California Psychological Inventory. In P. McReynolds (Ed.), *Advances in psychological assessment (Vol. 1).* Palo Alto, CA: Science and Behavior Books.

Green, Celia. (1968). *Lucid dreams.* London: Hamish Hamilton.

Greyson, B. (1982). Near-death, out-of-body and lucid experiences: Additional comments and data. *Lucidity Letter, 1*(3), 6.

Gur, R. C., & Gur, R. E. (1974). Handedness, Sex and eyedness as moderating variables in the relation between hypnotic susceptibility and functional brain asymmetry. *Journal of Abnormal Psychology, 83,* 635–643.

Gur, R. C., & Gur, R. E. (1980). Handedness and individual differences in hemispheric activation. In J. Herron (Ed.), *Neuropsychology of left handedness* (pp. 211–231). New York: Academic Press.

Hakstain, A. R., & Cattel, R. B. (1975). An examination of adolescent sex differences in same ability and personality. *Canadian Journal of Behavioral Science, 1*(4), 295–312.

Harris, L. J. (1978). Sex differences in spatial ability: Possible environmental, genetic, and neurological factors. In M. Kinsbourne (Ed.), *Asymmetrical function of the brain.* Cambridge: Cambridge University Press.

Hearne, K. M. T. (1978). *Lucid dreams: An electrophysiological and psychological study.* Unpublished doctoral dissertation, University of Liverpool.

Hearne, K. M. T. (1983). Features of lucid dreams: Questionnaire data and content analyses (1). *Journal of Lucid Dream Research, 1*(1), 3–20.

Hendricks, M., & Cartwright, R. D. (1978). Experiencing level in dreams: An individual difference variable. *Psychotherapy: Theory, Research and Practice, 15*(3), 292–298.

Hulfish, S. (1978). Relationship of role identification, self-esteem, and intelligence to sex differences in field independence. *Perceptual and Motor Skills, 47,* 835–842.

Irwin, H. J. (1985). *Flight of mind: A psychological study of the out-of-body experience.* Metuchen, NJ: The Scarecrow Press.

Kinsbourne, M., & Hicks, R. E. (1978). Mapping cerebral functional space: Competition and collaboration in human performance. In M. Kinsbourne (Ed.), *Asymmetrical function of the brain.* Cambridge: Cambridge University Press.

Kohr, R. L. (1980). A survey of psi experiences among members of a special population. *The Journal of American Society for Psychic Research, 74,* 295–311.

Kohr, R. L. (1982). Near death experience and its relationship to psi and various altered states. *Theta, 10,* 50–53.

Kueny, Sallie R. (1985). *An examination of auditory cueing in REM sleep for the induction of lucid dreams.* Unpublished doctoral dissertation, Pacific Graduate Schol of Psychology.

LaBerge, S. P. (1985). *Lucid dreaming.* Los Angeles: Jeremy Tarcher.

LaBerge, S. P., & Gackenbach, J. I. (1982). [Self-perception testing]. Unpublished raw data

Leftcourt, H. M., & Telegdi, M. S. (1971). Perceived focus of control and dependence as predictors of cognitive activity. *Journal of Consulting and Clinical Psychology, 37,* 53–56.

Ley, R. G. (1983). Cerebral laterality and imagery. In A. A. Sheikh (Ed.), *Imagery: Current theory, research, and application* (pp. 252–287). New York: Wiley.

McCabe, B. F., & Ryu, J. H. (1979). *Vestibular physiology in understanding the dizzy patient.* Rochester, MN: American Academy of Otolaryngology.

McCarley, R. W., & Hobson, J. A. (1979). The form of dreams and the biology of sleep. In B. B. Wolman (Ed.), *Handbook of dreams: Research, theories and applications.* New York: Van Nostrand Reinhold.

Megargee, E. I. (1972). *The California psychological inventory handbook.* San Francisco: Jossey-Bass.

Meskin, B. B., & Singer, J. L. (1974). Reflective thought, and laterality of eye movements. *Journal of Personality and Social Psychology, 30,* 64–71.

Milner, B. (1965). Visually-guided maze learning in man. *Neuropsychologia, 3,* 317–338.

Newcombe, S., & Russell, W. R. (1969). Disassociated visual, perceptual and spatial deficits in focal lesions of the right hemisphere. *Journal of Neurology, Neurosurgery, Psychiatry, 32,* 73–81.

Noppe, L. D., & Gallagher, J. M. (1977). A cognitive style approach to creative thought. *Journal of Personality Assessment, 41,* 85–90.

Nussdorf, G. E. (1975). *Sex, sex-role stereotypes and sex-role orientation as factors in risk-taking behavior.* Unpublished doctoral dissertation, Fordham University.

Ogilvie, R., Hunt, H., Kushniruk, A., & Newman, J. (1983). Lucid dreams and the arousal continuum. *Sleep Research, 12,* 182.

Ohrmacht, F. W., & McMorris, R. F. (1971). Creativity as a function of field independence and dogmatism. *Journal of Psychology, 79,* 165–168.

Owens, W., & Limber, J. (1983). Lateral eye movement as a measure of cognitive ability and style. *Perceptual and Motor Skills, 56,* 711–719.

Palmer, J. (1974). A community mail survey of psychic experiences. *Research in Parapsychology, 3,* 130–133.

Reed, Henry. (1977). Meditation and lucid dreaming: A statistical relationship. *Sundance Community Dream Journal, 2,* 237–238.

Richardson, A. (1969). *Mental imagery.* New York: Springer.

Rosenberg, E. S. (1976). Some psychological and biological relationships between masculinity and femininity and field dependence and field independence. *Dissertation Abstracts International, 36,* 5875B.

Shepard, R. N. (1978). The mental image. *American Psychologist, 32,*(2), 125–137.

Siegel, R. K. (1977). Hallucinations. *Scientific American, 237,* 132–140.

Snyder, M. (1974). Self-monitoring of expressive behavior. *Journal of Personality and Social Psychology, 30,* 526–537.

Snyder, T. J., & Gackenbach, J. I. (1981). Lucid dreaming and cerebral organization. *Sleep Research, 10,* 154.

Spence, J. T., & Helmreich, R. L. (1978). *Masculinity and femininity: Their psychological dimensions, correlates and antecedents.* Austin and London: University of Texas Press.

Spence, J. T., Helmreich, R., & Stapp, J. (1975). Ratings of self and peers on sex role attributes and their relation to self-esteem and conceptions of masculinity and femininity. *Journal of Personality and Social Psychology, 43,* 568–571.

Sporros, N. P., Stam, H. J., Radtke, H. D., & Nightingale, M. E. (1980). Absorption in imagining, sex-role orientation, and the recall of dreams by males and females. *Journal of Personality Assessment, 44,* 227–282.

Spotts, J. V., & Mackler, B. (1976). Relationship of field-dependent and field-independent cognitive styles to creative test performance. *Perceptual and Motor Skills, 24,* 239–268.

Stoner, J. A. F. (1961). *A comparison of individual and group decisions involving risk.* Unpublished master's thesis, Massachusetts Institute of Technology, Sloan School of Management.

Tart, C. (1972). *Altered states of consciousness.* Garden City, New York: Anchor Books.

Tart, C. (1975). *States of consciousness.* New York: E. P. Dutton.

Torrance, E. P. (1972). Predictive validity of the Torrance Tests of Creative Thinking. *Journal of Creative Behavior, 6*(4), 236–252.

Vandenberg, S., & Kuse, A. R. (1978). Mental rotations: A group test of three dimensional spatial visualization. *Perceptual and Motor Skills, 47,* 599–604.

Van Nuys, D. W. (1984). Lateral eye movement and dream recall II: Sex differences and handedness. *International Journal of Psychosomatics, 31*(3), 3–7.

Witkin, H. A., & Goodenough, D. R. (1981). *Cognitive styles: Essence and origins.* New York:]International Universities Press.

Witkin, H. A., Dyk. R. B., Faterson, H. F., Goodenough, D. R., & Karp, S. A. (1962). *Psychological differentiation: Studies in development.* New York: Wiley.

Witkin, H. A., Goodenough, D. R., & Oltman, P. K. (1979). Psychological differentiation: Current status. *Journal of Personality and Social Psychology, 37,* 1127–1145.

Zuckerman, M. (1979). *Sensation seeking: Beyond the optimal level of arousal.* Hillsdale, NJ: Erlbaum.

Zuckerman, M., Bone, R. N., Neary, R., Mangelsdorff, D., & Bustman, B. (1972). What is the sensation seeker? Personality trait and experience correlates of the sensation-seeking scales. *Journal of Consulting and Clinical Psychology, 39*(2), 308–321.

III

Personal Accounts and Clinical Applications

11

A Model for Lucidity Training as a Means of Self-Healing and Psychological Growth

PAUL THOLEY

The theoretical principles for the psychotherapeutic use of lucid dreaming are outlined in view of my own first lucid dream studies and experiences. These are based on the field theoretical assumptions of Gestalt psychology that the personality is capable of self-healing and growth. In this way, lucid dreams have proven to be helpful. I will point out that one can discern unconscious conflicts and contribute to solving them during these dreams through appropriate behavior of the dream ego. Conciliatory interaction with threatening dream figures seems to be important in diagnosis and therapy. For instance, the way in which the dream ego should react in order to deprive a threatening figure of its dangerous character will be examined. I will argue, in accordance with the theoretical assumptions that conciliatory interchange is the most effective principle.

Based on the findings of this and other empirical investigations, a self-healing program using lucid dreams was developed. This program was first tested by individuals not in psychotherapy. Because of the positive effects of the self-healing program on their dreaming and waking life, it was finally applied in psychotherapy. By referring to several case histories, I will explain how this program is suited to abolishing different emotional disorders, which are rooted in unconscious conflicts.

PAUL THOLEY • Psychological Institute, Johann Wolfgang Goethe University, Frankfurt, West Germany.

RETROSPECTIVE VIEW OF MY OWN WORK WITH LUCID DREAMS

My present research on lucid dreams goes back to 1959. I was previously unaware of the phenomenon of lucid dreaming. When I started studying psychology, I began to take an interest in the content of my dreams. It occurred to me that the dreams might be consciously experienced. I started with the basic assumption that if a subject in the waking state develops a critical-reflective attitude toward his or her momentary state of awareness by asking himself or herself if he or she is awake or dreaming, then this attitude can be transferred to the dream state. As a rule, the unusual nature of dream experiences makes it possible for the subject to recognize that he or she is dreaming.

Consequently, every day I repeatedly asked myself whether I was awake or dreaming. Four weeks later I had success. My first experience of being conscious that I was dreaming was when I realized that I had met my aunt, whom I knew to be deceased. Otherwise, everything in the dream seemed to be real. I was fascinated by this dream experience, especially because of the unbelievable authenticity of the scene and the phenomenal realness of my own body. However, after a while, I was overcome by a feeling of anxiety; indeed, I had never heard of such states of awareness. But, on my aunt's advice, I stared closely at a flower. This feeling faded, and then I woke up about 10 seconds later.

I was so impressed by this dream that I was really looking forward to experiencing other phenomena of that kind—of course, without the feeling of anxiety. Thus I had to find a method that would allow me to wake up from such dreams when desired. Moreover, I had read about the physiological findings regarding the association of REM sleep with dreaming (Aserinsky & Kleitman, 1953). Consequently, by also relying on supplementary assumptions, I presumed that one could end a dream by fixing one's gaze on a stationary point in the dream surroundings. I thereby remembered in my previously described dream, after staring at the flower, that I had awoken. This hypothesis proved to be correct in experiments with other subjects (Tholey, 1973, 1977, 1983a).

I had coined the German term *Klartraum* (which actually corresponds to the English term *clear dream*) to describe the phenomenon of conscious dreaming, and I later distinguished between seven aspects of clarity in these dreams. I only became aware of the term *lucid dream,* which was coined by van Eeden (1913), 10 years after my first experiments with this kind of dream, through reading Green (1968) and Tart (1969).

I called the method which I developed for inducing lucid dreaming the "reflection technique." In later research, I developed a number of other techniques for inducing dream lucidity (Tholey, 1982b, 1983b). My first experiments with other subjects who had learned lucid dreaming by using my reflection technique were especially useful in clarifying certain problems with perception, memory, thinking, and psychophysiological processes in the lucid dream state.

The foundation for my interest in psychotherapeutic applications of lucid dreaming was laid when I realized that threatening and helping figures could appear in lucid dreams. The main problem was to determine how to deal with these dream figures in order to obtain positive effects in the dreaming and waking life. I relied on my own dream experiences. To illustrate:

> After my father's death in 1968, he often appeared to me in my dreams as a dangerous figure, who insulted and threatened me. When I became lucid, I would beat him in anger. He was then sometimes transformed into a more primitive creature, like a dwarf, an animal, or a mummy. Whenever I won, I was overcome by a feeling of triumph. Nevertheless, my father continued to appear as a threatening figure in subsequent dreams. Then I had the following decisive dream. I became lucid, while being chased by a tiger, and wanted to flee. I then pulled myself together, stood my ground, and asked, "Who are you?" The tiger was taken aback but was transformed into my father and answered, "I am your father and will now tell you what you are to do!" In contrast to my earlier dreams, I did not attempt to beat him but tried to get involved in a dialogue with him. I told him that he could not order me around. I rejected his threats and insults. On the other hand, I had to admit that some of my father's criticism was justified, and I decided to change my behavior accordingly. At that moment, my father became friendly, and we shook hands. I asked him if he could help me, and he encouraged me to go my own way alone. My father then seemed to slip into my own body, and I remained alone in the dream.

This lucid dream had a liberating and encouraging effect on my future dreaming and waking life. My father never again appeared as a threatening dream figure. In the waking state, my unreasonable fear and inhibitions in my dealings with persons of authority disappeared. With regard to psychotherapeutic use of lucid dreaming, the aforementioned dream was a key experience. I came to the following conclusions about appropriate behaviors toward threatening dream figures:

1. It is useful to confront the threatening dream situation despite rising fears.
2. It is better to reconcile with the dream figure through constructive dialogue than to attack it aggressively.
3. After the dialogue, the threatening figure can be transformed into a friendly one, who can provide help.
4. The following dream brought me to the fourth conclusion. A constructive dialogue is not possible with some hostile dream figures. Therefore, it is useful to separate oneself from these figures.

Although I was able to effectively treat people suffering from nightmares with these basic therapeutic principles, my research on lucid dreaming was rejected by psychologists in West Germany. Also, my offer to be a subject in the sleep laboratory was declined. At this time, I had the following lucid dream:

> In the lucid dream state, I was flying over a street in which I wanted to land. Suddenly an ugly fellow appeared, who shouted up to me, "Nobody can fly! It's physically

impossible. It should be forbidden. I'm going to tell the police!'' When I asked him who he was, his head took on doglike characteristics and he said angrily, ''A top dog.'' When I tried to involve him in a dialogue, he screamed at me that he did not want to talk to me. It became clear to me that the dream expressed my conflict between the desire to research lucid dreaming and the fear of academic psychologists' negative sanctions. I decided during this dream to continue research and to make it public. At that moment, an enormous fence rose between me and the ''top dog.'' I then flew from the scene, at which point the other dream figure was transformed into a tiny pup, which finally disappeared.

In 1973 I presented an extensive report of my lucid dream research at the University of Frankfurt/Main. Some of my colleagues considered me to be a fantasist, whereas some of my students saw me as a guru. At that time, I had the following lucid dream:

> I met my brother [2 years older than me] in the lucid dream state. He insulted me and told me he had always been superior to me. He criticized me for playing the role of a guru in order to outdo him. He then brought my attention to a balloon in the form of an inflated Buddha. I knew that he identified me with this inflated Buddha, and I came to the conclusion that my brother was not entirely wrong in doing so. Then two hands appeared from heaven and clapped so that the balloon burst. After this, my brother approached me in a friendly manner.

It became clear to me, through this dream, that I was pursuing a secondary goal of superiority in my work. This goal, which had been unconscious to me until then, stemmed from a childhood rivalry with my older brother. The dream led me to a less ego-centered and more critical attitude toward myself. It also encouraged me to commit myself to goals, which I considered important, even though such a decision might damage my professional prestige.

Because of my own lucid dream experiences and similar experiences with other subjects, I became convinced that interaction with dream figures, whether they are human, animal, or mythical, has a special place in mental hygiene. For that reason, empirical tests were made as to which form of interaction with dream figures was most effective. Before these empirical studies are outlined, the theoretical foundations of our basic psychotherapeutic principles will be described.

BASIC THEORETICAL PRINCIPLES

In our research program, during interpretation of findings and for the psychotherapeutic application of lucid dreaming, we relied on the field theoretical approach of Gestalt psychology.[1] The field theory is based on a dynamic model

---

[1]Gestalt psychology was founded by Wertheimer, Koehler, Koffka, and Lewin. Meanwhile, it has developed to an elaborated theoretical system that extends to border areas of science (cf. Tholey, 1980d). Gestalt psychology should not be confounded with the so-called Gestalt therapy of Fritz Perls (1969) that has various theoretical weaknesses (cf. Henle, 1978; Tholey, 1984b).

of personality. As opposed to the psychoanalytical point of view, which is also based on a dynamic model, the field theory does not consider behavior as solely based on organismic drives but rather as dependent on the total psychological field (psychological person and psychological environment). The personality can be viewed as composed of many subsystems (i.e., drives, needs, goals, moral demands, social requirements), which are in dynamic interaction with one another. Based on experimental findings concerning symbol formation (for a survey, see Leuner, 1962), the dynamics of the personality can find expression in dreams. Because the unconscious facts are "projected" symbolically, Freud (1900) considers the dream as the *via regia* (the royal road) to the unconscious. However, the therapist is the leader along this road, so that the therapeutic effects may largely depend on his or her theoretical bias. Hence, we consider the use of lucid dreaming important as it enables the subject to find his or her own way to his or her unconscious and its integration into the personality.

Compared to nonlucid dreams, the lucid dream has the following advantages:

1. Because of the lucidity, the dream ego is less afraid of threatening dream figures or situations. For this reason, there is less resistance to confrontation with these figures or situations.
2. Using appropriate techniques for manipulating lucid dreaming, the dream ego can get in touch with places, times, situations, or persons that are important to the dreamer.
3. Especially in dialogue with other dream figures, the dream ego is able to recognize the present personality dynamics and their etiology (diagnostic function).
4. Through appropriate activity of the dream ego, a change of personality structure is possible (therapeutic or creative function).

In this way, the lucid dream is helpful for self-knowledge, self-healing, and self-actualization. This is possible because, according to the field theory, the symbolic dream events are in dynamic interaction with the symbolized psychological facts. For example, an interpsychic or psychosocial conflict can be expressed in threats from a hostile dream figure. On the other hand, the reconciliation with this dream figure can contribute to the resolution of the conflict.

EMPIRICAL RESEARCH SURVEYED

The following questions arise regarding: the psychotherapeutic applications of lucid dreaming:

1. How can one learn techniques for inducing and manipulating lucid dreaming?

2. How should the dream ego act within a lucid dream in order to obtain positive effects in dreaming and waking life?
3. How should the therapist and the client interact in lucid dream therapy?

Our empirical research has been based on these three questions. Because we described the techniques for inducing and manipulating lucid dreams in earlier articles (Tholey, 1982b, 1983b), we only briefly refer to them here. In our research, we realized that it was not the dream lucidity itself that induced the positive effects; rather, it was the dream ego's activity in the lucid dream. In lucid dreams, one may avoid dealing with conflicts that have arisen, or one can confront them and thus contribute to their solution (cf. LaBerge, 1981). It has become evident that the interaction of the dream ego with other dream figures is significant for both diagnosis and therapy. For this reason, we also investigated, in our empirical studies, how certain forms of interactions with dream figures affect (a) the events in the present lucid dream, (b) future dreaming, and (c) waking life.

Field theory is significant, not only for its theoretical structure but also for its methodological approach. Thus, in our exploratory studies, we used the method of stepwise approximation of theoretical and empirical work (Lewin, 1940), which is similar to the "dialectical approach" of Malamud (1978).

In our investigations, we used the so-called phenomenological-experimental approach (for a survey on this approach, see Kebeck & Sader, 1984; Tholey, 1986a). In contrast to traditional experimental research, the independent and/or dependent variables are of a subjective nature. In spite of this, the results of such experiments do possess a certain degree of intersubjective validity, provided that a sufficient number of individuals report, independent of one another, on identical experiences. In order to be able to speak of experiments, the independent variables must be varied in analog form as in objective experiments. In the phenomenological-experimental approach to lucid dream research, the experimenter instructs the subjects in the way in which they are to vary their behavior during lucid dreaming. It is also the experimenter's task to observe the effects that take place and to draw up reports for each subject after they have awoken (Tholey, 1980b). The variations may either concern the activity of different test groups and/or the activity of individual subjects. We carried out a number of investigations testing psychological and psychophysiological assumptions about lucid dreaming. Here we will describe only those phenomenological experiments in which the influence of the dream ego's activity on the expressions, appearances, statements, and behaviors of other dream figures was examined.

Based on this research, we developed a self-healing program using lucid dreaming. This program was tested by people not in psychotherapy. Because of the positive effects of this self-healing program on their dreaming and waking lives, the program was used in psychotherapy in the following case studies. In our program, we used the field theoretical method of reconstruction of single cases (for details see Kebeck, 1983). Due to space limitations, the empirical experiments can only be featured here in a shortened form. Consequently, details concerning the methodology and the findings are omitted.

PHENOMENOLOGICAL EXPERIMENTS ON INTERACTIONS WITH DREAM FIGURES

Problem

In phenomenological-experimental research on lucid dreaming, several difficulties can arise. Gillespie (1984) indicates 12 "problems related to experimentation while dreaming lucidly." However, he only mentions the awareness that one is dreaming as criterion for the lucid dream state (1983). For Tart (1984, p. 5), this is "a necessary but not a sufficient criterion for labeling a dream 'lucid.'" In my opinion, a dream can only be called "lucid," according to van Eeden's definition (1913) if, as well as being aware that one is dreaming, the dreamer also recalls one's waking life, is in full command of one's intellectual abilities, and has control over one's own activity. It is, however, this clarity about the possibility of controlling one's own activity that first alters entirely the nature of the dream (cf. Tholey, 1986b). Being able to recollect one's waking life, and having control over one's own activity are necessary requirements for the phenomenological-experimental approach to lucid dream research.

We took this fact into account in applying the various techniques for inducing lucid dreams. Subjects were instructed to carry out actions such as simple motions (cf. Tholey, 1983b)—actions planned in the waking life—on achieving lucidity. This would seem to explain why almost all of the subjects could recall their waking lives and were aware of the control over their own activity, so that several of the problems mentioned by Gillespie (1984) become irrelevant. The control of the dream ego over one's own activity does not mean that the dream ego is in a position to manipulate the entire dream; there are certain limitations to such manipulation (cf. also Tholey, 1983b; Gackenbach, 1986).

Our interest in these experiments was with the ability of the dream ego, when interacting with a hostile dream figure, to eliminate its threatening character. However, in our phenomenological experiments, difficulties arose. For example, it was necessary for the subjects to have lucid dreams in which hostile dream figures appeared. Indeed, experienced lucid dreamers have various means to facilitate their meeting such figures. Our experiments were limited by ethical concerns because, in our exploratory studies, some types of activities of the dream ego would lead to unpleasant effects; we noted destructive behavior toward a hostile dream figure (e.g., killing the figure) as well as totally submissive behavior toward the dream enemy's aggression (e.g., letting oneself be killed).

In the first case, feelings of euphoria as well as strong feelings of fear and guilt were aroused, and these continued even after awakening. In the second case, feelings of fear and discouragement were almost always noted. In this context, we should also emphasize that recent experimental findings (Tholey, 1985) suggest that some dream figures might have an independent awareness. They behave as if they possessed their own perceptual perspectives, cognitive abilities (memory and thought), and even their own motivations. Also, they might suffer pain. We concluded from this that we must treat dream figures as if they were real "beings." Nevertheless, in our early experiments on lucid dreaming, aggressive or submissive behavior of the dream ego was tolerated to a certain extent, in order to observe and analyze the influence of these forms of behavior on the threatening or hostile dream figures. In particular, in six separate phenomenological experiments, the appearance, statements, and behavior of the hostile dream figure's influence on the following was tested:

1. When the dream ego was inspired with fear or courage.
2. When the dream ego looked away from the dream figure, or looked at him openly.
3. When the dream ego conducted submissive or conciliatory dialogue.
4. When the dream ego conducted aggressive or conciliatory dialogue.
5. When the dream ego displayed submissive or conciliatory behavior.
6. When the dream ego displayed aggressive or conciliatory behavior.

Three forms of dialogue and three forms of behavior of the dream ego have been proposed. However, in each of the six experiments, only two forms of activity were tested in order not to demand too much from the subjects.

Method

The subjects were 38 male and female students who had learned to dream lucidly, using our techniques. Some of the students participated in more than one of the six experiments. To adapt their emotional, visual, verbal, and bodily activities while dreaming lucidly, according to the demands of the experiment in which they were taking part, the various forms of activities were explained to the subjects in detail. The subjects were told various techniques for inspiring feelings of fear and courage, techniques that I had developed in investigations in sports psychology. Furthermore, in conciliatory dialogue, the subjects were instructed that they should approach the hostile dream figures with friendly gestures. Instead of resorting to attack, they should protect themselves against the dream enemy's attacks. Finally, if possible, the subjects were instructed to end the lucid dream only after the dream figures had lost their threatening character.

In each experiment, an analysis was made of the subject's first lucid dream in which he or she was confronted by a hostile dream figure and acted according to his or her experimental instructions. If the subject observed the expected change in the threatening nature of the hostile figure, it would be considered a success; if not, a failure was registered.

Results and Conclusion

Our statistical inference is based on the Bayesian statistics, which have been argued to be superior to significance testing (for details see Tholey, 1980c, 1982a). The Bayesian approach renders possible the calculation of the probabilities of the hypotheses (for an introduction to elementary Bayesian methods see Hays, 1973, Chapter 19). It can be seen in Table 1 that the first five tested hypotheses have a very high probability of being correct. Thus it seems to be helpful if the dream ego approaches the hostile dream figure in a courageous manner, looks at him openly, conducts a conciliatory dialogue with him and shows his willingness for reconciliation.

The qualitative results show important details. In changing the dream ego's activity, the hostile dream figures displayed transformation processes of various kinds. If the dream ego courageously faced up to the hostile dream figure, this figure itself often began to shrink. If the dream ego alternatively allowed himself to be anxious, the hostile figure sometimes began to grow. While shrinking or growing, the dream figures sometimes changed their guise, so that, for example a snake became a worm and vice versa.

If the dream ego looked openly at the hostile dream figure, its appearance

Table 1. Effects of the Dream Ego's Activities on the Threatening Nature of Other Dream Figures

Dream ego's activities	n^a	r^b	$P(H)^c$
1. Inspiring with fear/courage	16	12	.98
2. Looking away/openly Dialogue	15	12	.99
3. Submissive/conciliatory	17	14	.99
4. Aggressive/conciliatory Behavior	15	12	.99
5. Submissive/conciliatory	18	15	.99
6. Aggressive/conciliatory	18	10	.67

[a]Number of subjects
[b]Number of successes (decrease of the threatening nature of other dream figures according to the hypothesis).
[c]Probability for the tested hypothesis H, that the probability for success $\pi > 5$, given the values for n and r. The values for $P(H)$ have been calculated according to the Bayesian statistics. We used the tables of Pearson (1968) for computation of these values.

often became less harmful. In this case, looking directly into the eyes of the hostile figure seems to have a special meaning. According to the reports of the subjects, the dream ego can keep a hostile figure at a distance by looking into his eyes. On the other hand, several dream figures were able to escape the gaze of the dream ego by jerking their heads, by putting on a cowl, or by attacking the dream ego from the rear (see also Tholey, 1985).

As with our exploratory studies, in our experimental research, the conciliatory dialogue proved to be the most effective principle. The friendly approach of the dream ego often caused progressive transformations of the hostile dream figures. It seems that these are changes from lower-order into higher-order creatures, that is, the transformation of an animal or mythological figure into a human being. These transformations and the dream figure's responses often allowed the subjects to immediately understand the meaning of the dream. This sometimes occurred with the defenseless attitude in a dream dialogue, that is, when the dream ego did not reject insults or threats. When the dream ego reverted to a verbal attack, regressive transformations of dream figures were sometimes observed. For example, a mother figure was transformed into a witch and finally into a beast.

Regressive transformations of dream figures were very often experienced after bodily attacks of the dream ego. In most cases, the dream ego conquered the dream enemy and subsequently experienced feelings of triumph or euphoria. Sometimes these feelings were mixed with anxiety or guilt. In the latter case, other dream figures sometimes appeared as "avengers." Defenseless behavior almost always led to unpleasant experiences of fear or discouragement, and hostile dream figures would often win out in size and strength. Depending on the dream ego's conciliatory behavior, the originally threatening dream figures would generally become more friendly in appearance and behavior.

The quantitative and qualitative results of the phenomenological experiments just described are consistent with our basic theoretical concepts and the resultant hypotheses on the effects of different types of interactions of the dream ego with threatening dream figures.

EMPIRICAL INVESTIGATION OF A SELF-HEALING PROGRAM USING LUCID DREAMS

Problem

Based on exploratory research in a study group and phenomenological experiments of the kind just described, we developed a self-healing program. This program contains guidelines (1) on the techniques for inducing and ending lucid dreams, (2) on methods for incubating and manipulating the contents of lucid dreams, (3) on the appropriate behavior regarding resistance (such as "defense" or "avoidance" mechanisms), and (4) on helpful principles for interaction with other dream figures. Examples were used to illustrate the program.

We consider the mere induction of dreaming lucidly as a step toward healing. The usual dream state, in which lucidity is not achieved, we regard as a form of consciousness disorder (Tholey, 1985).

The instructions for the incubation of the content of lucid dreams were similar to the ones used for nonlucid dreams (cf. Stephan, 1984). The subjects were advised that they could obtain help for special problems by thinking about their problem before falling asleep. Furthermore, the subjects were told how they could manipulate the dream content within certain limits while dreaming lucidly. It was stressed that the confrontation with unpleasant dream situations or figures is very important for the diagnostic and healing processes.

We recommended that the subjects should even purposely look for threatening dream situations or figures if these did not appear of their own accord. This is consistent with the work of Kuenkel, who argues that the true way to healing is through the "barking pack" of the "dogs of the unconscious" (Kuenkel, 1934, p. 225). If they do not appear spontaneously, they must be sought in their hiding places. Only through reconciliation with these "dogs" can emotional balance be obtained, according to Kuenkel. Based on our exploratory research, the subjects were instructed that the way to threatening dream situations and figures is as from the light into the dark (e.g., from an open field into a wood), from above to below (e.g., from the surface of a pond to the bottom of it), or from the present to the past (e.g., from adulthood into early childhood). Nevertheless, different forms of resistance can arise on the way to the unconscious. For instance, the dreamer can be responsible for his or her lack of success in achieving or retaining the lucid dream state (for examples, see Tholey, 1980b), sometimes resulting in a "false remaining awake" or a "false awakening" (Tholey, 1983b). Additionally, while dreaming lucidly, a resistance can be expressed in feelings of fear when approaching unpleasant situations. Furthermore, in the dream-environment, obstacles, like fences, locked doors, or invisible forces, can bar the way of the dream ego. Finally, dream figures can divert the dream ego by using warnings, threats, or bodily violence.

In our self-healing program, the different forms of resistance were explained. The subjects were advised to not seek out very threatening situations or figures in their first lucid dreams but to slowly confront unpleasant experiences. The subjects were also told that, while dreaming lucidly, one can look for an ally or a "pacemaker" (cf. Leuner, 1978), who in the early stages accompanies the dream ego on its way to the unconscious. Such a dream figure often appears in the role of an internal self helper (ISH) (cf. Sally, 1985).

At the core of our self-healing program was advice on how to deal with different situations with hostile dream figures. The following instructions were given to the subjects:

1. *Confrontation*: Do not attempt to flee from a threatening dream figure. Rather, confront him courageously, look at him openly, and ask him in a friendly way, "Who are you?" or "Who am I?"[2]

2. *Dialogue*: If it is possible to address the dream figure, try to come to a reconciliation with him through a constructive dialogue. If agreement is impossible, try to arrange the conflict as an open dispute. Moreover, refuse his insults or threats, but recognize his justified objections.

3. *Fight*: Do not surrender to an attack by a dream figure. Show your readiness to defend yourself by taking a defensive position and by staring at the dream figure in his eyes. If a fight is unavoidable, attempt to conquer the dream enemy but do not try to kill him. Offer reconciliation to the conquered enemy.

4. *Reconciliation*: Attempt to reconcile in thought, words and/or gestures with the hostile dream figure.

5. *Separation*: If a reconciliation does not seem possible, separate yourself from the figure in thought, words, and/or bodily withdrawal.

Sometimes you must also leave a dream figure with whom you have become reconciled. For example, if you recognize that this figure represents a person, who once meant a lot to you but is no longer attainable (whether because of death or the dissolving of a partnership), thank this person for his former accompaniment on your path of life before you leave him.

6. *Seek help*: After reconciliation with a dream figure, ask him whether he can help you. Then you can mention specific problems in your waking or dream life.

Method

A preliminary self-healing program using lucid dreaming was applied and, based on its findings, improved, according to the method of successive approximation. Then, in a corrected and elaborated form, the program was presented and discussed at a university and was featured in the German media. As a result, I received many letters from persons of different sex, ages, and occupations. The results discussed next refer mainly to reports from 62 male and female students, with whom we had contact over a period of at least one year after they had learned to dream lucidly. We asked them questions about their lucid dream contents and the effects of these dreams on their waking and dream life.

Results and Conclusion

The most important quantitative results concerning the contents of these subjects' lucid dreams are diagnosed in Figure 1. We examined only those lucid

---

[2]All guidelines refer basically to all kinds dream figures; thus instead of simply "him," one may always read "him, her, its," and so forth.

dreams in which there was real confrontation with a hostile dream figure. These included 282 lucid dreams from the 62 subjects. Overall, 77% of the hostile dream figures had been deprived of their threatening nature. Reconciliation was gained with 33% of them. In most cases, this was achieved by dialogue. The percentage of cases in which subjects obtained help from the dream figures after reconciliation is small. However, subjects more often had help from dream figures that had appeared friendly from the beginning. There were more reports of successful conciliatory activity compared to our earlier work where we had not given instructions concerning interactions with other dream figures.

To fully demonstrate the effectiveness of the self-healing program, a de-

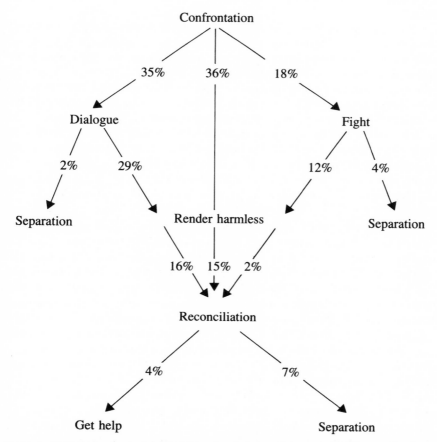

Figure 1. Percentage of principles in interaction between dream ego and threatening dream figures. (All percentages refer to the total number of 282 dreams. Missing percentages: dreamers who awoke.)

tailed description of single cases should be presented. Due to space limitations, we will only refer to our own lucid dreams and the case studies of six clients.

The majority of the clients reported positive effects on their subsequent dreaming and waking lives. "Normal" dreams were experienced as more pleasant and meaningful. Furthermore, 66% of the clients were able to resolve problems and conflicts of various kinds by means of their lucid dreams. In waking life, they felt less anxious (62%), more emotionally balanced (45%), more open-minded (42%), and more creative (30%). However, 22% of the participants reported transitory negative symptoms. In cases where a client, contrary to our instructions, fled from a threatening dream figure, feelings of discouragement appeared. After the confrontation, feelings of anxiety or guilt eventually arose if the client was still able to accept the gained insights. Sex differences were not found.

A more detailed analysis of the clients' self-reports and the continuous observations by the investigators led to the conclusion that the positive effects should not be interpreted as changes of the discrete dimensions of the personality but as consequences of a structural alteration of the personality. From the psychoanalytic perspective, an increase in ego strength would have been reported. However, we would prefer to use the term *confirmation of courage* (or self-reliance). The latter is an attribute of the entire personality. This courage (self-reliance) is gained by a confrontation with threatening situations or persons during lucid dreaming and, what is more important, from a recognition of needs or goals that had previously been denied and were working as isolated complexes in the personality. However, confrontation with threatening dream figures and conflicts requires a certain amount of courage as strong resistances have to be overcome.

Furthermore, confirmation of courage (self-reliance) is closely related to a change from an ego-centered attitude to a situation-oriented attitude. Ego-centeredness impedes perception, creative activities, shaping, and acting (cf. Wertheimer, 1959; Metzger, 1962) and is responsible for several emotional and psychosocial disorders (cf. Kuenkel, 1982; Metzger, 1976). An insight into the demands of the whole psychosocial situation is accomplished by overcoming ego centeredness. The person is now ready to behave courageously and in creative "freedom" (for theoretical and empirical details, cf. Metzger, 1962; 1976).

The results of other clinical research on the effects of lucid dreaming is consistent with our findings (e.g., Malamud, 1979). Malamud developed a self-healing program for the increase of lucidity in dreams, waking dreams, and in waking life. The increase of lucidity was associated with awareness, liberty, and safety, in the imaginal realm, and insight into dreaming and daydream imageries, the latter also being an important condition for personal growth and integration. She did not, however, discuss the principles of these changes. Research on the relation between the ability to dream lucidly and various personality dimensions is not directly comparable with our results because of the different methodological approaches. Nevertheless, it seems remarkable that frequent lucid dreamers were less tense, anxious, and neurotic, and more likely to have more ego strength, emotional and physical balance, creativity, and risk-taking ability; we here refer, above all, to the extensive research of Gackenbach (cf. Gackenbach, 1978, 1980; Gackenbach & LaBerge, 1984; see her chapter elsewhere in this book).

On the other hand, the results are inconsistent and puzzling, for example the "lack of a self-concept difference between the two lucid dreaming groups and the non-lucid dreamers" (Gackenbach, 1980, p. 258). In our opinion, these results might be better understood by examining how lucid dreams have been dealt with. Several subjects who spontaneously dreamed lucidly reported that their lucid dreams were only used for their delight, that is, for flying or for "sex and crime." Although there are no objections against enjoying lucid dreams for their own sake, for self-healing, a confrontation with one's own conflicts and experiences are indispensable conditions.

In the latter context, it is remarkable that we noted positive effects of lucid dreaming on athletic skills in our work with sport students. The sports involved used much physical balance (for this concept, see Tholey, 1984d) as well as risk taking, for example, skiing and skateboarding. Originally, we traced the positive effects of dreaming lucidly to improvements in the organization of the sensory field (Tholey, 1981). Elsewhere (Tholey, 1984c), we found a relationship between athletic ability improvement and a change from an ego-centered to a situation-oriented personal attitude. From a Gestalt psychological perspective (cf. Metzger, 1962), this change promotes sensitivity of perception and interpersonal courage. This is especially relevant for those sports in which quick and risky reactions to changing situational conditions are prevalent. Gestalt psychology and certain teachings in Zen Buddhism (Kohl, 1956; Metzger, 1962; Tholey, 1984c) support this relationship between the personality structure and athletic processes.

CASE STUDIES OF A PSYCHOTHERAPEUTIC PROGRAM USING LUCID DREAMS

Problem

The aforementioned study will now be supplemented by six clinical case histories of patients who sought psychotherapy. It is assumed herein that our self-healing program can be effective with clients who cannot resolve their own problems. We see it as the basic duty of the therapist to provide the patient with the means of self-help; to support him or her in a trustworthy way with our method; and to protect him or her from discouragement in the face of resistance. With a few patients, it was necessary to complement the described self-healing program with other therapeutic techniques.

Method

The program was offered by different therapists to patients who complained of the following symptoms: (1) recurring anxiety dreams or nightmares; (2) other anxiety or phobic symptoms, for example, fear of snakes, dogs, height; (3) symptoms of psychogenic depressions; (4) psychosomatic symptoms of various kinds, for example, blushing; (5) addiction symptoms, for example drug abuse, or (6) social adjustment difficulties, for example shyness, problems with partners. These symptoms did not generally occur separately but were combined within different syndromes, indicating various psychoneuroses.

The program was not offered in the following cases: (1) low intelligence (IQ below 90); (2) poor motivation; (3) psychotic or prepsychotic disorders, or (4) organic brain disorders. Depending on the type of disorder, the program was altered or complemented. Thus patients who complained of a disorder involving reality awareness were never offered the reflection technique for the induction of lucid dreams because the disorder could have been worsened with this technique. Follow-up therapy depended on the first lucid dreams, which were diagnostically significant for the patient as well as the therapist. In this context, it is important that the therapist conduct an interview with the participants upon their awakening. Reis (in preparation) has developed a special interview technique that allows both the therapist and the patient to attain more important information about dream content and above all about its dynamic course than is possible by means of self-reports. It remains the task of the therapist to eliminate the patient's resistance to regaining consciousness. The interview is also meant to enable the patient to later interpret his or her dreams alone. Lack of space prevents us from describing this important technique in any detail here.

Results and Conclusions

We chose only a few characteristic cases, which illustrate the therapeutic application of the lucid dream. The program proved to be very effective in eliminating unpleasant dreams. In most cases, patients also felt a liberating effect on their waking lives.

Case 1: A 28-year-old female student complained of recurrent nightmares. She was in a difficult personal situation at that time as she had disturbed relationships with her husband and her fatally ill father; she showed signs of anxiety and depression in her waking life.

A few days after the lucid dream technique was explained to her, she had the following dream:

She found herself in the house she had lived in as a child and was expecting a group of people, who intended to do something harmful to her. She remembered that this situation often occurred in her dreams, so she became lucid. Despite the fact that she was struck with fear and wanted to flee, she overcame this fear and courageously stood her ground. People in long robes approached. She looked at the first figure, a gigantic man with a cold, blue face and glowing eyes, and asked him, "What are you doing here? What do you want from me?" The man looked at her sadly, his expression became helpless as he said, "Why? You called us. You need us for your anxiety." Then the man shrank to normal size. His face became normal and his eyes stopped glowing.

Since this first lucid dream, for the last 5 years, the student has not had any more nightmares. She has also felt less anxiety in her waking life.

This student could not interpret her dream. In other case histories, as well, lucid dreams occurred in which the confrontation with hostile dream figures led to the abolishing of fear in the waking state, without the patients understanding their dream activity. The following possibilities may explain this behavior:

1. Because of the dynamic interaction between symbolic activity and symbolized psychological facts, the activity of the dream ego can exercise an immediate influence on the personality structure without a rational mediative process. In this way, the reconciliation with a hostile dream figure can result in the solution of an unconscious conflict, without having to make this conflict conscious. This is important, because due to a lack of intelligence and/or an inner resistance, it is often impossible to make some patients aware of certain conflicts.

2. The unpleasant symptoms may have been caused by traumatic or conflicting situations that no longer exist. They can be disposed of in a lucid dream in the same way as systematic desensitization in behavior therapy. This is an effective technique in abolishing phobic symptoms.

3. Finally, it seems that the courageous confrontation with unpleasantness in the dream can cause a positive transfer into similar situations while awake.

For this student, the first two hypotheses are plausible. According to her, the insight that she had beckoned her own fears was very important. Subsequently, she tolerated turns of fate courageously. Her lucid dreams as well as her usual dreams continued to help her. For instance, after the death of her father, he appeared to her in a dream. He was, however, not angry, as he had been toward the end of his long illness, but a friendly ally, as he had been in her childhood. The student was holding a candle in her hand. Both she and her father knew that when the candle went out, her father would go away forever. In spite of the fact that she knew her father would leave her and she would mourn, the dreamer accepted her father's going with calmness. She had rediscovered her healthy and friendly father during the dream and in her waking life as well.

It seems important to me that one can take leave of a dream figure, with whom one has become reconciled and from whom it is necessary to part, if one feels strong enough to cope with one's own problems. In this, one should be thankful for the positive things shared with the person in question and integrate these into the personality. After a series of helpful dreams, the student was told in her dream that her name should be changed from "Cordula" to "Laetitia." She learnt from her friends that the Latin word *laetitia* meant joy or happiness, whereas the word *cordula* (or sweetheart) had a childlike, timid quality. This new name, which she has since used with her friends, reflects the joy of living won in her dream. In the meantime, she has become a therapist herself and successfully uses dreams and especially lucid dreams.

Case 2: A 32-year-old manager sought help from a therapist because he suffered feelings of anxiety and various phobic symptoms. He felt that he was handicapped in his career by shyness and lacked perseverance. After approximately one week, he had his first lucid dream:

He was hiding in a pine wood, and saw people walking in the woods. He was overcome by the desire to throw pinecones at one of them from his hiding place. To his childish delight, he noticed that the pinecones exploded like hand gernades and that they killed or injured the people. He thought this was great fun. On awakening, he was shocked at discovering that he had an aggressive tendency, as he had always considered himself to be free of aggression. This dream showed clearly that aggressive behavior can have a cathartic effect over a short period of time, without however being therapeutic in the long run.

The next lucid dream the patient had was more helpful. He saw a burglar in his house, who had a vicious dog with him. Despite his great fear, he forced himself to approach the man and asked him his name. The burglar called a name (which the patient could no longer remember). Then he said that he stood by what he did. He explained to the dreamer that it is much worse not to accept the truth about oneself. The patient realized during the dream that the burglar symbolized his own aggressiveness that he had not admitted.

In another lucid dream, the patient recognized the reasons for his inhibitions with regard to his aggression. He saw his father behaving aggressively in different ways in a dream. After awakening, the patient realized that his father (also a manager), who claimed to be a peaceful person, was covertly very aggressive. Furthermore, he remembered that his father had strictly suppressed the patient's own aggressiveness in his childhood. It is of interest that the patient arrived at these conclusions without the help of the therapist and that he later trusted his own dreams more than the therapist's guidance. The latter was nevertheless able to help the patient deal therapeutically with these conclusions.

Apparently, the integrity of the patient's personality was damaged in two ways. The overstrict upbringing by his father induced a moral demand that represented a foreign body in the patient's own personality. At the same time, a basic personality need was isolated. The aggressiveness was then directed toward the patient himself, expressed in his fears and phobic symptoms. The patient made a step forward in the therapy, by distancing himself from his father as a model and admitting his own aggressiveness. The latter still had to be integrated into the personality. It should be noted that, according to the field theory, the so-called aggressive drive is originally a neutral need for activity, which, depending on the upbringing, can develop into a constructive drive for intellectual or active confrontation in the outside world, or a destructive drive, which can be directed against others or oneself (for experimental findings, see Metzger, 1962). Self-destructive tendencies develop when the natural drive for action is suppressed by an authoritarian upbringing, as in the patient's case.

The therapist's duty was not to change the self-destructive tendencies within the patient to aggressive tendencies toward others but to change them into a spirit of enterprise and perseverance in his business life. As the patient was judicious, he succeeded in doing this after a relatively short period of time. The unpleasant symptoms disappeared.

The lucid dream technique was no longer necessary in the patient's learning how to persevere, although it would have been apt as can be seen in the following case.

Case 3: A 16-year-old schoolgirl had been so suppressed in her childhood by her mother's lover that she had retreated into her shell. This behavior of hers led to another suppression on the part of her classmates, so that suicidal thoughts developed. After clinical treatment, she was relieved of her depressions. However, she continued to suffer dreams of fear in which she was oppressed as was the case in her waking life. By learning lucid dreaming, she was able to confront her suppression in dreams. She no longer remained silent when exposed to her classmates' attacks but argued well on her own behalf. She did this as well while awake. People who had known her as a submissive and passive girl were completely surprised by this alteration in her behavior. After changing classes, she had a positive, open relationship with her classmates and felt at ease. Her anxiety dreams disappeared completely. This example shows that through open dialogue in the lucid dream, not only can fears within the dream be abolished but that this dialogue (also as testing action) can lead to a meaningful change in waking behavior. It must be noted, however, that the schoolgirl was already aware of the reason for her problem.

Along with the suppression of aggression, suppression of the sexual drive can also lead to neurotic disorders. This can express itself in the persecution dreams of young women. The following case is a particularly instructive example:

Case 4: A 22-year-old female teacher, who was unable to deal with her pupils because of her shyness, suffered from persecution dreams. She had the following dream:

She found herself in a wood, where she suddenly discovered a large mushroom. When this was transformed into a snake, she became lucid. Although the snake crawled toward her, she remained standing. The snake acquired wings and was transformed into a large bird, which flew into the branches of a nearby tree. When she tried to look at this more closely, it changed into a handsome prince. It became painfully clear to her that because of the prince's rank and his position in the tree, he was unobtainable. At that moment, the prince was transformed into a dolphin, which jumped from the tree into a pond. The dreamer jumped in after him and played with him.

This dream clearly reflects her immature relationship to the opposite sex. In being threatened by the snake—mushrooms and snakes are often phallic symbols—her fear of sexuality was expressed. There was certainly a series of progressive transformations in the dream. But these transformations exceeded her goal, in that they did not lead to an attainable partner but to a prince. In this, the teacher's unrealistic infatuation is expressed. She comes, however, to the important conclusion, within the dream, that this infatuation is not enough and that she needs contact with a partner. The fact that this partner is a dolphin in the dream indicates that she is not yet mature enough for a real partnership with another person.

With regard to therapy, it is important that from the field-theoretical perspective, sexuality, like aggressiveness is not a chaotic drive, as Freud considered it to be, but that it can be made so by incorrect upbringing. If the sexual need is integrated into the personality by being satisfied in a love relationship, it contributes to the self-realization of a person (cf. Maslow, 1981). This young teacher had complained of no other symptoms apart from her shyness. She quickly gained insight about herself and is now happily married.

In working with further dreams, she lost all her shyness and became very self-assured. The following dream shows that additional energy was set free through the solution of her problems. She found herself in a place of power. There was a stone lying on the ground that seemed to exude enormous energy. When she decided to pick it up, in order to take it with her, a voice sounded from heaven, "You can't take the stone into the waking state, but you will keep the force that comes from it." According to the formerly shy teacher, this dream gave her enormous strength.

One can obtain help in an apparently hopeless crisis situation by using lucid dreams, where no unconscious dynamics are involved, as the following case will illustrate.

Case 5: A 38-year-old academic suffered from severe depression as a result of various external circumstances. Before going to sleep, he thought about the possibility of committing suicide. The following night he had a lucid dream, in which he met a man who grinned at him diabolically and asked, "Well, do you know the way to the Reaper [Death] now?" This dream disturbed the man to such an extent that he fell asleep the following day with the desire to obtain help in a further lucid dream. He had the following dream:

He was skiing and flew so high after a jump that he became lucid. He then unbuckled his skis to go to a hooded man, who was standing in front of a cave. As he came nearer, he noticed that a skull was looking at him. In his shock, he stabbed at Death with his ski stick, but he only stabbed between bones. He then realized that aggressive behavior in a lucid dream was pointless, and addressed the man, "Who are you?" The latter answered, "The plundering wolf!" Whereupon the dreamer asked, "Can you help me?" Death invited him to go into the cave with him. At the far end of the cave, they came to a vault, in which there was a tombstone. Death indicated a painted skeleton on the tombstone and said, "Look, this stands behind every man. But you are not dead, you are alive." He made it clear to the dreamer, in an impressive way, how unimportant his problems were in the face of death.

This was a key experience for the dreamer, which helped him to overcome later crises. In this dream, death may have represented the personification of his tendency toward self-preservation, which was still present. Moreover, this dream shows a surprising parallel (unknown to the dreamer) to a passage in Castaneda's book (1972), in which Death is considered to be the "wisest advisor."

With addiction disorders, the lucid dream technique can only be used as a supporting method. In this way, lucid dreams can impressively make alcoholics, who normally do not accept their illness, aware of the seriousness of the situation. It is characteristic of alcoholics to have dreams in which they are approached by figures who are drunk. The following case is typical.

Case 6: A 41-year-old male teacher who consumed alcohol and drugs had the following dream shortly after Elvis Presley's death:

While being in a lucid state, he met Elvis, who seemed to be completely high and drunk, on a street. He asked Elvis, "Who are you?" Thereupon, Elvis answered, "I belong to you, and you will soon be with me.'' Then Elvis invitingly offered the dreamer a bottle of whisky. When the disgusted dreamer refused the offer, Elvis was transformed into a monster, which approached the dreamer threateningly. The dreamer defended himself by stabbing at the monster with a knife. However, this had no effect. Laughing cynically, the monster said, "No one can conquer me! I will destroy anyone who comes near me!" Thereupon, the dreamer fled to the protection of his friends, where the monster could do him no harm.

The dream example is characteristic because the dreamer's addiction appears in personified form, tries to lead him astray, and finally threatens him. This lucid dream shocked the teacher about his illness so much that he shortly thereafter decided to enroll in a clinic. Lucid dreaming also helped him later in setting new goals, which were very important in freeing him from alcohol.

Within LSD therapy, some drastic cases of healing effects on alcoholism are also reported. The LSD experience can lead to negative "horror trips" as well as to positive peak experiences. In the latter case, the experience of being one with mankind and the universe is reported. This "cosmic experience" that can also occur during dreaming lucidly (cf. Gillespie, 1986; Tholey, in preparation) may lead to relief from addiction and to a deep personality change. This leads to discarding the ego-centered attitude, which, according to the field theory, is the greatest obstacle to the development of a harmonious and creative personality. Lucid dreamers occasionally mention such cosmic experiences.

We have little experience with the effect of lucid dream therapy on drug addicts. I am, however, aware that drug addicts have attended my seminars, in order to learn lucid dreaming as a precaution against further drug experiences. People experienced in drug taking report that taking imagined drugs in a lucid dream may not only induce a "high experience" but also intensify it compared to real drugs (Roos, 1984).

SUPPLEMENTS

The few case histories chosen for illustration already testify to the variety of therapeutic possibilities of the application of lucid dreaming. We believe that these possibilities are nowhere near being exhausted. Lucid dreaming is a new territory for scientific research, which still requires theoretical and experimental work. We are presently investigating a technique that involves the ego consciousness leaving the body of the dream ego and entering into the body of another dream figure. To illustrate this technique, which we might call "entering into another dream figure," we are including an example from a teenager. The girl was in love with a young man whose behavior was friendly and pleasant to her and yet reserved. Before going to sleep one night the girl spent some time wondering why the young man was so reserved toward her. That night she had the following dream:

> I was in the same room as the boy and we were both doing something or other; I can't remember now what it was. I do remember that we were talking, though. All at once I knew that I was dreaming. I asked myself again why he didn't return my feelings and wanted to get an answer to this question in the dream. It was then that I became aware

of my spirit, that is, that part of me I think of as my "self," detaching itself from my body and floating across to his body and then entering his body. In this bodiless state I was able to use all my senses to orientate myself, that is, seeing, hearing, feeling, etc. After I had left my body, I still saw it standing there, doing some sort of fiddly work and talking. In other words, you could not tell by looking at my body from the outside that I was no longer inside it. So I floated across to the boy and slipped into his body. As I did so, I had the feeling that I had taken over all his bodily functions without him being aware of it. And so I took over his vital bodily functions and his motoricity, in other words, everything the body needs to operate. To begin with, it felt really strange, everything was so different and so much more restricted than in my body, and so unfamiliar. It was the kind of feeling you have when you have driven a Mercedes for years, know the car inside out, and then suddenly change it for an Austin Mini.

As time went one, however, and I got used to being in his body and could handle it better, this feeling gradually grew weaker. I saw with his eyes, felt with his hands, and talked with his voice, and so on. And, with his eyes, I saw my body standing there engaged in some sort of activity. I also saw his spirit, his consciousness. I saw him thinking, without being able to remember how this had come about. So I observed his thoughts and actions but did not try to interfere with them because, as I have said, the boy did not know that I was in his body with him. I saw how he perceived me, the effect I had on him, and the feelings he had for me. I saw the conflict he was in—after all, he had, I suppose become aware of my feelings for him, and he was very fond of me, but he did not want to go out with me as such. When I had watched his thoughts and seen myself through his eyes, I understood why he had been so reserved with me, and I realized that he would never return my feelings. I knew exactly what he was thinking and why. At this point, I woke up out of the dream.

This dream was very important and helpful for the girl because it sorted out her feelings. She was satisfied with being the young man's friend and, in settling for his friendship, felt a certain relief because the tension that had existed between them previously vanished completely following the dream.

Our current findings suggest that the technique described in the preceding example is more effective than the previously mentioned technique involving interaction with other dream figures, but it generally requires more practice. Moreover, it is also possible to slip into different dream figures, one after the other, during lucid dreaming, *and* to conduct a dialogue with a dream figure that one has left with the ego consciousness (for example, see Tholey & Utecht, 1987; Tholey, in preparation).

Further research into lucid dreaming should investigate whether the lucid dreamer can communicate with the therapist while being in the lucid dream state. Not as a telepathic contact but rather a communication by means of apparatus. We use equipment that transmits subliminal tactile stimuli as signals dependent on certain eye movements of the dreamer (cf. Reis, 1983). This is possible before becoming lucid as well as after having gained lucidity. This means that the lucid dreamer could consciously cause feedback signals by eye movements and recognize them, although they were integrated into the dream events. Our investigations on the ability of rendering the dream figures conscious indicate that it seems possible that an outside observer who is following the signals can communicate not only with the dream ego but also with other dream figures (cf. Tholey, 1985).

Even more important than abolishing difficult personality disorders using lucid dreaming is the possibility that lucid dreaming can be used as a method allowing us to deal with psychological problems in their early stages. If one includes the other possibilities of lucid dreaming, it seems desirable to contribute to a general propagation of lucid dreaming. Considering that a human being spends about 4 years of his or her life dreaming, it is irresponsible not to do something about the quality of our dream life. This will become as stunted as waking experience if it is not practiced. It is time to put our energy into insisting that dreams and lucid dreams be attended to in families and schools. In my experience, children are interested in dreams and achieve lucidity more easily than adults.

REFERENCES

Aserinsky, E., & Kleitman, N. (1953). Regularly occuring periods of eye motility and concomitant phenomena during sleep. *Science, 118,* 273–274.

Castaneda, C. (1972). *Journey to Ixtlan: The lessons of Don Juan.* New York: Simon & Schuster.

Freud, S. (1900). *Die Traumdeutung.* Leipzig and Wien: Deuticke.

Gackenbach, J. I. (1978). *A personality and cognitive style analysis of lucid dreaming.* Unpublished doctoral dissertation, Virginia Commonwealth University.

Gackenbach, J. I. (1980). Lucid dreaming project. *A.R.E. Journal, 15,* 253–260.

Gackenbach, J. I. (1986). Speculations on healing with the lucid dream. *Lucidity Letter, 5*(2), 5–8.

Gackenbach, J. I., & LaBerge, S. P. (1984). The lucid dream: A dream whose time has come. *ASD Newsletter, 1*(1), 1–12.

Gillespie, G. (1983). Memory and reason in lucid dreams: A personal observation. *Lucidity Letter, 2*(4), 8–9.

Gillespie, G. (1984). Problems related to experimentation while dreaming lucidly. *Lucidity Letter, 4*(2 & 3), 1–3.

Gillespie, G. (1986). Ordinary dreams, lucid dreams and mystical experiences. *Lucidity Letter, 5*(1), 27–31.

Green, C. (1968). *Lucid dreams.* London: Hamish Hamilton.

Hays, W. L. (1973). *Statistics for the social sciences.* New York: Holt, Rinehart & Winston.

Henle, M. (1978). Gestalt psychology and Gestalt therapy. *Journal of the History of the Behavioral Sciences, 14,* 23–32.

Kebeck, G. (1983). Feldtheorie als Methodologie. Ueberlegungen zur Nuetzlichkeit Lewinscher Grundgedanken fuer die Allgemeine Psychologie und Methodenlehre. *Gestalt Theory, 5*(4), 247–266.

Kebeck, G., & Sader, M. (1984). Phaenomenologisch-experimentelle Methodenlehre. Ein gestalt-theoretisch orientierter Versuch der Explikation und Weiterfuehrung. *Gestalt Theory, 6*(3), 193–245.

Kohl, K. (1956). *Zum Problem der Sensumotorik.* Frankfurt am Main: Kramer.

Kuenkel, F. (1934). *Charakter Leiden und Heilung.* Leipzig: Hirzel.

Kuenkel, F. (1982). *Einfuehrung in die Charakterkunde.* Stuttgart: Hirzel.

LaBerge, S. P. (1981). Lucid dreaming: Directing the action as it happens. *Psychology Today, 15* 48–57.

Leuner, H. C. (1962). *Die experimentelle Psychose*. Berlin, Goettingen, and Heidelberg: Springer.

Leuner, H. C. (1978). Principles and therapeutic efficacy of Guided Affective Imagery (GAI). In J. L. Singer & K. S. Pope (Eds.), *The power of imagination: New Methods in psychotherapy* (pp. 125–166). New York, London: Plenum Press.

Lewin, K. (1940). Formalisation and progress in psychology. In University of Iowa studies. *Studies in child welfare, 16*, No. 3: *Studies in topological and vector psychology I*, 7–42.

Malumud, J. R. (1978). *The development of a training method for the cultivation of "lucid" awareness in fantasy, dreams, and waking life*. Unpublished doctoral dissertation, New York University.

Maslow, A. H. (1981). *Motivation and Persoenlichkeit*. Reinbeck bei Hamburg: Rowohlt.

Metzger, W. (1962). *Schoepferische Freiheit*. Frankfurt am Main: Kramer.

Metzger, W. (1976). *Psychologie fuer Erzieher I: Psychologie in der Erziehung*. Bochum: Kamp.

Pearson, K. (1968). *Tables of the incomplete Beta-function*. Cambridge: Cambridge University Press.

Perls, F. S. (1969). *Gestalt therapy verbatim*. Lafayette: Real People Press.

Reis, J. (1983). *Biofeedback—Induktion des Klartraums*. Unpublished doctoral dissertation, Johann Wolfgang Goethe-Universitaet, Frankfurt am Main.

Reis, J. (in preparation). Verlaufsaspekte von Klartraeumen. Entwicklung einer inhaltsanalytischen Methode zur Erfassung affektiv-szonischer Verlaufsphaenomen. Doctoral dissertation, Johann Wolfgang Goethe-Universitaet, Frankfurt am Main.

Roos, M. (1984). *Vergleichsstudie zwischen Klartaumerfahrungen und Erlebnisse unter dem Einfluss psychodelischen Drogen* Unpublished doctoral dissertation, Johann Wolfgang Goethe-Universitaet, Frankfurt am Main.

Sally, R. D. (1985). Dream work in a case of multiple personality. *ASD Newsletter, 2*(4), 1–4.

Stephan, C. (1983). Die Wirklichkeit der Seelenreisen. *Esotera, 34*(6), 511–518.

Stephan, C. (1984). Vom Nutzen der Traeume. In K. Schnelting (Ed.), *Hilfe, ich traeume* (pp. 178–190). Muenchen: Goldmann.

Tart, C. T. (1969). *Altered states of consciousness*. New York, London, Sydney, and Toronto: Wiley.

Tart, C. T. (1984). Terminology in lucid dream research. *Lucidity Letter, 3*(1), 4–6.

Tholey, P. (1973). *Die Ueberpruefung psychophysiologischer Traumtheorien mit Hilfe der Klartraumtechnik* (unpublished lecture, Johann Wolfgang Goethe-Universitaet, Frankfurt am Main).

Tholey, P. (1977). Der Klartraum: Seine Funktion in der experimentellen Traumforschung. In W. H. Tack (Ed.), *Bericht ueber den 30; Kongress der deutschen Gesellschaft fuer Psychologie in Regensburg 1976* (pp. 376–378). Goettingen: Hogrefe.

Tholey, P. (1980a). Erkenntnistheorie und systemtheoretische Grundlagen der Sensumotorik. *Sportwissenschaft, 10*, 7–35.

Tholey, P. (1980b). Klartraeume als Gegenstand empirischer Untersuchungen. *Gestalt Theory, 2*, 175–191.

Tholey, P. (1980c). Verwerfungsregeln fuer statistische Hypothesen. *Arbeiten aus dem Institut fuer Psychologie der Universitaet Frankfurt am Main, 15*.

Tholey, P. (1980d). *Gestaltpsychologie*. In R. Asanger & G. Wenninger (Eds.), *Handwoerterbuch der Psychologie* (pp. 178–184).

Tholey, P. (1981). Empirische Untersuchungen ueber Klartraeume. *Gestalt Theory, 3*, 21–61.

Tholey, P. (1982a). Signifikanztest und Bayessche Hypothesen-pruefung. *Archiv fuer Psychologie, 134*, 319–342.

Tholey, P. (1982b). Bewusstseinsaenderung im Schlaf: Wach' ich oder traeum' ich? *Psychologie heute, 9*(12), 68–78. Reprinted in Psychologie heute Redaktion (Ed.), *Grenzerfahrungen*, (pp. 95–102). Weinheim: Beltz.

Tholey, P. (1983a). Relation between dream content and eye movements tested by lucid dreams. *Perceptual and Motor Skills, 56,* 875–878.

Tholey, P. (1983b). Techniques for inducing and manipulating lucid dreams. *Perceptual and Motor Skills, 57.* 79–90.

Tholey, P. (1984a). Der Klartraum—Hohe Schule des Traums. In K. Schnelting (Ed.), *Hilfe ich traeume* (pp. 100–118). Muenchen: Goldmann.

Tholey, P. (1984b). Gestalt therapy made-in-USA and made-elsewhere. *Gestalt Theory, 6,* 171–174.

Tholey, P. (1984c). Sensumotorisches Lernen als Organisation des psychischen Gesamtfelds. In E. Hahn & H. Rieder (Eds.), *Sensumotorisches Lernen und Sportspielforschung: Festschrift fuer Kurt Kohl,* (pp. 11–26). Koeln: bps-Verlag.

Tholey, P. (1984d). Zur Gleichgewichtsproblematik im Sport. *Spprtpaedagogik, 8*(5), 13–16.

Tholey, P. (1985). Haben Traumgestalten ein Bewusstsein? Eine experimentell-phaenomenologische Klartraumstudie. *Gestalt Theory, 7,* 29–46.

Tholey, P. (1986a). Deshalb Phaenomenologie! Anmerkungen zur experimentell-phaenomenologischen Methode. *Gestalt Theory, 8* 144–163.

Tholey, P. (1986b). Letter to the editor. *Lucidity Letter 5*(2), 45–48.

Tholey, P., & Utecht, K. (1987). *Schoepferisch Trauemen. Der Klartraum als Lebenshilfe.* Niedernhausen: Falken Verlag.

Tholey, P. (in preparation). Die Entfaltung des Bewusstseins als Weg zur schoepferischen Freiheit. Vom Traeumer zum Krieger. In T. Metzinger & E. Waelti (Eds.), *Chrysalis. Ausserkoerperliche Erfahrungen.*

van Eeden, F. (1913). A study of dreams. *Proceedings of the Society for Psychical Reserach, 26,* 431–461.

Wertheimer, M. (1959). *Productive thinking.* New York: Harper.

12

Clinical Applications of Lucid Dreaming

Introductory Comments

PATRICIA GARFIELD

We explore in this chapter the *value* of lucid dreaming. For most of us, learning to dream lucidly requires supreme effort and highly focused attention. Why bother to make such exertions? What benefits can we hope to gain for our clients or ourselves?

Among the assorted values claimed, proponents say that lucid dreaming allows us to:

1. Develop greater self-awareness, asleep or awake.
2. Banish nightmares.
3. Resolve problems.
4. Test alternate behaviors in a safe environment; practice deliberate actions upon reflection, such as self-assertion.
5. Accelerate activity of the immune system for physical healing.
6. Enhance ability to change waking life.
7. Develop new elements of personality; understand oneself.
8. Integrate conflictual aspects of the self; synthesize the personality.
9. Explore the creative potential of the mind.
10. Differentiate more clearly between dreaming and waking.

Each of the authors in this chapter touches upon some of these values, emphasizing what has been most prominent in his or her experience. Keep in mind that the field of lucid dreaming is in its infancy. It is just learning to walk, to develop skills. The accounts given here are impressionistic; they contain personal descriptions and ideas that are subject to refining as the field becomes more mature. Think of them as rich ground for digging out hypotheses to test in the sleep laboratory.

Disciples who undergo diverse approaches to spiritual training often engage

PATRICIA GARFIELD • 191 24th Avenue, San Francisco, CA 94121.

in some practice of heightened self-awareness. This awareness is given different labels in different systems. In Buddhism, for instance, the practice is referred to as "mindfulness." Gurdjieff spoke of it as "self-remembering." Still others call it "staying conscious" or "being fully awake."

Lucid dreaming has become, for some adherents, yet another route to developing self-awareness. The superaware state may simply serve to enrich daily life, or, for a few, become a springboard to spiritual adventures. Whether we call the expanded inner awareness that becomes available in lucid dreaming "a contact with the creative source," the "higher self," or the divine, those dreamers who attain it are convinced of its worth.

I start the chapter by discussing the value of lucid dreams for *exploring one's creative potential*. Giving several personal examples, I show how lucid dreams have successfully provided titles, names, images, and novel experiences for my professional life.

Fellows, in his selection, highlights this value, referring to *development of increased awareness*. He points out that by learning to take the right action in the dream, by taking responsibility for dream experience and changing it when desirable, the dreamer increases self-confidence in waking life.

Not all readers will agree with Fellows that "the realization that one is dreaming seems to have little effect" on the emotion existing prior to becoming lucid. Many dreamers, including myself, find that lucidity can dispel an ongoing fear or allow a complete shift to a sense of delight. However, most lucid dreamers will join Fellows in his view that facing and overcoming a difficult situation in lucid dreams helps the dreamer change waking behavior.

Fellows also touches upon the value of *self-integration* through lucid dreams. His term *aspect integration* will be familiar to readers as a form of Gestalt dreamwork where each dream figure is understood to represent an aspect of the self. By resolving conflicts between dream figures, the dreamer is said to assimilate these conflictual aspects and so restore peace to the psyche.

I have known people who employ this technique of "merging with the enemy" while awake, despite life-threatening situations. One Quaker man, for example, facing an armed striker, declared, "You can't shoot me—I love you." He was, in fact, able to establish rapport, to persuade the striker to lay down his weapon and resolve their difference through discussion.

The whole field of T'ai Chi and some of the related martial arts are based upon the principle of "going with" the aggressor. By yielding, by providing no solid resistance, the intended victim can render an attacker helpless. He fails to get at a person who is so supple, so light, so quick, so "like water," that there is nothing to receive the brutal action. Exhausted, the attacker quits. We may not be brave enough—or depending on one's point of view—foolhardy enough, to attempt such "going with" a hostile figure while awake, but we are free to do so while asleep.

Fellows suggests resolving conflicts among figures in dreams by discussion, by empathy, or by "entering into" the character, adopting its "world view"—

much as LaBerge did with his ogre. Merging with the aggressive dream figure, Fellows says, creates a new level of understanding, and conflict ceases.

Touching upon the value of *exploring mind potential*, Fellows refers to the wise and mature part of the dreaming mind as the "Dreamspeaker." He makes the intriguing suggestion that, after dreamers have dialogued with a dream character, they attempt to merge with it and then reexperience the feelings of being the "Dreamspeaker" character while they are awake.

Halliday, in his selection, gives an example of how lucid dreaming can help to *banish nightmares*. He raises the importance of approaching major change in frightening dreams by small increments. Altering a minor condition in a recurrent nightmare—such as the color of an object—he finds, leads the dreamer to gain a sense of the possibility of control and so establish a foundation for further change. Making a minor change alone is sometimes sufficient to eliminate the nightmare.

Elsewhere (at the Lucid Dreaming Preconvention Symposium held at the annual meeting of the Association for the Study of Dreams in Charlottesville, Virginia, 1985), Halliday described how a client who was convinced she was unable to make any change in her life was greatly encouraged by changing a recurrent nightmare. After conquering her dream aggressor, the woman made significant improvements in her waking life. Halliday also mentioned that lucidity training was less useful for people who had secondary benefits from recurrent nightmares, such as a workman who was receiving disability payment and a woman who could control her husband by her "prophetic dreams from God."

In his article, Halliday points out that training in lucid dreaming may be useful for patients who confuse reality with the dream state. He describes a case where the application of tests for assessing whether one is waking or dreaming gave a client *better discrimination between both states*.

In the closing section of this chapter, Malamud has devoted much of her work so far to the development of techniques to train dreamers in lucidity. In her contribution, she summarizes several of her methods with some ties to the other chapter contributors' work.

To fully benefit from lucid dreaming, Malamud first points out, one must be aware of its implications. In her model, lucidity consists of three different elements: (1) the dreamer is the creative source of the dream; (2) the dream environment reflects the self; and (3) the dream state is an alternate reality. She explores each of these elements in depth.

1. Dreamers may be helped to recognize that they are the creative source of their dreams, according to Malamud, by fostering awareness of being creative in waking life. She encourages dreamers who want to learn lucidity to pay attention to their waking fantasies, to observe themselves in the act of creation by recording spontaneous daydreams, by inventing stories and dreams, by guiding fantasies, by improvisation of acting in groups, and by writing poetry.

By becoming lucid, dreamers begin to comprehend that they create their own symbolic language. A young man I know who kept an extensive dream journal while he was in therapy began to interpret his ongoing dreams. For instance, in a dream in which he saw himself urinating, he commented to himself in the dream, "I must be feeling 'pissied off,' " The act of urination, he recognized, was his metaphor for being angry.

For Malamud, becoming aware of the waking use of metaphor assists the dreamer in understanding his or her dream pictures. She suggests exercises that help *connect emotional feelings with imagery.*

2. By recognizing that the dream environment symbolizes aspects of the self, dreamers may become more aware of waking feelings and beliefs. The dream-self corresponds to the waking self-concept, Malamud suggests, whereas the dream environment parallels the subjective perception of the waking world. Becoming lucid, then, can lead to *self-discovery.*

3. By recognizing that the apparent reality of dreams is deceptive, we can become more alert to possible false impressions in waking life, Malamud tells us. She points out that when dreamers realize that dreams are subjective, options become available. Lucid dreams provide a safe, private *place to practice self-confidence and alternative experiences.*

Dreamers who know they are dreaming can enjoy adventures impossible in waking life—flying, instantaneous travel, encountering deceased persons or supernatural beings, and other adventures.

The lucid dreamer who learns to use this incredible freedom of the dream space is also able to use the creative process more freely while awake. Becoming lucid, dreamers are better able to tolerate their own mental activity, to be less defensive and fearful. Thus, dreams as well as waking fantasies become more available for *generating new ideas and creative solutions.*

In her final segment, Malamud describes her approaches to training lucidity. These revolve around reviewing a specific dream in waking fantasy, transforming it into a lucid one. Individual guidance and feedback, she states, are needed by many dreamers in order to achieve lucidity.

The potential values of lucid dreaming surveyed in this chapter represent only a beginning. New frontiers include the fascinating work of Andrew Brylowski on activating the immune system during lucid dreams.

Having persuaded ourselves that there are substantial benefits to be gained by learning the skill of lucid dreaming, our next question is how to reach these goals. Assuming we acquire lucidity, how do we reap its harvest?

The essence of the answer is, I believe, contained in the phrase "taking action." Once we are lucid, we need to do something—to act—to attain value from our special state of consciousness. Here the various theorists begin to part company. Each endorses certain actions over others.

There is, it seems to me, a hierarchy of responses. Initially, to convince the dreamer that it is possible to influence the course of an ongoing dream, I find it useful to teach "confronting and conquering" hostile dream figures. By fighting back and succeeding, dreamers learn that they have power within their dreams; they realize they have options other than running and hiding, or waking up, to escape.

Once this confidence is established, dreamers may derive benefit from simply challenging an aggressive dream figure with questions such as, ''Who are you? What do you want? What is your name? What do you symbolize?'' Conducting a dialogue with dream characters, in the knowledge that one can safely dispatch them if necessary, the dreamer can obtain much information. In his work (see Chapter 11), Paul Tholey underscores the importance of reconciliation at this stage.

Beyond the point of discussion with a dream attacker, it becomes easier to befriend it. Engaging in enjoyable activities with a formerly hostile dream figure can evolve into friendship. Pierre Étévenon has suggested, in personal communication, that the dreamer surround the would-be hostile figure with golden light. This approach could disarm villainous dream characters and allow friendly interaction.

Perhaps the highest step in the hierarchy of potential responses by the dreamer to a negative dream figure is that of merging with it. (In some cases— such as sexual abuse of the dreamer—merging with a hostile dream figure that represents a threat to the dreamer in waking life would be inadvisable.) By integrating the conflictual aspects of our dreaming mind, we may be able to unite our strengths and achieve an inner synthesis.

We have much to discover in the world of lucid dreaming: to learn its laws and its limitations; to define when its use is recommended and when it is contraindicated; to refine and correct our present knowledge; to test hypotheses; to devise questionnaires; to analyze dream diaries; to gather clinical and laboratory information; and to evaluate the dimensions of lucidity. We hope that the personal experiences and limited clinical applications presented here will serve as inspiration for contemporary and future dream scientists. Meanwhile, every dreamer's talent is needed. Let's pull on our dreamcaps and explore.

Creative Lucid Dreams

PATRICIA GARFIELD

What should I name my new book? It was a question that reverberated in my head for weeks. Having published two books previously, I knew the advantage of a catchy, clever title like *Creative Dreaming* and the handicap of an awkward one like *Pathway to Ecstasy: The Way of the Dream Mandala*. I was determined that this third book should, like a newborn, have a proper name.

Lists were made; friends and relatives were consulted; I tried all manner of shape and sound on my tongue. None were completely satisfying. Yet the time had come for a decision, so I chose *Dreamchild*.

That night I dreamt that a friendly woman said to me, with a touch of superiority, "Well, I would have called it *Your Child's Dreams*." "That's too bad," I thought on awakening, "I prefer *Dreamchild*." For months, as I polished off the final chapters, I referred to the manuscript by this label. It was short, simple, easy to say and write, and had, to my mind, a touch of poetry.

"Too much," said my editor, "Let's just call it *Children's Dreams*." I protested that several books already claimed this title. Mine was distinct, unique. It needed its own name. "Find another one that's better or go with our choice," was the ultimatum.

With only a weekend until the presses rolled, I recalled my dream. I made a new list of 10 titles, burying the dream suggestion among them. On Monday morning I telephoned my editor in New York to read the candidates. When I reached the dream title there was a momentary silence on the other end of the wire. "That's perfect! Any title with *your* in it sells well. It's just right." *Your Child's Dreams* transformed from a phrase spoken in the shadow of a dream into a book title. My dreaming mind had known better than my waking one what was needed.

Creative ideas that come to us in dreams deserve our respect. They are often

---

PATRICIA GARFIELD • 191 24th Avenue, San Francisco, CA 94121.

the synthesis of abundant experience. They include observations made outside our periphery of conscious experience as well as the sensations, emotions, and actions in our awareness. Recombined in a dream, given a new arrangement, these elements often form highly creative answers to knotty problems. Like an innovative seamstress, our dreaming mind can assemble a patchwork of life scraps into a brilliant new pattern.

Lucid dreamers can draw upon this power deliberately. By searching for solutions to their problems during a dream, amazingly "new" ideas may occur. Here's a brief sampling of some creative lucid dreams.

On one occasion, I was searching for a special image. I wanted to portray, in a children's story that I was illustrating, a "dream tiger" that had a special quality. He was to display a personality different from what other artists have depicted in their drawings of tigers. Again I made many attempts to rearrange the basic elements while awake. I sketched tigers first this way, than that, with no feeling of satisfaction. I determined that the next time I was lucid in a dream I would summon a dream tiger.

After a couple of abortive trials—one in which I was flying above polar bears and landed in a children's playground—I finally saw the object of my desire. The tiger was plump and sassy with strangely arched eyes that gave him a charming quizzical appearance. To my mind, he was the very creature I sought; I drew him with pleasure when I awoke.

Stephen LaBerge, a lucid dream expert and part-time artist himself, tells me that when he wants a visual idea, he sometimes places an empty picture frame beside his bed. Asleep and lucid, he "looks" at the frame that, in his dream, magically fills with a picture. On awakening, he proceeds to duplicate as much as possible the dreamed picture.

Lucid dreamers may find their skills at dream creativity have commercial value. A few months ago, I was hired by a leading advertising agency to assist their executives in "dreaming up" a new product name.

They had already tried brainstorming in a group as well as individual word play. They wanted something more. Our "naming team," as such groups are called, set to work on the project. Without revealing the product, or giving details, I can say that in three sessions we had fascinating results.

Knowing how dreams are based upon emotional experience, I first endeavored to arouse the participants' feeling-loaded memories that could be associated with the product. For a warmup, I had them engage in traditional word games. Then I asked them to close their eyes and follow a guided fantasy meant to link their childhood experiences with an aspect of the product. Serene, smiling faces and furtive tears assured me that emotional wells had been reached. Possible names were written down after these activities. The assignment was to induce a dream relating to the product as stimulated by their visualization.

At the second session, everyone reported dreams associated with the project in greater or less degrees. Even those executives who ordinarily did not dream or who thought dreams unimportant reported they had dreamed. A couple of these dreams were even lucid. Names were culled from all of the dreams.

We further stimulated dream activity by engaging the physical senses. My purpose was to provide *direct* experience with the product. Exercises were devised, involving sight, sound, touch, and even taste receptors. Before going to bed, each of the naming team was to choose the sensations that were most evocative for them and repeat them prior to sleep. By now, personal experience with the product had emotional and sensory components. At the end of this meeting, more names were suggested.

At our final session, more dream reports were shared. We engaged in a few further exercises and then summarized our findings. Beyond question, the most satisfying names were those tied to emotions and to dreams.

The naming team, along with others from the agency, went on to make an evaluation of all the names, picking a limited list of the best to be presented to the client. Several dream-derived names survived this final cut. Although the client selected a name that was not dream produced, the team felt tremendous benefit had evolved from the process.

Despite the fact that not every member was able to get good names from his or her dreams, each reported heightened awareness and positive product associations (which was not true prior to the experiment). The relaxation techniques and sense stimulation exercises, along with greater dream recall, helped them generate a broader range of names than usual. One member of the group reported that subsequent attempts at dream incubation helped her name another product. Using the dream state had enriched name production.

Examples like finding an innovative title for a book, an unusual name for a character in a novel or even for a commercial product, and an artistic image all show the ability of lucid dreamers to obtain specific answers.

Another approach to harvesting the creative fields in lucid dreams is more general. Some dreamers find their most fulfilling lucid dreams come in response to the statement, ''Tell me what I need to know!'' This open-ended request can lead to intriguing experiences that may be more inventive than a narrow demand.

In one such riveting lucid dream, I possessed two dream bodies, one that watched over and was in charge of the other. In the dream, ''I'' command ''myself'' to grow tinier with a wave of my hand until I almost disappear, and then I reverse the process, stretching myself back to full size, aware that I can grow further, to giant size if I wish. I realize that I am following the Tibetan Buddhist dream practice of ''making small things get bigger and big things small.'' I have a strange sense of protecting this other self and communicating special knowledge to it. Awake, I recognized the flexibility and caretaking of the dream were just what was needed in my waking life at that time.

Thus, whether we choose to ask our lucid dreams to provide precisely what we want or leave them free to tell us what we need to know at that particular moment, we have much to learn from them. Every night, the station is broadcasting. We need only turn on our lucid dream set, select a channel with a program sure to inspire us, or spin the dial to see if there is something more appealing. And these are magnificent shows—entertaining, apt, and always informative. Tune in and enjoy.

Working within the Lucid Dream

PETER FELLOWS

With the recognition of lucid dreaming came the realization of a powerful vehicle for self-exploration and discovery. The lucid dreamer finds himself or herself awake within the magical universe of his or her dreams. Conscious, he or she walks in wonder through a world that springs full blown from the intimate depths of his or her own psyche—where each creation, object, and event is complete and purposefully placed.

In its ephemeral nature lies the limitation of lucid dreaming as a reliable therapeutic tool. Spontaneous, fleeting moments of clarity during a dream, lucidity is for the most part, the talent of natural dream savants and trained oneironauts. For the naive dreamer, it remains an elusive art.

Fortunately, lucidity is a learnable skill. For the dedicated and persistant dream apprentice, a fair degree of competence can be attained. It is here that I begin with my clients and students. In and of itself, increasing awareness of one's thoughts, feelings, actions, and relationship to one's experience can have a beneficial effect in waking life as well as serving to increase the incidence of lucidity in dreams.

It is not necessary for the student or client to wait for a lucid dream before he or she begins to work with dreams. Actions that are, ideally, to be undertaken within the dream can be rehearsed in waking through the use of imagination. Although perhaps not as effective, this form of dreamwork still has validity.

There are three areas that my clients and students encounter as blocks in their dreaming. Sometimes a situation is frustrating, independent of any dream characters. An example of this would be machinery that will not work or being unable to find a lost object. Then there might be dreams in which an invisible force threatens or restrains the dreamer. And finally, there are the dreams in which there is interaction with other dream characters.

PETER FELLOWS • Centre for Inner Learning, Toronto, Ontario, Canada.

Lucid, the dreamer learns to take right action in the dream. If the situation is less than satisfactory, then the dreamer changes the dream. He learns to take responsibility for his experience and change it when necessary. Although this is not always possible in waking life, the action and attitude taken in the dream state builds self-confidence and a sense of mastery that carries over into waking life.

Perhaps the most common of the "invisible force" dreams are those in which the dreamer cannot move or cannot run fast enough. I had a dream of this ilk as I was experiencing writer's block with this material you are now reading. It seemed that in this dream I was walking through endless corridors, pursued by some unseen enemy. At one point, I came upon a table with an assortment of weapons upon it. None of the weapons was in a usable form; they sat in various stages of completion, their craftsman-maker nowhere to be found. Quickly, the enemy was upon me. I tried to run away but found that I could not move. Indeed, it seemed that the more I exerted myself, the closer I drew to my nemesis.

At this point, instead of awakening, I became lucid, which in itself is a kind of awakening. I purposefully became calm, reminding myself that this experience was of my own creation. Then, in a manner rather difficult to describe, I organized my scattered mind into one clear intention: to simply walk ahead. There was with this thought a corresponding sensation of clarity and rightness. Upon awakening, I was free of my writer's block, and I have been able to call back the same sensations and use them in the waking state to enhance my effectiveness.

Throughout the lucid dreams of my experience, there often occurs an interesting if paradoxical situation. Whatever the emotion prevalent before lucidity, the realization that one is dreaming seems to have little effect. If there is fear, then the fear remains, although the threat is recognized as an illusion. If there is love, the love remains, although the person is recognized to be only an imaginary character. This facet of lucid dreaming gives it tremendous therapeutic value. A situation faced and overcome in a lucid dream still has emotional validity and therefore is effective in self-change.

My students and clients want to more fully express their thoughts and feelings, they want to be more aware of them and reach out to other people, acting in positive and assertive ways. This is what I teach them to do in the dream state. Being conscious, they can reflect upon the situation and act with volition. As they do this more and more in the dream state, the effects begin to carry over into the waking state. As dreamers, they are given an opportunity to experience an alternative way of being in a safe environment.

Another exercise that some of my students and clients use, I call "aspect integration." The premise behind this is that each of the characters within a dream is only a projection of an aspect of the dreamer's personality. Through the process of aspect integration, the dreamer learns to assimilate the aspects of himself or herself and restore psychic harmony.

The means of accomplishing aspect integration are several. Many times the dreamer will simply resolve any conflicts with the aspect as one would with any person, through dialogue and understanding. Other times, the dreamer will actually enter into the character and adopt its "world view." This may serve to create a new level of understanding.

When a dreamer enters into a dream character, he or she experiences the world from that character's perspective. There is besides the intellectual outlook, a whole "feeling" attitude to be experienced. This goes beyond emotion. It is as if you have touched the unique "feeling identity" of that character. Such an experience is an intimate sharing. The dreamer senses the "rightness" of that personality aspect, and there ceases to be a conflict. When this occurs, the aspect has been fully assimilated, and the dreamer awakens feeling whole and privileged.

At this point, the reader may have noticed that I have not mentioned anything about dream interpretation. Although it is true that, in a lucid dream, the dreamer could question dream characters on the symbolic meaning of the experience, I never teach or do this. Time in a lucid dream is a precious commodity and I do not like to waste it. If, as I am dreaming, I become lucid at a point in the scenario where someone is sitting on my head, I do not begin to question him or her on the symbolic meaning of the experience. I act, and quickly.

When symbolic dreams "work" for us, a waking life conflict is acted out in symbolic guise and resolved. Somehow, that resolution is translated back into real life with real effect. What lucidity enables us to do is to ensure that the dream conflict gets resolved and to reap the benefits in self-confidence that come from doing so consciously. Interpreting the dream, knowing exactly what area of one's life the dream conflict was related to, is fine, but when the work is actually done, the result will be experienced whether or not the interpretation was correct.

Beyond resolving conflicts between different aspects of the self, the dreamer can begin to use the medium of the lucid dream to explore the potential of his or her own mind. Who is it that creates our dream experiences? What aspect of the Self has the capability and creativity to produce our nocturnal psychodramas? In dreams, we receive inspiration that solves problems, creates new inventions, answers questions, writes stories, plays, songs, and poetry. Dreams have proven to be an incredible source of creativity and information, but what portion of the psyche is it that speaks to us through our dreams?

I hesitate to designate the brilliant creation of a dream to something called the "unconscious." I prefer to personify this aspect of the Self as other aspects find personification in dreams. To this portion I give the name: Dreamspeaker.

Within the dream, my students and clients personify their Dreamspeakers as simply more wise or maturer versions of themselves. This is a level or perspective that we all can learn to make more conscious. In moments of great genius or inspiration, we touch that level. In the program I taught, students learned to first consult their Dreamspeaker in their dreams and then practiced aspect integration with that character. Back in the waking state, the students attempted to recreate the "feeling" of being the Dreamspeaker. The resulting experience seldom failed to be a profound one.

My purpose here has only been to introduce the reader to some areas of lucid dream exploration that I have found beneficial for myself, my students, and my clients. It is my hope that I may have provided some new areas for you to explore as you lucid-dream.

Lucid Dreaming
Use in Nightmares and Sleep–Wake Confusion

GORDON HALLIDAY

The following is a brief note concerning some of my work with patients involving lucid dreaming. Clinical lore on lucid dreaming is primarily anecdotal and oral at this point, and so limiting discussion to my own work allows a greater attention to limitations and cautions in the use of lucid dreaming techniques. The first part of the note describes helping persons modify nightmares. The second part describes the results of a case in which Hearne's 10 tests for differentiating dreams from the awake state showed clinical utility.

In treating a person who wants to get rid of nightmares, some training in lucid dreaming is one of several approaches that may be helpful. The well-regarded, nontechnical books by Garfield (1974) and Faraday (1974) have popularized the so-called "Senoi" method of banishing nightmares. In this method, people are trained to become aware that they are dreaming during the dream itself and to use that awareness to confront and conquer any monster or enemies in the nightmares. The Senoi, a primitive Malaysian people, were said by Kilton Stewart to have extensively used this confront-and-conquer method, a claim now generally discredited (Denton, 1986; Domhoff, 1985; Faraday & Wren-Lewis, 1984). Thus the confront-and-conquer technique should be considered experimental rather than proven, with an unknown range of applicability.

I have found that some patients cannot confront and conquer the objects of terror in their nightmares but that they can sometimes benefit from attempting smaller changes. For example, a person who had a recurrent traumatic nightmare about being run over by a tractor tried, on his own, to totally get rid of the tractor and failed. When, however, he was enouraged to try a smaller change (altering

GORDON HALLIDAY • The Center for Individual and Family Services, Mansfield, OH 44907.

the color of an item in the background), he then experienced a success (this case was previously reported in Halliday, 1982b). This type of success in dream alteration can provide an immediate feeling of being in greater control. It can also serve, if needed, as the basis for building additional changes into the nightmare, for shaping the nightmare into more pleasant dream behavior.

In a similar manner, a female patient in her 20s reported twice-nightly traumatic nightmares, primarily of her molestation as a child, for 6 months prior to the start of psychological therapy. She had weekly nightmares "for years" prior to that. Dream lucidity techniques were discussed with her at the second therapy session, particularly the idea of mnemonic cuing (e.g., "as soon as you see the doll on the bed, remember that you are dreaming and try to change the color of its dress." This is similar to LaBerge's MILD technique, as described in Price, Bouchet, Ripert, & Dane, 1986). She was uncomfortable with the idea of standing up to her attacker in her dream but was able to make use of the idea of changing one detail. Thus, in the third session, she mentioned she changed the color of a doll and of a bedspread in her abuse dream that made the dream not as bad. She explained that this change process caused her to focus on what she was doing, rather than just attending to the action of abuse. She accomplished this color change in two different dreams that week. At the seventh session, she mentioned she had had no recurrence of the traumatic molestation nightmare for about 2 weeks. Therapy then centered on other issues, with no further discussion of dreams. Given the severity of her nightmares, this initial improvement seems promising, although definitive conclusions cannot be reached as this case lacks an adequate follow-up.

The cultivation of lucid dreams is no panacea for nightmares but rather is one of a number of techniques that may help some patients (see Halliday, 1987). In fact, one patient reported that lucidity made her nightmares of drowning worse rather than better, as she knew it was a dream and panicked that she could not wake up (this may imply that therapy should sometimes aim for control in lucid dreams rather than just lucidity *per se*). For two female patients with a diagnosis of both depression and borderline personality disorder, the self-control techniques of lucidity have not proved of value for nightmare control—but neither have waking imagery dialogue, interpretation, or desensitization. With certain relatively healthy children, in contrast, improvement may be rapid and dramatic (see Garfield, 1984). Although many clinicians report using dream lucidity techniques to handle nightmares, including "Senoi" or confront-and-conquer techniques, flying to escape danger, calling on a dream friend, or use of magical weapons, there are few case reports and no controlled studies on the use of these techniques. More research, including case studies with adequate symptom frequency and follow-up data, as well as controlled experiments, are needed.

Hearne's (1982) tests for telling if one is dreaming or awake proved of value in treating a female patient who complained of having dreams that were so real that she later did not know if something really happened while she was awake or if it happened during a dream (this section of the note is taken from Halliday, 1982a). This confusion caused her some social difficulty in that, for example, when she saw somebody she knew, she did not know if she should continue a previous conversation with him or her—the earlier conversation may only have occurred in a dream.

During part of the second session with this client, Hearne's list of 10 tests for differentiating the dream from the waking state was gone over. She was also given a copy of the list for home study. When she was seen a week later, she reported no longer being confused or upset by her dreams. She noted she had been able to apply one of the tests (the test to look carefully at the surroundings and see if there is something that should not be there). Specifically, she thought she was awake and at work until she saw a gigantic rat. She knew the rat should not be there because the exterminator had come so frequently to her factory. She therefore knew she was dreaming.

The client canceled her following two appointments and did not respond to follow-up. Whether or not long-lasting change occurred, therefore, cannot be ascertained. The initial positive response to her use of Hearne's tests must nevertheless be considered encouraging. More research, with a variety of clients, is called for to delineate the benefits and liabilities of this approach.

REFERENCES

Denton, R. (1986, June). *A Discussion of Senoi dream theory*. Discussion presented at the meeting of the Association for the Study of Dreams, Ottawa, Canada.

Domhoff, G. (1985). *The mystique of dreams*. Berkeley: University of California Press.

Faraday, A. (1974). *The dream game*. New York: Harper & Row

Faraday, A., & Wren-Lewis, J. (1984). The selling of the Senoi. *Lucidity Letter, 3*(1), 1–3.

Garfield P. (1976). *Creative dreaming*. New York: Ballantine Books.

Garfield, P. (1984). *Your child's dreams*. New York: Ballantine Books.

Halliday, G. (1982a). Clinical utility seen in lucid dreaming ability. *Lucidity Letter, 1*(4), 6–7.

Halliday, G. (1982b). Direct alteration of a traumatic nightmare. *Perceptual and Motor Skills 54*, 413–414.

Halliday, G. (1987). Direct psychological therapies for nightmares: A review. *Clinical Psychology Review*.

Hearne, K. (1982). Ten tests for state assessment. *Lucidity Letter, 1*(3), 6–7.

Price, R., LaBerge, S., Bouchet, C., Ripert, R., & Dane, J. (1986). The problem of induction: A panel discussion. *Lucidity Letter, 5*(1) 205–228.

Learning to Become Fully Lucid
A Program for Inner Growth

JUDITH R. MALAMUD

My experience with lucidity workshop participants and dissertation research subjects (Malamud, 1980, 1982a,b) suggests that learning to become *fully* lucid in dreams may foster the acquisition of a broad range of psychological insights and abilities with clinical and self-help applications. What I mean by a "fully" lucid dreamer is one who not only has the knowledge that she or he is dreaming but who is also experientially aware of certain implications of that fact, that is, that she or he is the *creative source* (CS) of a *self-reflecting environment* (SE) which is an *alternate*, qualitatively different *reality* (AR) (LeShan, 1976) from that of waking life.[1] Because actual lucid dreamers rarely report full, continuous awareness of all these implications in any one dream (Garfield, 1974; Green, 1968; LaBerge, 1980; Saint-Denys, 1982; Sparrow, 1976; Tart, 1979; Van Eeden, 1969), my definition of full lucidity is a hypothetical maximum, intended for research and teaching purposes. I will suggest some hypotheses relating growth in awareness of these implications, CS, SE, and AR, to the development of particular kinds of insight and skill and conclude with some examples of how I work with students.

IMPLICATIONS OF THE FACT THAT ONE IS DREAMING

Dreamers Are the Primary Creative Sources of Their Dreams (CS)

Fully lucid dreamers are aware of creating their dreams. Teaching techniques that aim to bring about such awareness may also foster awareness of one's

[1]There are other possible interpretations of the nature of the dream state. Due to lack of space, I will not discuss them here.

JUDITH R. MALAMUD • 2555 Bainbridge Avenue, Bronx, NY 10458.

creative role in life generally, understanding of one's metaphoric "language," familiarity with one's repertoire of life themes, more skillful use of conscious volition, and increased sensitivity to one's ambivalent feelings.

Acknowledging One's Creative Role

In ordinary dreams, we find ourselves in situations that are *seemingly* not of our own making. Such dreams are ideally suited to nurture any frank or hidden beliefs we may have that we are helpless, powerless, or victimized. Lucid dreams gently challenge and nudge us toward greater satisfaction and pride in our actual roles as magnificent creators. Dreamers who have recognized their power to create a convincing world in their dreams may come to realize that they are more responsible than they had previously imagined for creating their experience of the waking world as well, even when that world seems to be a totally external, given fact (Green, 1976).

When we are awake, most of us would readily give at least intellectual assent to the notion that we create our dream worlds, but achieving emotional acceptance of this idea is not necessarily an easy task. Because many of our dreams impress us as bizarre, alien, or unflattering to our self-images, the idea that we are responsible for them can seem incredible or even repugnant. One way to help students get in touch with their roles as creators of their dreams is to help them directly sense their own creative process by catching themselves in the act of creating fantasies. Because one usually has little difficulty accepting that one is truly the creator of one's own waking reveries, fantasies provide an excellent introduction to the mind's creative power.

If unhindered by guilt or fear, one can have waking fantasies about almost anything. Some people fear a riotous invasion of incestuous, malevolent, greedy, or otherwise demonic fantasies if they unchain their minds. The grip of guilty fear can sometimes be loosened by fostering a relaxed, curious, observer attitude and a readiness to be entertained by the upwellings of spontaneous ideas and imagery. The ability to consciously direct one's imagery is also a valuable component of lucidity, but those who would feel too guilty, at first, to comfortably claim ownership of their own ideas need not be pressured into consciously choosing what they will imagine. Later on, conscious control of fantasy can be presented as a new kind of game, a way of testing the limits of one's imagination as a source of pleasure, excitement, and discovery. Examples of exercises for discovering one's imaginative creativity are: recording spontaneous daydreams, making up stories, making up dreams, improvising dramas in groups, experiencing guided fantasies, and writing poetry.

Intuitive Understanding of Metaphoric Language

Fully lucid dreamers intuitively understand what they intend to express via their symbolic, imagistic "language." Achieving such understanding in dreams may be facilitated by familiarity with *conscious* use of metaphoric language as a means of self-expression. Partial comprehension of metaphoric language is usually possible, even for the beginner, in the waking fantasy exercises mentioned before. Further strengthening of this capacity depends on willingness to suspend judgment of what particular images "should" or "must" mean, in favor of a relaxed attitude of listening to the *feelings* that arise unbidden when one experiences those images. One could also practice more specific exercises designed to connect feelings with "dream language." Examples:

> Sense how you are feeling right now. Think of an image that expresses this feeling.
>
> Allow an image to pop into your mind. What does this image suggest about what you feel, want, or do not want, right now?

This kind of practice lays the groundwork for understanding not only dreams and fantasies but also the vagaries of unconscious communication and symbol formation in waking life. The value of clarity about our creative roles in waking life becomes most emphatically apparent when we are in trouble, "trapped" in dreamlike melodramas such as the unfulfilling life scripts we enact, the self-defeating behaviors we choose unconsciously but blame on "circumstances beyond our control," or the self-improvement plans we embark on so enthusiastically but that often come to naught because of the interference of "inner saboteurs" we have relegated to unawareness. One can gain fresh insights by viewing such a situation as if it were one's richly symbolic dream and asking oneself, "What do I intend to express by creating this?"

Becoming Familiar with One's Repertoire of Themes

One technique for becoming lucid is, in itself, a means of becoming acquainted with recurrent themes among one's creations. This technique is simply to become familiar with one's repertoire of dream themes, characters, environments, actions, and so forth, by keeping and reviewing a dream journal. Waking familiarity with typical dream situations encourages recognition *during* a dream: "I've dreamed this before—Aha!—I must be dreaming *now*!" As we discover the kinds of realities we structure for ourselves in dreams, we inevitably begin to experience moments of resonance to our waking lives. I have found interesting correlations between my patterns of waking and dreaming creativity when I have kept a parallel journal of "most satisfying" and "least satisfying" experiences during the day and during my dreams.

Exercising Conscious Control

Fully lucid dreamers can decide consciously what will happen in their dreams. This phenomenon is often called "dream control," a term that can be misleading because it may be taken to imply that ordinarily the dreamer does *not* control the dream and that control is always a conscious process. If it is not the dreamer who controls the dream, who is it? The dreamer is always controlling, that is, choosing and creating, the dream experience: The question is, how *conscious* she or he is of doing so. Conscious dream control may merely reflect recognition of one's already ongoing creative activity, combined with awareness of one's freedom to choose among possible alternative experiences. Conscious practice in deciding what to imagine, either in dreams or in waking fantasy, may have a carryover effect of enhancing awareness of one's power to make choices in waking life. Fellows gives an example in this chapter: When he became lucid during a dream of being chased, he was enabled to choose effective action in the dream and found himself free of writer's block when he awakened.

Acknowledging Conflict and Ambivalence

Sometimes attempts at conscious dream control succeed. Very often, however, the dream will not conform to one's conscious plan. What does it mean when a lucid dreamer tries to create something and does not get it? Such "failures" may be pivotal points for insight because they suggest there may be some disagreement between conscious and unconscious intentions, due to opposing wishes, perceptions, or beliefs.

Success and failure at conscious control may have analogous implications in waking life. Can we succeed at achieving our waking-life goals only when those goals are not opposed by stronger, conflicting, unconscious motives? In the case of conflicting motives, the creation of a happy outcome requires that all sides of one's conflict be taken into account and a new synthesis achieved. Research is needed to determine whether efforts to create more satisfying outcomes in dreams could actually stimulate integration and growth in waking life.

Dreamers Can Recognize Aspects of the Self in the Dream Environment (SE)

Dreams, however realistically they may sometimes reflect the outer world, are also uniquely personal creations. Fully lucid dreamers are aware that conscious and unconscious aspects of themselves are mirrored in the seemingly external elements of their dream worlds. Techniques that foster such awareness may enhance awareness of one's beliefs, perceptions, feelings, wishes, and latent resources and also promote integration and synthesis of projected aspects of the self.

Inferring Characteristics of the Unknown Self

The self-character in the dream experiences itself as dwelling in a nonself environment but because the self-character and the dream environment are both creations of the dreamer, the self-character may have a "sibling" relationship to all the other elements in the dream, with whom it shares a "parent," namely the whole and partly unknown organism/self who generates them all. One therefore may discover much about the characteristics of one's whole organism, or larger self, by becoming acquainted with one's "siblings" in the dream. Dream behaviors stimulated by the desire for self-discovery may include observing, exploring, confronting, engaging in dialogue, sharing feelings or gifts, and giving or receiving help. These behaviors can be rehearsed in waking fantasy using Gestalt dreamwork techniques (Faraday, 1974; Perls, 1969) and approaches attributed to the Senoi people of Malaya (Stewart, 1969) or by "redreaming" a dream, in waking fantasy, from the viewpoint of another character in the dream.

Integrating Projected Aspects of the Self

Having become aware that other dream characters and parts of the dream environment may reflect unrecognized, disowned, or newly emergent aspects of the self, the lucid dreamer may move toward greater personal integration and harmony by befriending, negotiating, or merging with these dream elements, either during the dream itself, or subsequently, in waking fantasy. In this chapter, Fellows calls such work "aspect integration," and LaBerge (Chapter 2) gives an illuminating personal example of loving union with a dream "enemy" who presumably symbolized a previously denied part of himself. The hypothesis that such symbolic self-integration within dreams can have beneficial effects on the waking personality is certainly worthy of further study.

Identifying with the Larger Self

A further challenge in self-discovery is for the self-character in a lucid dream to directly sense the larger self who is creating not only the self-character but also all the other parts of the dream. This identification would involve sensing the feelings, conflicts, wishes, beliefs, perceptions, and so on, that inspire the dreamer to create each element of the dream. Waking exercises such as the following may facilitate identification with the larger self:

> Ask yourself, in regard to any element in a dream, "Can you sense, in your body, the feelings out of which you created this part of the dream?"
>
> Ask, in regard to unpleasant dream situations: "Can you sense that in some way you *wanted* to experience this situation, even though you found it unpleasant?"
>
> Have a "dream" (in fantasy) based on the possibilities your original dream excludes. Your attempt to create an alternative dream should begin to expose your investment of feelings, wishes, perceptions, and beliefs in the dream you originally created.

An analogy could be drawn between waking and dreaming experience, such that the waking *self-concept* would correspond to the dreamed *self-character*, and *subjective perception of the waking world* would correspond to the *dream environment*. The parallel lucidity challenges in waking life would then be (a) to discover one's wishes, feelings, and beliefs by examining one's impressions of the waking environment and (b) to directly sense one's larger self and why it chooses to foster one's particular conscious self-concept and subjective experience of the world.

The Dream World is an Alternate Reality (AR)

Fully lucid dreamers are aware that they are experiencing a reality that is qualitatively different, in its subjectivity, privacy, and imaginary nature, from the reality of waking life.[2] Techniques that teach this aspect of lucidity may also foster awareness that appearances can be deceiving, that options exist and new behaviors are possible, that it is safe to discover oneself as a unique being, apart from pressures to conform to one's social milieu, and that the mind can safely fly free of the limitations of the outer world.

Recognizing That the Apparent Reality of Dreams Is Deceptive

In our ordinary dreams, we take it for granted that we are experiencing the real world, but if we begin to question the reality of the apparent world, we stand a chance of becoming lucid. Similarly, hardly a day goes by when we do not fail to test our bedrock assumptions against actual experience and to question the validity of our highly questionable perceptions. Perhaps we may become more alert as questioners, more usefully skeptical, less rigid and less dogmatic, if we practice, both in dreams and waking life, noticing anything that contradicts our assumptions about reality. Halliday, in this chapter, describes a systematic approach to questioning the reality of the dream. Keepers of dream journals can become more alert to bizarre dream events that may lead to lucidity if they regularly underline all passages describing unrealistic or "dreamlike" happenings (Malamud, 1980). Surprising events in waking life offer analogous opportunities for reality testing. One may ask oneself: What assumption of mine was contradicted by this unexpected occurence? What new hypothesis can I formulate?

Recognizing That the Subjectivity of Dreams Allows Many Options

Because dream experience is subjective, it contains as many alternative possibilities as the dreamer is willing and able to create. Hence, fully lucid dreamers are aware that at any point during their dreams, they may choose to

---

[2]This is a useful but debatable assumption, contradicted by Eastern philosophies that hold that ordinary waking reality is a kind of dream.

experience a variety of possibilities. Halliday (this chapter) uses this principle to help clients ameliorate recurrent nightmares by instituting minor changes in the dream. I encourage students to try out alternative approaches with the aim of increasing their "satisfaction," however they each may define that concept, in their lucid dreams and waking dreams. Indeed, lucidity training can be a rewarding arena in which to learn confidence and persistence in generating alternatives, a skill that is also valuable in the less tractable world of waking life.

Recognizing That the Privacy of Dreams Provides Safe "Space" for Individuation

Although the occurrence of telepathically shared "mutual" dreams (Campbell, 1980) renders questionable an assumption of complete mental privacy, we can generally assume that others are not conscious of our dreams unless we report them. Although the usual privacy of mental behavior may seem obvious, most of us do not take this privacy for granted on an emotional or unconscious level. Learning to trust mental privacy allows one to think or imagine that which would be disapproved of by one's intimates and society and thereby permits the development of individual identity—the sense of emerging from the family and social matrix as a unique person. Lucidity training can specifically point out this privacy, for example: "You can do anything you want in your dream (or fantasy), and no one will know about it unless you tell them."

Recognizing That the Imaginary Nature of Dreams Provides Freedom and Safety.

Because dreams are imaginary, dream experience is not limited by laws governing the physical world. The dreamer can have adventures that are impossible or improbable in waking life, such as flying, experiencing the past or possible futures, traveling instantly, and encountering creatures, things, or people that are unknown or nonexistent in waking life. When lucidity training explicitly points out this freedom, it encourages the kind of wide-ranging, uninhibited, recombinatory mental activity that is characteristic of the creative process. Hence, lucidity training can be a form of creativity training.

A frequent obstacle to a liberated inner life is the fear of having "bad" thoughts, images, or dreams. This fear usually reflects one or more unconscious, nonlucid assumptions, such as (a) I am what I think; hence my self-concept and self-esteem are vulnerable to my every passing thought; (b) thinking something is the same as doing it; thoughts can kill; therefore I will shut out thoughts of anything I should not do; and (c) if I think something, I will automatically do it, thereby possibly causing harm in the outer world. However, a corollary of the imaginary quality of dream experience is that dreaming is *safe*, that is, regardless of what mayhem occurs in a dream: (a) The dream is *not* the dreamer but only one of the dreamer's many creations, and therefore the self-concept need not be vulnerable to passing dream phenomena; (b) dream actions may represent, but are not equivalent to, waking life actions, and there is no literal carryover of dream events to the waking world; and (c) having an idea, image, or fantasy does not compel one to act on it; action remains a choice. Some people dispute the idea that dreams are safe by pointing out, quite correctly, the dramatic and lingering impact nightmares can have on the emotions and physiology of dreamers. However, it is not the events in our nightmares that horrify us; it is our attitude of taking these events literally that scares the wits out of us. Once one realizes, "I am having a nightmare," one is no longer having a *nightmare*. Lucidity calms the mind and body and *makes* dreams safe. Learning that dreams are safe, involves, in effect, learning not to fear one's own mental activity. This fearlessness should lead to a relaxation of defensiveness in encountering oneself.

When students learn that the mind is a free, safe, and private "space," permitting many options, they may use dreams and fantasies to generate new ideas and solutions to problems. Garfield gives several fascinating examples of such creative dream incubation elsewhere in this chapter. Interchanges between the inner self and the outer world are never more likely to succeed than when one feels confident and free in considering one's options. For example, I might ask, "How could I express myself most effectively in this particular situation, with this particular person?" By consulting my repertoire of metaphoric images, I might come up with something most suitable for the occasion—a particular stance I once admired in a character from my dreams or daydreams or a delightful role I once dared play in a dream, having gained permission from unconscious sources of authority long hidden from daytime awareness because of frightening admonitions such as "act your age," "be a good girl," and "don't be such a spoiled brat!"

INDIVIDUALIZING LUCIDITY TRAINING

I have devised a tape-recorded guided fantasy that simulates a lucid dream (Malamud, 1982a), a lucidity checklist for journal work (Malamud, 1980), and a lucidity "card game" for group work (Malamud, 1982a). Each of these teaching devices spells out implications of the fact that one is dreaming and aims to prepare students for having "lucid waking dreams" in which they rehearse lucid dreaming in waking fantasy. I have found, however, that even when people are given detailed instructions, they have widely varying abilities to engage in lucid fantasy and tend to have individual blind spots and inhibitions. Because students usually need considerable individual feedback to comprehend and achieve each aspect (CS, SE, and AR) of lucidity, training programs in lucidity may be more effective if they include procedures for diagnosing and responding to individual differences.

In my doctoral dissertation study (Malamud, 1980), I worked with six young adult subjects to develop a lucidity training program that was carried on via written correspondence with each subject over a 12- to 17-week period. The main components of this program were lucidity checklist instructions for "re-dreaming" a dream lucidly in waking fantasy and my written feedback to each subject on his or her attempts to use these instructions. Following are some examples, quoted from this study, of the kinds of feedback I give to students of lucidity.

To a subject who questioned whether it was possible or even advisable to direct his or her fantasies consciously, rather than letting them flow spontaneously, I gave the following reply, which includes general instructions for having lucid waking dreams:

> In this program, the purpose of the lucid waking dream is to practice the lucid attitude in conjunction with the search for personal satisfaction. These "practice" aspects of the waking dream may often have to be done deliberately and actively, particularly in the early stages of learning.
>
> Before you begin the lucid waking dream, you will probably find it helpful to think through the implications of lucidity as they apply to your original dream. For example, you could remind yourself that "I could use magic to solve that problem," or, "I don't have to be afraid of that danger," or, "That character may reflect some of my own feelings," etc. You also may need to do some initial clarifying of what you *want* in the dream situation.
>
> With the dual framework of lucidity and satisfaction clearly in mind, you can begin the waking dream, allowing it to proceed spontaneously or deliberately, according to your preference. What happens then? You may remain thoroughly lucid and satisfaction-oriented right through to the end of your waking dream, or, you might not. In the latter case (e.g., if you become afraid of one of your characters, or you get bogged down in an unfulfilling situation) you can "stop the action" and consciously remind yourself of your freedom and safety in the waking dream state, or take time out to search among your feelings to find the lost thread of satisfaction. You might deliberately experiment with various responses to the dream situation until you find one that feels good. At that point, you could allow your waking dream to continue spontaneously (Malamud, 1980, p. 93).

Another subject was embarrassed, in her dream, to ask a stranger if they could go riding together as a favor to the subject. I pointed out that the privacy of dreams and fantasies brings freedom from the danger of social censure:

> You used your lucidity [in the waking dream] to change the girl into an old friend so you would feel comfortable asking to go riding. Sounds like that solution felt very good!
>
> Here is another thought: In dreams and fantasies, you don't have to worry about being considered impolite if you ask a stranger-image for a favor. In waking life, people might indeed think badly of you for such behavior, but in dreams and fantasies, *you* make the rules!
>
> When you're having a dream or fantasy, no one even knows what's going on inside your head, so you can imagine doing absolutely *anything* that pleases you without fear of offending any real people. In your lucid dreams or waking dreams, you

might still choose to behave according to the etiquette of waking life, if it gives you satisfaction to do so, but you don't *have* to (Malamud, 1980, pp. 126–127).

A third subject responded aggressively to an intruder in his dream and subsequent waking dream. In my response, I emphasized the internal, self-created, self-reflecting, and essentially harmless nature of images:

> It appears that you responded: (1) as if the image of the intruder were an external reality, and (2) as if you were actually in danger. These responses are perfectly valid choices, as long as you are clearly aware that, in dreams and fantasies: (1) all the images are inside you—your own creation—and therefore reflect your own feelings and perceptions, and (2) your images cannot actually hurt you and thus you are never in real danger.
>
> Just to get a feel for this, you could try having another waking dream based on these assumptions: "This intruder who seems to threaten my being is actually an image which I am creating right now. I am infusing this image with a feeling of threat; the threat is my own feeling which I am picturing as belonging to the intruder-image. No matter how viciously I have this intruder-image attack me," that is, my *image* of myself, *I* cannot be hurt (Malamud, 1980, p. 170).

Most of the many techniques for inducing lucid dreaming (Malamud, 1986) aim simply to teach dreamers to recognize *when* they are dreaming but do not systematically teach them to be aware of the empowering *implications* of the fact that they are dreaming. The full potential of lucidity training to foster awareness, insight, and skills can only be realized when lucid dreamers learn to understand and take advantage of these implications. What we need, if lucidity training is to become a broadly applicable method of personality development, are approaches to teaching lucidity that explicitly illuminate *what it means* to be dreaming and *what kind of reality* dreaming is. In addition, the recent development of a diverse assortment of training techniques now makes it possible to explore optimal matching of teaching methods to the needs and goals of individual students and clients.

REFERENCES[3]

Campbell, J. (1980). *Dreams beyond dreaming*. Virginia Beach: Donning.

Faraday, A. (1974). *The dream game*. New York: Harper & Row.

Garfield, P. L. (1974). *Creative dreaming*. New York: Simon & Schuster.

Green, C. (1968). *Lucid dreams*. Oxford: Institute of Psychophysical Research. (Distributed by State Mutual Book and Periodical Service, New York)

Green, C. (1976). *The decline and fall of science*. Oxford: Institute of Psychophysical Research. (Distributed by State Mutual Book and Periodical Service, New York)

LaBerge, S. P. (1980). Lucid dreaming: An exploratory study of consciousness during sleep. (Doc-

[3]The author's articles in *Lucidity Letter* and *Dream Network Bulletin* are available from the author, 2555 Bainbridge Avenue, #6B, Bronx, NY 10458.

toral dissertation, Stanford University). *Dissertation Abstracts International, 41,* 1966B. (University Microfilms Order No. 8024691).

LeShan, L. (1976). *Alternate realities: The search for the full human being.* New York: Evans.

Malamud, J. R. (1980). The development of a training method for the cultivation of "lucid" awareness in fantasy, dreams, and waking life. (Doctoral dissertation, New York University, 1979). *Dissertation Abstracts International, 40,* 5412B. (University Microfilms International Order No. 8010380)

Malamud, J. R. (1982a). Discovering lucidity: Experiential exercises for dream study groups. *Dream Network Bulletin, 1*(2), 1–3.

Malamud, J. R. (1982b). Training for lucid awareness in dreams, fantasy, and waking life. *Lucidity Letter, 1*(4), 7–11.

Malamud, J. R. (1986). Becoming lucid in dreams and waking life. In B. Wolman & M. Ullman (Eds.), *Handbook of States of Consciousness.* New York: Van Nostrand Reinhold.

Perls, F. S. (1969). *Gestalt therapy verbatim* (Compiled and Edited by J. O. Stevens). Lafayette, CA: Real People Press.

Saint-Denys, H. de. (1982). *Dreams and how to guide them* (M. Schatzman, Ed., and N. Fry, Trans.). London: Duckworth. (Original work published 1867)

Sparrow, G. S. (1976). *Lucid dreaming: Dawning of the clear light.* Virginia Beach: Association for Research and Enlightenment.

Stewart, K. (1969). Dream theory in Malaya. In C. Tart (Ed.), *Altered states of consciousness: A book of readings* (pp. 159–167). New York: Wiley.

Tart, C. T. (1979). From spontaneous event to lucidity: A review of attempts to consciously control nocturnal dreaming. In B. B. Wolman (Ed.), *Handbook of dreams: Research, theories and applications* (pp. 226–268). New York: Van Nostrand Reinhold.

van Eeden, F. (1969). A study of dreams. In C. Tart (Ed.), *Altered states of consciousness: A book of readings* (pp. 145–158). New York: Wiley. (Reprinted from *Proceedings of the Society for Psychical Research,* 1913, *26,* 431–461)

13

Personal Experiences in Lucid Dreaming

ALAN WORSLEY

PERSONAL HISTORY RELATING TO LUCID DREAMS

Childhood

My first lucid dream arose from my discovery as a child of 5 that I could wake myself from frightening dreams by trying to shout "Mother!" Having gained confidence through this discovery that I could escape from unpleasant dreams, I allowed them to continue longer than before. The first time I did this was in a dream in which I seemed to be falling. My instinct was to wake myself before I reached the ground, but, instead, I allowed the fall to go on; by now I was fairly sure that there was no real danger because it was only a dream. As I remember, the fall ended in no sudden bump, but, instead, the dream changed and turned out not to be unpleasant at all.

Over the next few years I had few lucid dreams. I cannot remember precisely, and I kept no records, but I estimate I dreamed lucidly once every few months.

Early Adolescence

I began to experiment with lucid dreams in my early teens. At the time, I called them "conscious dreams," not having yet heard the now accepted term *lucid dream* (van Eeden, 1913).

The author gratefully acknowledges the considerable editorial assistance of Morton Schatzmann in the preparation of this chapter.

ALAN WORSLEY • 35 Croftdown Road, London NW5 1EL, England.

I carried out my first experiment at the age of about 14. It concerned what I thought of at the time as visual acuity. In my dream, I was standing in a doorway that had a wooden frame. As a test of the extent to which visual detail is possible in dreams, I examined the wood to see if the grain was evident. The grain was evident, and I concluded that the appearance of fine detail in dreams was indeed possible.

Even before this specific experiment, I had experimented in a general way with various things that are possible in lucid dreams, such as flying. I tended to initiate flight, as I do even now, by jumping into the air. Jumping is a means of disengaging myself from contact with the "ground." This breaks the cycle of expectation and reinforcement that anchors me to the ground and normal modes of travel and so leaves me free to move in any direction. I do not recall ever trying to fly by moving my arms.

More recently, I learned how to regard "flying" as a matter of changing my point of view by driving the imagery in one direction or another, as if I was sitting in a chair, watching television, and had control of the camera. I no longer have to regard the imagery as stationary and myself as moving through it. Astral travelers do not seem to have this option and thus tend to interpret their experience as taking place in a real space of some sort. I tend to regard lucid dream imagery in general as real in the way a fascinating film is real, with the option to revert to regarding it as mere imagery, which I can ignore or change.

Late Adolescence and Early Adulthood

In my teens, I tried to learn about other strange experiences involving altered states of consciousness. I read books about subjects orthodox and occult, including telepathy, hypnotism, psychoactive drugs, astral projection, and ritual magic. Information obtained from this reading enabled me to refine my lucid dreaming techniques during my teens and 20s and no doubt influenced my expectations about what experiences were likely; nevertheless, I tried to keep an open mind and remained sceptical, for instance, about the status of claims concerning astral projection. I obtained a degree in psychology followed by several years' research in other areas, but not until 1969, when I was 32, did I discover from reading Celia Green's book *Lucid Dreams* (Green, 1968) that what I had been trying to investigate informally for so long was already an object of careful study.

FIRST LABORATORY EXPERIMENTS

In 1973, I met Keith Hearne, who had come to Hull to do an M.Sc. in psychology. His research topic, visual evoked responses, involved the use of an

EEG machine. He had previously studied hypnotic guided dreams and, as this seemed to be a subject closely related to lucid dreams, I told him of my experiments during lucid dreams and how potentially important they seemed as a method for studying the mind and brain. In 1975, after much discussion of lucid dreams and related subjects, we agreed to collaborate by combining the expertise he had now gained by using the EEG machine with my ability to control my dreams while they were happening. We decided to use the facilities of the psychology department of the university in Hull to investigate what changes, if any, would be evident in the polygraph record of my sleep at lucidity onset.

Signaling from Lucid Dreams

Our first problem was to mark the point at which I realized I was dreaming. Somehow or other, I had to signal that I had grasped the real situation—that I was sleeping in a laboratory and was taking part in an experiment. I had to move some part of my body deliberately in a recognizable way (according to an agreed pattern) that could be recorded by the machine.

Because eye movements were already being recorded as a matter of course in sleep laboratory experiments, and as eye movements seemed to have some relation to dream content, it occurred to us to use eye movements (under my voluntary control) as a means of easily recorded communication. This control might be achieved by my manipulating the content of my dream or at least by directing my gaze toward specific parts of the dream scene. Having already acquired the capacity to exert voluntary control of dreams while knowing I was dreaming, I was confident before we began the experiment that I could move my eyes from left to right a certain number of times, whether or not I looked back and forth at objects in the dream scene to my left and right. I was already sufficiently familiar with lucid dreaming to predict that once I had become lucid and thereby aware of my true situation, this eye-movement signaling routine would not be difficult. In fact, on the second night and with my first laboratory lucid dream, we succeeded with this simple technique for marking the onset of awareness of dreaming. This single instance in itself demonstrated that lucid dreams could occur in REM sleep, that the dreamer was able to remember a task and carry it out, that he or she was able to signal that he or she was doing so, and that he or she could count the eye movements and make them at the agreed rate. We carried out these first experiments in April 1975.

We began to use this new technique to do other experiments. We tried, for instance, to discover if various forms of external stimulations during REM sleep would help me to realize that I was dreaming. We tried water spray, which influenced the content of my dreams, but it did not make me realize that I was dreaming. We also tried verbal messages.

We further tried to see if, when I had signaled that I was lucid, I could distinguish various odors that were presented to me. We found that the odors influenced the dream content but that reliable detection and differentiation of odors during lucid dreams was difficult, though not impossible, for me.

Some of this work is reported in Keith Hearne's unpublished doctoral dissertation (Hearne, 1978) for which I was the main subject. Perhaps the greatest benefit of this research for me was that it vindicated to a considerable degree the reliability of my lucid dream reports. This meant that reports of experiments I performed at home could now be more readily accepted as valid. The disadvantage of laboratory work, particularly before I had discovered how to induce lucid dreams with a fair degree of reliability, was that it was slow, inconvenient, and expensive.

EXPERIMENTS AT HOME

Introduction

Factors Influencing Dream Content

The content of my lucid dream experiences is a product of many factors including my attitudes and prejudices about dreams and my circumstances at the time of the dream. It is conceivable that my ideas about the generation of dreams could influence both the content of my dreams and the means of their generation. I have therefore included these ideas as background material because I believe they constitute part of the data.

Control. An important point to make about the content of my lucid dreams is that my exercise of concurrent control over a dream implies changing the content from what it might have been. The data from dream experiments involving control therefore should be separated from data derived from uncontrolled dreams because, for purposes of analysis, each data set represents a different population.

Presleep Intentions. Sometimes the intention to carry out the experiment alters the content even before I become lucid, for instance, in cases where I might find the materials needed for the experiment on hand before I realize I am dreaming.

Attention. In the vast majority of dreams with the highest degree of lucidity, once I had realized I was dreaming I directed my attention toward introducing new content. In lucid dreams, I have succeeded in changing the content on so many occasions and in so many directions that I now feel that the notion of typical content, if applied to controlled lucid dreams, may be misplaced.

Experimental Method

Standard Procedure

The standard procedure that I have used now for over 2 years for producing, controlling, and recording lucid dreams at home is as follows.

Timing of Sleep Periods. When I am intending to carry out a lucid dream experiment, I settle down to go to sleep around 1.30 A.M. I sleep from about 2 A.M. to exactly 7.45 A.M. when the alarm sounds, about 5¾ hours, as this seems to produce the best results. I get up and remain awake, until about 9.30 A.M., eating breakfast, drinking tea, and reading a newspaper and any mail that has arrived.

Stating Intentions. About 9 or 9.30 A.M., before settling down to go to sleep, I write down in some detail the experiments I intend to carry out. In order to make the maximum use of the few minutes during which I am likely to be sufficiently lucid to carry out the experiment, I generally try to combine several experiments, as long as these do not interfere with each other. Some experiments are long-running, such as those in which I am trying to discover how to prolong or retrieve the lucid dream state. I aim to be back to sleep by about 10.00 to 10.30 A.M.

Sleep Position. As far as possible, I arrange to go to sleep in a face-down position because it seems to aid the induction of lucid dreams. (When I am not involved in lucid dream experiments I generally lie on one side or the other). Having my forearms under my chest and fists to cheeks also seems to help, possibly because it stops my arms moving. In this position, sometimes my arms go numb, which can become so uncomfrotable that I start to worry about the bad effects of restricting my circulation. Several times, because of this anxiety, I have terminated a long series of lucid dreams that seemed as if it might go on indefinitely. When I am fully awake, I am able to reassure myself that the harm I fear is unlikely.

Recording Results. When I wake, I record the results briefly in my diary. I do this whether I have a lucid dream or not. If there is much interesting material, I dictate my account into a tape recorder. If I have managed to carry out an intended experiment, I concentrate on recording the details relevant to that, unless something else seems more important. The result of this selectivity is that the contents of which I have a record represent a biased sample of the content of my lucid dreams.

Criteria of Lucidity

Degrees of Lucidity. In many dreams, I have sufficient awareness that I am dreaming to know it is safe to take liberties that I would not take during waking life. These might be considered lucid dreams, and yet I am diverted by the imagery away from the research objective upon which I have set my sights during waking. I may simply be attracted by the prospect of some simple pleasure. This is natural enough and does not necessarily imply a serious lack of lucidity—though in waking life I think I would assign a higher value to carrying out a new experiment in a dream than say, to merely fly for the fun of it in a dream.

If I am not very lucid, I might think that by flying I could enjoy another kind of pleasure, that of amusing or amazing people. In this case, I am treating the dream people as if they were real.

Lucidity as Content: Some Basic Characteristics of Lucidity. An understandable tendency among those whose knowledge of lucid dreams is very limited is to imagine that knowing you are dreaming must be an all-or-nothing affair. In my experience, how well I know I am dreaming varies from moment to moment within the same dream. This rapid change in the level of lucidity from one second to the next as one thought follows another might be expected to cause problems in deciding whether a whole dream, covering perhaps 2 or 3 minutes, should be regarded as lucid. In carrying out experiments, I find there may be momentary hitches, but if my mental function and awareness of the situation is generally adequate, the plan gets executed. If the lucidity is deficient, then I do not reach the goal of the experiment. I use "reaching the goal," not all the moments on the way to the goal, to decide whether I was lucid.

Once I have realized, even momentarily, that I am dreaming and have started to do an experiment, as long as I complete the attempt to do the experiment, I consider the dream to have been lucid even though I have not specifically thought again about whether I am dreaming.

In order to convince myself that I really understand my position when dreaming, I feel it unnecessary to check through a list of implications, such as "I also know I am at home asleep in bed." The single criterion that seems to divide the lucid dreams I have recorded into two equal groups is whether I remember to do the experiment I have arranged before sleep onset. I need not actually manage to carry out the experiment to satisfy this criterion because conditions might be too difficult.

If I think of a substitute experiment that I judge to be valid on waking, that will also satisfy my criterion. However. carrying out an experiment that does not make sense, such as writing something down so that I can read it when I wake, does not satisfy my criterion. In such a dream, I may have correctly felt free to take liberties without risking untoward consequences, but I have also taken liberties with the rules of logic, which may lead to interesting experiences but suggests that the degree of lucidity is too low (unless such liberties are taken deliberately in the clear knowledge that they are illogical). I may deliberately decide, in order to maintain the stability of the dream, to pretend that dream characters are real, which I could do from a position of high lucidity. That would be very similar to the suspension of disbelief while watching a play.

I think one can devote one's whole attention to some activity during a dream while presupposing, so to speak, the fact that one is dreaming. The question that should perhaps be asked is: Does such a dream come within the definition of lucidity as "knowing one is dreaming"?

Results

Television Experiments

I think perhaps the most interesting experiments I have done are my current (1984) "television experiments." The tasks I have set myself in these experiments are to find a television set, turn it on (if it is not already on), watch it, try to understand what I see, and experiment with the controls to change such things as the sound level and the color intensity. I have also pretended with some success that the television set will respond to voice control, thereby enabling me to interrogate it and to command it to display various images.

The idea for these television experiments grew out of a number of other lines of investigation, in particular those involving controlling imagery in one sensorimotor modality by taking action in another one (for example, trying to switch on a light in the dark). I have experimented with manipulating imagery, as if I were learning to operate by trial and error an internal computer video system (including "scrolling," "panning," changing the scene instantly, and "zooming"). Further, I have experimented with isolating part of the imagery or "parking" it, by surrounding it with a frame such as a picture frame or proscenium arch and backing away from it ("windowing").

A Spontaneous Variation on the Television Theme: Electronic Paintbox. In my search for a television set in order to begin the experiment, several times I have come across something similar to, but not the same as, a television set. For example, on one occasion I came across what I immediately realized was an electronic finger-painting device. (Such devices exist, but I had never actually used one.) In the dream, in one corner of the screen was an electronic palette displaying different colors into which one could dip one's finger, and then, having specified the color one wished to use, one could leave a trail of the color by drawing one's finger across the screen. In the dream, I played with this device for a few seconds but then reverted to my search for a normal television set, even though, in this case, it might have been more profitable to experiment further with the device that the dream had already produced.

Dispenser Television. I have also attempted to use a television set to dispense equipment that I need for experiments in dreams. My idea was to instruct the television verbally to display a desired object and then to open the glass front of the screen in order to retrieve the object from behind the screen, as if what I was seeing was not just a two-dimensional display but an actual object. In one such series of experiments, I attempted to use the television/dispenser as a means of obtaining a cannister of what I was calling "ESP gas." The idea was that if I raised my expectations sufficiently high by inhaling this "ESP gas," I would facilitate telepathy or remote viewing in the dream and thereby permit any such ability I might have to emerge more readily. I am not convinced that inhaling the "ESP gas" has produced any extrasensory perception.

In a more rewarding incident, while observing the rapidly changing three-dimensional display on one television/dispenser, I noticed that on an adjacent machine, chocolates were being displayed. I thought to myself that because I was dreaming, there would be none of the usual penalties if I ate some of these chocolates, so I allowed myself to be diverted on this occasion to an experiment with a sensory as well as an intellectual reward. I grabbed a handful of what I took to be orange-cream chocolates and started eating them. I noted the taste, which seemed to be both sharp and bitter, corresponding to two of the components in the taste of orange cream and bitter chocolate. However, other components such as a sweet taste and fruity fragrance were absent. On waking, which occurred a minute or two later, I realized I had a taste similar to this bitter sharpness in my mouth, perhaps partly as a result of having been lying on my back for an hour or two with my mouth open. This is consistent with an observation I have made in respect of other senses, notably hearing, that sometimes during a lucid dream I can apparently experience sensory information that arises from sources external to my brain (cf. electric stimuli in Chapter 8, Schatzman *et al*).

Body Image Experiments

Matter Penetration. One topic I have investigated in some depth is what I call "matter penetration." This generally takes the form of breaking in some way the normal expectation that solid objects cannot be penetrated by, for instance, one's hands. I have found that this expectation is not too difficult to alter, and being able to push my hands into solid objects has proved useful in my repertoire of techniques for controlling lucid dreams. I have used matter penetration as a means of escaping from a confined situation. As an alternative to walking through or sinking through a wall, I can carve a hole with my bare hands and then walk through it. Once, to amuse people in a lucid dream and to show them how adept I was, I carved large lumps out of a piano leg, but in my attending to the exhibitionistic aspects of the situation, my awareness that I was only dreaming and that my efforts were on behalf of an unreal audience weakened.

Pushing My Hand through Glass. On another occasion, I pushed my hand through a car windshield to see whether my hand would come through intact on the other side. I found that it did. While doing this, I felt as if I was pushing my hand through a hole that continuously changed shape to fit perfectly around my hand. I felt some drag but not so much as to be uncomfortable.

Sinking into the Ground. In another dream, instead of trying to move upwards off the ground and fly, I decided to try to move downwards, directly into the ground. That is possibly a more difficult task than flying because not only is it more unusual but because it is normally not possible to even start the movement: Solid ground, unlike air, cannot be jumped into. At first, for a few seconds, nothing much happened, but then I felt as if I was standing on a soft blacktop road surface, and I began to sink. The movement gathered pace, and I rapidly went below ground level. The sudden success of this after the slow start surprised me a little, and I was not prepared for what I should perhaps have expected to happen next. As my eyes passed ground level, it suddenly went dark. That is to say, the visual imagery disappeared. When this happens, I have found that unless I have prepared in my imagination a new visual image and am holding it ready, an entirely new visual image may appear; the transformation of the scene is often enough to cause loss of orientation and, perhaps as a consequence, loss of awareness that I am dreaming.

What happened in the case I am describing was that I had a false awakening. I dreamed that I was in bed in the house in which I used to live with my parents and that my mother came into the bedroom. I am calling this a false awakening because dreaming of suddenly finding oneself in bed is a situation in which one is likely to conclude that one has just woken, which is what I concluded. I did not realize that the situation was an unreal one as my mother had been dead for several years. It occurred to me afterwards that this fact may be connected with why, having just sunk into the ground, I then, "logically," met my mother.

Interpenetration of Parts of the Dream Body

An interesting variation on the "matter penetration" technique is penetrating one part of the dream body by another. For instance, on a number of occasions, I have passed one forearm through the other, again experiencing "drag." This interpenetration seems to me to be a rather unexpected thing to be able to do, even in a dream. I half expected there to be some sort of automatic blocking mechanism that would prevent this, rather like the automatic mechanisms on aircraft that prevent their gunners shooting at the wings. However, there seemed to be no such mechanism. For instance, I have passed a knife through my wrist.

The Solidity of Dream Objects. Yet solidity is present if required, as demonstrated by my being able to play the piano, walk up stairs, open a door, use tools, and snap my fingers quite realistically if I want to.

Once, during a short philosophical discussion in a lucid dream I banged on the table to emphasize how *solid* matter could be in a dream. I did this, tongue-in-cheek, knowing that my audience was not real and wondering whether my demonstration refuted or complemented Dr Johnson's famous "argument" of kicking a stone ("I refute it thus . . .") against the philosophy of Bishop Berkeley ("All the choir of heaven and furniture of earth—in a word, all those bodies that compose the mighty frame of the world—have not any subsistence without a mind").

Penetration of Head by Hands: Attempt to Locate Dreamer's Point of View

I have used this technique of penetrating one part of the body by another in an experiment where I was trying to locate my point of view in a dream as follows.

If one puts one's hands in front of one's eyes in a dream, then, the visual imagery usually duly disappears. It occurred to me to try to find the point in my visual field at which this effect begins by starting with my hands behind my eyes and moving them forward until it went dark. I pushed my hands into the sides of my head until my fingertips met in the middle. I checked that they had met and were aligned by clicking my fingernails together. I moved my hands forwards, so that they would emerge through my eyeballs and be in front of my eyes, and would then block my view. It seemed possible that they might block my view before that point. However, when my hands reached a point that I judged or sensed to be at the back of my eyeballs, I felt as if my hands were pressing against the backs of my eyeballs and that, if I moved by hands any further, I would pop my eyeballs out. Even though I knew that it was a dream, at this point I was in fact inhibited and have not tried that particular experiment again. The nearest I have got to doing so was to make my fingertips meet in the middle of my head, but I was distracted by what seemed to be an impenetrable lump that I felt below the penetrable lobes of my cerebral cortex, as if I had a brain within a brain.

Limb Extension Experiments

I have tried with considerable success to extend various body members including my nose, arms, and various artificial ones such as tentacles. The tentacles I have so far produced (from my forehead and my abdomen) have been visual only—observed in a mirror. I have extended my nose by willing it to do so and simultaneously gently pulling it out. This succeeded, but I have yet to develop any prehensile capacities in it. I have used the same extension techniques on my tongue with gratifying results.

The integration of the visual and haptic imagery involved in these extensions seems not to be reliable. I discovered that I seemed to have two dream arms—a visual arm and a haptic arm. I could make the visual arm grow to a considerable length by willing my arm to stretch, but the *haptic* arm did not stretch with it unless I made special arrangements to keep it congruent with the visual arm. In order to do this, as my arm extended, I crawled my hand along a surface so that I could feel it doing something at the end of the arm, as well as see it. Having developed this technique for integrated multisensory arm extension, I am now able to use it to retrieve distant objects in a dream.

Tabulated Results

The numbers of instances shown in Table 1 are generally small because I performed these experiments not to measure incidence but primarily for my own satisfaction to see if I could do certain things in dreams. In this respect, I regard dream activities as similar to waking activities, which do not have to be done more than once to prove that they are possible.

Table 2 shows the degrees of success I am currently achieving in my attempts to have lucid dreams and, in those cases in which I have achieved lucidity, in remembering to carry out a planned experiment. The figures show that I am able to have a lucid dream on about half the occasions on which I attempt to do so, and, of those occasions, I use more than half to carry out an experiment successfully. Thus on about one quarter of the occasions when I attempt to make specific changes in the content according to a prearranged plan, I succeed. In a high proportion of these occasions, I introduce content that I may never have experienced before.

For instance, before beginning the television experiments, results of which are shown in Table 1, I had never dreamed, to my knowledge, about watching television, although I had dreamed about things I had seen on television. I had never dreamed about pushing my hands into solid objects, and certainly not into the middle of my head, until I did this with some trepidation in a lucid dream. Making my arm and even totally artificial limbs several feet long was not part of my dream experience until I did it deliberately while lucid.

Discussion

Integration of Imagery in Different Modalities during Sleep-Onset Dreams

I have discovered a technique to produce sleep-onset lucid dreams with multisensory qualities. When I use this technique, the dreams often begin with

Table 1. Changing the Content of Lucid Dreams

Content of experiment	Difficulty rating			Successes/attempts		
	Easy	Moderate	Hard	Number	Total	%
Matter penetration						
Hand into wall or table	E			21	23	91
Carve with bare hand	E			8	10	80
Knife through wrist	E			2	2	100
One fore-arm through another	E			5	5	100
Fingers into head (some hesitation)	E			5	5	100
Other effects						
Create flames at finger tips by flicking like a						
cigarette lighter	E			7	10	70
Generating sound						
Turning on radio	E to M			3	5	60
Playing piano	E			5	6	83
Tapping hard object	E			4	5	80
Speaking	E			9	10	90
Receiving audible reply to spoken question			H	2	7	29
Reading						
Single words	E			9	10	90
Pairs of words	E			8	10	80
Short sentences		M		2	7	29
Long sentences			H	0	5	0
Visual experiments						
Looking left or right	E			100	100	100
Scrolling laterally (panning)	E			8	9	89
Scrolling down (like levitating)		M		3	6	50
Scrolling up (sink into ground)			H	2	5	40
Zoom backwards and forwards	E			7	8	88
Television experiments						
Turn on television	E			3	4	75
Change channel	E			8	9	89
Add sound		M		2	3	67
Add color	E			2	2	100
Take objects from screen		M		2	3	67
Integration of sensory modalities						
Haptic activation of visual imagery						
Turn light on in dark (no visual imagery)						
Instantaneously			H	0	13	0
After a 10-second delay		M		6	12	50
Turn light on in well-lit room						
(Instantaneously)	E			8	10	80
Visual/ visual imagery change						
Color of scene by filter	E			10	10	100
Haptic activation (sudden) of aural imagery						
Making gun or balloon bang		M		3	7	43

(continued)

Table 1. (Continued)

Content of experiment	Difficulty rating			Successes/attempts		
	Easy	Moderate	Hard	Number	Total	%
Limb lengthening Experiments						
Arm, seen and felt, no technique			H	0	8	0
Ditto by crawling hand technique		M		4	7	57
Extension of arm, visual only	E			7	8	88
Extend tentacle ex head (visual)	E			1	1	100
Flying experiments						
Levitating a few inches to check if really dreaming		M		23	48	48
Flying up to about 100 feet	E			98	112	88
Flying 100 feet to 500 high		M		23	54	43
Flying over 500 feet high			H	3	27	11

nonvisual imagery. I had one in which a strange creature like a mermaid seemed to slither over the bed until I could feel her scaly skin in contact with me. Although she was gentle, I soon discovered she had very sharp teeth. This made me a little anxious, but I knew from previous occasions that if I moved, I would wake up, and the experience would end.

I have this kind of dream rarely. That may be because the initial haptic imagery is so convincing that it tends to demand immediate action. This action tends to result in actual movement of my physical body. I believe that I can make this physical movement because at the haptic stage of these sleep-onset dreams, the inhibition of physical movement that applies during predominantly visual dreams—a later stage—has not yet taken effect. A movement in these circumstances seems to occur in both my dream body and in my physical body. It immediately terminates the dream, partly, I suppose, by attracting my attention to my physical situation. Thus my attention turns away from the dream imagery to "external" (originating outside my brain) body sensations, which results in

Table 2. Lucid Dream Induction Attempts (One per Day) and Successes and Frequency of Experiments in Lucid Dreams

Year	Trial days total	Successful days with lucid dreams in				Successful experiments in lucid dreams		
		Singles	Series	Total	%	Trials	Total	%
1982	226	37	78	115	51	115	69	60
1983	188	35	52	87	46	87	50	57

the dream imagery tending to fade away. However, if I ensure that I do not move, no matter what peculiar or frightening events appear to be taking place, then the dream imagery continues.

At first, the imagery is more often auditory, tactile, or kinesthetic than visual. I might hear a simple sound like a hiss or feel some change in pressure on my body, as if my bedclothes were moving. The two sensations might combine, so that I both hear and feel the bedclothes moving. The interpretation I put on such imagery while asleep may be that the bedclothes are slipping off the bed because of gravity or that someone is actually pulling them off or rearranging them.

Imagination in Dreams

During dreaming, I can experience visual imagery both in my imagination and as part of the dream. For instance, haptic imagery that appears initially by itself seems often to be translated into visual terms by first appearing in my imagination and then, after a few seconds, as part of the visual dream imagery. The dream imagery thus created maintains itself without further effort, whereas scenes voluntarily imagined require my continuous effort to hold them in view.

This new *visual* dream content tends to change my perspective on my situation, and lucidity may be lost, as I am taken in by the image my eyes apparently see.

During an experience of spontaneous kinesthetic sensations in my feet, I wondered what could be the explanation, and an image of a strange machine came to mind. Because, in the dream, I was lying face down, I was not in a position to see either my feet or the strange machine that I was imagining, but after a change in my position—I sat up and turned round—I saw the strange machine. The imagined visual imagery had transferred to the dream proper and appeared as part of the dream imagery.

There is a distinction between imagery in the imagination during dreaming and the dream imagery proper. If this is not understood by dreamers, their dream reports could be misleading. *Logically,* imagined scenes seem less likely to evoke eye movements than those "seen" in the dream proper as external. Imagined scenes are recognized more easily by the dreamer as being generated internally (as is the case with imagined scenes while awake) and therefore making scanning eye movements unnecessary. Conversely, I expect imagery that the dreamer believes originates externally would produce eye movements, as during waking observation of external scenes.

Eye movements may not be strictly necessary to scan the imagery, as there are alternative methods of driving the imagery around. I have experimented with shifting visual dream imagery without moving my eyes, by, for example, holding a mirror close to my eye in a dream, so that I can look at different parts of the dream scene by moving the mirror rather than by moving my eyes. Perhaps this method could eliminate, under some circumstances, some of the rapid eye movements from REM sleep. At least it might be possible to discover what movements, if any, would be left after eliminating those used by the dreamer to shift his or her gaze.

Superlucid Dreams

When spontaneous kinesthetic imagery occurs in a sleep-onset lucid dream, it is often so convincing that I tend to interpret it as real movement, even though I "know" that it is not. I am not used to illusory sensations of movement in, for example, my feet and therefore, when I feel my feet apparently moving spontaneously and I try to stop this movement, my willed act seems to predominate, and further spontaneous sensations cease.

If, while lying in bed, I hear an unexpected visitor come into the room, whether I am dreaming or not, my natural response is to feel alarmed and to investigate. Among other things that can happen or that actually have happened, while I lay in bed, are, falling out of bed, feeling the bedclothes slipping or someone putting them back, or a cat walking over the bed, or hearing the telephone ring, or someone coming into the room. Perhaps that is why these are the events that most commonly happen in haptic dreams of lying in bed.

I have found that these dreams develop in interesting ways if allowed to do so. They often combine auditory, tactile, kinesthetic, visual, and sometimes even olfactory and gustatory imagery. There is usually a high degree of awareness and of an ability to consider the situation. I believe these occur because of the continuity of consciousness from the waking state. This results in a powerful experience, and I am inclined to invent a new term to refer to such experiences—*superlucid dreams*. They seem to be comparable to out-of-the-body experiences, which are sometimes described as being "extremely real" and "unlike ordinary dreams," yet I interpret them as dreams, not as out-of-the-body experiences.

Out-of-the-body experiences, at least those occurring during sleep, may be a subcategory of a more general class of dreams of the kind I have been describing but that have not figured much in dream lore because they are normally accessible only by the use of special techniques such as those described by Monroe (1975).

In one recent superlucid dream, I felt myself lying in bed in the dark on my back (which I was in fact doing). I was aware of considerable downward pressure on my upper front teeth, which forced my head into the pillow. I could not tell what was causing this pressure. I felt rather uncomfortable, and my first impulse was to struggle. Remembering my resolve not to move or resist the imagery, I allowed it to continue. I felt as if I was at the dentist's.

I saw dimly above me a thin stream of clear liquid falling toward my face. Despite being lucid, I feared that I was in a torture chamber and that the liquid might be acid.

I knew the experience was not based on concurrent sensory input from the real world but that did not eliminate my concern about anticipated subsequent events, just as watching a play is normally emotionally involving even though one is not actually on stage and one knows the action is simulated.

Although I expected the liquid to be acid, it caused no discomfort. Two revolving, very soft brushes like woolen dusters descended onto my face and brushed the liquid away. The apparatus that was carrying out this procedure retracted, and I found myself lying in a dark tunnel of polished mahoganylike wood about as wide as my shoulders, three feet high, and curved at the top. I moved as if on a conveyor belt and emerged from the tunnel feet first. The scene brightened, and I sat up, swinging my legs to the floor. I saw a procession of people who were dressed as if to go to a ball. The women were in long pastel-colored dresses made of satinlike material, and the men wore simple fawn-colored military dress. They were parading past, rather like dolls. I gathered I was supposed to don one of these uniforms, which, with the help of an assistant, I did.

I took a step or two toward a mirror to examine my face to see what had happened to my teeth. (This shows that, although my attitude was still basically passive, I was able to act independently without apparently seriously disturbing the dream narrative.) I had been fitted with buckteeth!

I joined the procession with a female partner aged about 35, who also had buckteeth. We went into a larger room where an open train was waiting, consisting of small trucks that could each hold about six people, and we climbed into one. The train began to move toward a very large mirror. I was curious to know what would happen next. We crashed slowly and silently through this mirror, and the pieces hung in the air. I asked my partner what she thought was going on. By some kind of wordless communication, I gained the impression that she thought I was her husband, that we were all dead, and that she had been dead for some time. Then the dream ended.

The Light-Switch Phenomenon

The "light-switch" phenomenon (Hearne, 1981) is something I first noticed many years ago and that has been described by Green (1968). It is the nearly invariable failure of light switches to work in dreams where the dreamer is in darkness or in a dimly lit scene. I believe that to talk as if the light somehow really existed and the switch should actually work is based upon a misconception about the light-switch penomenon and perhaps the phenomenology of dreams in general. After all, dreams consist of images, not light waves, and simulate real things.

I have noticed that in dreams many things do not work entirely as expected, as in the television experiments previously noted. However, the light-switch phenomenon seems to be unusually consistent in its occurrence. In dreams in which I have experimented with this effect, lights have sometimes flickered or increased slowly in brightness but never come on instantaneously from pitch darkness to illuminate fully a whole scene. My impression is that it is very difficult or impossible to get the visual-imagery system running by willing it to appear but that, once it is running, it can be deliberately controlled.

Other experiments I have carried out to investigate the production of sudden effects (comparable to switching on a light) in one sensory modality by manipulating imagery in another sensory modality (for example, firing a gun) have often led to similarly feeble effects (a click instead of a bang). By contrast, attempts to produce overall effects *within* the visual modality, such as tinting the whole visual field by the use of a color filter, have been consistently successful.

Hearne (1981) may be right in suggesting that at any particular time there is an upper limit to the potential brightness of the visual imagery in a dream. This is most clear in the case where, because there is no visual imagery, there is no imagery brightness. I can produce a whole brightly lit scene from complete darkness but only under special circumstances, as follows. If, while looking at a scene, I close my eyes and thereby experience complete darkness but within a second or two open them, the dream scene will still be there. If I leave it longer, the scene may be difficult to retrieve. It is as if the "memory" that holds the visual image available for immediate "screening" decays rapidly unless I am looking at the scene and paying attention to it.

I have found that increasing existing brightness is generally much easier than producing any degree of brightness, starting from complete darkness. It is easy to put on additional lights or to increase the brightness of existing lights.

I have investigated other illumination-control mechanisms in dreams such as suddenly opening a door to let in light. The results have been similar to those obtained with switches. If there is no visual imagery to start with, it seems to be impossible for me to initiate it instantaneously. If there is some visual imagery, I can usually increase its brightness.

In order to begin to explain the light-switch phenomenon, we must understand how changes in dream content can be made voluntarily. One way in which new elements can be deliberately introduced into a dream is by the manipulation of expectation. Expecting something to happen in a dream is often enough to bring it about. Why, then, does expectation have no effect when the dreamer operates a switch in a dream and expects the room to be illuminated? The answer is perhaps as follows. If one's expectations of illumination appeared to be fulfilled, one would be creating imagery, not light. The correct question is not, "Why does the *light* not come on when the *switch* is operated?" but "Why does the visual *imagery* fail to appear when *expected?*"

Normally, in wakefulness and in dreaming, the visual system is basically passive: You see only what is already there. In switching on a light when awake, you actively will the switching but expect passively to see the scene. The willing applies only to the switching.

It appears that when a visual dream begins, the dreamer normally has no control of the activation of the visual imagery generating system. He or she can neither stop it nor start it.[1]

However, I have found that this is not always so. When I wake from a lucid dream, if I keep still and do not start to think, after about a minute I often have another lucid dream. I can arrange for this cycle to occur several times and thereby produce a whole series of lucid dreams. Each dream lasts about 3 or 4 minutes with about 1 minute of wakefulness in between. Usually the series is regular with the dreams evenly spaced, but sometimes if, for instance, I interact enthusiastically with the imagery, two or more cycles may run together and miss out the brief waking period. At the end of the series, I usually wake up, but I may fall back into dreamless sleep. However, it seems that the more sleep I have had, the more likely I am to wake at the end of the series because I cannot further subdue waking thoughts and the desire to move. The degree of lucidity during these dreams varies and seems to depend partly on how well I am maintaining the optimum balance between imposing my own will and ideas on the next dream and allowing the dream to emerge naturally.

At the beginning of each dream, I experience what I call REM reentry. I do not feel that I am deliberately initiating the next dream in the series so much as maintaining the conditions that are necessary for it to occur. I have to wait for it to happen. If I move or start thinking or open my eyes and look at something, this seems to terminate the condition, and the dream imagery does not return. I have found no method of abruptly initiating visual imagery at will.

Conclusion

These examples illustrate what I consider to be only the beginning of a whole range of experiences that can be produced when dreams are under one's conscious control. It would seem that even stranger exercises are required before the limits are reached. My lucid dream experience has convinced me that we are only at the beginning of the exploration of inner space.

Update

Large Voluntary Movements of the Physical Limbs in Dreams

In connection with the phenomenon of actual movement of the physical body during dreams (mentioned in the previous discussion and in Chapter 8), I

---

[1]As long ago as 1867 Hervey de Saint Denys had noted in his book *Les Rêves et les moyens de les diriger* (now published in translation and edited by Morton Schatzman as *Dreams and How to Guide Them* by Duckworth, London 1982) that if he closed his eyes in a visual dream the flow of visual images would cease for a moment but very soon more images would appear. It is in this sense that I mean that a dreamer cannot normally stop the dream (except by waking up).

have made further observations in both predominantly visual dreams and predominantly haptic dreams.

Normally, observation of haptic dreams may be rare because they are usually terminated within a few seconds of starting (for reasons given at the beginning of the previous discussion). It is possible that haptic dreams are often not recognized as dreams in view of (a) the frequent correspondence, in my case at least, between the haptic dream setting and my actual physical situation (usually lying in bed in both cases), (b) the brevity of such dreams when not observed under consciously controlled immobility, and (c) their lack of visual content. This may mean that the accepted view of the incidence of dreams classified according to dominant sensory mode may be distorted. This is perhaps especially so because there seems to be a tendency to regard stage-REM sleep and dreaming sleep as practically synonymous. There is, of course, good evidence for this, but it may be an artefact of both the classification system and the undisciplined physiology of the brain rather than something that is inevitable.

According to my personal observations, the initial dominant sensory mode of a dream seems likely to influence whether the dream will continue. The incidence pattern of dreams classified by dominant sensory mode seems likely, in view of the apparent shortness of haptic dreams, to vary according to the length of time a dream is defined as having to last to be considered as a dream at all. Furthermore, to the extent that rapid eye movements in dreams are a result of scanning the visual imagery, haptic dreams with no visual imagery would seem likely to exhibit less REM, though it is possible that scanning might take place "in the dark" in the hope of seeing what caused the nonvisual imagery.

A related demarcation problem can arise in connection with dreams in which vision is the dominant sensory mode. Occasionally, I have experienced an apparent ability while experiencing a visual dream to make large movements of my physical legs. This contradicts the accepted view that during stage-REM sleep only minor movements of limbs are possible (see Chapter 8).

From my limited experience of such movements and the mass of evidence suggesting that such movements do not occur, it seems to me to be necessary, if actual movement of the physical legs is to occur, that the dreamed movement be strongly willed, such as would be the case with a hard kick. The difficulty in establishing this is partly a matter of the criteria used to decide whether an event occurs in REM or while awake or is indeterminate. Although I believe I have demonstrated, while dreaming in the laboratory, the ability to make a large movement of the lower leg, the fact that this was followed within 1 second by my waking exposes my claim to be able to do this to the criticism that I was already waking anyway. The classification system of Rechtschaffen and Kales, developed before the second-by-second timing of dreams now made possible by lucid signaling, is based on a comparatively leisurely pace of events. Under that system, unless an event occurs at least several seconds before waking, it enters an indeterminate area where it could be part of the waking process. Its status as a genuine dream event is accordingly regarded as dubious.

What is required is an experiment in which the dreamer, having signaled that he or she is lucid, responds to a signal made at a randomly selected time, upon the detection of which the correct response is to make a large movement of one leg or the other, or not, depending on the signal. If the dreamer can demonstrate a consistent ability to stay asleep when the signal is received or to make a large movement, depending on the signal, then, even if waking occurs within a second of initiating the movement, not waking on the other occasions would suggest that it was the movement that caused the waking and not the waking that permitted the movement, or that the signal caused involuntary movement.

On the occasion on which I made a large movement of my leg while dreaming and sleep recording in the laboratory, I was lying face down. My legs were covered with a light quilt that was lying loose. Thus my lower legs were free to move by swinging upwards from the knee. In the dream, which was lucid (signal verified), I was deliberately kicking backwards with my right foot against a hard surface. Suddenly I woke and found that my right lower leg was in the air. (The large movement was recorded on the polygraph as high amplitude upper leg EMG followed in less than a second by the usual sudden increase in amplitude on other channels characteristic of waking.) It seemed obvious to me that the kick in the dream had caused a large real movement of my physical leg. Unfortunately, this occasion is the only one for which I have recorded hard physiological evidence.

On another occasion (February 8, 1987), not in the laboratory, I was lying on my left side. I was experiencing an ordinary (not lucid) visual dream. In this dream, which had a coherent narrative, I made a powerful Kung Fu side kick with my right leg. Again, my physical right leg was free to move, and it did so. Again, this large violent actual movement seemed to cause me to wake suddenly. I was quite convinced that that was what had happened. I felt a little shocked, partly because the situation in the dream had been tense, and I was still affected by that, but also because I was suddenly thrown out of the dream into my bedroom and it took me a second or two to ajust.

Such instances are very rare in my own personal experience in spite of having paid special attention to this phenomenon. I therefore think that it is unlikely that many other instances have been recorded and recognized.

Transfer of Technique from Lucid Dream Repertoire to Ordinary Dream Repertoire

On September 10, 1986, I observed, during what I would until that point have classified as a nonlucid dream, an instance of the use of a technique, that of arm lengthening to retrieve distant objects, which I had, as far as I know, used previously only in lucid dreams.

For many years, I have used various special techniques in ordinary, nominally nonlucid dreams. An example is a trick I have of descending stairs by slipping from the edge of one stair to that of the next as if my shoes were skis. I feel clever when I do this, and it became a habit. The strangeness of it never triggered lucidity.

In the September 10 dream, I was in a classroom of my old school. I had returned in the present with someone who wished to visit one of the masters. Being a bit bored while waiting, I used my arm-lengthening technique to reach out to take a cap from the head of one boy and put it on the head of another. Both were beyond my normal reach. Up to this point, I had been well behaved, acting as if the situation were real and impossible things could not happen. I do not remember however any sign of a thought such as "I can do this because I am dreaming."

On waking and recalling the dream, it struck me as interesting because as I have no experience of lengthening my arm while awake (apart from imagining it and remembering dreams in which I did it), there must be a possibility of transfer of technique from lucid dreams to less lucid dreams. This development may seem unsurprising because both are dreams. One might ask though, "How did I know I could do it if I had not realized I was dreaming?" Did I know at some other level that I was dreaming? Or had it now become some sort of state-specific habit and, if so, which state exactly?

Then I recalled the other techniques that I use in ordinary nonlucid dreams. It would be dangerous to use the slipping technique while awake, and I would not attempt it. On the other hand, I often seem to think I am awake in some sense when I use it in dreams; that is why I feel so clever when I do it. Somehow I must know it is safe in dreams.

Again, it appears that lucidity is not a simple matter.

REFERENCES

Green, C. (1968). *Lucid dreams*. London: Hamish Hamilton.

Hearne, K. M. T. (1978). *Lucid dreams: An electrophysiological and psychological study*. Unpublished doctoral dissertation, Liverpool University.

Hearne, K. M. T. (1981). A 'light-switch' phenomenon in lucid dreams. *Journal Of Mental Imagery, 5,* 97–100.

Monroe, R. (1975). *Journeys out of the Body*. London: Corgi.

van Eeden, F. (1913). A study of dreams. *Proceedings of the Society for Psychical Research, 26,* 431–461.

14

Without a Guru
An Account of My Lucid Dreaming

GEORGE GILLESPIE

As I came out of the jungle I approached a missionary bungalow. I seemed to be in either India or Africa. I told the couple who came to the door that I was only dreaming and wanted to know where I was before I woke up. They said nothing. I went into the house and looked for maps that might indicate where I was. I found some maps, but they were inconclusive. In another room, I found two old friends to whom I told my problem. They did not respond. I thought at the time, "You know, I can just open my eyes and make you disappear." Soon I woke up.

That, in 1975, was my first lucid dream. The experience of knowing I was dreaming interested me, and I recorded it. I had never heard of lucid dreams and had no notion of their significance or potential. I was 41. My wife, Charlotte, and I were American Baptist missionaries teaching at a theological college in Jorhat, a small town in India about 50 miles from the Burma border. As an ordained clergyman, teaching the history of religions (Hinduism, modern religious movements in India, and major religions of India) along with some Biblical courses, it did not occur to me to give the dream and the ones that followed any religious significance.

I saw lucid dreaming as an opportunity to study the nature of dreams. So after five lucid dreams I began to plan experiments to carry out when I knew I was dreaming. By planning and carrying out experiments in these earliest dreams, my pattern of approach to lucid dreams was established for years to come. I planned the experiments while awake, so that for every lucid dream I had an experiment ready to carry through if I could recall it. As my memory is poor

All examples of dreams are taken from the writer's journal, *Dreamer's progress: A record of experiments made while dreaming.* Unpublished manuscript.

GEORGE GILLESPIE • Department of Oriental Studies, University of Pennsylvania, Philadelphia, PA 19104.

while dreaming, I frequently did not recall the experiment. As I normally realized I was to do an experiment, when I could not think of the right one, at times I planned another spontaneously. The spontaneous experiment often made little sense as I cannot think very rationally while dreaming. I carried out each planned experiment in as many dreams as it required for me to feel satisfied with the results. Critical analysis after the dream has always been important to me. I felt an obligation to record every dream in detail. Occasionally while dreaming, the thought that what I do would be recorded has influenced my choice of action.

My earliest experiments included willing things to appear or disappear or to be changed. For example, in a dream I was running on air about a foot above the ground down a street from my childhood. People passed me but did not seem surprised. Then I realized from my being above the ground that I was dreaming. I had planned to find a house to make changes in but I didn't remember that. I chose a child dressed in white to change into a child's small wagon. I probably thought of red. I tried hard for perhaps half a minute, and all that happened was that the child's feet became round white wheels. I then woke up or dreamed something else.

In the early days, it did not occur to me to question whether the manipulation of dreams might defeat the purpose of having dreams. I had no idea of anyone else having such an opportunity to study dreams from the inside, and I felt it was important to do this. Besides, once lucid, I am to some degree detached from dream events, and I cannot proceed in any ordinary manner with the dream. I cannot imagine that I have ever spent more than 15 minutes at the most in a month in experimentation.

My lucid dreams became more frequent toward the end of 1976 and have since tended to occur at an average of five a month. By June 1986, I recorded 500 lucid dreams. In preparing some statistics on my first 282 lucid dreams, I saw that I either did not or probably did not wake up immediately after 8% of them. Of those for which I recorded a time for waking up afterward (207), 58% occurred between 5 and 9 in the morning,* 28% between 3 and 5, and 13% between midnight and 3. I have tended to go to bed about 10:00 P.M. Twice I had a lucid dream while napping in the afternoon. I do not often nap in the afternoon.

I could not say how I came to know I was dreaming in at least one-third of the dreams. Either I forgot how, or I came to know with no apparent cause. Sometimes I came to know by noticing that something in the dream was false or inconsistent or not possible, as when I saw my grandmother and remembered that she had died. Frequently, I recognized that what I was doing was common to my

---

*Van Eeden, in his account of his lucid dreams, said that, without exception, his lucid dreams occurred after 5 in the morning. (van Eeden, F. A study of dreams *Proceedings of the Society for Psychical Research* 26:431–461, 1913. Reprinted in C. Tart (Ed.), *Altered States of Consciousness: A Book of Readings.* New York: John Wiley, 1969.)

I questioned whether I was dreaming and tested to find out, for instance by trying dreams, as when I found myself wandering from room to room. Some few times to fly or by trying to pull someone in half. I have even realized I was dreaming by false reasoning. When I felt a book store did not have as many books as it had the last time I had been there, I thought that was an inconsistency and realized I was dreaming. However, upon waking reflection I realized that I had not been in the bookstore earlier.

In February 1977, after 17 lucid dreams and more than a year had passed since my first, I saw in the fourteenth edition of the *Encyclopaedia Britannica* under *dream* a reference to two men who told of knowing they were dreaming— Frederick William Henry Myers, founder of the Society for Psychical Research, and Frederik van Eeden, the Dutch poet and medical doctor. Their lucidity was not discussed at length in the article, but I believed that the reference must be to what I also had experienced. This was the first I knew of such dreams happening to others.

As I knew nothing of any literature on lucid dreams, I developed my own understanding of them and my own vocabulary for discussing them. I called them "known dreams." In August of 1977, soon after moving to the city of Hyderabad in South India to teach in an ecumenical seminary there, I found in a bookstore in the city Ann Faraday's *Dream Power*. For the first time, after 48 "known dreams," I found a discussion of lucid dreams. It was not until we arrived in the United States in the summer of 1979 and more specifically until I responded to Stephen LaBerge's article on lucid dreaming in *Psychology Today* (January 1981) that I came in touch with more literature on the subject and those who write it. My lack of familiarity with what was being said and done in the field of lucid dreams during those first five years of lucid dreaming resulted in an independent approach to understanding and dealing with them.

EXPERIMENTATION IN LUCID DREAMS

My experiments remained my focus of interest in lucid dreams. I tried changing the location of the dream, recalling a friend's address, which I had forgotten while awake, recalling where I was sleeping, composing brief portions of poetry, praying the Lord's Prayer, and putting into alphabetical order objects I saw while dreaming. While awake, I planned the plot for a dream that I would try to carry through when I knew I was dreaming. That included planning what I would do, what the dream environment should be, and what another person in the dream should do. I tried counting from the time I knew I was dreaming through the waking-up process in order to examine the continuity of my consciousness through waking up. I stopped my activity in the dream to watch what would happen when I became simply receptive. I examined objects in the dream for authentic duplication of waking objects. I tried to picture in my mind my grandmother's house, while keeping the ongoing dream environment in view. When I heard that other lucid dreamers had difficulty in repeating their name in a lucid dream, I tried repeating mine. In different manners, I tested the solidity and nonsolidity of dream objects. And finally, I tried to eliminate the process of dreaming while remaining asleep.

As I found my intended experiment often difficult to remember while dreaming, I occasionally used a system to help bring it to mind. When going to sleep or when falling back asleep in the middle of the night, I would repeat to myself silently something like, "I'm going to sleep. I will dream. I will realize I am dreaming. Then I will test solidity." The purpose of this was more to bring to mind the experiment should I discover I was dreaming than to encourage lucid dreaming itself, but it appeared to be as effective in encouraging lucidity. When I discovered I was dreaming, I would try to bring to mind the cue as to what I was to do. If I could bring to mind a phrase such as *test solidity*, then I remembered somewhat clearly what I was to do.

Normally I awaken from a lucid dream quite unwillingly and without having been lucid very long, though frequently long enough to carry through some experiment. It has often been a concern of mine during a dream that I not wake up. However, when I first experimented with the continuity of consciousness between dreaming and wakefulness, I unexpectedly had a problem waking up. When I realized I was dreaming, I began counting aloud (aloud in the dream), "1, 2, 3 . . ." at about the speed of one number per second. As I had a problem waking up, eventually I was counting in the 280s and finished with 300 soon after I awoke. It would seem I had counted for about 5 minutes except for some flaws in the experiment. While I counted, many things happened. I was in a beautiful old hotel listening to M. complain about something. I felt that it was about my counting continually. After I passed 100, I began counting again at 1, as I do when running in place during the day for exercise. Somewhere in the middle of the second hundred I stopped counting, possibly when I told someone I was counting until I woke up but that I couldn't wake up. Realizing I had stopped counting, I tried picking up counting again where I had left off. That way, I may have missed counting some numbers. Somewhere in there, my aunt asked my mother when we were leaving our house. Another time I came to a pond and thought for a moment that I would walk through it but decided it might feel too cold. I became conscious of counting very loudly and was afraid I might be heard by those awake. After the second 99, I began with 100, 101, and so forth, and remembered that it should be 200, 201, and so forth. Other events may have been forgotten.

I woke up gradually. I did not lose my pace of counting. Gradually I lost the feeling of my body's position in the dream and became aware of my body lying in bed. Gradually I lost the feeling that I was saying the numbers aloud and found myself only thinking them. When I knew I was awake, I thought to count a little more to be sure I had counted well into being awake. There was no discontinuity in the rhythm of my counting as I woke up. I noticed no "gap" or "bump" in my awareness, no moment of awakening, as I normally do when I wake up. The transition had gone smoothly. But I was left with the question of why I had trouble waking up.

Most of 1980 was spent with what I called my solidity experiments. Objects in dreams normally feel as they would when I am awake. This I called the "reality effect." When I intended to put my hand through an object, my hand usually went through it without resistance and without the object changing shape. But I always felt its texture. It was somewhat as when I pass my hand through water. My hand moves easily through, but I feel its substance strictly within the bounds of the object. I called this the "liquid effect." At times when I manipulated objects with the intention that they become pliable, I found them to have what I called the "putty effect." They lost their shape. They could easily be molded or stretched, often forming strings as with stringy cheese. I wanted to see whether I could pass my hand through something without feeling it at all. This I would call the "immaterial effect."

In November 1980, I did my last solidity experiment. I dreamed I was in another time and another place. I walked up a narrow cobblestone street. At the end of the street I entered someone's house to pass through to another street. Then I realized that I would not enter another's house when I don't know the person. Then I realized I was dreaming. Remembering the experiment, I looked around what seemed to be a small, stone-floored kitchen. A large square loaf of freshly baked bread, golden brown, sat on a stool. Using the loaf for my experiment, I felt it firmly with both hands. It felt a little springly like fresh-baked bread and firmly real. For the next part of the experiment, I passed my right hand through the loaf. I felt the loaf as my hand passed through it. It was the liquid effect. I thought of my desire to pass my hand through while feeling nothing at all. The bread puffed up a little before I tried. Then I passed my hand through but felt the liquid effect as before. Determinedly I passed my hand through several times more, but I always felt a texture to the loaf. Then I woke up. I reviewed the dream in the light of previous tests and felt that I had tried enough and always found that I felt the substance of what my hand passed through. The immaterial effect remained only theoretical. Things usually felt realistic. When I expected them to yield to my hand, either the putty or the liquid effect resulted, apparently determined by whether I expected to reshape the object or pass through it.

RELIGIOUS SIGNIFICANCE OF LUCID DREAMS

My lucid dreaming still did not have any particular religious significance for me. Even when praying the Lord's Prayer, though it was a sincere prayer, its primary function was as a test of rote memory. Because it was planned ahead, it lacked spontaneity. I also could not relate the words to reality because of my lack of memory of my current life situation.

As an ordained minister and a teacher of courses on the Bible and on Indian religions, I was familiar with Christian and Hindu theological concepts. I was particularly interested in the writings of Indian Christian theologians who discuss Christianity in Indian terms and such people as Swami Abhishiktananda, the French Benedictine monk, who as a Christian, found spiritual insight in the Upanishads. As I had been in India 20 years, my own theology had been formed in the Indian Christian context. It was natural that in November of 1980 I gave more attention to a Hindu concept that had interested me for years.

The earliest Upanishads speak of three states of consciousness—the waking state, dreaming, and dreamless sleep. Dreamless sleep, according to the Upanishads, is the state in which the delusion of both waking and dreaming is eliminated. In dreamless sleep the experiencer desires no desire and sees no dream. He knows nothing within or without, for there is no second thing for him to experience. Dreamless sleep is the state of nonduality, the experience of *brahman,* ultimate reality. The phrase *dreamless sleep* intrigued me. By then I had analyzed to my own satisfaction what the elements of dreaming were, and I felt that when I became lucid I could, through various means, try to eliminate dreaming while remaining asleep. It would not be true to say that I literally accepted what the Upanishads had to say or even that I really understood what was being spoken of. I wanted to see whether I could, in fact, produce dreamless sleep. This was not a religious quest. I had no idea what to expect. As it happened, my lucid dreams gradually moved into an entirely new direction.

My first attempt was to be the elimination of the nonbody dream environment. After 2 days, I dreamed I was at a restaurant table with Charlotte when I realized I was dreaming. I first thought of making some kind of test on a woman I saw at another table. Then I remembered the experiment I was to do. I closed my eyes. It became dark. I remained very much aware of sitting on a chair with my feet on the floor and leaning on the table. I wanted to remove these perceptions also. I pushed the table away, then raised my feet off the floor. I was hesitant to push the chair from under me. I willed the chair away. I remained with my legs raised and became unaware of the chair. I was first floating, then spinning, very much aware of my body. Charlotte came along and thought we should leave. So I got out of the chair. We gathered our things and left the restaurant. Then I woke up.

Eventually, in one dream, I did eliminate my awareness of all objects including of my dreamed body. I reached the point where nothing was left except my own consciousness in darkness, though I have no memory of maintaining that state. I was satisfied that I had reached the point of dreamless sleep, but I saw the state as literally only that—sleeping without dreaming. I did not see religious or philosophical meaning inherent in the experience.

Through the years that I worked on eliminating dream elements, many other novel experiences happened also, which I recognized as phenomena described in mystical literature. My intellectual ability was limited. I felt myself rise and float in the air. At times I felt myself projected at great speed involuntarily. I have often felt vibrations, occasionally heat, and once expansion of myself. I have seen impressive scenes, patterns of light, disks of light, and fullness of light. I have felt devotion and joy and "awareness" of the presence of God in the full light. But in my waking, critical reflection on these experiences, I saw them as dream experiences without theological or philosophical meaning. I could see these events in their dream context, explainable by talking about dreams. As, from the beginning, I had tried to analyze every lucid dream critically, this analytical attitude to these experiences was natural. I did not feel that I could suddenly forgo critical analysis just because these experiences began to include religious feelings.

THE EXPERIENCE OF LIGHT

At times I had seen areas of light that made me think I was waking up into the light of my room, but I would wake up in the dark. I also saw an occasional disk of clear light, which had no particular meaning for me. The habitual analytical attitude toward what were to me "only" dreams determined my earliest reaction to a greater experience of light, which, out of a dream context, would have been to me a rather startling incident. That first experience of the fullness of light was in January 1981, in my 254th lucid dream. I dreamed that I was in front of my childhood home. I wanted to show some people a high jump. When I jumped high in front of the house, I realized I was dreaming. I was far above the people. I descended. It became a fall. I remembered that I can fall in a dream without fear. I fell, not expecting to land on the ground. I just stopped below. Then I was flying again. I remembered to close my eyes and eliminate the visual environment. I did not remember to do any more. I remained floating with body awareness. I saw a bright light to my left. I remembered that a bright light does not need to mean that I am waking up. I was then surrounded by light. I seemed to float in the light and began to contemplate prayerfully what I was doing and might see. I called "Father" spontaneously, meaning God. I remained some time in this attitude and then woke up.

While dreaming, I accepted what was happening unquestioningly as an experience of God. Upon waking reflection, although I recognized the event as having the characteristics of a mystical experience, it did not occur to me at all that it had been an actual experience of God. In fact, in my journal, I recognized in this dream two breakthroughs—that I could fall in a dream without crashing or waking up and that I could become aware of a light in a dream without figuring that I must be seeing the light of my room and waking up, as had been my usual response.

By chance, the next day I was loaned Gregory Scott Sparrow's *Lucid Dreaming: Dawning of the Clear Light*. This book presented the experience of light in lucid dreams as more mystical than I was willing to accept. As there came more experiences of full light, never exactly the same, but always with the brightness and color of the sun and accompanied by varying degrees of devotional feelings and joy, the conflict grew between my assurance of God's presence that I felt during the light and my waking critical analysis. Meanwhile, I continued to feel that my first duty within a lucid dream was to continue my attempt to achieve dreamless sleep, not to experience the light which in any case I could not bring about.

Concentration came to play a large part in my attempts to eliminate dreaming. I recognized that my methods were influenced by my understanding of the methods of yoga. Concentration plays an important part in classical yoga's process for stopping the fluctuations of the mind. However, I never studied yoga other than through reading. I had begun regular exercise in 1976 with yogic postures in addition to Western exercises but only as exercise. I did not practice meditation and never studied with a guru. In fact, I felt that I should not study meditation because I did not want it to influence my dream study.

I am still wary about associating lucid dreaming with mystical meaning. All the extraordinary phenomena that have accompanied my lucid dreaming, even the religious feelings and awareness of God, no matter how self-validating they appear to be, can be explained in terms of dreaming. I feel that any belief that there is ontological or theological meaning in even ''an experience of God'' is a matter of faith, not of self-evidence.

I did, in fact, slowly reach that point of faith at which I accepted my experiences in the fullness of light to be what they appeared to be—experiences of God. I recognize that this faith is based on the insight of my intuitive self and not my rational self, for I will always be able to explain it away. Because of my devotional experiences in the light, because of my belief that phenomena described in mystical literature are explainable in terms of dreaming, particularly lucid dreaming, and because I see a relationship between meditation and lucid dreaming, my interest in lucid dreams has become largely religious. I had not intended that it become so. Now I use my lucid dreams for times of worship— prayer, praise, and singing. I cannot produce or predict the appearances of light, in which my devotion becomes more spontaneous and uncontrollable. As a dreamer, I cannot but uncritically accept what happens. Upon awaking, I still cannot but be the critic of both the dream and the dreamer. I am happy with this arrangement. As long as dreamer and critic can respect each other, the conflict is minimized.

IV

Theoretical Implications of This New Research

15

Out-of-the-Body Experiences and Dream Lucidity
Empirical Perspectives

HARVEY J. IRWIN

The objective of this chapter is to explore the possible relationship between proneness to lucid dreaming and the occurrence of a phenomenon known as the out-of-the-body experience (henceforth, OBE). In an OBE, the experient (or OBEr) has the impression that consciousness or the center of awareness is outside the physical body. Among the general public, the OBE commonly is regarded as a mystical phenomenon within which context it is known as astral projection or astral travel. Particularly in recent years, however, OBEs have attracted scientific interest among psychologists, parapsychologists, and psychiatrists so that there is a growing quantity of data as to the nature of the experience.

On the basis of phenomenological surveys by several researchers (for a review see Irwin, 1985), it is possible to offer a sketch of a typical OBE. Generally speaking, the experience arises under extreme levels of cortical arousal. Most commonly, this entails a state of complete mental and physical relaxation, but at the other extreme, a number of experiences do arise in the face of physical or mental trauma. In about a third of the cases, the onset of the OBE is reported to be characterized by distinctive physical sensations including percussive and other noises, vibration of the body, an impression of numbness or even complete immobility (catalepsy), and a momentary "blackout" or gap in the stream of consciousness. However, the majority of OBEs begin instantaneously: The experient suddenly becomes aware that consciousness seems

HARVEY J. IRWIN • Department of Psychology, University of New England, Armidale, NSW 2351, Australia.

to be outside the body. Almost invariably, this is accompanied by a perceptual-like impression (by some accounts, mental imagery) of the physical world. Thus the OBEr's consciousness reportedly looks down upon the immediate environment and "perceives" it in a seemingly realistic fashion; often the individual claims to have seen his or her own physical body from the exteriorized position. Occasionally, the OBEr mentally ventures to more distant settings, and in a small minority of cases, the experiences may relate to environs ajudged by the OBEr to be extraterrestrial, paradisal, or "astral." Between apparent changes of setting, there may be experienced a brief blackout or a sensation of passing along a dark tunnel-like structure, but such phenomena are relatively uncommon, being acknowledged by about a quarter of survey respondents. There are comparatively infrequent elements of OBE content associated particularly with experiences evoked upon confrontation with death: These include awareness of a bright light, various discarnate entities, and beautiful music. Psychologically, the out-of-body state is described by experients as one characterized by relaxed alertness, clarity, and emotional detachment or quiescence, even in OBEs arising under traumatic conditions.

While in the exteriorized state, many OBErs also have the impression that their consciousness is centered in some form other than the physical body; most commonly this so-called parasomatic form or "astral body" is a duplicate of the physical body. In some cases, the exteriorized self is said to have been connected to the physical body by a cordlike structure, known in occult circles as the astral cord or silver cord. Like the onset of the experience, the OBE in most instances ends instantaneously, with the experient suddenly realizing that the center of awareness once again is "in" the physical body, that is, perceptual experience has been restored to the perspective of the physical body. Nevertheless, in about a third of survey reports, sensations upon "reentering" the body are noted. Qualitatively, these correspond to the range of OBE onset sensations described earlier.

Of all features of the OBE, it probably is the reported realism of the experience's perceptual-like content that most encourages OBErs and occultists to interpret the phenomenon as one of astral projection or a literal separation from the physical body of a nonphysical element of human existence (e.g., the "mind" or the "soul"). It is important to note, however, that the characteristic of realism by no means negates the view that the OBE is an imaginal event. First, it could be that in an OBE an image of the environment is generated with an intended function of being maximally convincing. Second, the subjective realism of the experience frequently is assumed rather than critically evaluated. That is, if the OBE's content corresponds to the experient's memory of the actual setting, often the experience immediately is accepted as realistic; rarely is an attempt made to check the accuracy of intuitively acceptable content (Osis, 1979). Finally, there are instances of OBEs in which the perceptual-like content is known not to be veridical. For example, one OBEr noted that the pattern on the livingroom wallpaper during her OBE did not correspond to the actual pattern (Crookall, 1966, Case 111); another experient tried to direct his astral excursion outside his bedroom but found his way blocked by (imaginary) iron bars on the bedroom window (Crookall, 1972, Case 731). In drawing attention to these points, it is not the writer's intention to discount the separationist theory of OBEs but rather to caution that the role of imaginal processes in the OBE should not be overlooked. Such processes are of potential importance in the present context because lucid dreaming is, of course, an imaginal experience.

What then is the evidence that lucid dreams in some manner are linked with these impressions of a transitory exteriorized existence? Essentially, the evidence is of two kinds, that on the statistical association and that on a functional connection between the experiences. Each of these aspects will be reviewed in turn.

THE STATISTICAL ASSOCIATION

Although various OBE adepts had earlier suggested that a functional connection could exist between a state of lucidity and the induction of an OBE, the principal impetus for research on the statistical dependence between the phenomena was provided by Green's (1968b) hypothesis that these experiences were closely related. Green (1966), in fact, had surveyed a group of British university students for both OBEs and lucid dreams but did not proceed to a test of dependence between the two variables.

Although parapsychological interest in the OBE continued to grow in the following decade, it was not until the late 1970s that data on the OBE's association with proneness to lucid dreaming began to emerge. Table 1 presents a summary of the survey findings on the issue to date. For ease of comparison, the tabulated data are ordered in terms of both generality of sample and the country within which each study was conducted.

The study most nearly representing a survey of the general population was undertaken by Haraldsson in Iceland (Wiedmann & Haraldsson, 1981). Using that country's *National Registry,* Haraldsson randomly selected a group of residents between 30 and 70 years of age and dispatched questionnaires to them. Over 900 people returned usable data, a participation rate of 80%; although only 671 people completed the two items on the OBE and lucid dreams, it is likely that the sample was fairly representative of the Icelandic population within the surveyed age range. The only other tabulated study tapping the general population was Palmer's (1979a) mail survey of 700 residents of Charlottesville, Virginia. Potential participants were selected from the *City Directory* that lists residents over the age of 18. The response rate was 51%, which perhaps is a little low to ensure representativeness. Of the 354 respondents, 334 completed the two items pertinent to the issue.

Table 1. Surveys of the Dependence between Lucid Dreams and Out-of-the-Body Experiences

Source	Country	Sample	Sample size	Corrected χ^2 (1)	ϕ	p
Wiedmann & Haraldsson (1981)	Iceland	Adults ages 30–70 years	671	16.96	.16	.0001
Palmer (1979a)	USA	Charlottesville, VA residents	334	8.79	.16	.005
Kohr (1980)	USA	ARE members	406	33.93	.29	.0001
Gackenbach (1978)	USA	ARE members	75	5.43	.27	.02
Palmer (1979a)	USA	University of Virginia students	265	7.37	.17	.01
Myers (1982)	USA	St. Louis University students	202	1.63	.09	ns
Blackmore (1982a)	Britain	Surrey University students	157	4.73	.17	.05
Blackmore (1982a)	Britain	Bristol University students	114	2.58	.15	ns
Blackmore (1982b)	Netherlands	Amsterdam University students	189	7.19	.19	.01
Irwin (1983a,b)	Australia	University of New England students	89	10.39	.34	.005

Kohr (1980) and Gackenbach (1978) also surveyed adult populations, but their samples were not representative of the general population; they were comprised of members of the Association for Research and Enlightenment (ARE). The ARE is inspired by the teachings of the psychic Edgar Cayce, and its members are highly interested in parapsychological phenomena such as ESP and OBEs and in other topics generally described as concerning "human growth and potential." Thus, compared with Palmer's adult sample, the participants in Kohr's study showed a high incidence of OBEs and lucid dreams. Nevertheless, the rate of participation in ARE surveys usually is substantial.

The remainder of the investigations listed in Table 1 surveyed university students. Although the generalizability of these data to the population as a whole can be queried, student samples typically show a high participation rate and thereby are thought to yield comparatively reliable results. In a small way, the student surveys also provide an indication of the consistency of the relevant association across different countries, although it is regrettable that all of these investigations were set in Western nations.

The tabulation of results also warrants some explanation. The sample size shown in Table 1 for each study is the number of individuals who responded to the questions on both lucid dreams and OBEs. Because a few people do omit occasional items in questionnaires, the size of the sample stated in the original report may be slightly larger than the net figure given here. In addition to the corrected χ^2 statistic for the test of dependence between the two variables, the phi coefficient (ϕ) is included in the table as an index of the strength of the association. For the studies by Palmer, Kohr, and Blackmore, these statistics were not specified in the original reports and were ascertained through personal correspondence; the cooperation of these investigators is gratefully acknowledged.

The surveys summarized in Table 1 clearly evidence a statistical dependence between lucid dreams and OBEs. Eight of the 10 samples yielded a significant result, and 1 of the nonsignificant studies, that of Myers (1982), claims a significant correlation between OBEs and a more detailed categorization of the frequency of lucid dreams ($r_{pb} = .17, p < .05$). Further, all sets of data are in the same (positive) direction. A meta-analysis of the 10 survey results confirms the level of empirical testimony to the relationship. Using the Stouffer technique (Rosenthal, 1978), the combined significance level of the cited findings is of the order of 10^{-16}. The association is also highly stable in Strube and Hartmann's (1983) sense that the future inclusion of a few currently unknown and unpublished null results would not negate the conclusion that a relationship exists between dream lucidity and OBEs; indeed, by Rosenthal's (1979) index, if the association was a truly chance one, every one of some 250 additional studies would have to generate a null effect before the overall significance level fell to .05.

By the same token the tabulated values of ϕ suggest that the association between lucid dreams and OBEs is not strong. In Irwin's (1983a,b) survey, where the relationship was at its strongest, less than 12% of the variance between the two variables is explained. The meta-analysis of the 10 results also puts the combined effect size at $\phi = .20$ only. Thus, although the association between the occurrence of the two experiences is statistically significant and a fairly reliable finding, it is of meager predictive value.

A FUNCTIONAL CONNECTION

Long before any statistical assessment of the association had been attempted, a few OBE adepts had posited a functional connection between lucid dreams and OBEs. On the basis of self-experimentation, these individuals claimed that the state of lucidity during a dream could be used as a springboard for an OBE: That is, on realizing that one is dreaming, it is possible to manipulate consciousness in such a way as to evoke the impression of literal exteriorization.

The first to explore this notion in some detail was a British psychic, Hugh Callaway, who wrote under the nom de plume of Oliver Fox. His use of dream lucidity for the induction of OBEs was described initially in a series of papers published in the *Occult Review* (Fox, 1920a,b; 1923); these accounts were expanded into the monograph *Astral Projection* published in 1938 or 1939 (Fox, 1962). The initial phase of Fox's technique entailed the achievement of a state of lucidity during a dream. Various suggestions were made for the development of this skill. One was to learn to interpret an incongruity or inconsistency in a dream as a cue to the fact that one is dreaming, thereby making it a "dream of knowledge." Another means of activating the "critical faculty," Fox claimed, was to dream that one was waking up while actually remaining asleep; in this "state of false awakening," lucidity could be realized. The second phase of the technique was to use the state of dream lucidity to elicit an OBE. According to Fox, this was simply a matter of being in a position during lucidity to direct dream imagery to the desired end. Here, one might either mentally sit up from the supine physical body or mentally hurl oneself out of the body (Fox, 1962). By such means, the center of awareness may be perceived to have left the body and then may be guided to any chosen setting. Fox did outline other modes of OBE induction, but these did not rely upon the vehicle of lucid dreams.

An American OBE adept, Sylvan Muldoon, described a similar technique in *The Projection of the Astral Body,* first published in 1929 (Muldoon & Carrington, 1968). Muldoon's procedure for producing lucidity was to focus on hypnagogic images at the point of going to sleep and to try to maintain into sleep the feeling of being aware that one is dreaming. Muldoon states that with due practice, this would develop an aptitude for lucid dreaming. Once ludicity is achieved, the dreamer may imagine being engaged in some enjoyable activity that is analogous to the process of exteriorization. For example, one might engineer a dream of going up in a balloon or an elevator. While the individual concentrates on the sensation of moving upward, the "astral self" may step out of the physical body and an OBE begins. The techniques of both Muldoon and Fox require much rehearsal in order to be effective. Not only must susceptibility to lucid dreaming be increased, but also there is a need for some practice in manipulating the dream to effect an OBE.

Other occult commentators (e.g., Denning & Phillips, 1979; Moser, 1974; Ophiel, 1961) have discussed the functional connection between dream lucidity and OBEs, but they have little to add to the basic methods proposed by Fox and Muldoon. Perhaps the more recent accounts give greater emphasis to the use of dream diaries in order to instill an appreciation that we do dream every night; this in turn may make the preliminary objective of dream control appear more attainable. In any event, there seems to be some general acknowledgment in the occult literature that dream lucidity can be employed as a vehicle for the OBE. Unfortunately, parapsychologists and lucidity researchers have not sought to establish the functional connection in more scientific terms. This is not to say that Fox and Muldoon were deluded or deceitful but merely that we cannot say for whom the connection is functional. Both Fox and Muldoon were able to induce OBEs by various other means, and hence it is feasible that their technique of manipulation of a lucid dream is viable only for those who have a more broadly founded ability to evoke an OBE. Until psychologists examine the connection with more representative samples of experimental participants, it is advisable not to overgeneralize from the autobiographical comments of OBE adepts.

For this reason, the reported statistical association between lucid dreams and OBEs cannot be explained by the functional connection promoted in the occult literature. That is, on the evidence presently available, the statistical association cannot justifiably be attributed to the notion that lucidity is an ideal context for consciously evoking an OBE. The inadequacy of such an account also is indicated by the fact that the vast majority of OBErs who have participated in surveys did not induce their OBE deliberately but rather had an experience that arose spontaneously or without premeditation. Thus, there is more to the statistical association between lucid dreams and OBEs than the intentional manipulation of dreams toward an OBE.

BASES OF THE STATISTICAL ASSOCIATION

The Theory of Phenomenological Equivalence

According to some researchers (e.g., Faraday, 1976; Honegger, 1979; Salley, 1982), the statistical association evidenced in Table 1 is due to the phenomenological equivalence of lucid dreaming and an OBE. Specifically, an OBE might be construed as a lucid dream in which one just happens to be conjuring up images in an out-of-body perceptive.

There are several arguments against the proposition of the phenomenological equivalence of the two experiences. One is that the strength of the association between lucid dreams and OBEs (as indexed by the phi coefficient in Table 1) is so low that it offers little empirical comfort for this view. One essential element of the smallness of ϕ is that some OBErs do not report having lucid dreams. This is a curious situation. If the OBE is nothing other than a lucid dream with an out-of-body perspective, why should all "lucid dreams" of this particular group of OBErs only occur in an exteriorized perspective? In short, the theory of phenomenological equivalence demands a much stronger association between the two variables than has been evidenced in past surveys.

Other evidence also suggests that the equivalence theory must be taken in at least a slightly broader sense. It simply is the case that not all OBEs occur during sleep. According to survey data (Green, 1968a; Poynton, 1975; Twemlow, Gabbard, & Jones, 1982), some 62 to 88% of experients were not asleep at the time of their OBE. The majority of OBEs induced in the laboratory also have been achieved with waking participants (e.g., Palmer, 1978). Clearly, there are many waking OBEs that it is not possible to construe as lucid dreams, as Salley (1982, p. 157) himself admits. Indeed, even OBEs that arise in sleep are claimed by experients to be distinguishable from any sort of dream (e.g., Twemlow et al., 1982, p. 453). It is not clear why such phenomenological elements such as percussive noises at the onset should be found in the "lucid dreams" with the out-of-body perspective yet not in "other" (non-OBE) lucid dreams. Therefore, the notion of strict phenomenological equivalence must be relaxed somewhat and reformulated as the view that the lucid dream and the OBE are each an experience in which the individual observes or critically reflects upon the contents of mind in a detached manner. Elements of this approach can be found in Green's (1976) description of the two phenomena.

Yet, even this weaker or more general form of the equivalence theory is open to question. This formulation maintains that both experiences represent a state of lucidity. But is the experient lucid in an OBE? During an OBE, the individual typically regards the out-of-body setting and the actions of the exteriorized self as real, just as one does in a nonlucid dream or some such absorbing fantasy. Unlike lucid dreaming, there is no objective reflection that the mind is engaged in fantasy during the OBE. Further, if lucid dreams and OBEs are equivalent by their lucidity, the occurrence of the OBE should correlate with proneness to the realization of lucidity in other altered states of consciousness (ASC). In a test of this implication, I surveyed the OBE and 10 different ASC encountered by 121 mature-age psychology students at the University of New England. There was no significant tendency for the report of OBEs to be positively related to a proneness towards lucidity in any of the ASC or to load on any general "Lucidity Proneness" factor. It is doubtful that the OBE necessarily has an intrinsic "Lucidity factor" that it shares with the lucid dream. This is not to deny that during the experience, the OBEr is aware that consciousness has an out-of-body perspective, but this may represent awareness of the contents of the experience rather than lucidity itself.

Therefore, there is insufficient evidential support for the notion that the association between OBEs and proneness to lucid dreaming can be attributed to the phenomenological equivalence of the two experiences.

The Possibility of Neurophysiological Equivalence

It is possible that a given physiological state may be interpreted by the individual in phenomenologically different ways, according to the context in which the state arises. In the present context, although a lucid dream and an OBE may be experienced to be distinct from one another, they might well have the same neurophysiological representation. Assessment of this possibility requires examination of the reported neurophysiological correlates of each of the experiences.

In relation to lucid dreams, most of the neurophysiological research effort has been devoted to determining whether the individual is actually asleep or momentarily awake at the time of lucidity and at what stage of the sleep cycle lucid dreaming occurs. Evidently, lucidity is initiated occasionally in moments of transitory wakefulness, although even here the subsequent lucid dream does take place in sleep; nevertheless, the majority of lucid dreams are both initiated and enacted in sleep, almost always REM sleep (LaBerge, Nagel, Taylor, Dement, & Zarcone, 1981; LaBerge, Levitan, Gordon, & Dement, 1983; Ogilvie, Hunt, Tyson, Lucescu, & Jeakins, 1982; Price & Cohen, 1983).

As noted earlier, there is substantial survey evidence suggesting that the majority of OBEs do not occur during asleep. Nevertheless, some neurophysiological studies of OBEs in sleep have been conducted by Tart (1967, 1968), and the results of these should permit an apt comparison with the previously mentioned data on neurophysiological correlates of lucid dreaming. Tart's (1968) first experimental participant exhibited slowed alpha activity and an absence of REMs during the OBE. In the second study, another subject showed some slowing of alpha activity, but this was not as persistent as in the previous case; REMs also were reported, although Blackmore (1978, pp. 14–15) has argued that the ocular activity in Tart's second subject might not have constituted REMs because it may have taken place during Stage 1 sleep. Although a greater quantity of data on OBEs in sleep would be desirable, there is little in Tart's research to suggest a clear neurophysiological equivalence between OBEs and lucid dreams. Neither is the standing of the equivalence theory improved when waking OBEs are taken into account. Research on the physiological correlates of waking OBEs (e.g., Hartwell, Janis, & Harary, 1975; Mitchell, 1973; Morris, Harary, Janis, Hartwell, & Roll, 1978; Osis & Mitchell, 1977; Palmer, 1979b; Whitton,

1974) simply has not established the existence of a physiologically distinct OBE state; there is scant conformity to the corresponding data on lucid dreaming.

Although the data admittedly are meager, the association between lucid dreams and OBEs would not appear to be a reflection of the neurophysiological equivalence of the phenomena.

The Search for Common Factors

In the absence of convincing evidence that OBEs and lucid dreams are either phenomenologically or neurophysiologically equivalent, it is appropriate to consider the various factors that might make an individual jointly prone to lucid dreaming and OBEs.

Demographic variables will be given first consideration here, not because they are of primary interest but because such factors could have a bearing on the interpretation of the phenomenon's relationships with other psychological variables. The two major OBE surveys that sampled a wide range of demographic information are those by Palmer (1979a) and Kohr (1980). Surveys of lucid dreams do not seem to have tapped demographic variables to the same extent, but Gackenbach (1978) took some account of such factors, and Kohr, at my request, has calculated correlations between demographic factors and two lucid dream variables included in his original survey of ARE members (Kohr, 1980). Generally, it seems that neither lucid dreams nor OBEs vary consistently with age, race, educational level, or religiosity. In the sample of Charlottesville residents, Palmer (1979a) found a higher incidence of OBEs among respondents who were either separated or divorced, but no such trend was found by Kohr; marital status did not correlate with lucid dreams in the studies by Kohr and Gackenbach. Political orientation had an influence on the report of OBEs in Kohr's survey but not in either of Palmer's samples; this factor was unrelated to responses on Kohr's lucid dream items. The individual's sex has received more empirical attention.

Reports of a dependence of OBEs upon the experient's sex are variable, sometimes with a relatively higher incidence among females (e.g., Kohr, 1980) and in other cases more commonly among males (e.g., Blackmore, 1982b). However, in 16 samples known to the author, only 4 yielded a significant correlation between OBEs and sex; two of these favored females and two favored males. Thus, OBEs do not exhibit an unequivocal relationship with sex of respondent (Irwin, 1985). No relationship between sex and occurrence of lucid dreams was observed by Kohr (1980), Palmer (1979a), and Gackenbach (1978). A higher frequency of such dreams among females was found in student samples surveyed by Gackenhach (1987) and Hearne (1978), whereas a higher incidence among male students was reported by Blackmore (1982b). Generally, the occurrence of lucid dreams and that of OBEs is not a function of demographic characteristics. It might be said that research on the role of the respondent's sex has yielded inconsistent findings. It is possible also that sex may interact with other variables pertinent to the phenomenon, as we shall see in discussing personality correlates.

Given that the content of both lucid dreams and OBEs typically is described as very vivid, it is pertinent to explore the contribution of skills in visual imagery to each of the phenomena. Several questionnaire measures of vividness of visual imagery have been administered to groups of OBErs and nonOBErs without any indication of the OBErs' superiority in this respect (see Cook & Irwin, 1983, and Irwin, 1985, for a detailed review of this literature). Little work of this kind has been conducted in relation to lucid dreams, but two such studies (Blackmore, 1982a; Hearne, 1978) failed to reveal any significant contribution of imagery vividness to the occurrence of lucid dreams. Again, given that the content of lucid dreams and OBEs can be controlled to some degree, it is feasible that the skill in control of visual imagery would make an important contribution to the occurrence of each of these phenomena. But empirical study also fails to substantiate this notion (Blackmore, 1982a; Cook & Irwin, 1983; Hearne, 1978; Irwin 1985). Nevertheless, some recent work suggests that spatial skills may have some relevance. Thus, a greater aptitude for manipulation of specifically three-dimensional images has been established among OBErs (Blackmore, 1983; Cook & Irwin, 1983). Similarly, lucid dreaming has been linked to spatial abilities (Gackenbach, 1978), although there may be some interaction effects with sex here (Gackenbach *et al.*, 1981; Gackenbach, Prill, & Westrom, 1983).

This is not to say that spatial skills necessarily play the same role in OBEs as in lucid dreams. Manipulation of three-dimensional images might serve the purpose of enhancing the sense of realism in the OBE, whereas in a lucid dream, such manipulation might not be directed at realism but rather used in confirmation of the impression of lucidity, that the dreamer knows he or she is dreaming and hence can maneuver its thematic development by volitional effort. Nevertheless, the fact remains that superior spatial skills may make some individuals more open to both lucid dreams and OBEs. Hence, the association between the two experiences could be attributable in part to this factor.

Because lucid dreams and OBEs are reported by only a part of the population, researchers have considered the personality dimensions in their investigations of each phenomenon. The most substantial program of research into the personality correlates of lucid dreaming is that by Gackenbach (1978, 1983). Her 1978 survey of ARE members included administration of several personality scales including Cattell's Sixteen Personality Factor Questionnaire (16PF). Factor analysis of the data established 10 personality dimensions by which members of the sample could be described. The incidence of lucid dreams was related to only one of these factors, termed by Gackenbach "Self Concept." Thus, people who acknowledged having frequent lucid dreams were inclined to have a relatively positive self-concept. Further analysis suggested that lucid dreamers had a tendency to "try new things" or to experiment. In Gackenbach's (1983) second study, a sample of college students completed the 16PF, and here a rather more complex pattern of results emerged, possibly because the ARE group was self-selected and on average somewhat older. Female students who had frequent lucid dreams were found to be practical, relaxed,and subdued. The male lucid dreamers, in this sample, were inclined to be conscientious and anxious yet also depict themselves as assertive and happy-go-lucky. An experimenting proclivity, again, was characteristic of lucid dreamers of either sex. Another study to look into personality characteristics associated with lucid dreaming is that by Hearne (1978). His sample of English students did not evidence any relationship between the occurrence of lucid dreams and either extraversion or neuroticism. Several similar investigations have yielded either null (e.g., Belicki, Hunt, & Belicki, 1978) or contradictory results (see Gackenbach & LaBerge, 1986).

As some psychologists (e.g., Rawcliffe, 1959) have interpreted the OBE as a psychotic episode, much of the research on personality correlates of the OBE has focused on the traits of psychoticism, neuroticism, and mental health. Typically, these studies have not established any evidence of personality disturbance amongst OBErs (Gackenbach, 1978; Jones, Twemlow, & Gabbard, 1980; Myers, 1982). The survey by Jones et al. did suggest that OBErs were less "danger seeking" than a control group of nonexperients, but such a trend was not found in Irwin's (1980) study and is not accorded much significance by Jones and his colleagues. Gackenbach (1978) reports that the frequency of OBEs among her ARE respondents was associated with the personality factors of Independence (an unrestrained, imaginative, tender-minded exploratory approach to life) and Bohemia (a tendency toward undisciplined self-conflict and radicalism). These results are only partly consistent with Gackenbach's characterization of lucid dreamers as having an experimenting disposition. Myers (1982) found that OBErs rated more highly in Complexity and Breadth of Interest than did non-OBErs. Comparison of her figures with normative data for college students suggests that the results say as much if not more about the personality of the Jesuit-college nonexperients than they do about the experients (Irwin, 1985). In short, apart from some limited data yielded by Gackenbach's (1978) self-selected ARE sample of OBErs, there is scant evidence of an integral personality profile that is conducive to lucid dreams and OBEs alike. Nevertheless, there certainly is scope for further research on this issue.

The individual's needs may also have a bearing on each of the experiences. The long-term needs or need dispositions of lucid dreamers do not appear to have been researched. A study by Irwin (1981a) surveyed the need dispositions of OBErs and found these people as a group to exhibit a relatively high need for Intraception, a need that in part entails a concern with and attention to one's mental processes. With regard to immediate needs, it is likely that these shape the content of both lucid dreams and OBEs. For example, a pressing desire to be with a particular person may influence the content of the OBE or lucid dream to that end. Apart from general effects upon cortical arousal (to be discussed later), the pertinence of such needs to the actual occurrence of each experience is uncertain. Certainly psychological set may be influential in this respect. Thus LaBerge *et al.* (1981) report that an intention to recognize one is dreaming is important to the occurrence of lucid dreams, and the nature of many induction techniques for lucid dreams (e.g., Garfield, 1974; LaBerge, 1981) is consistent with this interpretation. Similarly, Palmer and Lieberman (1975) have demonstrated the role of a psychological set in their laboratory technique for inducing OBEs. Although a psychological set may facilitate the induction of both lucid dreams and OBEs, it is a moot point that this dimension has a major bearing on the occurrence of spontaneous cases of each of these experiences. In most cases, the individual is unable to recall any prior resolution that could be construed to have evoked their experience. Nevertheless, although an intention to have either one of the experiences may influence their individual occurrence, it has little promise as a factor accounting for the association between lucid dreams and OBEs.

Cognitive style is another area that has been given some scrutiny in this context. Gackenbach (1978; Gackenbach, Heilman, Boyt, & LaBerge, 1985) reports that people who have lucid dreams are inclined to be field independent, at least in the case of men; that is, male lucid dreamers are relatively adept in isolating and acting upon a particular piece of information that is embedded in a complex stimulus array. Palmer and Lieberman (1975) found no correlation between field dependence and the success of an OBE induction technique. However, their field-dependent subjects did report greater feelings of psychological detachment during the session. Admittedly, the experiment by Palmer and Lieberman was concerned with induced OBEs rather than spontaneous cases; nonetheless, their data and those of Gackenbach do not indicate a consistency between lucid dreams and OBEs in this regard. The only other study incorporating a measure of cognitive style was that by Irwin (1980). This did not reveal any significant trend for OBErs to adopt the cognitive style of a visualizer rather than that of a verbalizer (see also Cook & Irwin, 1983). The visualizer–verbalizer dimension (Paivio, 1971; Richardson, 1977) does not seem to have been utilized in lucidity research.

Possibly allied to cognitive style is the psychological dimension of Absorption, the capacity to become totally engrossed in ongoing mentation or activity and to be oblivious to distracting stimuli (Tellegen & Atkinson, 1974). Several phenomenological features of the OBE and the circumstances of its occurrence suggest that capacity for psychological absorption may have a strong bearing on the instigation and maintenance of the impression of an exteriorized state, and indeed a series of investigations (Irwin, 1980, 1981b; Meyers, 1982) has shown that OBErs have a substantially higher absorption capacity than non-OBErs. Further, in Irwin's (1981b) study, students with high Absorption scores were more susceptible to an experimental OBE induction procedure than were low

Absorption scorers. The induced experiences of the former group were judged to be qualitatively more like spontaneous OBEs than were those of the low scorers. In two unpublished surveys by Irwin, there also was a significant relationship between absorption capacity and each of two phenomenological characteristics of the OBE, namely the exteriorized self's apparent possession of a form or body of its own and the report of definite sensations upon "reentering" the physical body at the end of the experience. Clearly, the dimension of absorption has an important role to play in the OBE. On the other hand, there is doubt that this relationship extends to the phenomenon of dream lucidity. Gackenbach (personal communication, April 1982) found no significant difference in the Absorption scores of lucid and nonlucid dreamers. In another unpublished study of a sample of 73 students, Irwin included both OBE and dream lucidity as variables in an analysis of variance of Absorption scores and observed that whereas OBErs and non-OBErs again differed substantially in mean capacity for absorption ($p < .0005$), the variable of dream lucidity did not account for a further substantial proportion of the variance ($p > .08$). It is conceivable that the latter relationship could reach significance in a survey of a very large sample. On the current evidence, the size of the effect for lucidity would be so minor in comparison with that for OBEs that the dimension of Absorption emerges as another major discriminator between lucid dreams and OBEs. This result questions the view that the two experiences are phenomenologically equivalent.

Another correlate that may prove to differentiate the two types of experiences is susceptibility to migraine, although the direction of such differentiation may not have been anticipated correctly in much of the literature. Several commentators on the OBE (e.g., Comfort, 1982; Eastman, 1962) have argued that the occurrence of OBEs is related to susceptibility to migraine headaches; Lippman's (1953) work is often cited in support of this view. However, none of these writers provide any statistical information to document the proposed relationship. What seems to have been the first attempt to procure relevant data was reported by Irwin (1983b). Across four samples of university students, an average of 50% of OBErs claimed a history of migraine, whereas only 24% of non-OBErs did so. At this point, the data seemed in clear support of a relationship between proneness to migraine and OBEs. Nevertheless, this impression was queried by a further study undertaken to see if lucid dreaming also was linked with the migraine factor. Here, susceptibility to migraine was more clearly related to dream lucidity than to OBEs, and a canonical correlation of the two phenomena against migraine yielded coefficients of .90 for lucid dreams and only .22 for OBEs. This strongly suggests that the much quoted relationship between the OBE and migraine is largely an artifact of each of these variables' independent correlation with lucid dreaming. Therefore, the association of dream lucidity with proneness to migraine attacks is emerging as a characteristic distinguishing between lucid dreams and OBEs. Further investigation along these lines is warranted, with future studies incorporating a thorough medical assessment of participants' migraine history rather than the self-report measures used in the aforementioned research.

Now a possible basis for the link between lucid dreams and a history of migraine is that some instances of lucidity might be evoked by a subclinical migraine attack; that is, by a physiological state that is not sufficiently marked to be perceived as a migraine headache but that nonetheless constitutes acute stress during sleep. This raises the issue of the role of physiological stress or more generally of high cortical arousal in dream lucidity and in OBEs. With regard to lucidity, LaBerge et al. (1983) have provided strong evidence that the initiation of lucid dreams is dependent upon a relatively high level of cerebral activation. Similarly, Garfield (1975) and Hearne (1978) report lucid dreams often follow a day of high arousal and activity. Gackenbach, Curren, and Cutler (1983) also note that lucid dreams tend to occur following a day of unpleasant interpersonal interactions and unhappy emotions. Evidently, high cortical arousal is an important element in the realization of dream lucidity. This appears somewhat at odds with the findings of neurophysiological studies of the OBE (e.g., Morris et al., 1978), but it must be remembered that, in these experiments, participants invariably employed techniques of mental relaxation to induce their OBE. Although the distinct majority of spontaneous OBEs also appear to arise in such a psychological state, there are many cases in which high cortical arousal is a prominent feature of the circumstances of the OBE's occurrence. Perhaps the clearest instances of the latter are OBEs associated with a sudden threat of imminent danger to life. Thus, OBEs may spring from either extreme of cortical arousal (Irwin, 1985), with just a minority of spontaneous cases associated with a high level of cerebral activation.

In the present context, it is the existence of this minority class of OBE that accrues some importance because it suggests that the association between dream lucidity and the OBE in some way reflects a style of response to states of stress. For example, many lucid dreams and certain OBEs could be interpreted as responses to circumstances that require a reassurance of the integrity of the self. During a dream, when the individual largely is out of touch with reality, such reassurance might be achieved either by waking or through lucidity. The latter, in many instances, may be quite sufficient for the realization that all is well and that, for example, one is "only dreaming." In a life-threatening or other arousing circumstance, an OBE (be it a literal event or a fantasy) likewise could provide assurance that at least the self, if not the physical body, remains intact. To function effectively in this regard, both the lucid dream and the OBE may have to call upon certain spatial and other skills, but these would be of secondary importance to our understanding of the association between the phenomena. That the common defensive reaction entails the reinforcement of a conviction in the self's well-being is a moot point and is discussed here principally for purposes of illustration. Whatever the actual basis of the reaction, the present proposal is that instances of the OBE and dream lucidity can represent responses to cues of stress. Thus, to the extent that certain individuals in the population tend to rely on this general defensive reaction to high cortical arousal, dream lucidity and OBEs may be encountered among the same people: That is, a limited statistical association between the phenomena may be evident.

It must be reiterated that not all OBEs (nor perhaps all lucid dreams) serve a defensive function. That only a minority of OBEs are a defensive response to high cortical arousal or to be more precise, that only a minority of OBErs have the disposition to have the experience when faced with a stressful situation could account for the fact that the association between the phenomena, although statistically significant and fairly reliable, has relatively low strength (as indexed by the phi coefficient). Additionally, it may be possible to accommodate, within this framework, the reported success of some adepts in using dream lucidity as a vehicle for an OBE. In achieving a state of lucidity, the adept may increase cortical arousal to one of the extreme levels necessary for the occurrence of an OBE. This, in conjunction with the individual's expectations and possibly also some independently developed capacities for OBE induction, may be the basis of the eventual realization of the impression of exteriorization in such a context.

Having outlined one interpretation of the association between lucid dreams and OBEs, it is essential to enter a caveat to the effect that the account is no more than a speculation based on relatively limited empirical foundations. Much is still to be learned of the correlates and the modus operandi of the two phenomena, and other major variables may be found to link the phenomena. It is probable that such variables will be identified not in investigation of the association between lucid dreams and OBEs but rather through study of each experience in its own right. Nevertheless, an understanding of the association is important particularly to OBE research because, through dream lucidity, a more reliable laboratory technique for induction of the OBE may be devised. In this regard, continued interaction between researchers in the two fields should prove fruitful.

REFERENCES

Belicki, D. A., Hunt, H., & Belicki, K. (1978). An exploratory study comparing self-reported lucid and non-lucid dreamers. *Sleep Research, 7,* 166.

Blackmore, S. (J.) (1978). *Parapsychology and out-of-the-body experiences.* London: Society for Psychical Research.

Blackmore, S. J. (1982a). Out-of-body experiences, lucid dreams, and imagery: Two surveys. *Journal of the American Society for Psychical Research, 76,* 301–317.

Blackmore, S. J. (1982b). Have you ever had an OBE?: The wording of the question. *Journal of the Society for Psychical Research, 51,* 292–302.

Blackmore, S. J. (1983). Imagery and the OBE. In W. G. Roll, J. Beloff, & R. White (Eds.), *Research in parapsychology 1982* (pp. 231–232). Metuchen, NJ: Scarecrow Press.

Comfort, A. (1982). Out-of-body experiences and migraine. *American Journal of Psychiatry, 139,* 1379–1380.

Cook, A. M., & Irwin, H. J. (1983). Visuospatial skills and the out-of-body experience. *Journal of Parapsychology, 47,* 23–35.

Crookall, R. (1966). *The study and practice of astral projection.* New York: University Books.

Crookall, R. (1972). *Case-book of astral projection, 545–746.* Secaucus, NJ: University Books.

Denning, M., & Phillips, O. (1979). *The Llewellyn practical guide to astral projection.* St Paul, MN: Llewellyn.

Eastman, M. (1962). Out-of-the-body experiences. *Proceedings of the Society for Psychical Research, 53,* 287–309.

Faraday, A. (1976). *The dream game.* Harmondsworth, England: Penguin.

Fox, O. (1920a). The pineal doorway: A record of research. *Occult Review, 31,* 190–198.

Fox, O. (1920b). Beyond the pineal door: A record of research. *Occult Review, 31,* 251–261.

Fox, O. (1923). Dream-travelling: Some additional notes. *Occult Review, 38,* 332–338.

Fox, O. (1962). *Astral projection: A record of out-of-the-body experiences.* New Hyde Park, NY: University Books.

Gackenbach, J. (1978). *A personality and cognitive style analysis of lucid dreaming.* Unpublished doctoral dissertation, Virginia Commonwealth University.

Gackenbach, J. (1983). Personality differences between individuals varying in lucid dreaming frequency. *Manuscript under editorial consideration.*

Gackenbach, J., & LaBerge, S. (1986). An overview of lucid dreaming. In A. Sheikh (Ed.), *International review of mental imagery: Vol. 2* (pp. 57–89). New York: Human Sciences Press.

Gackenbach, J., Snyder, T. J., McKelvey, K., McWilliams, C., George, E., & Rodenelli, B. (1981). Lucid dreaming: Individual differences in perception. *Sleep Research, 10,* 146.

Gackenbach, J., Curren, R., & Cutler, G. (1983). Presleep determinants and postsleep results of lucid versus vivid dreams. *Lucidity Letter, 2*(2), 4–5.

Gackenbach, J., Prill, S., & Westrom, P. (1983). The relationship of the lucid dreaming ability to mental imagery experiences and skills. *Lucidity Letter, 2*(4), 4–6.

Gackenbach, J., Heilman, N., Boyt, S., & LaBerge, S. (1985). The relationship between field independence and lucid dreaming ability. *Journal of Mental Imagery, 9*(1), 9–20.

Garfield, P. (1974). *Creative dreaming.* New York: Simon & Schuster.

Garfield, P. (1975). Psychological concomitants of the lucid dream state. *Sleep Research, 4,* 183.

Green, C. E. (1966). Spontaneous 'paranormal' experiences in relation to sex and academic background. *Journal of the Society for Psychical Research, 43,* 357–363.

Green, C. E. (1968a). *Out-of-the-body experiences.* London: Hamish Hamilton.

Green, C. E. (1968b). *Lucid dreams.* London: Hamish Hamilton.

Green, C. E. (1976). *The decline and fall of science.* London: Hamish Hamilton.

Hartwell, J., Janis, J., & Harary, B. (1975). A study of the physiological variables associated with out-of-body experiences. In J. D. Morris, W. G. Roll, & R. L. Morris (Eds.), *Research in parapsychology 1974* (pp. 127–129). Metuchen, NJ: Scarecrow Press.

Hearne, K. M. T. (1978). *Lucid dreams: An electro-physiological and psychological study.* Unpublished doctoral dissertation, University of Liverpool, England.

Honegger, B. (1979). Correspondence. *Parapsychology Review. 10*(2), 24–26.

Irwin, H. J. (1980). Out of the body Down Under: Some cognitive characteristics of Australian students reporting OOBEs. *Journal of the Society for Psychical Research, 50,* 448–459.

Irwin, H. J. (1981a).The psychological function of out-of-body experiences: So who needs the out-of-body experience? *Journal of Nervous and Mental Disease, 169,* 244–248.

Irwin, H. J. (1981b). Some psychological dimensions of the out-of-body experience. *Parapsychology Review, 12*(4), 1–6.

Irwin, H. J. (1983a). Migraine, out-of-body experiences, and lucid dreams. *Lucidity Letter, 2*(2), 2–4.

Irwin, H. J. (1983b). The association between out-of-body experiences and migraine. *Psi Research*, 2(2), 89–96.

Irwin, H. J. (1985). *Flight of mind: A psychological study of the out-of-body experience*. Metuchen, NJ: Scarecrow Press.

Jones, F. C., Twemlow, S. W., & Gabbard, G. O. (1980, May). *The out-of-body experience: II. Psychological profile*. Paper presented at the annual meeting of the American Psychiatric Association, San Francisco.

Kohr, R. L. (1980). A survey of psi experiences among members of a special population. *Journal of the American Society for Psychical Research, 74*, 395–411.

LaBerge, S. P. (1981). Lucid dreaming: Directing the action as it happens. *Psychology Today, 15*(1), 48–57.

LaBerge, S. P., Nagel, L. E., Taylor, W. B., Dement, W. C., & Zarcone, V. P. (1981). Psychophysiological correlates of the initiation of lucid dreaming. *Sleep Research, 10*, 149.

LaBerge, S. P., Levitan, L., Gordon, M., & Dement, W. C. (1983). Physiological characteristics of three types of lucid dream. *Lucidity Letter, 2*(2), 1.

Lippman, C. W. (1953). Hallucinations of physical duality in migraine. *Journal of Nervous and Mental Disease, 117*, 345–350.

Mitchell, J. L. (1973, April). Out-of-the-body vision. *Psychic*, 44–47.

Morris, R. L., Harary, S. B., Janis, J., Hartwell, J., & Roll, W. G. (1978). Studies of communication during out-of-body experiences. *Journal of the American Society for Psychical Research, 72*, 1–21.

Moser, R. E. (1974). *Mental and astral projection*. Cottonwood, AZ: Esoteric Publications.

Muldoon, S. J., & Carrington, H. (1968). *The projection of the astral body*. London: Rider. (Original work published 1929)

Myers, S. A. (1982). *Personality characteristics as related to out-of-body experiences*. Unpublished master's thesis, St Louis University.

Ogilvie, R. D., Hunt, H. T., Tyson, P. D., Lucescu, M. L., & Jeakins, D. B. (1982). Lucid dreaming and alpha activity: A preliminary report. *Perceptual and Motor Skills, 55*, 795–808.

Ophiel (1961). *The art and practice of astral projection*. New York: Weiser.

Osis, K. (1979). Insiders' views of the OBE: A questionnaire survey. In W. G. Roll (Ed.), *Research in parapsychology 1978* (pp. 50–52). Metuchen, NJ: Scarecrow Press.

Osis, K., & Mitchell, J. L. (1977). Physiological correlates of reported out-of-body experiences. *Journal of the Society for Psychical Research, 49*, 525–536.

Paivio, A. (1971). *Imagery and verbal processes*. New York: Holt, Rinehart & Winston.

Palmer, J. (1978). ESP and out-of-body experiences: An experimental approach. In D. S. Rogo (Ed.), *Mind beyond the body* (pp. 193–217). New York: Penguin.

Palmer, J. (1979a). A community mail survey of psychic experiences. *Journal of the American Society for Psychical Research, 73*, 221–251.

Palmer. J. (1979b). ESP and out-of-body experiences: EEG correlates. In W. G. Roll (Ed.), *Research in parapsychology 1978* (pp. 135–138). Metuchen, NJ: Scarecrow Press.

Palmer, J., & Lieberman, R. (1975). The influence of psychological set on ESP and out-of-body experiences. *Journal of the American Society for Psychical Research, 69*, 193–213.

Poynton, J. C. (1975). Results of an out-of-body survey. In J. C. Poynton (Ed.), *Parapsychology in South Africa* (pp. 109–123). Johannesburg: South African Society for Psychical Research.

Price, R., & Cohen, D. (1983). Auditory biofeedback as a lucidity induction technique. *Lucidity Letter, 2*(4), 1–3.

Rawcliffe, D. H. (1959). *Illusions and delusions of the supernatural and the occult*. New York: Dover. (Original work published 1952)

Richardson, A. (1977). Verbalizer–visualizer: A cognitive style dimension. *Journal of Mental Imagery, 1*, 109–126.

Rosenthal, R. (1978). Combining results of independent studies. *Psychological Bulletin, 85*, 185–193.

Rosenthal, R. (1979). The 'file drawer problem' and tolerance for null results. *Psychological Bulletin, 86*, 638–641.

Salley, R. D. (1982). REM sleep phenomena during out-of-body experiences. *Journal of the American Society for Psychical Research, 76*, 157–165.

Strube, M. J., & Hartmann, D. P. (1983). Meta-analysis: Techniques, applications, and functions. *Journal of Consulting and Clinical Psychology, 51*, 14–27.

Tart, C. T. (1967). A second psychophysiological study of out-of-body experiences in a gifted subject. *International Journal of Parapsychology, 9*(3), 251–258.

Tart, C. T. (1968). A psychophysiological study of out-of-the-body experiences in a selected subject. *Journal of the American Society for Psychical Research, 62*, 3–27.

Tellegen, A., & Atkinson, G. (1974). Openness to absorbing and self-altering experiences ('Absorption'), a trait related to hypnotic susceptibility. *Journal of Abnormal Psychology, 83*, 268–277.

Twemlow, S. W., Gabbard, G. O., & Jones, F. C. (1982). The out-of-body experience: A phenomenological typology based on questionnaire responses. *American Journal of Psychiatry, 139*, 450–455.

Whitton, J. L. (1974). 'Ramp functions' in EEG power spectra during actual or attempted paranormal events. *New Horizons, 1*, 174–183.

Wiedmann, K.-D., & Haraldsson, E. (1981). *Some results concerning reported OBEs in Iceland.* Unpublished manuscript, University of Iceland, Reykjavik.

16

A Theory of Lucid Dreams and OBEs

SUE BLACKMORE

INTRODUCTION

Lucid dreams have much in common with out-of-body experiences, or OBEs. Harvey Irwin has described, elsewhere in this book, the empirical evidence for similarities and statistical relationships between the two experiences. I believe these relationships are important: so much so that any theory of one experience must also be able to account for the other.

Existing theories of the OBE leave much to be desired and mainly fall into one of two categories. On one hand, there are the "ecsomatic" theories, which postulate that a soul, astral body, spirit, or whatever leaves the body temporarily in an OBE and permanently at death (see e.g., Crookall 1961; Muldoon & Carrington 1929; Rogo 1978). On the other hand, there are psychological theories of the OBE that deny that anything leaves the body and posit that the experience is one of the imagination (Blackmore, 1982a; Irwin, 1985; Palmer, 1978). Rogo (1983) has recently exposed some of the drawbacks and limitations of existing psychological theories. They provide little insight into the phenomenology of the experience and lead to few testable predictions.

As far as lucid dreams are concerned, neither theory has much to contribute. The first type may say that lucid dreams are astral projection during sleep or even that all dreams are actually "out of the body." But this is hardly an explanation and provides no testable predictions. The psychological theories can offer no improvement beyond the obvious point that dreams are also products of the imagination. Neither type of theory really makes sense of the special relationship between lucid dreams and OBEs. Therefore this relationship provides a chal-

SUE BLACKMORE • Brain and Perception Laboratory, University of Bristol, Bristol B58 1TD, England.

lenge to existing theories of the OBE and indeed to theories of altered states of consciousness (ASCs) in general.

I propose to offer a framework for ASCs that provides a new approach to understanding both OBEs and lucid dreams. Although it is speculative, it leads to new questions and testable predictions.

There are several notable similarities and differences between OBEs and lucid dreams that I think should be explicable on a theory of the phenomena.

1. As noted by Irwin, the same people tend to report both experiences. The correlation appears to be reliable, but small.
2. The two experiences can be initiated in very different ways (see Blackmore, 1982a; Green, 1968a,b; Gackenbach & LaBerge, 1986), but one way of achieving an OBE is through the lucid dream.
3. Consciousness is often reported as extremely clear in both.
4. In both, perception can be described as clearer and more vivid than in normal perception (Blackmore, 1982c; Gackenbach & Schillig, 1984; Green, 1968a,b).
5. Both are sometimes described as being profound and life-altering experiences (e.g., Blackmore 1982a; van Eeden, 1913).
6. People often strive to have more of them.
7. The simplifications, distortions, and additions found in the experienced world can be similar in both experiences (Blackmore 1982a; Monroe 1971; Muldoon & Carrington 1929).
8. In both, imagining or thinking about changes in the environment can bring about those changes.
9. Flying is common in both (van Eeden 1913; Muldoon & Carrington 1929).
10. In both, there are oddities of lighting such as self-illumination of objects and the difficulty of switching lights on (Fox 1962; Green 1968b).
11. There is an interesting difference. Lucid dreamers are (by definition) aware that they are dreaming and therefore assume that the surroundings are not real, whereas OBErs are often convinced that their surroundings *are* real.

Two other phenomena seem to be linked with OBEs and lucid dreams. These are the flying dream in which one dreams of being able to fly, float, soar or swoop in the air, and the false awakening in which one dreams one has woken up. The comparison is interesting. In a false awakening, one dreams that one is awake; in a lucid dream, one dreams that one is dreaming.

The false awakening is like an OBE in that one seems to be in the normal world, but without the usual physical restraints. One also has a duplicate body, apparently lying in bed or getting up, but unlike some OBEs, there are not usually two bodies at once. In false awakenings, as in OBEs, the lighting is often eerie or strange, and electric lights unresponsive. Unlike the other experiences, false awakenings are often unpleasant or at least mildly wierd.

Irwin has detailed the evidence suggesting that the same people tend to report OBEs and lucid dreams. There is less research on these other experiences, but what little there is suggests that they are related (Blackmore 1982a). For example, in surveys Blackmore (1982b, 1984a) found that the same people tended to report OBEs, lucid dreams, and flying dreams.

These are just some of the features that need explanation and which I shall deal with in the following account.

MODEL BUILDING

Man is a self-modeling system. Indeed the main task of the cognitive system is constructing models, or representations, of our world and of ourselves in it. I suggest that a better understanding of lucid dreams and OBEs is initially to be gained by seeking explanations at the level of these models, rather than at physiological or other lower levels of explanation.

Two types of models are of particular relevance here. First, there is the stored mental representation of the world; the "cognitive map." This is a long-term model in memory that incorporates much of our knowledge about the places we have experienced. It is this that enables you to imagine your own town on a map of the world, your own house in its position in the town, or your bed positioned in your house. Its structure is inferred from behavior that displays knowledge of places, although only parts of the information are used at any one time.

Of course, it is not like a map on a piece of paper but is a mental representation with properties that reflect this. For example, it is often wrong, that is, judged by comparison with the physical world. Much is left out or systematically simplified. For example, you may be able to "see" objects in your image but not to count them; to "see" writing but not to read it (Liben, Patterson, & Newcombe 1981).

In addition to this stored information (and based partly upon it), there is an immediate and ever-changing model of self in the world. This is constructed in perception and continually updated. The process of perception is not a passive process of observing the world "as it really is." After all, there is no world "as it really is." Rather, perception is a process of analysing features of the visual image (or input from other senses) and constructing models, or hypotheses, about the outside world on the basis of this analysis. The process starts with a viewer-centered representation of the world, as in the visual image, and progresses to derive a relatively more object-centered representation that is less dependent on the exact viewing position (see, e.g., Marr, 1982). In this way, you end up perceiving plates as round, oranges as spherical, tables as square, and rooms as rectangular, regardless of your position relative to them. However, you never let go of the fact that you are perceiving these things from the position of your body.

Memory plays a crucial role in perception, to the extent that the processes of memory and perception cannot be separated. Information from memory is used all the time in the construction of perceptual models. So when I see the keyboard in front of me, I am using a lot of information about keyboards I have seen in the past as well as sensory input, in constructing my model of what I see, feel, and hear. When I glance up at the far wall,I seem to see it in detail because memory and guesswork fill in the gaps. I can even imagine the room beyond, as well as the parts in view, because of the information in my cognitive map. This makes for efficient and stable perception and accounts for the well-known importance of expectation in perception. There is nothing new in this, I am only emphasizing the fact that perception is a process of constructing representations or models of the world.

As well as input from outside, there is somatosensory input from the body that is integrated into the "body image." This is essential to carrying out coordinated actions. Errors and distortions of the body image are associated with derealization, depersonalization, and some types of psychosis. They also occur in epilepsy and migraine (Critchley 1950).

The body image and perceptual representation are usually discussed quite independently, but here they are best treated together. After all, I am always aware that someone is perceiving. I not only see the keyboard, but I am conscious of myself sitting at it. My model of the world naturally includes a model of myself in it, and that self has a specific location. The perceptual model and body image together form one representation that one may call the "model of reality."

It is this "model of reality" that we take to be the real world with ourselves in it. If we argue (following Yates, 1985) that the contents of awareness are a model of the world, then normally it is this "model of reality" that is primary in our consciousness.

Let us consider what this "model of reality" is like. First "we" always seem to have a specific position. Most people will tell you "they" seem to be either in their head, behind their eyes, or perhaps in the forehead (Blackmore,1987). This is not to say that any "thing" is located at this spot, but rather that, in the process of building perceptual models, it is helpful to construct them from a perspective coincident with the body. In our imagination we can "see" from any position we like. With eyes closed different people can do this with greater or lesser ease, but, with our eyes open, it is very hard, and we are almost inevitably governed by the actual viewing position. Because vision is the predominant sense in humans, it makes sense that most of us, most of the time, seem to be somewhere in the head looking out through the eyes. This is part of our model.

It is interesting to compare this with other models we build, both viewer and object centered. For example, we may recall a scene from memory, or construct an imaginary scene, in many different ways (Siegel, 1977). It may be "seen" as though from eye level in a view comparable to a perceptual experience. Alternatively, we can "see" it from another location, often directly above and looking down, a position from which we have never actually seen it. This may be a particularly useful way to represent detailed layouts. It involves a complex transformation from any original input, but this is the sort of transformation the cognitive system does all the time. It is very good at it. The result is a flexible and economical representation. Finally, we may model the scene without "seeing" from any specific location at all. Rather, we seem to be "in" the whole scene at once. This provides a kind of 360-degree vision and an identification with the imagined objects. This kind of abstract representation may preserve essential information about the relationships of objects in the scene, without having to reconstruct any of the features of directional viewing. Some people are more used to using this kind of representation than others.

To summarize: We create all the time a model of self in the world. It is continuously built up from and checked against sensory information and backed up by memory. The result is that we seem to be a person located inside a body, perceiving a stable external world. In other words, we have an effective "model of reality."

REALITY

We take it for granted that what we see is "really" there. However, this is not necessarily obvious as far as the brain is concerned. In building plausible models of external "reality," it must make decisions about what is noise, what is imagination, and what is genuinely "out there." It is important to note that the separation of information based on input and that from memory is not trivial. Information from external and internal sources is amalgamated very early in perceptual processing. In vision, it may even occur in the retina. Clearly, this information is used to construct successive representations through the system, and no tagging of what began where would be feasible. Yet in the end, at the highest levels of representation, it must be clear what is "really" out there and what is imagination. My fingers have to touch the keys on the keyboard, not the plants in the garden of my imagination.

I suggest, and this is the central proposition of my theory, that this decision is taken at a very late stage in processing. At any time, the cognitive system constructs many high level models, but one, and only one, is taken as representing "reality." In other words, it makes the sensible assumption that there is only one "reality." This provides a useful constraint to apply to the modeling process. The chosen model is assigned the status of "reality"—its contents seem "real." Any other models being worked on at the same time can be rejected as failed models of reality or accorded the status of "imagination" or "thinking." In this way, we can be perceiving a stable external world, imagining something else and planning our next activity, all at once without getting confused as to what is "real." I suggest that only one model is assigned reality status at once and that there must always be one such model. So how is this model chosen?

Most of the time, the choice is easy. One model is complex, detailed, stable, and constantly being confirmed by sensory input. Others are attempts at modeling the same thing but are not so good at predicting input and are abandoned. Still others are not directly related to input at all. The former is labeled *reality* and behavior based on it; the second type is rejected; and any others are labeled "thinking" or "imagining." It is not essential to the theory that any particular criteria be used for selecting the "model of reality." However, I have argued elsewhere (Blackmore 1984b) that stability is the most likely candidate. In other words, the most stable model at any time is taken to represent "reality."

Updating reality models is obviously a crucial process, but it is expensive in terms of processing. Just how good a model is made may depend not only on the complexity of the input but on all sorts of internal constraints on available processing capapcity. A criterion may be involved here, of the sort familiar in signal detection theory. With a strict criterion, even slight descrepancies between the existing model and new input are unacceptable and force updating and improvement of the model. This means a lot of processing, but it provides a very accurate model of "reality." With a lax criterion, larger discrepancies are accepted. This means more errors in perception are likely, for the sake of savings in processing. At the most extreme criterion, the model could shift away from input entirely, as increasingly large discrepancies are ignored.

Changes in criterion may be deliberate, in order to devote attention to something else. For example, external events may go unnoticed when you are reading or thinking hard. Or changes may be enforced by unavoidable constraints. Tiredness may force a laxer criterion to save processing. Increasing arousal may shift it to be stricter. Other factors may push the criterion in either direction, and this determines to what extent the model of "reality" is input-controlled.

Interestingly, the capacity for absorption (Tellegen & Atkinson, 1974) may be seen as an ability to shift to a laxer criterion. We should therefore note that OBErs have been found to have a higher capacity for absorption (Irwin 1981).

Altered States of Consciousness

The reason I have dwelt at such length on "models of reality" is because they may help us to understand altered states of consciousness (ASCs). I propose that we look at ASCs as alterations in the type of model being constructed. This means aiming at a higher level of explanation than is traditional in accounts of ASCs. If this can ultimately be reduced to lower level explanations in terms of physiology or neuronal processes, all well and good, but we need to start at the level of "models of reality." This means we must ask questions relevant to these models—questions like what will happen to the model when taking drugs or going to sleep, when sensory input drops, or when processing capacity or arousal change. In trying to answer these questions I believe we gain insights into the lucid dream, the OBE, and other ASCs.

In sleep, both arousal and sensory input are reduced. In certain drug states, a lot of noise is mixed with input, and some techniques of meditation or isolation deliberately reduce sensory input while maintaining arousal. What effect would we expect these changes to have on the "model of reality"? According to the theory so far outlined, we would expect interesting results in all these cases. Changes in sensory input and changes in arousal are expected to have different results. So let us first consider changes in sensory input.

If for some reason sensory input falls, it will become harder and harder to make a detailed and accurate model of "reality." With insufficient input, ambiguities may arise so that more than one model can be fitted to the input. If a strict criterion is in force, the ambiguities will be unacceptable, and different models may be tried out in the attempt to reduce discrepancies. These attempts to find a match may be successful, and a good model be reinstated. However, if there is insufficient input, the modeling may take off on a wrong tack and get so far away from the "correct" model that it is hard to reconstruct it.

This may also happen if there is too much noise. It will be impossible to fit the input to the model without some discrepancies. One way of coping would be to shift to a laxer criterion—allowing greater discrepancies between input and model, but the danger is, of course, that the model will drift away from input control.

However, assuming that arousal is high enough, there must still be models of various kinds. And (according to the theory), one of these must still be labeled *reality*. This model could be of something quite bizarre, with resulting hallucinations; it might be something of particular significance as in mystical and religious experience, or it might be something more closely approximating the normal physical world. The kind of model that takes over will depend on the circumstances and demands at the time and will in turn determine the kind of experience that ensues.

I have already made explicit the assumption that experience depends entirely upon the current "model of reality." However, this raises awkward questions like why is one model in the system "in awareness," whereas others are not? In other words—what is the awareness? A somewhat radical approach solves such problems. Assume that all mental models are conscious, or rather, that consciousness is what it is like being a mental model (see Blackmore, 1986a). In this view, all representations constructed at any stage in processing give rise to awareness. Why then am "I" apparently conscious of some and not others? Because "I" am only a model like everything else. Any models that form part of the model of self at the time are in "my" awareness. Others are only in their own awareness, which may be fleeting and ephemeral. Looked at in this way, we can see that in normal states of consciousness, there is one overriding model of self in the world or "model of reality." But, in extreme ASCs, this may break down entirely, to be replaced with other "models of reality", or even with chaos, or stillness. In this sense, ASCs can and do profoundly affect the self. In some ASCs, one can even gain insight into the constructed, or illusory, nature of the self. So to understand ASCs, we must always ask, what is the "model of reality" like?

Out-of-the-Body Experiences

There are many circumstances that can induce a change from the normal "model of reality." For example, accidents, acute stress, certain drugs, sensory deprivation, sleep deprivation, and so on may disrupt the normal waking state. In such circumstances, one may be deprived of adequate information about the world and unable to maintain a good input-controlled model. Nevertheless, there are very good reasons for trying (in spite of the difficulty) to maintain a model of self in the world and to keep trying to get back to input control. The dangers of slipping off into hallucinations are obvious.

So, what is the best strategy? It may be to try to build the best approximation to "reality" that is possible on the evidence available. This means using information from memory and the cognitive map as well as what is available from the input. The model may not have a terribly good match with external facts but will be the best the system can manage. If the problem does not last long, you may never notice the lapse from input control, but, if it continues, more and more of the details will have to be constructed from memory instead of from sensory input. As we have seen, representations in memory are less viewer-centered. So if the system tries to reconstruct a model of self, doing whatever you knew yourself to be doing and wherever you remember you were, then this representation may not be from the eye-level viewpoint. Like many representations from memory, it may be from a bird's eye view or not really from a specific location at all. If a model like this is built, then your apparent viewpoint will not coincide with actual bodily position. *In other words, an OBE has occurred.*

I suggest that an OBE occurs when it is not possible (or perhaps desirable) to construct a predominantly input-controlled model of reality from the normal viewpoint. A model is still constructed and still seems real. It includes all the likely facts known about one's position at the time, along with any derived from the limited sensory input still available. There is a body image as usual, and the model includes a version of the world around you. The only difference is that it is largely memory- or imagery-controlled, not input-controlled and "you" are in the wrong position.

This explains why everything seems so real in an OBE. It is "reality" in exactly the same sense as the contents of any other model that has been assigned that status. This erroneous model may go on for some time having that status because it will be rich, detailed, and convincing in spite of its lack of fit with input. It may even incorporate some input without switching back to the "correct" position. For example, auditory input is less specific as to location than is visual information. This may explain the incorporation of correct details in OBEs near death or in accidents, when hearing is the last sense to be lost even when a person is behaviorally unconscious.

With time, the new model may begin to break down, and some other model may gain the ascendant. If this is a fantasized scene, one will be hallucinating, and indeed this does follow some OBEs. With deliberate control of the imagery, it is possible to shift to other ASCs and even to transcendent or mystical experiences. Alternatively, sensory input may reassert itself. In this case, a new correct model will be constructed, will take over from the incorrect one, and the OBE will end abruptly. There cannot be two "reality" models at once, and so the switch will be sudden.

If the incorrect (OBE) model is highly discrepant from input (that is, predicts it badly), then input cannot easily be incorporated, and the OBE may continue for a long time. If it is only slightly wrong, a match is more likely to occur by chance or by modifying it. A model that is only slightly out of coincidence is therefore unstable, whereas a very different one is more stable. This may account for the apparent discreteness of the OBE.

Other features of the OBE are also explicable. The common position looking from above and behind oneself may be a result of the fact that this is a convenient position from which to imagine scenes. For instance, try imagining your own bedroom or recall the last time you were walking in the countryside. Where are "you" in this scene? You may well find that you imagine at least some scenes from a bird's-eye perspective.

The fact that the out-of-body world is often more abstract and stylized than the real world reflects its origin in models constructed from memory. The kinds of "errors" often reported in OB vision are exactly what is expected. They are the same errors that are found in using cognitive maps. For example, Green (1968b) cites the case of a man who rose through the roof of his house and saw a chimney stack that, when he checked the next day, he found was not there. In my own experience (Blackmore 1982a), I saw tiles of quite the wrong type and color on the roofs of Oxford. I floated over a "star-shaped island with 100 trees" and saw coastlines greatly simplified as compared to the real thing. I suggest that this is exactly what we should expect and that people only report that all the details were accurate because they see what they are expecting, and, on the whole, they do not bother to check the facts afterwards (Blackmore 1984a).

Many writers have puzzled over the existence of clothes, carriages, or railways in the out-of-body world—or the problem, as Tart (1974) puts it, of where the pajamas come from. But this is no problem if the OB world is truly thought created.

More generally, all the effects of thought on the OB world are predictable. Several adepts have noted that movement is effected by thought (e.g., Fox 1962; Monroe 1971), and Muldoon and Carrington declare that "thought creates in the astral. . . . In fact the whole astral world is governed by thought" (1929 p. 46). Clearly, these writers would not agree with my interpretation, but it does fit extremely well with their descriptions. A constructed model like this can only be affected by thought. This fact provides the freedom to fly or to do anything you can think of, but it also provides the limitations of thought. For example, the difficulty of turning on lights may reflect the difficulty of constructing a complete change in the scene all at once. Similarly, other oddities of behavior such as things falling slowly or sounds coming a long time after events are seen may also result from limitations of processing. Even something like Muldoon's three traveling speeds (Muldoon & Carrington, 1929) makes sense because these may result from the different ways one can, by thought, move viewpoint in a constructed model. I believe that an exploration of the limitations of change in modeling will provide great insight into the nature of the out-of-body world.

Lucid Dreams

We may now come to lucid dreams. As one falls asleep, both sensory input and arousal fall. The input-controlled model of reality gets less and less input and less and less demands on it. Other trains of thought may temporarily become stronger and even briefly take over "reality" status (producing the familiar experience of realistic hypnagogic imagery), but, as arousal drops and sleep ensues, all the models become weaker. The input-controlled model disappears, and only vague trains of thought remain. This state may persist through NREM (or ordinary) sleep. If one is woken, one may report some kind of thinking or nothing at all.

In dreaming sleep arousal increases, but hardly any sensory input is processed. This means that, although complex models may be constructed, they cannot be based on input. Therefore, no good input-controlled model is available. However, we have postulated that the dominant model at any time will seem real. The model that now takes on reality status (and seems real) is therefore whichever one happens to be the most convincing at the time. This could be anything at all that imagination can create, and I suggest that this is why dreams are both so bizarre and yet so convincingly real. You are effectively stranded in a mental world without a stable model of who and where you are. This is surely the familiar experience of dreaming. You have lots of adventures, see all sorts of things, but you are not aware of your name, the date, or the fact that you are dreaming. Indeed, "you" are whatever self is constructed in the dream. Although the waking "you" may not remember it very clearly, to the dream self, the dream seems real.

Of course, if memory in dreams were as accurate and efficient as it is in waking, then presumably it would be possible to remember who you are; that you had gone to sleep, and so on, and so to construct a self much like the waking one with a reasonable reality model. However, memory is not that good in ordinary dreams—perhaps just because arousal is still too low.

We may then wonder whether, under some circumstances, it should not be possible to become aware of these things. According to this theory, this would mean building a model of self as a dreamer, asleep, knowing the relevant facts about your name, the day, where you went to bed, and so on. If such a model could be created and were sufficiently stable and coherent, then it could achieve reality status. Possibly, it would be easier to recall on waking because the constructed self would be more similar to the normal waking self.

So how could this come about? It may be that, in the course of ordinary dreaming, something occurs that raises the idea of dreaming. This may be, for example, a recurrent dream motif or theme. It may be a dream of going to bed or lying down. It may be that something so bizarre happens that you question its status. Whichever it is, the result is the same. That is, a model is tried out that says that this is a dream and that you are asleep. However, this model does not usually stand much of a chance. There is so little sensory input that it cannot be confirmed by normal reality testing, and it may have no other advantages over other trains of thought. Indeed, it is probably a lot less interesting than the lion chasing you, the cliff you are about to leap off, or the fact that your Rolls Royce will not start. In this case, it fails to achieve reality status and is dropped. At best, it is a prelucid dream.

However, this sort of model might gain the advantage if enough information from memory were available. If you could only remember who you are and that you are dreaming and keep these facts stable in the new model, then it might be possible to maintain it long enough for it to achieve reality status. The result would then be a shift of reality status to the new model and the realization that you are actually dreaming. In other words, a lucid dream would occur.

It can be seen that memory is crucial here in providing stability for the lucid model. If we suppose that the efficiency of memory is a function of arousal (at least at these low levels of arousal in sleep), then this theory would predict that lucid dreams will occur when arousal is relatively high. There is, in fact, mounting evidence that this is the case (see Gackenbach & LaBerge, 1986).

Once lucidity is established, several possibilities open up. First one can continue with the previous dream imagery but maintain the realization that it is a dream. This is very hard because the dream imagery will typically involve a model of yourself as involved in the action, rather than as someone who is dreaming it. So there is always the danger that this "action" model will take over again and lucidity be lost. However, concentrating on rational thoughts, such as "I know I am dreaming," will help, while allowing yourself to get involved in the action, and consequent emotions will hinder the maintenance of lucidity. These effects have been described,for example by Fox (1962) and Hearne (1978).

Second, you may choose to create a model of yourself lying in bed asleep and dreaming as though from the position of a spectator. Such a model is unlikely to be an accurate one in the absence of sensory input, but it will be plausible. You will seem to be a second self, looking at your body in bed. This is exactly the same situation as in the OBE already described. The only difference is that you are aware that it is a dream. If you realize what is happening or have recalled prior intentions, you may then fly or do anything else you want in your thought-created body. It has already been noted that lucid dreams can provide a stepping stone to the OBE (Rogo 1983). This route may be easier for people who find it especially hard to ignore sensory input, but the danger is always that it will lapse back into ordinary dreaming. This will happen if the new model of self as dreamer is not sustained and one of the other dream images takes over "reality,"

A final alternative is that the search for sensory input to back up the new model may result in your waking up, achieving the sensory input in the process, and so ending the state.

A rather different kind of model that may be created during dreaming is one of yourself in bed but looking from the position of the body as you do when waking up. This may be easier to construct than other eye-level views because of its familiarity. If this achieves reality status, you may not realize it is any different from normal, and, in this case, a false awakening has occurred. This approach to the false awakening suggests that it should more often occur in familiar surroundings, when the eye-level view is a very well-known one, and to people who habitually use eye-level views in imagery.

In this way, lucid dreams, false awakenings, and OBEs can all be seen as the natural result of our normal modeling process coming up with models of reality that are not predominantly input-driven.

We can now answer at least some of the questions about the relationships between lucid dreams and OBEs. As Irwin concluded, they are not phenomenologically the same. According to this analysis, they are both ways of entering a world of thought and memory unconstrained by sensory input and the restrictions of the body, but they are bounded by different constraints. The lucid dream depends on a unstable model, just as the OBE does. However, in OBEs, there is likely to be too much sensory input, and the model is likely to slip back into normal (or correct) perspective. On the other hand, in lucid dreams, there is likely to be too little sensory input and too little information from memory, and it is more likely to drift into dream imagery. This means that for sustaining an OBE, the most important factors are those that block sensory input, whereas sustaining a lucid dream requires more arousal and better memory. This explains why the two experiences are related but not more closely so.

We should now ask whether this theory leads to any testable predictions for the OBE or lucid dream.

First, one would not predict a simple relationship between imagery and OBEs. As explained elsewhere (Blackmore, 1984b, 1986b), in a spontaneous OBE, the external circumstances do the work of cutting off sensory input, and an OBE may even be avoided in people whose imagery is good enough to restore the normal model. However, for a deliberate OBE, good imagery is needed to construct the alternative viewpoint. This makes sense of data showing variable relationships between OBEs and imagery (Blackmore,1982b; Irwin, 1981). Further research is needed to test whether people having deliberate OBEs have better imagery, as predicted. As for the lucid dream, the ability to recall information across different states is more important than imagery. Indeed, no correlation between imagery skills and lucid dreams has been found (Blackmore 1982b). State-specific recall has yet to be tested,but clearly dream recall is a kind of corollary of recalling waking from dreams and indeed lucid dreaming and dream recall are highly correlated (Blackmore 1984).

We can now see that deliberate OBEs have more in common with lucid dreams than spontaneous ones do. For this reason, a higher correlation between lucid dreams and deliberate, not spontaneous, OBEs is predicted. Also, dream control skills would be expected to correlate with having deliberate but not spontaneous OBEs. Both these predictions were confirmed in a recent survey. A higher proportion of people reporting deliberate OBEs also reported lucid dreams and various dream control skills (Blackmore 1986b).

Final predictions concern the use of viewpoints in imagery, OBEs, and lucid dreams. According to the theory presented here, it is the change of imaginary viewpoint that is essential to the OBE. We should therefore expect OBErs to be better at using a bird's-eye, or observer, viewpoint in imagery, to use it habitually in recall, and to be better at switching viewpoints. Because viewpoint is not important to the lucid dream, we should not expect such relationships. These predictions were confirmed in three studies (Blackmore 1985, 1987). OBErs more often used observer viewpoint in recall of dreams, though not in recalling waking situations. They reported more vivid imagery from different viewpoints and were consistently better at switching viewpoints in imagery. Lucid dreamers did not use observer viewpoint more often, but they were better at switching viewpoints. This may reflect a skill or kind of control that is useful in having lucid dreams. It was also predicted and confirmed that unpleasant dreams should more often be recalled in observer perspective.

Selfless States

This theory can also be applied to other altered states of consciousness. There are many other states in which the normal sensory-based model is given up and other models are created almost entirely out of information from memory. The world experienced in these states should therefore reflect the properties of mental constructions and mental limitations rather than the physical world. In all these states, one is free from the restrictions not only of sensory input but of bodily actions. One is constrained only by imagination. This is why flying is possible, and in fact anything you can imagine is possible. I think it is a reflection of most people's lack of imagination that most OBEs involve such mundane scenes and even replica bodies. Of course, in many OBEs, there is still some sensory input and therefore some restriction. The lucid dream is freer in this respect but is still limited by the fact that arousal and access to memory are only just high enough. And even in lucid dreams there is typically heavy dependence on a model of self.

One can see that in some types of meditation, where sensory input is ignored and arousal kept high, one can enter a state that is further along the continuum of unrestricted states than either the OBE or the lucid dream. With training and practice in the skills of concentration and modeling, the potential for altered states is vast (as mystics have long tried to tell us).

Finally, there is really no need for the system to construct a "self" at all, with all its attendant cravings and illusions. A selfless model, a selfless state of consciousness is quite possible. Indeed, there is a whole world of "models of reality" that we have hardly begun to explore. Lucid dreams and OBEs are just first steps.

REFERENCES

Blackmore, S. J. (1982a). *Beyond the body: An investigation of out-of-the body experiences*. London: Heinemann.

Blackmore, S. J. (1982b). Out of body experiences, lucid dreams, and imagery: Two surveys. *Journal of the American Society for Psychical Research, 76*, 301–317.

Blackmore, S. J. (1982c). Have you ever had an OBE?: The wording of the question. *Journal of the Society for Psychical Research, 51*, 292–302.

Blackmore, S. J. (1984a). A postal survey of OBEs and other experiences. *Journal of the Society for Psychical Research, 52*, 225–244.

Blackmore, S. J. (1984b). A psychological theory of the OBE. *Journal of Parapsychology, 48*, 201–218.

Blackmore, S. J. (1985). Lucid dreams and viewpoints in imagery: Two studies. *Lucidity Letter, 4*, 34–42.

Blackmore, S. J. (1986a). Who am I? Changing models of reality in meditation. In G. Claxton (Ed.), *Beyond therapy*. London: Wisdom.

Blackmore, S. J. (1986b). Spontaneous and deliberate OBEs: A questionnaire survey. *Journal of the Society for Psychical Research, 53*, 218–224.

Blackmore, S. J. (1987). Where am I? Perspectives in imagery and the out-of-body experience. *Journal of Mental Imagery, 11*(2), 53–66.

Crookall, R. (1961). *The study and practice of astral projection*. London: Aquarian Press.

Fox, O. (1962). *Astral projection*. New York: University Books Inc.

Gackenbach, J., & LaBerge, S. (1986). An overview of lucid dreaming. In A. Sheikh (Ed.), *International Review of Mental Imagery (Vol. 2)*. New York: Human Sciences Press.

Gackenbach, J., & Schillig, G. (1984). Lucid dreams: The content of conscious awareness of dreaming during the dream. *Journal of Mental Imagery, 11*(2).

Green, C. E. (1968a). *Lucid dreams*. London: Hamish Hamilton.

Green, C. E. (1968b). *Out-of-the-body experiences*. London: Hamish Hamilton.

Hearne, K. M. T. (1978). *Lucid dreams: An electrophysiological and psychological study*. Unpublished doctoral dissertation, University of Liverpool.

Irwin, H. J. (1981). Some psychological dimensions of the out-of-body experiences. *Parapsychology Review, 12*, 1–6.

Irwin, H. J. (1985). *Flight of mind*. Metuchen, NJ and London: Scarecrow Press.

Liben, L. S., Patterson, A. H., & Newcombe, N. (Eds.). (1981). *Spatial representation and behaviour across the life span*. New York: Academic Press.

Marr, D. (1982). *Vision*. San Francisco: Freeman.

Monroe, R. A. (1971). *Journeys out of the body*. New York: Doubleday.

Muldoon, S., & Carrington, H. (1929). *The projection of the astral body*. London: Rider & Co.

Palmer, J. (1978). The out-of-body experience: A psychological theory. *Parapsychology Review, 9*, 19–22.

Rogo, D. S. (1978). *Mind beyond the body*. New York: Penguin.

Rogo, D. S. (1983). *Leaving the body*. Englewood Cliffs, NJ: Prentice-Hall.

Siegel, R. K. (1977) Hallucinations. *Scientific American, 237*, 132–140.

Tart, C. T. (1974). Out-of-the-body experiences. In E. Mitchell (Ed.) *Psychic exploration* (pp. 349–373). New York: G. P. Putnams Sons.

Tellegen, A., & Atkinson, G. (1974). Openness to absorbing and self-altering experiences (Absorption), a trait related to hypnotic susceptibility. *Journal of Abnormal Psychology, 83*, 268–277.

van Eeden, F. (1913). A study of dreams. *Proceedings of the Society for Psychical Research, 26*, 431–461.

Yates, J. (1985). The content of awareness is a model of the world. *Psychological Review, 92*, 249–284.

17

Lucid Dreams in Their Natural Series

Phenomenological and Psychophysiological Findings in Relation to Meditative States[1]

HARRY T. HUNT and ROBERT D. OGILVIE

> Phenomena are best understood when placed in their series, studied in their germ and in their over-ripe decay, and compared with their exaggerated and degenerated kindred. . . . [This] method of serial study is so essential for interpretation that if we really wish to reach conclusions we must use it. . . . We renounce the absurd notion that a thing is exploded away as soon as it is classed with others, . . . refusing to consider [its] place in any more general series and treating [it] as if [it] was outside of nature's order altogether. . . . The only novelty I can imagine this course of lectures to possess lies in the breadth of the apperceptive mass.
>
> William James, *The Varieties of Religious Experience* (1920)

INTRODUCTION

James's method of "placing things in their series"—so akin to Wittgenstein (1979) on the descriptive rendering of features along multiple lines of "family resemblance" and its recent formalizations within social science—provides the methodological context for our approach to lucid dreams, both in terms of their descriptive phenomenology and psychophysiological processes. By considering the striking interrelations and overlap among dream lucidity and control, highly bizarre dreams, mundane true-to-daily-life dreams, out-of-body experience,

[1]The authors would like to thank Kate Ruzycki for her careful reading and editorial assistance.

HARRY T. HUNT and ROBERT D. OGILVIE • Department of Psychology, Brock University, St. Catharines, Ontario, Canada.

"near-death" epidsodes, and the range of meditative experiences and techniques, it becomes clear that prototypical lucid dreams can be seen as a species of
spontaneously realized meditative state, and this in their phenomenological,
physiological, and cognitive aspects.

Phenomenologically considered, lucid dreams show the same kind of intensified or broadened "self-reference" found in the "insight" or "mindfulness"
meditative traditions, and physiologically we find the same mixed or transitional
state reported with a variety of meditative techniques. So much is this the case
that we could even speculate that systematic meditation might have been "in-
vented" as an attempt to attain within wakefulness the sort of mental clarity,
exhilaration, and simultaneously detached openness that emerges as lucid dreaming. What sort of "state" or "intelligence" is thereby manifested will occupy us
after this overlap has been established.

THE PHENOMENOLOGY OF LUCID DREAMS AND RELATED PHENOMENA: THE QUALITATIVE SERIES

Dream Lucidity in Relation to Normative Dreaming and Dream Bizarreness

Knowing one is dreaming while dreaming and ongoing control of dream
content (with or without the full sense of lucidity) represent rare but theoretically
important transformations of ordinary dreaming. Variously depicted by van
Eeden (1913/1969), Fox (1975), Whiteman (1961), and Green (1968), the lucid
dream shows a modification of the peculiar insulation of dreams from each other
and from the totality of previous waking experience that Rechtschaffen (1978)
has termed their *single mindedness* and Hunt (1982) has likened to a clouding of
consciousness or confusional state within the dream. Lucidity seems to be the
opposite of this tendency to "disorientation for time and place."

That said, however, we are left with two very different but not necessarily
competing ways of classifying these phenomena: The first alternative, surely true
up to some point, is to restrict lucidity to a transformation that is necessarily
unique to the dreaming process (whether in REM, NREM, or hypnagogic states).
Certainly, if we follow the lead of Hughlings-Jackson (1958) on the primacy of
"negative symptoms" and ask what is typically missing or absent from dream
experience, it is just the sort of mnemic and/or intellectual clarity that would lead
us to lucidity. After all, a fully coherent reflection on the bizarre hallucinatory
elements of a dream would inevitably cue us to the fact that we are dreaming, and
even the most realistic of dreams could, in principle, still lead us to the realization that the last thing we recall before "all this" was going to bed.

Similarly, Green, in her classic work (1968), speaks of the "perceptual realism" of lucid dreams and the absence of those visual-spatial distortions that, since Freud (1900/1965), have been taken as manifest indicators of the symbolic aspects of dream formation. In our previous work (Hunt *et al.*, 1982), we found that dream bizarreness is generally based on the intrusion of relatively unlikely visual content (usually plausible in some other setting than the one actually dreamt) along with various aspects of cognitive clouding (such as sudden shifts of scene, confusional thinking, and difficulties in reasoning within the dream situation, memory distortions within the dream, and, of course, related difficulties in recall upon awakening).

Because Dorus, Dorus, and Rechtschaffen (1971) and Snyder (1970) have demonstrated the relative realism of most people's dreams, it might seem tempting to place lucid dreams at one potential extreme of a linear biazarreness–realism continuum—as a within- dream breakthrough into a near-waking cognitive capacity. At the other end would be the sort of rare psychedelic/archetypal transformations typical of the dreams of Jung (1961) and the more extreme altered states of consciousness.

Yet there are serious problems with any approach that leaves lucidity as a sort of mental waking up within and unique to the dream. First, it seems likely that the approximation of lucid dreams to our waking faculties is only partial. Not only can "lucidity" create its own kinds of confusions (Green, 1968), but there is often a failure to draw the obvious consequences of one's situation even with experienced lucid dreamers (Gillespie, 1984). Despite the *relative* attenuation of abstract intelligence within most dreams, their typical nonlucidity may actually mirror a formally identical failure to develop our full potential sense of context and perspective within wakefulness as well, thus making lucidity about equally different from both ordinary dreaming *and* ordinary wakefulness.

Second, the relation between lucidity and bizarreness seems to be complex and nonlinear. Indeed, dream incongruity and "dreamlikeness" are common triggers for lucidity, and we will see later a striking association between various categories of bizarreness and prelucidity (the specific uncertainty whether or not one is dreaming that often precedes full lucidity). Although some lucid dreamers have emphasized their "realism," other anecdotal and cross-cultural accounts (Chang, 1963) show that more developed lucidity/control can be associated with extreme forms of dream bizarreness rarely seen in normal samples.

A comparative perspective suggests the beginning of a solution: What Green describes as "realism" is distinct from the true-to-daily-life "realism" of most dreams and wakefulness. Rather, she seems to be describing a "special" feeling of immediacy and vividness—a "felt reality"—"everything was so real, clear, and somehow present." Such clarity and exhilaration come only at our "peak" moments (Maslow, 1962) and are based on a transformation of the way we normally attend to things. It is that special experiential quality of lucidity that must now be located.

Lucid and Control Dreams in Their Natural Series: Out-of-Body Experience, Near-Death Experience, Autoscopic Hallucinations, Hypnagogic Autosymbolism, and the Structure of "Mindfulness" Meditation

Our comparative phenomenology of lucid dreaming, releasing us from the strict confines of dream psychology and REM psychophysiology, allows a more inclusive alternative classification of the material: Lucid dreaming is not merely (or even primarily) the *intellectual* awareness that one is dreaming ("Am I? Oh well, I guess so. Isn't that quaint?"), nor can it be exhaustively described as a cognitive awakening within REM—although both characterizations are partially correct. However, they make it seem as though the state of mind in lucid dreams would be unique to the REM and/or dreaming state, and that does not seem to be the case.

In prototypical lucid dreaming we find the development of a simultaneous capacity for detached observation or self-reflection along with a continued "dreamt" participation. This development of a capacity for sustained self-reflection for its own sake, and the difficulty of its integration with complex ongoing involvements, also describes the goal and difficulties of the "mindfulness" or "insight" meditative traditions—typified by Zen (Luk, 1964), Theravada Buddhism (Thera, 1962), and Tibetan Mahamudra practice (Chang, 1963). In both mindfulness meditation and lucid dreams, this tenuous balancing of a detached "receptive" attitude with ongoing participation is associated with strong feelings of exhilaration, freedom, and release, along with a special cognitive clarity and sense of "presence." Other ways of describing this state of mind include an unusually broad sense of context and perspective, a "balance" of normally contradictory attitudes, and the felt sense of one's own existence (that special "I am" or "being" experience common to Maslow, 1962, on "peak experience" and Gurdjieff on "self remembering", Walker, 1965).

What, then, of the lucid dream's other near relatives? What of the "series" that would connect lucidity and meditation? In this regard, the descriptive phenomenology of out-of-body experience (OBE) (Green, 1973) is crucial to our approach, because it seems to provide a more concretely realized form of this balance between detached observation and engaged participation. In "naturalistic" terms, the OBE is a very vivid, generally hyperrealistic "dreamt" version of one's actual physical setting, except that, at least in the first stages, it includes the imagined construction of one's body position as if seen from outside (usually as unconscious or sleeping). It is hard to describe the phenomenon in cognitive terms other than as an imaginal reversibility of perspective closely related to Piaget's "decentering" as well as Mead's "taking the role of the imaginary other." Yet this form of "taking the role of the other" is expressed here in "presentational" not "representational" symbolism (Edelson, 1975). Although representation conventionalizes and subordinates the medium of expression to its message (i.e., language), in presentational meanings the crucial symbolic operations are directly conveyed in the phenomenal properties of the medium itself (i.e., aesthetics).

If the dreamt-imaginal "reality construct" in OBE, generally emerging from the hypnagogic period, deep meditation, psychedelics, or from traumatically overwhelming waking stress, is to carry with it a specially broadened sense of context and/or self-reference, it will have to include this startling, directly sensed form of "lucidity," that is, seeing oneself as if from outside. It is as if a dreaming sequence starts, but, atypically, awareness of one's actual setting in time and space is not dislodged as in most dreams, so that the out-of-body structure becomes the emergent compromise, thereby integrating the imaginal participation of dream with a detached self-awareness that knows one's actual context for what it is. (The felt "accuracy" of many OBEs and some lucid dreams, only sometimes confirmed afterwards in normal awareness, would rest on a genuinely astonishing capacity to imaginatively intuit what would be going on at a friend's house and, for the immediate physical setting, on the specifically human cross-modal or synaesthetic capacity (Geschwind, 1965) for direct visual translation of actual auditory and somatic cues.)

Both prototypical out-of-body experiences and lucid dreams show the same tenuous, balanced duality of attitude and ihe same concommitant sense of release, exhilaration, and clarity. Although there are relative differences between them, these differences, with their numerous transitional cases and exceptions, actually reemphasize the underlying similarities—implying that the differences result primarily from the different originating settings (i.e., REM versus unusually high or low arousal within wakefulness), giving rise to ultimately common cognitive processes.

For instance, following some of Green's distinctions, the out-of-body state—at least in its initial stages—includes seeing one's own physical form, unlike typical lucid dreaming. Yet both lucid and nonlucid dreams can, on occasion, include the dreamt version of one's own body "as if" from an external perspective. Similarly, the OBE, often, but certainly not always, entails a felt disembodiment, that is, there is no "second body" felt as looking down on the first, just a nonembodied visual locus or view. Again, both lucid and nonlucid dreams can have this same disembodied, purely observational structure—as if the detachment component were exaggerated, with a resulting balance that is more stable but also more one-sidedly nonparticipatory. Finally, the typically superior realism, accurate intuition, and control of the OBE accounts is even more obviously relative, admitting of numerous crossovers and exceptions.

It seems especially important that actual empirical cases illustrating these continuous transitions between the typical OBE and typical lucidity patterns are easily found in the literature, supporting the notion of a continuum based on common processes—in addition to statistical associations between the two experiences (Gackenbach, Prill, & Westrom, 1983; Harroldson, 1982). Green reports several examples that are genuinely indistinguishable between the two "types," whereas van Eeden, Whiteman, and Castaneda (1974) describe experiences in which lucid dreams end with a "reverse" out-of-body sensation (the dreamt phenomenal body "slipping into" the visually perceived sleeping position) and out-of-body patterns can turn into standard lucid dreams. One of our own subjects reported that her commonly lucid dreams sometimes ended, on subjective awakening, in an out-of-body condition during which she looked down on her phenomenal sleeping form and, usually with some discomfort, had to finish the awakening process by willing a small movement of her visually perceived, but not felt, hand—after which she "came to" lying in bed.

Following a more formal line of thought, as soon as a phenomenally "embodied" out-of-body subject works up the courage to leave the setting of his or her bedroom and venture "outside", he or she is in the phenomenal situation of the lucid dreamer—whether he or she is "flying" or in a more normal physical stance. In other words, such a subject is in an ostensibly real, yet dreamt situation (realistic or not) while simultaneously knowing that he or she is actually "at home" and asleep. Correspondingly, if the lucid dreamer deliberately dreams his or her return to the actual bedroom setting, then we have the essential structure of the OBE—assuming, of course, that the dreamt bedroom includes one's own sleeping form. Castaneda (1979) describes just such an episode. Finally, and most strikingly, if the out-of-body subject leaves the bedroom setting and participates in an external dream environment and *then* manages to get caught up in the situation and forgets that it is a dream, we have the basic structure of ordinary nonlucid dreaming. Contrary to the implication of the more fantastic out-of-body literature, it does seem that some OBEs end in just that way.

To complete this "series" and further solidify its common basis in an intensified self-reference emerging within presentational symbolism (i.e., as a natural if rare symbolic process), we can briefly mention near-death experience, autoscopic hallucinations, and the autosymbolic features of hypnagogic imagery.

Near-death accounts (Ring, 1980) are particularly intriguing if we try to take them in this naturalistic cognitive sense. They occur in a context of ultimate life crisis, when some "overview" of one's immediate situation and life as a whole would be appropriate, and seem to involve an intensification of the cognitive self-reference that both Mead (1934) and Van Dusen (1972) make criterial to all symbolic intelligence. Their usual mode of initiation is the out-of-body pattern, with its enhanced self-reference and sense of broadened context, a context that is also obvious in the "life review" imagery scintillations, and the ultimately "numinous," all-encompassing perspective of the "white light" experience. Similarly, the threshold symbolism of "the return"—often moving back from a fence or a path into "life"—is typical of autosymbolic imagery during awakening as detailed by Silberer (1909/1951). Near-death accounts fuse an intensified self-reference with the more traditionally psychedelic geometric form constants (the tunnel, mandalalike patterns, and the "white light of the void"). We have tried to show elsewhere that such geometric-imaginal forms, typical with meditation and psychedelics but rare in dreaming, show a development of abstract presentational thought that is consistent with Arnheim's (1969) approach to the bases of all thinking in geometric imagery (Hunt et al., 1982, 1984).

Autoscopic hallucinations, although comparatively rare even in this rarified collection of phenomena, offer a further empirical brdige along our continuum of heightened self-reference, released for its own sake and no longer subordinated to pragmatic usage. These reports involve features that seem almost equally related to OBE and those relatively infrequent observational dreams in which one sees oneself as if from outside during ongoing active involvement in the dream setting. In autoscopic hallucinations occurring during wakefulness (Lukianowicz, 1958), the person sees his or her "double"—sometimes with a "peculiar" physical sensation very much like out-of-body reports as the perceived double steps out from one's actual physical-motor "location" and then turns to face the startled viewer. This "second self" can be completely realistic, semi-transparent, or just an invisible "sense" of presence. Speaking in constructionist, "naturalistic" terms, it is as if the conditions for an OBE were primed (self-reference was to be markedly enhanced within an immediate presentational symbolism), but there was intense resistance to such a "loss." The result would be the autoscopic phenomenon—a compromise formation based on a defensive holding on to the concrete perceptual-motor setting.

Finally, the hypnagogic period provides more "elements" that overlap with our general series. Not only is sleep onset a common setting for OBE in persons so prone, but geometric form constants, body image transformations, imagery scintillations, and "white light" experiences are also reported. Some recent statistical support for the association of hypnagogic experience with dream lucidity and OBE has been provided by Hearne (1983) and Gackenbach, Prill, and Westerom (1983). Most important, Silberer (1909/1951) and Van Dusen (1972) have shown that hypnagogic phenomena are often based on a striking "autosymbolic," self-referential capacity in which the immediately preceding content of thought or actual features of background cognitive processes are metaphorically reflected in imagery.

Here we gain an important clue to the question whether near-death experience, OBE, and even lucid dreams might not occur far more often than reported, but typically be forgotten. Probably not. When Foulkes and Vogel (1965) took average sleep lab subjects and awakened them during normal sleep onset—and we need to keep in mind that classical hypnagogic reports tend to be spontaneously self-arousing—they did not find these classical hypnagogic-psyche-delic effects but rather brief "dreamlets" that showed considerable variation in realism-bizarreness. These brief dreams would have been forgotten without the artificial interruption of sleep onset. Given that physiological studies of classical hypnagogic experience find concomitant sudden EEG arousals and/or un-usually stabilized "transitional" alpha/theta records preceding these reports (Os-wald, 1962; Schacter, 1976), it seems likely that hypnagogic autosymbolism is a cognitive enhancement and energization that will be remembered when it occurs. Accordingly, it would be most likely that the OBE, lucidity, and near-death accounts are similarly based on intensification of abstract awareness (self-refer-ence for its own sake expressed within immediately given presentational imag-ery)—a "developmental advance" within any setting or state (awake, asleep, or in between). The perceptual and cognitive clarity and "felt reality" of these states is such that they should override the usual state specificity of recall. In other words, the cognitive processes manifested within the lucid dream, OBE, and near-death experience are such that if you have one, you will remember it.

Indeed, Nigro and Neisser (1983) have shown that memories of events high in self-awareness and emotionality tend to be in an "observer" mode (i.e., a broad reconstruction centered on the "objective circumstances" of the recalled situation, including one's own appearance as it could have been seen by an outside observer.) They note that although such memories imply a greater than usual cognitive assimilation, important events may also be directly experienced in the observer mode.

Further Parallels between Lucidity and Meditation

It is crucial for our approach that lucid dreaming is *not* a unitary phe-nomenon. Even beyond the variations in its degree of stabilization and in the potential integration of lucidity awareness and deliberate control, there are fur-ther shadings and subtypes. Their full range actually helps to confirm the mutual assimilation of lucidity and meditation because the latter traditions show for-mally identical variations.

For instance, consider the complexly "nested" or recursive structure of some prelucid dreams (false awakenings and dreams within dreams), where each "coming to" within one dream setting is successively "contained" or encom-passed by a subsequent more inclusive dreamt setting. These phenomena are quite reminiscent of trying to meditate in the mindfulness traditions where "con-sciousness" is approximated in more and more inclusive states that nonetheless fall short of full realization. Both prelucidity and mindfulness illustrate the basic and paradoxical features of the "self-reference" that Mead (1934), Neisser (1976), and Hofstadter (1979) have made criterial for human intelligence, which operates by the attempt to turn around on itself and so can never be completed—

except possibly when a kind of interior exhaustion may lead to an ongoing acceptance and tolerance of the openness and uncertainty in all our experience ("clear yet void" as the Tibetan Buddhist might say.)

Going further along these comparative lines, just as meditative practice can "go wrong" as a withdrawn, stuporously encapsulated state (Chang, 1963), reversing the sought enhancement of "felt reality" and "release," we have encountered a few informants who have lucid dreams and hate them. They realize "it is only a dream," but that means to them that "it is not *real* and so nothing that happens here matters at all and I'm trapped within pointlessness." The dreaming (and life episodes) that these people value and that may be correspondingly infrequent are those in which they can "lose themselves" in non-reflective spontaneity. It is interesting that these few subjects tend to see themselves and to be seen by others as quite analytic and controlling. Here a genuinely integrated balancing of action and receptive detachment would have to be accented more toward outward expressiveness.

We have put aside, until now, the relation between lucidity and dream control. Dream control can vary considerably, from deliberate "magical" alterations of ongoing dreams (flying) (and this with or without the full lucidity "sense") to presleep dream incubation or suggestion influencing later, nonlucid dream content. Although, at some levels of attainment, lucid awareness and control may become indistinguishable (LaBerge, Nagel, Dement, & Zarcone, 1981), lucidity is often destroyed by attempts at specific control—with the sustained effort and concentrated involvement leading either to awakening or to "magical transformations" so engrossing that the actual setting is quickly forgotten. Similarly, in their first phase of potential integration, one can usually detect a leaning toward one or the other type. Special development of dream control often ends up being accompanied by a merely vestigal, liminal sense of lucidity, having no experiential impact in itself but merely serving as a platform for further efforts at dream transformation (Arnold-Foster, 1921). Correspondingly, the lucidity *sense* can be so powerful that the dreamer has no desire to change things at all but instead lives out the dream, contemplatively, as a "given."

These trade-offs, with their potential for eventual overlap and integration, do seem identical to the formal relationship between the insight/mindfulness meditative traditions (Soto Zen, Tibetan Mahamudra) and concentrative mind control methods (classical Yoga). Both are based on an enhanced capacity for sustained attention, but mindfulness practice seeks the broadened receptivity of the "passive witness" set, without any attempt at control or change, whereas concentrative meditation develops from an intensified narrowing and fixing of attention. Goleman (1972) emphasizes that practice within either tradition leads to the same basic transformations of consciousness, and, exactly like lucidity and dream control, the full development of either tradition tends to elicit the other ability as well. In establishing these formal parallels between the qualitative features of meditation and lucidity, it is especially striking when even the standard variations of each phenomenon turn out to be so closely coordinated.

Perhaps the main difficulty in comparing dream lucidity to insight meditation is that, whereas the tenuous integration of receptivity awareness and ongoing activity is clear in the former, meditation might seem to the reader as something more purely passive and nonparticipatory. Where is the integration of awareness and action in the meditative traditions? In fact, the "witness set" is sufficiently against the grain of everyday life that it can only develop in its early stages within a setting of radically reduced and simplified participation—namely in the immediate here and now of "just sitting" and "just breathing." Yet the stated goal of many of these systems is to bring the receptivity set, thereby established into other organismic settings—to extend it into deep sleep (for which Banquet, 1973, offers some striking evidence), dreaming, and then finally into the maximally demanding involvements of the everyday social order. The most persuasive evidence in favor of our equation of insight meditation and dream lucidity is that the meditative traditions themselves seek to extend meditative awareness into dreams and discuss what the West terms "lucid dreams" as the form of meditation that is available within dreaming sleep (Chang, 1963). Once the meditator in the Tibetan Buddhist tradition has attained a relatively stable dream lucidity, he may practice confronting fearsome dieties or use the opportunity to deepen his meditative absorption in preparation for "lucidity" during Bardo (i.e., while actually dying.)

The best illustration of the attempt to be lucid during normal wakefulness can be found in the system and methods of Gurdjieff (Walker, 1965). His methods seek a continuous "self-remembering" (the *sense* "I am here now in this place doing . . .") in the midst of everyday participations. The Gurdjieff–Ouspensky system minimizes the importance of classical meditation, providing instead initially simple observational exercises in simultaneous doing and self-awareness and then testing and extending that ability in ever more emotionally demanding situations. Gurdjieff, along with other meditational traditions, stresses that we are typically caught up in the events of our lives in such a way that we lose ourselves in them and literally forget or never notice that we *are* alive and that some day we will die. This is the full human context to which, on rare occasions, we spontaneously "wake up" in the form of the "I am" or "being" awareness. In terms of common underlying processes indicated by the shared phenomenology of dream lucidity and such meditative realization, the formal parallel to the directly felt "this-is-a-dream" within REM is the fully sensed "this-is-a-life-and-some-day-it-will-end" within everyday living. It, too, can have quite an impact.

The tenuous unstable quality of this "coming to" within daily living is formally identical to the instability of most dream lucidity. Indeed, it seems likely that the reason lucidity may be more available during dreams is that the actual nonparticipatory basis of REM sleep (with its inhibitory paralysis) would be more open to the development of a simultaneous contextual awareness. In psychophysiological terms, REM may be the ideal precursor for the sort of waking lucidity sought within the meditative traditions.

PSYCHOPHYSIOLOGICAL AND PHENOMENOLOGICAL INVESTIGATIONS OF LUCID DREAMS: THE QUANTITATIVE CONTINUUM WITH MEDITATION

First Study: Lucidity, Prelucidity, Dream Bizarreness, and EEG Alpha in Laboratory Subjects Trained for Lucidity

This work, relating dream lucidity (in its access or preliminary stages) to enhanced EEG Alpha within REM (Ogilvie, Hunt, Tyson, Lucescu & Jeakins, 1982; Tyson, Ogilvie, & Hunt, 1984), grew out of our earlier report (Ogilvie, Hunt, Sawicki, & McGowan, 1978)—the first to describe the "capture" of lucid dreams in the laboratory—in which we showed, consistent with the work of LaBerge and Hearne, that lucid dreams do occur within the REM state and are not artifacts of arousal. In addition we found that lucid dream reports emerging from spontaneous self arousal were preceded by high alpha activity. This link was important in the light of research indicating that alpha enhancement is associated with the special sense of clarity and concentration prominent in subjective accounts of meditation, biofeedback (Woolfolk, 1975), and even creative thought (Whitton, 1978). This coincidence of phenomenological and physiological criteria seems to support the view that the lucid capacity for simultaneous detachment and active dream participation could be considered as a naturally occurring meditative state during REM. Accordingly, we were led to a more systematic attempt to study REM alpha in relation to dream lucidity and dream bizarreness.

Method

It is important to emphasize that, from the beginning, we took a somewhat different, yet hopefully complementary, approach from that of LaBerge and Hearne—who tend to investigate few highly developed lucid dreamers capable of sustained laboratory lucidity and concommitant within-REM signaling. Our approach has been to look more at "access" lucidity in subjects whose development, although falling short of that in some studies, may provide clues to the full range and variation of the phenomenon. Accordingly, our 10 subjects (5 males and 5 females, ranging in age from 19 to 31 years) were selected primarily as good dream recallers (five or more dreams per week), with some previous laboratory experience and relatively high amounts of alpha (both awake and in

REM). All subjects reported at least occasional lucid dreaming, ranging from one or two in several subjects to near nightly episodes in one participant.

A Nihon-Kohden Model ME-175E EEG machine was used to record 17 channels of physiological information. EEG recorded from the right central derivation was filtered for alpha (8–13 HZ). Subjects were told they would be awakened four times during REM sleep during each of their 2 nights in the lab (twice when alpha levels were at highest amplitude and density and twice when alpha was relatively absent). Arousals were made after a minimum of 5 minutes in stage REM, with a coin toss determining whether the first arousal was made during high or low alpha activity. The experimenters sought periods in excess of 30 seconds that were artifact free (unambiguous REM) and contained highest or lowest alpha levels for that subject. The filtering for alpha was crucial in that the usual unfiltered recordings were insufficient to identify the normal fluctuations of within-REM alpha.

On awakening, all subjects were first requested to describe their immediately prior mentation and only then were asked whether they had been in a lucid, prelucid, or control dream and what portion of the dream had been involved. Although such self-reports lack the precision of concurrent in REM signaling, they are consistent with standard laboratory approaches to dream content variables. Blind to the arousal condition and not yet provided with the answers to the lucidity questions, HTH rated the dream narratives in terms of the bizarreness scales developed in Hunt et al. (1982)—a series of "altered state" transformations in dreams that can be considered separately or combined into hallucinosis (i.e., predominantly "out of place" visual intrusions) and clouding-confusion (i.e., sudden scene shifts, confused thinking, difficulties in recall) as two composite factors. These categories have been studied in various normative and unusual samples and can be taken as empirical indicators of the classical notions of dream symbolism.

Subsequent to these ratings, the same experimenter, again blind to arousal conditions, arranged the subjects' lucidity responses along a 7-point continuum from no lucidity, to prelucid or control reports, to full lucidity, in terms of whether each lucidity or prelucidity/control episode was a brief moment, a definite narrative component of the dream, or throughout the dream. In the context of the transitional or "access" levels of lucidity occurring in this study, the judge could tell only infrequently from the dream narrative alone whether the episode had been labeled lucid, prelucid, or control.

Results

Once again, it was clear that lucid and prelucid/control dreams were REM-specific and could not be interpreted as artifacts of arousal. Fluctuations of alpha within ongoing REM have long been part of the REM literature (Rechtschaffen & Kales, 1968); alpha is potentially associated with reflective-intellectual dream activity (Goodenough, Shapiro, Holden, & Steinshiben, 1959). Predominance or absence of alpha was associated here with significant differences in lucidity ($f_{1,8}$ = 7.28, $p < .05$)—mean lucidity ratings following high alpha REM arousals were 2.60 and, following low alpha arousals, was .95. Subsequent more precise EEG spectral analysis (see Tyson, Ogilvie, & Hunt, 1984) has shown that it is the prelucidity subtype that is largely responsible for this association—consistent with the possibility that we were picking up something at the initial developmental level of dream lucidity, much as the case with enhanced alpha in meditation. (Tyson, Ogilvie, and Hunt also found significant positive associations between the composite bizarreness categories and REM alpha.) Correspondingly, it was the prelucidity reports that were the most bizarre in terms of composite hallucinosis and clouding ratings—strikingly so in contrast to previous laboratory studies with the same scales. Full lucidity showed a tendency to return to the more normatively realistic nonlucid dreams ($N = 4$, $df = 6$, clouding: $\chi^2 = 14.1$, $p < .05$; hallucinosis: $\chi^2 = 13.4$, $p < .05$).

Because the totals for lucid versus nonlucid and the specific subcategories of dream anomalies are small, it seemed most appropriate to compare this entire sample to previously established (Hunt et al., 1982) laboratory norms for bizarreness (keeping in mind that these transformations cluster in the prelucid reports). This group of good recallers asked to be lucid does show an overall enhancement of dream bizarreness, most obvious in auditory and somatic "hallucinatory" intrusions, sudden changes in scene, and more awareness of gaps in waking recall, and an observational/detached attitude. (For composite factors, $N = 212$, $df = 2$; clouding: $\chi^2 = 6.13$, $p < .05$; hallucinosis, N.S.).

Discussion

The significant association of enhanced alpha with both dream lucidity (especially transitional prelucidity) and dream bizarreness is especially interesting given the importance of alpha rhythms in meditation. We gain a view of a possible continuum between nonlucid dreams and the sort of developed, stabilized lucidity to be found in accounts from the meditative traditions and in the recent work of LaBerge. Indeed, his laboratory studies with highly developed lucid dreamers have not shown enhanced alpha. Yet, quite apart from the likely importance of specific filtering for alpha activity, which others have not yet done, we have concentrated on a less spectacular level of lucidity and have included in our data all mentation reports from all arousals—rather than concentrating on a selection of least ambiguous instances. Both approaches are needed, and it seems especially important that we, too, could reject the possibility of arousal artifact accounting for lucidity, because no arousals were made following movement artifacts and subsequent reanalysis showed that other signs of arousal (EMG, eye blinks, or sudden changes in heart rate and respiration) were absent from experimental arousals.

Finally, we seem to have picked up part of the continuum between dream bizarreness (symbolic transformations of normative dream realism) and the more explicitly reflective attitude of lucidity. Although, anecdotally, we know that high bizarreness can return with fully stabilized lucidity and, at lower levels of lucid development, that it is often the "trigger" for the realization of lucidity and pre-lucidity, here we find statistical evidence that transitional lucidity goes with very high bizarreness that then drops away with the push into full lucidity. (In this study, all lucidity episodes had elements of prelucidity as well, indicating a progressive scale of lucidity.) Given findings showing the association of dream bizarreness and waking creativity (Sylvia, Clark, & Munroe, 1978) and Gackenbach, Curren, LaBerge, Davidson, and Maxwell's (1983) linkages of lucidity with spatial abilities and creativity, this suggests that bizarreness and lucidity develop together up to a point as part of a spatial-imaginative, symbolic-presentational transformation of ordinary dreaming. The final push to lucidity will initially "use up" or subordinate bizzarreness, suggesting that they are both based on common cognitive processes—with bizarreness pushing forward first and then reflection-lucidity. Similarly, within developing meditative practice (Kornfield, 1979), we seem to have evidence of a sequence alternating between increasing detachment (witness set) and spontaneous and intensified psychedelic/archetypal transformations of focal awareness—a sort of "conversational" interchange within the presentational aspect of symbolic intelligence.

Second Study: Psychophysiology in Some Experienced Lucid Dreamers (Lucidity as a Transitional or Mixed Organismic State)

Our most recent laboratory study was an attempt to apply the same physiological and content-psychological methods to newspaper-recruited, frequent lucid dreamers (more than one per week), thus moving more toward the kind of sample used in other laboratory studies. In addition, we cued subjects for lucidity within REM and asked them to respond to the awareness of ongoing dreaming with the sort of eye-movement signals utilized by LaBerge and others. Thus, in contrast to our first study, where subjects were selected for dream recall and high amplitude alpha during relaxed wakefulness, these subjects were selected exclusively for lucidity. The immediate result, not attributable to cuing alone (see Table 2) was an increase in fully lucid dream recall from the 22% of scorable laboratory awakenings in the first study to 57% in the present study.

Method

Eight subjects spent 1 to 4 nights in the laboratory. They were trained to give three sets of large horizontal eye movements when they were aware of dreaming and told that if, after approximately 15 minutes in REM, they had not signaled spontaneously, an auditory cue would be given that would remind them to become aware of their dreaming. They were to give three sets of eye-movement signals immediately after that cue was heard and to signal again after approximately 30 seconds if they were aware of being in a dream at that point (because the first answering signals might only indicate receptivity to the stimulus rather than lucidity itself). The episode was considered a cued lucid dream (rather than a spontaneously signaled lucid dream or a spontaneous arousal) if two sets of signals were given, separated by at least 30 seconds of REM sleep and followed by a lucid report. In addition, half of the auditory cues were given during relatively high-REM alpha and half during low-REM alpha. Arousals were made within 1 to 2 minutes of all potential lucidity signals (spontaneous or elicited), and our standard interview procedure followed—with subsequent blind scoring by HTH for content and lucidity evaluations.

Results

From Table 1, we see that almost all spontaneous signaling occurred from REM, and the dreamer usually remained in REM until awakened—as one would expect from our own previous work and that of LaBerge and Hearne, demonstrating the REM specificity of lucid dreaming. The picture is quite different, if fortuitously so, with the experimenter-cued episodes. Despite attempts to adapt subjects to the cue during pretesting and allowing each subject to select a comfortable level, cuing typically either awakened the subject directly or left a mixed record, showing both REM and arousal indexes. Waking was seen almost immediately in 44% of the auditory cuing in high-alpha REM. Although such arousals often disrupted REM and although virtually all lucid dream reports were initiated during unambiguous recordings, lucid and/or nonlucid dreaming often continued whether the subject was physiologically awake or asleep. In other words, the EEG record could clearly indicate physiological arousal, but the subjective report need not have reflected that discontinuity.

One is reminded of the dissociation between subjective and objective indicators at sleep onset (Oswald, 1962) and more generally of the "transitional" or "mixed" indicators that characterize many altered state settings, that is, normative inconsistencies between different physiological measures and subjective and behavioral reports.

Along these lines, one of our more curious findings was the occurrence of "contentless" REM lucidity, predominantly but not entirely from one subject. Here, the cue elicited an awareness of "being in REM" as a kind of physical state but without ongoing dream content (although the subject sensed that isolated imagery sequences could easily develop into ordinary dreaming). About half of these episodes, reminiscent of Lewin's (1958) "blank dreams", occurred in unambiguous REM and about half in physiological (but not psychological)

Table 1. Electrophysiological Data

		Presignal state (%)			Postsignal prearousal state (%)				Dream reports				
	(n)	REM	A	R–A	REM	A	R–A	R–II	% Lucid	% Preld	% Nonld	X̄ Clouding	X̄ Hallucination
Spontaneous signal	(14)	86	7	7	86	14			64	27	9	1.1	1.3
Cued hi alpha	(16)	88	6	6	19	44	31	6	43	21	36	1.4	2.6
Cued low alpha	(15)	100			20	27	47	6	69	12	19	1.1	1.8
Spontaneous arousal	(4)	100							50	0	50	3.5	4.5
Unscorable	(2)				Present study					51	21	22	
					Ogilvie et al. (1982)					22	38	40	

wakefulness. It was as though the potential trade-off between lucid self-awareness and dream participation went to the extreme of lucidity at the price of no content whatsoever.

Whether because our subjects now approximated the sort of "star" lucid dreamers most typically studied in other laboratory work or because of the effects of cuing and the concentration on signaling, the alpha level during REM did not discriminate lucid from nonlucid dream reports in this study. Indeed, the spontaneous signaling episodes show lucidity and content profiles that are most similar to the cued low-alpha arousals. Consistent with our previous work, however, high alpha was associated with dream bizarreness—although here the relation between hallucinosis and alpha tended to be bimodal ($N = 47$, $df = 2$, hallucinosis: $\chi^2 = 6.82$, $p < .05$; clouding: $\chi^2 = 6.06$, $p < .05$). The relations between lucidity and bizarreness were not significant in this study, although the most extremely bizarre dreams here tended to be fully lucid.

Again, when we compared the combined dreams from this highly lucid sample to previous nonlucid laboratory norms in terms of our specific categories of bizarreness, it was apparent that this entire sample also shows enhanced bizarreness, especially in the more extreme visual transformations and intrusions, unlikely somatic and auditory content, memory anomalies within the dream, awareness of gaps in waking recall, and observational/detached attitude (for composite factors, $N = 213$, $df = 2$, clouding: $\chi^2 = 7.52$, $p < .05$; hallucinosis: $\chi^2 = 4.64$, $p < .10$). The shift toward dream lucidity seems to entail the sort of content transformations associated with both waking altered states, imaginative creativity, and classical notions of dream symbolism.

Discussion

It seems relevant that, as our subject selection and signaling procedures approximate more closely to the laboratory work of others while still concentrating on the full range of the resulting nonlucid and lucid records, a new picture of the psychophysiology of lucidity emerges. It suggests a broader natural series for lucid dreaming.

Most lucid dreams developed in the REM state (although 14% of our spontaneous signaling came from wakefulness or REM transitional to wakefulness). Yet we should not forget the commonly described phenomenological and physiological instability of lucid dreams, at least short of that rare degree of laboratory stabilization shown in studies by LaBerge. Most lucid dreaming probably does end in slipping back into ordinary dream realism or premature arousal. It is this tenuous, transitional quality, itself so reminiscent of the subjective difficulties of meditation practice where the meditator struggles back and forth between drowsiness and ordinary everyday obsessions, that we have now located psychophysiologically. Cued as opposed to spontaneous lucidity was especially characterized by this fragmented mixture of waking and REM indexes, with dream lucidity typically continuing into transitional wakefulness. Spontaneously signaled lucid episodes were less transitional between states (86% continued as REM as opposed to only 19.5% following auditory cuing). The cued transition that stops just short of full wakefulness (unlike the more disruptive effect in high-alpha REM) may in itself help trigger lucidity (69 versus 43%), to the extent that the lucid dreamer is normally closer to wakefulness.

This broader transitional context for lucidity is not only consistent with the meditative traditions (where a lucidity-type mentation is definitely not linked to REM) but fits with hypnagogic/sleep-onset research, suggesting that lucid dreams (Tholey, 1983) and out-of-body phenomena (Green, 1973) can occur in any prolonged transition between waking and sleep. Current attempts (Ogilvie & Wilkinson, 1984) to sharpen the sleep onset/offset definition, based on behavioral and respiratory measures, should be important for future lucidity research.

The failure of other laboratories to report the alpha effect may have been further clarified: As mentioned, specific filtering for the alpha–theta bands is crucial (Tyson, *et al.,* 1984), and the effect *may* be developmentally linked to subjects whose predominant style of dreaming is prelucid. But the disruption of REM sleep with cuing (more so in high alpha) must remind us that, at present, we have no idea how methodologies based on concurrent signaling and cuing may affect lucid REM physiology, especially because lucid dreamers often have to strive against the tendency toward full awakening to hold onto their tenuous lucidity. Quite conceivably, the special effort involved in signaling alone could modify the background conditions leading to lucidity, inadvertently creating hybrid laboratory forms.

Only studies that directly compare the LaBerge-type concurrent signaling methods with more standard, noninterventionist postwaking interview methods, using a broad range of lucid and nonlucid subjects, will be able to assess the methodological artifacts to which both methods may be vulnerable (unintentionally narrowing the range of REM available for lucidity versus any demand features of laboratory postwaking interviews). Until both approaches are pursued with separate groups in the same experiment, any specific physiology of lucid REM (let alone non-REM lucidity) remains problematic.

Yet we have seen how the broader range of lucidity emerges from a state or setting that is a transitional, unusually prolonged mixture of normally discrepant physiological, behavioral, and subjective indexes. In differing combinations, meditation, the hypnagogic state, night terrors, catatonic states, and even hypnosis (with its EEG of normal wakefulness combined with behavioral indications of detached immobility and spontaneous hypnagogiclike imaginative phenomena) all show such a transitional or "trance" stabilization of typically discordant criteria. In fact, meditation research shows a wide variability in EEG—from the most common finding of unusually prolonged alpha/theta recordings to unusually stabilized beta and sleeplike delta patterns—often mixed with autonomic indexes of markedly low arousal, behavioral detachment, and subjective "lucidity'' (Woolfolk, 1975). Altered states of consciousness seem to emerge from such transitional states, varying considerably in terms of whether mentation is narrowed and concentrated or broadened and ''lucidly'' opened and whether the overall configuration is avoidant/defensive or an enhancement/intensification of a positive symbolic capacity. It remains to address later how it would be that the prolonged, transitional mixture of the sleep/wakefulness organizations could make contact with a normally masked ''mentality'' based on abstract presentational symbolism.

Our second study, then, descriptively locates lucidity within a broader psychophysiological context than has been seen in previous laboratory studies. Stabilized lucid dreaming can occur entirely within REM, yet Green's phenomenological accounts emphasize the more transitional, shifting state that we have here located physiologically. By examining all episodes of cued and spontaneous arousal in subjects who had a developed lucid capacity, the present study captured more of the natural range of lucid dreams and reaffirmed—in this broader psychophysiological context—its close analogy with meditational states.

Third Study: Dream Bizarreness and Lucidity in Long-Term Meditators[1]

In this study, the first author, with Barbara McLeod, looked more directly at our postulated relationship between meditative involvement, dream bizarreness, and the lucidity continuum in long-term meditators who were asked to keep a dream diary over a 30-day period. Previous studies have found increased dream recall with long- and short-term meditative practice (Buzby & DeKoninck, 1980; Reed, 1978), along with enhanced ratings of bizarreness (Buzby & DeKoninck, 1980; Faber, Saayman, & Touyz, 1978), but none have looked for the interrelation of bizarreness, lucidity, and meditation that is crucial to any view that lucidity *is* a form of meditation and that dream bizarreness also reflects an aspect of the imaginal-presentational intelligence involved in that development. We have already cited evidence (qualitative and quantitative) for a complex curvilinear relation between the lucidity continuum and bizarreness, and, like Hoffman and McCarley (1980), we found significantly enhanced bizarreness categories in our laboratory prelucid dreams (Study 1). Here we tried to move closer to the notion that to be lucid in one's dreams is to meditate, and vice versa.

Method

307 dreams were collected from 18 long-term meditators (14 females and 4 males, average age 36.1, range 24–50). They had spent an average of 5.1 years

[1] We would like to thank Venerable Khenpo Karthar Rinpoche of Karma Triyana Dharmachakra, Woodstock, NY, and Cho Je Lama Namse Rinpoche of Karma Kargyu Buddhist Meditation Centre, Toronto, Ontario, for their permission to conduct this study.

in some form of meditative practice (7 months to 17 years)—10 subjects in the Karma Kargyu lineage of Tibetan Buddhism and the rest in a variety of Yogic and Zen groups. These subjects were asked to rate each dream as in whole or part, lucid, control/prelucid, or nonlucid and to provide estimates of their total lucid, control, and prelucid dreams over the past year. Each reported dream was assigned to the 7-point lucidity rating continuum presented in Study 1. (In retrospect, as will be seen later, it would have been better to add further levels for control alone and a highest stage of lucidity combined with control.) Following Gackenbach's (1978) suggestions on "balance" in lucid dreams, subjects also rated each dream on whether they recalled felt limb movement, voices, and nonverbal sounds. They also rated the overall meaningfulness and interest of their dreams and whether, within or outside meditative practice, they had made any attempts to modify their dreams. All dreams were rated in terms of the bizarreness categories first presented in Hunt et al. (1982) and so can be compared to the normative data therein. Ratings were done by the first author and Barbara McLeod, and doubtful cases were arbitrated.

Results

Initially, the question arises whether these subjects have enhanced dream lucidity compared to nonmeditating control groups. The answer seems to be a guarded "yes." We compared the past-year estimates of our subjects with those of a sample of 61 subjects from a previous study of dream bizarreness. Although the latter were preselected in terms of good dream recall (three or more dreams per week), there were no significant differences in dream recall between these two groups. Our meditating group estimated 42.8 fully lucid dreams, 18.4 pre-lucid, and 56.1 control (without lucidity) over the past year compared with 34.1, 34.0, and 24.6 for the nonlucid good recallers. Although the meditators' lucidity was not significantly greater than that of the good recallers ($t = 1.59$), their estimated control dreams, which during the diary period were mostly lucid as well, were significantly greater ($t = 5.19$, $p < .01$) and their prelucid significantly less than the good recallers ($t = 2.93$, $P < .01$). Given the correlational findings to be reported later, showing stronger relations between control and bizarreness and control and meditation than for lucidity, this pattern of difference between meditators and controls in terms of the lucidity continuum does suggest that our meditators have developed further along that continuum than the good dream recallers.

Table 2 shows the profile of dream bizarreness categories for the meditation sample. Because we had a large enough sample of dreams, it is possible for this study to consider the subcategories of bizarreness more specifically and to separate lucid from prelucid/control reports. These can now be compared to a range of "home recall" samples, that is, normative dream diaries, the most fantastic dreams recalled by normative subjects, and the dreams of Jung. Because no

Table 2. Categories of Dream Bizarreness in Lucid and Nonlucid Dreams: Percentage of Dreams with One or More (and Two or More) Anomalies

Scoring categories	Total Meditation sample (N=307) 18 subjects		Lucid (N=71)		Prelucid and control (N=79)		Nonlucid (N=157)		Normative home recall (N=479) 47 subjects		Most fantastic (N=35) 35 subjects		Jung's (N=34)	
	1	(2+)	1	(2+)	1	(2+)	1	(2+)	1	(2+)	1	(2+)	1	(2+)
Hallucinosis: Percept Transformations														
Visual														
Form[a]	26	(9)	38	(17)	24	(8)	21	(6)	13	(2)	43	(14)	24	(9)
Content 1[b]	28	(6)	25	(4)	35	(6)	25	(6)	26	(7)	43	(3)	15	(3)
Content 2	18	(3)	14	(3)	15	(1)	21	(3)	14	(1)	34	(11)	53	(12)
Content 3	48	(25)	38	(18)	42	(25)	56	(28)	27	(8)	54	(26)	32	(12)
1,2,3 combined	65	—	49	—	67	—	72	—	47	—	86	—	80	—
Somatic														
Form	10	(3)	20	(7)	10	(3)	4	(1)	4	(0)	9	(0)	0	
Combined content	23	—	17	—	17	—	30	—	10	—	43	—	9	—
Auditory														
Content and form	30	—	35	—	23	—	32	—	14	—	26	—	32	—
Clouding/confusion														
Abrupt change in scene, gaps	33	(11)	28	(7)	23	(3)	43	(18)	20	(6)	51	(14)	18	(3)
Confusion in thought[c]	60	(24)	61	(28)	54	(20)	63	(25)	41	(17)	54	(31)	35	(9)
Memory within[d]	31	(5)	44	(6)	30	(5)	33	(11)	15	(1)	29	(9)	12	(3)
Memory about[e]	29	(3)	17	(1)	23	(5)	40	(5)	30	(4)	31	(14)	9	(0)
General														
Uncanny emotion	5	(0)	9	(0)	3	(0)	4	(0)	4	(0)	17	(0)	38	(0)
Mythic/overinclusive thought	12	(4)	14	(6)	15	(6)	8	(1)	3	(0)	26	(6)	38	(6)
Bizarre personification[f]	10	(0)	18	(0)	8	(0)	8	(0)	4	(0)	34	(9)	53	(9)
Observational attitude	17	(0)	24	(0)	10	(0)	23	(0)	10	(0)	20	(3)	15	(0)

[a] Psychedelic transformations of formal properties of vision (Klüver).
[b] Content 1, 2, and 3 represent degrees of unlikeliness in objects perceived, without formal distortion.
[c] Disorganization and confusion in reasoning, irrational insights.
[d] Anomaly of memory within the dream.
[e] Difficulties in detailed recall after awakening.
[f] Uncannily fascinating or terrifying others, strange creatures, animism.

single statistic encompasses all these samples, we will proceed descriptively and consider only the more obvious variations.

Considering the combined dreams of the entire meditation sample, it is clear that our meditators report strikingly bizarre dreams. These dreams often exceed the level of our second laboratory study and are comparable in most categories only to the single most fantastic dreams recalled by normative subjects and to the psychedelic/archetypal dreams of Jung in his autobiography, *Memories, Dreams, Reflections*. Especially noteworthy are the elevations in the most qualitatively bizarre or transformed categories within the overall "hallucinosis" factor—visual and somatic form (based on Klüver-type (1966) transformations of light and shape, geometricizations, multiplications, and condensations), somatic form (similar formal changes in body perception, including flying), and the most extreme type of out-of-place "content" intrusions (level 3), including normatively infrequent auditory anomalies (recalled dialogue inappropriate to or unlikely in the dream setting). Within the composite clouding-confusional dimension of bizarreness, our sample shows striking elevations in sudden changes of scene (gaps), anomalies and confusions in thinking, and anomalies of recall *within* the ongoing dream.

Separating lucid, prelucid/control and nonlucid dreams tells a still more specific and important story—especially with the psychedelic/archetypal transformations that, we have argued elsewhere (Hunt *et al.*, 1982), show a radical intrusion of abstract, visual-spatial imaginative processes into the fabric of normative dreaming. Here, it is the fully lucid dreams that show a marked elevation in visual and somatic form, both of which are especially rare in all dream samples (lucid and nonlucid) hitherto investigated and far more typical of psychedelic drugs. Other intrinsically bizarre categories (i.e., descriptions of uncanny-numinous feeling, mythic-metaphysical preoccupations, and the presence of archetypal/parataxic beings in the dream) seem unusually prominent in the lucid dreams of the meditators, whereas the more "normative" hallucinations (content intrusions levels 1, 2, 3) are now more characteristic of their nonlucid dreams. (It should be noted that, in previous studies, all these categories normally vary together.) The unusually high degree of clouding-confusion in the sample now divides between sudden scene shifts (gaps) and difficulties in postwaking recall, which are characteristic of nonlucidity, and memory anomalies within the ongoing dream that go with lucidity.

These differences and the interesting lack of differentiation between lucidity and nonlucidity in terms of confusional thinking confirms our earlier suggestion (Hunt *et al.*, 1982) that, in the context of incipient lucidity, "clouding" anomalies can be of two sorts: the "normal" delirium of nonlucid dreams and the confusions *caused* by the shift toward lucidity. Cognitive anomalies associated here with lucidity comprise sudden intuitive knowings without any natural basis in the dream setting and those mnemic effects where the dreamer reports being in "a" house or "a" school, possibly with dream-specific false memories to explain the location but generally with the alien setting accepted without question (rated under memory within). Both these effects have the sort of "bare presencing" or "crystalline" quality described in meditative and peak experience and confirm the need for a further separation of the subcategories of dream clouding because pro- and antilucidity phenomena are included in the same groupings. Certainly it seems clear that lucid dreams are not based on an approximation to the cognitive orientation of wakefulness (see also Gillespie, 1984).

Pearson correlations based on average ratings for each subject fall into two clusters, one organized around years spent in meditative practice and the other around hours spent meditating per day, which were in turn orthogenal to each other. Thus, past-year lucidity estimates and lucidity ratings in the dream diary were significantly associated ($N = 18$, $r = .63$, $p < .01$). The former went significantly with meditation in years ($r = .67$, $p < .002$) and the latter marginally ($r = .45$, $p < .06$). Lucidity ratings correlate significantly with visual form (.51), somatic form (.58), and significantly against gaps ($-.48$) and marginally negative with combined visual content ($-.43$). Meditation in years also correltaed significantly with visual form (.56) and somatic form (.62). Likewise, the past-year lucidity estimates went significantly with visual form (.47) and somatic form (.67). Contrary to our previous practice of combining control with prelucidity but consistent with our earlier discussion of this sample, past-year dream control estimates correlated better with meditation and psychedelic transformations (visual and somatic form) than lucidity *per se*. However, neither control nor lucidity estimates were related to prelucidity. Lucidity estimates did not correlate significantly with attempts to become lucid or to change one's dreams, either within meditative practice or in general. This suggests that whatever dream changes long-term meditation may bring cannot be explained in terms of any attempt to so modify one's dreams. Lucidity and heightened bizarreness would come as an automatic effect of long-term practice.

On the other hand, time spent in daily meditation tended to correlate with all measures of sensory detail. Thus, time in daily practice was significantly related to our own category of sensory detail (specific mention of nonanomalous but vivid color, shadows, other details of "perceptual grain") (.66) and to diary ratings of sounds other than voices (.49) but not to lucidity or years of meditation.

A varimax rotated factor matrix on a somewhat reduced list of variables confirmed these two patterns: a Clarity-Detail factor, including hours per day of meditation and Gackenbach's content indexes of "balance" (46% of variance), and a Lucidity/Years in Meditation/Psychedelic Content factor (39% of variance). It does seem that different aspects of Green's initial phenomenology of lucid dreaming can be isolated and will be associated with various features of meditative practice. A third factor (15% of variance) seemed to show that, for a group of subjects, the longer one meditates per day, the less meaningful one's dreams and the more readily they are forgotten on awakening. These associations may reflect the observation (Reed, 1978, and anecdotal reports here) that, for some subjects, possibly where dreaming is typically more troubled and confusing, meditation can initially decrease dream recall and reduce bizarreness.

Discussion

Of course, a correlational study cannot show that lucidity *is* a meditative state, but we do seem to have picked up evidence of the close relation between actual meditative practice and dream lucidity, along with indications (across our three studies) of the curvilinear relation between lucidity and dream bizarreness already implied in the anecdotal literature. Among our good recallers, it was prelucidity that was associated with elevations in the more standard bizarreness categories, but that relation (confirmed also by Hoffman and McCarley) drops out with the high-lucidity subjects of our second laboratory study. Finally, long-term meditators show an enhancement of the lucidity continuum and an association of that lucidity with bizarreness categories almost never encountered in normative dreaming. Still, it does not follow from our equation of lucidity and meditative states that meditators alone would show high degrees of dream lucidity: The spontaneous unfolding of lucid and control dreams makes sense as a specific, often unsought, form of that transformation that also constitutes the more general aim of the meditative traditions.

In keeping with our view that the lucid dream is the equivalent of a spontaneous meditative balance involving a mixed or transitional organismic state (Goleman's "fifth state"), not only did our meditators report rare archetypal/psychedelic dream transformations, but their dreams were actually more difficult to rate than average, stretching and challenging the scoring system for dream anomalies. Indeed, some of these subjects were simply not sure themselves how to categorize certain of their dreams, which were often about meditating or receiving teachings from their guru. They could not tell in retrospect whether they were awake and meditating or having what we had defined for them as a "lucid dream."

CONCLUSIONS: THE COGNITIVE BASES OF THE LUCIDITY CONTINUUM IN THE DEVELOPMENT OF PRESENTATIONAL-METAPHORIC THINKING

Self-Reference and Transitional Organismic States

The phenomenal series we have been considering—from the lucidity continuum to the varieties of meditation and including OBE, near-death experience, autoscopic hallucinations, and the autosymbolism of the hypnagogic period—

seems to involve a marked enhancement of "self-reference" (Neisser's "turning around on the schemata," Mead's "taking the role of the other," Hofstadter's "recursion"). This self-reference is not subordinated to the more predominant, socially "adaptive" uses of our symbolic capacity but develops for its own sake as one side of an abstract presentational symbolism.

An initial challenge for this cognitive approach comes from the fact that the lucidity series seems to rest on a change in organismic state or arousal, with subtypes emerging from those very high *or* very low levels of physiological arousal that are "transitional" to literal unconsiousness. So striking are the somatic and physiological correlations of these states that neurophysiological-arousal models have always proved especially tempting in the altered state literature.

Yet a fully developed cognitive perspective also *entails* such physiological features. Self-reference, for its own sake, goes against the pragmatic grain of the "everyday life world," and the predominance of representational symbolism in the latter seems to obtain primarily within an "average" range of waking physio-logical arousal. The shift to a broader awareness of the expressive properties of context would thus be favored by levels of very high or low arousal that inhibit the functional bias of the organism. Such "extreme" organismic situations, just short of unconsciousness, would allow the direct release of what, in all societies, constitutes a nondominant but culturally significant use of *intelligence*. The more diffuse and global ("microgenetically primitive," see Hunt & Chefurka, 1976; Hunt, 1984) the resulting expressive patterns, the more potentially abstract and encompassing their presentational meaning. This sequence would culminate in the "white light of the void" of classical mysticism, felt as symbolically encom-passing and meaning "everything." The functional, generally conventionalized reference of representational symbolism is turned (so to speak) "inside out," and the normally embedded and tacit presentational-imaginal aspect of all sym-bolism (Arnheim, 1969) will stand forth in its own right. This makes "altered states" of decided relevance for general cognitive theory.

Dream Bizarreness and Lucidity as Exteriorizations of "Conversational Roles" in the Imaginal Dialogue of Presentational Symbolism

On the one hand, we can distinguish between two sides of symbolism: the relatively pragmatic, automatized, and representational and the more immediate-ly "sensed," presentational, and imaginal, which in the present context includes both dream lucidity and dream bizarreness and is generally more explicitly self-referential or autosymbolic (Van Dusen, 1972).

However, following Mead on "taking the role of the other" or "self-reference'' as the basis for *all* symbolic operations, we can also distinguish two "phases'' or "roles'' within the "interior conversation'' of thought (whether its medium is verbal or imaginal-gestural). Any conversation alternates between two roles—one receptive or receiving and the other actively articulated or sending. The latter requires an ongoing self-referential monitoring that is specific and inevitably narrowing, so that we necessarily lose context. The receptive role, although inevitably more detached, allows a broader sense of perspective, because self-reference is not subordinated to managing active communication.

We can certainly see the lucidity series as the unfolding of the "receptive'' role or "observing self'' (Deikman, 1982) within presentational symbolism. But we can go further in these terms and address the developmental interaction between lucidity and bizarreness demonstrated over our studies: Overt dream and altered state bizarreness, which show the structures of symbolic imagination, would constitute the relatively less self-conscious, actively communicating role. The transformation of dreaming by abstract presentational symbolism would develop like any conversation, showing phases of mutual facilitation, competition, alternation, and final integration between the receptive role of lucidity and the actively articulated patterns of specific bizarreness. Prelucidity and bizarreness develop together, with a competition at the initial point of lucidity—as if both lucidity and bizarreness were aspects of the same visual-spatial imaginative process. Yet, with fully stabilized lucidity and dream control (here, as a potential function of years of meditative practice), levels of enhanced bizarreness/ symbolization return that are qualitatively distinct from normative dream anomalies. "Sending'' and "receiving'' thus alternate, with the stabilized witness set of lucidity functioning like an exaggeration of the waiting, receiving role in any conversation, and so calling forth a maximum answering expression from the "other'' (as the various mandala and luminosity patterns that constitute the highest abstraction within the presentational mode). These stages of presentational cognition, probably more accessible in dreaming than wakefulness, have the structure of a conversation that may develop over a lifetime.

Lucidity and the Meditative Attitude

Lucid dreams and their related series, with their balance of detached self-reference and active imaginal involvement, can be most parsimoniously understood as brief and often spontaneous realizations of the state of mind sought within the meditative traditions. The lucid dreamer is living within the dream in the released, detached manner, with its sense of full "felt reality'' and "being there,'' that is the goal within wakefulness of "insight'' meditative practice. Consideration of lucid dreams in terms of phenomenal content, psychophysiology, and cognitive process all lead to and confirm this conclusion. In turn, these meditative traditions can be understood as exemplifications of the development open to an abstract form of presentational symbolism—both "receiving" (lucidity) and "sending" (white light experiences), unfolding toward a more and more inclusive sense of "context." Whether our narrowly functional age specifically lacks this contextual intelligence is an empirical question. It is certainly a possibility.

REFERENCES

Arnheim, R. (1969). *Visual thinking*. Berkeley: University of California Press.

Arnold-Foster, M. (1921). *Studies in dreams*. London: Allen & Unwin.

Banquet, J. (1973). Spectral analysis of the EEG in meditation. *Electroencephalography and Clinical Neurophysiology, 35,* 143–151.

Buzby, K., & DeKoninck, J. (1980). Short-term effects of strategies for self regulation on personality dimensions and dream content. *Perceptual and Motor Skills, 50,* 751–765.

Castaneda, C. (1974). *Tales of power*. New York: Simon & Schuster.

Chang, G. (Ed. & Trans.). (1963). *Teachings of Tibetan Yoga*. New York: University Books.

Deikman, A. (1982). *The observing self: Mysticism and psychotherapy*. Boston: Beacon Press.

Dorus, E., Dorus, W., & Rechtschaffen, A. (1971). The incidence of novelty in dreams. *Archives of General Psychiatry, 25,* 364–368.

Edelson, M. (1975). *Language and interpretation in psychoanalysis*. New Haven: Yale University Press.

Faber, P., Saayman, G. S., & Touyz, S. (1978). Meditation and archetypal content of nocturnal dreams. *Journal of Analytical Psychology, 23,* 1–22.

Foulkes, D., & Vogel, G. (1965). Mental activity at sleep onset. *Journal of Abnormal Psychology, 70,* 231–243.

Fox, O. (1975). *Astral projection*. Secaucus, NJ: Citadel.

Freud, S. (1965). *The interpretation of dreams*. New York: Avon. (original work published 1900)

Gackenbach, J. (1978). *A personality and cognitive style analysis of lucid dreaming*. Unpublished doctoral dissertation, Virginia Commonwealth University.

Gackenbach, J., Curren, R., LaBerge, S., Davidson, D., & Maxwell, P. (1983, June). *Intelligence, creativity, and personality differences between individuals who vary in self-reported lucid dreaming frequency*. Paper presented at the annual meeting of the American Association for the Study of Mental Imagery, Vancouver, BC.

Gackenbach, J., Prill, S., & Westrom, P. (1983). The relationship of the lucid dreaming ability to mental imagery experiences and skills. *Lucidity Letter, 2*(4), 4–6.

Geschwind, N. (1965). Disconnection syndromes in animals and man. *Brain, 88,* 237–297, 585–644.

Gillespie, G. (1984, March). *Problems related to experimentation while dreaming lucidly*. Paper presented at the annual meeting of the Eastern Psychological Association, Baltimore, MD.

Goleman, D. (1972). The Buddha on meditation and states of consciousness. *Journal of Transpersonal Psychology, 4,* 1–44.

Goodenough, D., Shapiro, A., Holden, M., & Steinschriben, L. (1959). A compairson of "dreamers" and "nondreamers": Eye movements, electroencephalograms, and the recall of dreams. *Journal of Abnormal and Social Psychology, 59,* 295–302.

Green, C. (1968). *Lucid dreams*. London: Hamish Hamilton.

Green, C. (1973). *Out-of-the-body experiences*. New York: Ballantine.

Harroldson, E. (1982). Out-of-body and lucid experiences. *Lucidity Letter, 1*(3),6.

Hearne, K. (1983). Features of lucid dreams: Questionnaire data and content analyses. *Journal of Lucid Dream Research, 1,* 3–20.

Hoffman, E., & McCarley, R. (1980). Bizarreness and lucidity in REM sleep dreams. *Sleep Research, 9,* 134. (Abstract)

Hofstadter, D. (1979). *Gödel, Escher, Bach: An eternal golden braid.* New York: Basic Books.

Hughlings-Jackson, J. (1958). Evolution and dissolution of the nervous system. In J. Taylor (Ed.), *Selected writings of John Hughlings-Jackson. Vol. 2* (pp.45–75). London: Staples Press.

Hunt, H. (1984). A cognitive psychology of mystical and altered state experience. *Perceptual and Motor Skills, 58,* 467–513.

Hunt, H., & Chefurka, C. (1976). A test of the psychedelic model of altered states of consciousness. *Archives of General Psychiatry, 33,* 867–876.

Hunt, H. (with Ogilvie, R., Belicki, K., Belicki, D., Atalick, E.). (1982). Forms of dreaming. *Perceptual and Motor Skills, 54,* 559–633.

James, W. (1902). *The varieties of religious experience.* Garden City, NJ: Dolphin Books.

Jung, C. G. (1962). *Memories, dreams, reflections.* New York: Pantheon.

Kornfield, J. (1979). Intensive insight meditation. *Journal of Transpersonal Psychology, 11,* 41–58.

Klüver, H. (1966). *Mescal and mechanisms of hallucination.* Chicago: University of Chicago Press.

LaBerge, S., Nagel, L., Dement, W., & Zarcone, V. (1981). Lucid dreaming verified by volitional communication during REM sleep. *Perceptual and Motor Skills, 52,* 727–732.

Lewin, B. (1958). *Dreams and the uses of regression.* New York: International Universities Press.

Luk, C. (Ed. and Trans.). (1964). *The secrets of Chinese meditation.* New York: Samuel Weiser.

Lukianowicz, N. (1958). Autoscopic hallucinations. *Archives of Neurology and Psychiatry, 80,* 199–220.

Maslow, A. (1962). *Towards a psychology of being.* Princeton: Van Nostrand.

Mead, G. H. (1934). *Mind, self, society.* Chicago: University of Chicago Press.

Neisser, U. (1976). *Cognition and reality.* San Francisco: Freeman.

Nigro, G., & Neisser, U. (1983). Point of view in personal memories. *Cognitive Psychology, 15,* 467–482.

Ogilvie, R., & Wilkinson, R. (1984). The detection of sleep onset: Behavioral and physiological convergence. *Psychophysiology, 21,* 510–520.

Ogilvie, R., Hunt, H., Sawicki, C., & McGowan, K. (1978). Searching for lucid dreams. *Sleep Research, 7,* 165. (Abstract)

Ogilvie, R., Hunt, H., Tyson, P., Lucescu, M., Jeakins, D. (1982). Lucid dreaming and alpha activity: A preliminary report. *Perceptual and Motor Skills, 55,* 795–808.

Oswald, I. (1962). *Sleeping and waking.* New York: Elsevier.

Rechtschaffen, A. (1978). The single-mindedness of dreams. *Sleep, 1,* 97–109.

Rechtschaffen, A., & Kales, A. (Eds.). (1968). *A manual of standardized terminology, techniques, and scoring system for sleep stages of human subjects.* University of California at Los Angeles: Brain Information Service/Brain Research Institute.

Reed, H. (1978). Improved dream recall associated with meditation. *Journal of Clinical Psychology, 34,* 150–156.

Ring, K. (1980). *Life at death.* New York: Coward, McCann, & Geoghegan.

Schacter, D. (1976). The hypnagogic state: A critical review of the literature. *Psychological Bulletin, 83,* 452–481.

Silberer, H. (1951). Report on a method of eliciting and observing certain symbolic hallucination-phenomena. In D. Rapaport (Ed.), *Organization and pathology of thought* (pp. 195–207). New York: Columbia University Press. (Original work published 1909).

Snyder, F. (1970). The phenomenology of dreaming. In L. Madow & L. Snow (Eds.), *The psychodynamic implications of the physiological studies in dreams* (pp. 124–151). Springfield, IL: Thomas.

Sylvia, W., Clark, P., & Monroe, L. (1978). Dream reports of subjects high and low in creative ability. *Journal of General Psychology, 99,* 205–211.

Thera, N. (1962). *The heart of Buddhist meditation.* London: Rider.

Tholey, P. (1983). Techniques for inducing and manipulating lucid dreams. *Perceptual and Motor Skills, 57,* 79–90.

Tyson, P., Ogilvie, R., & Hunt, H. (1984). Lucid, prelucid, and nonlucid dreams related to the amount of EEG alpha activity during REM sleep. *Psychophysiology, 21,* 442–451.

Van Dusen, W. (1972). *The natural depth in man.* New York: Harper & Row.

Van Eeden, F. (1969). A study of dreams. In C. Tart (Ed.), *Altered states of consciousness* (pp.145–158). New York: Wiley. (Original work published 1913).

Walker, K. (1965). *A study of Gurdjieff's teaching.* London: Joanathon Cape.

Whiteman, J. (1961). *The mystical life.* London: Faber & Faber.

Whitton, T. (1978). EEG frequency patterns associated with hallucinations in schizophrenics and "creativity" in normals. *Biological Psychiatry, 13,* 123–133.

Wittgenstein, L. (1979). *Remarks on Frazer's Golden Bough.* Atlantic Highlands, NJ: Humanities Press.

Woolfolk, R. (1975). Psychological correlates of meditation. *Archives of General Psychiatry 32,* 1326–1333.

18

Action and Representation in Ordinary and Lucid Dreams

WYNN SCHWARTZ and MARY GODWYN

INTRODUCTION TO CONCEPTS

When we dream, we experience a world of various objects, processes, events, concepts, and relationships. These experiences occur in a context or realm of fantasy. When we are awake, we also experience objects, processes, events, concepts, and relationships, although these experiences happen in the more inclusive context of the real world. Objects, processes, events, concepts, and relationships are what constitute a world, whether fantasized or real, created or discovered (Ossorio, 1978). This chapter will explicate the special case of the lucid, or self-aware, dream. Self-awareness is possible in a lucid dream because the dreamer is able to recognize the context of fantasy within the context of the real world; the dreamer therefore recognizes the dream as a dream. Furthermore, the dreamer has the potential to reflect on his or her own motivations for deciding on courses of action within the dream. Within the lucid dream, the dreamer can act self-consciously. We will outline the distinguishing features of both the realm of fantasy and the more inclusive context of the real world. Although it may seem tempting to explore these concepts from the perspective of a dual world conceptualization (that is, two independent and coexisting worlds: one of fantasy and one of reality), it has been apparent, at least since the writings of Hume (1739/1978) and more recently Wittgenstein (1953), that it is the real world that begets the world of fantasy. Fantasy requires the foundation of reality.

WYNN SCHWARTZ • Department of Psychiatry, Harvard Medical School at the Cambridge Hospital, Cambridge, MA 02139. MARY GODWYN • Boston, Massachusetts.

The real world is inherently a domain of both formal (logical) and empirical (factual) constraints. These constraints are shared in that they are common to all people. Words, meanings, and actions maintain their relative stability because they have the potential to be shared, that is, to have a place in social practice and to allow for public disclosure. The intrapersonal worlds of dream and fantasy logically require a foundation of meaning in the real world to lend them meaningful, communicable, or interpretable content. Systems of meaning arise from social practice whether an individual chooses to disclose his or her meanings or not. The intrapersonal worlds of dream and fantasy require the public and social worlds for their meaningful content and *not* the other way around. This is the familiar reminder of the analytic philosopher that there are no private unsharable languages. Hence, the "real world," as defined for this chapter, is the realm of the public or the potentially sharable and common.

A convention adopted in descriptive psychology (Ossorio, 1978) is to use the concept *reality* to refer to the full range of possible objects, processes, events, and other states of affairs (see also Wittgenstein, 1921/1971). The concept *real world* refers to the actual historical and empirical manifestations of reality's possibilities. The real world, as the context of meaningful representation, is therefore the context in which behavior occurs. In the world of waking action, we sometimes pick and choose our way across the landscape; to the extent we employ the appropriate pragmatic, historical, and conventional limits, we experience the real world. It is on this basis that we recognize or interpret situations and measure our ability to create or change situations. This is implicit in reality testing. The limits present in the social world are different from those in intrapsychic experience of which ordinary dreams are an example. This is not to say that historical or pragmatic constraints have no influence on dreams; but dreams, unlike waking action, are not necessarily limited by pragmatic constraints and often ignore or violate them.

As argued here it is a person's actions in the real world that define his or her meanings and utterances. The real world is the primary context for the development of meaningful expression. The realm of fantasy, like the realm of poetry and art, allows for a range of representation beyond possible real world action; this includes the impossible, the absurd, and the nonsensical. *Where the real world's forms of representation are limited pragmatically, the realms of dream and fantasy are limited only by the semantic and pictorial potential of the dreamer's language and imagery.* Real world representation is shaped by the actor's intrinsic concern with effective and realistic action; such constraints are lacking during the dream. This difference in forms of representation corresponds somewhat to what psychoanalysts mean by the primary- and secondary-process modes of cognition. This is a theme we will return to later because the lucid dream appears to be a special case that sometimes involves both pragmatic real world recognition (reality testing) and semantic-pictorial freedom.

INTENTIONAL AND DELIBERATE ACTION

Lucid dreams appear to overlap some of the categories of action, and, with this in mind, we will explore several key concepts of action. A concern with consequence and effectiveness provides waking action with a different signifi- cance from those actions represented in ordinary and lucid dreams. To clarify these distinctions, we will employ Ossorio's (1981) conceptualization of inten- tional and deliberate actions.

Intentional action is the general case of goal-directed or purposeful behav- ior. Deliberate action is a special case of intentional action in which the actor chooses his or her goals and behaviors from the available options. In the basic case of intentional action, only a goal must be desired, distinguished, and sought. Deliberate action involves a choice among ways of achieving the goal. In order to act deliberately, one must see that there are additional ways of reaching a goal. Deliberate action involves a choice among ways of achieving a goal; therefore the actor may have the eligibility to question his or her motivations, values, and priorities as well as the repercussions of the action before actually acting.

Ossorio (1981) has described persons as intentional actors who are able to observe and describe their actions. Further, they are able to criticize, sometimes deliberately, their actions and descriptions and hence modify their actions. Os- sorio has formed a conceptualization of persons as individuals who are eligible to engage in three interrelated roles of actor, observer-describer, and observer- critic. These three roles make up a self-correcting feedback loop and is what I refer to as a linguisitic self-regulation (Schwartz, 1982). In ordinary waking behavior, the observer–critic role is employed when significant options are en- countered and recognized, that is, when choices are to be made; otherwise, such critical behavior is not generally relevant and, if overemployed, may be a sign of obsessional pathology. But although the wakeful actor may seldom or only occasionally want or need to critique and choose, he or she is always eligible to do so because the role of observer-critic is a basic standing condition of human personality. The eligibility to criticize may be a hallmark of the experience of reality *as* reality. Within the dream, the dreamer has the ability to appraise and criticize; however, this criticism is not in recognition of the broader context of the real world. Such appraisals or criticisms that do recognize the pragmatic and empirical constraints of the real world are referred to by Plotkin and Schwartz (1982) as final-order appraisals. Final-order appraisals are basic to reality testing and employ the temporal structure of episodic memory as the basic context. We will return to this point because this eligibility usually diminishes during sleep except in the special case of the lucid dream.

Final-order description and critique are special cases of intentional action (i.e., a variety of cognizant deliberate action) potentiated by language or lan-guagelike representation (grammar-governed images). Intentional action occurs in nonlinguisitic beings and is the general form of goal-directed animal behavior. Deliberate action, however, is the form of intentional behavior specific to peo-ple. People use language or language-governed images to represent, appraise, and critique the available behavioral options. Because language provides infinite representational possibilities, we may consider the novel, the fantastic, the not-present, and the not-yet or never-to-be-encountered. Of course, language "on holiday" can also allow for a consideration of the nonsensical and the absurd. The central point here is that language or language-governed imagery enables a person to perform "experiments in acting" without having to otherwise perform the deed. With such an attribute, a person can represent to himself or herself both what is there and what is absent, what might be performed and what might not.

Again, in the general case of intentional action, only a goal must be desired, distinguished, and sought. In deliberate action, a choice in ways of achieving the goal is recognized, and various versions, conflicts, and repercussions of the action can be considered; the deliberate actor can act self-consciously. In deliber-ate action, a person may choose not to pursue the goal. Renunciation is a form of deliberate action.

Intentional action involves, in its paradigm case, the performance and achievement that follow from the specific standing conditions of the actor's motivation, knowledge, and skill. The motivation, knowledge, and skill may be unconscious and may correspond to what are sometimes referred to as drives and unconscious fantasies and wishes, insofar as these have actual motivational status. Intentional action is goal-directed action that may be consciously, pre-consciously, or unconsciously performed. Deliberate action involves a choice among appraised alternatives and is usually cognizant behavior.

SELF-AWARENESS AND RESPONSIBILITY

When people engage in a deliberate action, they have the potential to be self-aware. Because deliberate action is action in which the actor chooses on the basis of the merits of alternative behaviors, these actions may often involve self-awareness in that the actor is proceeding with a consideration of his or her own reasons to behave one way rather than another. Of course, people are often mistaken about the nature of their motives and situations, but, in any case, they proceed in relation to what they take their reasons and circumstances to be. But, although deliberate action is conscious behavior, it might not be self-conscious or cognizant (Ossorio, 1981). Note that the consideration of one's motives *as one's motives* is conceptually separate from the desire for a given goal and the actions taken to achieve that goal. Self-awareness is often, though not neces-sarily, present in the deliberate actor. It is conceivable that, in some or perhaps most instances, a person could avoid recognizing his or her values and motives in the choosing of one alternative over another. Deliberate action, then, potentially but not necessarily, involves self-awareness. Although, by definition, deliberate action involves a choice among alternative paths and consciousness aids in presenting the various versions of the actions, such activity can be performed without people paying heed to the fact that the consciousness, the choice, and the motivations are their own.

The capacity to engage in self-conscious deliberate action is, however, a major anchor to the concept of personal responsibility (Schwartz, 1984). We expect that people can regularly act deliberately, and we often hold them responsible for doing so whether they do so or not. Failures to act deliberately are often construed as failures to act in a responsible manner. Although people are not always engaged in deliberate action, in many situations they are expected to be; in such circumstances, they are held accountable by both themselves and others for their actions. Furthermore, whether or not the ordinary dreamer's action is construed to be intentional or deliberate, the dreamer will not be held responsible for this action as one would be held responsible for an act committed in waking life, or possibly, for an act committed in a lucid dream. Above and beyond the fact that an action within a world of fantasy does not hold the same significance as an actual happening, the dreamer is not held culpable for actions within ordinary dreams for two reasons: First, there is a diminished sense of choice regarding the action and the circumstances in which the action is committed, thus reducing the possibility for the dreamer to question and determine his or her own reasons or motivations for action; second, the dreamer does not act self-consciously. The dreamer is unable to compare and contrast the context of the ordinary dream world to the context of the real world, again barring the possibility for the dreamer to consider the realistic boundaries of his or her personality as it may influence the action. The ordinary dreamer is not self-aware. It is not clear in the case of a lucid dream, however, whether the dreamer is culpable. If one dreams lucidly, one may be able to act deliberately, that is, to choose among alternatives, and one is self aware, that is, able to recognize one's circumstances and values.

The recognition of the context of the real world and the ability to act deliberately create both the categories of the culpable and the negligent. Hence, deliberate action is central to part of our experience of blame, shame, and guilt. These considerations will be helpful in illustrating the special freedoms sometimes associated with the lucid dream. Insofar as dreamers hold themselves responsible for their personal characteristics, they may also feel responsible for the content of their dreams, whether or not the dreams are lucid. There is a conceptual difference between responsibility for the chosen and responsibility for one's personal attributes (Schwartz, 1984). One significant difference between the lucid dream and the waking consciousness is that there is more primary-process thinking during the lucid dream. After all, it is a dream and as difficult as it is to control reality during waking action, it is even more difficult to control the primary process of dreaming. But, because our behavior and our dreaming necessarily reflect our personal characteristics, there is always potential for blame.

ORDINARY DREAMS

We expect that people can regularly act deliberately and that the outcome of deliberate actions depends upon the depth and breadth of awareness and the ability to employ relevant pragmatic considerations. Deliberate action usually involves attempted recognition of effective and appropriate courses of behavior. A deliberate action may lead to self-recognition or some critical observation of one's personal values. Usually in waking behavior, Ossorio's "observer–critic" role is the role that is manifested in deliberate action.

In the ordinary dream, the dreamer's ability to critique is diminished. This deficit of deliberate thought and action in ordinary dreams is descriptive of what Freud acknowledged about dreaming when he wrote that "the renunciation of the voluntary direction of the flow of ideas cannot be disputed" (1900/1975, p. 590). In ordinary dreams, we pursue goals with a diminished sense of choice or deliberation, and our actions usually appear represented as nondeliberate intentional actions.

In ordinary dreams, the deficit in deliberation occurs in a correspondence with a diminished concern with the real world, although the dreamer does experience his or her actions as within a world (i.e., a dream world or a world of fantasy). For the duration of the ordinary dream, the dreamer is not aware that the world depicted in the dream is not the real world. In the ordinary dream, the dreamer is presented with constraints and limitations that seem to be out of his or her own control, much like the constraints and limitations inherent in the real world. However, in the world of the ordinary dream, the dreamer often faces these limitations without the sense of choice regarding his or her actions within the dream world. Where the wakeful actor is potentially self-aware and can perform both deliberate and nondeliberate intentional acts, the ordinary dreamer has a diminished or nonexistant potential to act deliberately.

In dreams of all sorts, intentional actions are not limited by pragmatic real-world constraints but only by the semantic and pictorial possibilities inherent in the dreamer's imagination. Deliberation, in contrast, as a waking activity, usually occurs in relation to a sense of the pragmatic constraints of the real world. A person's actions would be hazardous or ineffective if they were not so constrained. The dreamer, on the other hand, is able to operate safely because the issues that generate deliberate thought are less prudently significant when one is asleep. Sleep's temporary freedom from the constraints of reality allows the dreamer to develop a wide range of representation. The range of representation may include the nonsensical and the absurd by virtue of what psychoanalysts call condensation, displacement, and symbolization. The dreamer may act in a context that is a juxtaposition of the imaginary and the real; he or she is not required to attend to reality in order for a dream action to have its intended results.

LUCID DREAMS

The paradigm case of the lucid dreams is as follows: A lucid dream is a dream in which first, the dreamer is self-aware that he or she is acting in the context of a dream, and second, the dreamer is aware that he or she is able to choose or construct alternatives in circumstances and action. Notice that self-awareness and choice are related but separate conditions. In the lucid dream, self-awareness is primary, and choice may follow. Choice and self-awareness are related in that, when we choose, we do so "more or less" in recognition of our personal values, skills, and goals. The crucial difference, then, between the ordinary and the lucid dream is that in the lucid dream the dreamer is self-aware and may be able to act deliberately, that is, with a sense of personal choice, and with the knowledge that he or she is acting within a context of personal creation. It is important to remember that choice and deliberation do not guarantee a successful action even in waking life; consequently, although choice may be one of the hallmarks of the lucid dream, it is secondary to the defining sense of cognizance or self-awareness. And choice is especially problematic in the domain of the primary process. It makes sense, then, that the first critical step in generating a lucid dream or in transforming an ordinary dream into a lucid one is the experience within the dream of some state of affairs that calls attention to the context of the self or of the dream. Lucid dreams are generated when the dreamer is aware that his or her choices can be made in the context of self or dream. Either the perceived *necessity* for choice or the forced recognition of self could generate lucidity.

The limited empirical literature on the lucid dream suggests that they most often occur in the dream setting of anomalies, inconsistencies, and anxieties (Hearne, 1982). This is exactly what we would expect, if there is an important relationship between self-awareness and deliberation. The recognition of an anomaly or an inconsitency presupposes the recognition of a context; an anomaly can only occur within the context of the normal, whether this be the context of the world or of the self (Plotkin & Schwartz, 1982). To recognize a personal anomaly or inconsistency *is* to be self-aware; to recognize an "environmental" anomaly or inconsistency is to be aware of the world.

Similarly, an anxiety may precipitate a lucid dream because to be anxious or in perceived danger is to be in a condition that ordinarily gives a person reason to try to do something else, that is, to choose circumstances that are different from those occurring or impending. Anxiety also makes us self-aware in that it tends to call attention to aspects of ourselves that are threatened. The same circumstances that make us feel threatened, defensive, or awkward, should we encounter them in waking life, may make us lucid when we encounter them when we dream. We are not suggesting that those circumstances that generate unconscious defensive activity and block awareness in waking life will make us lucid when we are asleep but rather that those threats that we already are aware of may create the lucid dream. The interesting possibility that, at times, unconsciously perceived threats may generate lucidity seems reasonable if it is also true that, when we are asleep, our defensive activity wanes. This last possibility opens a door of great psychotherapeutic promise. Could we encounter and do battle in our lucid dreams with those issues we are blind to by day?

Consistent with the preceding formulations, another possible instigator of the lucid dream is for a dream situation to simultaneously present a variety of personally significant objects or goals. The opportunity to achieve the greatly valued goal that is in conflict with another equally important desire may make us lucid. Varied and conflicted opportunity may be as powerful a generator of self-awareness as is recognized threat.

CONCLUSIONS

Three basic ideas have been developed. The first is that, although the general case of action in both waking and dream life is intentional, only in waking life and in the lucid dream do we experience self-awareness and do we act deliberately. The second key distinction is that the observer–critic role of reality testing the effectiveness of an action is generally restricted to waking life but may also characterize the lucid dream. The third point is that the central difference between dreaming and waking activity is that action and representation in the dream are limited semantically or pictorially. In waking life, our choices have to be more or less realistic and must involve historically particular and real subjects, objects, processes, and so on. But, in the lucid dream, the dreamer has both the potential for choice and the freedom of the imaginary. The lucid dreamer may experience the freedom of the "unrealistic" choice. Not only is the lucid dreamer not by necessity bounded by social recognition and consequence, but he or she may create or discover elements and opportunities that the real world does not provide. Because the real world does have choices forbidden by social consequence, the lucid dreamer may entertain those actions even if they can only be enjoyed when they are left in the utter privacy of the dream.

REFERENCES

Freud, S. (1975). The interpretation of dreams. *Standard edition of the complete psychological works of Sigmund Freud* (Vols. 4 & 5). (J. Strackey, Ed. & Trans.). London: Hogarth Press. (Original work published 1900)

Hearne, K. M. T. (1982). Settings and causes of lucidity. *Lucidity Letter, 1,* 2–3.

Hume, D. (1978). *Treatise of human nature* (L. A. Selby-Bigge, Ed.). Oxford: Oxford University Press. (Original work published 1739)

Ossorio, P. G. (1978). *What actually happens.* Columbia, SC: University of South Carolina Press.

Ossorio, P. G. (1981). Outline of descriptive psychology for personality theory and clinical applications. In K. E. David (Ed.), *Advances in descriptive psychology* (Vol. 1) (pp. 57–81). Greenwich, CT: JAI Press.

Plotkin, W. B., & Schwartz, W. R. (1982). A conceptualization of hypnosis: Exploring the place of appraisal and anomaly in behavior and experience. In K. E. Davis (Ed.), *Advances in descriptive psychology* (Vol. 2) (pp. 139–199). Greenwich, CT: JAI Press.

Schwartz, W. R. (1982). The problem of other possible persons: Dolphins, primates, and aliens. In K. E. Davis (Ed.), *Advances in descriptive psychology* (Vol. 2, pp. 31–55). Greenwich, CT: JAI Press.

Schwartz, W. R. (1984). The two concepts of action and responsibility in psychoanalysis. *Journal of the American Psychoanalytic Association, 32.*

Wittenstein, L. (1971). *Tractatus logico-philosophicus.* (D. F. Pears & B. F. McGuiness, Trans.). New York: The Humanities Press. (Original work published 1921)

Wittenstein, L. (1953). *Philosophical investigations* (G. E. M. Anscombe, Trans.). New York: Macmillan.

19

Dream Psychology
Operating in the Dark

ALAN MOFFITT, ROBERT HOFFMANN, JANET
MULLINGTON, SHEILA PURCELL, ROSS PIGEAU,
and ROGER WELLS

The questions we want to address concern the scientific significance of lucid dreaming, especially for our understanding of the function of dreaming. There is an emerging consensus that scientific dream psychology has not lived up to the potential that motivated much of the research following the discovery of REM sleep in 1953 (see Antrobus, 1978). Foulkes, for example (1978, 1982, 1983a,b, 1985) has claimed that the three foundation disciplines of dream psychology (psychoanalysis, psychophysiology, and evolutionary biology) have contributed very little to a scientific understanding of dreaming. Similarly, Fiss (1983, 1986) has argued that the scientific study of dreaming has failed to develop a clinically relevant psychology of dreaming.

One important reason for this apparent lack of fruitfulness is the traditional exclusion of lucid dreaming from the central concerns of dream psychology. Ogilvie (1982) has aptly observed that lucid dreaming has been consigned to the "wasteland of parapsychology" until quite recently. However, these habits are changing with the demonstration by a number of researchers that lucid dreaming

Drawn from a paper originally presented at the Lucid Dreaming Symposium, held in conjunction with the annual meeting of the Association for the Study of Dreams, June 1985, Charlottesville, Virginia.

ALAN MOFFITT and ROBERT HOFFMANN • Department of Psychology, Carleton University, Ottawa, Ontario, Canada K1S 5B6.   JANET MULLINGTON • Department of Psychology, City College of New York, New York, NY 10013.   SHEILA PURCELL • Department of Psychology, Carleton University, Ottawa, Ontario, Canada K1S 5B6.   ROSS PIGEAU • Human Factors, Defense and Civil Institute of Environmental Medicine, Toronto, Ontario, Canada M3M 3B9.   ROGER WELLS • Department of Psychology, Carleton University, Ottawa, Ontario, Canada K1S 5B6.

is a scientifically real phenomenon (Dane, 1984; Fenwick, Schatzman, Worsley, & Adams, 1984; Hearne, 1981, 1983; LaBerge, 1980a,b; LaBerge, Nagel, Dement, & Zarcone, 1981; Ogilvie, Hunt, Tyson, Lucescu, & Jeakins, 1982; Tholey, 1983; Tyson, Ogilvie, & Hunt, 1984). "Scientifically real" in this context means that researchers such as Worsley and LaBerge have been able to show that prearanged signaling is possible during lucid dreaming from stage REM sleep without the intervention of a transition to the waking state (see, for example, LaBerge, Levitan, & Dement, 1986). In effect, the dreamer is simultaneously awake and asleep. The significance of this finding has not been fully appreciated within scientific dream psychology in particular or cognitive psychology more generally.

What is meant by the phrase *lucid dreaming*? There is obviously no single definition of lucid dreaming covering the full range of phenomena that have been reported by skilled lucid dreamers (see the preceding references and, in addition, Brown, 1936; Gackenbach, 1978; Garfield, 1979; Gillespie, 1984; Green, 1968; Reed, 1978; van Eeden, 1972). Some researchers only attribute lucidity to the dreamer when cognitive abilities during dreaming appear to be approximately equivalent to those of the waking state (Tart, 1979). We prefer a minimalist definition: the emergence while dreaming of the awareness that one is experiencing a dream. Other cognitive capabilities of the dreamer need not be altered in any way. We prefer such a definition because people who participate in our studies usually are not skilled lucid dreamers. We recognize, of course, that lucid dreaming represents a continuum of content and process from the minimalist to the elaborate and sustained. However, for most of the issues to be considered in this chapter the fact of simple lucidity is as important as its more complex forms. In our research, occurrences of lucidity are generally brief and unstable, usually followed by a return to nonlucid dreaming or a transition to the waking state (Purcell, Mullington, Moffitt, Hoffmann, & Pigeau, 1986). Our research also indicates that lucidity of the minimalist type occurs spontaneously on about 1% to 2% of experimental laboratory awakenings of adult dreamers not selected for lucid dreaming ability. This figure is similar to the results of other experimental studies with ordinary dreamers (Hoffman & McCarley, 1980; McCarley & Hoffman, 1981).

The significance for cognitive science of the occurrence of spontaneous or intentional lucid dreaming in the laboratory situation has not been fully appreciated. It leads to the conclusion that dreaming shares a fundamental property of all cognitive systems, specifically emergent self-reference and self-reflection (Hofstadter, 1985; Humphrey, 1983; Jantsch, 1983; Maruyama, 1963; Maturana & Varela, 1982; Prigogine & Stengers, 1984). It is now widely recognized in psychology that language, cognition, and ordinary waking experience all have these properties (Flavell, 1977; Humphrey, 1983; Paillet & Dugas, 1982; Suls & Greenwald, 1982/1983). Maturana and Varela use the term *autopoiesis* to call attention to the recursive, self-referential, and self-reflective character of the self-organizing activity of the human nervous system. These characteristics are recognized as fundamental developmental emergents during human ontogeny (Fishbein, 1976; Flavell, 1977; Laughlin & D'Aquili, 1974). The scientific verification that lucid dreaming does exist as a denotable state rather than as an error of perception and/or cognition on the part of the dreamer suggests that self-organizing and self-regulating processes occur within dreaming as well as waking.

The term we use to characterize these important collections of properties and processes is *self-reflectiveness*. Our quantification of the term is based on the work of Rossi (1972) and is presented in Table 1. He has outlined a developmental sequence in which dreaming of various sorts is involved in the growth of personality. Although we do not necessarily agree with the details of Rossi's theoretical position, his developmental sequence is empirically testable. In addition, it is based on his careful observation of the dynamics of dreams and dreaming in the growth and development of personal competence in clinical situations, possibly adding face validity to the scale.

The scale of dream self-reflectiveness that we derived from Rossi's work is a 9-category scale with Level 1 representing unfamiliar images without the dreamer present in the dream and Level 9 representing minimalist lucid dreaming. Table 2 presents the ordinal values of the self-reflective scale and our understanding of the terminology of others working in this area. This table is useful in clarifying otherwise problematic terms such as Rechtschaffen's (1978) concept of the single-mindedness of dreams, or the categories used by Hunt and

Table 1. Self-Reflectiveness Scale Categories in Abbreviated Form[a,b]

Category	Process level
1	Dreamer not in a dream; objects unfamiliar; no people
2	Dreamer not in dream; people or familiar objects present
3	Dreamer completely involved in dream drama; no other perspective
4	Dreamer present predominantly as observer
5	Dreamer thinks over an idea or has definite communication with someone
6	Dreamer undergoes a transformation of body, role, emotion, age, etc.
7	Dreamer has multiple levels of awareness: simultaneous participating and observing; dream within a dream; noticing oddities while dreaming
8	Dreamer has significant control in, or control over dream story; can wake up deliberately
9	Dreamer can consciously reflect on the fact that he or she is dreaming.

[a]For Rossi, dream control, prelucidity, and lucidity are all examples of dreams with multiple levels of awareness (here, category 7). We have assigned these dreams additional categories (8 and 9) because of our research interests.

[b]We have restricted our use of bizarreness to those oddities that are recognized by the dreamer within the dream. We have similarly restricted transformations (category 6) to those in the dreamer only, excluding those in the environment or of other dream characters.

Table 2. The Self-Reflectiveness Continuum: Process and Theory Terms

Scale level	Organization of consciousness	Process terms			Theory terms
1	Unfamiliar images	Seeing		Single mindedness or nonlucid dreaming	
2	Familiar images				
3	Participation	Perception/action dimension	Normative dreaming		Endogenous autopoietic operativity
4	Looking/watching	Reflection			
5	Language and thought	Self-representation			
6	Transforms of self-identity				
7	Transforms of awareness	Prelucid		Self-reflection	
8	Control				
9	Fleeting lucidity	Godel crisis			
10	Sustained lucidity	Recursive autopoiesis			
n	Action lucidity				Endogenous metapoietic operativity
o	Experimental lucidity	(Self-) reflective autopoiesis			
p	?				

his colleagues of nonlucid, prelucid, and lucid dreaming (Ogilvie *et al.*, 1982; Tyson, *et al.*, 1984). Table 2 also indicates the possibility, indeed the necessity, of extending the self-reflectiveness continuum to include more complex forms of lucidity.

We have found that dream reports can be classified reliably by the self-reflectiveness scale. Dream reports of random samples of dreamers are more or less normally distributed along the scale. Dream reports from stage REM sleep are more self-reflective than dream reports from Stages 2 and 4, which in turn do not differ. The dream reports of frequent dream recallers are more self-reflective than those of infrequent dream recallers, and the development of higher levels of dream self-reflectivess on the scale appears to be a skill that can be learned (Purcell *et al.*, 1986). Thus, both self-reflectiveness and lucidity have important implications for our understanding of dreaming and of the relation of dreaming to waking experience.

For us, the most important implication is that all experience is potentially self-reflective, not just waking experience. This strongly implies the existence and operation of common recursive mechanisms in the organization and production of experience within and between the dreaming and the waking states. Furthermore, because lucidity represents a correct judgment concerning the current contents of awareness during sleep, any scientific interpretation that views the organization of consciousness during dreaming as *necessarily* derivative in relation to normal waking consciousness probably will have to be modified, especially those classic interpretations of contemporary dream psychology that see dreaming as necessarily hallucinatory and/or regressive (Hartmann, 1973; Koukkou & Lehmann, 1983; Koukkou, Lehmann, & Angst, 1980; Rechtschaffen, 1978). Similarly, the assumption that dreaming represents the result of only random processes, as proposed in some neurophsyiological and psychophysiological theories of dreaming, can be seen to be unlikely (Hinton & Sejnowski, 1986; McCarley, 1983; McCarley & Hobson, 1979). Random processes may have a role to play in theories of dreams, dreaming, and dreamers. However, the story of the role of randomness in the organization and function of dreaming is likely to be much more complicated than suggested by theorists such as Hobson and McCarley when they characterize dreaming as the cortex making the best of a bad job. Instead, we conclude that dreaming, like waking cognition and language, is an epigenetic system showing complex forms of self-reflectiveness. This suggests that Crick's assertion that dreaming results from a failure of adaptation at the neurophysiological level is not likely to be generally correct, as others have noted (Crick & Mitchison, 1983, 1986; Hinton & Sejnowski, 1986).

Our research indicates that many lucid episodes are "triggered," often by noticing bizarreness in the dream. In addition, some episodes of lucidity appear to be spontaneous. As far as we can tell, they just happen. Thus awareness in the dream can be both self-reproductive and self-organizing. The stream of consciousness can lead to consciousness of the stream in dreaming as well as in waking. Further levels of self-reproductive organization of awareness are, of course, possible, as both experimental research and phenomenological descriptions have demonstrated (see the preceding references). We conclude, therefore, that dreaming, in general, and lucid dreaming, in particular, are self-organizing, self-reflective, and self-reproductive semiautonomous processes. Both cognition and language share these features. Such features define generative dissipative systems, systems that are both open and creative (London & Thorngate, 1981; Prigogine, 1976; Prigogine & Stengers, 1984). However, unlike Foulkes (1982), we do not believe that dreaming is to be understood as equivalent to either cognition or language. They may share common mechanisms, but they are not identical. Neither normal waking cognition nor language contains an exact biopsychological homologue to lucid dreaming, even with a minimalist definition; analogs yes, but not homologues.

We may now approach the important question of function. What is the function of dreaming? Why do we dream? Why do we dream the way we do? Numerous answers have been proposed to these questions, and, in the long run, none of them has been very convincing to scientific dream psychologists. It is clear that dreaming is a sufficiently complex activity that it can support any interpretation whatsoever with respect to function, including none at all (Haskell, 1986; Moffitt & Hoffmann, 1987a,b). Indeed, the dominant scientific interpretation of the function of dreaming since the logical positivists has been that dreaming serves no function at all (Dennett, 1981; Fodor, 1981; Malcom, 1959).

The question that must now be considered is whether lucid dreaming in particular and dream self-reflectiveness more generally have anything to contribute to our understanding of the function of dreaming. Why would a form of conscious awareness evolve during sleep that is capable of giving a correct description of its own state while in that state? We think the answer is fairly simple and follows from the preceding characterization of dreaming as self-organizing, self-reproductive, self-referential, and self-reflective. Waking consciousness also has these characteristics (Humphrey, 1983; Laughlin & D'Aquili, 1974; Laughlin, McManus, Rubinstein, & Shearer, 1986; Maturana & Varela, 1982). Moreover, as Hunt (1982, 1984, 1985) has noted, waking consciousness frames the experience of dreaming. One function of dream content, therefore, is to call attention to itself, to be noticed. Normally this noticing occurs across a major transition in the physiological organization of state, and we speak of *dream recall* under these circumstances. We may then question the nature of conscious experience in the sleeping and waking states, comparing and contrasting their similarities and differences. Such a process appears to be important in the differentiation of children's notions of reality (Shweder & LeVine, 1975).

In the case of lucid dreaming, we notice that we are dreaming without a major transition in the physiological organization of state. Consequently, when we recall a lucid dream, we notice that we noticed that we were dreaming. The result when awake is that we are obliged to question what it means to be awake in any state. The function of lucid dreaming for the waking state therefore is to render our understanding of what it means to be awake relative rather than absolute (Chang, 1974; Gyatso, 1975). In other words, the function of dream self-reflectiveness in general and lucidity in particular is epistemic and meta-epistemic (Kitchener, 1983). It requires us to revise our understanding of what it means to be asleep and to be awake (see, for example, Malcom, 1959), and how we make and justify assertions about our knowledge of such states. It is this consequence that is likely to result in considerable resistance within cognitive psychology to the assimilation of dream psychology. Until recently, scientific cognitive psychology has generally avoided questions of self-reflective consciousness and awareness with all their problematic implications (however, see Marcel, 1983; Shepard, 1984). Lucid dreaming is exactly the sort of anomalous datum that Kuhn (1970) has suggested illustrates the need for a new paradigm. We look forward, therefore, to the assimilation of dream psychology into cognitive psychology as proposed by Foulkes and Antrobus. Foulkes (1982) has argued that dream psychology should become assimilated with cognitive psychology, and Antrobus (1978) has suggested an assimilation with cognitive neuropsychology. When and if this happens, the character of cognitive psychology and cognitivie neurospychology will be permanently altered, possibly in the direction of a better understanding of the function of both waking and sleeping mentation.

One such alteration is that the meaning of the expression *being awake* can no longer be regarded as univocal. Cognitive psychology can no longer make the assumption that being awake has a clearly defined univocal meaning (see Fodor, 1981; Moffitt & Hoffmann, 1987a). The immediate consequence of this multiplicity of meaning is that the problem of awareness must emerge as a central concern of any revisionist cognitive psychology or cognitive neuropsychology that purports to include dreaming within its doman (see Shepard, 1984). For example, Hinton and Sejnowski (1986) refer to internally generated model construction resulting from the autonomous activity of internal units as ''folie a deux'' (p. 297). Moreover, they assert, quite incorrectly in our opinion, that a random dreaming process is necessary ''to make the system maximally responsive to regularities present in the environment and to prevent the system from using its capacity to model internally generated regularities'' (p. 298). The learning of self-reflectiveness and lucidity makes such claims less plausible than they might have seemed before the work of Worsley and LaBerge. Thus, if dream psychology is to play a role in the development of cognitive neuroscience, it is fundamentally important that self-reflectiveness and lucidity be included in dream psychology as a legitimate area of research and thought. Otherwise, cognitive psychology and dream psychology will both be the poorer. Two important recent neurocognitive texts on ''higher mental processes'' and the frontal lobes do not mention sleep, REM, or dreams in their indexes, yet both discuss self-consciousness and self-awareness (Perecman, 1987; Stuss & Benson, 1986). Cognitive neuropsychology and cognitive psychologists might benefit from their encounter with the modern sleep laboratory, just as contemporary dream psychology has been stimulated by its encounter with modern cognitive and neurocognitive psychology.

There is another, equally important consequence of lucidity for cognitive psychology, and it bears directly on the nature of the altered character of a cognitive psychology that has been broadened to include dreaming and lucid dreaming. Lucidity enables the further development of intentional action within the dream state. In effect, one can develop a new form of competence, a form of skill not available during the waking state. The observations of many skilled lucid dreamers suggest that this skill is of a different order than those found in the waking state. It is different, not derivative. This is the case because the affordances of perception and of action are not the same in the dream state as in the waking state. Consequently, we do not agree with claims such as those made by Koukkou and Lehmann (1983) that we necessarily regress to a concrete operational mode of functioning in the dream state. Many of the operational skills of more advanced lucid dreaming are of a different form in comparison to either concrete or formal operational intelligence during the waking state. These skills represent a form of human competence that are *sui generis,* of their own type. They depend initially upon the simple but difficult act of noticing that one is dreaming while dreaming. This noticing, when cultivated, enables the development of unique forms of perception and action in the dream state. This type of competence defines an internal ecosystem with unique affordances with respect to the self-referential dynamics of perception and action (Gibson, 1970, 1977, 1979). Cognitive psychology and cognitive developmental psychology have ignored or understated the contribution of dream self-reflectiveness and lucid dreaming to human development. The functions of such competence are analogous to the functions of cognitive, meta-cognitive, and epistemic competence during the waking state: the creation of knowledge based on experience and of experience based on knowledge. As Humphrey (1983) has suggested, ''we lack even the bare bones of a good story about consciousness in human beings'' (p. 46). For us, dream self-reflectiveness and lucid dreaming are an essential part of that story. They must not be left out of the integration of dream psychology into cognitive neuropsychology, experimental phenomenology, or what Humphrey has called *natural psychology.*

REFERENCES

Antrobus, J. (1978). Dreaming for cognition. In A. Arkin, J. Antrobus, & S. Ellman, (Eds.), *The mind in sleep.* (pp. 569–581). Hillsdale, NJ: Lawrence Erlbaum Associates.

Broughton, R. (1982). Human consciousness and sleep/waking rhythms: A review and some neuropsychological considerations. *Journal of Clinical Neuropsychology, 4,* 193–218.

Brown, A. (1936). Dreams in which the dreamer knows he is asleep. *Journal of Abnormal and Social Psychology, 31,* 59–66.

Chang, G. (1974). *Teachings of Tibetan yoga.* Secaucus, NJ: The Citadel Press.

Crick, F., & Mitchison, G. (1983). The function of dream sleep. *Nature, 30,* 111–114.

Crick, F., & Mitchison, G. (1986). REM sleep and neural nets. *The Journal of Mind and Behavior, 7,* 229–249.

Dane, J. (1984). *A comparison of waking instructions and post-hypnotic suggestion for lucid dream induction.* Unpublished doctoral dissertation, Georgia State University.

Dennett, D. (1981). *Brainstorms: Philosophical essays on mind and psychology.* Cambridge: The M.I.T. Press.

Fenwick, P., Schatzman, M., Worsley, A., & Adams, J. (1984). Lucid dreaming: Correspondence between dreamed and actual events in one subject during REM sleep. *Biological Psychology, 18,* 243–252.

Fishbein, H. (1976). *Evolution, development and children's learning.* Pacific Palisades, CA: Goodyear.

Fiss, H. (1983). Toward a clinically relevant psychology of dreaming. *Hillside Journal of Clinical Psychiatry, 5,* 147–159.

Fiss, H. (1986). An empirical foundation for a self-psychology of dreaming. *The Journal of Mind and Behavior, 7,* 161–191.

Flavell, J. (1977). *Cognitive development.* Englewood Cliffs, NJ: Prentice-Hall.

Fodor, J. (1981). Methodological solipsism considered as a research strategy in cognitive psychology. In J. Haugeland (Ed.), *Mind design: philosophy, psychology, artificial intelligence* (pp. 307–358) Cambridge: The M.I.T. Press.

Foulkes, D. (1978). *A grammar of dreams.* New York: Basic Books.

Foulkes, D. (1982). A cognitive-psychological model of REM dream production. *Sleep. 5,* 169–187.

Foulkes, D. (1983a). Cognitive processes during sleep: An evolutionary perspective. In A. Mayes (Ed.), *Sleep mechanisms and functions in humans and animals: An evolutionary perspective.* London: Van Nostrand Reinhold.

Foulkes, D. (1983b). Dream ontogeny and dream psychophysiology. In M. Chase & E. Weitzman (Eds.), *Sleep disorders: Basic and clinical research. Advances in Sleep Research. Vol. 8.* New York: Spectrum Publications.

Foulkes, D. (1985). *Dreaming: A cognitive-psychological analysis.* Hillsdale, NJ: Lawrence Erlbaum Associates.

Gackenbach, J. (1978). A personality and cognitivie style analysis of lucid dreaming. Unpublished doctoral dissertation, Virginia Commonwealth University.

Garfield, P. (1979). *Pathway to ecstasy.* New York: Holt Rhinehart & Winston.

Gibson, J. (1970). On the relation between hallucination and perception. *Leonardo, 3,* 425–427.

Gibson, J. (1977). The theory of affordances. In R. Shaw & J. Bransford (Eds.), *Perceiving, acting and knowing.* (pp. 67–82.) Hillsdale, NJ: Lawrence Earlbaum Associates.

Gibson, J. (1979). *The ecological approach to visual perception.* Boston: Houghton Mifflin.

Gillespie, G. (1984). Problems related to experimentation while dreaming lucidly. *Lucidity Letter, 3,* 1–3.

Green, C. (1968). *Lucid dreams.* Oxford: Institute of Psychophysical Research.

Gyatso, T. (1975). *The Buddhism of Tibet and the key to the middle way.* London: George Allen & Unwin, Ltd.

Hartmann, E. (1973). *The functions of sleep.* New Haven: Yale University Press.

Haskell, R. (1986). Cognitive psychology and dream research: Historical, conceptual and epistemological considerations. *The Journal of Mind and Behavior, 7,* 131–159.

Hearne, K. (1981). A "light-switch phenomenon" in lucid dreams. *Journal of Mental Imagery, 5,* 97–100.

Hearne, K. (1983). Lucid dream induction. *Journal of Mental Imagery, 7,* 19–23.

Hinton, G. E., & Sejnowski, T. J. (1986). Learning and relearning in Boltzman Machines. In D. E.

Rumelhart J. L. McClelland (Eds.), *Parallel distributed processing. Volume 1.* (pp. 282–317). Cambridge: The M.I.T. Press

Hoffman, E., & McCarley, R. (1980). Bizarreness and lucidity in REM sleep dreams: A Quantitative evaluation. *Sleep Research, 9,* 134.

Hofstadter, D. (1985). *Metamagical themas.* New York: Basic Books.

Humphrey, N. (1983). *Consciousness regained.* Oxford: Oxford University Press.

Hunt, H. (1982). The forms of dreaming. *Perceptual and Motor Skills,* Monograph Supplement, 1-V54.

Hunt, H. (1984). A cognitive psychology of mystical and altered-state. *Perceptual and Motor Skills,* Monograph Supplement, 1-V58, 467–513.

Hunt, H. (1985). Cognition and states of consciousness. *Perceptual and Motor Skills,* Monograph Supplement, 1-V60, 239–282.

Jantsch, E. (1983). *The self-organizing universe.* New York: Pergammon Press.

Kitchener, K. (1983). Cognition, meta-cognition and epistemic cognition. *Human Development, 26,* 222–232.

Koukkou, M., & Lehmann, D. (1983). Dreaming: The functional state-shift hypothesis. *British Journal of Psychiatry, 142,* 221–231.

Koukkou, M., Lehmann, D., & Angst, J. (Eds.). (1980). *Functional states of the brain: Their determinants.* Amsterdam: Elsevier/North Holland Press.

Kuhn, T. (1970). *The structure of scientific revolutions* (2nd ed.). Chicago: The University of Chicago Press.

LaBerge, S. (1980a). Induction of lucid dreams. *Sleep Research, 9,* 138.

LaBerge, S. (1980b). Lucid dreaming as a learnable skill: A case study. *Perceptual and Motor Skills, 51,* 1039–1042.

LaBerge, S., Nagel, L., Dement, W., & Zarcone, V. (1981). Lucid dreaming verified by volitional communication during REM sleep. *Perceptual and Motor Skills, 52,* 727–732.

LaBerge, S., Levitan, L., & Dement, W. (1986). Lucid dreaming: Physiological correlates of consciousness during REM sleep. *The Journal of Mind and Behavior, 7,* 251–258.

Laughlin, C., & D'Aquili, E. (1974). *Biogenetic structuralism.* New York: Columbia University Press.

Laughlin, C., McManus, J., Rubinstein, R., & Shearer, J. (1986). The ritual transformation of experience. In N. Denzin (Ed.), *Studies in Symbolic Interaction, 7,* Part A (pp. 107–136). Greenwich, CT: JAI Press.

London, I., & Thorngate, W. (1981). Divergent amplification and social behavior: Some methodological considerations. *Psychological Reports,* Monograph Supplement 1-V48.

Malcom, N. (1959). *Dreaming.* London: Routledge & Kegan Paul.

Marcel, A. (1983). Conscious and unconscious perception: An approach to the relations between phenomenal experience and perceptual processes. *Cognitive Psychology, 15,*238–300.

Maruyama, M. (1963). The second cybernetics: Deviation amplifying mutual causal processes. *American Scientist, 51,* 164–179.

Maturana, H., & Varela, F. (1982). Autopoiesis and cognition. *Boston Studies in the Philosophy of Science 42.* Dordrecht, Holland: D. Reidel.

McCarley, R. (1983). REM dreams, REM sleep, and their isomorphisms. In M. Chase & E. Weitzman (Eds.), *Sleep disorders: Basic and clinical research. Advances in Sleep Research* (Vol. 8, pp. 363–392). New York: Spectrum Publications.

McCarley, R., & Hobson, J. (1979). The form of dreams and the biology of sleep. In B. Wolman (Ed.), *Handbook of dreams* (pp. 76–130). New York: Van Nostrand Reinhold.

McCarley, R., & Hoffman, E. (1981). REM sleep dreams and the activation-synthesis hypothesis. *American Journal of Psychiatry, 138,* 904–912.

Moffitt, A., & Hoffmann, R. (1987a). On the single-mindedness and isolation of dream psychophysiology. In J. Gackenbach (Ed.), *A sourcebook on sleeping and dreaming.* pp. 145–186. New York: Garland.

Moffitt, A., & Hoffmann, R. (1987b). *On the question of the functions of dreaming.* Paper presented at the Symposium on the Functions of Dreaming at the Annual Meeting of the Association of Professional Sleep Societies, July, Copenhagen, Denmark.

Ogilvie, R. (1982). Is dream lucidity work another Reich's Orgone box. *Lucidity Letter, 1,* 2.

Ogilvie, R., Hunt, H., Tyson, P., Lucescu, M., & Jeakins, D. (1982). Lucid dreaming and alpha activity: A preliminary report. *Perceptual and Motor Skills, 55,* 795–808.

Paillet, J-P., & Dugas, A. (1982). Approaches to syntax. *Linguisticae Investigationes Supplementa,* Vol. 5. Amseterdam/Philadelphia: John Benjamins.

Perecman, E. (Ed.). (1987). *The frontal lobes revisited.* New York: IRBN Press.

Prigogine, I. (1976). Order through fluctuations: Self-organization and social system. In E. Jantsch & C. Waddington (Eds.), *Evolution and consciousness: Human systems in transition.* (pp. 93–126) Reading, MA: Addison-Wesley.

Prigogine, I., & Stengers, I. (1984). *Order out of chaos.* Boulder: Shambhala.

Purcell, S., Mullington, J., Moffitt, A., Hoffmann, R., & Pigeau, R. (1986). Dream self-reflectiveness as a learned cognitive skill. *Sleep, 9,* 423–437.

Rechtschaffen, A. (1978). The single-mindedness and isolation of dreams. *Sleep, 1,* 97–109.

Reed, H. (1978). Meditation and lucid dreaming. *Sundance Community Dream Journal, 2,* 237–238.

Rossi, E. (1972). *Dreams and the growth of personality.* New York: Pergamon Press.

Shepard, R. (1984). Ecological constraints on internal representation: Resonant kinematics of perceiving, imagining, thinking and dreaming. *Psychological Review, 91,* 417–447.

Shweder, R., & LeVine, R. (1975). Dream concepts of Hausa children. *Ethos, 3,* 209–229.

Stuss, D., & Benson, D. (1986). *The frontal lobes.* New York: Raven Press.

Suls, J., & Greenwald, A. (Eds.). (1982/1983). *Psychological perspectives on the self* (Vols. 1 & 2). Hillsdale, NJ: Lawrence Earlbaum Associates.

Tart, C. (1979). From spontaneous event to lucidity. In B. Wolman (Ed.), *Handbook of dreams.* (pp. 226–268) New York: Van Nostrand Reinhold.

Tholey, P. (1983). Techniques for inducing and manipulating lucid dreams. *Perceptual and Motor Skills, 57,* 79–90.

Tyson, P., Ogilvie, R., & Hunt, H. (1984). Lucid, prelucid and nonlucid dreams related to the amount of EEG alpha activity during REM sleep. *Psychophysiology, 21,* 442–451.

van Eeden, F. (1972). A study of dreams. In C. Tart (Ed.), *Altered states of consciousness.* (pp. 147–160) New York: Anchor Books.

Index